Puerto Rico

Randall Peffer

LONELY PLANET PUBLICATIONS
Melbourne · Oakland · London · Paris

18°30'N
67°W
66°45'W
66°30'W

18°30'N
Isla
Desecheo
67°30'W

ATLANTIC OCEAN

Cavernas del Río Camuy
Third-largest cave network in
the world, with ample rappelling
and spelunking adventures

Rincón
Surfing mecca with
thriving expat community
and winter whale-watching

18°30'N
Punta Sardina
Punta Borinquen
Isabela
Punta
Las Tunas
Punta
Puerto Nuevo
Puerto del
Tortuguero
Camuy   Hatillo
Puerto
Arecibo
112
Quebradillas
Arecibo   Barceloneta   (toll)
Aguadilla
2
22
2
Manatí
Punta
Gorda
Cordillera Jaicoa
Río Camuy
Montañas
Guajonex
Río Tanamá
Río Grande de Arecibo
149
Río Culebrinas
129
Río Grande de Manatí
Río Cibuco
Punta
Higüero
Rincón
Lares
Ciales
La Cadena
Río Grande de Añasco
123
Cerro Los
149
18°15'N
Montañas
119
10
Tres Picachos
de Uroyan
124
Utuado
3953ft
Cordillera Central
Mayagüez
105
(under
construction)
Cerro de Punta
Aibonito
Ruta Panorámica
Río Yagüez
Maricao
135   525
Adjuntas 4389ft
143   Ruta Panorámica
2
120
366   365
10
Reserva Forestal
Toro Negro
Laguna
de Joyuda
Cordillera   Central
Río Guanajibo
100
San
Germán
(under
construction)
Coamo
101
116
Sabana
10
14
Grande
Yauco
(toll)
Río Loco
Sierra
Bermeja
Río Yauco
Guayanilla
149
52
Guánica
2
Ponce
1
SALINAS
Cabo
Rojo
Bosque
Estatal de
Guánica
Playa
Ponce
52
Santa Isabel
Cayo
Berberia
Cayos de
Ratones
Bosque
Estatal
de Guánica
Punta Brea
Punta
Cabullónes
CARIBBEAN SEA
Bahía de
Tallaboa
Isla Caja
de Muertos
17°45'N

Río Guanajibo

Bosque Estatal de Guánica
Rare subtropical dry forest with
extensive hiking and a wild
coast ideal for exploration

Ponce
Treasure trove of 19th-century
architecture and the island's
most spectacular Carnaval

Reserva Forestal Toro Negro
Cloud forest with 4000-foot
peaks and the island's most
rugged hiking and camping

68°W   67°45'W
Isla
Mona
Pasaje de la Mona
18°N

Isla Mona
Wildlife refuge home to
giant iguanas, caves and
world-class diving

0   50   100 km
0   30   60 miles

Isla
Desecheo
Isla
Mona
PUERTO RICO
Culebra
Vieques
18°N
66°30'W
66°W
67°W
68°W

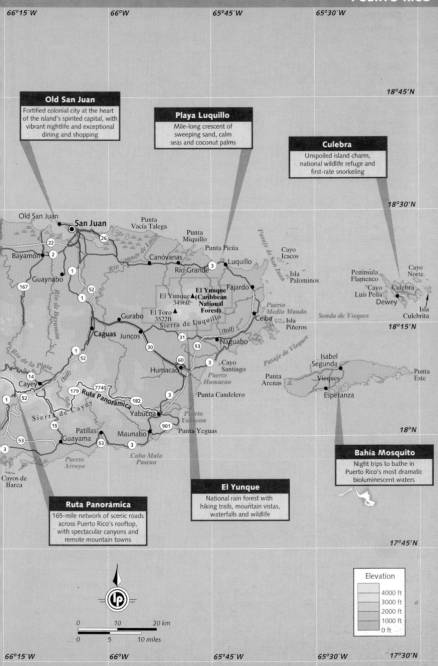

PUERTO RICO

Old San Juan
Fortified colonial city at the heart of the island's spirited capital, with vibrant nightlife and exceptional dining and shopping

Playa Luquillo
Mile-long crescent of sweeping sand, calm seas and coconut palms

Culebra
Unspoiled island charm, national wildlife refuge and first-rate snorkeling

Bahía Mosquito
Night trips to bathe in Puerto Rico's most dramatic bioluminescent waters

El Yunque
National rain forest with hiking trails, mountain vistas, waterfalls and wildlife

Ruta Panorámica
165-mile network of scenic roads across Puerto Rico's rooftop, with spectacular canyons and remote mountain towns

18°45'N
18°30'N
18°15'N
18°N
17°45'N
17°30'N

66°15'W
66°W
65°45'W
65°30'W

Old San Juan
San Juan
Punta Vacía Talega
Punta Miquillo
Punta Picúa
Bayamón
Guaynabo
Canóvanas
Río Grande
Luquillo
Fajardo
Cayo Icacos
Isla Palominos
Península Flamenco
Cayo Luis Peña
Cayo Norte
Culebra
Dewey
Isla Culebrita
Pasaje de San Juan
El Yunque 3496ft
El Yunque (Caribbean National Forest)
El Toro 3522ft
Gurabo
Caguas
Juncos
Sierra de Luquillo
Ceiba
Puerto Medio Mundo
Isla Piñeros
Sonda de Vieques
Naguabo
Cayo Santiago
Punta Candelero
Isabel Segunda
Vieques
Punta Este
Pasaje de Vieques
Punta Arenas
Esperanza
Humacao
Puerto Humacao
Cayey
Ruta Panorámica
Yabucoa
Puerto Yabucoa
Punta Yeguas
Patillas
Guayama
Maunabo
Sierra de Cayey
Puerto Arroyo
Cabo Mala Pascua
Cayos de Barca
Río Grande de Loíza
Río de Bayamón
Río de la Plata

22 26 2 1 167 52 1 31 53 30 60 3 3 3 14 52 1 52 7740 179 182 901 15 53 3

(toll)

Elevation
- 4000 ft
- 3000 ft
- 2000 ft
- 1000 ft
- 0 ft

0   10   20 km
0   5   10 miles

Puerto Rico
1st edition – October 1999

Published by
Lonely Planet Publications Pty Ltd A.C.N. 005 607 983
192 Burwood Rd, Hawthorn, Victoria 3122, Australia

Lonely Planet Offices
Australia PO Box 617, Hawthorn, Victoria 3122
USA 150 Linden St, Oakland, CA 94607
UK 10a Spring Place, London NW5 3BH
France 1 rue du Dahomey, 75011 Paris

Photographs
Tony Arruza, Mark Bacon, Tom Bean, Kevin R Downey, Thomas R
Fletcher, Robert Fried, Dave G Houser, Joan Iaconetti, Bob Krist, Bob
Krist/Puerto Rico Tourism Company, Randall Peffer, James P Rowan,
Steve Simonsen, David Zingarelli

Some of the images in this guide are available for licensing from
Lonely Planet Images.
email: lpi@lonelyplanet.com.au

Front cover photograph
Masquerader at Carnaval, Ponce (Bob Krist)

ISBN 0 86442 552 X

Contents

2   Contents

EAST COAST   190

SOUTH COAST   212

WEST COAST   244

NORTH COAST   275

CENTRAL MOUNTAINS   294

SPANISH VIRGIN ISLANDS   309

SPANISH FOR TRAVELERS   336

Map Index

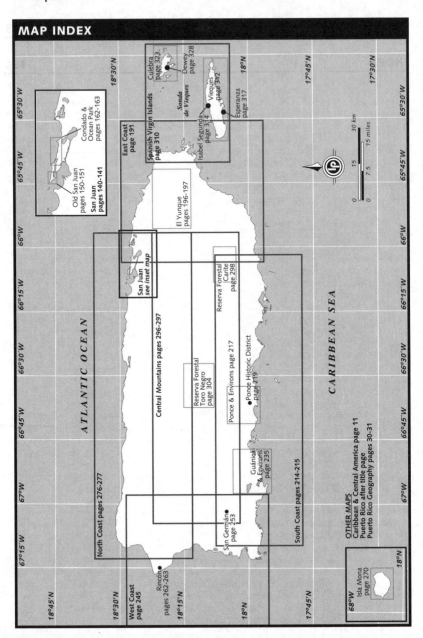

MAP INDEX

San Juan see inset map

Old San Juan pages 150-151
Condado & Ocean Park pages 162-163
San Juan pages 140-141

East Coast page 191

Spanish Virgin Islands page 310
Culebra page 323
Dewey page 328
Sonda de Vieques
Vieques page 312
Isabel Segunda page 314
Esperanza page 317

El Yunque pages 196-197

ATLANTIC OCEAN

North Coast pages 276-277

Central Mountains pages 296-297

Reserva Forestal Toro Negro page 304

Reserva Forestal Carite page 298

Ponce & Environs page 217
Ponce Historic District page 219

Guánica & Environs page 235

West Coast page 245
Rincón pages 262-263

San Germán page 253

South Coast pages 214-215

CARIBBEAN SEA

OTHER MAPS
Caribbean & Central America page 11
Puerto Rico after title page
Puerto Rico Geography pages 30-31

Isla Mona page 270

30 km
15
7.5
15 miles
0

The Author

Randall Peffer

As a boy Randy hopped a freight train out of Pittsburgh, Pennsylvania, his home town, in search of the King of the Hoboes. He's been traveling ever since. Those travels have taken him into jobs as a commercial pilot, Chesapeake Bay waterman, research schooner captain and teacher in a naval prison.

His romance with Puerto Rico started on a sailing cruise through the Caribbean in the 1970s. He has returned regularly to *la isla* during the last 20 years to foster long-standing friendships with Puerto Rican mariners, surfers, divers, hikers, gardeners, cooks, writers and various figures of the night.

A widely published feature writer, Randy has contributed to *National Geographic, Smithsonian, Islands, Travel Holiday, Sail, Reader's Digest* and most of the major metro dailies in the US. Randy is the coordinating author of Lonely Planet's 2nd-edition guide to *Washington, DC & the Capital Region* and author of National Geographic's driving guide to New York, New Jersey and Pennsylvania. His book *Watermen* (Johns Hopkins), about Chesapeake fishermen, won the *Baltimore Sun's* Critic's Choice award. A new nonfiction memoir about a maritime exploration of the Massachusetts coast and its history, *Logs of the Dead Pirates Society* (Sheridan House), has a spring 2000 publication date.

Currently Randy lives with his wife, Jackie, and sons, Noah and Jacob, at Phillips Academy in Andover, Massachusetts, where he teaches literature and writing.

FROM THE AUTHOR

First of all, thanks to senior editor Carolyn Hubbard, whose trust, encouragement, insight, guidance and friendship have shepherded this project from a gleam in my eye to the volume at hand. Thanks also go to project editor David Zingarelli and his editorial colleagues Laura Harger, Robert Reid and Rachel Bernstein – all fine editors with sharp eyes for both details and phrases gone astray. Cartographer Alex Guilbert and his minions have proven themselves wizards at their tasks. Equally valuable are the talents these people have shown for painstaking thoroughness, patience and good humor. They are the epitome of the successful collaboration that is at the very heart of producing a book like this.

Thanks also go to a number of my colleagues at Phillips Academy who have supported this project with their expertise. In particular, I would like to thank Susan Noble and her staff of research librarians at the Oliver Wendell Holmes Library for their magical ability to unearth rare and valuable sources with lightning speed. Then there is the respected Cuban poet and novelist Emilio Mozo, who shared his lifetime of insight about Spanish-Antilles culture and literature with me over *café con leche* on a lot of cold winter mornings in

Massachusetts while we were Caribbean dreaming. In this regard, my Puerto Rican colleague Aida Orenstein Cardona and our Puerto Rican students Diana Calderón and Hans Hertell were also invaluable in unfolding to me the peculiar secrets of their island, culture and language in advance of my recent travels to their island home.

On the island, many Puerto Rican friends and acquaintances gave their time freely to assist me in the researching and writing of this book. Chief among those friends is the fiery, erudite and amusing editor-in-chief of publications for the Instituto de Cultura Puertorriqueña, Henry Cobb, a true Puerto Rican patriot. His insightful critiques of all things linguistic and cultural in this manuscript have been simply priceless. Sonya Marrero and Cristina Junquera at the Compañía de Tourismo Puertorriqueño provided nearly endless logistical support and local knowledge for my travels and research in the field. Joyce Martin of Hill and Knowlton also provided contacts and primary source material.

In addition, my family and I were the beneficiaries of nearly endless Puerto Rican hospitality in spite of living on the island during and after the most devastating hurricane of the 20th century. Especially generous were our new friends María and Juan Casalduc, our landlord Michael Giessler and our neighbor Joe Carroll.

This list of acknowledgments would not be complete without thanks to my department chair, Craig Thorn; Phillips Academy's Dean of Faculty, Philip Zaeder; and Dean of Studies, Vincent Avery, for granting me a sabbatical as a means to completing this project.

Finally, and most importantly, I must thank my wife, Jackie, and infant son, Jacob, for enduring thousands of miles of traveling around the island – and living for weeks on the island without water and electricity in the aftermath of Hurricane Georges – without complaint. The adventure of writing this book would have been hollow indeed without having my family to share it with.

Muchas gracias a todos.

This Book

FROM THE PUBLISHER

This 1st edition of *Puerto Rico* was produced in Lonely Planet's Oakland office. David Zingarelli was the coordinating editor. Text and maps were edited by Robert Reid, Rachel Bernstein and David, with help from senior editors Laura Harger and Carolyn Hubbard. Tara Duggan, Rebecca Northen, David Peterkofsky, Kevin Anglin, Laura and David proofed the text and maps. Sandra Bao helped with fact checking. David Zingarelli indexed the book. Maps for this book were produced by Jenny King with assistance from Bart Wright and Tim Lohnes and oversight from Alex Guilbert and Amy Dennis. Mary Hagemann deftly worked the maps into their final form and saw them through layout. Design and production were executed by Wendy Yanagihara, who laid out the book and designed the special section on traditional arts, with guidance from Margaret Livingston. Laura, Henia Miedzinski and Mary helped out with layout review. Beca Lafore designed the colorwraps and guided pre-production with oversight from Margaret. Illustrations were created by Hayden Foell, Mark Butler, Rini Keagy, John Fadeff, Hugh D'Andrade and Wendy. Rini designed the book's cover. Richard Wilson lended his technical expertise. Warm thanks to senior editor Carolyn Hubbard for her guidance at the onset of the project, and to Laura Harger, who so skillfully and gracefully took over the role of senior editor and helped shepherd this book through production.

Foreword

ABOUT LONELY PLANET GUIDEBOOKS

The story begins with a classic travel adventure: Tony and Maureen Wheeler's 1972 journey across Europe and Asia to Australia. Useful information about the overland trail did not exist at that time, so Tony and Maureen published the first Lonely Planet guidebook to meet a growing need.

From a kitchen table, then from a tiny office in Melbourne (Australia), Lonely Planet has become the largest independent travel publisher in the world, an international company with offices in Melbourne, Oakland (USA), London (UK) and Paris (France).

Today Lonely Planet guidebooks cover the globe. There is an ever-growing list of books, and there's information in a variety of forms and media. Some things haven't changed. The main aim is still to help make it possible for adventurous travelers to get out there – to explore and better understand the world.

At Lonely Planet we believe travelers can make a positive contribution to the countries they visit – if they respect their host communities and spend their money wisely. Since 1986 a percentage of the income from each book has been donated to aid projects and human-rights campaigns.

Updates Lonely Planet thoroughly updates each guidebook as often as possible. This usually means there are around two years between editions, although for more unusual or more stable destinations the gap can be longer. Check the imprint page (following the color map at the beginning of the book) for publication dates.

Between editions, up-to-date information is available in two free newsletters – the paper *Planet Talk* and email *Comet* (to subscribe, contact any Lonely Planet office) – and on our website at www.lonelyplanet.com. The *Upgrades* section of the website covers a number of important and volatile destinations and is regularly updated by Lonely Planet authors. *Scoop* covers news and current affairs relevant to travelers. And, lastly, the *Thorn Tree* bulletin board and *Postcards* section of the site carry unverified, but fascinating, reports from travelers.

Correspondence The process of creating new editions begins with the letters, postcards and emails received from travelers. This correspondence often includes suggestions, criticisms and comments about the current editions. Interesting excerpts are immediately passed on via newsletters and the website, and everything goes to our authors to be verified when they're researching on the road. We're keen to get more feedback from organizations or individuals who represent communities visited by travelers.

> Lonely Planet gathers information for everyone who's curious about the planet – and especially for those who explore it firsthand. Through guidebooks, phrasebooks, activity guides, maps, literature, newsletters, image library, TV series and website, we act as an information exchange for a worldwide community of travelers.

Research Authors aim to gather sufficient practical information to enable travelers to make informed choices and to make the mechanics of a journey run smoothly. They also research historical and cultural background to help enrich the travel experience and allow travelers to understand and respond appropriately to cultural and environmental issues.

Authors don't stay in every hotel because that would mean spending a couple of months in each medium-size city and, no, they don't eat at every restaurant because that would mean stretching belts beyond capacity. They do visit hotels and restaurants to check standards and prices, but feedback based on readers' direct experiences can be very helpful.

Many of our authors work undercover; others aren't so secretive. None of them accept freebies in exchange for positive write-ups. And none of our guidebooks contain any advertising.

Production Authors submit their raw manuscripts and maps to offices in Australia, the USA, the UK or France. Editors and cartographers – all experienced travelers themselves – then begin the process of assembling the pieces. When the book finally hits the shops, some things are already out of date, we start getting feedback from readers and the process begins again....

WARNING & REQUEST

Things change – prices go up, schedules change, good places go bad and bad places go bankrupt – nothing stays the same. So, if you find things better or worse, recently opened or long since closed, please tell us and help make the next edition even more accurate and useful. We genuinely value all the feedback we receive. Julie Young coordinates a well-traveled team that reads and acknowledges every letter, postcard and email and ensures that every morsel of information finds its way to the appropriate authors, editors and cartographers for verification.

Everyone who writes to us will find their name in the next edition of the appropriate guidebook. They will also receive the latest issue of *Planet Talk*, our quarterly printed newsletter, or *Comet*, our monthly email newsletter. Subscriptions to both newsletters are free. The very best contributions will be rewarded with a free guidebook.

Excerpts from your correspondence may appear in new editions of Lonely Planet guidebooks, the Lonely Planet website, *Planet Talk* or *Comet*, so please let us know if you *don't* want your letter published or your name acknowledged.

Send all correspondence to the Lonely Planet office closest to you:

Australia: PO Box 617, Hawthorn, Victoria 3122
USA: 150 Linden St, Oakland, CA 94607
UK: 10A Spring Place, London NW5 3BH
France: 1 rue du Dahomey, 75011 Paris

Or email us at: talk2us@lonelyplanet.com.au

For news, views and updates, see our website: www.lonelyplanet.com

HOW TO USE A LONELY PLANET GUIDEBOOK

The best way to use a Lonely Planet guidebook is any way you choose. At Lonely Planet, we believe the most memorable travel experiences are often those that are unexpected, and the finest discoveries are those you make yourself. Guidebooks are not intended to be used as if they provided a detailed set of infallible instructions!

Contents All Lonely Planet guidebooks follow the same format. The Facts about the Country chapters or sections give background information ranging from history to weather. Facts for the Visitor gives practical information on issues like visas and health. Getting There & Away gives a brief starting point for researching travel to and from the destination. Getting Around gives an overview of the transport options available when you arrive.

The peculiar demands of each destination determine how subsequent chapters are broken up, but some things remain constant. We always start with background, then proceed to sights, places to stay, places to eat, entertainment, getting there and away, and getting around information – in that order.

Heading Hierarchy Lonely Planet headings are used in a strict hierarchical structure that can be visualized as a set of Russian dolls. Each heading (and its following text) is encompassed by any preceding heading that is higher on the hierarchical ladder.

Entry Points We do not assume guidebooks will be read from beginning to end, but that people will dip into them. The traditional entry points are the list of contents and the index. In addition, however, some books have a complete list of maps and an index map illustrating map coverage.

There may also be a color map that shows highlights. These highlights are dealt with in greater detail later in the book, along with planning questions and suggested itineraries. Each chapter covering a geographical region usually begins with a locator map and another list of highlights. Once you find something of interest in a list of highlights, turn to the index.

Maps Maps play a crucial role in Lonely Planet guidebooks and include a huge amount of information. A legend is printed on the back page. We seek to have complete consistency between maps and text, and to have every important place in the text captured on a map. Map key numbers usually start in the top left corner.

Although inclusion in a guidebook usually implies a recommendation, we cannot list every good place. Exclusion does not necessarily imply criticism. In fact, there are a number of reasons why we might exclude a place – sometimes it is simply inappropriate to encourage an influx of travelers.

Introduction

Every Friday and Saturday night, music teases crowds into the streets of Old San Juan. Chic young people in polo shirts and sheer dresses parade along the cobblestones. Perfecting their night moves, they sashay up the hill past the centuries-old Casa Blanca, ancestral home of the family of Juan Ponce de León – seeker of the legendary Fountain of Youth.

Throngs gather on Calle San Sebastián, the street that rises above the sea and the restorations of the fortified city that has been the commercial hub of the Caribbean for more than 450 years. Here, wandering groups of musicians and dozens of bars, restaurants and clubs pump the sounds of *salsa* into the tropical night. Everyone moves to the syncopated rhythm of bongos, congas, maracas, cowbells, trumpets and song. And an island celebrates the fusion of elements that gave birth to a place, a culture, a race and a spirit that the world calls 'Puerto Rico' but islanders still know as Borinquen – the name the Taíno Indians

gave their island home before the arrival of Christopher Columbus in 1493.

Like the island's famous salsa – a spicy blend of Afro-Caribbean rhythms and big-band jazz – almost everything about Puerto Rico stands out as a dramatic and original yoking of opposites. Here, travelers will find strong and recognizable vestiges of Amer-indian ancestors, Spanish *conquistadores* and West African slaves, as well as the polit-ical and economic influence of the USA – the Commonwealth of Puerto Rico's legal step-parent. The fusion of these strains is so distinctive that neither the place nor the culture can be mistaken for any other, and Puerto Rico claims a vitality and reputation that far exceed the island's diminutive size.

Just 35 miles wide and 100 miles long, Puerto Rico is the smallest of the Greater Antilles and stands as the keystone between the larger islands to the west and the long arch of the Lesser Antilles to the east. In many ways this location makes Puerto Rico the 'gatekeeper' of the Caribbean Sea, and

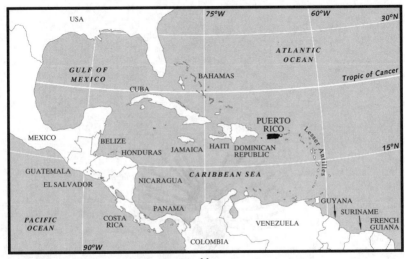

the island's strategic position as a cross-roads has fired her character. Not only can you see the fusion of Native America, Africa and Europe in the faces of her people, but you can also hear the synthesis of Spanish and English (spiced with Taíno and African words) in islanders' speech in this officially bilingual commonwealth. Diners taste the merger of the fields of Europe, the spices of Africa and the fish of the Caribbean in traditional cuisine such as *asopao,* a hearty stew. Drinkers here in the rum capital of the world find magic in the spirits distilled from sugarcane and mixed with pineapple and cream of coconut in the popular piña colada or blended with tart lime juice in a daiquiri.

In Puerto Rico, poets become politicians and spiritual wayfarers embrace elements of Catholicism and African Santería. Songs with rhythms to make stones rise up and dance carry lyrics about heartbreak. Slums and mansions stand side by side, and simple guesthouses languish in the shade of resort hotels. Ford Mustangs adorned with extra chrome, blazing paint jobs and tinted glass travel the backroads with herds of wild horses. Street vendors selling *tostones* (fried plantains) share the block with Burger King, while the warships of the US Navy keep company with local sailboats.

No doubt, travelers will find the most dramatic signs of fusion in the landscape itself. Contemporary Borinquen is a place where the green peaks of the Cordillera Central press the high-rises of modern San Juan to the edge of the sea. The ancient fortresses and walled Spanish city of Old San Juan stand nearly adjacent to the casinos, condominiums and resorts of the newer Condado district. Cane fields surround golf courses, soulless housing developments mask the way to pristine ocean coves, and the world's most luminescent phosphorescent bay lies next to a proving ground for military maneuvers. Broad beaches lie almost in the shadow of the verdant mountain slopes of El Yunque, the national rain forest.

And in spite of – or perhaps *because* of – these dramatic contrasts, the music never stops on this island whose anthem, 'La Borinqueña,' praises Puerto Rico as a 'flowering garden of exquisite magic…the daughter of the sea and the sun.'

Facts about Puerto Rico

HISTORY
Early Peoples

From discoveries of conch shells and hatchets in a limestone cave at Loíza Aldea, east of San Juan on the north coast of the island, archaeologists have traced human habitation of Puerto Rico to the 1st century AD. Generally known as Los Arcaicos (the Archaics), these first settlers belonged to the same racial group of Indians that populated the North American continent after crossing the Bering Strait. It is speculated that they reached Puerto Rico after voyaging south from present-day Florida in large rafts hewn from trees. Like many nomadic peoples, the Arcaicos seem to have had little time to develop specialized activities such as pottery making, canoe building or farming.

A more advanced group of nomads, the Igneris, of the Arawakan linguistic group, arrived at Puerto Rico in about 300 AD after traveling up the chain of the Lesser Antilles from the Orinoco River basin of Venezuela in swift, mammoth canoes that could carry up to 100 people. The Igneris settled coastal Puerto Rico, bringing with them well-developed skills in pottery making, fishing and canoe building.

A second wave of Arawaks, a subgroup called the Taínos, reached the island's shores in about 600 AD. These wayfarers were less skilled at pottery but adept at agriculture and better than their predecessors at grinding tools and procuring jewels from stones. Archaeological evidence and reports from the first European explorers indicate that the Taínos traveled throughout the West Indies, establishing scattered settlements as they went. Eventually, the Taínos centered their civilization in Hispaniola and Puerto Rico, where they emulated the crafts and customs of the Igneris and evolved a sophisticated culture of their own on the island they named Borinquen.

Early Spanish chroniclers described the Taínos as short people with straight dark hair, high cheekbones and muscular, copper-colored bodies. Except in the case of the caciques and married women – who wore apronlike garments called *naguas* – most of the Taínos wore no clothes. The copper coloring of their skin was actually a body paint made from plant and mineral dyes. In addition to these dyes, the Taínos favored red, white and black hues for their faces. While the body paints were considered fashionable to some degree, they primarily functioned as protection against insects, the tropical sun and evil spirits.

But no body paint could protect the Taínos from the invasion of the Caribs. Master mariners and ruthless warriors, this tribe of Indians left the northern shoulder of South America during the 15th century and launched a reign of terror, wiping out the Taínos as the invaders moved north through the Lesser Antilles. By the fall of 1493, the Caribs were raiding the southeastern coast of Borinquen. Whole Taíno communities took refuge in the Cordillera Central, the island's mountainous interior, and the battle line between the Taínos and Caribs was drawn along the eastern threshold of the island.

Enter Columbus

Following his first 'voyage of discovery' to the New World in 1492, Christopher Columbus returned to the court of King Ferdinand and Queen Isabella of Spain with excellent news: By sailing 33 days east from the Azores, he had discovered the 'Indies,' a land where it was perpetually summer and the rivers flowed with gold.

Upon hearing his report, the Spanish monarchs vested Columbus with the title 'Admiral of the Ocean Sea' and bid him assemble a fleet for a second voyage for the glory of Spain. So off he went with 17 ships and more than 1200 pilgrims, mariners and soldiers – all men – under the flagship nicknamed *Maríagalante*. The fleet departed the Spanish port of Cádiz on September 25, 1493, and sighted land on November 3: an island in the Lesser Antilles that Columbus

Christopher Columbus

named 'Dominica' because it came in sight on Sunday morning.

In subsequent weeks the Spanish fleet worked its way north through the Leeward Islands, where they encountered the Caribs. While the fleet was anchored off the island of Guadeloupe, an exploratory party went ashore and got lost in the jungle, and when they returned they told tales of hastily abandoned Indian villages with huts stocked with human limbs and choice cuts of human flesh. The explorers also found captive Taínos – emasculated boys being fattened for slaughter and serving at a coming feast and '12 very beautiful plump girls from 15 to 16 years old.' The Spaniards brought these Taínos to the fleet to serve as interpreters, coast pilots and sex slaves.

The fleet met more Indians on November 14, when the Spanish vessels anchored off Salt River Bay at Santa Cruz (St Croix) island. When a landing party of 25 men headed for a Carib village on shore, the inhabitants scattered. But as the Spanish rowed back to their flagship, they surprised a Carib canoe coming around the point. The Caribs – four men and two women – let loose a flock of arrows on the Spaniards in their open boat. Arrows wounded two sailors – one mortally – before the Spaniards rammed the Carib canoe, forcing the Indians to swim. But the Caribs swam to a rock and fought on. At last the Spaniards succeeded in taking the Caribs as prisoners, and gained a respect for these fierce warriors.

In subsequent days, the Taíno captives guided Columbus west along the southern coasts of the present-day US Virgin Islands, the island of Vieques and eventually Puerto Rico. On November 19, 1493, the Spanish ships gathered off a broad bay (possibly that of present-day Boquerón or Aguadilla) on the west coast of the island and waited out a night at sea before setting anchor in the bay on November 20. Here, Columbus gave the island its first European name – San Juan Bautista (St John the Baptist) – after a saint popular in his home of Genoa, Italy. Landing parties went ashore to make contact with the Indians. But the Taínos fled, leaving the parties to procure fresh water and explore an abandoned village of 12 well-made huts staged around an open space, and one great square house with turrets laden with vegetation, not unlike the arbors of Valencia. The Spaniards speculated wrongly that this village was a summer resort for the Caribs. Meanwhile, one of admiral's shipmates, Juan Ponce de León, tasted the cool water from the dark-green mountains, sniffed the fragrant air, admired the wide beach, noted the plentiful fish and vowed to return.

The Search for El Dorado

Columbus and the fleet sailed on to establish a colony on Hispaniola and explore Cuba and Jamaica before returning to Spain to plan the third and fourth New World 'voyages of discovery' under the pennant of the Admiral of the Ocean Sea. Three years later, the great explorer founded the city of Santo Domingo on Hispaniola, one of the islands on which the Indians cryptically suggested he might find a city of gold. So began the oldest permanent settlement in the Americas and what would be the center of Spanish colonial government for centuries.

But colonial life on Hispaniola proved to be no fiesta. After a few years of quasi-enslavement of the Taínos by the Spaniards – who controlled the Indians through

The Taínos

Historical estimates put the Taíno population at about 30,000 when Christopher Columbus (Cristóbal Colón in Spanish) encountered Borinquen on his second trip to the New World, in 1493. What the first Europeans in the Americas discovered was an island scattered with dozens of separate Taíno communities called *yucayeques*, each with about 300 to 600 inhabitants living within a sharply defined social structure presided over by a *cacique* (chief). Each village was composed of a collection of large circular shelters called *bohíos*, which were built of trees and straw and clustered around an open space called the *batey*. Here the Taínos staged their ceremonial dances and played a ball game involving 10 to 30 players, somewhat similar to that played by the Mayans of Mexico's Yucatán Peninsula. Scholars disagree as to whether the ball game involved human sacrifices, as the Mayan game did, but there seems to be little question that the competition was more than simple sport: Victories or defeats were most likely viewed as messages to or from the gods about community concerns such as the yam harvest.

Within Taíno villages, multiple or extended families shared the bohíos, sleeping in *hamacas* (hammocks) strung between support poles. The families also used the shelters for cooking and weaving. Often a large, square bohío housed the village cacique and his mates.

Inhabitants of Taíno villages bent to the rule of the cacique and the *bohíque* (shaman), who presided over religious rites and community celebrations called *areytos*, or fiestas. Both leaders were usually male. Not only did the leaders enjoy the privilege of taking many mates, but they also sidestepped the normal hunting, fishing, farming and construction tasks common to most of the other men in the community. A small aristocracy called *nitaynos*, who were mostly relatives of the cacique, lived a life of relative comfort with multiple mates and few obligations. The *naborias* were the common folk who did most of the work in the community, including the tending of the *conucos* (fields), where they grew a potatolike tuber called *yautías* as well as yams, corn, cotton, chili pepper and cassava. Of course, when it came to doing the real grunt work, slaves captured in battle were called upon.

The Taínos worshipped a pantheon of deities – called *cemíes* – and paid tribute to many of them by idolizing natural objects believed to be inhabited by powerful spirits. Such idols typically consisted of a rock, a shell, a piece of wood or even gold carved in a human likeness. Each of these spirits individually governed heavenly bodies such as the moon and the stars, as well as the earth and all living things. At the top of this pyramid of gods stood Yocahú, the invisible creator. Next in power were Yukiyú, the male god of positive forces, and his female companion. Jurakán controlled the forces of evil from the Lesser Antilles, where his anger grew into hurricane winds. The Taínos also believed in a plethora of lesser spirits, such as those of their ancestors as well as spirits who lived in trees and other features of the landscape.

starvation as well as physical and sexual abuse – the Taínos rebelled, slowing the search for El Dorado (City of Gold) and mining operations on Hispaniola. Frustrated and poor in Santo Domingo, Ponce de León struck a secret accord with the Spanish governor of the Caribbean for mining gold on the uncolonized island of San Juan Bautista.

It was with dreams of riches that Ponce de León and 50 colonists set sail in July of 1508.

The Conquest

Like Ponce de León's first visit to San Juan Bautista, this trip took him to the southwest coast of the island. Upon their arrival, the Spaniards encountered hospitable Taínos whose cacique, Agueybaná, cut his wrist and invited Ponce de León to do the same so that the men could accomplish the ritual mixing of blood that made them 'blood brothers.' It's likely that Agueybaná feared the invading Caribs and saw the Spaniards as useful allies. But whatever the cacique's motives, he guaranteed Ponce de León's men safe passage as they explored the north coast of the island. Finally, in 1509, the adventurers established a settlement called Caparra a few miles from the Atlantic Ocean on a branch of the Río Bayamón. Shortly thereafter, a political and commercial rival named Cristóbal Sotomayor founded the settlement of San Germán near the southwest corner of the island.

From these outposts the Spaniards began their pursuit of gold. At first, they tried bartering with the Taínos, but negotiations did not go well as the Indians showed little desire for the meager European goods the Spanish offered in trade. Driven by greed to more desperate measures, the Spaniards decided to mine for nuggets of alluvial gold in the hills and streams. But there was just one problem: The conquistadores, their priests and the colonists felt themselves

Women Warriors

Conventional portraits of Caribbean Indian culture have imagined a male-dominated civilization, but in his book *The Islands* (1974), Stan Steiner cites anthropological evidence for the existence of a matriarchal structure in at least some indigenous communities. Steiner's case stems from an assemblage of first-hand impressions by Spanish *conquistadores* and thoughtful scholarship by Puerto Rican anthropologists.

Fernando Colón, the biographer son of Christopher Columbus, tells how 'a multitude of women armed with bows and arrows and with plumes on their heads' charged a group of Spanish sailors when they tried to come ashore on a Caribbean island. Later, the captured leader of this group told the Spaniards that 'the whole island belonged to women.' Colón writes that 'the Admiral believed it on account of what he had seen of the women, and because of the energy and strength they had displayed.'

A few years later, when Spanish explorer Juan Ponce de León led settlers to Puerto Rico, the Spaniards found a Taíno community at the mouth of the Río Grande de Loíza, the island's largest river, dominated by a female cacique whom the Spanish named 'Luisa.' Known as Hayamano, this community was believed by the Taínos to be home to some of the island's most powerful spirits. One of these was the 'Mother Goddess,' ruler of the water, winds, earth and life, and consort of the male fire god. In Luisa's domain, women played alongside and even against men in the ball games staged on the batey. Following the birth of a child, fathers suffered postnatal trauma and ritually acted out the pain of delivery by retreating to their hammocks, abstaining from work and fasting. One Spanish priest of the time observed the equality of the genders wherein 'men and women alike choose their mates and live as they please' – a distinctly different situation from that of male-dominated feudal Spain in the 15th century.

Steiner points to the persistent independence of modern Puerto Rican women as a legacy of their Indian ancestors. During the 20th century, women of the island have held prominent places on the Commonwealth's Supreme Court, as well as in the professions of medicine, law, education and politics. Some of these distinguished women include Felisa Rincón de Gautier, San Juan's beloved mayor from 1946 to 1968; 'Cucusa' Hernández, the longtime Speaker of the House of Representatives; and Sila Calderón, the present mayor of San Juan.

above manual labor. The solution was an ordinance called the Repartimiento de Indios (Distribution of the Indians), which gave the Spaniards authority to subdue the indigenous populations of Spain's 16th-century New World colonies, convert them to Christianity and impress them into forced labor. Under the pretense of enforcing this ordinance, Ponce de León appointed more than 40 *hidalgos* (minor nobles) to 'protect' and Christianize villages of Indians. What this system meant in fact was that the Spaniards coerced the Indian men to do all the dirty work and took advantage of the Taíno women. In the meantime, Spanish priests scurried around trying to clothe the Indians. The priests also began to bless intermarriage between Spaniards and Taínos, perhaps as a way of legitimizing the common colonial practice of keeping Indian mistresses.

Soon the Taínos had enough. Some fled to other islands, while others resisted by killing their newborn babies to save them from Spanish exploitation or joining mass suicide rituals. But by 1511, even such drastic passive resistance to the conquistadores was not enough, and the Taínos formed an alliance with their old Carib enemies to attempt to drive the Spaniards off the island. The attack began on the south side of San Juan Bautista at San Germán, where the Indians killed village founder Cristóbal Sotomayor and some of his family. When word of the rebellion reached the outpost at Caparra, Ponce de León mounted a militia of 120 men to march into the Indian strongholds of the island's interior and seize the offensive. The Spaniards made a sneak attack on a Taíno village, slaughtering 200 Indians with no loss to the attackers. Fired up by this victory, the Spaniards went on to burn other villages and destroy their inhabitants. Finally, after the death of Taíno rebel leader Guaybana at the hands of the Spaniards, the Indians withdrew from further warfare.

Two more Indian rebellions broke out in 1513 and 1518, but the Spanish repressed them quickly with efficient crossbows, firearms and a scorched-earth policy. As the violence spread, many more Taínos fled the island, while those who remained perished at alarming rates from the smallpox and whooping cough epidemics brought to their island by the Europeans. By the middle of the 16th century, most of the Taínos – except for a few communities hidden in the Cordillera Central – had vanished from the island, while the migratory Caribs retreated to the Lesser Antilles. Borinquen now belonged to the Spaniards and their children, known as *mestizos* for their mixed European and Amerindian ancestry.

Puerto What?

As the production of gold from the mining operations dwindled to a trickle, the Spanish settlers took stock of the situation in Ponce de León's 'capital' of Caparra and were soundly dismayed. Built on a marshy plain, Caparra found itself wide open to Indian attack and – even worse – vulnerable to swarms of malaria-carrying mosquitoes that wiped out settlers at about the same rate that new ones arrived. Clearly, Ponce de León had to move his minions if the colony was to survive.

Perhaps as early as 1511, settlers began evacuating Caparra in favor of a small island with a dramatic headland guarding the entrance to a large, protected bay on the north shore of the island. Originally, the colonists called their new settlement Puerto Rico, meaning 'Rich Port,' but eventually usage and a cartographic mix-up applied this name to the island as a whole. The little fortified town became known as San Juan, after the original Spanish name for the island.

But the Spaniards were faced with more problems than maintaining their health and defense and naming their new colony. Poverty and a labor shortage loomed large. With the gold rush a fading memory, settlers turned to agriculture for profit. In short order, they began growing bananas, rice, plantains, ginger, oranges, lemons and sugarcane, many of which were introduced from Europe or from other Spanish colonies. The settlers also began tending all manner of livestock. Sugarcane flourished, presenting the possibility of profits never before realized by the colonists. But large-scale cane plantations were impossible without the forced labor of the dwindling Taíno population, until Portuguese and Dutch slave traders began arriving in San Juan with West Africans for sale in 1518.

By 1530, West African slaves – including members of the Mandingo and Yoruba tribes – numbered about half the population of 3000 in Puerto Rico. The Spanish colonists subdued this workforce in the same two ways that had proven effective with the Taínos: interbreeding and religion. Unlike the Dutch, French and English colonists elsewhere in the Americas, the Spaniards always acknowl-edged their slaves as capable of religious salvation. This point of view made interracial coupling spiritually and socially acceptable to hordes of lonely Spanish and mestizo men, who proceeded to have children by as many of the female slaves as they could.

Wolves at the Door

Throughout the mid-16th century, Puerto Rico struggled to survive devastating hurricanes, disease, and the boom-bust cycles of primary cash crops such as sugar and ginger. To the degree that the colony flourished,

Chronology of Puerto Rican History

100 AD – Puerto Rico's earliest known inhabitants, Los Arcaicos (the Archaics), migrate to the island
300 – Igneri Indians settle coastal Puerto Rico
600 – Taíno Indians establish settlements on Puerto Rico
1493 – invading Carib Indians reach Puerto Rico's shores; Christopher Columbus claims the island for Spain
1508 – Juan Ponce de León leads Spanish colonists to Puerto Rico in search of gold
1509 – Ponce de León's colonists establish the settlement of Caparra
1511 – Taínos and Caribs form an alliance against the Spaniards; settlers at Caparra move their community to a defensible island
1518 – first West African slaves are brought to Puerto Rico
1521 – colonists begin the fortification of San Juan
1538 – French forces raid San Germán; construction on the monumental Fuerte San Felipe del Morro begins in San Juan
1595 to 98 – English naval forces launch a series of offensives against San Juan; all fail

1625 – Dutch forces take San Juan, but withdraw due to disease and guerrillas
1626 to 1759 – Puerto Rico flourishes as a haven for smugglers and pirates
1791 – slave revolt in Haiti sends white planters fleeing to Puerto Rico; modernization of the island's sugar industry begins
1798 to 1810 – sugar, rum and coffee trade between Puerto Rico and the fledgling USA burgeons
1800 – population swells to 155,000; island painter José Campeche reaches the height of his career
1810 to 1822 – revolutions throughout Spain's American colonies cause an influx of Spanish loyalists to Puerto Rico
1838 – Spanish government quells a movement led by Buenaventura Quiñones to liberate Puerto Rico from colonial status
1849 – Manuel Alonso writes El Gíbaro, giving a face to the island's personality
1850 to 1867 – Puerto Rican liberation movement gathers strength under Ramón Emeterio Betances
1868 – revolutionaries take the town of Lares and declare a Puerto Rican republic, but the uprising fails
1873 – slavery is abolished

its growth came largely as a consequence of the island's strategic position. During this time, Spanish government officials described Puerto Rico as 'the entrance and key to all of the Indies' and 'the strongest foothold of Spain in America.' Almost invariably, the great fleets of treasure ships that Spain sent to the Americas made their first landfall at Puerto Rico; the ships then proceeded through the Pasaje de la Mona (Mona Passage) and veered south to claim Inca gold at the Isthmus of Panama, or west for Mexican silver at Veracruz.

French corsairs such as François LeClerc and English privateers such as John Hawkins and Francis Drake knew that the waters off Puerto Rico were perhaps the best place of all to disrupt or even paralyze Spanish shipping. Aware of this threat, the Spanish government began subsidizing the citizens of San Juan to fortify their town as early as 1521, when descendants of Ponce de León began building a stone-block house known as the Casa Blanca (White House). Shortly thereafter, inhabitants of the town began construction of a larger stone stronghold,

Chronology of Puerto Rican History

1895 – island-born painter Francisco Oller gains international acclaim

1897 – Spain charters Puerto Rico as an autonomous state under a Spanish governor

1898 – US forces invade Puerto Rico, ending the Spanish-American War; Spain cedes Puerto Rico to the US

1900 – US Congress passes the Foraker Act, granting a US-run civil government to Puerto Rico; island population exceeds 1 million

1917 – the Jones Act grants islanders US citizenship

1937 – student *independentistas* clash with police on Palm Sunday; 19 people die in the 'Masacre de Ponce'

1938 – Luis Muñoz Marín establishes the Partido Popular Democrático (PPD) to promote social and economic reform

1943 – Muñoz Marín and US President Roosevelt develop 'Operation Bootstrap,' a plan to industrialize Puerto Rico

1947 – with US Congressional approval, Puerto Ricans craft their own constitution and elect their first governor, Muñoz Marín

1950 – members of the new Partido Independentista Puertorriqueño (PIP) attack the governor's mansion; 27 people die

1951 – Puerto Rico becomes a US commonwealth; gunmen for the *independentista* movement attempt to assassinate US President Truman

1955 – the Instituto de Cultura Puertorriqueña begins a campaign to preserve and foster island arts

1956 – cellist Pablo Casals retires to the island to establish his world-famous music festival

1950 to 1960 – more than 1 million Puerto Ricans migrate to the US, primarily settling in New York City

1967 – Puerto Rico holds its first plebiscite to test public sentiment on the issue of Puerto Rico becoming a US state

1968 – the pro-statehood Partido Nuevo Progresista (PNP) is formed

1980 – island population passes 3 million

1989 – Hurricane Hugo devastates the island

1993 – the island's second referendum on statehood fails by a narrow margin

1998 – Hurricane Georges rakes the island, causing US$15 billion in damage; voters reject the referendum for US statehood in third islandwide plebiscite

La Fortaleza (the Fortress), designed to be the seat of Spanish colonial government. Today, La Fortaleza remains in use as the residence of the governor of Puerto Rico and is the oldest occupied executive mansion in the Americas.

After a French raid on San Germán in 1538, even La Fortaleza did not seem like adequate defense against a foreign invasion. So Spain drummed up funds from its richer colonies in the Americas and from the royal coffers to finance the construction of the monumental fortress of San Felipe del Morro – known simply as 'El Morro,' meaning 'the Headland' – on the cliffs guarding the entrance to Bahía de San Juan (San Juan Bay). Eventually, this military construction boom found total financing from the Mexican government, which paid Puerto Rico an annual *situado* (protection fee) to keep the sea lanes open and build more fortresses at San Juan, thereby assuring the safe passage of treasure fleets to and from Mexico. In a sense, Puerto Rico had a nice little protection racket going until Spain's enemies grew bold enough to put San Juan's fortifications to the test.

Following the outbreak of war between Spain and England in 1585 and Sir Francis Drake's defeat of the Spanish Armada in the English Channel in 1588, England's Queen Elizabeth hatched a plot to seize Puerto Rico. Led by veteran privateers John Hawkins and Drake, the English attacked El Morro on November 22, 1595. But the Spanish repelled the three-day onslaught with gusto, killing Hawkins and two other captains before forcing the invaders to retreat.

The English tried again three years later. The Earl of Cumberland, George Clifford, led a fleet of 20 ships to the north shore of Puerto Rico. But this time the English steered clear of the awesome firepower of San Juan's fortifications and made their assault over land from the beaches of Loíza. Eventually, Cumberland's forces drove the Spanish back to El Morro, burned San Juan and hammered at the fortress with cannons until the walls began to crumble and the island's governor surrendered. But the English only stayed in command for 65 days: An epidemic of dysentery wracked the British troops and local guerrillas harassed the invaders until Cumberland withdrew, fearing the arrival of Spanish reinforcements.

Apparently having not read their history lessons very well, the Dutch repeated the English debacle in 1625. Once again an enemy burned San Juan and secured a surrender, only to retreat in the face of disease and guerrilla attacks. Immediately, San Juan's citizens rebuilt and redoubled their fortifications, eventually turning their city into a walled bastion. Troops and administrators from Spain still dominated Puerto Rico's sociopolitical landscape, but the growing number of island-born colonists were a tough bunch. No foreign power would challenge them again for more than 150 years; none would succeed until 1898.

Outlaw Island

Like all of Spain's colonies in the Americas during the 17th century, Puerto Rico labored under the restrictions of a military dictatorship and Spain's tightfisted mercantile economy. During this century, Spain barred islanders from participation in their own government, restricted their movement around the island and limited their commerce with the outside world to trade with Spain, specifically the Compañía de las Indias in the Iberian port of Seville. Like it or not, Puerto Rican colonists had to send all their raw goods – particularly sugar and leather – in trade to Seville, where they were sold at prices set by Spanish accountants. In return (sometimes), the company sent a shipload of high-priced, heavily taxed finished goods such as clothes and furniture to the island for the few consumers who could afford such luxuries. Feeling doomed to poverty, many of the island's more adventuresome residents slipped away to join the gold rush in South America. Others, wedded to their island home, conspired to create an alternative to poverty through smuggling.

The political reality in Europe and the colonies was that Spain had been slipping into the role of a second-class power as the 17th century unfolded. The costly war with England, the defeat of the Armada, political corruption and intrigue, spendthrift monarchs, outrageous taxes and inept or half-hearted farming all left Spain with few resources to develop and maintain its colonies. Consequently, England, France and Holland claimed former Spanish colonies throughout the Lesser Antilles, as well as Jamaica and western Hispaniola (French Saint-Domingue). On Puerto Rico, Spain's declining power – and the fear that it would soon lose control of Mexico and the South American trade – compelled the mother country to direct obsessive attention and effort toward making San Juan a military fortress and naval harbor of the first magnitude. Such a concentrated focus on the colony's capital, of course, left the rest of the island unattended. So islanders living beyond the watchful eyes of Big Brother in San Juan began to trade with English, Dutch, French and North American colonists who called on obscure ports such as Cabo Rojo on the west coast, Ponce on the south coast and Fajardo on the east coast.

Eventually, the smuggling trade gave rise to a collection of freewheeling prosperous ports used for shipping everything from cane and corn to coffee and cattle. Finally, even the city's government officials, clergy and ambitious citizens became *contrabandistas* (smugglers). By the time the king of Spain sent his tough, Irish-born commissioner Alejandro O'Reilly to establish order in the 1760s, the colony was in economic disarray with virtually all of the island's 45,000 citizens involved in some way with smuggling. The legitimate economy of the colony was totally impoverished, as was the island's labor force. This included some 5000 African slaves and many more free itinerant laborers. Meanwhile, Puerto Rico completely lacked roads, bridges and schools. Lastly, islanders no longer thought of themselves as colonists: They were *puertorriqueños*.

In response to a 150-year legacy of Spanish neglect, corruption and economic anarchy, O'Reilly recommended a series of solutions: further strengthening the island's defenses; dropping trade restrictions between the island and the rest of the Spanish colonies; lowering taxes; building roads; shifting away from cattle raising in favor of increased cane farming; building better schools; and creating an incentive plan (including free land) to encourage literate, educated people to immigrate. The implementation of these measures more than tripled the island's population – from nearly 45,000 in 1765 to 155,000 by 1800. Eighteen new towns sprang up. Roads and schools were built. Island arts and music began to flourish, and people spoke proudly to one another in a home-grown dialect of Spanish infused with the Taíno and African words and expressions of more than two centuries. Puerto Ricans began to feel legitimate, cultivated and proud of their island and their emerging identity. Furthermore, they were not giving up the personal freedoms to which they had become accustomed during more than a century of neglect by the mother country. For the men of the island, freedom meant the right to feel like the kings of their own private fiefdoms – large or small – without interference from the government or the Catholic Church. For Puerto Rican women, the gains were smaller, especially for those who were members of the island's upper-class society, which mimicked Spain's cloistering of aristocratic women. Underclass women felt less fettered: The island's chronically short-handed labor pool meant jobs and the relative freedom that came with earning wages of their own.

Yanqui Dollars

When the US cast off its colonial shackles by defeating the British in the Revolutionary War in 1781, the victory spawned independence movements in Europe and the Americas. In 1789, the French became the first to join the revolutionary fury, and the resulting instability sent shock waves throughout the western world.

In the 18th century, Spain had become a satellite of France after the French installed relatives of their Bourbon monarchs in Madrid. Now, at the end of the century, Spain found itself caught up in a succession of European wars brought on by the revolution in France, the French-English rivalry for European dominance and Napoleon's imperial ambitions. Spain's monarchs began changing with each turn in the tides of war in Europe. And if bloodshed and lack of consistent leadership were not enough to hobble Spain, the English destruction of the Spanish fleet (along with the French) at the Battle of Trafalgar in 1805 clearly brought the former world power to its knees. This whipping nearly severed commercial relations between Spain and her colonies, including Puerto Rico.

The first effect of this European turmoil on the Caribbean colonies came in 1791, when French-owned slaves took advantage of the revolution in the mother country to rebel against the tyrannical European regime in Saint-Domingue, on western Hispaniola. Eventually, the self-liberated slaves succeeded in killing or driving many Europeans off the island and establishing the independent nation of Haiti. But the slave revolt was a protracted event that devastated the island's lucrative sugar trade.

The revolution on Hispaniola had positive consequences for Puerto Rico. Now traders – particularly those from the fledgling US – turned to Puerto Rico to supply the sugar and rum no longer available on wartorn Hispaniola. Meanwhile, white planters escaped Hispaniola to set up shop on Puerto Rico, and in so doing introduced much more efficient means of raising sugarcane and producing rum. For the first time in the island's modern history, Puerto Rico prospered. This fact was not lost on the English, who sent a fleet of 60 ships and 9000 redcoats to seize the island in April 1797. But in spite of the magnitude of the British assault force, island militias eventually drove the invaders back to sea and Puerto Rico resumed its trade with the US. This trade was sometimes legal or illegal depending on the changing regimes in Spain, but Puerto Rican dock workers kept hoisting the sacks of sugar and barrels of rum aboard US merchant ships, and the *yanqui* (Yankee) dollars kept flooding in.

But while the Puerto Ricans celebrated their new-found prosperity, the island's sister colonies saw Spain's loss of power in the Americas as a moment ripe for revolution. Between 1810 and 1822, liberal New World-born leaders such as Venezuelan Simón Bolívar led revolts that ousted the Spaniards from all their American colonies, from Argentina in the south to Mexico in the north. By the mid-1820s, Cuba and Puerto Rico were all that remained of Spain's huge New World empire.

Freedom Fever

Fearing it would lose Puerto Rico and Cuba as well, the Spanish Crown quickly set about dismantling the last vestiges of mercantilism by reducing tariffs, easing shipping regulations and opening more ports for foreign trade. To further guard against revolution in Puerto Rico, the Spanish king appointed a series of tyrannical military governors who ruled for 42 years with absolute power. One notorious governor, Miguel de la Torre, pacified the islanders with a regime dedicated to *los tres b's* (three b's): *baile, botella, baraja* (dancing, drinking, gambling). Meanwhile, Puerto Rico's sugar trade with the US grew by a factor of 10, with the States sending slaves and finished goods from its factories in exchange for the island's favors.

With economic growth, the island's population blossomed from about 155,000 at the end of the 18th century to 681,000 in 1872. By the end of the 19th century, that number had grown to nearly 1 million citizens. Unlike most other Caribbean islands, including Cuba, Puerto Rico did not increase its population through a massive influx of slaves. In fact, statistics show that the number of slaves actually decreased slightly, from 32,200 in 1827, in the early years of the economic boom, to 31,600 in 1872, the year before the Spaniards finally abolished slavery on the island. Rarely in the island's history did the slave population constitute more than 11% of the whole. Few Puerto Ricans could afford slaves, and the slave revolts on Hispaniola and elsewhere largely turned public sentiment against the barbaric institution.

During the mid-19th century, the number of white islanders doubled to almost 329,000, mostly due to an influx of Spanish loyalists fleeing revolutions in former Spanish colonies. Drawn to Puerto Rico by offers of free land for plantation developers, these refugees formed the bulk of an emerging agrarian aristocracy whose *haciendas* (agricultural estates) not only fueled the island's sugar boom but also made the production and export of coffee and tobacco big-money industries.

The number of free nonwhites also increased significantly during the mid-19th century, doubling to 257,700 as many people of color came to Puerto Rico from other Caribbean islands seeking jobs. These immigrants formed the primary labor source for the haciendas. These 'free laborers' – who became known as *agregados* – were 'squatting' on Crown lands, and after 1824 the government began evicting them in order to create a landless peasantry that had no choice but to seek employment on the haciendas or to enter sharecropping arrangements in order to secure food, shelter and clothing.

The thriving economy, draconian laws and a huge influx of conservative refugees loyal to the Crown subdued the revolutionary enthusiasm that might have otherwise spread over the island from liberation movements abroad. Nevertheless, democratic-minded Puerto Rican liberals dreamed of freedom from Spanish colonial rule. In 1838 the colony's government got wind of a revolutionary plot led by island-born Buenaventura Quiñones, executed some of the organizers and drove others into exile. But the lust for independence could not be stifled, and by the 1850s the Puerto Rican independence movement had found a passionate leader in Ramón Emeterio Betances. Born to an affluent family in Cabo Rojo, Betances studied in France and came to Mayagüez in the 1850s to practice medicine and promote island independence and social reforms such as the abolition of slavery. Betances formed a secret society to promote these goals, but the government discovered the group and forced Betances into exile in France.

Eventually the libertarian returned to Puerto Rico, but in 1867 government pressure forced him to flee to New York, where he joined Cuban revolutionaries in plotting the overthrow of the Spanish colonial governments on both islands. The following year, Betances traveled to Santo Domingo to establish a revolutionary committee for Puerto Rican freedom, purchasing 500 rifles, six cannons and a small ship to support revolutionary chapters on Puerto Rico. But once again the Spanish colonial government infiltrated the movement and began arresting the leaders.

The revolutionaries rallied their troops in frustration, and on September 23, 1868, several hundred men took action without the leadership of Betances, who had been detained by the English on St Thomas. The revolutionaries surprised a garrison of Spanish troops and seized the town of Lares, in the western interior of the island, shouting *¡Viva Puerto Rico Libre!* ('Long Live Free Puerto Rico!'). This rallying cry came to be known as the Grito de Lares (Cry of Lares) and continues to symbolize the Puerto Rican liberation movement.

The revolutionaries proclaimed a Puerto Rican republic, elected a provisional president and even got a priest to bless the new government, but the movement sputtered

The Grito de Lares lives on in modern mural art.

as moderate intellectuals and the working classes failed to rally under a banner proclaiming *'Libertad ó Muerte'* (Liberty or Death). Six weeks after it began, the revolution expired with most of the rebels dead or in jail, along with a large number of innocent people labeled as sympathizers.

But the Grito de Lares was not a cry in the wilderness. A few days after the capture of Lares, military leaders in Spain overthrew the monarchy of Queen Isabella II. On October 10, revolution broke out in eastern Cuba spawning a 10-year civil war. In response to these events, the new republican government in Spain made a number of concessions in subsequent years to the liberal demands of the colonies. The Spanish government abolished slavery and granted freedom of the press, the right to petition, the opportunity for Puerto Rico to send representatives to the Spanish Cortés (House of Representatives) and allowed the formation of elected municipal councils on the island. These events gave rise to the first political parties in Puerto Rico's history.

During the next two decades, changing regimes in Spain eventually dismantled many of the islanders' newly won freedoms, but political momentum for some form of self-government continued to gain strength among Puerto Ricans. In 1895, Cuban patriot-poet Jose Martí launched a second revolution to liberate his country. Shaken by the Cuban uprising and internal politics, the conservative government in Spain fell to liberals. A new spokesperson for Puerto Rican autonomy, Luis Muñoz Rivera, immediately went before the Spanish government to plead for Puerto Rican independence, and won. In 1897, Spain chartered Puerto Rico as an autonomous state under a Spanish governor and gave the island the right to self-govern according to laws made by elected officials of a bicameral parliament. Finally, Puerto Rico appeared to be on the brink of sovereignty.

Spanish-American War

Since the outbreak of the second revolutionary war in Cuba, in 1895, US economic interests on that island and sensational journalism

Luis Muñoz Rivera

highlighting Spanish atrocities against the Cubans pitched a strong case to the American government and citizenry for US intervention to 'liberate' Cuba. Initially, US leaders resisted the propaganda, but after the US battleship *Maine* exploded and sunk mysteriously in Havana's harbor on February 15, 1898, cries of 'Remember the *Maine!*' swayed US sentiment. Two months after the *Maine* disaster (for which the US blamed a Spanish mine), US President William McKinley approved a Congressional resolution calling for the immediate withdrawal of the Spaniards from Cuba. Spain responded by declaring war on the US.

On July 17, 1898, the inaugural date of the first Puerto Rican Parliament (with Muñoz Rivera at its head), Spanish troops surrendered to US forces at Santiago de Cuba. Eight days later, American troops landed at Guánica, on Puerto Rico's south coast, where they quickly subdued flaccid Spanish resistance. Some witnesses described the American invasion of Puerto Rico as a 'triumphant march,' not a battle. The Spanish government sued for peace, and the Puerto

Rican Parliament dissolved. At the Treaty of Paris in December, Spain ceded Puerto Rico to the US.

Cynics have long claimed that the US – with imperialist ambitions of its own – precipitated the Spanish-American War by asserting a military presence in the territorial waters of the Spanish colonies. As a result of its victory over Spain, the US solidified its sphere of influence in the Caribbean and secured strategic military, fueling and trading outposts for its merchant and naval fleets.

Struggling under Uncle Sam

For the next two years, US generals governed Puerto Rico – surprising a significant number of its inhabitants who believed that the Americans had arrived to free the island from colonial tyranny. Under the military regime, the government limited the freedom of the press and dissolved centuries of linkage between the Catholic Church and the government. This separation left hundreds of priests and nuns without salaries and ended the church's control over education on the island. American instructors and Protestant missionaries arrived to fill the void and begin teaching English to the population. American corporations moved in to buy out the haciendas and take over the island's sugar and tobacco industries. At the same time, the military government tried to anglicize the name of the island to 'Porto Rico' for easier pronunciation. Adding to islanders' disenchantment, a deadly hurricane hit in 1899, destroying the year's coffee crop – a setback from which the industry has never fully recovered. The good news about US rule was that the army distributed food to the needy, virtually eliminated yellow fever by improving sanitation conditions, vaccinated the islanders against smallpox and built roads.

Faced with popular uprising in the Philippines and realizing that martial law in Puerto Rico might promote similar troubles, the US Congress passed the Foraker Act in 1900 to grant civil government to the island. Under this proviso the island gained the right to elect an Executive Council, a House of Delegates and a Resident Commissioner as a nonvoting delegate to the US House of Representatives. The US president appointed the governor and judges of the Supreme Court of Puerto Rico. Islanders were taxed according to American laws but were not granted US citizenship. Much of the freedom that Puerto Rico had won from Spain in the 1897 charter of autonomy had disappeared.

Caught in the midst of a deepening identity crisis, Puerto Ricans chafed under US rule. During the first decades of the 20th century, the island reeled from labor strikes in the tobacco and cane industries while political parties gained passionate followings. Island political leaders such as Luis Muñoz Rivera kept up the pressure on the US for greater Puerto Rican freedom, and finally – just before the US entered WWI – Congress passed the Jones Act to expand the island's legislature and grant US citizenship to all residents of Puerto Rico.

During the first three decades of US rule, American investment nearly tripled the amount of land available for sugar production, and the cigar and textile industries began to grow as well. Wages improved, though they were still lower than those in many other Caribbean countries producing similar goods. In the same era, the population grew by 60% as modern medicine addressed traditional island plagues such as hookworm. The number of children enrolled in schools increased from 8% to 50%, and each year the Universidad de Puerto Rico (founded in 1903) expanded its facilities and student body.

But just as many Puerto Ricans were beginning to improve their individual circumstances, two hurricanes and the depression of the 1930s devastated the island's economy. By 1933, only 35% of the population had jobs. In the midst of this misery, Puerto Ricans blamed the US for their problems and began fervently championing a host of political parties. During the mid-1930s, Puerto Ricans looked back on nearly two decades of their political history with dismay: They saw that Puerto Rico and its friends in the US Congress had petitioned and proposed numerous bills asking the US to grant the island independence, autonomy or statehood, but the pleas had come to nothing.

Political demonstrations became commonplace in Puerto Rico by the second half of the 1930s. An encounter between members of the Partido Nacionalista Puertorriqueño (PNP; the Puerto Rican Nationalist Party) and the police in 1936 ended in the deaths of four citizens. In retaliation, nationalists assassinated the colonel of the insular police. The US colonial government responded by sentencing the leaders of the party to six to 10 years in US prisons. Nevertheless, remnants of the Nationalist Party continued to stage street demonstrations. In 1937, one of these marches was staged on Palm Sunday in Ponce, then the island's second-largest city. A conflict between marchers and police ensued and 19 people died in what came to be called the 'Masacre de Ponce' (Ponce Massacre).

Rising from the Rubble

A strong and reasonable voice emerged from the political chaos of the 1930s: that of Luis Muñoz Marín, son of the deceased political leader Luis Muñoz Rivera. In 1938, Muñoz Marín founded the Partido Popular Democrático (PPD; Popular Democratic Party) to advocate social and economic reform, promising 'bread, land and liberty.' Adopting the straw hat of the *jíbaro* – Puerto Rico's traditional mountain dweller and farmer – as its symbol, the party seemed like something of a joke to political insiders in San Juan and Washington, DC. But with a pledge to focus on improving the quality of island life rather than simply argue over Puerto Rico's status as a colonial protectorate, Muñoz Marín and his *populares* won the support of the island's poor, who voted the PPD to victory in every major election between 1940 and 1964.

With Muñoz Marín leading the island from a number of political positions and support from a succession of four US presidents, the PPD ushered the island through a series of massive changes in the next 25 years. In the early 1940s, the PPD developed a plan to shift the island's economic base from agriculture to manufacturing and tourism, gaining support in this effort from US President Franklin Roosevelt. This project,

which became popularly known as 'Operation Bootstrap,' aimed to kickstart the island's economy by encouraging US manufacturers to take advantage of the island's labor pool and invest in Puerto Rico, where all revenues were free from US income tax. Simultaneously, the PPD pressed for more political autonomy, and in 1947 the US granted Puerto Ricans the right to elect their own governor for the first time in the island's history. That leader, of course, was Luis Muñoz Marín.

Commonwealth Status

In the eyes of some islanders, Muñoz Marín sold out to the establishment by ceasing to push for Puerto Rican independence, and some of his most liberal supporters broke away from the PPD to form the Partido Independentista Puertorriqueño (PIP; Puerto Rican Independent Party). While the PIP clamored for island freedom from US colonial shackles, the US Congress passed a law in 1948 to grant the island a constitutional government. After a four-month constitutional convention, island leaders produced a constitution that designated a new relationship between Puerto Rico and the US: Puerto Rico became an *estado libre asociado* (associated free state), a commonwealth of the US. Voters approved the constitution and their new status by a margin of three to one on July 4, 1951. This new status meant that Puerto Rico superficially resembled a US state. However, islanders could not vote in US presidential elections, nor were they represented in the US Congress, except by a nonvoting Resident Commissioner in the US House of Representatives. One benefit of this special status was that islanders paid no US income taxes.

But through the evolution of Puerto Rico's relationship with the US during the early 1950s, militant groups continued the struggle for island independence. In 1950, a group of *independentista* militants attacked the governor's mansion in San Juan; guards fired back and 27 people died. A year later, Puerto Rican nationalists tried to assassinate US President Harry Truman in Washington, DC. In 1954, liberation gunmen opened fire

on a session of the US House of Representatives, shouting '¡Viva Puerto Rico Libre!' –
the famous Grito de Lares – wounding five
lawmakers. Despite the violence, pragma-
tists realized that, like it or not, the island's
economic welfare depended on continuing
its 'special relationship' with the US.

Best of Both Worlds?
The recent history of Puerto Rico is largely
the story of fitful but amazing economic
growth and cultural cross-pollination between the island and the 'Mainland' (the US).
Operation Bootstrap brought more than
2000 factories to the island before Muñoz
Marín retired from the governorship in
1964. By this time, manufacturing was well
on its way to dominating the island's gross
domestic product. But while manufacturing
produced hundreds of thousands of jobs,
large numbers of Puerto Ricans left the
island for better opportunities spawned by
the economic boom in the US resulting from
the Korean War. By 1960, almost a million
Puerto Ricans were living on the mainland,
many of them in New York's boroughs, especially El Barrio – 'Spanish Harlem' – on
Manhattan's Upper East Side.

Back on the island, school attendance, literacy rates, life expectancy and wages continued to improve. With this increased buying
power, Puerto Ricans moved to San Juan and
the other northern towns in droves, where
many bought TVs and cars at an astonishing
rate as signs of their new affluence.

With the flow of travel between the island
and the mainland, the wholesale importa-
tion of American pop culture, and the service of tens of thousands of the island's
young men in the US war in Vietnam, more
and more Puerto Ricans began to consider
US statehood desirable. In 1967, the island
government held the first plebiscite to test
local sentiment. The proposal for statehood
failed, but in 1968 the desire for it generated
a new political party, the Partido Nuevo
Progresista (PNP; New Progressive Party),
which continues to be a consistent voice for
statehood.

During the 1970s, the '80s and early '90s,
the PPD continued to endorse maintaining
the status quo – Puerto Rico's status as a
commonwealth of the US – while the new
PNP attracted more support for statehood.
The two parties traded the leadership of the
island's government back and forth several
times. During these decades, the population
ballooned to more than 3.5 million. The
island continued to draw outside investors
(mostly from the US) under a permutation
of Operation Bootstrap called Section 936,
the clause in the US Internal Revenue Code
that exempts manufacturers from paying
federal income tax on their operations in
Puerto Rico. Recent years have seen a stam-
pede of US and foreign banks to set up shop
in San Juan, and the US military presence –
particularly at the huge naval complex at
Roosevelt Roads on the island's east coast –
has been expanded to protect US interests
in the Caribbean as well as Puerto Rico's
economic dynamo.

Growing Pains
The end of the 20th century has seen Puerto
Rico wrestling with overpopulation, high
crime rates, chronic traffic problems, an
AIDS epidemic and persistently high unemployment. Nevertheless, Puerto Ricans seem
optimistic about the island's future. Under
the governorship of Pedro Rosselló, the
PNP called for an islandwide 'nonbinding'
plebiscite on US statehood in 1993. The push
for statehood failed by a narrow margin:
48.4% against, 46.2% in favor and 4.4% for
independence. Undaunted, Governor Rosselló and his party called for another plebiscite in 1998.

Those in favor of statehood (the PNP)
argued that it was time to end the island's
status as a colony, allow Puerto Ricans to
enjoy all the rights of other US citizens and
give the island access to federal money that
only full states enjoy. The PDP promoted a
continuation of the status quo, arguing that
the island needed to recognize and nurture
its 'special relationship' with the US, but
that full statehood would mean enforced
education in the English language and an
erosion of the island's Spanish culture.
Members of the marginal but vocal independent party wanted to throw off the

shackles of colonialism once and for all to let the island and its people stand proud and independent.

In anticipation of the plebiscite, Rosselló's PNP spent US$10 million in a campaign to promote Puerto Rican statehood on the island and among members of the US Congress, many of whom had consistently expressed resistance to the idea. The PNP got its message across. In March of 1998, the US House of Representatives voted in favor (by one vote) of recognizing Puerto Rico's right to hold the first-ever federally authorized plebiscite on the future of the island. However, the bill was bogged down in the US Senate.

Governor Rosselló announced that another nonbinding plebiscite would be held on December 13, 1998. But one element that galvanized opposition to the governor's pro-statehood campaign was the referendum's wording (as drafted by the PNP): According to the text describing each of the choices on the ballot, the island's present commonwealth status could be revoked at any time by the US Congress. Pro-commonwealth factions claimed that this was a scare tactic on the part of pro-statehood factions to induce people to vote against maintaining Puerto Rico's status as a commonwealth.

In reaction to the ballot text, the pro-commonwealth and pro-independence representatives in Puerto Rico's legislature formed a coalition. They forced the inclusion of the so-called fifth-column option on the ballot, which allowed citizens to vote for 'none of the above.'

On election day, 80% of the electorate turned out to vote. The fifth column won with 51%, the pro-statehood option garnered 46.5% and independence 3%. Governor Rosselló claimed victory for his pro-statehood forces and promised to take the vote as a mandate to persuade the US Congress to endorse Puerto Rican statehood. But the governor's bravura fooled no one: The majority vote for the fifth column was clearly a vote for the status quo. The number of voters in favor of Puerto Rico remaining a commonwealth had increased by more than 2% since the 1993 plebiscite.

As San Juan's present pro-commonwealth mayor, Sila Calderón, stated:

Commonwealth status is perfect for us. It gives us a union with the United States and allows us to maintain US citizenship, which we cherish, but also allows us to maintain our own identity, our fiscal autonomy, our language and our Olympic team.

For the moment, Sila Calderón speaks for the majority, and she may be in the governor's office as Puerto Rico enters the new millennium. In the meantime, Puerto Rico's legal 'adoption' process remains incomplete.

GEOGRAPHY

Cartographers group Puerto Rico with the Caribbean's three largest islands – Cuba, Jamaica and Hispaniola – in the so-called Greater Antilles. But at 100 miles long and 35 miles across, Puerto Rico is clearly the little sister, stuck off to the east of Hispaniola at about 18° north latitude, 66° west longitude. With its four principal satellite islands – Islas Mona and Desecheo to the west, Culebra and Vieques to the east – and a host of cays hugging its shores, Puerto Rico claims approximately 3500 sq miles of land, making the Commonwealth slightly larger than the Mediterranean island of Corsica or the second-smallest state in the US, Delaware. The perimeter of the island measures 311 miles, but the ragged texture of the coast gives Puerto Rico about 750 miles of tidal shoreline.

Like almost all the islands ringing the Caribbean Basin, Puerto Rico owes its existence to a series of volcanic events that took place along the dividing line between the North American and Caribbean Plates. These eruptions built up layers of lava and igneous rock and created an island with four distinct geographical zones: the central mountains, karst country, the coastal plain and the coastal dry forest. At the heart of the island, running east to west, stands a spine of steep, wooded mountains called the Cordillera Central. The peak of Cerro de Punta rises 4389 feet near the center of the island to mark the highest point in Puerto Rico; at the eastern end of the Cordillera Central,

3496-foot El Yunque (the Anvil) gathers a miasma of clouds to its slopes and creates a setting for the dramatic tropical rain forest of the same name. Monte Guilarte, Cerro Maravilla and Cerro Los Tres Picachos are other prominent peaks rising out of the western and central cordillera.

The lower slopes of the cordillera give way to foothills, comprising a region on the island's north coast known as 'karst country.' In this part of the island, erosion has worn away the limestone, leaving a karstic terrain of dramatic sinkholes, hillocks and caves.

The northern fringe of the island spreads out into a coastal plain between 8 and 12 miles wide, while the coastal plain on the south side of the island is only a few miles wide. These plains were traditionally the site of sugarcane plantations and cattle ranches, but with the industrialization of the island, factories and towns have filled in a lot of the plains along the northwest coast between San Juan and Aguadilla.

The southwest corner of the island sustains an unusual desert wilderness called the coastal dry forest, which is home to a rich collection of trees, cactus and migratory birds found nowhere else on the island (and only rarely in tropical maritime settings worldwide).

Forty-five nonnavigable rivers and streams rush from the mountains and through the foothills to carve the coastal valleys, particularly on the east and west ends of the island, where sugarcane, coconuts and a variety of fruits are cultivated. The island's longest river is the Río Grande de Loíza, which flows north to the coast. Other substantial rivers include the Río Grande de Añasco, the Río Grande de Arecibo and the Río de la Plata.

Surprisingly there are no large natural lakes on the island, although there are 12 artificial reservoirs to supply Puerto Rico with adequate drinking water and water-power for hydroelectricity. An array of coral reefs – particularly off the south and east coasts – supports a small fishing industry.

Little of the island's virgin forest remains, but second- and third-growth forests totaling 140 sq miles now comprise significant woodland reserves, mostly in the center of the island. One-third of Puerto Rico's land is suitable for agriculture, but after centuries of use, only about 5% of this land is truly fertile. The mineral resources of the island represented, of course, the island's main draw to the Spaniards back in 1508, but the gold has long since disappeared. Today, the island supports profitable copper, phosphate, cement-making, glass-making and marble industries. San Juan, Ponce and Mayagüez constitute Puerto Rico's major seaports.

CLIMATE

Near-constant pleasant weather sets the tempo for life on Puerto Rico.

Temperature

Daily temperatures on the coast average about 73°F during the coolest months, January and February; during the hottest months – July, August and September – the mercury climbs to an average of 80°F. While high humidity is a fact of life here as in most tropical maritime climates, persistent easterly trade winds and local sea breezes make the air feel much fresher than that of other tropical regions such as Southeast Asia or nearby Central America. 'Continentals' drawn to the northwest coast of the island for world-class surfing have often compared Puerto Rico's climate to that of Southern California, Hawaii and the Pacific beaches of Oaxaca, Mexico. Of course, the mountains can be much cooler than the beaches, and night-time temperatures sometimes dip below 50°F at the higher elevations.

Rainfall

The mountain slopes of the Cordillera Central average more than 100 inches of rain per year, which accounts for the brilliant green of the vegetation, the rain forest environment of the Caribbean National Forest (commonly known as El Yunque) and the lush growing conditions for coffee. Rainfall in the north coastal region averages 60 to 80 inches a year. The driest region of the island is the southern coastal lowland, particularly west of Ponce, where only about 37 inches of rain fall per year. In contrast, the wettest area on the island is – not surprisingly – the

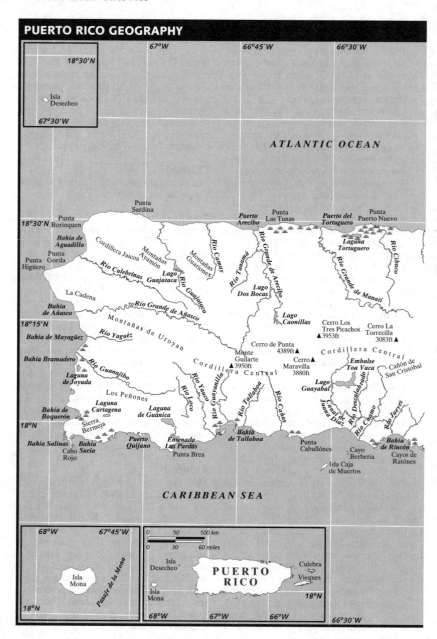

PUERTO RICO GEOGRAPHY

PUERTO RICO GEOGRAPHY

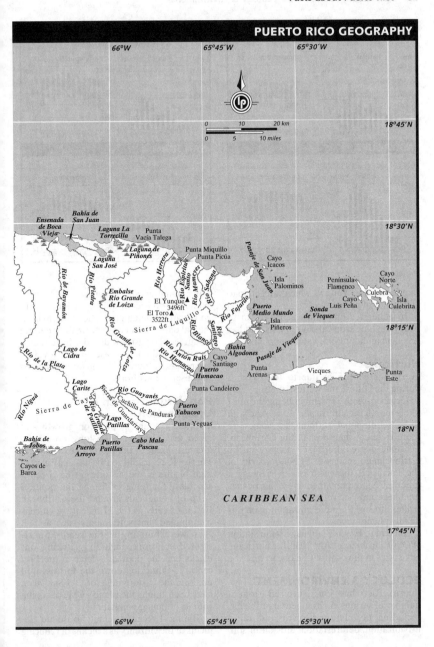

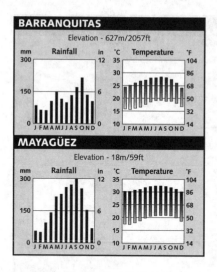

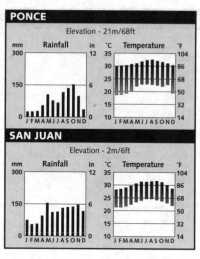

rain forest of El Yunque, which can get up to 200 inches of rain per year.

In general, rain comes in the form of heavy daytime tropical cloudbursts that last less than an hour before sun reappears.

Hurricanes

Hurricane season in Puerto Rico comes during the hottest and wettest months – July to October – with September being the most likely month for a hurricane strike. And with the onset of global warming, hurricanes are more frequent than ever in the Caribbean. To some degree, hurricane activity in the Caribbean correlates to El Niño activity in the Pacific: If the earth is experiencing a quiet El Niño year, then more hurricanes are likely, and vice versa. See the boxed text 'Killer Storms' for more information on this deadly phenomenon.

Tune in to English-language radio station WOSO San Juan, at AM 1030, for hurricane advisories in the central Caribbean.

ECOLOGY & ENVIRONMENT

Puerto Rico has long suffered from a number of serious environmental problems, including population growth and rapid urbanization, deforestation, erosion of soil, water pollution and mangrove destruction. While Puerto Ricans still have a long way to go toward undoing generations of environmental damage and preserving their natural resources, the past few decades have seen a general gradual increase in the level of awareness, resources and action dedicated to conservation efforts.

Population Growth & Urbanization

Without a doubt, population growth and rapid urbanization have long posed the greatest threat to the island's environment. Puerto Rico traditionally has had a very high birthrate and historically has been a sanctuary for refugees fleeing the political strife of homelands around the Caribbean Basin. As early as the 17th century, citizens complained that settlements such as San Juan were bursting at the seams. Short-sighted solutions, including locking out blacks and the poor or – later in the 19th century – knocking down the fortress wall marking the eastern edge of Old San Juan, have been among the island's ways of coping with its booming population.

The most recent attempts to isolate elements of the citizenry as a means of reducing

Killer Storms

The word 'hurricane,' denoting fierce cyclonic storms with winds in excess of 75mph, comes to English and Spanish from the language of Puerto Rico's Taíno Indians and their god of malevolence, Jurakán. This fact is warning enough that Puerto Rico lies along one of the most frequently traveled paths of these vicious tropical storms. Generally, the 'seeds' of these storms begin to grow off the west coast of Africa near the Cape Verde Islands, then migrate across the equatorial girdle of the Atlantic to the southern Caribbean as upper-atmospheric disturbances driven by the easterly trade winds. Here they linger and pick up moisture and energy until the Coriolis effect of Earth's spinning propels the growing storms north through the Caribbean and/or the Gulf of Mexico. Eventually, many of these storms pose a threat to the southern and eastern US coasts.

Puerto Rico suffered devastation from three storms – Hugo, Marilyn and Hortense – in the 10 years preceding 1998. Just when islanders were beginning to think that enough was enough, the so-called storm of the century, Georges, struck a direct blow. On September 21, 1998, Georges tore into Puerto Rico with sustained winds of more than 110mph, raking the island from east to west and causing damages estimated in excess of US$15 billion before going on to pulverize the Dominican Republic, Haiti, Cuba, the Florida Keys and the US Gulf Coast.

But the island was ready. Fewer than a half-dozen people were killed. Most telephone service was uninterrupted. Shipping and air traffic began flowing in and out of the island within 24 hours, and all major roads were cleared of debris. Meanwhile, hotels kept their guests healthy, cool and happy with auxiliary generating systems and water supplies. Amazingly, the government restored water and electricity to more than half of the island within five days (the less-powerful Hurricane Hugo had disrupted basic services for more than two weeks in 1989).

Good, long-range storm predictions (broadcast widely on TV and radio and in newspapers), thorough preparation and the nearly universal practice of building new houses and public and commercial buildings of cement block or reinforced concrete went a long way toward reducing casualties and property damage. A month after Georges cut its swath through the Caribbean, life for most Puerto Ricans and travelers to the island was back to normal. Unfortunately, Puerto Rico's poorer and less-prepared neighbors – the Dominican Republic, Haiti and Cuba – suffered from a lack of shelters and basic services, while mourning the more than 500 people who lost their lives.

RANDALL PEFFER

In the wake of Georges

population density have included the development of large, low-income federal housing projects called *caserios*. While Puerto Rico's population has virtually doubled to 3.8 million during the past 50 years, these caserios have become overcrowded hellholes suffering from crime and drug abuse.

As recently as 10 years ago, sociologists identified the caserios as a nightmare vision of the island's future. They saw Puerto Rico's population density approaching that of Singapore and projected that the expansion of metropolitan San Juan would envelope virtually all land within a 20-mile radius of the old city.

All this has come to pass, but over the same decade the birthrate on the island has fallen from almost four children per mother to two. At the onset of the new millennium, the current birthrate puts the island on track for zero population growth within the decade.

Without a doubt, the island's north coast is densely populated, and this density has caused a constellation of woes ranging from polluted estuaries to massive traffic jams. But urban planners are beginning to realize their dreams for an urban rail transit system to reduce highway traffic (see the San Juan chapter for specifics). Planners are also changing community zoning laws to promote clusters of multifamily housing rather than allowing the remaining open space to be gobbled up by single-family homes.

Deforestation & Soil Erosion

During the late 19th and early 20th centuries, massive logging operations denuded much of the island. Consequently, untold acres of rich mountain topsoil have eroded away to clog the mouths of rivers and streams. But in the 1920s and '30s, thoughtful islanders and forward-looking conservationists in the island's US colonial government began to set aside and reforest an extensive network of wilderness reserves, mostly in karst country and the Cordillera Central.

Today these reserves are mature forests, and nearly the entire central part of the island – about one-third of Puerto Rico's landmass – is sheltered by a canopy of trees.

While the creation of wilderness reserves and reforestation have retarded Puerto Rico's erosion problems, much damage has been done by clearing hillside land for housing subdivisions in places such as Guaynabo and Trujillo Alto, both suburbs of San Juan. Consequently, when heavy rains and hurricanes strike, mudslides and hillside streets that turn into rivers threaten life and property.

Water Pollution

Reforestation, the creation of wilderness reserves to preserve mountain watersheds and generally thoughtful creation of mountain reservoirs have gone a long way toward assuring that the island's freshwater resources remain pollution-free. Nevertheless, streams, rivers and estuaries on the coastal plain have long been polluted by agricultural runoff, industry and inadequate sewer and septic systems. And while a number of environmental groups lobby for the cleanup of these cesspools, little has been accomplished. Currently, visitors should not be tempted to swim in rivers, streams or estuaries near the coast (including Bahía de San Juan) – nor should they eat fish or shellfish from these waters – because of the risk of disease and chemical pollutants.

Mangrove Destruction

As with the island's other environmental problems, mangrove destruction was at its worst decades ago when Operation Bootstrap and the rush to develop business and housing lots saw the devastation of vast mangrove swamps, particularly along the island's north shore in the vicinity of Bahía de San Juan. Small bays such as Laguna Condado, now lined with hotels, homes and businesses, were rich mangrove estuaries just 50 years ago.

Environmentalists began fighting to preserve the island's remaining mangrove estuaries in the mid-1970s, and the late '90s have brought a number of significant victories in this arena. Environmentalists won a court battle in 1998 to preserve most of the land at the western end of Laguna de Piñones, long slated for development as resort property, as wilderness. Environmentalists have won a similar battle to protect the mangroves around La Parguera, on the island's southwest shore. The recent creation of the huge 2883-acre Reserva Nacional de Investigación Estuarina de Bahía de Jobos (National Estuarine Research Reserve at Bahía de Jobos; see Aguirre & Bahía de Jobos in the South Coast chapter) assures the preservation of the island's largest mangrove estuary, although one power plant stands on the fringe and a second may be coming.

Recycling

Although Puerto Rico now has a government recycling campaign, there are very few receptacles in public places for the recycling of aluminum cans or other materials. The Solid Waste Management Authority collects cans, glass, paper and plastic on the second Saturday of every month as if recycling day is simply another religious feast day to observe and forget. Meanwhile, about 8000 tons of garbage overwhelm island landfills to the point that many have been stuffed to capacity and closed.

Conservation Groups

To combat the mounting destruction of the island's environment, citizens in many municipalities have formed local environmental action groups, while a number of organizations lead the fight islandwide. Contact one of these groups if you see a problem or – even better – want to collaborate with professionals and volunteers to help save the island:

Campers Association of Puerto Rico
☎ 787-760-1422

Caribbean Environmental Information
☎ 787-751-0239

Conservation Trust of Puerto Rico
☎ 787-722-5834

Environmental Coalition of Puerto Rico
☎ 787-765-4303

Natural History Society of Puerto Rico
☎ 787-726-5488

Puerto Rican Association of Water Resources
☎ 787-729-6951

Puerto Rican Conservation Foundation
☎ 787-763-9875

FLORA

Puerto Rico has an unusually varied topography for such a small area, and this has made the island a rich garden. Thousands of tropical plant varieties grow here, and a short drive can transport a nature lover between entirely different ecosystems. Mangrove swamps and coconut groves dominate the north coast, while El Yunque's rain forest at the east end of the island supports mahogany trees and more than 50 varieties of wild orchid. Giant ferns thrive in the rain forest as well as in the foothills of karst country, while cacti, mesquite forest and bunchgrass reign on the dry southwest tip of the island, which has the look of the African savanna.

Exotic shade trees have long been valued in this sunny climate, and most of the island's municipal plazas spread beneath canopies of magnificent *ceibas* or *kapoks* (silk-cotton tree), the *flamboyán* (poinciana) with its flaming red blossoms, and the African tulip tree. Islanders often adorn their dwellings with a profusion of flowers such as orchids, bougainvillea and poinsettias, and tend lovingly to fruit trees that bear papaya, *uva caleta* (sea grape), *carambola* (star fruit), *panapen* (breadfruit) and *plátano* (plantain). Of course, sugarcane dominates the plantations of the coastal lowlands, while farmers raise coffee on the steep slopes of the Cordillera Central.

FAUNA
Land Mammals

Very few of the land mammals that make their home on Puerto Rico are native to the island; most mammal species have been either accidentally or intentionally introduced to the island over the centuries. Among the most distinctive of these is the Paso Fino horse, which is a small-boned, easy-gaited variety. The Paso Finos have been raised on the island since the time of the Spanish conquest, when they were introduced to the New World to supply the conquistadores on their expeditions throughout Mexico and the rest of the Americas. These horses may be seen in any number of parades and can be rented from stables offering rides at nature attractions such as El Yunque or at popular beaches. But the horses are most dramatic on the island of Vieques, off Puerto Rico's east coast, where they roam in wild herds on vast tracts of land owned by the US Navy.

Not far from Vieques lies the 39-acre Cayo Santiago, where a small colony of rhesus monkeys introduced for scientific study in 1938 has burgeoned into a community of more than 700 individuals. The island is off-limits to all but scientists from the Universidad de Puerto Rico, but a tourist boat brings the curious to snorkel on adjacent reefs, and the monkeys always flock to trees on the water's edge for a good view of their odd-looking cousins with the masks and flippers.

Other prevalent land mammals that a visitor will likely encounter include the mongoose and numerous species of bat. The mongoose was introduced to control the rat population in the days of the sugarcane plantations and has since overrun the island.

Reptiles & Amphibians
Puerto Rico is home to more than a dozen species of snake (none of which are poisonous), including the Puerto Rican boa, which grows to more than 7 feet in length. Into this mix goes a host of small and not-so-small lizards – including the 3-foot-long giant iguanas of Isla Mona and the large anoles. Another giant anole (more than 2 feet long), called the *culebra*, has long been associated with the island of the same name. Scientists still believe that the culebra haunts the island's mountainous wildlife reserves, but there have been no documented sightings of the lizard during the last 30 years.

The largest reptiles on the island are a species of alligatorlike caiman, which was introduced to the island during the 1970s in the form of exotic pets released into the wild. These animals have actually become a plague in the vicinity of Laguna Tortuguero, on the island's north-central coast, where locals hunt the animals for meat (see the boxed text 'Look, Mom, No Hand!' in the North Coast chapter for more on this).

Numerous species of toad and frog populate the island. The *sapo concho* is an endangered toad that inhabits the dry forest of the

southwest coast; scientists regularly monitor this toad's ability to reproduce and thrive as a measure of the health of the dry forest ecosystem. Then there is the de facto national animal, the distinctive *coquí*, a species (with many subspecies) of tiny tree frog found nowhere else on earth. The coquí's signature evening song forms a perfect musical seventh. These frogs live naturally in a variety of habitats, from the rain forest to the coastal plain. But Puerto Ricans are so charmed by the tiny creatures that they have captured them and introduced them to city parks and suburban flower gardens.

Puerto Rico's beloved mascot, the *coquí*

Recently, some tour guides at El Yunque have reported that poisonous snakes have been introduced to the forest as a result of people freeing exotic pets into the wild. We cannot confirm this as fact, but given the island's centuries-old tradition of releasing exotic animals such as the wild Paso Fino horses of Vieques and the caimans of Laguna Tortuguero, the snake story has plenty of historical precedent. Hikers and campers should inquire about snake threats with local rangers, brush up on their snake identification skills and be prepared.

Birds & Insects
More than 60 species of bird inhabit the rain forest of El Yunque, including the greenish-blue, red-fronted Puerto Rican parrot, which is on the edge of extinction. The coastal dry forest of Guánica features more than 130 bird species, largely songbirds. Some of these are

migratory fowl, such as the prairie warbler and the northern parula. Many are native species, including the lizard cuckoo and the endangered Puerto Rican nightjar. One of the joys of winter beachcombing is watching the aerial acrobatics of brown pelicans as they hunt for fish.

The island also has an ample supply of unusual flying and crawling insects, including a large tropical relative of the firefly called the *cucubano*, and a centipede measuring more than 6 inches in length with a sting that can kill.

Marine Life

Terrestrial species represent only a small part of Puerto Rico's animal life. Much of what thrills nature lovers about the island swims here. Puerto Rico's mangrove estuaries and vast coral reefs are the nurseries and feeding grounds for hundreds of species of tropical fish. And not just sergeant majors, angel fish, groupers and lobsters – Puerto Rico is one of the best places in the world for divers to come face-to-face with large barracudas, manta rays, octopus, moray eel and plentiful nurse sharks. Endangered giant sea turtles such as the hawksbill, green and leatherback nest on Puerto Rican beaches, particularly on the island of Culebra. Game fish such as tuna and blue marlin patrol the deep. Schools of porpoise play in the bow waves of boats off Fajardo, manatees wallow in the shallows and estuaries (especially on the south shore), pilot whales frolic between the islands of Culebra and Vieques, and humpback whales spout and sing their mating songs each winter within view of the island's west coast.

Coral Ecology A coral is a tiny animal with a great gaping mouth, surrounded by tentacles for gathering food, at one end. The polyps, which resemble flowers or cushions upholstered with plush fabric, live protected by external skeletons, the production of which is dependent upon algae that live inside the polyps' tissue. The creatures live in vast colonies that reproduce both asexually by budding, and sexually through a synchronous release of spermatozoa that turns the surrounding sea milky. Together they build up huge frameworks – the reefs.

A reef is usually composed of scores of species of coral, each occupying its own niche. However, all corals can flourish only close to the ocean surface, where they are nourished by sunlight in clear, unpolluted waters above 70°F. Each species has a characteristic shape – bulbous cups bunched like biscuits in a baking tray for the star coral; deep, wending valleys for the well-named brain coral. Deeper down, where light is scarcer, massive corals flatten out, becoming more muted in color. Deeper still, soft corals – those without an external skeleton – predominate. These lacy fans and waving cattails look like plants, but a close perusal shows them to be menacing animal predators that seize smaller creatures, such as plankton.

Coral reefs are the most complex and sensitive of all ecosystems. Taking thousands of years to form, they are divided into life zones gauged by depth, temperature and light. When a coral polyp dies, its skeleton turns to limestone that another polyp may use to cement its own skeleton. The entire reef system is gnawed away by parrotfish and other predators.

Until now, Puerto Rico's coral reefs have been spared the wholesale devastation that has been typical of reefs in places such as Bermuda, the Bahamas and even nearby Hispaniola. During the 20th century, local fishing fleets have preyed upon the reefs of these islands, often pouring bleach into the water to drive fish out of hiding and killing the coral as a result. In Puerto Rico, the combination of a traditional diet not heavily dependent on seafood and the availability of imported fish has kept the inshore fishery a true cottage industry that has had little effect on the island's vast reef system.

Likewise, tourism in the form of careless divers, snorkelers and cruising yachts has been less of a threat to Puerto Rican reefs than in the neighboring US Virgin Islands, for the simple reason that wind and wave conditions are rougher in Puerto Rico. As a result, far fewer novices unaware of environmental concerns now tend to visit Puerto

Rico's reefs. For the most part, diving in Puerto Rico is an offshore experience that involves a substantial commitment of time and money, the benefit of which is making the trip in the company of professionals well-versed in conserving the island's undersea resources.

Only in recent years have casual snorkelers discovered the easily accessible fringe reefs of Culebra, Vieques and the nature reserve of Las Cabezas de San Juan. These reefs have now begun to show areas of dead coral resulting from careless divers, souvenir collectors and poor anchoring techniques.

For more information on the fragile reef ecology, pick up Dr William S Alevizon's superb *Caribbean Reef Ecology* (Pisces Books).

Cruelty to Animals

Cockfights are a popular sport on Puerto Rico. The owners and trainers of gamecocks often regard their birds with profound affection and respect. They truly do not want their animals to die. But no one can effectively argue that lashing spurs to an animal and teaching it to use them to slice another animal to death *isn't* an act of cruelty. See the boxed text 'Bloody Birds' in the Facts for the Visitor chapter for more on this popular pastime.

PARKS & RESERVES

One of the features that distinguishes Puerto Rico from its Caribbean neighbors is its collection of more than a dozen well-developed and protected wilderness areas, which offer an array of exploration and camping opportunities. Most of these protected areas are considered *reservas forestales* (forest reserves) or *bosques estatales* (state forests), although these identifiers are often treated interchangeably in government-issued literature and maps. See the regional chapters for more details on the areas mentioned below.

The best-known of these preserves is the 43-sq-mile Caribbean National Forest, generally referred to as **El Yunque**, which dominates the cloudy yet sun-splashed peaks at the east end of the island. A second large tract of forest, the **Reserva Forestal Toro Negro**, dominates the central section of the cordillera and encompasses the island's highest peak (Cerro de Punta).

Reserva Forestal Carite, Bosque Estatal de Guilarte and Bosque Estatal de Maricao are all on the slopes of the cordillera. The **Bosque Estatal de Río Abajo** covers 5780 acres in karst country near the Observatorio de Arecibo (Arecibo Observatory). **Bosque Estatal de Guajataca** is a slightly smaller preserve near the northwest corner of the island, while **Bosque Estatal de Guánica**, on the southwest coast, is home to a desertlike tropical dry forest ecosystem on the edge of a rugged coast.

Another coastal preserve is the 316-acre **Reserva Natural de las Cabezas de San Juan** (Cabezas de San Juan Nature Reserve), at the northeast corner of Puerto Rico, where El Faro (the Lighthouse) stands guard over the offshore cays. Eighteen miles east of here lies the island of Culebra, 7 miles long and 4 miles wide. Much of the island has been designated the Culebra National Wildlife Refuge under the control of the US Fish and Wildlife Service.

Some 300 acres of wilderness make up the **Parque de las Cavernas del Río Camuy** (Camuy River Caves Park), near Lares in karst country; the park marks the entrance to one of the largest known cave systems in the world and is also the site of one of the world's largest underground rivers.

The most isolated of Puerto Rico's nature sanctuaries, **Isla Mona**, lies about 50 miles east of Mayagüez across the often turbulent waters of Pasaje de la Mona. This tabletop island is sometimes called Puerto Rico's Galápagos – or more recently, Jurassic Park – because of its isolation and total lack of development, 200-foot limestone cliffs, honeycomb of caves and giant iguanas.

Commonwealth or US federal agencies administer most of the natural reserves on the island, and admission to these areas is generally free. Private conservation groups own and operate a few of the nature preserves, including Las Cabezas de San Juan; visitors to these places should expect to pay an entrance fee (usually under US$5).

GOVERNMENT & POLITICS

Puerto Rico has been a US commonwealth since 1951, operating as a representative democracy much like the 50 states of the Union. Like both federal and state governments in the US, Puerto Rico's constitution (1951) provides for three branches of government: executive, legislative and judicial. Islanders elect their governor for four-year terms, with no term limits. The legislature has two houses: The Senate normally includes 27 members and the House of Representatives has 51 members. Citizens from eight senatorial districts and 40 representative districts elect their legislators to serve four-year terms. The governor holds the right to appoint Supreme Court judges as well as judges on all the lesser courts, with the exception of judges serving on the Federal District Court, who are appointed by the US president. Seventy-eight *municipios* with mayors and assemblies manage the island's town and city governments.

Like the 50 'full' states in the Union, Puerto Rico has the right to govern itself in all matters of internal affairs but yields to the US government when it comes to defense, foreign affairs, postal service and customs regulations. Citizens of the island are also US citizens, and men over 18 years old are eligible for military conscription in the US armed forces. However, Puerto Ricans do not enjoy the right to vote in US presidential elections, and the island has no voting members in the US Senate or House of Representatives. The island's only voice in the federal government is that of its Resident Commissioner, a nonvoting member of Congress. This lack of representation has been a driving force for both advocates of full statehood and those favoring total independence. See the History section, earlier in this chapter, for more on recent events in Puerto Rico's struggle for consensus on the island's future.

Puerto Rico has a number of political parties, but only two of them have enough clout to gain a majority in the island's government. The Partido Popular Democrático (PPD) is the party that Luis Muñoz Marín began in the late 1930s, and it dominated island politics until the 1970s. This party favors the island remaining a commonwealth. The Partido Nuevo Progresista (PNP) favors statehood and has controlled the government for most of the 1990s under the leadership of Governor Pedro Rosselló. The small but vocal Partido Independentista Puertorriqueño (PIP) keeps up a constant clamor for island independence. The Partido Nacionalista Puertorriqueño (PNP) was the militant group behind the 1951 assassination attempt on US President Harry Truman and the attack on the US House of Representatives in 1954 (see the History section, earlier in this chapter).

ECONOMY

For nearly 450 years, Puerto Rico staggered under a colonial economy based on supplying agricultural products and raw materials to Spain and then the US. The island began a dramatic economic shift toward a manufacturing-based economy during the 1940s under the auspices of Operation Bootstrap. This transition was also aided by a new agency of the island government called Fomento (Encouragement), which was established to promote economic development. By the end of the 20th century, Puerto Rico's economy had totally changed its face from an agricultural to an industrial and service-oriented base. During this metamorphosis, the island's gross domestic product (GDP) increased from US$759 million to US$23 billion, taking Puerto Rican workers from the ranks of the poorest in Latin America to the richest, with an annual per-capita income of about US$8000. Nevertheless, this figure represents only one-third of the average income in the US. Still, at the onset of the 21st century, Puerto Rico is clearly the economic hub of the Caribbean.

Economic Sectors

Today, manufacturing accounts for more than 40% of Puerto Rico's GDP, with 2000 factories employing over 160,000 people. Dominating this sector of the economy are chemical-producing factories; pharmaceutical production is at the heart of this industry. Presently there are about 100 drugmakers on the island – representing many of the world's major pharmaceutical companies – with most of the factories concentrated along the coastal plain east and west of San Juan. Puerto Rico is also a major producer of electrical machinery, scientific instruments and rum (83% of the rum sold in the US is made here). Rubber and plastic products are also important exports. Currently, agriculture only represents 1% of the island's GDP.

Service industries as a whole account for more than 55% of the GDP. The finance, insurance and real estate sectors lead the growth as the 'Golden Mile' of San Juan's Hato Rey business district continues to burgeon as a major international banking capital. Tourism accounts for 7% of the GDP and employs more than 60,000. Retail and wholesale businesses contribute a similar number of jobs. Construction, mining, transportation and utilities provide employment for some 110,000 islanders. Government is the second-largest employer on the island with almost a quarter-million workers.

Despite the economic growth, unemployment rates are somewhere between 13% and 30%. Many families depend on the federal food stamp program, and nearly half of Puerto Rico's 20,000 farms produce only a subsistence income for those who operate them. Fishing is another subsistence-level industry that adds little to the economy. The one exception in this sector is the tuna industry centered in Mayagüez, which ships more than US$400 million worth of canned tuna to the US each year.

POPULATION & PEOPLE

Long a pastoral oasis, Puerto Rico has become one of the most densely populated places on earth during the second half of the 20th century. Currently more than 3.8 million people live on the island. Estimates place the island's population density at more than 100 people per sq mile – denser than any state in the US and just short of the density found in Taiwan and South Korea. A high birthrate and dramatic increases in life expectancy owing to better health care have been principal factors in the island's rapid population growth. Puerto Rico's popula-

tion figures include tens of thousands of recent immigrants from economically troubled Cuba and the Dominican Republic.

These statistics can be deceptive, however, because the bulk of the island's population has migrated to a handful of urban areas. At least 1.6 million people live in metropolitan San Juan, while the cities of Caguas, Ponce, Mayagüez, Aguadilla and Arecibo account for another million citizens. Beyond the *tapones* (traffic jams) that result from the cities' endless arrays of traffic lights and narrow streets, Puerto Rico remains a place of windy peaks, quiet cane fields and empty beaches.

Class Structure

Most ethnologists agree that Borinquen's Taíno Indians disappeared as an identifiable group by the beginning of the 17th century. The Taínos succumbed to diseases brought from Europe, racial mixing and cultural assimilation with the Spanish conquistadores and the African slaves who were brought to the island during the first century of Spanish conquest (see the History section, earlier in this chapter). During the next 300 years of the colony, Spaniards, *criollos* (island-born people of European descent) and new immigrants from places such as France, Italy and the Canary Islands evolved a rigidly stratified class system – especially in San Juan – more or less identical to those of Spain's other American colonies. While wealth figured as part of the equation, bloodlines were at least as important in determining social status. Pure-blooded Europeans and their criollo descendants topped the pyramid of power and social acceptability. Beneath this aristocracy, Puerto Ricans lined up according to the percentage of European or 'white' blood they could claim.

The *mestizos* – people of European, Taíno and African ancestry – pursued their traditional lives on the coffee, sugar and tobacco plantations of the island's hinterlands. These rural islanders became known as *jíbaros* (country persons), and over time their music, crafts and folkways – even their typical straw hats, called *pavas* – became associated with the essence of Puerto Rican culture.

Today, most Puerto Ricans share a synthesis of Amerindian, African and European ancestry. In contrast, the community of Loíza, east of San Juan, remains a proud black community whose strong links to its African heritage remain intact and are celebrated. In a few circles of San Juan society, old criollo families still brag of the *pureza* (purity) of their Spanish blood. See Society & Conduct, later in this chapter, for more on the function of this hierarchy in contemporary Puerto Rican society.

EDUCATION

Just as Puerto Rico's economy has undergone a total metamorphosis during the 20th century, so has its education system. When the US wrenched control of the island away from the Spanish in 1898, only 23% of Puerto Ricans could read and write, and the Catholic Church ran virtually all the schools. Today, 85% of school-age children (nearly 800,000 students) attend public schools, and the population's literacy rate has jumped to more than 90%. In fact, Puerto Rico claims a higher percentage of students graduating from high school than any state in the US. While Spanish is the principal language of the schools, the island is officially bilingual and all students study English as well.

Given the island's clear commitment to education, it is hardly surprising that more than a third of Puerto Rico's young people pursue post-high-school education. Almost 190,000 students go to technical schools, and more than 100,000 students attend the island colleges. Fifty thousand students enrolled at the Universidad de Puerto Rico in 1999; the institution's principal campuses in the Río Piedras district of San Juan and in Mayagüez feature a panoply of graduate programs including schools of medicine, law and library science. The private Universidad Católica in Ponce attracts 10,000 students.

Universidad Interamericana is now the largest private university in the Western Hemisphere, enrolling tens of thousands of students. It started in San Germán and has branch campuses in San Juan, Arecibo, Barranquitas, Bayamón, Fajardo, Guayama and Ponce.

ARTS

Puerto Rico overflows with riches in the arts. Since its establishment in 1955, the Instituto de Cultura Puertorriqueña, a government agency, has nurtured island culture and is constantly finding new ways of showcasing it to the world. The 1990s have seen the flowering of many such projects, including the ongoing historic restorations of colonial San Juan and Ponce. At the threshold of the 21st century, Puerto Rico is arguably the cultural center of the Caribbean.

Wandering the narrow streets of Old San Juan, you'll find a host of art galleries and small museums dedicated to the visual, musical and literary arts. One of these is the Museo de Casals (Casals Museum), packed with memorabilia illustrating the life of acclaimed cellist Pablo Casals, who made his final home in San Juan and gave his name to the most celebrated classical music festival in the Caribbean. On a grander scale, the brand new Museo de Arte de Puerto Rico (Puerto Rican Art Museum), in San Juan's Santurce district, includes three centuries of art by Puerto Rican masters such as José Campeche. The Museo del Arte de Ponce (Ponce Art Museum), known as the 'Parthenon of the Antilles,' houses the most complete collection of art in the Caribbean, with works representing all the major periods in western and island visual arts, from the Renaissance to the Pre-Raphaelites and beyond.

The arts thrive at the Luis A Ferré Center for the Performing Arts, more commonly known as Bellas Artes, in Santurce. Bellas Artes is a venue for performances by the Puerto Rican Symphony Orchestra, the Ballet de San Juan and other dance troupes, chamber music ensembles and visiting artists from around the world. Bellas Artes is also among the performance sites for the famous Festival Casals in June (see Special Events in the Facts for the Visitor chapter). One of the most recent additions to the long list of performing-arts celebrations is the Fiesta de Película – San Juan (San Juan Cinema Fest), staged each fall with competitive screenings of Caribbean films and independent offerings from around the world (see the San Juan chapter for details).

You don't have to go to the art palaces to find signs of a vibrant and expressive culture at work. Along the backroads and quiet beaches of the island lie the studios of the traditional weavers of *mundillo*, a traditional Spanish-style lace; the carvers of *santos*, figurines reputed to have magical properties; and the designers of *caretas*, masks representing many-horned diabolical figures, worn at many island festivals. The byways of Puerto Rico lead to crafters of all manner of guitarlike instruments, including the *cuatro*, and to more than a few practitioners of oil and watercolor painting who fill canvases with surrealistic images and the bright colors of *tropicalismo*, a contemporary art movement celebrating the flora and fauna of the tropics. But you never have to search for the music of the island. Classical, folk and *salsa* rhythms fill the air. See the Traditional Arts section for additional information on the art forms described above.

Traditional Arts

Puerto Rico's artistic heritage is a centuries-old weave that draws upon the belief systems and musical and visual-arts traditions of Spain, Africa and indigenous America. Many of these traditions date back centuries before the arrival of the first Spaniards.

Music & Dance

The Taínos had a rich tradition of music and dance, but because of their subjugation by the Spaniards and rapid assimilation into the colonial culture, little of their music survived. One exception is the ceremonial dance and associated fiesta known collectively as the *areyto,* performed to the rhythms of percussion instruments. One such instrument, the *bastón* – an ornamented stick struck heavily on the ground – has virtually disappeared from the island music scene. But two other traditional Taíno instruments, both made from gourds, are crucial to traditional island music as well as modern salsa: the *maracas,* which are shaken like a rattle, and the *güiro,* an elongated gourd slit open to create sound chambers and rasped with a stick. Over nearly five centuries, these Taíno instruments were synthesized with African rhythms and instruments, the guitar of the Spanish colonial troubadours and the traditional instrumental, dance and vocal forms popular in Spain to give Puerto Rican music its distinctive sound and vigor.

Left: Traditional Taíno *maracas* live on in island music such as salsa.

When Ponce de León and his colonists arrived on Puerto Rico in 1508, they brought their ecclesiastical and military music with them. In these early days, the sounds of organ recitals echoed from the chapels, while drums and bugles set the rhythm for

life in the garrisons of La Fortaleza and El Morro in San Juan. The Spaniards also developed homemade variations of the guitars they had left back in Europe – the *tiple,* the *tres* and the popular *cuatro,* with either four or five double courses of strings. Slaves from Africa re-created their own musical instruments – *tambores* (congas), tall barrel-like drums held together by metal hoops; *bongos,* a pair of small round drums joined by a piece of wood; and *claves,* two sticks struck together to rap out a rhythm.

African rhythms inspired a musical form and dance called the *bomba,* which evolved on the lowlands of the island's north coast. While the musicians set up call-and-response dialogues among themselves, singers jumped into the musical conversation. Dancers – alone or as couples – swirled within a circle of participants and let their bodies 'interpret' the music. Over the years, the bomba, which has many similarities to the Cuban *rumba,* has evolved into an ever-growing number of rhythmic variations.

A different musical form developed during the 19th century on the south coast around Ponce. *Plenas* unfold to distinctly African rhythms beat out with maracas, *panderos* (tambourines), claves and güiros. At the heart of a plena is a singer who delivers a short narrative somewhat in the style of the traditional Spanish *romance,* but plena lyrics almost always describe the news of the day and have a satirical edge. Curiously, the earliest plenas may have been sung in English by black immigrants to Ponce from the Virgin Islands, but contemporary lyrics are always in Spanish and sung with high, plaintive voices.

A very different-sounding folk music derives from the jíbaro culture of the island's mountains. Known as the *seis,* this form of music uses the usual collection of island percussion and string instruments with the addition of the cow bell to create a syncopated background for improvisational lyrics by the singer, who weaves a tale or collection of verbal images in a manner somewhat similar to contemporary rap artists. Family celebrations and community festivals in Puerto Rico are often punctuated by a *seis de controversia,* in which two singers compete in creating flamboyant images of love or beauty. As pure music, the seis inspires a host of folk dances.

During the Christmas season, visitors are likely to hear groups singing *aguinaldos,* variations of Spanish *villancicos,* lyrical carols sometimes accompanied by a cuatro.

Top: *Tambores,* tall barrel-like drums

Bottom: *Bongos,* small round drums

Puerto Ricans are so proud of their traditional music that visitors will inevitably see advertisements for performances staged in the casinos and swank hotels. These performers are generally top-notch, but nothing beats the authentic experience of listening to a seis contest or plena singers at one of the countless local fiestas.

Folk Art

Four forms of folk art have held a prominent place in the island's artistic tradition since the early days of the colony. Some of the island's folk art draws upon the artistic traditions of the Taínos as well.

Cemíes & Santos

The Taínos' 1- to 2-foot-high statues of minor gods, called *cemíes,* were the first icons of island culture. Crafted from stone, wood or even gold, the idols were prized for the power they were believed to bestow on their owners. Visitors can see collections of the simple, primitive-looking cemíes at a number of museums on the island, including the Museo del Indio in Old San Juan (see the San Juan chapter). Shortly after the arrival of the Spaniards in 1508, the Taínos and their civilization were assimilated. But the islanders' affection for magical statuary did not vanish. Instead, the Indians and their immediate descendants – who were quickly converted to Christianity – found a new outlet for their plastic arts in the colonial Spaniards' attachment to small religious statues called *santos* (saints). Like the cemíes, santos represent religious figures and are enshrined in homes to bring spiritual blessings to their keepers. Importing the santos from Spain was both difficult and expensive, so islanders quickly began making their own.

Initially, the island santos mimicked the elaborately detailed imports from Spain. But over the centuries, Puerto Rican carvers called *santeros* have evolved highly individualized styles that are simultaneously more dramatic and simpler than their European antecedents. But despite the santeros' liberties with form and expression, the carvers always stay true to the traditional symbols, such as a blue robe or a sword, that identify individual saints.

Icons of La Virgin (Virgin Mary) in all her incarnations – including the black Virgin of Montserrat – are perennially popular. Figures of the Magi, the Holy Family and Sta Bárbara are also favorites. The carving art reached its peak in the late 19th century, then slipped into decline. But a renewed interest in the figures on the part of upscale collectors has brought new energy to the art, and today hundreds of santeros are at work on the island. The santos carved by three generations of the Cabán family, Don Zoilo Cajigas (1855-1961) of Aguada, and Carmelo Soto are highly regarded works of art. There is a valuable collection of antique santos in the Capilla de Cristo in Old San Juan. Santos of

MARK BACON

Left: *Santero* Carmelo Soto, Lares

varying quality are widely available in galleries and craft markets around the island, but none are cheap. And cursed be the person who fails to provide a santo with a cozy shrine or altar.

Mundillo

Mundillo is a type of lace made only in Spain and Puerto Rico. The weaver makes the cloth with delicate designs such as flowers and spiders by manipulating bobbins of thread at lightning speed to form different kinds of stitches.

The tradition came to the island with the early nuns, who practiced the art in order to finance schools and orphanages. Over the 17th, 18th and 19th centuries, the nuns perfected the art in their schools and convents, but the intricate process was almost lost in the face of mass-produced textiles during the 20th century. Renewed interest in island folk arts, generated by the Instituto de Cultura Puertorriqueña, has revived the process. The Centro de Artes Populares at the Convento los Dominicos in Old San Juan has a display on mundillo as well as information about shops that make and sell the lace. Another good place to see mundillo is in the workshops of Moca, a community on the island's northwest coast, or at the Festival del Tejido (Weaving Festival), held at the end of April in Isabela.

Musical Instruments

When the first Spaniards arrived on the island bereft of their beloved guitars, for which there had been no room aboard the Spanish galleons, the colonists quickly set about making their own. A number of indigenous variations of this instrument developed on the island, but the most

Top: Leonides Lopez, traditional lacemaker, Moca

Bottom: *Cuatro* students perfect their technique.

enduring is the *cuatro* (see Music & Dance, above). No doubt the original cuatro had four strings, but over time it developed into a 10-string instrument played in the mode of a classical Spanish guitar. But the cuatro is significantly different from a guitar in construction: Its body is hollowed and shaped from a single piece of wood. For contemporary cuatros, prices start in the hundreds of dollars and rise into the thousands.

Masks

Sometimes simply called *máscaras* (masks) and otherwise known as *caretas*, the frightening and beautiful headpieces traditionally worn at island fiestas have become popular pieces of decorative folk art in recent years. The tradition of masked processions goes back to the days of the Spanish Inquisition and perhaps earlier, when masqueraders known as *vejigantes* brandished balloonlike objects (called *vejigas*) made of dried, inflated cow's bladders and roamed the streets of Spanish towns as 'devils' bent on terrifying sinners into returning to the fold of the church.

Spaniards brought their tradition to Puerto Rico, where it merged with masking traditions of the African slaves. Red-and-yellow papier-mâché masks with a multitude of long horns, bulging eyes and menacing teeth are typical of the headpieces created for the February Carnaval celebrations in Ponce.

In the distinctly African community of Loíza Aldea, maskers wear headpieces fashioned from coconut husks to celebrate the Fiesta de Santiago and honor the African god Changó in July. Hatillo sponsors the Día de las Máscaras in December. Most decorative masks in these styles cost between US$15 and US$85 at one of the many arts-and-crafts stores in Old San Juan or Ponce.

Bottom: Raul Ayala carves a mask out of a coconut husk, Loíza

TONY ARRUZA

Music & Dance

Classical A lot of tourist literature about Puerto Rico gives the impression that island culture was bereft of classical music before Pablo Casals, the most famous cellist of the 20th century, moved to Puerto Rico in 1956 to spend his old age in his mother's homeland. Without a doubt, the maestro's contributions have been monumental in the founding of the Puerto Rican Symphony Orchestra, the Puerto Rican Conservatory of Music and the Festival Casals – one of the great musical events of the Americas. It's likely that this native of Catalonia, Spain, found such fertile ground for his projects in Puerto Rico because they fit into an already rich tradition.

One way for European colonists to stay in touch with their culture was to practice and perfect the symphonic music that Europe exported during the baroque and romantic periods. San Juan had a municipal theater for performances of classical music as early as 1824. Within eight years, the island had its own philharmonic society and developed a music academy and orchestra to mount concerts, operas and *zarzuelas* – comic operas.

During the 19th century, island composers such as Felipe Gutiérrez, Juan Morel Campos and Manuel Tavárez composed operas, zarzuelas, *fantasias*, overtures and an important species of piano music called *danza*. Originally a highly stylized social figure-dance of the 19th century, with roots in Spain, danza developed into sophisticated compositions for concert pianists, woodwinds and strings in the hands of Puerto Rican composers. Contemporary island composers such as Rafael Aponte Ledée and Ernesto Cordero synthesize eclectic mixtures of European classical modes with elements of island folk music.

Salsa Everyone knows *salsa* when they hear it. It is the up-tempo dance music featuring fast, syncopated call-and-response between bold, sassy horns, a vocalist and a smoldering rhythm section. But salsa has so many permutations that it has always been tricky to define. Older aficionados hear salsa simply as jazzed-up versions of the music played by the *mambo* and *son* bands popular in Cuba in the 1940s and '50s. Others believe salsa is the sound of Puerto Rico, a synthesis of the rhythms of the bomba with the lyrics of the plena.

Ethnomusicologists claim that salsa is a distinctly modern fusion of big-band jazz and Afro-Caribbean music, and that both its lyrics and rhythms make endless references to Santería and the worship of African gods such as Changó and Yemayá (see Religion, later in this chapter). Cosmopolitan observers note that salsa transcends even this regional geography, drawing much from Brazil and enjoying strong practitioners and large followings in places such as northern Europe and Japan. But everyone agrees that salsa *is* the contemporary sound of Latin American communities from Miami to Medellín – music with an attitude…and a breathless energy.

This most eclectic and best-known hybrid of all the strains of Puerto Rican music is the one that did not really begin – at least commercially – on the island at all. Salsa started in that offshore colony of Puerto Ricans and Cubans known as El Barrio: the Latin Quarter, Spanish Harlem, New York City. In the euphoria following the end of WWII, New York's nightclub scene bloomed as dancers came in droves to the Palladium on 52nd St to bump and grind to the sound of the mambo bands they heard – or dreamed of hearing in the casinos of Havana, Cuba. At the time, the music carried a basic Latin syncopated beat and relied heavily on a horn section typical of the great swing bands of Stan Kenton and Count Basie.

Then a young Puerto Rican drummer named Tito Puente came into the picture. After serving three years in the US Navy and attending New York's Juilliard School of Music, Puente began playing and composing for Cuban bands in New York City. He quickly became notorious for spicing up the music with a host of rhythms that came from endless combinations of Puerto Rican bomba. Soon Puente had his own band, the Latin Jazz Ensemble, that was going way beyond the old Cuban templates.

By the late 1950s, Puerto Rican musician-producer Johnny Pacheco took this new

Tito Puente

sound out of the clubs and put it on Fania Records along with updates of some Puerto Rican classics. Into this mix came innovative Puerto Rican trombonist Willie Colón, who gave more syncopation to the brass riffs in the new music, added Brazilian songs, incorporated the plaintive vocals of the plena, introduced the cuatro as a lead instrument and secured the talents of the inimitable Cuban vocalist Celia Cruz. During the 1960s, this synthesis produced a megahit called 'Birimbau,' and Fania sold millions of records. Imitators began popping up all over Latin America, and the craze was on. Legend has it that a Venezuelan disc jockey coined the term 'salsa' to describe the music in the early 1970s. And everybody agrees that 'salsa' is exactly the right word: It means a spicy or piquant sauce, a catalyst to foods or fiestas, and – in Latin jazz circles – a flashy solo.

The rest is epic. During the past three decades, Puente, Colón and Fania Records have led the way, and hundred of *salseros* from all over the Latin American diaspora and beyond have taken up the torch, continually modifying and synthesizing traditional and disparate elements. Everyone has their favorites, but Puente, Colón, the late Héctor Lavoe, Eddy Palmieri, Gilberto Santa Rosa,

El Gran Combo de Puerto Rico and La Sonora Ponceña are the enduring superstars from the island. They join Cubans such as Beny Moré and Celia Cruz (the 'Queen of Salsa') and Panamanian Rubén Blades at the top of salsa's pantheon. Puerto Ricans Rafael Cortijo and Ismael Rivera are among the superstars whose deaths have earned them virtual sainthood among their fans. Today, Puerto Rican Marc Anthony is one of the new bright lights on the salsa scene, gaining recent recognition for his performance on the sound track of the Hollywood film *Zorro*.

Literature

Writing during the early 20th century from exile in Cuba, the revolutionary poet Lola Rodríguez de Tió described her native Puerto Rico as being joined with Cuba's fight for freedom 'like two wings of a bird.' In his poem 'Indiana' (1913), Luis Felipe Dessús proclaims:

I am Indian and African:
Puerto Rican
in whom fiery races fuse:
I am life, I am the flame.

The voices of these two poets highlight two major motifs in a vibrant island literature: defiance and rebellion on one hand, and an attraction to (or even idolizing of) nature on the other. What binds these works together is the third and most prevalent theme in Puerto Rican literature – a deep affection for the island's geography and culture that translates into a fervent pride in being Puerto Rican.

The island began inspiring writers in the earliest years of the Spanish colonial period. In 1535, Spanish friar Gonzalo Fernández de Oviedo wrote the *Historia general y natural de las Indias* (General and Natural History of the Indies), in which he painted a lush portrait of the island Ponce de León and his company found. About 100 years later, two thorough accounts of colonial life on the island came from the pen of the Bishop of Puerto Rico, Fray Damián López de Haro, and that of Diego Torres Vargas.

To Dance with the Saints – Salsa from Puerto Rico & Beyond

Most salsa bands include a multinational collection of artists, demonstrating the music's traditional bridging of Latino-Caribbean cultures. Here's an eight-pack salsa sampler to spice up any party.

Viva Salsa This anthology features all of the Fania team, with lots of Tito Puente and Johnny Pacheco (four-CD set, Fania, US/Charly, UK).

Salsa Superhits Here is a one-CD version of Fania's greats, including Tito Puente, Ray Barreto and Willie Colón (Charly, UK).

Fania All Stars Live at Yankee Stadium, Vols I and II The title says it all. This is a monster album that not only includes Puente, Colón and company, but Celia Cruz, Rubén Blades, cuatro player Jomo Toro and saxman Manu Dibango (Fania, US).

Introducing Celia Cruz This is the Queen of Salsa's greatest hits CD, including songs such as 'Santa Barbára' and 'Cúcala' (Charly, UK).

Grandes Exitos Here is a fine collection of two decades of music from Willie Colón, with vocals by Celia Cruz and jíbaro-voiced Héctor Lavoe (Fania, US).

Siembra This is Rubén Blades at his romantic best (Fania, US).

Buscando América Blades gets political and pan-Latino...and pulls it off (Electra, US).

Riquiti This CD features Venezuelan superstar Oscar D'León backed up by some of the most outrageous trombonists in the business (TH-Rodven, US).

Videos

For a video, check out *Celia Cruz and the Fania All Stars Live in Kinshasa, Africa* (BMG, 1974). The musicians are all fired up, and the crowd goes over the top!

Then, of course, you could rent Hollywood's hit film *The Mambo Kings*, with Armand Asanti and Antonio Banderas singing and playing along with Tito Puente and Celia Cruz.

Puerto Rico was without a printing press until 1807, and Spain's restrictive administrative practices inhibited education and kept literacy rates extremely low on the island during almost 400 years of colonial rule. But an indigenous literature developed nonetheless, particularly in the realms of poetry – which was memorized and declaimed – and drama. The 19th century saw the rise of a number of important writers in these fields. Considered the father of Puerto Rican literature, Alejandro Tapia y Rivera (1826-82) distinguished himself as the author of poems, short stories, essays, novels and plays. His long, allegorical poem, the *Sataniada,* raised islanders' eyebrows with its subtitle, 'A Grandiose Epic Dedicated to the Prince of Darkness.' Tapia y Rivera's play *La cuarterona* (The Quadroon) depicted the struggles of a biracial woman in San Juan.

In 1849, Manuel Alonso wrote *El Gíbaro,* a now-classic collection of prose and poetry vignettes that delineate the cockfights, dancing, weddings, politics, race relations and belief in *espiritismo* (spiritualism) that characterize the island jíbaro. This work led to the collective view of the jíbaro – clever, cordial and generous, but also distrustful and mysterious – as the archetypal Puerto Rican. Working in this same vein of romantic literature, known as *costumbrismo* (local color), were poets such as Lola Rodríguez de Tió, José Gautier Benítez and 'El Caribe' – the pen name of José Gualberto

Padilla. Manuel Zeno Gandía's novel *La charca* (The Pond) gave a new twist to costumbrismo with its depiction of the chronic poverty of coffee workers living in feudal conditions amid the sublime landscapes of the Cordillera Central. Written in 1894, this work distinguished the author as the father of the *naturalismo* movement in Puerto Rico.

When the US claimed the island as a territory in 1898, scores of island writers responded with protest literature. In the 1930s, a professor of Hispanic studies named Antonio S Pedreira wrote *Insularismo*, an eloquent indictment of the effects of American imperialism on his island. In the same decade, Puerto Rico's first important novelist, Dr Enrique Laguerre, published a novel in the vein of Pedreira's protest. *La llamarada* (Blaze of Fire) takes place on a sugarcane plantation, where a young intellectual wrestles with the destitution of his island in the wake of US corporate exploitation. Following this achievement, Laguerre wrote seven other novels that examine the sociological damage wrought by imperialism and frustrated Puerto Rican nationalism. Critics often identify *La resaca* (The Undertow) as the best of these works. During this epoch of intellectual foment, the architect of the modern Puerto Rican commonwealth, Luis Muñoz Marín, was composing poetry and sowing the seeds of his Partido Popular Democrático.

Expressions of protest and declarations of Puerto Rican pride continued with the next generation of writers, who came of age following WWII. Dramatist René Marqués rocked both island and international theaters with the 1951 production of *La carreta* (The Ox-Cart). Translated into several languages, this play portrays the crumbling lives of a rural Puerto Rican family that migrates first to an urban island slum and then to a New York barrio in search of the good life. Francisco Arriví plumbed the depths of Puerto Rican identity in his 1958 play called *Vejigantes* (Masqueraders).

As more islanders migrated to the US in the 1950s, the Puerto Rican 'exiles,' known as 'Newyoricans,' became grist for fiction writers. One of the most successful authors to take on this subject is Pedro Juan Soto, whose 1956 short-story collection *Spiks* (a racial slur aimed at Newyoricans) depicts life in the New York barrios with the hardbiting realism that the musical *West Side Story* could only hint at. Almost always dealing with characters caught in a clash between Anglo-American and Puerto Rican-Hispanic cultures, Soto's novels – including *Usmaíl* and *El francotirador* (The Sniper) – are existential bombshells.

In recent decades, the release of works by Puerto Rican authors in both Spanish and English has extended their readership. Luis Rafael Sánchez's novel *Macho Camacho's Beat* (1976) has won the author popular success as well as critical acclaim from diverse quarters. More recently, Esmerelda Santiago's 1986 memoir, *Cuando era puertorriqueña* (When I Was Puerto Rican), has become a standard text in many US schools.

Readers interested in a variety of island literature should dig into *Borinquen: An Anthology of Puerto Rican Literature,* edited by María Theresa Babin.

Architecture

The most dramatic architectural achievements of Old San Juan are the fortresses of El Morro and San Cristóbal, the stone ramparts surrounding the city and the mammoth seaside entry gate – all built from sandstone gathered from the shore. These 16th-century military monuments stand guard over about 4 sq miles of historically significant buildings, designated a UNESCO World Heritage Site. Within the city's walls are a few 16th- and 17th-century buildings, including the Convento de los Dominicos, the Iglesia de San José and the ancestral home of the Ponce de León family, the Casa Blanca.

Parts of the interiors of La Fortaleza (the governor's mansion) and the Catedral de San Juan (Cathedral of St John) also date to the 16th century. But for the most part, walking the shady cobblestone streets of the city, travelers feel immersed in the 19th century. The delicate wrought-iron balconies, columned entrances and symmetrical windows of the neoclassical style mix with porticos, pillars, arches and domes typical of

Spanish-baroque architecture. The plaza designs blend neoclassical symmetry with the ornamentation and fountains typical of the baroque style. The Paseo de la Princesa, with its royal palms, skirts the harbor side of the city in the style of world-class promenades such as the Piazza San Marco in Venice.

A visit to Puerto Rico's important southern city of Ponce brings visitors to an equally large trove of historical architecture. During the last decade, government and private sources have financed the restoration of a 66-block area of central Ponce at the cost of nearly US$500 million. The project includes more than 1000 buildings; most of the architecture dates from the 19th century, when Ponce flourished first as a locus for smuggling, then as a center for rum production and finally as the intellectual center of the island. Wandering the gaslit streets that fan out from the central Plaza Las Delicias, visitors see virtually endless examples of a distinct variation of neoclassical architecture known as Ponce criollo, with columned balconies built around interior patios. Examples of nearly every other variation of 19th-century architecture can be found here as well.

Ponce is the place to come for those who like house tours. The city's aristocrats left behind a number of monuments that are now open to the public. Among the must-sees is the Casa Salazar, which houses the Museo de la Historia de Ponce. The Casa Salazar combines neoclassical and Moorish styles with rich decorative detail including stained-glass windows, mosaics, pressed-tin ceilings and iron columns. Castillo Serrallés is a Spanish-revival castle that looks down on the city from the peak of El Vijía. Another home associated with the Serrallés family, creators of the Don Q rum empire, is the Casa Serrallés, which is being restored to its neoclassical elegance as an art studio and gallery. Ponce's vaulting red-and-black Parque de Bombas (firehouse), in the historic district's Plaza Las Delicias, is nothing short of a Victorian fantasy.

Travelers eager for a more rural evocation of colonial Puerto Rico should head for the town of San Germán, near the southwest corner of the island. San Germán is Puerto Rico's second-oldest town, and the main architectural attractions are its two churches. Iglesia Porta Coeli (Heaven's Gate) dates to 1606 and has undergone several restorations. While the whitewashed church is by no means monumental, it is nonetheless a dramatic backdrop to the pristine, terraced plaza at its entrance. This is one of the few truly Gothic churches in the Americas and includes an altarpiece painted by Puerto Rico's first great artist, José Campeche (see Visual Arts, below). The other church in town is the Catedral de San Germán de Auxerre, largely a 19th-century creation with a neoclassical steeple that serves as the focal point of the picturesque town.

One of the often-missed architectural treats on the island is the 19th-century hacienda architecture typical of the wealthy coffee and sugarcane plantations. A number of these haciendas are now open to the public as living-history museums or *paradores* (inns). The Hacienda Buena Vista, outside Ponce, is the most thoroughly restored of these estates. Standing on 80 acres of rural land, the hacienda includes not only a grand manor house but also a trove of 19th-century farm machinery – including waterwheels – all restored to working condition. Hacienda Esperanza, a sugar plantation west of San Juan in Manatí, will soon open as another living-history museum under the auspices of the Conservation Trust of Puerto Rico.

Visual Arts

Historians frequently suggest that the word, not the image, has always dominated Puerto Rican culture. These commentators see Puerto Rico as a nation of singers and poets rather than visual artists. A survey of the wealth of island music and literature might lead to this conclusion, but only if one overlooks the less-dramatic yet persistent creation of icons on the island, which dates back centuries before the arrival of the first Spaniards (see Traditional Arts, earlier, for more information).

While folk arts flourished during the early centuries of the Spanish colony, poverty and a lack of exposure to the materials and traditions of Europe's pictorial arts slowed the development of the indigenous Puerto Rican painters. But during the second half of the 18th century, the self-taught painter José Campeche (1752-1809) burst onto the scene. Masterpieces such as *Lady on Horseback* and *Governor Ustauriz* demonstrate Campeche's mastery over the genres of landscape and portraiture as well as his most frequent subject – the story of Jesus. Despite the fact that he worked with homemade paints and never saw more than a few prints from the European masters, Campeche gave nothing away in the realms of composition, form or color to his 18th-century European and North American contemporaries.

Despite Campeche's success, he did not engender a school of followers, and the next great Puerto Rican artist, Francisco Oller (1833-1917), did not gain recognition until the second half of the 19th century. Oller was a very different artist than Campeche; he studied in France under Gustave Courbet and felt the influence of acquaintances such as Paul Cézanne. Works such as *Hacienda Aurora* and *El Velorio* show a richness in color, a keen sense for dramatic subjects and a touch of impressionism. And like his mentor Courbet, Oller dedicated a large body of his work to the portrayal of scenes from humble, everyday island life. Courbet called this choice of everyday rural scenes 'realism.' The Spanish term is *costumbrismo*, and Oller's pride in his native culture parallels the focus of the island literature of the time. Over the years, his art found its way into the hands of Spanish royalty as well as the Louvre in Paris.

Oller's work spawned a school of impressionists in Puerto Rico. One of these figures was Ramón Frade, whose paintings (such as *El Jíbaro*) showed the island's 20th-century artists that traditional island scenes have the power to liberate both the artist's mind and hand. A similar theme emerges from the work of Juan A Rosado.

When US control of the island troubled local writers of the first half of the 20th century, Puerto Rico's artists began to obsess over political declarations of national identity. During this period, the island government funded extensive printmaking, commissioning artists to illustrate preexisting literary texts. Poems, lines of prose, memorable quotations and political declarations all inspired poster art. Among the best of these practitioners have been Mari Carmen Ramírez, Rafael Turfiño and, perhaps most notably, Lorenzo Homar. In Homar's masterworks, such as *Unicomio en la Isla*, a poster becomes a work of art, as it has in the hands of some of his students, including Antonio Martorell and José Rosas.

In the midst of the storm of poster art that covered the island in visual and verbal images during the 1950s and '60s, serious painters such as Julio Rosado de Valle, Francisco Rodón and Myrna Báez – as well as Homar himself – evolved a new aesthetic in Puerto Rican art, one in which the image rebels against the tyranny of political and jingoistic slogans and reigns by itself. Recent international shows of Puerto Rico's new artists at places such as El Museo del Barrio in New York City and the Museum of Fine Arts in Springfield, Massachusetts, have highlighted the lush, dreamy images of Myrna Báez as well as the dark symbolism of the tortured dogs in the work of Jaime Carrero. The abstract assemblages of Carlos

Francisco Oller

Dávila Rinaldi stand in opposition to the haunting self-portraits of Enrique Castellanos. The bright paintings of Mari Mater O'Neill look like tropical Marc Chagall. Then there are the intentionally primitive gouaches of Nick Quijando, which capture the serene private moments of daily life such as bathing, taking a siesta or embracing in the aftermath of lovemaking.

SOCIETY & CONDUCT

Generalizing about national character is always dangerous, and Puerto Ricans have suffered from unfortunate stereotypes rooted in the popular musical *West Side Story* and the ethnic rivalries of New York City's neighborhoods. The stereotype of Puerto Rican men as *chulos* – knife-carrying gang members addicted to drugs and the music of blaring trumpets and wild bongo beats – is so strong that many first-time visitors to the island are more than a little surprised by the complex people and culture they find.

One of the best places to meet the islanders and get a feel for their lives is to do a little shopping in the local *colmados* (convenience stores). Generally run by gregarious souls, these stores attract a clutch of neighbors who buy *café con leche* (coffee with milk), a soft drink or a Medalla beer and linger at tables or benches outside to discuss the news of the day…especially politics. It is at the colmado that one can get an answer to all of one's questions about island mysteries, catch a few laughs, hear the shop owner's newest salsa tapes and sense the cultural pride that infuses Puerto Ricans. At the colmado, you pick up on an island value system that places a high priority on family, friends, the time to enjoy them and the courtesy of looking good for them.

As the statistics show, part of 'looking good' means having a car that reflects a person's individuality and pride. Puerto Ricans may not have the most expensive cars in the world, but they may have the shiniest – replete with accessories that range from magnesium wheels to woofer speakers that fill up the entire backseats of sedans. For anyone enchanted with the possibilities of personal expression open to a person with a fertile imagination and an auto parts catalog, Puerto Rico is the place to come.

In contrast to the islanders' love affairs with their cars and an attachment to fashionable clothing, Puerto Ricans generally place a low priority on other possessions – including their housing. No doubt centuries of hurricane devastation have taught islanders some bitter lessons about investing too much money or psychic energy in their dwellings: The houses that islanders – even the wealthy – live in today bear more than a slight resemblance to concrete bunkers and look almost uniformly modest. 'It is not wise to show off your wealth,' islanders tell one another. 'When you show off, you are just tempting fate…or the criminals.'

Gringos (a term used on the island to describe Americans exclusively) and other visitors to Puerto Rico may find traditional island customs and attitudes that differ significantly from those at home. As in many Latin cultures, Puerto Ricans seem to have a strong need to please, and this can lead to people promising you things that they have neither the time nor the means to deliver. After being disappointed a few times, some people tend to judge Puerto Ricans as unreliable and possibly manipulative. But nothing could be farther from the truth. If travelers knew that the average Puerto Rican constantly struggles to 'look like life is a breeze' while juggling obligations to loved ones, children, an extended family, a vast network of friends, a career and the spirit world, they wouldn't expect islanders to deliver on generous but unrealistic promises, which are made in an effort to make guests feel good. As one Puerto Rican says, 'On my island you must always be ready to forgive people for their good intentions.' Indeed, anyone who deals successfully and genially with island culture *always* brings multiple sets of contingency plans to any situation.

In addition to navigating a culture in which people like to do things *a la buena* (the genteel way) – even if promises are more hopes than commitments – travelers of both genders may find that this traditionally male-dominated society is a bit difficult to get used to. Stereotypes of reckless and cavalier

This Thing Called *Machismo*

For many people, the word conjures leather-tough gunslinger images from Clint Eastwood movies, but the etymology of *machismo* leads in a different direction. *Macho* behavior is rooted in the confluence of Roman and Islamic cultures that struggled and merged in Spain during the Middle Ages. Both cultures asserted the absolute superiority of the male gender in virtually all legal and social situations.

This belief in male dominance evolved into a complicated code of chivalry with the rise of knighthood in Spain. At its heart lay the idea that a man is his own master: Nothing and nobody can dominate him. According to the code of machismo, personal honor is of premier importance. Feats of *bravura* (daring) in love and confrontations are the surest signs of a macho man – as one thoughtful contemporary Puerto Rican male says, 'I grow angry and fierce when I feel afraid.' Real conquistadores and their sons, as well as literary heroes such as Miguel Cervantes' Don Quixote, grew addicted to the code.

After 500 years of such role models in Puerto Rico, the behavior persists, particularly in the dominance games drivers play with each other on the highways, but occasionally in social and business situations as well. In this context, a translation of the *Velázquez Dictionary* definition of the word 'macho' offers food for thought: '1. A male animal; in particular, a he-mule or he-goat. 2. A masculine plant. 3. A piece of some instrument that enters into another. 4. Hook to catch in an eye. 5. Screw pin. 6. An ignorant fellow. 7. Pillar of masonry to support a building. 8. Sledge hammer.' The Spanish noun 'macho' relates to the verb *machacar*, 'to pound, to break anything into small pieces.'

behavior have been pinned on Puerto Rican males (see the boxed text 'This Thing Called *Machismo*'), and it might be said that the stereotypes have some roots in fact. If you are the type of person who sees social interactions as dominance games, you may eventually have difficulty with Puerto Rican males' *machismo*.

Does this mean that Puerto Rican males are pugnacious, sexist bullies? No. They are often gentle, kind, inordinately generous and even sentimental. You will find that they make loyal and engaging friends if you do not try to give them a lesson in your home country's concept of political correctness.

If you look below the surface of this apparent 'man's world,' you will discover an essential truth: Puerto Rican women can be every bit as self-confident and fiercely independent as the island's males.

Some sociologists would go so far as to say that Puerto Rican culture is a virtual matriarchy in which women, not men, hold the power in the areas of primary importance to a Puerto Rican's happiness – romance and family. Calling island culture a 'matriarchy' may be stretching it, but no one should look at the five-year-old girls with pierced ears and skirts practicing their salsa steps and imagine that they are rehearsing to be some macho's trophy wife. Nevertheless, gender discrimination persists. As in most industrialized countries, women in Puerto Rico have moved into the old male bastions of business, law, medicine and science in great waves, but few have pierced the so-called glass ceiling.

Race & Class Issues

Throughout 400 years of Spanish colonial domination, the notion of *limpieza de sangre* (blood purity) – with origins in the Spanish effort to rid the Iberian peninsula of the Jews and the Moors – was the critical factor in establishing a person's place in the social pecking order. Over the centuries, upper-class families regularly conducted 'trials' to test whether individuals could document 100% European ancestry before being permitted to marry within the upper classes. As recently as 100 years ago, families regularly hired lawyers to document the purity of their blood. This practice was of course wide open to corruption, and more than a few wealthy families on the island were rumored to have 'bought' their whiteness. During this long colonial epoch, Puerto Rico (like many other Caribbean colonies) evolved an extensive vocabulary consisting of more than 20 words to describe an individual's skin tones and racial features.

While the entire concept of limpieza de sangre is both hideous and silly, the old colonial prejudice in favor of white or European appearance has not vanished from the island, despite the fact that almost all Puerto Ricans represent a racial mix of Amerindian, European and African genes. Even today, you will hear islanders use racist terms such as *mulato* (half-black), *trigueño* (wheat-colored) and *jabao* (not quite white) in reference to other islanders. Furthermore, many dark-skinned Puerto Ricans have found it difficult to rise out of poverty, traditionally denied opportunities on an island where meaningful work has always been hard to find. This painful fact also resonates with the descendants of the landless free laborers (agregados), who have flocked to the cities to accept the questionable benefits of more than 330 government-subsidized housing projects and food stamps.

Dos & Don'ts

What can a traveler do to maximize the chances of a rewarding, hassle-free interlude in this complex society? Probably the best advice from veteran travelers and the islanders themselves is to live by the code of *a la buena;* in other words, relax when problems occur and make it your highest priority to make Puerto Ricans feel your respect for them and their culture.

As noted earlier in this section, Puerto Rican culture offers and expects a more formal and genteel approach to dress and social interactions than some travelers associate with Caribbean travel. The bottom line is that Puerto Rico is not Margaritaville: If you dress and act like you are at a beach party,

you will find yourself shunned. Neat and fashionable clothing, good grooming, a readiness to laugh at misfortune and a few respectful Spanish phrases such as *con su permiso* (with your permission, or more commonly, excuse me) and *perdóneme* (pardon me) will go a long way toward winning you favor among Puerto Ricans. If you practice your Spanish with a smile, so much the better. However, even if your Spanish is excellent, be prepared to be spoken to in English and treated like a guest, not a comrade.

RELIGION

The religious traditions of Puerto Rico reach back centuries to the Taínos, who worshipped a pantheon of deities – called cemíes – represented in carvings of wood, shell, stone or gold. (See the History section, earlier in this chapter, for more on the Taíno belief system.)

Like most of Spain's colonies after 1500 AD, Puerto Rico found its native traditions submerged beneath the state-sponsored religion of the conquistadores: Roman Catholicism. Some island historians contend that the Catholic Church had an enormous impact on developing island culture, but the true picture of Puerto Rican Catholicism is more complicated. When Christopher Columbus sailed to the New World, he was accompanied by priests chosen and paid for by the king and queen of Spain to tend to the spiritual needs of the explorers and convert the Amerindians to Catholicism. Likewise, Ponce de León brought priests with him when he began his Puerto Rican colony in 1508, and in 1519 Puerto Rico garnered the distinction of being the first papal see – a religious province under the leadership of a bishop – in the Americas. Later in the same century, Puerto Rico temporarily held the post as New World headquarters for the Inquisition.

As in all other Spanish overseas colonies, the church's primary mission was to convert the indigenous people to Christianity, enforce ethical values in the community, care for the sick and educate the children of the rich and powerful. But unlike the situation in colonies such as Mexico and Peru, where vast landholdings and profits from gold and silver mining made the church enormously rich and

Concerning Spirits

Slaves brought from West Africa between the 16th and 19th centuries carried with them a system of animistic beliefs that they passed on through generations of their descendants. Anyone with a passing knowledge of West African religions and their New World permutations, such as Santería, Voodoo, Candomblé and Obiah, will recognize some signs of African spirituality in Puerto Rican culture. You can hear it in the cadences of the African drums in traditional music like bomba and, more recently, in salsa. You also hear Africa in dance names like *rumba* and in variations on 'Changó,' the name of the Yoruba god of fire and war, like *machango, changuero, changuería* and *changuear* (all are island words that relate people, things and behavior to Changó). Virtually every Puerto Rican can tell you that island lore identifies the community of Guayama on the southeast coast as the 'town of sorcerers,' because the inhabitants held tight for centuries to their ancestors' mystical beliefs. The Fiesta de Santiago, held in Loíza Aldea in July, is in reality an African tribute to Changó.

Then there are the virtually endless references to African gods that occur in salsa titles and lyrics. True, many of these references come from Cuban singers whose lives and history are profoundly rooted in African spiritual traditions, but today's salsa is encouraging more and more Puerto Ricans to rediscover and – more importantly – learn to value Africa's contributions to their own culture.

The largest Afro-Caribbean religion is an amalgam of Catholic and Yoruba beliefs known as Santería. This religion flourishes in Cuba, where virtually everyone on the island is familiar with Santería's gods and practices. The worship and understanding of Santería per se is not nearly as widespread in Puerto Rico (at least outside the island's black and Cuban communities). But Santería is an important traditional thread in Puerto Rico's spiritual weave, and a working knowledge of this religious tradition can help unlock some of the mysteries concerning Puerto Rican spirituality.

In Santería, Catholic saints and incarnations of the Virgin are associated with Yoruba deities, or *orishas*. During Spanish colonial rule of the island, the Europeans outlawed all forms of worship except Catholicism. Much like the Taínos before them, the slaves developed this scheme of religious syncretism to mask the worship of their traditional deities. Unlike the Catholic saints whose names they bear in Santería, the orishas do not represent perfection; in fact, they have many human frailties. Yet the concepts of original sin and a final judgment are unknown. Instead, ancestral spirits are celebrated, frailties and all.

Among the most important orishas is the androgynous creator god Obatalá, who is always dressed in white and associated with Christ or Nuestra Señora de la Merced (Our Lady of Mercy). Odudúa, Obatalá's wife and goddess of the underworld, is also associated with the Virgin. Obatalá's son, Elegguá (St Anthony), is the god of destiny. Yemayá, the goddess of the ocean and mother of all orishas, is identified by the color blue and associated with Nuestra Señora de Regla. Changó, the Yoruba god of fire and war, lives in the tops of the royal palm trees and controls the thunder and lightning. His color is red; he carries a sword and stands by a castle. Changó is usually associated with Sta Bárbara, but in Puerto Rico's Afro-Caribbean community of Loíza Aldea he seems to be linked to Santiago (St James). His son Aggayú Solá, god of land and protector of travelers, is associated with San Cristóbal (St Christopher). Ochún, wife of Changó and companion of Yemayá, is the goddess of love. As might be expected, she's a very powerful orisha and is associated with Cuba's patroness, the

Concerning Spirits

Virgin de la Caridad del Cobre (whose color is yellow). Ogún is associated with San Juan Bautista (St John the Baptist). Babalú Ayé (St Lazarus) is the orisha of disease.

The rites of Santería are controlled by a male priest called a *babalawo* or *babalao,* who is often consulted for advice, to cure sickness or to grant protection. Offerings are placed before a small shrine in the babalawo's home. Although the figures of Catholic saints mounted on the shrines represent a variety of orishas, the real power resides in necklaces of stones and colored beads called *collares* or *elekes,* which drape the statues. The stones and beads are believed to harbor the spirits of the orishas, and they must be fed with food, herbs, rum and blood. Animals such as chickens, doves and goats are sacrificed during rituals.

The little wooden santos figurines that have been staple products of Puerto Rican artists for centuries descend to some degree from Santería beliefs in the powers of the saints (although many Puerto Ricans may not be aware of the sources of this worship). Many Puerto Ricans keep a collection of their favorite santos enshrined in a place of honor in their homes, similar to shrines the Yoruba keep for the orishas. Puerto Rican people have traditionally cultivated relationships of obligations – called *promesas* – with their santos in which the supplicants promise to offer up anything from rum or money to a beautiful comb to a santo who grants a favor. This practice precisely mirrors that of Yoruba people in West Africa. It seems no accident that the artists who carve the santos are called *santeros,* which is another name for babalawos, even though these carvers are not practicing mystics.

Not surprisingly, belief in the magical properties of small carved gods also harks back to the island's early inhabitants, the Taínos, evidenced in their worship of the little stone cemíes and in their respect for *jupías,* spirits of the dead who roam the island at night to cause mischief.

After centuries of keeping spirit worship away from the prying eyes of imperial moralists and the Catholic Church, Puerto Ricans today are still shy when it comes to talking about what is most commonly referred to as *espiritismo* (spiritualism) and *brujería* (witchcraft). Nevertheless, tens of thousands of islanders consult with *curanderos* (healers) or *espiritistas* – yet other names for babalawos – when it comes to problems with love, health, employment, finance and revenge. Islanders also spend significant amounts of money in *botánicas,* shops that sell herbs, plants, charms, holy water and books on performing spirit rituals.

Travelers are welcome to visit botánicas, and if you show genuine interest and respect you may get a chance to inspect household shrines and attend ceremonies. Distinct Santería worship occurs mainly within the island's large population of Cuban immigrants, most of whom have arrived here since the Cuban Revolution of the late 1950s. If you attend a Santería ceremony at a private residence, you probably will be expected to leave a few dollars for the saint (and the babalawo) on the altar.

powerful, the church in Puerto Rico always remained poor and dependent on a financially strapped government for funds. This dilemma left the island's priests and nuns with little to do but preach a blind allegiance to the Spanish Crown (which paid their paltry salaries) and, in later years, to exercise censorship and discourage Puerto Ricans from attending schools in North America, where they might be exposed to secular thoughts.

Few funds flowed to the church for the development of hospice and education facilities. In consequence, all but the wealthiest people of the island led short, squalid lives well into the 20th century. With the end of Spanish rule in 1898 came separation between church and state. During the last 100 years, Protestant missionaries have worked fervently to establish congregations on the island, and in recent years Jewish and Muslim communities have developed in San Juan. Nevertheless, 85% of Puerto Ricans consider themselves Roman Catholics, and feast days for local patron saints continue to be some of the most important holidays on the island calendar.

Roman Catholicism may be the island's principal religion, but it's fused with spiritualism and centuries of Indian and African folkloric traditions. See the boxed text 'Concerning Spirits' for more on this.

LANGUAGE

Puerto Rico has been officially bilingual since 1898, when the US won control of the island in the Spanish-American War. One hiccup in this position occurred in 1991, when Governor Rafael Hernández Colón of the PPD eliminated the use of English as an official language, giving 'cultural heritage' as

the reason for his decision. His choice won applause from nationalist factions (as he intended) and from the Spanish government, but it outraged many of the island's middle class and educators, who believed Puerto Rico's future to be intrinsically linked – for better or worse – with the US and the English-speaking world, as well as with Spain and her former New World colonies. Colón's opponents urged Puerto Ricans not to tamper with the special bilingual role they enjoy as interlocutors between the English-speaking and Spanish-speaking cultures of the Americas. Standing firmly behind this argument, Governor Pedro Rosselló reinstated English as an official language alongside Spanish in 1993. An estimated 100,000 opponents gathered in the streets of San Juan to protest.

Nevertheless, Puerto Rico remains an officially bilingual culture at the onset of the 21st century, and while many well-educated people on the island are fluent in two languages, Spanish is *always* the language in which island-born Puerto Ricans speak to one another, as a matter of cultural pride. Many older citizens and Puerto Ricans living outside areas frequented by English-speaking travelers and businesspeople speak only Spanish.

One of many unique elements of Boricua – the language of Borinquen – is the linguistic mixing that stems from the influence of English. Even in the more remote parts of the island, elements of US English filter in from Puerto Rican barrios on the mainland and from TV, radio, film and advertising. Puerto Ricans have taken the stems of many English words and turned them into Spanish-sounding verbs and nouns. See the Spanish for Travelers chapter for more on this.

Facts for the Visitor

THE BEST & THE WORST

Value judgments are always risky, but Puerto Rico is such a dynamic island that it can't help but produce strong emotions in travelers. The following likes and dislikes are the author's own subjective take on this place that the Taínos called Borinquen.

Top 10

Old San Juan Monumental fortresses, a dozen museums, galleries, restaurants, boutiques, shady cobblestone streets, a textbook collection of Spanish colonial architecture and 500 years of history beckon the traveler.

Vieques Otherwise known as La Isla Nena (Little Girl Island), this 21-mile-long mountainous island off the east end of Puerto Rico remains largely undeveloped because the US Navy controls about 70% of the land. But generally, the Navy opens the land (with miles of backroads for biking and dozens of beaches) to citizens and travelers. The phosphorescent bay here may be the most luminescent in the world, and the island has a low-key, vibrant expatriate and travelers' scene for anyone who fancies the undiscovered Caribbean. See the Spanish Virgin Islands chapter for more information.

Culebra This is the other major island in the so-called Spanish Virgin Islands. Culebra is smaller, farther offshore from Puerto Rico and more scalloped with bays and coves than Vieques. Much of the island is a designated wildlife refuge, and the fringe of the island has countless world-class snorkeling sites.

El Yunque This rain forest and anvil-like mountain peak on the east end of the island is a highly touted tourist attraction, and for good reason. On an overpopulated, overdeveloped island, the 28,500 acres of this national forest provide an extensive sanctuary for rare birds including the Puerto Rican parrot. Although you can catch views of almost half the island from the summits, you can literally get lost in the valleys. See the East Coast chapter for information.

Ponce Although lacking the dramatic seaside geography of Old San Juan, the historic center of Ponce has more square footage of historic buildings and plazas than the capital. The Plaza Las Delicias (Plaza of Delights), with its cathedral and fanciful firehouse, ranks as a truly elegant example of a traditional urban center. Carnaval here in February is outrageous.

Bosque Estatal de Guánica Ever heard of a tropical dry forest? This example of the rare ecosystem is one of the best. You will find great vistas of the rugged landscape and seashore here on the southwest end of the island as you hike the trails or find a sandy niche along the rocky coast for swimming. See the South Coast chapter for details.

Ruta Panorámica There is no better way to escape the island's tropical heat, crowds and sprawl than to head west on this scenic drive along a chain of roads that follow the island's spine. Along the route you can see the deep, volcanic rift called Cañón de San Cristóbal, the mountain town of Barranquitas and the tallest peaks on the island. More information about the Ruta Panorámica can be found in the Central Mountains chapter.

Parque de las Cavernas del Río Camuy This is one of the three largest cave systems in the world, replete with deep sinkholes, an underground river and subterranean 'cathedrals.' The government of Puerto Rico has done an excellent job of preserving the natural integrity of the caves and the surrounding wilderness. Adventure tour operators offer rappelling, spelunking and body-rafting trips here. See the North Coast chapter for more information.

Hacienda Buena Vista The Conservation Trust and the Smithsonian Institution have spent decades returning this 19th-century coffee plantation and corn mill to its former glory. Located in a pristine valley, this farm has a water-driven mill with functioning 19th-century machinery, as well as a fully restored manor house. See the South Coast chapter for details.

Isla Mona There is probably no other Caribbean island this large – 14,000 acres – that remains uninhabited. Mona lies 50 miles west of Mayagüez, between Puerto Rico and the Dominican Republic. A longtime pirate lair, Mona became a wildlife preserve early in the 20th century and now offers spectacular diving, caving and trekking expeditions. Keep an eye out for wild goats, pigs and giant iguanas. See the West Coast chapter for more information.

Bottom 10

Automobile Saturation Puerto Rico is overrun with more than 1.5 million cars – a car for just about every two humans here. In spite of the addition of many expressways, island roads remain clogged with cars. Municipal governments such as San Juan's gave up enforcing parking regulations years ago, making driving conditions even worse.

Aguadilla This seaside town on the northwest tip of Puerto Rico has some of the most dramatic seaside cliffs and beaches on the island. Unfortunately, it was one of the first towns to buckle to commercialism when the US Air Force located its huge Base Ramey here and developed it as a center for the Strategic Air Command in the 1950s and '60s. Today, the base (which has been turned over to the people of Puerto Rico) and the surrounding collection of tawdry strip malls stand as monuments to US imperialism, commercialism and thoughtless development.

Bayamón This historic small town on the western border of San Juan has ballooned into a city of more than 200,000 citizens due to an influx of light and medium industry. Construction of buildings, highways and

the Tren Urbano (rapid transit) clogs the landscape, and auto dealerships reproduce like viruses along the roads.

Cataño 'Poor Cataño,' sigh the *sanjuaneros* (residents of San Juan) as they look across Bahía de San Juan at the little town on the far shore. Controlling waterfront real estate on the west side of the bay with fabulous views of the old city, Cataño nevertheless remains a depressed area of unkempt homes and businesses. Recent municipal governments, however, have thrown a lot of energy and money into giving Cataño a new image. This includes building a library that looks like a futuristic Egyptian pyramid.

Highway 2 on the North Coast There is less traffic on Hwy 2 now that Hwy 22 has come on line, but Hwy 2 remains a slow-moving conduit of traffic lights, tire stores, restaurants and roadhouses, comparable to US 1 along the East Coast of the USA.

Highway 3 on the East Coast This road has all the unpleasant scenery of Hwy 2 but with more modern roadside attractions and frustrating traffic jams. And there is no toll-road alternative. To avoid this madness, consider a secondary road, Hwy 187, which meanders along the coast.

Salinas Jam-packed with flimsy vacation homes and dirty restaurants, this 'resort' village smells of sewage and rotting garbage. The area is a textbook example of how the human impulse to have waterfront property can ruin a perfectly good mangrove estuary.

El Combate The same forces that created Salinas have developed this crowded, rowdy shambles of a vacation community on the southwest coast.

Puerto Real/Playa Fajardo The port area in Fajardo where you catch the ferries to the Spanish Virgin Islands gets a regular battering from passing hurricanes. Each new storm drives more fishing boats, tugs and yachts ashore and blows away parts (or all) of local buildings. During the last 15 years, no one seems to have made an effort to clean up any of this accumulating debris.

Squatters If you go prying into the property records on the island, you will find that every municipality has its share of squatters who have built houses on land to which they have no title. This is a centuries-old tradition on the island and throughout Latin America. While squatters' dwellings are usually associated with the most impoverished citizens of a country, on Puerto Rico some of the most outrageous squatting has been perpetrated by the upper middle class. In places such as Culebra and La Parguera, you see the squatters' vacation homes built along waterfront that's ostensibly protected from development by commonwealth and/or federal agencies.

SUGGESTED ITINERARIES

Even though Puerto Rico seems relatively small at 100 miles by 35 miles, its rugged terrain and – in some places – traffic make travel take about twice as long as it does in the USA, Canada, Australia or Western Europe. Keeping this in mind, independent travelers with only a week or two to spend would do best to explore only one or two regions. Unless, of course, driving is your idea of exploring.

Even if you crave sun and surf, plan on spending a minimum of two days with the historic sites, museums, shops and vibrant social life in Old San Juan and other neighborhoods of the capital, such as Río Piedras or Condado, Ocean Park and Isla Verde, with their urban beach scene.

After exploring the capital, you can take one of the most popular routes for short-term explorers, heading east out of the capital for a visit to the mountain rain forest at El Yunque. After a trek along the forest trails, you can *disfrutar* (chill out) on the beaches at Luquillo or Fajardo. More adventurous travelers catch the ferry from Playa Fajardo for Culebra or Vieques to lose themselves in the wilderness and laid-back expat communities on those islands.

A second option is to head into the mountains south of San Juan and follow the Ruta Panorámica (a network of highways) to mountain villages and several forest reserves where you can hike and camp. The second half of this trip should include a day exploring the museums, mansions and historic restoration of colonial Ponce. Then head off for a low-key beach experience in the Guánica area, perhaps punctuated with a visit to historic San Germán.

A third option, traveling west from San Juan, gives the traveler a chance to see some of the most spectacular natural scenery on the island, including the peaks and sinkholes of karst country, which holds the Cavernas del Río Camuy, the Observatorio de Arecibo and several forest reserves. Adventurers might want to wind their way into the high mountains of the Cordillera Central to cool off at an old coffee plantation turned *parador* (inn) in Utuado or Maricao. When you come down from the mountains, the city of Mayagüez waits with its commerce and expansive university campus. Travelers can take off from here to find a little piece of paradise along the west coast, where rugged headlands and palm-fringed beaches shelter a wide variety of resort options, from the exclusive Horned Dorset Primavera to the surfers' bungalows in Rincón.

More time? Mix and match the above recommendations.

PLANNING
When to Go
Puerto Rico has one of the most congenial year-round climates in the world, so there is no bad time to visit. There are only 'good' and 'better' times. Daily temperatures range from the low 70s in January and February to the low 80s from July to September. The hottest months are also the rainiest, and while the heat and humidity are not as wilting as what you find in a place like Bangkok, the combination can be daunting if you are not cooled by the easterly trade winds, fans or air conditioning. Hurricane season runs from July to October (see the Climate section in the Facts about Puerto Rico chapter).

For most travelers, weather is far less important a factor in planning a trip to Puerto Rico than is successfully navigating the tourist season. 'The Season' runs from Christmas week until late April. During these months, squadrons of charter and regularly scheduled flights deposit crowds of sun-loving gringos from Europe, the USA and Canada at Aeropuerto Internacional de Luis Muñoz Marín in San Juan. Many of these travelers are here on package tours that disperse them among resort hotels around the island or launch them aboard one of the 28-plus cruise ships that call San Juan 'home port' during the winter.

Outside of these popular months, you should still expect to find plenty of Puerto Rican families drawn to resort areas on holiday weekends such as Easter, Memorial Day, July 4th, Labor Day, etc. Lots of islanders take their summer vacations in July and August: During these months, the camping areas in the forest reserves as well as many seaside accommodations are busy or full. For their own getaways, Puerto Ricans often head toward the south or west coasts, where the weather is generally sunnier and drier, travelers on package tours are fewer and prices for meals and accommodations are lower than in the San Juan/north coast areas.

One of the charms of the island is that this crush of tourists and vacationers – more than 4 million in recent years – is apparent in few places other than the airport. While hotels and camping areas may be full during 'the Season,' beaches, restaurants and the major tourist attractions in Old San Juan and at El Yunque rain forest never seem overrun with the huge crowds you'd find during the same months in places like Cancún, Mexico, or Nassau in the Bahamas. The one exception to this is on days (generally Saturday through Tuesday) when a lot of cruise ships unleash their passengers and crews on Old San Juan.

For the independent traveler, the problem with the Season is that accommodations can be difficult to come by during the peak winter months, and they're 30% more expensive than at other times of the year. This situation is not likely to change in the near future. While the island has recently begun to build new hotels in both the luxury and the moderately priced categories, and more

guesthouses and apartment rentals are popping up, Puerto Rico's accommodations industry is far from overdeveloped when compared with such tourist destinations as Spain's Costa del Sol or Portugal's Algarve. Of course, this lack of development is exactly what makes Puerto Rico attractive to independent travelers. Just be aware that if you are planning to visit the island during the winter tourist season, you should make reservations a minimum of three months in advance to get a decent selection and price. Off-season travelers (those visiting in May and June or September and October) will find great weather – barring a fall hurricane – and deep discounts on things such as hotel rooms and rental cars.

What Kind of Trip

Depending on whether you want to spend most of your time at the beach or exploring towns, cities, mountains and remote islands, you will want to book a particular type of flight to Puerto Rico. If your main purpose in coming to Puerto Rico is to vacation for a week or two with sun and surf, you will find it significantly cheaper and easier to book a package tour that includes flights, transfers, accommodations and some meals.

If you have the time and inclination to explore, purchase a super-APEX fare in one of the 'shoulder season' months such as May or November. You may be able to negotiate a good rate for a multiday stay in one of the guesthouses in Old San Juan or Ocean Park/ Condado (San Juan) and use this site as your base to shop for the best deal from a host of rental-car agencies (a car is essential for exploration; see the Car section in the Getting Around chapter for details).

When you have had enough bright-lights-big-city, take off to explore the country. Note: You will save yourself a lot of aggravation if you avoid the traffic jams of Puerto Ricans leaving San Juan on Saturday mornings for the mountains or the beaches and returning on Sunday evenings. Once on the highway, use this book to pique your interest and lead you to campsites, beaches, rustic inns, distinctive hotels and a host of eating and recreational opportunities. Don't be surprised if some mountain village or seaside hideaway catches your fancy and you feel the urge to turn in the rental car, lease an apartment and become part of the scenery. Communities such as Rincón and Boquerón on the west coast, as well as Dewey on Culebra and Esperanza on the south side of Vieques, have charmed more than a few lotus-eaters into becoming permanent residents.

Maps

Rand McNally publishes a good fold-out road map for Puerto Rico that includes detailed city maps of Aguadilla, Arecibo, Caguas, Mayagüez, Ponce and San Juan, as well as the islands of Culebra and Vieques. The map is widely available at bookstores and newsstands around the island for about US$3.

A similar map produced by Map Supply of Lexington, North Carolina, is readily available at many island bookstores. It opens to 3 feet by 5 feet and is easier to read because of its use of color. Beware, though: The map lacks some detail you get in the Rand McNally and is sometimes wrong. The maps that you get from rental-car vendors such as Avis will get you around the island's principal sites, but they lack detail when it comes to backroads and city streets.

If you want something even more detailed – right down to housing plots – pick up Metro Data's *Guía Urbana* for San Juan and Ponce (more than US$10) in most San Juan bookstores. The US Geological Survey (USGS), an agency of the US Dept of the Interior, publishes very detailed topographic maps of the USA and Puerto Rico, at various scales up to 1:250,000. Maps at 1:62,500, or approximately 1 inch = 1 mile, are ideal for backcountry hiking and backpacking. Some private cartographers produce updated versions of old USGS maps at 1:62,500. Many bookstores and outdoor equipment specialists on the island carry a wide selection of topographic maps.

What to Bring

Not much, really. One of the great joys of Puerto Rico's tropical climate and status as a US commonwealth – as well as its position as the economic center of the Caribbean – is

that travelers do not need to lug in a lot of clothes, gear, supplies, medicines, favorite foods, etc.

Light cotton clothes and a couple of bathing suits will meet almost all of your daily garment needs. But you might bring along a somewhat fancier dress, sport shirt, jacket or slacks if you plan on strutting your stuff with the young and beautiful in Old San Juan on a Saturday night, or if you want to make the casino scene. Of course, comfortable walking shoes are essential for exploring the cobblestone streets of Old San Juan and the trails of the forest reserves. You will definitely want a sweater or fleece pullover for cool or windy nights on the coast or in the mountains.

An inexpensive plastic rain jacket (or at least a travel umbrella) can come in handy during tropical showers, and a flashlight is always useful for dark nights. So pack some toiletries, a good book, a sketch pad and a beach towel. If you forget something, buy it on the island. It may cost you a little more than what you'd pay in the USA but less than what you'd pay in many other countries.

RESPONSIBLE TOURISM

At the cusp of the 21st century, with overpopulation and corollary threats to the global environment leading the list of problems confronting humans (particularly on Puerto Rico), the need to protect the environment should not be news to travelers or island residents. Puerto Rico suffers from many environmental troubles (see the Ecology & Environment section of the Facts about Puerto Rico chapter), and visitors must be careful not to contribute to these problems.

Travelers should remember that discarded fishing line, plastic bags and six-pack rings entangle and kill birds and endangered sea creatures. Avoid buying jewelry made from endangered species such as black coral and sea turtles, which threatens the existence of the remaining animals.

Divers' etiquette teaches that standing on, hanging from or carrying away live coral all cause damage to reef ecosystems that takes decades for nature to repair. Boaters must not travel at high speeds over seagrass beds, to avoid hitting or even killing endangered turtles and manatees. Discharge of fuels, oils and cleaning bleaches kill all kinds of marine organisms and the birds that feed on them. Remember too that taking plants or animals as souvenirs from a forest reserve is stealing. When possible, recycle – failure to recycle paper, plastic containers, bottles and aluminum cans destroys global resources just as surely as a logging operation in a rain forest.

TOURIST OFFICES
Local Tourist Offices
The Puerto Rico Tourism Company (PRTC; www.prtourism.com) is the commonwealth's official tourist bureau and a very good source for thorough brochures on island accommodations, sports, shopping, dining and festivals. The PRTC also sponsors a variety of folk and fine-arts shows around the island. From abroad, you can call any of the PRTC offices worldwide and request a tourist information packet. On the island, call the offices or stop by for up-to-date information and calendars of current events. PRTC offices on the island include the following:

San Juan
(☎ 787-721-2400, 800-223-6530)
Paseo de la Princesa No 2, La Princesa Bldg, Old San Juan, San Juan, PR 00901
(☎ 787-791-2551)
Aeropuerto Internacional de Luis Muñoz Marín

Aguadilla
(☎ 787-890-0022)
Aeropuerto Rafael Hernández

Cabo Rojo
(☎ 787-851-7070)
Hwy 100, Km 13.7

Ponce
(☎ 787-840-5695)
Fox Delicias Mall, 2nd floor

Tourist Offices Abroad
All of the following are also Puerto Rico Tourism Company offices:

Argentina
(☎ 1-314-2347)
Esmerelda 847, piso 9, 1007 Buenos Aires

Canada
(☎ 416-368-2680)
41-43 Colbourne St, suite 301, Toronto, ON M5E 1E3

France
(☎ 01 44 77 88 00)
Express Conseil, 5 bls rue Louvre, 75001 Paris

Germany
(☎ 611-977-23-12)
Abraham Lincoln Strasse 2, 65189 Wiesbaden

Mexico
(☎ 5-202-1844 ext 13)
Av de las Palmas No 735, Lomas de Chapultepec, Piso 10, Despacho 1001, 1101 Mexico City, DF

Spain
(☎ 1-431-2128)
Calle Serrano No 1, 2 Izquierda, 28001 Madrid

USA
(☎ 213-874-5991, 800-874-1230)
3575 W Cahuenga Blvd, suite 405, Los Angeles, CA 90068
(☎ 305-445-9112, 800-815-7391)
901 Ponce de León Blvd, suite 604, Coral Gables, FL 33134
(☎ 212-599-6262, 800-223-6530)
575 Fifth Ave, 23rd floor, New York, NY 10017

Venezuela
(☎ 582-959-2601)
CCCT-Primera Etapa ENT Oeste, Oficina 619, Chuao, Caracas

VISAS & DOCUMENTS
As a US commonwealth, Puerto Rico subscribes to all the laws that apply to traveling and border crossing in the USA. Foreign visitors to the island (other than Canadians) must bring their passports. All travelers should bring their driver's licenses and any health insurance or travel insurance cards.

You'll need a picture ID to show that you are over 18 to buy alcohol or gain admission to bars or clubs (make sure your driver's license has a photo on it, or else get some other form of ID). It's a good idea to make a photocopy of your passport and international ID to carry around instead of the original. There's nothing worse than losing your identity on a trip.

Canadians must have proper proof of Canadian citizenship, like a citizenship card with photo ID or a passport. Visitors from other countries must have a valid passport, and many visitors are also required to have a US visa. Check the US State Dept Internet site (travel.state.gov/visa_services.html) for detailed current information about visa requirements, immigration, etc.

Passport & Visas

Apart from Canadians and those entering under the Visa Waiver Pilot Program (see below), all foreign visitors need to obtain a visa from a US consulate or embassy. In most countries the process can be done by mail or through a travel agent.

Your passport should be valid for at least six months longer than your intended stay in Puerto Rico, and you'll need to submit a recent photo ($1^1/_2$ sq inches) with the application. Documents of financial stability and/or guarantees from a US resident are sometimes required, particularly for those from developing countries.

Visa applicants may be required to 'demonstrate binding obligations' that will ensure their return back home. Because of this requirement, those planning to travel through other countries before arriving in Puerto Rico are generally better off applying for their US visa while they are still in their home countries, rather than while on the road.

The most common visa is a Non-Immigrant Visitors Visa, B1 for business purposes, B2 for tourism or visiting friends and relatives. A visitor's visa is good for one or five years with multiple entries, and it specifically prohibits the visitor from taking paid employment in Puerto Rico or the USA. The validity period depends on what country you're from. The length of time you're allowed to stay in the USA is ultimately determined by US immigration authorities at the port of entry. If you're coming to Puerto Rico to work or study, you will probably need a different type of visa, and the company or institution that you're going to should make the arrangements. Allow six months in advance for processing the application.

Visa Waiver Pilot Program Citizens of certain countries may enter Puerto Rico or the USA without a US visa, for stays of 90 days or less, under the Visa Waiver Pilot Program. Currently these countries comprise Andorra, Argentina, Australia, Austria,

HIV & Entering the USA

Anyone entering the USA who isn't a US citizen is subject to the authority of the Immigration & Naturalization Service (INS). The INS can keep someone from entering or staying in the USA by excluding or deporting them. This is especially relevant to travelers with HIV (human immuno-deficiency virus). Though being HIV-positive is not grounds for deportation, it is a 'ground for exclusion,' and the INS can invoke it to refuse admission.

Although the INS doesn't test people for HIV at customs, it may try to exclude anyone who answers 'yes' to this question on the non-immigrant visa application form: 'Have you ever been afflicted with a communicable disease of public health significance?' INS officials may also stop people if they seem sick, are carrying AIDS/HIV medicine or, sadly, if the officer happens to think the person 'looks gay,' though sexual orientation is not a legal ground for exclusion.

It's imperative that visitors know and assert their rights. Immigrants and visitors who may face exclusion should discuss their rights and options with a trained immigration advocate before applying for a visa. For legal immigration information and referrals to immigration advocates, contact the National Immigration Project of the National Lawyers Guild (☎ 617-227-9727), 14 Beacon St, suite 506, Boston, MA 02108; or the Immigrant HIV Assistance Project, Bar Association of San Francisco (☎ 415-782-8995), 465 California St, suite 1100, San Francisco, CA 94104.

Belgium, Brunei, Denmark, Finland, France, Germany, Iceland, Ireland, Italy, Japan, Liechtenstein, Luxembourg, Monaco, the Netherlands, New Zealand, Norway, San Marino, Slovenia, Spain, Sweden, Switzerland and the UK. Under this program, you must possess a roundtrip ticket that is non-refundable in the USA, and you will not be

Embassies & Consulates

US Embassies & Consulates

The US embassies and consulates represent the Commonwealth of Puerto Rico, so all matters should be directed to a US office.

Australia
(☎ 2-6270-5000)
21 Moonah Place,
Yarralumla, ACT 2600

(☎ 2-9373-9200)
Level 59 MLC Center,
19-29 Martin Place,
Sydney, NSW 2000

(☎ 3-9526-5900)
553 St Kilda Rd,
Melbourne, VIC

Austria
(☎ 1-313-39)
Boltzmanngasse 16,
A-1091 Vienna

Belgium
(☎ 2-513-38-30)
Blvd du Regent 27,
B-1000 Brussels

Canada
(☎ 613-238-5335)
100 Wellington St,
Ottawa, ON K1P 5T1

(☎ 604-685-1930)
1095 W Pender St,
Vancouver, BC V6E 2M6

(☎ 514-398-9695)
1155 rue St-Alexandre,
Montreal, QC

France
(☎ 01 42 96 12 02)
2 rue St-Florentin,
75001 Paris

Germany
(☎ 228-33-91)
Deichmanns Aue 29,
53179 Bonn

Ireland
(☎ 1-687-122)
42 Elgin Rd,
Ballsbridge, Dublin

Italy
(☎ 6-46-741)
Via Vittorio Veneto
119a-121, Rome

Japan
(☎ 3-224-5000)
1-10-5 Akasaka Chome,
Minato-ku, Tokyo

Mexico
(☎ 5-211-0042)
Paseo de la Reforma 305,
Cuauhtémoc, 06500
Mexico City, DF

Netherlands
(☎ 70-310-9209)
Lange Voorhout 102,
2514 EJ The Hague

(☎ 20-310-9209)
Museumplein 19,
1071 DJ Amsterdam

New Zealand
(☎ 4-722-068)
29 Fitzherbert Terrace,
Thorndon, Wellington

Norway
(☎ 22-44-85-50)
Drammensvein 18, Oslo

Russia
(☎ 095-252-2451)
Novinskiy Bulivar 19/23,
Moscow

Spain
(☎ 1-577-4000)
Calle Serrano 75,
28006 Madrid

UK
(☎ 020-7-499-9000)
5 Upper Grosvenor St,
London W1

(☎ 31-556-8315)
3 Regent Terrace,
Edinburgh EH7 5BW

(☎ 028-90328-239)
Queens House,
Belfast BT1 6EQ

Your Own Embassy or Consulate

As a tourist, it's important to realize what your own embassy or consulate – that of the country of which you are a citizen – can and can't do.

Generally speaking, it won't be much help in emergencies if the trouble you're in is remotely your own fault. Remember that you are bound by the laws of the country you are in. Your embassy will not be sympathetic if you end up in jail after committing a crime locally, even if such actions are legal in your own country.

Embassies & Consulates

In real emergencies you might get some assistance, but only if other channels have been exhausted. For example, if you need to get home urgently, a free ticket is highly unlikely – the embassy would expect you to have insurance. If all your money and documents are stolen, it might assist in getting a new passport, but a loan for onward travel is out of the question.

Embassies used to keep letters for travelers or have a small reading room with home newspapers, but these days the mail-holding service has been stopped and even newspapers tend to be out of date.

Consulates in Puerto Rico

Most nations' principal diplomatic representation is in Washington, DC. To find out the telephone number of your embassy or consulate in DC, call ☎ 202-555-1212.

In addition, many nations with 'interests' in Puerto Rico maintain consulates and honorary consulates on the island. Addresses and phone numbers of official foreign diplomatic representatives can be found in the yellow pages of the local telephone directory under *Consulados*. Honorary consulates change with great frequency and thus are not listed here, but the foreign consulates in Puerto Rico were as follows when this book went to press (all are in San Juan or the surrounding suburbs):

Argentina
(☎ 787-756-6100)
Royal Bank, Hato Rey

Austria
(☎ 787-766-0799)
Plaza Las Américas,
Río Piedras

Belgium
(☎ 787-725-3179)
Banco de Ponce, Santurce

Brazil
(☎ 787-754-7983)
286 Muñoz Rivera, Hato Rey

Canada
(☎ 787-790-2210)
107 Cereipo Alturas,
Guaynabo

Chile
(☎ 787-735-6365)
1509 Lopez Landrau,
Santurce

Colombia
(☎ 787-754-6885)
Mercantil Plaza, Hato Rey

Costa Rica
(☎ 787-282-6747)
1732 Yenisey,
Río Piedras Heights

Dominican Republic
(☎ 787-725-9550)
Edificio Avianca, Santurce

Ecuador
(☎ 787-724-2356)
301 Recinto Sur, San Juan

France
(☎ 787-753-1700)
Mercantil Plaza, Hato Rey

Guatemala
(☎ 787-783-3797)
22-A Serrania Urb,
Garden Hills, Pueblo Viejo

Haiti
(☎ 787-764-1392)
654 Muñoz Rivera,
Hato Rey

Honduras
(☎ 787-764-2206)
Mercantil Plaza, Hato Rey

Mexico
(☎ 787-764-0258)
Bankers Finance, Hato Rey

Netherlands
(☎ 787-764-2886)
Scotia Bank Plaza, Hato Rey

Norway
(☎ 787-725-2532)
400 Comercio, San Juan

Philippines
(☎ 787-762-2855)
Avenida 65th Infantry,
Km 9.7, Carolina

Spain
(☎ 787-758-6090)
Mercantil Plaza, Hato Rey

UK
(☎ 787-721-5183)
American Airlines Bldg,
Santurce

Venezuela
(☎ 787-767-5760)
601 Avenida Ponce de
León, Hato Rey

allowed to extend your stay beyond 90 days. Check with the US embassy in your home country for any other requirements.

Visa Extensions If you want, need or hope to stay in Puerto Rico and/or the USA longer than the date stamped on your passport, go to the local INS office (call ☎ 800-755-0777 or look in the local white pages telephone directory under 'US Government') before the stamped date to apply for an extension. Going any time after that will usually lead to an unamusing conversation with an INS official who will assume you want to work illegally. If you find yourself in that situation, it's a good idea to bring a US citizen with you to vouch for your character. It is also a good idea to have verification that you have enough money to support yourself.

Travel Insurance

No matter how you're traveling, make sure you take out travel insurance. This should cover you not only for medical expenses and luggage theft or loss, but also for cancellations or delays in your travel arrangements, and you should be covered for the worst possible case, such as an accident that requires hospital treatment and a flight home. Coverage depends on your insurance and type of ticket, so ask both your insurer and your ticket-issuing agency to explain the finer points. STA Travel (☎ 800-777-0112) and Council Travel (☎ 800-226-8624) offer travel insurance options at reasonable prices. Ticket loss is also covered by travel insurance. Make sure you have a separate record of all your ticket details – or better still, a photocopy of the tickets. Also make a copy of your policy in case the original is lost.

Buy travel insurance as early as possible. If you buy it the week before you fly, you may find, for instance, that you're not covered for delays to your flight caused by strikes or other industrial action that may have been in force before you took out the insurance.

Insurance may seem very expensive – but it's nowhere near the cost of a medical emergency in the USA or Puerto Rico. (For more details, see Health Insurance in the Health section, later in this chapter.)

Driver's License & Permits

An International Driving Permit is a useful accessory for foreign visitors in Puerto Rico and the USA. Local traffic police are more likely to accept it as valid ID than an unfamiliar document from a foreign country. Your national automobile association can provide one for a small fee. They're usually valid for one year.

If you plan on doing a lot of driving in the USA/Puerto Rico, it would be beneficial to join your national automobile association (see Useful Organizations, later in this chapter, for information).

Hostel Card

There are currently no youth hostels in Puerto Rico, so your card will not help you on the island. But it will help you on an extended multicountry trip. Most hostels in the USA are members of Hostelling International/American Youth Hostel (HI/AYH), which is affiliated with the International Youth Hostel Federation (IYHF). You can purchase membership on the spot when checking in, although it's advisable to purchase it before you leave home. Most hostels allow nonmembers to stay but charge them a few dollars more.

Student & Youth Cards

If you're a student, get an international student ID card or bring along a school or university ID card to take advantage of the discounts available to students, which include theater/museum tickets and public transportation.

Seniors' Cards

All people over the age of 65 get discounts throughout Puerto Rico and the USA. All you need is ID with proof of age should you be carded. There are organizations such as the AARP (see Senior Travelers, later in this chapter) that offer membership cards for further discounts and extend coverage to citizens of other countries.

CUSTOMS

US Customs allows each person over age 21 to bring 1 liter of liquor and 200 cigarettes duty free into Puerto Rico or the USA. US citizens are allowed to import, duty free, US$400 worth of gifts from abroad, while non-US citizens are allowed to bring in US$100 worth. US law permits you to bring in or take out as much as US$10,000 in US or foreign currency, traveler's checks or letters of credit without formality. Larger amounts of any or all of the above – there are no limits – must be declared to customs.

MONEY
Currency
Puerto Rico uses US currency. The US *dolar* or *peso* (dollar) is divided into 100 cents (¢). Coins come in denominations of 1¢, called the *centavo* or *chavito* (penny); 5¢, called the *villon* or *ficha* (nickel); 10¢ (dime); 25¢, called the *peseta* (quarter); and the seldom-seen 50¢ (half dollar) coin. Quarters are the most commonly used coins in vending machines and parking meters, so it's handy to have a stash of them. Notes, commonly called bills, come in US$1, US$2, US$5, US$10, US$20, US$50 and US$100 denominations – US$2 bills are rare but perfectly legal. There is also a US$1 coin that the government has tried unsuccessfully to bring into mass circulation; you may get them as change from ticket and stamp machines. Be aware that they look similar to quarters.

Exchange Rates
At press time, the exchange rates were as follows:

country	unit		dollar
Australia	A$1	=	US$0.65
Canada	C$1	=	US$0.68
euro	€ 1	=	US$1.05
France	FF10	=	US$1.60
Germany	DM1	=	US$0.54
Hong Kong	HK$10	=	US$1.29
Japan	¥100	=	US$0.82
New Zealand	NZ$1	=	US$0.54
UK	UK£1	=	US$1.60

Exchanging Money
Most banks on the island will exchange cash or traveler's checks in major foreign curren-cies, though banks in outlying areas don't do so very often, and it may take them some time. It is probably less of a hassle to exchange foreign currency in San Juan. Additionally, Thomas Cook, American Express and ex-change windows in airports offer exchange (although you'll get a better rate at a bank).

Cash & Traveler's Checks Though carry-ing cash is more risky, it's still a good idea to travel with some for the convenience; it's useful to help pay all those tips, and some smaller, more remote places may not accept credit cards or traveler's checks. Traveler's checks offer greater protection from theft or loss and in many places can be used as cash. American Express and Thomas Cook are widely accepted and have efficient replace-ment policies.

It's vital that you keep a record of the check numbers and the checks you have used, in case you have to replace lost checks. Keep this record separate from the checks themselves.

You'll save yourself trouble and expense if you buy traveler's checks in US dollars. The savings you *might* make on exchange rates by carrying traveler's checks in a foreign currency don't make up for the hassle of ex-changing them at banks and other facilities. Restaurants, hotels and most stores accept US-dollar traveler's checks as if they were cash, so if you're carrying traveler's checks in US dollars, the odds are you'll rarely have to use a bank or pay an exchange fee.

Take most of the checks in large denomi-nations. It's only toward the end of a stay that you may want to change a small check to make sure you aren't left with too much local currency.

ATMs ATMs – called ATHs in Puerto Rico for *a todos horas* (at all hours) – are a con-venient way of obtaining cash from a bank account back home (from the mainland USA or from abroad). Even many small-town banks in the middle of nowhere have ATMs. They are common in most shopping areas and are often available 24 hours a day.

There are various ATM networks, and most banks here are affiliated with several.

Exchange, Accel, Plus and Cirrus are the predominant networks. For a nominal service charge, you can withdraw cash from an ATM using a credit card or a charge card. Credit cards usually have a 2% fee with a US$2 minimum, but using bank cards linked to your personal checking account is usually far cheaper. Check with your bank or credit card company for exact information.

Credit & Debit Cards Major credit cards are accepted at hotels, restaurants, gas stations, shops and car-rental agencies throughout Puerto Rico. In fact, you'll find it hard to perform certain transactions, such as renting a car or purchasing tickets to performances, without one.

Even if you loathe credit cards and prefer to rely on traveler's checks and ATMs, it's a good idea to carry one for emergencies. If you're planning to rely primarily upon credit cards, it would be wise to have a Visa or MasterCard in your deck, since other cards aren't as widely accepted.

Places that accept Visa and MasterCard are also likely to accept debit cards. Unlike a credit card, a debit card deducts payment directly from the user's checking account. Instead of an interest rate, users are charged a minimal fee for the transaction. Be sure to check with your bank to confirm that your debit card will be accepted in Puerto Rico – the debit cards from large commercial banks can often be used worldwide.

Carry copies of your credit card numbers separately from the cards. If you lose your credit cards or they get stolen, contact the company immediately (contact your bank if you lose your ATM card). Following are toll-free numbers for the main credit card companies:

American Express	☎ 800-528-4800
Diners Club	☎ 800-234-6377
Discover	☎ 800-347-2683
MasterCard	☎ 800-826-2181
Visa	☎ 800-336-8472

International Transfers You can instruct your bank back home to send you a draft. Specify the city, bank and branch to which you want your money directed, or ask your home bank to tell you where a suitable one is, and make sure you get the details right. The procedure is easier if you've authorized someone back home to access your account.

Money sent by telegraphic transfer should reach you within a week; by mail, allow at least two weeks. When it arrives it most likely will be converted into local currency – you can take it as cash or buy traveler's checks.

You can also transfer money by American Express, Thomas Cook or Western Union, though the latter has fewer international offices.

Security
Carry your money (and only the money you'll need for that day) somewhere inside your clothing (in a money belt, a bra or your socks) rather than in a handbag or an outside pocket. Put the money in several places. Most hotels provide safekeeping, so you can leave your money and other valuables where you're staying. Hide or don't wear any valuable jewelry. A safety pin or key ring to hold the zipper tags of a day pack together can help deter theft.

Costs
The cost of accommodations on Puerto Rico varies seasonally, between the cities and the countryside, and between resorts and everywhere else. Rates are higher in summer and between the December holidays and the end of the spring holidays (which include Easter, Passover, public school vacations and colleges' 'spring break'). The cheapest rates are usually in the US$50 to US$60 range, but on rare occasions you will find a place for about US$25. Rustic camping is inexpensive, US$10 or less per night, but you may have to pay more at camping areas with amenities like hot showers.

Food prices are about 15% higher than what you pay in the USA but are still very reasonable in comparison to the prices on many other islands, particularly in the Caribbean. The occasional splurge at a first-rate restaurant will cost anywhere from US$20 to US$50 depending on where you are, but plenty of good meals in restaurants can be found for less than US$10 – or even half that for some lunch specials. If you purchase food and alcoholic beverages at markets and large supermarkets, you can get by significantly more cheaply.

Public transportation in Ponce and San Juan is relatively inexpensive; city buses cost anywhere from 25¢ to US$1.50 depending on distance and the system. *Públicos* (public vans) generally charge less than 50¢ per mile.

In many areas of the island, a car is the only way of getting around; weeklong rentals can cost less than US$200. Gasoline costs about the same as it does in the USA but a fraction of what it does in Europe and most of the rest of the world. For more information on renting and operating a car, see the Getting Around chapter.

Tipping

On the island, tipping is in order in restaurants and better hotels. Taxi drivers, hairdressers and baggage carriers also expect tips. In restaurants, waitstaff receive minimal wages and rely upon tips for their livelihoods. Tip 15% unless the service is terrible (in which case a complaint to the manager is warranted) or up to 20% if the service is great. Never tip in fast-food, take-out or buffet-style restaurants where you serve yourself.

Taxi drivers expect 10% and hairdressers get 15% if their service is satisfactory. Baggage carriers (skycaps in airports and attendants in hotels) get US$1 for the first bag and 50¢ for each additional bag. In budget hotels (where there aren't attendants anyway), tips are not expected.

Taxes

Almost everything you pay for in Puerto Rico is taxed. Frequently, the tax is included in the advertised price. This is the case for plane tickets, gas, drinks in a bar, entrance tickets for museums or theaters, restaurant meals and most purchases in retail shops and food stores. Tax rates for these things vary from item to item, and almost no one on the island except the tax collectors can tell you the difference between the tax included in the cost of the shirt you buy

versus the tax on the round of piña coladas you bought at the bar.

There are, however a couple of exceptions. There is an additional 5% tax on jewelry sold on the island. If you stay in a hotel with a casino, you will pay a 15% tax above and beyond the advertised room rate. For other accommodations, the tax is 9%. When inquiring about hotel or motel rates, be sure to ask whether taxes are included.

Unless otherwise stated, the prices given in this book don't reflect local taxes.

Special Deals

The USA – including its associated free state of Puerto Rico – is probably the most promotion-oriented society on earth. Though the bargaining common in many other countries is not generally accepted in the USA, you can work angles to cut costs. For example, at hotels in the off-season, casually and respectfully mentioning a competitor's rate may prompt a manager to lower the quoted rate. Artisans may consider a negotiated price for large purchases. Discount coupons are widely available – check circulars in Sunday papers and at supermarkets, tourist offices and chambers of commerce.

POST & COMMUNICATIONS
Postal Rates

Postage rates increase every few years. Currently, rates for 1st-class mail within the USA are 33¢ for letters up to 1oz (22¢ for each additional ounce) and 20¢ for postcards.

International airmail rates (except to Canada and Mexico) are 60¢ for a half-ounce letter, US$1 for a 1oz letter and 40¢ for each additional half ounce. International postcard rates are 50¢. Letters to Canada are 46¢ for a half-ounce letter, 52¢ for a 1oz letter and 40¢ for a postcard. Letters to Mexico are 40¢ for a half-ounce letter, 46¢ for a 1oz letter and 35¢ for a postcard. Aerogrammes are 50¢.

The cost for parcels airmailed anywhere within the USA is US$3 for 2lb or less, increasing by US$1 per pound up to US$6 for 5lb. For heavier items, rates differ according to the distance mailed. Books, periodicals and computer disks can be sent by a cheaper 4th-class rate.

Sending Mail

If you have the correct postage, you can drop your mail into any blue mailbox. However, to send a package that's 16oz or heavier, you must bring it to a post office. If you need to buy stamps or weigh your mail, go to the nearest post office. Larger towns have branch post offices and post office centers in some supermarkets and drugstores. Addresses for main local post offices are given in this book. For the address of the nearest branch, call the main post office listed under 'Postal Service' in the US Government section in the white pages of the telephone directory.

Usually, post offices in main towns are open 8 am to 5 pm weekdays and 8 am to 1 pm Saturday, but it all depends on the branch.

Receiving Mail

You can have mail sent to you, addressed as 'c/o General Delivery,' at any post office that has its own zip (postal) code. Mail is usually held for 10 days before it's returned to the sender; you might request that your correspondents write 'hold for arrival' on letters. Alternatively, have mail sent to the local representative of American Express or Thomas Cook, which provide mail service for their customers.

Telephone

All phone numbers within Puerto Rico consist of a three-digit area code – 787 – followed by a seven-digit local number. If you are calling locally, just dial the seven-digit number. If you are calling long distance, dial ☎ 1 + the seven-digit number. To call the island from the USA, dial ☎ 1 + 787 + the seven-digit number. Call the island from any other overseas destination the same way, after dialing the appropriate code for an international line in your country.

For directory assistance on the island, dial ☎ 411. For US directory assistance outside the Puerto Rico area code, dial ☎ 1 + the three-digit area code of the place you want to call + 555-1212. For example, to obtain directory assistance for a toll-free number, dial ☎ 1-800-555-1212 or 1-888-555-1212.

Area codes for places outside Puerto Rico are listed in telephone directories. If you need Puerto Rican directory assistance while you're outside the country, dial ☎ 1-787-555-1212. Be aware that due to sky-rocketing demand for phone numbers (for faxes, cellular phones, etc), some metropolitan areas of the USA are being divided into multiple new area codes. These changes are not reflected in older phone books. When in doubt, ask the operator.

The 800 and 888 area codes are designated for toll-free numbers within the USA and sometimes from Canada as well. These calls are free (unless you are dialing locally, in which case the toll-free number is not available). It's common for organizations and businesses to change their 800 or 888 numbers, so if you try a number that's no longer in service or that has been picked up by another company, call ☎ 800-555-1212 and request the company's new number.

The 900 area code is designated for calls for which the caller pays a premium rate, such as phone sex, horoscopes, jokes, etc.

Local calls cost 10¢ at island pay phones. Long-distance rates vary depending on the destination and which telephone company you use – call the operator (☎ 0) for rate information, and ask if you can speak in English if you are not comfortable speaking in Spanish (all Puerto Rican operators are bilingual). Don't ask the operator to put your call through, however, because operator-assisted calls are much more expensive than direct-dial calls. Generally, nights (11 pm to 8 am), all day Saturday and 8 am to 5 pm Sunday are the cheapest times to call (60% discount). Evenings (5 to 11 pm Sunday to Friday) are mid-priced (35% discount). Day calls (8 am to 5 pm weekdays) are full-price calls within the USA.

Many businesses use letters instead of numbers for their telephone numbers in an attempt to make them snappy and memorable. Sometimes this works, but sometimes it is difficult to read the letters on the keyboard. If you can't read the letters, here they are: 1 doesn't get any letters, 2 – ABC, 3 – DEF, 4 – GHI, 5 – JKL, 6 – MNO, 7 – PRS, 8 – TUV, 9 – WXY. Sorry, no Qs or Zs.

International Calls To make a direct international call from Puerto Rico, dial ☎ 011, then the country code, followed by the area code and the phone number. You may need to wait as long as 45 seconds for the ringing to start. International rates vary depending on the time of day and the destination. Call the operator (☎ 0) for rates. The first minute is always more expensive than extra minutes.

Hotel Phones Hotels hike up the price of local calls by almost 200%, and long-distance rates are raised between 100% and 200%. Many hotels (especially the more expensive ones) add a service charge of US50¢ to US$1 for each local call made from a room phone, and they also add hefty surcharges for long-distance calls. Public pay phones, which can be found in most lobbies, are always cheaper. You can pump in quarters, use a phone debit card or make collect calls at pay phones.

Phone Debit Cards A new long-distance alternative is the phone debit card, which allows purchasers to pay in advance for access through a toll-free 800 number. In amounts of US$5, US$10, US$20 and US$50, these are available from Western Union, machines in some supermarkets and some other sources.

When using phone debit cards, be cautious of people watching you dial in the numbers – thieves might memorize numbers and use your card to make phone calls to all corners of the earth.

Fax & Telegraph

Fax machines are easy to find in Puerto Rico at shipping companies like Mail Boxes Etc. You can also find fax machines at Insti-Print photocopy service shops and hotel business-service centers, but be prepared to pay high prices (more than US$2 a page). Telegrams can be sent from Western Union (☎ 800-325-6000).

Email & Internet Access

A lot of individuals and businesses are online on the island, but Internet access for travelers has been slow to arrive. Since most of the accommodations on the island cater to vacation travelers, the hotels are only gradually adding Internet connections as standard features in rooms. Although in Europe cybercafés are a typical way to access your email account, at the time of this book's publication there were no cybercafés on Puerto Rico. To see if one has opened recently on the island, check out www.netcafeguide.com for an up-to-date list of cybercafés worldwide. You may also find public Net access in libraries, better hotels or universities, but this can entail a significant search. At this time, major Internet service providers (ISPs) such as AOL (www.aol.com), CompuServe (www.compuserve.com) and IBM Net (www.ibm.net) do not have dial-in nodes in Puerto Rico.

No doubt it's only a matter of time before travelers gain better access to the Internet while visiting Puerto Rico, so here are some tips for getting online while traveling.

It's best to download a list of your ISP's dial-in numbers before you leave home. If you access your Internet email account at home through a smaller ISP or your office or school network, your best options are to either open an account with a global ISP, such as those mentioned above, or to rely on cybercafés and other public access points to collect your mail.

To use cybercafés, you'll need to carry three pieces of information that enable you to access your Internet mail account: your incoming (POP or IMAP) mail server name, your account name and your password. Your ISP or network supervisor will be able to give you these. Armed with this information, you should be able to access your Internet mail account from any Net-connected machine in the world, provided it runs some kind of email software (remember that Netscape and Internet Explorer both have mail modules). It pays to become familiar with the process for doing this before you leave home. A final option when collecting mail through cybercafés is to open a free Web-based email account, such as HotMail (www.hotmail.com) or Yahoo! Mail (mail.yahoo.com). You can then access your mail from anywhere in the world from any Net-connected machine running a standard Web browser.

Traveling with a portable computer is a great way to stay in touch with life back home, but unless you know what you're doing, it's fraught with potential problems. If you plan to carry your notebook or palmtop computer with you, remember that the power supply voltage in Puerto Rico or other countries you visit may vary from that at home, and thus you'll risk damage to your equipment. The best investment is a universal AC adapter for your appliance, which enables you to plug it in anywhere without frying the innards. You'll also need a plug adapter for each country you visit – often it's easiest to buy these before you leave home.

Also, your PC-card modem may or may not work once you leave your home country – and you won't know for sure until you try. The safest options are to buy a reputable 'global' modem before you leave home or buy a local PC-card modem if you're spending an extended time in any one country. Keep in mind that the telephone sockets in each country you visit will probably be different from those at home, so ensure that you have at least a US RJ-11 telephone adapter that works with your modem. You can almost always find an adapter that will convert from RJ-11 to the local variety. For more information on traveling with a portable computer, see www.teleadapt.com or www.warrior.com.

INTERNET RESOURCES

The World Wide Web is a rich resource for travelers. You can research your trip, hunt down bargain airfares, book hotels, check on weather conditions or chat with locals and other travelers about the best places to visit (or avoid!).

There's no better place to start your Web explorations than the Lonely Planet website (www.lonelyplanet.com). Here you'll find succinct summaries on traveling to most places on earth, postcards from other travelers and the Thorn Tree bulletin board, where you can ask questions before you go or dispense advice when you get back. You can also find travel news and updates to many of our most popular guidebooks, and the subWWWay section provides you with links to the most useful travel resources elsewhere on the Internet.

With thousands of sites cropping up in Puerto Rico, you can spend days – not necessarily productively – exploring the virtual island unless you have some key landmarks. At publication time, these websites were taking the cyber-voyager fast and far:

Discover Puerto Rico
  www.prtourism.com
  An introduction to the island via the homepage and links of the Puerto Rico Tourism Company

Escape to Puerto Rico
  Escape.toPuertoRico.com
  Provides all kinds of links for travelers

Institute for Puerto Rican Policy
  www.iprnet.org/IPR/
  Brings you up to speed on the political maneuvering around the independence-versus-statehood issue when political debates heat up on the island, but it can go flat once island elections are over

Let's Dine Puerto Rico
  www.letsdine.com
  A decent and growing list of places to eat

The Puerto Rican Hall of Fame
  www.angelfire.com/biz/chago/puertorros.html
  A biographical site that also provides great links to information on travel, sports, accommodations, etc

Puerto Rico Online Magazine
  www.prmag.com
  Another good source of information on island news and entertainment options

Where to Stay in the Caribbean
  www.where2stay.com
  One of the better online accommodations services for the island

BOOKS

Most books are published in different editions by different publishers in different countries. As a result, a book might be a hardcover rarity in one country while it's readily available in paperback in another. Fortunately, bookstores and libraries can search by title or author, so your local bookstore or library is the best place to find out about the availability of the following recommendations. If you find that a title is out of print, a good used bookstore or your library may still have copies.

Lonely Planet

If you are combining your visit to Puerto Rico with travels to other Caribbean islands, check out Lonely Planet's *Cuba*, by David Stanley; *Jamaica* and *Bahamas, Turks & Caicos*, both by Chris Baker; *Dominican Republic & Haiti*, by Scott Doggett and Leah Gordon; and *Eastern Caribbean*, by Glenda Bendure and Ned Friary. If you are traveling to Miami, our guide to the city, by Nick Selby, will prove indispensable, as will Nick and Corinna Selby's *Florida*. Finally, if your Spanish is not what it used to be, take along a copy of Lonely Planet's *Latin American Spanish Phrasebook*, by Sally Steward.

Guidebooks

Among the guidebooks to Puerto Rico, Insight Guides' *Puerto Rico* is a book that goes into depth on the island's culture and history, and it does so with the kind of photo layouts that make the book a coffee-table attraction.

Activity Guides

Contemporary mariners will want *Street's Cruising Guide to the Eastern Caribbean*, by Don Street, as well as Jerrems C Hart and William T Stone's *A Cruising Guide to the Caribbean and the Bahamas: Including the North Coast of South America, Central America, and Yucatan*.

Take a look at *Yachtsman's Guide to the Virgin Islands and Puerto Rico* by Van Ost and Kline (see ordering information in Sailing, later in this chapter). If you plan on sailing extensively around the islands of Culebra and Vieques, try to get your hands on Bruce Van Sant's *Cruising, Snorkeling & Diving Guide to the Spanish Virgin Islands*. There are good sketch charts of the anchorages, GPS coordinates and pages of local knowledge (see Boating under Vieques in the Spanish Virgin Islands chapter). Aviators should carry a copy of Paul Fillingham's *Pilot's Guide to the Lesser Antilles*.

Birders will not want to leave for the island without *A Guide to the Birds of Puerto Rico and the Virgin Islands*, by Herbert Rafaela. Snorkelers and divers should look into Eugene Kaplan's *A Field Guide to the Coral Reefs of the Caribbean and Florida* (Peter-sen's Guides) or the boxed *Reef Set*, by Paul Humann. This collection of three books is full of color pictures useful in identifying coral, fish and other reef creatures with loads of information about abundance, distribution, life-cycles, etc. Pisces' *Diving & Snorkeling Guide to Puerto Rico*, by Steve Simonsen, is an essential book for anyone contemplating an underwater adventure in these seas, as is Pisces' *Guide to Caribbean Reef Ecology*, by William S Alevizon.

History, Politics & Sociology

To picture Puerto Rico and the Caribbean through the eyes of the conquistadores and read about the tribulations and joys of the European discovery of the Americas, pick up Samuel Eliot Morison's *Admiral of the Ocean Sea* and *Caribbean the Way Columbus Saw It.*

Puerto Rico's tortured colonial history has long fascinated social scientists. For the basics, take a look at Morton Golding's *A Short History of Puerto Rico*. The in-depth look at the island's indigenous culture, *The Taínos: Rise & Decline of the People Who Greeted Columbus*, by Irving Rouse, will break your heart. Equally poignant and articulate studies of later epochs in Puerto Rican history are *Puerto Rico: A Political and Cultural History*, by Arturo Morales Carrión; *Puerto Rico: An Unfinished Story*, by Denis Hauptly; and *The Disenchanted Island: Puerto Rico and the United States in the 20th Century*, by Ronald Fernández.

Requiem on Cerro Maravilla: The Police Murders in Puerto Rico and the US Government Cover-Up, by Manuel Suárez, tells the story of the 1978 political murders of two *independentistas* and the ensuing cover-up, which kept island politics in turmoil for a decade (see the Central Mountains chapter for details). *The Puerto Rican Woman*, by Edna Acosta-Belen, has become a little dated since its publication in 1986, but it remains a powerfully evocative study of a strong and resourceful group of women.

Traveler's Chronicles & Literature

During the 1960s, Oscar Lewis published his famous chronicle of Puerto Rican life,

La Vida: A Puerto Rican Family in the Culture of Poverty – San Juan and New York. Since then a raft of other good books by travelers about the island have appeared. Stan Steiner's *The Islands: The Worlds of the Puerto Ricans* stands out for its vivid evocation of islanders and their anecdotal histories. *The Other Puerto Rico*, by Kathryn Robinson, depicts the island through the eyes of a keen naturalist.

To see the Caribbean through the lens of a master fiction writer, grab a copy of *Middle Passage: The Caribbean Revisited.* James Baldwin's novel *If Beale Street Could Talk* explores the agony and the ecstasy of Puerto Rican life on the island and in New York City.

See the Literature section in the Facts about Puerto Rico chapter for books written by Puerto Rican authors.

Flora & Fauna

Arboles comunes de Puerto Rico y las Islas Virgenes, by Elbert Little, Frank Wadsworth and José Marrero, is your guide to plant life on the island, while *The Amphibians of Puerto Rico*, by Juan Riviera, tells you everything you ever wanted to know about turtles and frogs (of which there are many on the island).

General

Anyone interested in the wealth of island architecture should pick up José Fernandez' *Architecture in Puerto Rico. Puerto Rican Cookery*, by Carmen Aboy Valldejuli, has a mammoth collection of succulent recipes. Billy Bergman's 1984 treatise on popular Latino music, *Hot Sauces: Latin and Caribbean Pop*, stands up to the test of time after a decade and a half.

Teachers looking for a good resource book on Puerto Rican culture – including music, traditions, labor struggles and lifestyles – ought to check out the *Caribbean Connection Series: Puerto Rico*, edited by Deborah Menkart and Catherine Sunshine, for grades seven through 12. Get *Natural History of the West Indies*, by Gonzalo Fernández de Oviedo, to learn about how Puerto Rico and the ring of islands forming the Caribbean Basin came into existence and thrived.

FILMS

During the last 20 years, filmmaking in Puerto Rico has become big business, with more than 60 productions on the island over these two decades and annual contributions to the local economy in the range of US$14 million. With careful nurturing by the Puerto Rican Film Commission, the number of productions per year has steadily increased as both Hollywood and independent producers have realized that the island's weather, geography, historic architecture and modern infrastructure allow Puerto Rico to double for settings as diverse as Vietnam and Miami Beach.

Some recent films, such as *Contact,* with Jodie Foster – the opening scenes of which take place at and around the Observatorio de Arecibo – make a point of letting viewers know the action is taking place in Puerto Rico. But most of the time Puerto Rico 'stands in' for some other tropical setting. The island seems to be a favorite choice of directors shooting tropical thrillers. Clint Eastwood started the trend by shooting parts of *Heartbreak Ridge* here in 1986.

OJ Simpson worked on *Frogmen* in Puerto Rico shortly before the murder of his ex-wife. The island's recent contributions to the world of suspense drama include *Species*, *Golden Eye, Terminal Force II* and *Executive Decision.*

Antonio Banderas and Sylvester Stallone touched off a tidal wave of celebrity worship in Puerto Rico when they filmed *Assassins* here in 1995. Steven Spielberg used the fortresses of El Morro (a lot) and San Cristóbal (a little) as sets in *Amistad. Swiss Family Robinson*, with Jane Seymour, used Puerto Rico as a double for Paradise.

For an island-based comedy about the ins and outs of tropical yacht charters, catch *Captain Ron*, with Kurt Russell.

NEWSPAPERS & MAGAZINES

Two daily papers cover news and current events in Spanish. In *El Nuevo Día* (The New Day), writers get into the meat of the political, social, economic and environmental issues facing the island, with a somewhat establishment (or right-wing) point of view.

El Vocero (The Speaker) is a sensational tabloid paper popular with Puerto Rico's proletariat – it features huge photos and scant articles depicting the victims of gang violence, drug deals and the like.

The *San Juan Star* comes out in Spanish and English. It prints stories from international wire services but also includes some accurate reportage by local writers. You can get good English-language economic coverage in the weekly *Caribbean Star*. The monthly *Tropical Times* caters to the yachting crowd, who gather at the east end of the island.

Travelers will find a complete supply of overseas papers in the better hotels and *papelerías* (paper stores). Most readers believe that the Caribbean edition of the *Miami Herald* gives the most thorough and thoughtful coverage of regional, US and international news.

Check out *San Juan*, a 'city magazine' published every six weeks, to get a bead on the capital's movers, shakers and beautiful people. To get an absolutely up-to-date list of restaurants, accommodations and attractions, pick up the Puerto Rico Tourism Company's *Qué Pasa*, a comprehensive bimonthly magazine for Puerto Rico-bound travelers. There are great photos here, too, so you can picture the best of the island.

RADIO & TV

Puerto Rico has more than 110 radio stations, 60% AM and 40% FM. Most of these radio stations feature Spanish-speaking announcers and callers and music in Spanish, but at the east end of the island you can pick up English stations transmitting from the Virgin Islands. San Juan's WOSO, at 1030 AM, has national/international news and commentary in English. Generally, these stations have a range of less than 50 miles – less if you are in the mountains – and FM stations depend on 'line-of-sight' communication, so expect to find stations fading in and out as you travel the country. In and near the major cities, stations crowd the airwaves with a wide variety of music, from pop to classical and salsa. In rural areas, be prepared for a predominance of salsa music, local news and talk radio.

Puerto Rico has eight local TV stations and all the usual cable channels – many of which carry a rather fatuous selection of US programming, some dubbed in Spanish. While watching Bugs Bunny and Jean-Claude Van Damme movies in Spanish may not stretch your aesthetic sensibilities, you can pick up a lot of everyday Spanish from logging an hour a day with the tube. Many *colmados* (convenience stores) have a TV going for neighbors who come to loaf and pass the news of the day. Travelers who like connecting with a community may enjoy the social aspects of sipping Medalla beer and watching US baseball or World Cup soccer with the gang at the colmado.

PHOTOGRAPHY & VIDEO
Film & Equipment

Print film is widely available at supermarkets and discount drugstores. Color print film has a greater latitude than color slide film; this means that print film can handle a wider range of light and shadow than slide film. However, slide film, particularly the slower speeds (under 100 ASA), has better resolution than print film. Like black-and-white film, slide film is rarely sold outside of major cities, and when available it's expensive, as is all film sold on the island.

Film can be damaged by excessive heat, so don't leave your camera and film in the car on a hot summer's day, and avoid placing your camera on the dash while you are driving.

It's worth carrying a spare battery for your camera to avoid the disappointment of your camera dying in the middle of nowhere. If you're buying a new camera for your trip, do so several weeks before you leave, and practice using it.

Drugstores are a good place to get your film cheaply processed. If you drop it off by noon, you can usually pick it up the next day. A roll of 100 ASA 35mm color film with 24 exposures will cost about US$6 to get processed.

If you want your pictures right away, you can find one-hour processing services in the yellow pages under 'Photo Processing.' The prices tend to creep up to near US$11, so be prepared to pay dearly. Many one-hour photo finishers operate in San Juan, and a couple can be found right on the Plaza de Armas in Old San Juan.

Video Systems

The USA uses the National Television System Committee (NTSC) color TV standard, which is not compatible with other standards (Phase Alternative Line, or PAL; Systeme Electronique Couleur avec Memoire, or SECAM) used in Africa, Europe, Asia and Australia, unless converted.

Airport Security

All airline passengers have to pass their luggage through X-ray machines. Today's technology doesn't jeopardize lower-speed film, so you shouldn't have to worry about cameras going through the machine. If you are carrying high-speed (1600 ASA and above) film, you may want to carry film and cameras with you and ask the X-ray inspector to visually check your film.

TIME

Puerto Rico is on Atlantic Standard Time. This time zone is an hour behind the Eastern Standard Time zone, which encompasses such US cities as New York, Boston, Washington, DC, and Miami. During Daylight Saving Time in those cities – from 1 am on the first Sunday in April until 2 am on the last Sunday of October – the time is the same in Puerto Rico. There is no Daylight Saving Time on the island.

When it is noon in Puerto Rico, it is 4 pm in London, 8 am in Los Angeles and 2 am in Sydney.

ELECTRICITY

As in the USA proper, voltage in Puerto Rico is 110V and plugs have two (flat) or three (two flat, one round) pins. Plugs with three pins don't fit into a two-hole socket, but adapters are easy to buy at hardware stores and drugstores.

WEIGHTS & MEASURES

Puerto Rico is a bit confusing around these issues. Like the rest of Latin America, the island uses the metric system to measure the volume of gasoline and highway distances. The US influence shows up in the posting of highway speed limits in miles per hours, but distance is posted on the highways in kilometers (Km 7, etc).

Generally, distances are in feet, yards and miles; volume is measured in ounces for containers of beer and other beverages. Depending on where you are, you will find the weight of grocery items such as meat measured either in *onzas/libras* (ounces/pounds) or the metric kilogram.

In this book, US measurements are used, except for highway markers. You'll find a conversion table inside the book's back cover.

LAUNDRY

There are self-service, coin-operated laundry facilities in most towns of any size and in better campgrounds on the island. Washing a load costs about US$1 and drying it another US$1. Some laundries have attendants who will wash, dry and fold your clothes for you for an additional charge. To find a laundry, look under *Lavandarías* (Laundries) or 'Laundries – Self-Service' in the yellow pages of the telephone directory, which is in both Spanish and English. Dry cleaners are also listed under 'Laundries.'

HEALTH

For most foreign visitors, no immunizations are required for entry to Puerto Rico, though cholera and yellow fever vaccinations may be required of travelers from areas with a history of those diseases. There are no unexpected health dangers on the island; excellent medical attention is readily available and the only real health concern is that a collision with the medical system can cause severe injuries to your finances.

San Juan alone has 14 private hospitals and a university medical school. You will find hospitals, medical centers and walk-in clinics in virtually every municipality on the island, as well as many *farmacias* (pharmacies) – some open 24 hours a day.

In a serious emergency, call ☎ 911 for an ambulance to take you to the nearest hospital's emergency room. But note that ER charges are usually incredibly expensive unless you have valid medical insurance.

Predeparture Preparations

Make sure you're healthy before you start traveling. If you are embarking on a long trip, make sure your teeth are in good shape. If you wear glasses, take a spare pair and your prescription. You can get new spectacles made up quickly and competently for well under US$100, depending on the prescription and frame you choose. If you require a particular medication, take an adequate supply and bring a prescription in case you lose your medication.

Health Insurance A travel insurance policy to cover theft, lost tickets and medical problems is a good idea, especially in the USA/Puerto Rico, where some hospitals will refuse care without evidence of insurance. There are a wide variety of policies; your travel agent will have recommendations. International student travel policies handled by STA Travel and other student travel organizations are usually a good value. Some policies offer lower and higher medical expense options, and the higher one is chiefly for countries that, like the US, have extremely high medical costs. Check the fine print.

Some policies specifically exclude 'dangerous activities' such as scuba diving, motorcycling and even trekking. If these activities are on your agenda, avoid this sort of policy.

You may prefer a policy that pays doctors or hospitals directly rather than making you pay first and claim later. If you have to claim later, keep *all* documentation. Some policies ask you to call back (reverse charges) to a center in your home country for an immediate assessment of your problem.

Check whether the policy covers ambulance fees or an emergency flight home. If you have to stretch out, you will need two seats, and somebody has to pay for it!

Travel Health Guides Take a look at *Travelers' Health: How to Stay Healthy All Over the World*, by Dr Richard Dawood. The text is comprehensive, easy to read, authoritative and generally highly recommended.

Medical Kit Checklist

Consider taking a basic medical kit that includes the following:

❏ **Aspirin** or **paracetamol** (acetaminophen in the US) – for pain or fever.

❏ **Antihistamine** (such as Benadryl) – a decongestant for colds and allergies, eases the itch from insect bites or stings, and helps prevent motion sickness. Antihistamines may cause sedation and interact with alcohol, so care should be taken when using them; take one you know and have used before, if possible.

❏ **Antibiotics** – useful if you're traveling well off the beaten track, but they must be prescribed; carry the prescription with you.

❏ **Lomotil** or **Imodium** – to treat diarrhea; prochlorperazine (eg, Stemetil) or metaclopramide (eg, Maxalon) is good for nausea and vomiting.

❏ **Rehydration mixture** – to treat severe diarrhea; particularly important when traveling with children.

❏ **Antiseptic**, such as povidone-iodine (eg, Betadine) – for cuts and scrapes.

❏ **Multivitamins** – especially useful for long trips when dietary vitamin intake may be inadequate.

❏ **Calamine lotion** or **aluminum sulfate spray** (eg, Stingose) – to ease irritation from bites or stings.

❏ **Bandages** and **Band-Aids**

❏ **Scissors, tweezers** and a **thermometer** (note that mercury thermometers are prohibited by airlines)

❏ **Throat lozenges** and **cold and flu tablets** – pseudoephedrine hydrochloride (Sudafed) may be useful if flying with a cold, to avoid ear damage.

❏ **Insect repellent, sunscreen, Chapstick** and **water purification tablets**

Unfortunately, it's rather large to lug around. You might read it before your trip and make copies of the sections you anticipate needing while you're away.

Food & Water

A crucial health rule is to take care in what you eat and drink. Stomach upsets are the most common travel-related health problem (between 30% and 50% of travelers in a two-week stay experience one), but the majority of these upsets will be relatively minor. In Puerto Rico, standards of cleanliness in places serving food and drink are generally high.

Bottled drinking water, both carbonated and noncarbonated, is widely available on the island. Tap water is usually OK to drink, but ask locally.

Everyday Health

Normal body temperature is 98.6°F or 37°C; more than 4°F or 2°C higher indicates a 'high' fever. The normal adult pulse rate is 60 to 80 per minute (children 80 to 100, babies 100 to 140). You should know how to take a temperature and a pulse rate.

Respiration (breathing) rate is also an indicator of illness. Count the number of breaths per minute: Between 12 and 20 is normal for adults and older children (up to 30 for younger children, 40 for babies). People with a high fever or serious respiratory illness (such as pneumonia) breathe more quickly than normal. More than 40 shallow breaths a minute usually means pneumonia.

Travel & Climate-Related Problems

Motion Sickness Eating lightly before and during a trip will reduce the chance of motion sickness. If you are prone to motion sickness, try to find a place that minimizes disturbance; for example, near the wing on aircraft or near the center on buses. Fresh air usually helps. Commercial anti-motion sickness preparations, which can cause drowsiness, have to be taken before the trip commences; once you feel sick, it's too late. Ginger, a natural preventative, is available in capsule form from health-food stores.

Jet Lag This condition is experienced when a person travels by air across more than three time zones (each time zone usually represents a time difference of one hour). It occurs because many of the functions of the human body are regulated by internal 24-hour cycles called circadian rhythms. When we travel long distances rapidly, our bodies take time to adjust to the 'new time' of our destination, and we may experience fatigue, disorientation, insomnia, anxiety, impaired concentration and/or a loss of appetite. These effects will usually be gone within three days of arrival, but there are ways of minimizing the impact of jet lag:

- Rest for a couple of days prior to departure; try to avoid late nights and last-minute dashes for traveler's checks or your passport.

- Try to select flight schedules that minimize sleep deprivation; arriving in the early evening means you can go to sleep soon after you arrive. For very long flights, try to organize a stopover.

- Avoid excessive eating (which bloats the stomach) and alcohol (which causes dehydration) during the flight. Instead, drink plenty of noncarbonated, nonalcoholic drinks such as fruit juice or water.

- Make yourself comfortable by wearing loose-fitting clothes and perhaps bringing an eye mask and ear plugs to help you sleep.

- Avoid smoking, as this reduces the amount of oxygen in the airplane cabin even further and causes greater fatigue.

Sunburn Most doctors recommend the use of sunscreen with a high protection factor for easily burned areas such as your shoulders and, if you'll be on nude beaches, areas not normally exposed to sun.

Heat Exhaustion Dehydration or salt deficiency can cause heat exhaustion. Take time to acclimatize to high temperatures, and make sure that you get enough liquids. Salt deficiency is characterized by fatigue, lethargy, headaches, giddiness and muscle cramps. Salt tablets may help. Vomiting or diarrhea can also deplete your liquid and salt levels. Anhydrotic heat exhaustion, caused by the inability to sweat, is quite rare, but unlike the other forms of heat exhaustion, it is likely to strike people who have been in a hot climate for some time rather than newcomers. Again, always carry – and use – a water bottle on long trips.

Heat Stroke Long, continuous periods of exposure to high temperatures can leave you vulnerable to this serious, sometimes fatal, condition, which occurs when the body's heat-regulating mechanism breaks down and body temperature rises to dangerous levels. Avoid excessive alcohol intake or strenuous activity when you first arrive in a hot climate to help prevent heat stroke.

Symptoms include feeling unwell, lack of perspiration and a high body temperature of 102°F to 105°F (39°C to 41°C). In extreme cases, hospitalization is essential, but meanwhile get victims out of the sun, remove their clothing, cover them with a wet sheet or towel and fan them continually.

Fungal Infections These infections, which occur with greater frequency in hot weather, are most likely to occur on the scalp, between the toes or fingers (athlete's foot), in the groin (jock itch or crotch rot) and on the body (ringworm). You get ringworm (which is a fungal infection, not a worm) from infected animals or by walking on damp areas such as shower floors.

To prevent fungal infections, wear loose, comfortable clothes, avoid artificial fibers, wash frequently and dry carefully. If you do get an infection, wash the infected area daily with a disinfectant or medicated soap and water, and rinse and dry well. Apply an antifungal powder and try to expose the infected area to air or sunlight as much as possible. Change underwear and towels frequently and wash them often in hot water.

Infectious Diseases

Diarrhea A change of water, food or climate can all cause the runs; diarrhea caused by contaminated food or water is more serious. Despite all your precautions, you may still have a mild bout of traveler's diarrhea from exotic food or drink. Dehydration is the main danger with any diarrhea, particularly for children, in whom dehydration can occur quite quickly. Fluid replacement remains the mainstay of management. Weak black tea with a little sugar, soda water, and soft drinks diluted 50% with water are all good. With severe diarrhea, a rehydrating solution is necessary to replace lost minerals and salts. Such solutions, like Pedialyte, are available at pharmacies.

Hepatitis This is a general term for inflammation of the liver. There are many causes of this condition: poor sanitation, contact with infected blood products, drugs, alcohol and contact with an infected person are but a few. The symptoms are fever, chills, headache, fatigue, and feelings of weakness and aches

Nutrition

If your food is poor or limited in availability, if you're traveling hard and fast and therefore missing meals, or if you simply lose your appetite, you can soon start to lose weight and place your health at risk.

Make sure your diet is well balanced. Cooked eggs, tofu, beans, lentils and nuts are all safe ways to get protein. Fruit you can peel – bananas, oranges or mandarins, for example – is usually safe and a good source of vitamins. (Melons can harbor bacteria in their flesh and are best avoided.) Try to eat plenty of grains (including rice) and bread. Remember that although food is generally safer if it is cooked well, overcooked food loses much of its nutritional value. If your diet isn't well balanced or if your food intake is insufficient, it's a good idea to take vitamin and iron pills.

Make sure you drink enough in hot climates – don't rely on feeling thirsty to indicate when you should drink. Not needing to urinate or small amounts of very dark-yellow urine are danger signs. Always carry a water bottle on long trips. Excessive sweating can lead to salt loss and therefore muscle cramping. Salt tablets are not a good idea as a preventative, but in places where salt is not used much, adding salt to food can help.

Dastardly, Debilitating Dengue

This insect-borne disease may be the biggest threat to your health in Puerto Rico. With the onset of the 21st century, the island has been experiencing an epidemic of more than 24,000 cases of dengue per year.

A particular species of daylight mosquito spreads the disease. The best way to avoid dengue is to use mosquito repellents liberally, since there is no treatment for the disease once it is in your system. A sudden onset of fever and muscle and joint pains are the first signs of the disease before a rash starts on the trunk of the body and spreads to the limbs and face. Hospitals can treat your symptoms, so by all means seek medical attention if you suspect that you have contracted dengue.

The normal pattern of the disease calls for the fever and other symptoms to begin subsiding after a few days. Serious complications are not common, but persisting weakness, returning fever and fits of depression can last a month or more.

and pains, followed by loss of appetite, nausea, vomiting, abdominal pain, dark urine, light-colored feces and jaundiced skin. The whites of the eyes may also turn yellow. Hepatitis A is the most common strain. You should seek medical advice, but there is not much you can do apart from resting, drinking lots of fluids, eating lightly and avoiding fatty foods. People who have had hepatitis should avoid alcohol for some time after the illness, as the liver needs time to recover. Viral hepatitis is an infection of the liver, which can have several unpleasant symptoms or no symptoms at all, and the infected person may not even know that he or she has the disease.

HIV/AIDS HIV, the human immunodeficiency virus, develops into AIDS, acquired immune deficiency syndrome, which is a fatal condition. Any exposure to blood, blood products or body fluids may put the individual at risk. The disease is often transmitted through sexual contact or dirty needles – vaccinations, acupuncture, tattooing and body piercing can potentially be as dangerous as intravenous drug use.

Fear of infection by HIV should never preclude treatment for serious medical conditions. A good resource for help and information is the US Center for Disease Control AIDS hotline (☎ 800-342-2437, 800-344-7432 in Spanish). On the island, call the Commonwealth's AIDS hotline (☎ 787-765-1010) for information and assistance.

Cuts, Bites & Stings
Coral Wounds & Scratches Skin punctures can easily become infected in hot climates and heal slowly. Treat any cut by first washing it with soap and fresh water, then cleaning it with an antiseptic such as Betadine. Finally, smear the wound with triple-antibiotic salve to prevent the further introduction of infection. When possible, avoid bandages and Band-Aids, which can keep wounds wet.

Bites & Stings The stings of bees and wasps and nonpoisonous spider bites are usually painful rather than dangerous. Calamine lotion will give relief, and ice packs will reduce the pain and swelling.

If you get caught in jellyfish tentacles, peel off the tentacles using paper or a towel to protect your fingers. Then wash the area with alcohol (rum works). To alleviate the itchy sting, cover the affected area with meat tenderizer, ammonia (bleach) or urine.

Ticks These parasitic arachnids may be in brush, forest and grasslands, where hikers often get them on their legs or in their boots. The adults suck blood from hosts by burying their head into skin, but they are often found unattached and can simply be brushed off. However, if one has attached itself to you, pulling it off and leaving the head in the skin increases the likelihood of infection or disease, such as typhus, Rocky Mountain spotted fever or Lyme disease.

Always check your body for ticks after walking through a high-grass or thickly forested area. To remove an attached tick, use a pair of tweezers, grab it by the head and gently pull it straight out – do not twist it. (If no tweezers are available, use your fingers, but protect them from contamination by using a piece of tissue or paper.) Do not touch the tick with a hot object such as a match or cigarette – this can cause it to regurgitate noxious gut substances into the wound. Don't rub oil alcohol or petroleum jelly on it. If you get sick in the next couple of weeks, consult a doctor.

WOMEN TRAVELERS

Men may interpret a woman drinking alone in a bar as a bid for male company, whether you intended it that way or not. If you don't want the company, most men will respect a firm but polite 'no thank you.'

Dressing for the public in Puerto Rico can be problematic for women travelers. If you wear comfortable shorts, a sleeveless top and walking shoes, you will be stereotyped as a cruise-ship passenger and treated to persistent badgering from touts and street people. Salespeople and restaurant staff may assume that you have bundles of money you can't wait to give them.

On the other hand, if you try to dress like many local women, you may cause problems for yourself as well. Tight, short dresses and skirts are a persisting trend with Puerto Rico's fashionable women. Sure, these women turn a lot of heads, but you will not see or hear many men harassing them because over the centuries, island women have developed a reputation for being fierce. If you are traveling among Puerto Rican women, you can

dress like this, too, if you want. But it is a sad fact of life that when you put on the same lipstick, dress and heels as your island counterpart and head out on the town alone or in the company of other women travelers, the local radar screens will spot you in a second and cruising men will soon be in your face.

A lot of Puerto Rican women who are spending a day of leisure at the galleries, museums, shops and restaurants avoid these extremes of dress and go with loose, comfortable cotton slacks, a matching top and sandals. Lots of younger women wear jeans, but you might find them hot until your body acclimates to the tropical temperature and humidity.

Women find themselves most vulnerable to harassment when they're working out. If you are jogging, power walking or roller blading along public thoroughfares, you must prepare yourself to get whistles, cat calls, clapping and the like from local men. It can get pretty annoying when you have to hear this kind of thing 10 or 15 times on a simple 30-minute jog around the perimeter of Old San Juan. But the only way to avoid such displays of male chauvinism is to exercise in a setting where other people are exercising as well. One such place is the fields of El Morro (in San Juan), where you will find joggers, walkers and mountain bikers working out between 7 and 8 am and after 5 pm. If you must take to the sidewalks and roads, you probably know the drill with these hecklers: never acknowledge their pathetic bids for attention, turn up the volume on your Walkman and go, girl.

Safety Precautions

Women often face different situations when traveling than men do. If you are a woman traveler, especially a woman traveling alone, it is a good idea to travel with a little extra awareness of your surroundings.

In general, you must exercise more vigilance in large cities than in rural areas. Try to avoid the 'bad' or less safe neighborhoods or districts; if you must go into or through these areas, it's best to go in a private vehicle (car or taxi). It's more dangerous at night, but crimes also occur in the daytime. Solo women travelers and small groups should avoid isolated beaches at any time of the day or night. If you are unsure which areas are considered less safe, ask at your hotel or telephone the tourist office for advice. Tourist maps can sometimes be deceiving, compressing areas that are not tourist attractions and making the distances look shorter than they are. In Puerto Rico, high-crime areas turn up with surprising frequency right next to vibrant tourist zones. For example, the lawless La Perla barrio lies right outside the northern wall of Old San Juan.

While there is less to watch out for in rural areas, women still may be harassed by men unaccustomed to seeing women traveling solo. Try to avoid hiking or camping alone, especially in unfamiliar places. Hikers all over the world use the 'buddy system,' not only for protection from other humans, but also for aid in case of unexpected falls or other injuries or encounters with potentially dangerous wildlife.

Women face the extra threat of rape, which is a problem not only in urban but also in rural areas, albeit to a lesser degree. Conducting yourself in a commonsense manner will help you to avoid some problems. For example, you're more vulnerable if you've been drinking or using drugs than if you're sober; you're more vulnerable alone than if you're with company; and you're more vulnerable in a high-crime urban area than in a 'better' district.

Don't hitchhike in Puerto Rico, and don't pick up hitchhikers if you're driving alone. If you get stuck on a road and need help, it's a good idea to have a pre-made sign to signal for help. At night, avoid getting out of your car to flag down help; turn on your hazard lights and wait for the police to arrive. Be extra careful at night on public transit, and remember to check the schedule of the last bus or train before you go out at night.

To deal with threats, many women protect themselves with a whistle, mace, cayenne-pepper spray or some self-defense training. If you do decide to purchase a spray, contact a Puerto Rican police station to find out about local laws, regulations and training classes. One law that doesn't vary is carrying sprays on airplanes – because of their combustible nature, it is a federal felony to carry them on board.

If you are a victim of violence or rape on the island, call the rape crisis center at ☎ 787-765-2285. The chances are high that the person on the other end of the phone will speak only Spanish, so if you can't bridge the language barrier or if you want to talk to the police, call ☎ 911. In some rural areas where 911 is not active, dial ☎ 0 for the operator. City telephone directories list rape crisis centers and women's shelters that provide help and support; if they're not listed, the police should be able to refer you to them.

Resources & Organizations

Bookstores, found in the yellow pages under *Librerías*, are good places to find out about gatherings, readings and meetings. The university campuses are also good sites to network, and their social centers often have bulletin boards where you can find or place travel and short-term housing notices.

One international organization with an affiliate office in Puerto Rico is Profamilia (Planned Parenthood; ☎ 787-767-6960), 117 Padre Las Casas, El Vedado, San Juan. The staff here can refer you to clinics and offer advice on medical issues. Another good source is the government office for the Comisión Para Los Asuntos de Mujer (Commission for Women's Affairs; ☎ 787-722-2857), 151 Calle San Francisco, Old San Juan.

GAY & LESBIAN TRAVELERS

Puerto Rico is probably the most gay-friendly island in the Caribbean. San Juan has a well-developed gay scene, especially in the Condado district, for Puerto Ricans and visitors. Other cities, such as Ponce, Mayagüez and Aguadilla, have gay clubs and gay-friendly accommodations as well. And the island of Vieques has become a popular resort destination for an international mix of gay and lesbian expatriates and travelers. In the cities and in major resort areas, it is easier for gay men and women to live their lives with a certain amount of openness. As you travel into the middle of the island, it is more difficult to be out. Gay travelers should be careful, *especially* in the rural areas where even being seen holding hands might not be safe.

Resources & Organizations

On the island, pick up a copy of the *Puerto Rico Breeze* (☎ 787-724-3411), a bilingual tabloid of events and listings for accommodations, restaurants, clubs, etc, for gay men and lesbians. Also, check with the staff at the Atlantic Beach Hotel (☎ 787-721-6900) in Condado, which is a gay venue, or visit nearby Scriptum Books (☎ 787-724-1123), 1129B Avenida Ashford, for information on current events in the lesbian and gay community.

If you are a student, check out the campus of the Universidad de Puerto Rico at Río Piedras and Mayagüez, where gay support groups are finally out of the closet.

The Damron Women's Traveller, with listings for lesbians, and *Damron Address Book*, for men, are both published by Damron Company (☎ 415-255-0404, 800-462-6654), PO Box 422458, San Francisco, CA 94142-2458. Ferrari's *Places for Women* and *Places for Men* are also useful. These can be found at any good bookstore, as can guides to specific cities.

Another good resource is the Gay Yellow Pages (☎ 212-674-0120), PO Box 533, Village Station, NY 10014-0533, which has a national edition and regional editions. Also check out the website *Puerto Rico Gay/Lesbian Guide* (woofbyte.com/puertorico), which gives you information about the club scene and gay-friendly accommodations and restaurants.

Try these US resource numbers:

Lambda Legal Defense Fund
  ☎ 212-995-8585 in New York City
  ☎ 213-937-2728 in Los Angeles

National AIDS/HIV Hotline
  ☎ 800-342-2437

National Gay and Lesbian Task Force
  ☎ 202-332-6483

DISABLED TRAVELERS

Public buildings (including hotels, restaurants, theaters and museums) are required by law to be wheelchair accessible and to have available restroom facilities. Public transportation services (buses, trains and taxis) must be made accessible to all, including those in wheelchairs, and telephone companies are required to provide relay operators for the hearing impaired. Some banks now provide ATM instructions in Braille, and you will find audible crossing signals as well as dropped curbs at busier roadway intersections.

Larger private and chain hotels have suites for disabled guests. Main car rental agencies offer hand-controlled models at no extra charge. All major airlines allow service animals to accompany passengers and frequently sell two-for-one packages when seriously disabled passengers require attendants. Airlines also provide assistance for connecting, boarding and deplaning the flight – just ask for assistance when making your reservation. Airlines must accept wheelchairs as checked baggage and have an on-board chair available, though some advance notice may be required on smaller aircraft.

Of course, the more populous the area, the greater the likelihood of facilities for the disabled, so it's important to call ahead to see what is available.

Resources & Organizations

A number of organizations and tour providers specialize in the needs of disabled travelers:

Mobility International USA
  (☎ 541-343-1284, fax 343-6812, info@miusa.org) PO Box 10767, Eugene, OR 97440. Advises disabled travelers on mobility issues. It primarily runs an educational exchange program.

Moss Rehabilitation Hospital's Travel Information Service
  (☎ 215-456-9600, TTY 456-9602) 1200 W Tabor Rd, Philadelphia, PA 19141-3099

Society for the Advancement of Travel for the Handicapped (SATH)
  (☎ 212-447-7284) 347 Fifth Ave, No 610, New York, NY 10016

Twin Peaks Press
  (☎ 360-694-2462, 800-637-2256) PO Box 129, Vancouver, WA 98666. A quarterly newsletter; also publishes directories and access guides.

Wheelchair Gettaways Rent-A-Car
  (☎ 787-726-4023, 800-868-8028) Provides livery service as well as tours.

A good website to find access information is www.access-able.com.

SENIOR TRAVELERS

Though the age when discounts begin varies with the attraction, travelers 50 years old and older can expect to receive cut rates and benefits. Be sure to inquire about such rates at hotels, museums and restaurants.

Visitors to national parks, such as the forts in Old San Juan, and to campgrounds can cut costs greatly by using the Golden Age Passport, a card that allows US citizens aged 62 and over (and those traveling in the same car) free admission nationwide and a 50% reduction on camping fees. You can apply in person for the card at any national park or regional office of the US Forest Service or National Park Service (see Useful Organizations, below).

Resources & Organizations

Some national advocacy groups that can help in planning your travels include the following:

American Association of Retired Persons (AARP; ☎ 800-424-3410) 601 E St NW, Washington, DC 20049. Advocacy group for Americans 50 years old and older; a good resource for travel bargains. US residents can get one-year/three-year memberships for US$8/20. Citizens of other countries can get the same memberships for US$10/24.

Elderhostel (☎ 617-426-8056) 75 Federal St, Boston, MA 02110-1941. Nonprofit that offers seniors the opportunity to attend academic college courses throughout the USA and Canada. Programs last one to three weeks, include meals and accommodations, and are open to people 55 years old and older and their companions.

Grand Circle Travel (☎ 617-350-7500, fax 350-6206) 347 Congress St, Boston, MA 02210. Offers escorted tours and travel information in a variety of formats and distributes a useful free booklet, *Going Abroad: 101 Tips for Mature Travelers.*

National Council of Senior Citizens (☎ 202-347-8800) 1331 F St NW, Washington, DC 20004. Membership (you need not be a US citizen to apply) gives access to added Medicare insurance, a mail-order prescription service and a variety of discount information and travel-related advice. Fees are US$13/30/150 for one year/three years/lifetime.

TRAVEL WITH CHILDREN

All four of Puerto Rico's mega-resorts offer full-day, camp-style programs for children three to 15; these are the Hyatt Dorado Beach Resort & Casino (in Dorado on the north coast), the Hyatt Regency Cerromar Resort & Casino (also in Dorado), El Conquistador Resort & Country Club (near Fajardo on the east coast) and the Wyndham Palmas del Mar Resort (near Humacao on the east coast). Refer to the relevant regional chapters for further information on these resorts.

Motorists should note that Puerto Rican law requires that children younger than four be restrained in an approved child's seat while traveling in an automobile. For information on enjoying travel with young ones, read *Travel With Children,* by Lonely Planet cofounder Maureen Wheeler.

USEFUL ORGANIZATIONS

See also the organizations listed above for women, gays and lesbians, seniors and disabled travelers.

American Automobile Association

For its members, AAA provides great travel information, distributes free road maps and guidebooks and sells American Express traveler's checks without commission. The AAA membership card often gets you discounts on accommodations, car rental and admission charges. If you plan to do a lot of driving – even in a rental car – it is usually worth joining AAA. Membership costs US$56 for the first year and US$39 for subsequent years.

Members of other auto clubs, such as the Automobile Association in the UK, are entitled to the same services if they bring their membership cards and/or a letter of introduction.

AAA also provides emergency roadside service to members in the event of an accident or breakdown or if you lock your keys in the car. Service is free within a given radius of the nearest service center, and service providers will tow your car to a mechanic if they can't fix it. The US toll-free roadside assistance numbers are ☎ 800-222-4357, 800-AAA-HELP.

In Puerto Rico, call ☎ 787-764-4913 for emergency service. All major cities and many smaller towns have an AAA office where you can start membership.

National Park Service & US Forest Service

The National Park Service (NPS), part of the US Dept of the Interior, oversees the use of parks such as El Morro fortress. The US Forest Service (USFS) is a part of the Dept of Agriculture and manages the use of forests like the one at El Yunque. National forests are less protected than parks, allowing commercial exploitation in some areas (usually logging or privately owned recreational facilities).

Current information about national forests can be obtained from ranger stations. (Ranger station contact information is given in this book.) National forest campground and reservation information can be obtained by calling ☎ 800-280-2267. General information about federal lands is also available from the Fish & Wildlife Service (see below).

Fish & Wildlife Service

Each state and commonwealth (including Puerto Rico) maintains regional Fish & Wildlife Service (FWS) offices that can provide information about viewing local wildlife. Their phone numbers appear in the white pages of the local telephone directory under 'US Government, Interior Dept,' or you can call the Federal Information Center (☎ 800-688-9889).

DANGERS & ANNOYANCES
Drugs & Drug Trafficking

As in many nations, Puerto Rico's *barrios* of the poor have become havens for lawlessness and drug trafficking. To address the problem, Governor Pedro Rosselló called up the National Guard in 1993 and moved troops into housing projects in all the major urban areas. As a result, many of these communities have taken on the look of prisons, with fences and bulletproof guard towers.

Meanwhile, many wealthy neighborhoods have turned themselves into walled compounds with guards. Some estimates speculate that US$20 billion of cocaine reaches Puerto Rico annually. While most of these drugs are bound for the US, more than enough is left behind to upset the lives of islanders. Recent statistics cite drugs as the cause of more than 60% of all crimes in Puerto Rico.

Personal Security & Theft

Even though Puerto Rico lacks the slums of Mexico City or the *favelas* of Rio, there are more than a few desperate people on the island. A recent year saw more than 800 homicides. Most of these murders were related to drug and gang turf wars, but the traveler should be aware that a significant percentage of the island population carry weapons and may be prone to violence when it comes to resolving a dispute. House break-ins have become epidemic. Muggings are commonplace on popular beaches after dark; personal articles left out on the beaches are never safe.

However, even though street crime is a serious issue in large urban areas, visitors need not be obsessed with security. A few commonsense reminders should help keep you secure.

Always lock cars and put valuables out of sight, whether you're leaving the car for a few minutes or longer, and whether you are in a town or in the remote backcountry. Rent a car with a lockable trunk. If your car is bumped from behind in a remote area, it's best to keep going to a well-lit area or service station. Never allow yourself to get in a conflict with another driver on Puerto Rican roads: 'Road rage' is common here, and more than a few antagonized drivers have been known to retaliate with gunfire.

Be aware of your surroundings and who may be watching you. Avoid walking on dimly lit streets at night, particularly when alone. Walk purposefully. Avoid unnecessary displays of money or jewelry. Divide money and credit cards to avoid losing everything. Aim to use ATM machines in well-trafficked areas.

In hotels, don't leave valuables lying around your room. Use safety-deposit boxes or at least place valuables in a locked bag. Don't open your door to strangers – check the peephole or call the front desk if unexpected guests try to enter.

Discrimination

Since most Puerto Ricans trace their genetic and cultural heritage to a mix of Taíno, European and African ancestors, the island has been a multicultural community for more than 400 years. Today you are much more likely to see people of different skin tones and features living, working and relaxing together in Puerto Rico than you are in many parts of the USA. Nevertheless, the old colonial prejudice favoring white males has not died here when it comes to workplace promotions and admission to elite clubs.

Street People

The USA and Puerto Rico have a lamentable record in dealing with their most unfortunate citizens, who often roam the streets of large cities in the daytime and sleep by storefronts, under overpasses or in alleyways and abandoned buildings.

This problem is less acute in the mostly rural areas than in urban centers on the coasts, but it is certainly not absent. Street people and panhandlers may approach visitors in San Juan or Ponce as well as on some beaches, such as the urban Condado; nearly all these people are harmless. It is an individual judgment call whether it is appropriate to offer them money or anything else.

Guns

The USA and, by extension, Puerto Rico, have a widespread reputation as dangerous places because of the availability of firearms. While partly true, this image is also propagated and exaggerated by the media. Residents of rural areas sometimes carry guns, but they most often target animals or isolated traffic signs rather than humans. Do be careful in the woods during the fall hunting season, when unsuccessful or drunken hunters may be less selective in their targets than one might hope.

Recreational Hazards

In wilderness areas the consequences of an accident can be very serious, so inform someone of your route and expected return.

Shark Bites?

Many of Puerto Rico's serious recreational hazards lie in the sea. Water conditions around Puerto Rico are perfect for the growth of coral, and Puerto Rico offers divers and snorkelers a plethora of fringe, ribbon, barrier and bank-type coral reefs. But remember that coral is an animal whose beautiful, calcified shell can cut easily and cause painful infections. Fire coral – the rust-colored branches with the white tips – actually packs a sting. Other animals that swimmers and divers might see – and should keep at a distance – are the moray eel, a fierce biting denizen of the reef; sting rays, which like to bury themselves beneath the sand in shallow areas (such as popular beaches); and the spotted scorpion fish that lurks around the bottoms of reefs and rocks. Spiny black sea urchins have the power to pierce a swim fin when stepped on.

Small sharks and large barracuda are plentiful in Puerto Rican waters, and swimmers should be cautious not to attract these predators with jerky movements or flashy metallic watches and jewelry. But as threatening as the razor-toothed fish look, they account for far fewer injuries to humans than the innocent-looking jellyfish. The chief villain of this group is the Portuguese man-of-war, whose whiplike stinging tentacles can extend 40 feet or more from the animal's balloon-shaped float. And these tentacles can still sting hours after they have detached from the animal's body or washed up on the beach. Watch where you swim and where you plant your feet on the beach during jellyfish season (August through October).

Wildlife As more and more people spend time in the backcountry or impinge on wildlife habitat, attacks on humans and pets are becoming more common. Some of these animals may seem very attractive to visitors, but they are nuisances and potentially hazardous. Wild horses, for example, roam parts of the vast US Navy land on Vieques, and although they look gentle and placid while grazing on the tropical underbrush, they can kick, bite and trample. Even small animals are capable of inflicting serious injury or even fatal wounds on unsuspecting tourists. Some carry rabies. Keep your distance from all wild animals. The monkeys on some of the cays off the south coast can be downright fierce, as can the iguanas.

Pests Like every tropical island, Puerto Rico has its share of pests, and islanders will debate long and hard about which they detest the most. Mosquitoes are ubiquitous – and they do not restrict their activities to the hours around sunset. In fact, one type of daylight mosquito carries dengue fever (see the boxed text under Health, earlier in this chapter). The only good thing that can be said about the island's mosquitoes is that they do not carry malaria. Another flying pest is a nearly microscopic sandfly, the 'no-see-um,' which penetrates screens and sets off sharp little itches every time it lands on bare human skin. Traveling in Puerto Rico without an arsenal of your favorite bug repellent is tantamount to offering up your body as a human sacrifice to the Lord of the Flies (the 1963 version, incidentally, was filmed on Vieques).

Hookworm – which can be contacted by simply walking barefoot through infected sand or dirt – once plagued the island. And while public health initiatives have reduced the prevalence of the disease, the possibility of catching it still exists; frequent bathing and the use of footwear is the best prevention.

EMERGENCY
Throughout Puerto Rico, dial ☎ 911 for emergency service of any sort. This is a free call from any phone. A few rural phones might not have this service, in which case you should dial ☎ 0 for the operator and ask for emergency assistance – it's still free. Other emergency phone numbers to keep on hand include the following:

Police	☎ 787-343-2020
Fire	☎ 787-343-2330
Ambulance	☎ 787-343-2550
Medical assistance	☎ 787-754-3535

Carry a photocopy of your passport separately from your passport. Copy the pages with your photo and personal details, passport number and US visa. If it is lost or stolen, this will make replacing it easier. In this event, you should call your local consulate or embassy. You can find your consulate's telephone number by dialing information on the island (☎ 411). To reach your embassy, call directory assistance for Washington, DC (☎ 202-555-1212).

Similarly, carry copies of your traveler's check numbers and credit card numbers separately. If you lose your credit cards or they are stolen, contact the company immediately (see Credit & Debit Cards, earlier in this chapter, for company phone numbers). Contact your bank if you lose your ATM card.

LEGAL MATTERS
If you are stopped by the police for any reason, bear in mind that there is no system of paying fines on the spot. Attempting to pay the fine to the officer is frowned upon at best and may compound your troubles by resulting in a charge of bribery. For traffic offenses, the police officer will explain your options to you. Should the officer decide that you should pay up front, he or she can exercise their authority and take you directly to the magistrate instead of allowing you the usual 30-day period to pay the fine.

If you are arrested for more serious offenses, you are allowed to remain silent. There is no legal reason to speak to a police officer if you don't wish, but never walk away from an officer until given permission. All persons who are arrested are legally allowed (and given) the right to make one phone call. If you don't have a lawyer or family member to help you, call your embassy. The police will give you the number upon request.

Drinking Laws

The drinking age is only 18 on the island – three years younger than in the USA! Legally you need an ID (identification with your photograph on it) to prove your age. Servers and police on patrol have the right to ask to see your ID and may refuse service or arrest you if you are drinking without an ID. In Puerto Rico, minors are not permitted in bars and pubs, even to order nonalcoholic beverages. Ostensibly, this prohibition means that most dance clubs are also off-limits to minors, but door guards seem to make liberal exceptions for pretty young women.

As recently as 1998, drinking in the streets of Old San Juan while bar-hopping was a favorite pastime of sanjuaneros on weekends. But now the city council has enacted a stiff law to stop the drinking in the streets. If you get caught, you will be fined US$500. The establishment that served you the drink will be charged US$1000. Furthermore, you could incur stiff fines, jail time and penalties if caught driving under the influence of alcohol. During fiestas, holidays and special events, roadblocks are frequently set up to deter drunk drivers.

Nevertheless, alcohol is much more a part of the social scene on the island than it is in many parts of the USA and Europe. Unlike the USA, Puerto Rico has few 'blue laws' prohibiting the times and places where alcohol can be consumed. This means that drinking (even underage drinking) is rampant during fiestas – as it is every Thursday to Sunday in San Juan and beach resort towns when islanders are in party mode. There are a lot of police on the streets of Puerto Rico's entertainment zones these days, patrolling for underage drinkers as well as the drunk or disorderly. Let the traveler beware!

Driving under the influence of alcohol or drugs is a serious offense in the US, subject to stiff fines and even imprisonment. For more information on driving and road rules, see the Getting Around chapter.

BUSINESS HOURS

Businesses are open 8 am to 5 pm, but there are certainly no hard and fast rules. Shops are usually open 9 or 10 am to 5 or 6 pm (often until 9 pm in shopping malls and on Friday evening), except on Sunday, when hours are 11 am to 5 pm (often later in malls). Post offices are open 8 am to 4 or 5:30 pm weekdays, and some are open 8 am to 1 pm Saturday. Banks are usually open 8 am to 2:30 pm weekdays, 9:45 am to noon on Saturday. Sometimes hours are decided by individual branches, so if you need specifics, give the branch a call.

PUBLIC HOLIDAYS

US public holidays are celebrated along with local holidays in Puerto Rico. Banks, schools and government offices (including post offices) are closed and transportation, museums and other services are on a Sunday schedule. Holidays falling on a weekend are usually observed the following Monday.

New Year's Day
    January 1

Three Kings Day (feast of the Epiphany)
    January 6

Eugenio María de Hostos' Birthday (honors the island educator, writer and patriot)
    January 10

Martin Luther King Jr Day
    3rd Monday in January

Presidents' Day
    3rd Monday in February

Emancipation Day (island slaves were freed on this date in 1873)
    March 22

Palm Sunday
    Sunday before Easter

Good Friday
    Friday before Easter

Easter
    A Sunday in late March/April

Jose de Diego Day
    April 18

Memorial Day
    Last Monday in May

Independence Day/Fourth of July
    July 4

Luis Muñoz Rivera's Birthday (honors the island patriot and political leader)
    July 18

Constitution Day
July 25

Jose Celso Barbosa's Birthday
July 27

Labor Day
1st Monday in September

Columbus Day
2nd Monday in October

Veterans' Day
November 11

Thanksgiving Day
4th Thursday in November

Christmas Day
December 25

Besides the above holidays, the USA and Puerto Rico celebrate a number of others. Here are some of the most widely observed ones (note that businesses do not close on these days):

February
Valentine's Day – the 14th. No one knows why St Valentine is associated with romance in the USA and Puerto Rico, but this is the day to celebrate.

March
St Patrick's Day – the 17th. This holiday celebrates the patron saint of Ireland and has become the occasion for major-league pub crawling in the US. Puerto Ricans' Irish connection began in the 18th century with the appearance of Alejandro O'Reilly as the king of Spain's special emissary to the island.

May
Mother's Day – the 2nd Sunday. Children send cards and flowers and call Mom. Restaurants are likely to be busy.

June
Father's Day – the 3rd Sunday. Same idea, different parent.

December
New Year's Eve – the 31st. People celebrate with few traditions other than dressing up, taking to the streets of Old San Juan and drinking champagne.

SPECIAL EVENTS
Every Puerto Rican town honors its patron saint annually. These *fiestas patronales* occur throughout the year and generally begin on a Friday 10 days before the saint's day. The fiestas usually take place in the town's central plaza and have the carnival atmosphere typical of such celebrations throughout Latin America. Salsa bands and more traditional music stir seas of dancers and gawkers. Gambling stalls attract crowds. The air fills with the scent of *lechón asado* (roast pork). The sky pops with fireworks. Beer and rum lubricate every gesture of the celebration. And auto traffic snarls to a crawl.

The fiestas climax with a parade on the Sunday nearest the saint's day in which parishioners of various churches carry large wooden effigies of the saint through the streets. Frequently, the music, dance and rituals associated with the parade blend African and some Taíno traditions with Roman Catholic protocol. For a complete and up-to-date list of these fiesta patronales, contact the Puerto Rico Tourism Company at ☎ 787-721-2400.

Below is a list of other island events that have cultural as well as entertainment value. The telephone numbers listed will connect travelers with event organizers or local tourist offices.

February
Coffee Harvest Festival, Maricao – mid-month. This is like a fiesta patronal but with demonstrations on traditional coffee making and local crafting. The rugged mountain setting of the town is sublime, and the fresh air fills with the scents of roasting beans. For details, call ☎ 787-838-2290.

Coffee Harvest Festival, Yauco – 2nd weekend. This festival is much like the one above; it's just staged in a different town. ☎ 787-856-1345

Carnaval, Ponce – six days preceding the beginning of Catholic Lent. During this time, Catholics and folks who love to party come to Ponce to celebrate and give themselves up to food, alcohol and romance before Lent begins. During Lent, they deny themselves the pleasures of the body until after Easter. While this event is not up to the standards of Rio de Janeiro's Carnaval or New Orleans' Mardi Gras, it is a hopping good time in the tradition of put-on-a-mask (or just pretend), wear funny clothes (cross-dressing is always cool) and party 'til you drop. This is one of the great places to see parades of *vejigantes*, the traditional horned maskers. ☎ 787-841-8044

March

Feria Dulce Sueño, Guayama – generally the 1st weekend of the month. This is the place for horse lovers to view an upscale competition among the island's famous Paso Fino, the smooth-gaited horses. ☎ 787-834-1988

April

Festival de Mavi, Juana Diaz – date varies. Like a fiesta patronal, this event may have special appeal to aficionados of strange brews. Crowds gather in the square of this south-coast town to imbibe a fermented beverage called *mavi* that comes from the bark of the ironwood tree. ☎ 787-837-2185 ext 2001

Festival de Azucar, San Germán – late in the month. With all the usual trappings of local fiestas, this event gives travelers a chance to see exhibitions on cane farming past and present. You could see the same thing by visiting a living-history museum, but you'd miss the chance to drink so much of the distilled essence of cane (rum), the national beverage. ☎ 787-892-5574

May

Fiesta Nacional de la Danza, Ponce – mid-month. This event features a week of music and dance concerts that celebrate the stately music of string quartets and the 19th-century ballroom dance that was the hallmark of island sophistication in the days when elegance and manners were more important. ☎ 787-284-4141

June

Festival Casals, San Juan – most of the month. This celebration of orchestral music is the premier musical event in Puerto Rico, and probably all of the Caribbean. Founded by the great cellist Pablo Casals, who retired in Puerto Rico, the festival is now more than 40 years old and draws world-class conductors and musicians for two weeks of concerts. Concert tickets can cost US$20 to US$40, but students, seniors and disabled persons can get a 50% discount. ☎ 787-721-2400 or 800-223-6530

Fiesta de San Juan Bautista Day, San Juan – the 21st. Here you have the big enchilada, the fiesta patronal of the island capital. You will find the narrow streets of Old San Juan filled with a crush of party animals. At midnight, legions of people walk backward into the sea (or sometimes fountains) three times to demonstrate their loyalty to the saint of Christian baptism and gain his blessing for the coming year. ☎ 787-721-2400

Festival de Flores, Aibonito – end of the month. You can see acres of roses, carnations, lilies, begonias, etc, come to life in the fresh air of this attractive mountain town. ☎ 787-735-2871

July

Fiesta de Santiago, Loíza Aldea – end of the month. Loíza is the place to come if you want to see one way that Puerto Ricans of African descent keep their ties to Africa alive. This is a fiesta worthy of Bahía in Brazil – parades, fabulous drum ensembles, masks and costumes revive saints, such as Santiago, who according to the traditions of Santería are incarnations of West African gods. ☎ 787-876-3570

November

Jayuya Indian Festival, Jayuya – mid-month. Although all pure-blooded Taínos have been gone for about 400 years, this festival does a decent job of reviving the games, costumes, food and music of the original islanders. As with almost all Puerto Rican fiestas, there is a beauty pageant, this time with young women in Indian dress. ☎ 787-828-5010

December

Hatillo Masks Festival, Hatillo – the 28th. Here is the island's third major festival of maskers. This one features masked devils prowling the streets as incarnations of the agents of King Herod, who sent his soldiers into the streets of Judea to find and kill the Christ Child. Kids think it is great fun to run and hide from the maskers.

ACTIVITIES

Puerto Rico's tropical climate and variety of land/seascapes make the island a mecca for outdoor activities – this is a place where you could spend a lifetime at play.

See the Getting Around chapter for a listing of tour operators who provide activity-oriented trips on the island. See the regional chapters for more information on the activities described below.

Swimming

With about 750 miles of coastline, Puerto Rico offers travelers a host of swimming beaches. Public beaches, called *balnearios*, feature lockers, showers and parking at nominal rates but do not necessarily provide professional lifeguards. These beaches are closed on Monday, Election Day (usually in early November) and Good Friday. Hours are 9 am to 5 pm in summer, 8 am to 5 pm in winter. For a complete list, contact the Dept of Recreation and Sports (☎ 787-722-1551).

All the balnearios are in lovely settings, but travelers should beware: These beaches can be packed on weekends when island families flee their urban apartments, and some of the beaches draw unsavory crowds. In contrast, some of these beaches look like ghost towns during the week. On one visit to Vieques, we found the Sombé (Sun Bay) balneario unattended for days except by a wild horse with a broken leg.

In general, if a beach and its clientele do not seem safe to you, they probably are not. Many travelers find it worth paying a hotel concessionaire a few dollars to rent beach chairs and an umbrella for the relative security of a resort's beach and facilities.

See Recreational Hazards, earlier in this chapter, for information about things to watch out for in and around the ocean.

Diving & Snorkeling

While freshwater run-off from tropical rains makes Puerto Rico's seawater a bit more cloudy than in other places in the Caribbean, diving and snorkeling here are world-class. Water temperatures hover around 80°F – eliminating the need for a wetsuit – while visibility is usually 70 feet or farther. Fringe, ribbon and bank reefs all lie off the Puerto Rican coast. Almost all the major types of coral – from brain to seafans to giant elkhorn – flourish on Puerto Rican reefs and attract rich collections of sea life. Parrotfish, clownfish, puffers, mullets, rays, groupers, sharks and barracuda are plentiful. You may also see octopus, moray eels and manatees.

You will find a good collection of snorkeling reefs off the coasts of Vieques, Culebra and Fajardo. If you have a boat, head for the unspoiled reefs off the small cays east of Fajardo, such as Palominos and Icacos. The cays off the south and east coasts, including Isla Caja de Muertos, Cayo Cardona and Cayo Santiago (where all the monkeys live), also have good shallow reefs. Although the waters off the north and east coasts are often rough, on calm days you can snorkel the fringe reefs off Condado and Isla Verde as well as Rincón's Little Malibu.

More than a dozen dive operators run day trips out of the major ports and resort hotels around the island (see the regional chapters for more details). If you are in the San Juan area, consider a dive trip to the caves and overhangs at Horseshoe Reef, Figure Eight or the Molar. There's great diving along the chain of islands called 'La Cordillera,' east of Las Cabezas de San Juan (in the Fajardo area). Catch the Drift or the Canyon off Humacao. Spectacular wall dives lie 6 miles out of La Parguera on the south coast. From the Rincón area, consider a trip to the fringe reefs and caves at Isla Desecheo. If you're not limited by money and true adventure diving is your thing, you must take a multiday diving trip to the virgin reefs 50 miles west of Mayagüez at uninhabited Isla Mona. See the West Coast chapter for information about guided hiking and diving trips to Isla Mona.

Travelers planning a dive expedition should get Steve Simonsen's *Diving & Snorkeling Guide to Puerto Rico* (Pisces) and request the useful 24-page booklet called *Puerto Rico Scuba Guide* from the Puerto Rico Tourism Company (☎ 800-223-6530). These volumes have lists of dive sites and dive operators around the island.

Surfing

Since the 1968 world surfing championships at Rincón, surfers the world over have known that Puerto Rico ranks with a few sites in Mexico (such as Puerto Escondido, Oaxaca) and Costa Rica for some of the biggest and best winter surfing in all of the Americas. The island has plenty of surf shops and beach concessions that will rent you a board for about US$20 a day, so don't worry if you didn't bring your *tabla*.

If you stay close to San Juan, you will find the *surferos'* scene at the beaches eastward from Isla Verde. But for the big stuff, you need to make a pilgrimage to Rincón, which hosts numerous important competitions each year. Stop at the West Coast Surf Shop (see Rincón in the West Coast chapter). Here you can get the current information on where it's breaking, as you might find great breaks off beaches all along the coast, from Rincón to Isabela. Most of the breaks are north of town. Note: These breaks are for seasoned surfers only, as there are hazards such as submerged rocks, undertows and surf that can often go way over 12 feet during the winter months. If you want to get stoked before you go, try to get a copy of the island-made surf video *La Bruja Puerto Rico* (The Puerto Rican Witch).

Windsurfing

Puerto Rico played host to the Ray Ban Windsurfing World Cup in 1989, and the sport has been booming here ever since. Hotdoggers head for the surfing beaches at Isla Verde or – better yet – the rough northwest coast. Some of the favorite sites here

Considerations for Responsible Diving

The popularity of diving is placing immense pressure on many sites. Please consider the following tips when diving, and help to preserve the ecology and beauty of reefs.

Do not use anchors on reefs, and take care not to ground boats on coral. Encourage dive operators and regulatory bodies to establish permanent moorings at popular dive sites.

Avoid touching living marine organisms with your body or dragging equipment across the reef. Polyps can be damaged by even the gentlest contact. Never stand on corals, even if they look solid and robust. If you must hold onto a reef, touch only exposed rock or dead coral.

Be conscious of your fins. Even without contact, the surge from heavy fin strokes near the reef can damage delicate organisms. When treading water in shallow reef areas, take care not to kick up clouds of sand. Settling sand can easily smother delicate reef organisms.

Practice and maintain proper buoyancy control. Divers who descend too fast and collide with a reef can do major damage. Make sure you are correctly weighted and that your weight belt is positioned so that you stay horizontal. If you have not dived for a while, have a practice dive in a pool before taking to the reef. Be aware that buoyancy can change over the period of an extended trip. Initially, you may breathe harder and need more weight; a few days later you may breathe more easily and need less weight.

Take great care in underwater caves. Spend as little time as possible within them, as your air bubbles may be caught within the roof and thereby leave previously submerged organisms high and dry. Taking turns to inspect the interior of a small cave lessens the chances of damaging contact.

Resist the temptation to collect or buy corals or shells. Aside from the ecological damage, taking home marine souvenirs depletes the beauty of a site and spoils others' enjoyment. The same goes for marine archaeological sites (mainly shipwrecks). Respect their integrity; some sites are even protected from looting by law.

Ensure that you take home all your trash and any litter you may find as well. Plastics in particular are a serious threat to marine life. Turtles can mistake plastic for jellyfish and eat it.

Resist the temptation to feed fish. You may disturb their normal eating habits, encourage aggressive behavior or feed them food that is detrimental to their health.

Minimize your disturbance of marine animals. In particular, do not ride on the backs of turtles, as this causes them great anxiety.

include Crash Boat Beach in Aguadilla and Playas Shacks, Jobos and Wilderness near the town of Isabela.

If you are just getting started, try the Laguna Condado in San Juan, where the wind is constant and there are no waves. The protected waters off El Conquistador Resort & Country Club and the Wyndham Palmas del Mar Resort on the east coast are great for novices, as are the bays at La Parguera and Boquerón. All the shoreside resort hotels have board rentals and instruction.

Sailing

The semiprotected waters off the east end of Puerto Rico, which include the so-called Spanish Virgin Islands of Culebra and Vieques, provide the setting for racing and cruising aboard sailboats. Out here you can count on the trade winds blowing 12 to 25 knots out of the east almost every day. A number of marinas meet sailors' needs in the Fajardo area. The largest is the massive Puerto del Rey Marina (☎ 787-860-1000), with 750 slips and room for vessels up to 200 feet long. A number of yachts carry passengers on picnic/snorkeling/sailing day charters out of Puerto del Rey and the four other marinas in the area (see Fajardo and Palmas del Mar in the East Coast chapter). These trips cost about US$55 per person for a six-hour sail and offer a good value if you want to enjoy a day of the cruisers' life.

More serious cruisers may want to rent a 'bareboat' (sail-it-yourself) from Sun Yachts (☎ 787-863-4813, 888-772-3500, sunyacht@prtc.net), at Puerto del Rey Marina in Fajardo. Sun Yachts has 36-foot to 51-foot boats for US$1680 to US$5390 per week for experienced sailors who want to cruise the islands. For additional information on chartering boats, see the Boat section in the Getting Around chapter.

If you are planning a bareboat adventure, book five or six months in advance and get a copy of the *Yachtsman's Guide to the Virgin Islands and Puerto Rico* from Tropic Island Publications (☎ 305-893-4277), PO Box 611141, North Miami, FL 33161. See Books, earlier in this chapter, for other good cruising guides.

Fishing

Puerto Rico hosts many deep-sea fishing tournaments, including the prestigious International Billfishing Tournament (in August/September), which is the longest-held billfish tournament in the world (see the San Juan chapter for more information). The quarry here is the giant blue marlin – as in Hemingway's *The Old Man and the Sea* – but 'big blue' is only one of the major game fish that patrol the thermoclines along the deep drop-offs along the north, west and south coasts of the island. You can fish for tuna all year long. Marlin is a spring/summer fish, sailfish and wahoo run in the fall and dorado show up in the winter.

Many charters run from the San Juan Bay Marina; see the San Juan chapter for details. You can also charter out of docks in Fajardo, Palmas del Mar, La Parguera and Puerto Real.

If you bring your own equipment, you can fish for large-mouth bass, sunfish, catfish and tilapia in the island's freshwater lakes. For more information, contact the Depto de Recursos Naturales (Dept of Natural Resources; ☎ 787-722-5938).

Golf

With 10 championship golf courses on the island, Puerto Rico has earned the reputation of being the 'Scotland of the Caribbean.' The top courses on the island are the four 18-hole courses designed by Robert Trent Jones at the Hyatt Regency Cerromar Resort & Casino, in Dorado on the north coast, and the nearby Hyatt Dorado Beach Resort & Casino (☎ 787-796-1234 for both resorts). The Dorado courses feature ocean vistas and some of the most challenging holes in the Caribbean.

Gary Player designed the 18-hole course at the Wyndham Palmas del Mar Resort (☎ 787-285-2256), near Humacao on the east end of the island, where holes 11 to 15 have been called the 'toughest five successive holes in the Caribbean.' Also on the east end of the island, golfers will find a challenge with the 200-foot changes in elevation on the course at the El Conquistador Resort & Country Club (☎ 787-863-1000) in Fajardo, and two courses by Greg Norman and Tom and George Fazio at the Westin Río Mar Beach Resort and Country Club (☎ 787-888-8811). The Bahía Beach Public Golf Course and the Berwind Country Club course are also in this area (see the East Coast chapter for contact details).

If you are on the west coast and craving a game, consider the Club Desportivo del Oeste (☎ 787-851-8880) at Cabo Rojo, or the Punta Borinquen Golf Club (☎ 787-890-2987) in Aguadilla.

Greens fees for most of these courses start at about US$65, and for nonguests they soar higher than US$100 at resort courses such as the Hyatt Dorado Beach. The exceptions are the courses in Aguirre and Aguadilla, where you can get in a game for less than US$20.

Tennis

Puerto Rico boasts well over 100 tennis courts, with more than 20 each at the mega-resorts of Hyatt Dorado Beach (on the north coast) and Wyndham Palmas del Mar (on the east coast). As you would expect, virtually all of the island's resorts have private courts (for guests only) and most have pros as well. But court fees are pricey, starting at US$15 and climbing to US$22 for prime time (6 to 8 pm). If you are addicted, consider booking a special tennis package through one of the resorts. There are a few public courts in San Juan, Ponce and Maya-güez. Some of the island's inns have courts that charge minimal fees.

The island hosts a number of tournaments annually, including the Puerto Rican Open and the Bud Light Tennis Classic.

Hiking

Among both tourists and islanders, the most popular hiking area in Puerto Rico is the national rain forest at El Yunque, with about 23 miles of hiking trails, including the steep ascent to El Toro peak (3522 feet). You can get trail maps at El Portal Tropical Forest Center. For more information on El Yunque, see the East Coast chapter.

While there is absolutely nothing second-rate about adventuring in El Yunque rain forest – people have actually gotten lost here for days – even wilder hikes await experienced trekkers in the heart of the high mountains of the Cordillera Central. If you want a serious challenge, pick up a trail map at the visitors center for the Reserva Forestal Toro Negro (Black Bull Forest Reserve) on Hwy 143 and make the rugged hike to Cerro de Punta (4389 feet, the highest point on the island) or to Salta Inabón. But don't expect to always have dramatic vistas, as clouds often shroud the peaks and keep the trails and flora damp. See the Central Mountains chapter for further details. All the commonwealth's *reservas forestales* (forest reserves) offer good hikes, as does the dry forest in Guánica.

Two great ways to make a trek in the company of Puerto Rican hikers with local knowledge is to take the hike through the Cañón de San Cristóbal; it leaves at 8:30 am most Saturdays from La Piedra restaurant (☎ 787-735-1034) in Aibonito – reservations are required (see the Central Mountains chapter for details on the canyon). You can also call the Fondo de Majoramiento (☎ 787-759-8366) and ask to join one of its day trips. These hikes cover the entire length of the island from east to west along the Cordillera Central in successive weekend day trips. A hike usually costs US$6/3 for individuals/students.

Horseback Riding

The Wyndham Palmas del Mar Resort (☎ 787-852-6000 ext 10310) in Humacao has the island's largest equestrian facility, Rancho Buena Vista, which serves the public with more than 40 horses. Here you will find instruction, a good mix of trail rides and even schooled hunters for jumping. Riders should also check out the Centro Equestre de Dulce Sueño (☎ 787-725-0937), at the Old Naval Base in San Juan; Tropical Trail Rides (☎ 787-872-9256), in Isabela on Hwy 4466 at Km 1.8; and Hacienda Carabaldi (☎ 889-5820), in Mameyes near Luquillo at the east end of the island. Horses at these stables will cost you more than US$20 an hour, but you will sometimes find local farm boys at popular beaches – particularly on

Vieques – with horses for hire for less than US$15 an hour if you bargain.

Bird-Watching
The best sites for birding are El Yunque, Maricao and the Guánica dry forest. If you want a guided tour, check with the ecotour companies listed under Organized Tours in the Getting Around chapter.

Bicycling
The high density of automobiles on the island makes bike touring difficult, particularly on the thickly settled north coast of the island. And rugged terrain and frequently slick turf (from tropical showers) on the prime mountain biking trails of the Cordillera Central make freelancing one of these trails risky. Since there is safety in numbers, most travelers do their touring or mountain biking through one of the adventure tour operators (see Organized Tours in the Getting Around chapter).

The best area for cycle touring is along the secondary roads on the south coast of the island, through the gently rolling hills of the coastal plain around Guánica, Cabo Rojo and Sabana Grande. Sabana Grande is the site of the International Cycling Competition each May.

For more information, contact the Cycling Federation (☎ 787-721-7185) or bike shops in San Juan such as Puerto Rico Bikes (☎ 787-761-5560) and the Bike Stop (☎ 787-782-2282). These shops know the touring and trail riding scenes out on the island, but they can point you to an expanding network of safe bike routes around San Juan as well.

If you really want to feel comfortable just tooling around on a bike from day to day, head to the less densely populated islands of Vieques or Culebra, where the terrain is gentle, the roads are open and the scenery is rural. You can rent bikes through guesthouses and vendors; see the Spanish Virgin Islands chapter for details.

LANGUAGE COURSES
The Universidad de Puerto Rico at Río Piedras (San Juan) offers many courses in conversational Spanish through the Multi-lingual Institute (☎ 787-763-4122). Courses start in August, January and June. During the fall and spring sessions, classes usually meet twice a week for two hours. The summer course has more intensive training for a month. You can choose between beginning, low intermediate, high intermediate and advanced classes. Most courses cost less than US$200.

WORK
With more than 13% unemployment, Puerto Rico is clearly a place that has more human resources than its economy needs, and jobs are scarce. Nevertheless, travelers with skills – such as diving instructors or those with a US commercial captain's license or forestry credentials – can sometimes find seasonal work in the national forests and other tourist sites. If you are looking to squat for a while and replenish the travel kitty, consider out-of-the-way beach areas where there are relatively few Puerto Ricans who should rightly get the low-key resort jobs first. The village of Esperanza on Vieques is one such site, as are Rincón and the island of Culebra. If you are good at carpentry, you might find work as a 'handyman' helping with the restoration of apartment buildings in Old San Juan. Many of these operations are the dreams of young American entrepreneurs, so check out their after-work haunts, such as some of the bars on Calle San Sebastián like Nono's. Experienced cooks, bartenders and salespeople may also find work in the tourist areas of San Juan.

If you are not a US citizen, you need to apply for a work visa from the US embassy in your home country before you leave. The type of visa varies depending on how long you're staying and the kind of work you plan to do. Generally, you'll need either a J-1 visa, which you can obtain by joining a visitor-exchange program, or a H-2B visa, which you get when sponsored by a US/Puerto Rican employer. The latter can be difficult to obtain (since the employer is required to prove that no US citizen or permanent resident is available to do the job); the former is issued mostly to students for work in summer camps.

ACCOMMODATIONS

Lodging rates in Puerto Rico vary significantly (sometimes more than 30%) from season to season and even from day to day, as hotels adjust rates according to the perceived demand. In general, rates are highest from December 15 through the end of May. They are also high during June, July and August, when many island families take their vacations. Rates are lowest from September 1 to December 14. Because prices change so frequently, the rates listed in this book include a range for each place unless otherwise noted. The prices given in this

---

Considerations for Responsible Hiking

The popularity of hiking, trekking and bushwalking is placing great pressure on the natural environment. Please consider the following tips when hiking, and help to preserve the ecology and beauty of Puerto Rico.

Trash

Carry out all your trash. If you've carried it in, you can carry it out. Don't overlook easily forgotten items such as silver paper, orange peel, cigarette butts and plastic wrappers. Empty packaging weighs very little anyway and should be stored in a dedicated trash bag. Try to carry out trash left by others.

Never bury your trash: Digging disturbs soil and ground cover and encourages erosion. Buried trash will more than likely be dug up by animals, who may be injured or poisoned by it. It may also take years to decompose.

Minimize the waste you must carry out by taking minimal packaging and taking no more food than you need. If you can't buy in bulk, unpack small-portion packages and combine their contents in one container before your trip. Take reusable containers or stuff sacks.

Don't rely on bought water in plastic bottles. Disposal of these bottles is creating a major problem, particularly in developing countries. Use iodine drops or purification tablets instead. Sanitary napkins, tampons and condoms should be carried out despite the inconvenience. They burn and decompose poorly.

Human Waste Disposal

Contamination of water sources by human feces can lead to the transmission of hepatitis, typhoid, and intestinal parasites such as giardia, amoebas and roundworms. Contamination can cause severe health risks not only to members of your party, but also to local residents and wildlife.

Where there is a toilet, please use it. Where there is none, bury your waste. Dig a small hole 6 inches deep and at least 270 feet from any body of water. Consider carrying a lightweight trowel for this purpose. Cover the waste with soil and a rock. Use toilet paper sparingly and bury it with the waste.

If the area is inhabited, ask locals if they have any concerns about your chosen toilet site.

Ensure that these guidelines are applied to a portable toilet tent if one is used by a large trekking party. Make sure everyone uses the site.

Washing

Don't use detergents or toothpaste in or near bodies of water, even if they are biodegradable.

For personal washing, use biodegradable soap and a water container (or even a lightweight portable basin) at least 135 feet away from the body of water. Disperse the wastewater

book do not reflect room taxes, which are 15% at hotels with casinos, 9% elsewhere.

Note that if you are planning to visit the island during the winter tourist season, you should make your reservations a minimum of three months in advance to get a decent selection and price. You should also reserve several months in advance for the summer season. Unless otherwise stated, the prices given in this book don't reflect local taxes.

Camping
Camping is the cheapest, and in many ways the most enjoyable, approach to a vacation.

Considerations for Responsible Hiking

widely to allow the soil to filter it fully before it finally makes it back to the body of water. Wash cooking utensils 135 feet away from bodies of water, using a scourer or sand to clean them instead of detergent.

Erosion
Hillsides and mountain slopes are prone to erosion. It is important to stick to existing tracks and avoid shortcuts that bypass a switchback. If you blaze a new trail straight down a slope, it will turn into a watercourse with the next heavy rainfall and eventually cause soil loss and deep scarring.

If a well-used track passes through a mud patch, walk through the mud; walking around it will increase the size of the patch. Don't remove the plant life, which keeps topsoil intact.

Fires & Low-Impact Cooking
Don't depend on open fires for cooking. In popular trekking areas, cutting wood for fires can cause rapid deforestation. Cook on a lightweight kerosene, alcohol or Shellite (white gas) stove. Avoid those powered by disposable butane gas canisters.

Use local accommodations that do not use wood fires to heat water or cook food.

If you do light a fire, use an existing fireplace rather than creating a new one. Don't surround fires with rocks, as this creates a visual scar. Use only dead, fallen wood. Remember the adage 'the bigger the fool, the bigger the fire.' Use minimal wood, just what you need for cooking.

Ensure that you fully extinguish a fire after use. Spread the embers and douse them with water. A fire is only truly safe to leave when you can comfortably place your hand in it.

Wildlife Conservation
Do not engage in or encourage hunting, or buy items made from endangered species. Don't assume that animals in huts are vermin and attempt to kill them. In wild places, they are likely to be protected native animals.

Discourage the presence of wildlife by not leaving food scraps behind you. Place gear out of reach and tie packs to rafters or trees. Do not feed wildlife, as this can lead to animals becoming dependent on hand-outs, to unbalanced populations and to diseases.

Camping & Walking on Private Property
Seek permission to camp from landowners. They will usually be happy if asked but may be confrontational if not.

Trekking in Populated Areas
Respect social and cultural considerations (see the Facts about Puerto Rico chapter) when interacting with the local community.

Visitors with a car and a tent can take advantage of dozens of private and public campgrounds and RV parks around the island. And many camping areas are near the beaches. Prices run about US$10 per night at most areas, but permits for camping in the Caribbean National Forest at El Yunque are free.

Public Campgrounds These are on public lands such as national forests and commonwealth *reservas forestales* (forest reserves). To camp in one of the reserves, contact the Depto de Recursos Naturales (☎ 787-724-3724) at least 15 days in advance for reservations and a permit or visit their office near the Capitolio on Avenida Fernández Juncos in Puerta de Tierra. If you want to camp at one of the *balnearios* (public beaches), for reservations and information call the Compañía de Fomento Recreativo (☎ 787-722-1551, 722-1771), Apartado Postal No 3207, San Juan, PR 00904. To make a reservation, you must pay with Visa, MasterCard or Discover Card.

There is no fee or reservation necessary to camp in El Yunque, but you must get a permit at the Catalina Work Center (☎ 787-888-1880) in the forest, and it might be a good idea to call ahead for current conditions.

Information and detailed maps are available at local ranger stations (addresses and telephone numbers for ranger stations are given in this book) and may be posted along the road. All campers in Puerto Rico must set up their tents in designated camping areas, as no off-trail (dispersal camping) is legally permitted on the island. Designated camping areas usually have toilets, drinking water, fire pits (or charcoal grills) and picnic benches. While most areas have drinking water, it is always a good idea to bring a few gallons of water when venturing out to the boonies.

More developed areas may have showers or RV hookups and will cost you several dollars more than the price of a basic site. The national forest campgrounds tend to be less developed, while commonwealth-run forest-reserve campgrounds are more likely to have showers or RV hookups available.

The less-developed sites are often on a first-come, first-served basis, so plan on an early arrival, preferably during the week, as sites fill up fast with islanders on Friday and weekends. Many areas – such as the forest reserves – may accept or require reservations; see the regional chapters for details.

Costs given in this book for public campgrounds are per site. A site normally accommodates up to six people (or two vehicles). If there are more of you, you'll need two sites. Public campgrounds often have seven or 14-night limits.

Private Campgrounds These are on private property and are usually close to or in a town. Most are designed with RVs in mind; tenters can camp but fees are several dollars higher than in public campgrounds. Fees given in this book are for two people per site. There is usually an extra-person charge of US$1 to US$3 each. However, they may offer discounts for week or month-long stays.

Facilities can include hot showers, coin laundry, a swimming pool, full RV hookups, a games area, a playground and a convenience store.

Guesthouses

Puerto Rican guesthouses offer alternatives to the high prices and insularity that come with rooms in resort hotels in the tourist zones. Nevertheless, visitors should be aware that Puerto Rican guesthouses are not always the casual, inexpensive sort of accommodations found under the name of 'guesthouse' or 'B&B' in Europe. While most guesthouses are family-run, they generally require advance reservations, though some will be happy to oblige the occasional drop-in.

Since Puerto Rico has no strict definitions for types or classes of accommodations, places calling themselves 'guesthouses' can differ vastly from one to another. While some guesthouses may have as few as two rooms for travelers, others may boast as many as 25. While one guesthouse may look like a roadside motel on the US model, another may be a charming beach house with a pool, bar and restaurant. Some guesthouses are actually small colonies of free-standing cabins.

The cheapest establishments, with rooms in the US$25 range, may have clean but unexciting rooms with a shared bathroom. Pricier places have rooms with private baths and balconies, sundecks and public dining rooms with extensive menus and table service (at extra cost). They may be in a modern structure, quaint country home or urban beach house. Rooms at most guesthouses fall in the US$60 to US$100 price range, but some cost more than US$100. The best are distinguished by friendliness and attention to detail from the owners/hosts, who can provide you with local information and contacts and other amenities.

Hotels

There are only a few accommodations on the island with rooms for less than US$40, and almost all of these are found in small towns or unsavory neighborhoods of the cities. As is the case the world over, these hotels are often magnets for romantic trysts and prostitution. Rooms are usually small, and beds may be soft or saggy, but the sheets should be clean. A minimal level of cleanliness is maintained, but expect scuffed walls, atrocious decor, old furniture and strange noises from your shower. Even these places, however, normally have a private shower and toilet and a TV in each room. Most have air con.

With the addition of the Hampton Inn at Isla Verde, Puerto Rico has begun to add a few more moderately priced rooms to its hotel stock, but for the most part island hotels categorize themselves as 'luxury' or 'deluxe' establishments and rooms run more than US$150 per night unless you have a tour package. Of course, prices drop 30% or more between early June and mid-December (prices are at their lowest September 1 to December 14), but that often means that a room that costs US$220 in March still costs US$165 in September. The island has a couple of truly world-class hotels, such as the Horned Dorset Primavera near Rincón and El San Juan Hotel & Casino in Isla Verde, but not all of these places live up to their self-appointed ratings. In other words, do not expect the lavish services or fanciful

architecture in most Puerto Rican resort hotels that you'd get for the same price in places such as Cancún and Ixtapa, Mexico.

The exceptions to this caveat are the island's mega-resorts: the Hyatt Dorado Beach Resort & Casino and the Hyatt Regency Cerromar Resort & Casino (both 18 miles west of San Juan); El Conquistador Resort & Country Club (near Fajardo); the Westin Río Mar Beach Resort and Country Club (near Luquillo) and the Wyndham Palmas del Mar Resort (near Humacao). These resorts are self-contained fantasy worlds of 500 to 2500 acres with championship golf courses, restaurants, spas, tennis courts and a complete array of water sports.

Because of changing marketing strategies and seasons, the prices in this guide can be only an approximate guideline at best. Also, be prepared to add the 7% to 9% room tax, and probably add a 10% service charge as well, to quoted rates. Children are often allowed to stay free with their parents, but rules for this vary. Some hotels allow children under 18 to stay free with parents; others allow children under 12 to stay free; others may charge a few dollars per child. You should call and inquire if traveling with a family. Remember too that phone calls placed from a hotel tend to be very pricey (see Telephone, earlier in this chapter, for details).

The prices advertised by hotels are called 'rack rates' and are not written in stone. If you simply ask about any specials that might apply, you can often save quite a bit of money. Booking through a travel agent can also save you money. Members of AARP or AAA can qualify for a 'corporate' rate at several hotel chains.

Reservations Special events and conventions can fill up a town's hotels quickly, so call ahead to find out what will be going on. The local visitors center or tourist office is always a good resource.

The cheapest places may not accept reservations, but at least phone from the road to see what's available; even if they don't take reservations they'll often hold a room for an hour or two.

Inns

Thirty-five years ago, the Puerto Rico Tourism Company adopted the Spanish idea of creating a network of government-endorsed country inns for islanders and travelers looking for retreats in charismatic natural settings.

Today, the PRTC endorses 18 *paradores* (inns) as *paradores puertorrinqueños*, but not all these places refer to themselves as 'paradores.' To further confuse the matter, quite a few hotels and guesthouses on the island use the name 'parador' but are not endorsed by the PRTC (though that's not necessarily a condemnation). Both the endorsed paradores and those without the PRTC's stamp of approval are scattered over the island and range considerably in style from modern seaside-resort clones to rustic conversions of historic coffee plantations to simple guesthouses.

Prices for rooms in both the endorsed and nominal paradores are generally comparable to the cost of rooms in the self-proclaimed guesthouses. But you might be able to get a better deal if you offer to stay multiple nights during midweek, when upscale Puerto Rican couples and families (who tend to be the most frequent guests) have gone back to their homes in the cities and suburbs for work and school.

If you visit a parador puertorriqueño on the weekend, be prepared to be serenaded by live local music, particularly during the Sunday *cena* (elaborate family lunch). During the week, when nothing moves but the wind in the trees and the only noises are the melodies of songbirds, one of these old coffee plantations in the mountains can make you feel like you've gone back in time 150 years. For reservations, a complete list and pictures of the government-endorsed paradores, contact Paradores Puertorriqueños (☎ 800-443-0266 in the USA, 800-462-7575 in Puerto Rico).

Note: Since the term 'parador' represents so many different kinds of places to stay, this book does not use it as a category when listing accommodations, and you will find inns claiming to be paradores listed under 'Guesthouses' and 'Hotels.'

Vacation Centers

In addition to the paradores puertorriqueños, the Commonwealth of Puerto Rico maintains clusters of rental cottages around the island in Arroyo, Boquerón, Añasco, Humacao and Maricao. These *centros vacacionales* are popular with island families on weekends, holidays and summer vacations. Some areas have rather basic wooden cabins on the beach, but recent years have seen a massive redevelopment at the centers. Now, most of the accommodations are two-bedroom condos in attractive new duplex structures. These units are available to 'bona fide family groups' only, so don't show up with three college-age couples and expect to be welcomed. There is a minimum stay of two nights, a maximum stay of seven. Short-term rates run about US$65 a night for a unit that sleeps six, but you may get a special weekly rate from September 1 to May 31 (when island kids are in school). Bring your own sheets, or be prepared to rent them for US$15 per set. Kitchen gear is not included in the price.

Reserve up to 120 days in advance through the Oficina de Reservaciones (☎ 787-724-2500, 722-1771, 722-1551, 888-767-4732), Compañía de Fomento Recreativo, Apartado Postal No 3207, San Juan, PR 00904.

Rental Accommodations

This is the fastest-growing segment of the accommodations business in Puerto Rico, and consequently offers travelers on both short and extended stays some of the best value for their money if they are willing to settle down in one place for a week or more. We have seen rates for such rentals as low as US$35 a night and as high as US$300. But whatever you pay, you will be getting a lot for your money – perhaps even a housekeeper or cook.

During the last 20 years, Puerto Rico has seen a boom in vacation condo/villa construction in coastal areas such as Dorado, Palmas del Mar, Luquillo, Fajardo and Rincón. More than 20 luxury condo highrises have sprouted along the beach at Isla Verde in San Juan near the international airport. Since the owners use these condos/villas for only a fraction of the year, renting them is a way to defray expenses. In the off-season (generally May or June to mid-December), there is a buyers' market for these rentals. Most of the properties are in prime resort areas and include an attractive, well-furnished home with spectacular views. Culebra and Vieques also have active villa/apartment rentals, as do the Condado and Isla Verde beach areas of San Juan. You can even find some short-term apartment rentals in Old San Juan (for details, see Places to Stay under individual towns' sections).

Searching the Internet for 'Puerto Rico vacation rentals' will turn up pages of offerings, mostly from booking services that cover the entire Caribbean and beyond. Many of these services have good reputations and a long history of satisfied customers. Nevertheless, having a local agent can be useful when you want a comprehensive survey of the market or you have a problem.

Here are some island real estate agencies specializing in villa/apartment/condo vacation rentals:

San Juan
    Century 21 (☎ 787-728-6124)
    Condado Properties (☎ 787-724-4121)
    La Caleta (☎ 787-646-9667), Old San Juan
    Roca Realty (☎ 787-722-3966), Old San Juan
Fajardo
    BV Real Estate (☎ 787-863-3687)
Luquillo
    Playa Azul Apartments Realty (☎ 787-889-3425)
Palmas del Mar
    Caldwell Banker, Diana Marster, Inc
    (☎ 787-850-3030)
Rincón
    Island West Properties (☎ 787-823-2323)
    PRWest (☎ 787-727-4752, 888-779-3788)
Spanish Virgin Islands
    Laurel Real Estate (☎ 787-741-6806), Vieques
    Pelican Enterprises (☎ 787-742-0052), Culebra

FOOD

Usually eaten between about 7 and 9 am, typical Puerto Rican breakfasts are light and simple, except on weekends and holidays when people have more time to cook egg dishes such as *tortilla española* (Spanish omelette) or French toast. You can get American breakfasts at chains like Denny's...and many Puerto Ricans do. More traditional islanders stop at a *repostelería* (bakery) for a long sweet cup of *café con leche* (a blend of coffee and steamed milk) and a couple of slices of *pan criollo* (a bit like French bread) with butter or *queso de papa* (a mild island cheese). Folks with more of an appetite may get a sandwich. Those with a sweet tooth favor a *mallorca* (sweet pastry covered with powdered sugar).

Lunch is available between 11:30 am and 2 pm. Puerto Ricans usually go cheap on this event, flocking to fast-food outlets for burgers and the like or gathering around street vendors selling a variety of fried finger foods (see Snacks, below). To a large degree, islanders avoid leisurely luncheon meals in upscale restaurants, and you will find the noon meal the best time of day to sample good Puerto Rican cooking because the restaurants are not crowded and you can often find fixed-price specials for as little as US$6.

Dinners, served between about 6 pm and 10 pm, are more expensive, and a legion of prosperous islanders have developed a tradition of going out to restaurants – especially on Thursday, Friday and Saturday – as a prelude to a long 'night on the town.' Be prepared to wait for a table if you do not call ahead for reservations at popular spots (some of the better restaurants require reservations). The same is true for the big Sunday afternoon *cena* (lunch) at resort destinations near the beach, in the mountains or at a parador. Dinner specials may also be available, but they are usually quite a bit more expensive than virtually the same lunch specials.

Travelers who want to take some of the risk out of sampling island cuisine can take advantage of the Mesones Gastronómicos program, sponsored by the Puerto Rico Tourism Company. This program has identified a collection of restaurants around the island that feature Puerto Rican cuisine and has screened those restaurants according to the highest standards of quality. The PRTC publishes a list of these restaurants in their bimonthly magazine, *Qué Pasa*.

Most food shoppers patronize the large, US-style supermarkets such as the Pueblo chain around the island, but if you like the sights and smells of an open-air bazaar, grab a string bag and head to the Mercado de Río Piedras (San Juan) for the freshest fruit on the island, as well as an array of other foodstuffs, dry goods and clothing. Miramar, Ponce and Mayagüez have smaller markets.

Snacks

If you are worried about counting your calories or your cholesterol levels, watch out for Puerto Rican finger foods. Most of them are deep-fried in animal fat and taste like your next addiction. *Amarillos* are fried ripe plantains – an island staple – coated with a sugar, cinnamon and wine sauce. *Mofongo* is another traditional low-budget island snack, made from plantains. This time the plantains are mashed and mixed with pork rind and spices before they are fried. Want something more filling? Try an *empanadilla*, which is a

The Island Menu

Below is a handy list of common Puerto Rican menu items. See the Spanish for Travelers section at the back of this book for other useful Spanish words and phrases.

Entradas (Appetizers)
almejas frescas (cherrystone clams)
coctel de camarones (shrimp cocktail)
coctel de carrucho (conch salad)
coctel de pulpo (octopus salad)
pastelillos de chapin (fried dumplings of trunkfish)

Ensaladas (Salads)
ensalada de aguacate (avocado salad)
ensalada de camarones (shrimp salad)
ensalada de langosta (lobster salad)
ensalada mixta (mixed salad)
ensalada verde (green salad)

Sopas (Soups)
caldo de gallina or *sopa de pollo criollo* (creole chicken soup)
sopa de ajo (garlic soup)
sopa de cebolla (onion soup)
sopa de mariscos (seafood soup)
sopa de pescado (fish soup)
sopa de vegetales (vegetable soup)

Arroz (Rice)
arroz con habichuelas (rice and beans)
arroz con pollo (rice and chicken parts)
asopao de camarones (rice stew with shrimp)
asopao de langosta (rice stew with lobster)
asopao de pollo (rice stew with chicken)
asopao de pulpo (rice stew with octopus)

Aves (Poultry)
chicharrones de pollo (chicken crisps)
guineas al vino (guinea hen in wine)
pollo a la parilla (grilled chicken)
pollo al ajillo (chicken in garlic sauce)
pollo asado (roasted chicken, generally seasoned with sofrito)

Carnes (Meats)
bifstec pizzaola (breaded beef cutlets)
chicharrón (crisp pork rind)
chuletas (pork chops)
churrasco (charcoal-broiled Argentinean steak)
filete a la criolla (creole steak)
filete a la parrilla (broiled steak)
lechón asado (roast pig)
medallon de filete (beef medallions)
parrillada (spicy grilled steak)

Pescados y Mariscos (Fish & Seafood)
bacalaítos (fried codfish fritters)
bacalao a la Viscaina (codfish stewed in a tomato sauce)
camarones a la plancha (grilled shrimp)
camarones al ajillo (shrimp garlic style)
camarones enchiladas (broiled shrimp with creole sauce)
camarones fritos (fried shrimp)
camarones mariposa (shrimp butterfly style)
carrucho a la vinagreta (conch meat in vinegar sauce)
carrucho guisado (stewed conch meat)
chapin (trunkfish)
chillo al horno (oven-baked red snapper)

pocket of plantain or yucca dough stuffed with any number of meats. A sweeter version of the same concept is a *pastel,* with a stuffing of raisins, beans, fish or pork. *Pastelillos* are a smaller variation on this theme; meat and cheese are stuffed into the little darlings. You will no doubt see beach vendors selling *piononos,* deep-fried cones made from plantains stuffed with cheese (or cooked meat) and coated with egg batter.

Slightly healthier choices in the finger food department are popular sandwiches such as the *medianoche* (midnight), which has ham, pork and cheese on pan criollo, or the *cubano,* with chicken, ham and cheese on the same fresh bread.

Main Dishes
Soups and stew are staples in *cocina criolla* (Puerto Rican cooking), and in these brews

---

The Island Menu

jueyes (land crabs)
mero a la criolla (seabass creole style)
mero a la parrilla (broiled seabass)
mero a la plancha (grilled seabass)
ostiones (small local oysters)
sierra al horno (oven-baked kingfish)
sierra frito (fried kingfish)

Plátanos (Plantains)
alcapurrias (fish, pork or crab fried in a batter of ground plaintains)
amarillos en dulce (ripe plaintains fried in sugar, red wine and cinnamon)
mofongo (balls of mashed plaintains mixed with pork rind and spices and fried; sometimes stuffed with crab or lobster)
tostones (twice-fried plantains, sometimes coated with honey)

Postres (Desserts)
bien-me-sabe (a coconut sauce over sponge cake)
dulce de leche (candied milk)
flan (custard)
tembleque (pudding made from coconut)

Sandwiches
cubano (chicken, ham and cheese, lettuce, tomato and special sauce grilled in a long piece of local bread)

medianoche (the 'midnight'; contains ham, pork and cheese on pan criollo)

Cocina del Kiosko (Food-Stand Offerings)
empanadillas (plantain or yucca dough stuffed with meat or fish and fried)
limber (homemade Popsicle)
maní (peanuts)
natilla (ice cream)
pionono (cone of mashed plantains stuffed with seasoned ground meat, deep-fried in batter)
piragua (cup of shaved ice covered with a fruity syrup in the tradition of a US snow cone)

Snow cone stand, Old San Juan

BOB KRIST

you can taste a fusion of Taíno, European and African recipes and ingredients. Many soups use unique island vegetables to add texture, taste and vitamins. Some of these vegetables, such as *yautía* (tanier), *batata* (sweet potato), *yuca* (cassava), *chayote* (squash), *berzas* (collard greens) and *grelos* (turnip greens) might seem odd to North Americans and Europeans. But you'll learn to love these sprouts and tubers when the greens are simmering in a *caldero* (iron/aluminum kettle) with a peculiar mix of criollo spices. *Sancocho* (Caribbean soup) is a blend of many of the vegetables mentioned above, along with plantains – peeled and diced – and coarsely chopped tomatoes, green pepper, chili pepper, cilantro leaves, onion and corn kernels. To this mix the cook

Tastes of the Islands

The following are the author's own variations on traditional Puerto Rican recipes, representing just a few of the island's enticing culinary delights.

Mofongo
A plantain treat in the Afro-Caribbean tradition (for 4)

4 ripe plantains	Juice from half a lime
Fine olive oil for frying	12oz crisp *chicharrón* (fried pork
4 large garlic cloves	rind)

After peeling the plantains, cut them into 1-inch diagonal slices and soak for 10 minutes in water with a pinch of salt. Drain.

Heat olive oil to 350°F and fry the plantain slices for about 12 minutes. Take them out before they brown. Pat dry with paper towels.

In a large mortar, crush garlic cloves with 1tbs of olive oil and the lime juice, then remove.

Now use the mortar to crush some of the slices of fried plantains and the crisp pork rind together. As you crush this mixture, stir in crushed garlic, lime juice and olive oil until all the ingredients have been crushed into a sticky mash.

Roll the mash into balls the size of a small lime and serve hot.

For something more exotic, stuff the mofongo balls with crab or lobster meat.

Asopao de Pollo
Chicken stew (for 4)

4lb whole chicken	1 peeled onion, chopped
Adobo sauce*	9 cilantro leaves, ground or chopped
3 cups white rice	1 4oz can tomato sauce
10 cups water	2 chopped tomatoes
Pinch of salt	10 stuffed olives
3tbs fine olive oil	1 Spanish sausage, cut in 1/4-inch rounds
1oz salt pork, diced	2tbs capers
1oz lean ham, diced	2tbs achiote coloring
1 green pepper, chopped	1lb green peas
1 sweet chili pepper, chopped	1 bunch asparagus, tips only

Divide chicken and wash, reserving carcass and giblets. Lather all chicken parts with adobo sauce. Wash rice and soak under cover for a half hour.

adds water, some tomato sauce, chopped beef and a few pork ribs for flavoring before cooking it over a low heat.

Perhaps the best-known island concoction to come from a simmering caldero is *asopao de pollo*. This is a rich and spicy chicken stew that is fragrant with the ever-present and distinctive seasoning called *adobo* (garlic, oregano, paprika, peppercorns, salt, olive,

lime juice and vinegar crushed into a paste for seasoning meat). Adobo comes from Spain and exists in many Spanish-inspired cuisines, including Phillipine, with which it's most often associated.

In addition to adobo, another seasoning that infuses the taste of many criollo dishes is *sofrito*. You can now buy this seasoning on the spice shelves of Pueblo supermarkets,

Tastes of the Islands

Combine water, pinch of salt, carcass and giblets in an 8qt pot. Cover and boil over medium heat for 20 minutes. Reduce heat and cook for 30 minutes.

In a frying pan, heat the olive oil and rapidly brown the pork and ham. Reduce heat to low and sauté the green pepper, chili pepper, onion and cilantro for 5 minutes.

Add tomato sauce, chopped tomatoes, stuffed olives, sausage rounds, capers and achiote coloring. Cook 5 minutes.

Add chicken parts and mix over moderate heat until boiling. Cover this and cook for 40 minutes over moderate heat.

Add broth and giblets. Heat rapidly to a boil.

Drain rice, add to the stew along with the peas and the asparagus and cook over moderate heat until boiling. Reduce heat to low and cook until rice reaches soupy consistency.

Serve in stew bowls.

*You can buy commercially prepared adobo sauce, or make your own with 2tbs of vinegar, 3 peppercorns, 2 garlic cloves, 1tsp of dried oregano, $1/4$tsp of paprika, 2tsp of salt, and 1tsp of olive oil, all crushed and mixed in a mortar.

Piononos
Stuffed cones of plantain (for 4)

1lb ground beef	Small pinch of salt
Taco seasoning or equivalent	$1/2$tbs flour
2 large plantains	$1/2$tbs water
1 egg	Fine olive oil for frying

Pan fry the ground beef with seasoning, drain and let cool, reserving the remaining oil in the pan.

Peel the plantains and cut them each into 4 long slices. Reheat the frying pan and the oil in which you cooked the beef, and rapidly brown the plantains. Remove and pat dry on paper towels.

Roll each slice into a cone. Hold it together with a toothpick.

Beat the egg and salt together, then mix in the flour and water.

Fill the cone with ground beef and cover with the egg batter. Fry in hot oil with the stuffing face down. When the batter is golden, remove the cones and drain on paper towels. Take out the toothpicks and serve.

but discerning diners say there is nothing like the taste of sofrito made from scratch. Certainly the smells that waft from the preparation are enough to make the effort worth it to many cooks as they brown a mix of garlic, onions, and pepper in olive oil and cap the mix with *achiote* (annato seeds).

Puerto Ricans claim that the modern barbecue descends from the pork roast that the Taínos called *barbicoa*. In this vein, *lechón asado* (roast suckling pig), cooked on a spit over a charcoal fire, is the centerpiece of fiestas and family banquets, particularly at holiday gatherings. Of course, this barbecued pig has been liberally seasoned with adobo, and cooks baste it with achiote and the juice from *naranjas* (the island's sour oranges). When cooked to crispness, the meat is served with *ajili-mójili* (a tangy garlic sauce).

For less festive occasions, Puerto Rican dinners will almost always include the staples of *arroz con habichuelas* (rice and beans) and *tostones,* which are fried green plantains or *panapen* (breadfruit). To these staples, the cook almost always adds a meat dish such as roasted *cabro* (kid goat), *ternera* (veal), *pollo* (chicken) or *carne mechada* (roast beef) – all seasoned with adobo.

Surprisingly, Puerto Ricans do not eat a lot of fish. But one of the most popular ways to prepare a variety of fish – from *pulpo* (octopus) to *mero* (sea bass) – is *en escabeche*. This technique yields a fried then chilled seafood pickled in vinegar, oil, peppercorns, salt, onions, bay leaves and lime juice. Fried fish generally comes with a topping of *mojo isleño* (a piquant sauce of vinegar, tomato sauce, olive oil, onions, capers, pimentos, olives, bay leaves and garlic). Land crabs – *jueyes* – have long been a staple of poor islanders who can simply gather the critters off the beaches. An easy way to enjoy the taste is to eat *empanadillas de jueyes,* in which the succulent crab meat has been picked from the shells, highly seasoned and baked into an empanadilla of *casabe* paste. Of course, grilled or boiled *langosta* (local tropical lobsters without claws) is a pricey delicacy for both islanders and travelers alike. Also try the *ostiones* (miniature oysters) if you like shellfish.

Fish lovers should also try a bowl of *sopón de pescado* (fish soup), with its scent of onions and garlic and subtle taste of dry sherry.

Desserts

While the caramel custard *flan* – a mainstay of dessert eaters throughout the Spanish-speaking world from Spain to Argentina – is a popular after-dinner food among Puerto Rican cooks and diners, the island has some other offerings. Consider the *quesito*, a sweet, baked shell stuffed with a soft sugary cheese like an Italian cannoli and topped with honey. Then there is *tembleque*, which is a puddinglike concoction of coconut milk and cinnamon. *Mil hojas* (a thousand leaves) appeals to pastry lovers with layers of thin crust divided by a paste of honey and almonds. Order *bien-me-sabe* if you fancy a coconut delight served over ladyfingers.

Fruit

The plantain is, of course, the staple fruit of Puerto Ricans' diet, and like virtually all the fruits on the island, it was first introduced as an exotic import. Thanks to the nearly perfect tropical climate and enterprising Spanish traders during colonial times, Puerto Rico is a fruit-lover's paradise today. In addition to the many varieties of bananas planted here as seeds or seedlings from places as diverse as Asia and Africa, Puerto Rico can boast of oranges descended from China, pineapples from the South Pacific and coconuts from the Cape Verde Islands. Other exotic fruits include the *tamarindo* (tamarind) of the Middle East, the *níspero* (sapodilla) of Mexico and *panapen* (breadfruit) of Tahiti.

Local delicacies include the *carambola* (star fruit), the *lechosa* (papaya), *mamey* (mammee apple), the *acerola* (West Indian cherry) and *guanábana* (soursop), which yields a popular juice that mixes like ambrosia with rum. Islanders' small yards often feature *limones* (lime trees) – and *naranjas* (orange trees) – for decoration, fragrance and consumption. Highway vendors will sell you *chupones* from their trucks: These are the peeled, sweet *china* oranges.

Vegetarian

You can live a veggie lifestyle on the island, but you may have to work at it. The problems are the popularity of meat dishes and meat flavoring among Puerto Ricans, as well as the use of animal fat to cook the many fried foods. Even when cooks use high-quality vegetable oils for frying, they are likely to fry your food in the same oil they used for pork or beef.

Creative vegetarian cooks can find ways of using the island's fruits – and seasonings like adobo and sofrito – to spice up basic platters of rice and beans. If you are eating out, you will discover a number of Asian restaurants that can meet your preferences. In addition, a growing number of establishments feature vegetarian cooking (in the tourist areas of Condado, Ocean Park and Isla Verde) or at least offer vegetarian alternatives.

DRINKS
Nonalcoholic Drinks

As a part of the USA, Puerto Rico has all of the soft drinks and many of the juices found in mainland supermarkets and restaurants – which means that travelers could miss trying the beverages that are unique to the island. Two of these are the carbonated and noncarbonated versions of guanábana juice. Other local favorites are carbonated and noncarbonated cans of piña colada (the creamy mix of pineapple juice and coconut cream that can form the basis for a rum drink). *Mavi* is something like root beer, made from the bark of the ironwood tree. Many health-conscious islanders drink bottles of a nonalcoholic, vitamin-fortified malt beverage called Malta. While this is carbonated and looks like dark beer, the taste is sweet and nothing like the alcohol-free beer produced in the USA. As in much of the tropics, beach and street vendors sell chilled green coconuts – *cocos fríos* – to the thirsty.

No doubt the most popular drink on the island is *café con leche*. Most islanders take their café con leche with several spoonfuls of raw sugar when the brew is 'warm as wind, smooth as skin and sweet as sin.' In general, you can't go wrong with Puerto Rican coffee.

Alcoholic Drinks

Because Puerto Rico is a major producer of alcoholic beverages – and since the government has not levied outlandish taxes on alcohol – Puerto Rico is clearly one of the cheapest places to drink in the Caribbean, and perhaps the world. And make no mistake, alcohol plays a major role in island social life.

People younger than 18 (minors) are prohibited from consuming alcohol in Puerto Rico. Carry a driver's license or passport as proof of age to enter a bar, order alcohol at a restaurant, buy alcohol or – yes – drink on the beaches as well as streets of a lot of towns (but not in Old San Juan, where public drinking is illegal).

Rum The importance of this beverage to Puerto Rico can hardly be exaggerated. Simply put, *ron* (rum) is the national drink. Puerto Rico is the largest producer of rum in the world, and the distilleries bring hundreds of millions of dollars into the island economy. The industry is based on the sugarcane that Columbus brought here on his second voyage to the New World. The headquarters for the famous Bacardi Rum Factory is in Cataño (see the San Juan chapter) and the island also produces many other internationally known brands like Don Q, Ronrico, Castillo and Captain Morgan (spiced rum).

With at least 20 brands marketed on the island, a drinker might be overwhelmed by the choice of rums. But you can take a lot of the ambiguity out of the offerings by realizing that the Mature Spirits Act guarantees quality across the board. Beyond brand-name preferences, the choice of which Puerto Rican rum to drink boils down to three options: white, gold or *añejo* (aged). Dark rums are largely the product of Jamaica and other former British colonies such as Barbados.

White rums are the lightest, distilled and aged for as little as a year and often mixed with orange or tomato juice (a Puerto Rican Bloody Mary). Gold rums must be distilled and aged for three years, and this beverage is often an ingredient in the piña colada and the *cuba libre* (rum and Coke with a wedge of lime). The longest-aged, most flavorful and

Guide to Sweet, Cool Fire

Daiquiri
(for 2)
4oz white rum
3tsp fresh lime juice
2tsp sugar

Shake all ingredients with cracked ice. Strain into chilled cocktail glasses.

Piña Colada
(for 4)
8oz gold rum
8oz canned cream of coconut
8oz canned pineapple juice

Mix thoroughly with about 4 ice cubes in a blender. Spoon into chilled cocktail glasses.

expensive rums are añejo. These amber beverages are often sipped straight or *con hielo* (on the rocks) and can be 'called' by a patron in a bar who wants to show a touch of class.

Adventuresome drinkers may want to take a risk and imbibe a bit of *cañita* or *pinchita*. These are homemade, illegal rums that can be either blinding firewater or the smooth, treasured drinks of connoisseurs. The rule of thumb here is to be wary and not drink anything unless you know and trust the person offering you the beverage. On the other hand, the chance to sip a little cañita before dinner in a private home is tantamount to being welcomed into the fraternity of islanders, and it has ritualistic connotations equivalent to sharing *yaqona* (kava) with Fijians.

Beer You can get most American, Mexican, Canadian and European beer *(cerveza)* with ease in Puerto Rico, but of course the price goes up for anything that has to be shipped to the island. Fortunately, there are two island-brewed beers that often cost no more than US$1 to US$1.50 in local bars. The India brand has been around for years; Medalla is a popular light pilsner that quite a few islanders drink like water. One distinctive feature of beers on the island is that they come in 10oz cans instead of the regular 12oz cans you find in most of the world. This package was originally designed to preserve the market for local breweries and keep out American competition. Now, of course, Budweiser and Coors have their own 10oz canning plants on the island.

Presidente is a flavorful, strong, bottled premium beer imported from the neighboring Dominican Republic. It has a lot of snob appeal, and costs about five times as much here as it does in the Dominican Republic, 100 miles away.

ENTERTAINMENT

The passion that pulsates through Puerto Rico's salsa music says it all: Here is a culture that loves to share a good time. In fact, it sometimes seems like there are so many ways for people to entertain one another on the island that it's a wonder that anybody has time to work.

Casinos

San Juan is not Las Vegas, but with about a dozen casinos in the San Juan area alone and others in Ponce, Humacao and Mayagüez, casino gambling is clearly big business. The San Juan Grand Beach Resort & Casino in Isla Verde, for example, packs more than 200 slot machines, 15 blackjack tables, craps, roulette wheels and minibaccarat into a 10,000-sq-foot gaming palace. All island casinos are associated with resort hotels. To a large degree, vacationers on package tours are the most frequent patrons of these casinos, while most islanders exercise their passion for gambling by playing the legal Lotto or the illegal *bolita*. Others bet next week's paycheck on the horse races, baseball pools or cockfights.

Most casinos are open between noon and 4 pm and 8 pm to 4 am. All these establishments expect their patrons to be well dressed, and many require jackets for men. You must be at least 21 to enter a casino.

Nightclubs

Puerto Rico – especially San Juan – offers a vast selection of nightclubs for every age.

social subgroup and desire. So the problem is not finding a place to help you burn your dollars, but finding the one that makes you love every minute of the experience.

The major resort hotels in Condado and Isla Verde offer Las Vegas-style shows, and surprisingly these spots can also be some of the best places to find the hottest salsa bands on the island for dancing. Unfortunately, you may not see the smoothest dancing here, as the crowds are largely made up of tourists working on the basic steps to the rumba and merengue that they learned in their hotel dance classes or on the cruise ships.

A younger, upscale, mostly Puerto Rican crowd heads for Old San Juan, which is on the verge of being overpopulated with clubs for everyone from gays to yuppies. Until very recently, most of these clubs featured disc jockeys and recorded music, a lot of it imported from the club scene in New York and Miami. But beginning in the late '90s San Juan's bars and club owners started rediscovering the island's longtime love affair with and contributions to the world of jazz and salsa. Now many venues in the old city as well as elsewhere feature live music from the island's great tradition of musicians. And even when the music is not traceable to Tito Puente, Willie Colón or Eddie Palmieri, make no mistake, you will see some steamy Latin dancing in these clubs, particularly when the crowds get warmed up after midnight. Condado is the center for gay nightlife. Some of the sleazier clubs are in the Condado, Miramar and Santurce districts and include strip shows, prostitution and all of the associated bad actors. You will find many of the upscale clubs in Old San Juan and Isla Verde.

Ponce and Mayagüez also have club scenes, which cater to their large college-age populations, singles, gays and tourists.

Bars

Puerto Rico is both a social and drinking culture, so the bar scene here is every bit as lively as it is in London, Sydney, Rio, New York or Caracas. But unlike the bars in most other places, Puerto Rican bars almost always open themselves to the outdoors with patios and plenty of plant life – so the cigarette smoke may not rot your lungs as fast. Through the dissipating smoke, people seem to come and go like moths on a summer night – both men and women, almost always smiling. And surprisingly, few people seem noticeably drunk.

Like the clubs, each bar has its own feel and attracts a different crowd, so look under the Entertainment sections in this book's regional chapters to find a place where you might fit in. Or just walk the length of Calles Cristo, San Sebastián or Fortaleza in Old San Juan and wander in and out of the bars until you discover a group of people who look like they might be fun to meet.

Classical Music, Opera & Ballet

The Luis A Ferré Center for the Performing Arts in San Juan hosts concerts by the Puerto Rican Symphony Orchestra as well as by international stars such as the Budapest Strings under the Pro Arte Musical series. Opera and ballet companies also perform here during the fall/winter season. For details, see the Music section in this book's Facts about Puerto Rico chapter and the Entertainment section in the San Juan chapter.

Traditional Music & Dance

The best way to see performances of traditional criollo music and dance is to participate in the LeLoLai program sponsored by the Puerto Rico Tourism Company (☎ 800-866-7827, 787-723-3135). Through LeLoLai, you can buy discount tickets to see a number of different kinds of traditional performances.

Theater

The Universidad de Puerto Rico, the Teatro Tapia and the Ferré Center for the Performing Arts, all in San Juan, are the places to check out for both avant-garde and Broadway-style productions, in Spanish and English.

Cinemas

Just as in the USA, the movie scene in Puerto Rico is rooted in an array of big multiplex cinemas scattered around the island's major population centers. These theaters show Hollywood first-run films in Spanish and English. As in the USA, many of the multiplex cinemas are in malls or shopping centers around the island.

SPECTATOR SPORTS
Baseball

Like Cuba and the Dominican Republic, Puerto Rico is an island that takes its *béisbol* very seriously. During the 1960s, Roberto Clemente, the great right-fielder for the world-champion Pittsburgh Pirates, became a hero for a whole generation of Puerto Ricans, citizens of the Spanish Caribbean

and people of color in the USA. Since those days legions of island men have seen baseball as a route out of poverty. Looking at the roster of the major-league teams in the USA today, one can easily see the distinctive presence of Puerto Rico ball players. The island has two professional teams playing in the Caribbean League (see Spectator Sports in the San Juan chapter).

Basketball

Call the Federación de Baloncesta (☎ 787-721-4823) for up-to-date information on the popular games between the 16-team amateur league or the new, six-team professional league.

Bloody Birds

Coming under the heading of 'Spectacle of Blood,' *peleas de gallos* (cockfights) cater to the dark side of Puerto Ricans' passion for gambling and competition. The 'sport' of placing specially bred and trained *gallos de pelea* (fighting cocks) in a pit to battle each other for the delight of humans goes back thousands of years to ancient Persia, Greece and Rome. But the spectacle was outlawed in most of Europe as well as most of the USA during the 19th century by moralists who judged the event as unusually cruel to the birds and evocative of barbaric displays of human emotions, like greed and blood lust.

Long a popular pastime in Puerto Rico and the rest of Latin America, the spectacle was outlawed upon the American occupation of the island in 1898. After almost four decades underground, cockfighting was once again legalized on the island in the 1930s. Today Puerto Ricans support more than 130 *galleras* (fighting pits), six alone in cosmopolitan San Juan.

The gallera or *club gallistico* is usually a steeply banked, circular arena presided over by bookies who give odds and take bets with lightning speed – like auctioneers – before and during each contest. Fighting cocks come from years of careful breeding for fierceness, strength, agility and resolution. A bird is paired off face to face with another bird of equivalent breed, size and weight. During the 20-minute fight – an utterly graphic display of the male impulse to dominate – the cocks try to peck and slash each other to pieces with sharpened natural spurs, or with steel or plastic spurs taped or tied to their feet. Feathers fly. Blood splatters. Meanwhile the crowd drinks, bets and screams unrepeatable words. The fight usually ends with one bird mortally wounded or dead. Then the *aficionados* (fans) collect their winnings or plunk down more money – to get even – on the next fight. Betting usually starts at US$100 and goes well into the thousands. Some estimates assert that galleras draw more than a million people a year to these spectacles. Aficionados claim that cockfights are refreshing – like a bullfight.

Gabriel García Márquez gives a graphic comic/ironic treatment of the peleas de gallos in his novel *El coronel no tiene quien le escriba* (No One Writes to the Colonel).

Volleyball

Volleyball fans head to the beaches of Puerto Rico during the last weekend of May and each weekend of June to watch the two-on-two National Beach Volleyball Tournament. The last weekend of the tournament, teams from around the world participate for the championship. July sees more competition as three-player, pro and amateur teams compete in the Return to Sand Volleyball Tournament each weekend of the month. The Caribbean Beach Volleyball Tournament follows in late summer. For times and locations, contact the Federación Puertorriqueña de Volleyball (☎ 787-282-7525).

Marathons

With at least five major long-distance running events – both over and under true marathon distance – the island seems almost as crazy about this sport as it is about baseball and volleyball. The February running of the 20K San Blas Marathon in Coamo is the premier event, attracting a strong group of international competitors. To qualify for this event, Puerto Rican runners must compete in the Enrique Rimírez Marathon in Lajas.

November brings athletes from 30 countries to run in the Women's Marathon, a 12K event in Guayanilla. During the same month, runners can compete in the modest Carrión in Juncos or push themselves to the limit in the 40-mile La Guadalupe marathon in Ponce.

Bicycling Competitions

During the second week in May, 100 to 120 cyclists from clubs around Puerto Rico and the Caribbean compete in the International Cycling competition in Sabana Grande. Cyclists also flesh out the ranks or the Tour Gigante de Puerto Rico. For information, contact the Federación Puertorriqueña de Ciclismo (☎ 787-723-0140, 721-8755).

Horse Racing

Thoroughbred racing draws a crowd to cheer and bet the odds at El Comandante (☎ 787-724-6060) track in Canóvanas, to the east of San Juan. Post time is usually 2:30 pm on Wednesday, Friday, Saturday and holidays.

SHOPPING

Shoppers will find a lot of tempting, pretty things in the shops of Old San Juan, Condado and Ponce, but few bargains. Puerto Rico is not a duty-free port. The only economic advantage to shopping in Puerto Rico is that there is no sales tax and purchasing in US dollars makes it easier for many shoppers to keep track of exactly how much their spree is costing them relative to their traveling budget.

Travelers looking for souvenirs are drawn to the island's folk arts (see Traditional Arts in the Facts about Puerto Rico chapter). *Santos* are probably the most popular purchase, but these carved religious figures can cost well over US$100. *Mundillo*, the intricately woven island-made lace, is also a popular purchase, as are woven hammocks like the ones Columbus admired when he first stopped at Borinquen. You can also pick up *vejigantes*, masks typical of those worn in the fiestas at Ponce and Loíza. Island-made macramé and ceramic items are also widely available in the shops catering to tourists. Noches de Galerías (Gallery Nights), sponsored by the PRTC, are held from 6 to 9 pm on the first Tuesday of the month, February to May and September to December in Old San Juan.

Since Puerto Rico is the leading producer of rum in the world, you would be right to expect that many travelers find this beverage the one thing they must buy on the island. You will not only find a dizzying variety of rum in Puerto Rico (see Alcoholic Drinks, earlier in this chapter), but you'll also discover that it is significantly cheaper here than in the USA. Most bottles cost between US$4 and US$10, depending on size and quality. And there is no limit to how much you can take out of Puerto Rico when you return home.

The second most popular consumable among island travelers is the rich, mountain-grown coffee. Both Adjuntas and Rioja are popular premium products with fancy labels and packaging, but islanders say that Puerto Rican coffee is of such high quality that you cannot go wrong buying the local supermarket brands.

If you need a mall fix, visit Plaza Las Américas, at Avenida FD Roosevelt and Expreso Las Américas in Hato Rey, which has 200 stores and is the largest mall in the Caribbean (see the San Juan chapter). There are smaller shopping plazas in Carolina and Río Piedras. Mayagüez has the Mayagüez Mall. In Ponce, shopping addicts head for the Centro del Sur, and new malls are popping up all over the island.

Getting There & Away

AIR

Airfares to Caribbean destinations such as Puerto Rico vary tremendously depending on the season you travel, the day of the week you fly, the length of your stay and the flexibility the ticket allows for flight changes and refunds. Still, nothing determines fares more than demand, and when things are slow, regardless of the season, airlines will lower their fares to fill empty seats. There's a lot of competition, and at any given time any one of the airlines could have the cheapest fare.

Airports

San Juan's Aeropuerto Internacional de Luis Muñoz Marín – commonly shortened to 'LMM' – lies just 2 miles beyond the eastern border of the city in the beachfront suburb

Warning

The information in this chapter is particularly vulnerable to change: Prices for international travel are volatile, routes are introduced and canceled, schedules change, special deals come and go, and rules and visa requirements are amended. Airlines and governments seem to take a perverse pleasure in making price structures and regulations as complicated as possible. You should check directly with the airline or a travel agent to make sure you understand how a fare (and any ticket you may buy) works. In addition, the travel industry is highly competitive and there are many hidden costs and benefits.

The upshot of this is that you should get opinions, quotes and advice from as many airlines and travel agents as possible before you part with your hard-earned cash. The details given in this chapter should be regarded as pointers and are not a substitute for your own careful, up-to-date research.

of Isla Verde. This large airport with its new, state-of-the-art terminal is the international air hub for the Caribbean; half of all flights to/from the Caribbean pass through this facility. San Juan is the Caribbean hub for American Airlines, which has the largest number of daily flights in and out of the region by a significant margin and offers easy access to/from its US domestic network.

The Commonwealth of Puerto Rico has spent a lot of money in recent years to make this airport a world-class facility with all the amenities, partially in reaction to the old terminal, looming large as a bad joke for decades of Caribbean travelers. Today everything is new, clean and air-conditioned, with dining, shopping and currency exchange facilities equal to those at other US ports of entry.

Chances are that you will be arriving and departing from San Juan, but two other airports on the island offer occasional service to/from the US: Ponce's Aeropuerto de Mercedita on the south coast, and the bomber strip at Aguadilla's Aeropuerto Rafael Hernández, on the former Base Ramey on the island's northwest tip. Until recently, KIWI International Air Lines operated daily flights from Miami and New York to Aguadilla, but at the time this book went to press the carrier had suspended its service indefinitely.

San Juan's original airport at Isla Grande, on the Bahía de San Juan in the Miramar district, services private aircraft and the bulk of the commuter flights to the Spanish Virgin Islands; see the Getting Around chapter for details.

Airlines

Puerto Rico is the most accessible island in the Caribbean. In addition to being a major hub for American Airlines, San Juan is served by a number of other North American carriers that fly between Puerto Rico and a score of mainland US cities; Miami has the most frequent flights. British Airways has services from London, Iberia flies from Madrid and

Lufthansa's subsidiary Condor provides travelers with a link from Frankfurt.

The following list includes some of the more popular airlines serving Puerto Rico from abroad (the 800 and 888 numbers are toll-free calls from the US, Canada, Mexico and the Caribbean):

ACES	☎ 800-846-2237
Aerolíneas Argentinas	☎ 800-333-0276
Air Calypso	☎ 800-253-0020
Air Canada	☎ 800-776-3000
Air France	☎ 800-237-2747
Air Guadalupe	☎ 787-253-0933
Air Jamaica	☎ 800-523-5585
Air St Thomas	☎ 800-522-3084
ALM Antillean Airlines	☎ 800-327-7230
American Airlines	☎ 800-433-7300
British Airways	☎ 800-247-9297
Canadian Airlines	☎ 800-426-7000
Caribbean Air Express	☎ 800-283-2426
Condor (Lufthansa)	☎ 800-524-6975
Continental Airlines	☎ 800-525-0280
COPA	☎ 787-722-6969
Delta Air Lines	☎ 800-221-1212
Hill Aviation & Helicopter	☎ 787-723-3385
Iberia	☎ 800-722-4642
Isla Nena Air Service	☎ 888-263-6213
KIWI	☎ 800-538-5494
KLM	☎ 800-374-7747
LACSA	☎ 800-225-2272
LIAT	☎ 787-791-3838
Martinair Holland	☎ 800-627-8462
Mexicana	☎ 787-788-4100
Northwest Airlines	☎ 800-225-2525
Tower Air	☎ 800-221-2500
TWA	☎ 800-221-2000
United Airlines	☎ 800-241-6522
US Airways	☎ 800-842-5374
Vieques Air Link	☎ 888-901-9247

Buying Tickets

Rather than just walking into the nearest travel agent or airline office, it pays to do a bit of research and shop around before purchasing your airline ticket. If you are buying tickets in the US, the *New York Times*, *Los Angeles Times*, *Chicago Tribune*, *San Francisco Examiner*, *Boston Globe* and other major newspapers all produce weekly travel sections with numerous travel agents' ads. Council Travel (☎ 800-226-8624, www.counciltravel.com) and STA Travel (☎ 800-777-0112, www.sta-travel.com) have offices in major cities nationwide. The magazine *Travel Unlimited* (PO Box 1058, Allston, MA 02134) publishes details on the cheapest airfares and courier possibilities.

Those coming from outside the US might start by perusing the travel sections of magazines such as *Time Out* and *TNT* in the UK, or the Saturday editions of newspapers such as the *Sydney Morning Herald* and *The Age* in Australia. Ads in these publications offer cheap fares, but don't be surprised if they happen to be sold out when you contact the agents: They're usually low-season fares on obscure airlines with conditions attached.

Your plane ticket will probably be the single most expensive item in your budget, and buying it can be intimidating. It is always worth putting aside a few hours to research the current state of the market. Start shopping for a ticket early – some of the cheapest tickets must be bought months in advance, and some popular flights sell out early. Talk to recent travelers, contact a few travel agents and watch newspapers and magazines for special offers. You can also use the Internet to hunt for low fares (see the 'Buying Tickets Online' boxed text).

Phoning a travel agent is still one of the best ways to dig up bargains. However, airlines have started to cater more to budget travelers and can sometimes offer the same deals you'll get with a travel agent. Airlines often have competitive low-season, student and senior citizens' fares. Find out about the fare, the route, the duration of the journey and any restrictions on the ticket.

Note that high season in Puerto Rico is mid-December to late April (winter). The lowest rates for travel to/from the island are found from May 1 to about December 20.

Cheap tickets are available in two distinct categories: official and unofficial. Official tickets have a variety of names including advance-purchase, APEX, budget or promotional fares. Unofficial tickets are simply discounted tickets that the airlines release through selected travel agencies (not through airline offices). The cheapest tickets are often nonrefundable and they require an extra fee for changing your flight (usually US$50 or more). Many insurance policies will cover this loss if you have to change your flight for emergency reasons.

Roundtrip (return) tickets are usually cheaper than two one-way fares – sometimes *much* cheaper.

Use the fares quoted in this book as a guide only. They are approximate and based on the rates advertised by travel agencies and airlines at press time. Quoted airfares do not necessarily constitute a recommendation for the carrier.

In some places, especially the UK, the cheapest flights are advertised by obscure bucket shops whose names haven't yet reached the telephone directory. Many such firms are honest and solvent, but some will take your money and disappear. If you feel suspicious about a firm, don't give them all the money at once – leave a deposit of 20% or so and pay the balance on receiving the ticket. If they insist on cash in advance, go elsewhere. Once you have the ticket, call the airline to confirm that you are booked on the flight.

You may decide to pay more than the rock-bottom fare by opting for the safety of a better-known travel agent. Established firms such as STA Travel and Council Travel (see contact information above), both of which have offices internationally, and Travel CUTS/Voyages Campus in Canada (☎ 800-667-2887, www.travelcuts.com) offer good prices to most destinations.

Once you have your ticket, make a copy of it and keep the copy separate from the original ticket. This will help you get a replacement if your ticket is lost or stolen. Remember to buy travel insurance as early as possible to protect yourself against any penalties for an unavoidable cancellation (see Travel Insurance under Visas & Documents in the Facts for the Visitor chapter for details).

Buying Tickets Online

Most airlines have their own websites with online ticket sales, often discounted for online customers. The airlines may sell seats by auction, offer last-minute specials or simply cut prices to reflect the reduced cost of electronic selling. To buy a ticket via the Web, you'll need to use a credit card – this is straightforward and secure, as card details are encrypted. Commercial reservation networks offer airline ticketing as well as information and bookings for hotels, car rental and other services. Networks include the following:

Atevo Travel
www.atevo.com
Biztravel.com Inc
www.biztravel.com
CNN Interactive's Travel Guide
www.cnn.com/Travel
Excite Travel by City.Net
www.city.net
Internet Travel Network
www.itn.net
Microsoft Expedia
www.expedia.com
Preview.Travel
www.previewtravel.com
Priceline
www.priceline.com
Travelocity
www.travelocity.com

A number of online travel agencies also specialize in cheap fares:

1-800-Airfare
www.1800airfare.com
Cheap Tickets
www.cheaptickets.com
LowestFare.com
www.lowestfare.com
Yahoo Travel
travel.yahoo.com/destinations/bargains/

Air Travel Glossary

Baggage Allowance This will be written on your ticket and usually includes one 44lb (20kg) item to go in the hold, plus one item of hand luggage.

Bucket Shops These are unbonded travel agencies specializing in discounted airline tickets.

Bumped Just because you have a confirmed seat doesn't mean you're going to get on the plane (see Overbooking).

Cancellation Penalties If you have to cancel or change a discounted ticket, there are often heavy penalties involved; insurance can sometimes be taken out against these penalties. Some airlines impose penalties on regular tickets as well, particularly against 'no-show' passengers.

Check-In Airlines ask you to check in a certain time ahead of the flight departure (usually one to two hours on international flights). If you fail to check in on time and the flight is over-booked, the airline can cancel your booking and give your seat to somebody else.

Confirmation Having a ticket written out with the flight and date you want doesn't mean you have a seat until the agent has checked with the airline that your status is 'OK' or confirmed. Meanwhile you could just be 'on request.'

Courier Fares Businesses often need to send urgent documents or freight securely and quickly. Courier companies hire people to accompany the package through customs and, in return, offer a discount ticket that is sometimes a phenomenal bargain. In effect, what the companies do is ship their freight as your luggage on regular commercial flights. This is a legitimate operation, but there are two shortcomings: the short turnaround time of the ticket (usually not longer than a month) and the limitation on your luggage allowance. You may have to surrender all your allowance and take only carry-on luggage.

Full Fares Airlines traditionally offer 1st class (coded F), business class (coded J) and economy class (coded Y) tickets. These days there are so many promotional and discounted fares available that few passengers pay full economy fare.

ITX An ITX, or 'independent inclusive tour excursion,' is often available on tickets to popular holiday destinations. Officially it's a package deal combined with hotel accommodations, but many agents will sell you one of these for the flight only and give you phony hotel vouchers in the unlikely event that you're challenged at the airport.

Lost Tickets If you lose your airline ticket, an airline will usually treat it like a traveler's check and, after inquiries, issue you another one. Legally, however, an airline is entitled to treat it like cash; and if you lose it, it's gone forever. Take good care of your tickets.

MCO An MCO, or 'miscellaneous charge order,' is a voucher that looks like an airline ticket but carries no destination or date. It can be exchanged through any International Association of Travel Agents (IATA) airline for a ticket on a specific flight. It's a useful alternative to an onward ticket in those countries that demand one, and is more flexible than an ordinary ticket if you're unsure of your route.

No-Shows These are passengers who fail to show up for their flight. Full-fare passengers who fail to turn up are sometimes entitled to travel on a later flight. The rest are penalized (see Cancellation Penalties).

Air Travel Glossary

Onward Tickets An entry requirement for many countries is that you have a ticket out of the country. If you're unsure of your next move, the easiest solution is to buy the cheapest onward ticket to a neighboring country or a ticket from a reliable airline that can later be refunded if you do not use it.

Open-Jaw Tickets These are roundtrip tickets on which you fly out to one place but return from another. If available, these can save you backtracking to your arrival point.

Overbooking Airlines hate to fly with empty seats, and since every flight has some passengers who fail to show up, airlines often book more passengers than they have seats. Usually excess passengers make up for the no-shows, but occasionally somebody gets bumped. Guess who it is most likely to be? The passengers who check in late.

Point-to-Point Tickets These are discount tickets that can be bought on some routes in return for passengers waiving their rights to a stopover.

Promotional Fares These are officially discounted fares, available from travel agencies or direct from the airline.

Reconfirmation At least 72 hours prior to departure time of an onward or return flight, you must contact the airline and 'reconfirm' that you intend to be on the flight. If you don't do this, the airline can delete your name from the passenger list and you could lose your seat.

Restrictions Discounted tickets often have various restrictions on them – such as advance payment, minimum and maximum periods you must be away (eg, a minimum of two weeks or a maximum of one year), and penalties for changing the tickets.

Round-the-World Tickets RTW tickets give you a limited period (usually a year) in which to circumnavigate the globe. You can go anywhere the carrying airlines go, as long as you don't backtrack. The number of stopovers or total number of separate flights is decided before you set off, and they usually cost a bit more than a basic roundtrip flight.

Standby This is a discounted ticket on which you only fly if there is a seat free at the last moment. Standby fares are usually available only on domestic routes.

Transferred Tickets Airline tickets cannot be transferred from one person to another. Travelers sometimes try to sell the return half of their ticket, but officials can ask you to prove that you are the person named on the ticket. This is less likely to happen on domestic flights, but on an international flight tickets are compared with passports.

Travel Agencies Travel agencies vary widely and you should choose one that suits your needs. Some simply handle tours, while full-services agencies handle everything from tours and tickets to car rental and hotel bookings. If all you want is a ticket at the lowest possible price, then go to an agency specializing in discounted tickets.

Travel Periods Ticket prices vary with the time of year. There is a low (off-peak) season and a high (peak) season, and often a low-shoulder season and a high-shoulder season as well. Usually the fare depends on your outward flight – if you depart in the high season and return in the low season, you pay the high-season fare.

Visit USA Passes Almost all domestic carriers offer Visit USA passes to non-US citizens. The passes are actually a book of coupons – each coupon equals a flight. Typically, the minimum number of coupons is three or four and the maximum is eight or 10, and they must be purchased in conjunction with an international airline ticket anywhere outside the USA, Canada or Mexico.

Coupons cost anywhere from US$100 to US$160, depending on how many you buy. Most airlines require you to plan your itinerary in advance and to complete your flights within 60 days of arrival, but rules can vary among individual airlines. A few airlines may allow you to use coupons on standby, in which case call the airline a day or two before the flight and make a 'standby reservation.' Such a reservation gives you priority over all other travelers who just appear and hope to get on the flight the same day.

Travelers to Puerto Rico should note that while these passes will help if you plan inexpensive air travel in the continental US and Canada, they generally will not cover travel to Puerto Rico, Alaska, Hawaii, Bermuda or Mexico unless you specify that you want a 'preferred' air pass to cover one or more of these offshore destinations.

Round-the-World Tickets Round-the-world (RTW) tickets can be a great deal if you want to visit other regions as well as the US and Puerto Rico. Although San Juan does not presently qualify as a stopover point on any carrier's round-the-world itinerary, RTW ticks are often real bargains and can get you to Miami (the nearest US entry point).

RTW tickets can be no more expensive – or even cheaper – than an ordinary round-trip ticket. Prices start at about UK£850, A$2399/2699 (low/high season) or US$2500. RTW tickets are of most value for trips that combine the USA with Europe, Asia and Australia or New Zealand. RTW itineraries that include South America or Africa are substantially more expensive.

Official airline RTW tickets are usually put together by a combination of two or three airlines and permit you to fly to a specified number of stops on their route systems as long as you do not backtrack. Other restrictions are that usually you must book the first sector in advance and cancellation penalties apply. Also, there may be restrictions upon the number of stops permitted, and tickets are valid for a fixed period – usually 90 days to one year. An alternative type of RTW ticket is one put together by a travel agent using a combination of discounted tickets.

Most airlines restrict the number of sectors that can be flown within the USA and Canada to three or four, and some airlines 'black out' a few heavily traveled routes (like Honolulu to Tokyo). In most cases, a 14-day advance purchase is required. After the ticket is purchased, dates can usually be changed without penalty, and tickets can be rewritten to add or delete stops for US$50 each.

The majority of RTW tickets restrict you to just three airlines. British Airways, US Airways and Qantas Airways offer a RTW ticket called the Global Explorer that allows you to combine routes (maximum six flights) on these airlines to a total of 28,000 miles for US$3100 or A$3192 (high season).

Qantas also flies in conjunction with American Airlines, Delta Air Lines, Northwest Airlines, Canadian Airlines, Air France and KLM. Qantas RTW tickets with any of the aforementioned partner airlines cost around US$3100/3300 (A$3079/3192) in the low/high season.

Canadian Airlines offers numerous RTW combinations ranging from C$3100 up to C$3600. Air Canada's base fare is C$3287. This is with two other carriers; as you add more, the price goes up.

Continental, TWA and Northwest also offer round-the-world fares. Your best bet is to find a travel agent that advertises or specializes in RTW tickets.

Getting Bumped
Airlines routinely overbook and count on some passengers canceling or not showing up. Occasionally, almost everybody does show up for a flight, and then some passengers must be 'bumped' onto another flight.

Getting bumped can be a nuisance because you have to wait around for the next flight, but if you have a day's leeway, you can turn this into an advantage.

On oversold flights, the gate agent will first ask for volunteers to be bumped in return for a later flight plus compensation of the airline's choosing. (If there aren't enough volunteers, some passengers will be forced onto a later flight. Each airline has its own method of choosing which customers will be bumped.) When you check in at the airline counter, ask if the flight is full and if there may be a need for volunteers. Get your name on the list if you don't mind volunteering. Depending on how oversold the flight is, compensation can range from a discount voucher toward your next flight to a fully paid roundtrip ticket or even cash. Be sure to try to confirm a later flight so you don't get stuck in the airport on standby. If you have to spend the night, airlines frequently foot the hotel bill for their 'bumpees.' You don't have to accept the airline's first offer; you can haggle for a better deal.

However, be aware that, due to this same system, being just a little late for boarding could get you bumped with none of these benefits.

Baggage & Other Restrictions

On most domestic and overseas flights to Puerto Rico, you are limited to two checked bags, or three if you don't have a carry-on. There could be a charge if a bag exceeds the airline's size limits. It's best to check with the individual airline if you are concerned about this. On some international flights, the luggage allowance is based on weight, not size; again, check with the airline.

If your luggage is delayed upon arrival (which is rare), some airlines will give you a cash advance so that you can purchase necessities. If sporting equipment is misplaced, the airline may pay for rentals. Should your luggage get lost, it is important to submit a claim. The airline doesn't have to pay the full amount of the claim; rather, they can estimate the value of your lost items. It may take them anywhere from six weeks to three months to process the claim and pay you.

Smoking Smoking is prohibited on all domestic flights within the US, and this includes Puerto Rico. Many international flights are following suit, so be sure to call and find out. Many airports in the US and Puerto Rico also restrict smoking.

Illegal Items Items that are illegal to take on a plane, either checked or as carry-on, include aerosols of polishes, waxes, etc; tear gas and pepper spray; camp stoves with fuel; and divers' tanks that are full.

Travelers with Special Needs

If you have special needs of any sort – a broken leg, dietary restrictions, dependence on a wheelchair, responsibility for a baby, fear of flying – you should let the airline know as soon as possible so that it can make arrangements accordingly. You should remind the airline when you reconfirm your booking (at least 72 hours before departure) and again when you check in at the airport. It may also be worth calling several airlines before you make your booking to find out how they can handle your needs.

Airfares

Below are estimated costs of flights to San Juan, Puerto Rico, from overseas destinations:

destination	high/low season
New York	US$469/174
Miami	US$504/271
Los Angeles	US$940/588
Chicago	US$735/298
Houston	US$821/527
Boston	US$783/394
Montreal	C$1007/582
Toronto	C$1007/582
London	UK£609/499
Paris	FF10,351/3500
Madrid	P163,117/107,386
Frankfurt	DM1936/1299

Airports and airlines can be surprisingly helpful, but they do need advance warning. Most international airports can provide escorts from check-in desk to plane, and there should be ramps, lifts, accessible toilets and reachable phones. Aircraft toilets, on the other hand, are likely to present a problem; travelers should discuss this with the airline at an early stage and, if necessary, with their doctor.

Guide dogs for the blind often have to travel in a specially pressurized baggage compartment with other animals, away from their owners, though smaller guide dogs may be admitted to the cabin. Guide dogs are not subject to quarantine as long as they have proof of being vaccinated against rabies.

Deaf travelers can ask that airport and in-flight announcements be written down for them.

Children younger than two travel for 10% of the standard fare (or for free on some airlines) if they don't occupy a seat. They don't get a baggage allowance with this deal, either. 'Skycots' should be provided by the airline if requested in advance; these will hold a child weighing up to about 22lb. Children between two and 12 years old can usually occupy a seat for one-half to two-thirds of the full fare and do get a baggage allowance. Strollers can sometimes be taken on as hand luggage.

Sometimes there is a child's rate on a discounted fare, sometimes not. It can be cheaper for a child to fly on an adult discounted fare than on a child's fare at two-thirds of the full adult rate. For pricing purposes, the child's age is reckoned at the time of departure on the first leg of the flight.

Arriving in the USA/Puerto Rico

Even if you are continuing immediately to another city, the first airport that you land in is where you must carry out immigration and customs formalities. Although your luggage may be checked from, say, London to San Juan, you will still have to take it through customs in Miami if that is where you land first.

If you have a non-US passport with a visa, you must complete your Arrival/Departure Record (form I-94) before you go to the immigration desk. It's usually handed out on the plane, along with the customs declaration. It's a rather badly designed form, and lots of people take more than one attempt to get it right. Some airlines suggest you start at the last question and work upward. Answers should be written *below* the questions. For question 12, 'Address While in the United States,' give the address of the location where you will spend the first night. Complete the Departure Record too (the lower part of the form), giving exactly the same answers for questions 14 to 17 as for questions 1 to 4.

The staff of the Immigration & Naturalization Service (INS) can be less than welcoming. Their main concern is to exclude those who are likely to work illegally or overstay, so visitors will be asked about their plans and perhaps about whether they have sufficient funds for their stay. If they think you're OK, a six-month entry is usually approved.

It's a good idea to be able to list an itinerary that will account for the period for which you ask to be admitted, and to be able to show you have US$300 to US$400 for every week of your intended stay. These days, a couple of major credit cards will go a long way toward establishing 'sufficient funds.' Don't make too much of having friends, relatives or business contacts in the US – the INS official may decide that this will make you more likely to overstay.

For details on customs allowances and the procedure for foreigners entering the USA/Puerto Rico, see the Facts for the Visitor chapter.

Departure Tax

In Puerto Rico, a US$12 airport departure tax is charged to all passengers. Passengers entering Puerto Rico or the US are charged an additional US$12 North American Free Trade Agreement (NAFTA) tax. These taxes are normally included in the cost of tickets bought in the US (thus they're 'hidden' taxes added to tickets' purchase price). Tickets purchased abroad may not or may not include these taxes.

The USA

The most popular routings to Puerto Rico from the USA are via New York and Miami, but direct flights from about a dozen other cities in the continental US also serve the island. Most major US carriers – including American, Continental, Delta, Northwest, United and US Airways – fly to Puerto Rico, which allows you to use their frequent-flyer and other discount programs. American Airlines has the most frequent service to and from the island, with more than 40 scheduled flights a day. Recently, US Airways has been beefing up its service with new flights to the island from places such as Philadelphia and Providence, Rhode Island.

For toll-free telephone numbers of airlines serving Puerto Rico from the US, see the Airlines section, earlier in this chapter.

Discount Tickets Many discount ticket agencies sell reduced-rate tickets to the Caribbean. One of the leading brokers specializing in the area is Pan Express Travel (☎ 212-719-9292), 25 W 39th St, New York, NY 10018.

Other leading discount agencies include the following:

Express Discount Travel
   (☎ 619-283-6324, 800-266-8669)
   5945 Mission Gorge Rd No 2, San Diego, CA 92120

The Vacation Store
   (☎ 212-465-0707, 800-825-3633, fax 212-594-6711)
   101 W 31st St, New York, NY 10001

Charter Flights Charter flights generally offer the lowest fares for confirmed reservations (sometimes one-third or more off airline prices) and can be booked through most travel agencies. You can sometimes book one-way tickets with charter airlines for less than half the roundtrip fare. Often the charter price is for a package that includes accommodations. Charter flights are usually direct, without the hub stop common on standard airlines. Few charters are listed in airline reservations systems, as they're operated by wholesale tour operators with whom you or your travel agent will have to deal directly.

However, there are drawbacks to this mode of travel. Although you can buy the ticket without an advance-purchase requirement, you do have to fix your departure and return dates well in advance, and a substantial fee may apply for any changes or cancellations. Consider cancellation insurance to protect yourself in the event of illness (see Travel Insurance under Visas & Documents in the Facts for the Visitor chapter). Also, seating on charter flights may be more cramped as planes tend to be full, and flights are often at inconvenient hours. And while US charter operators are bonded with the US government, if the tour operator or airline defaults, you may have difficulties getting your money back. Finally, charter airlines are often less organized than standard carriers, and processing at airport counters tends to be more confused and time-consuming, even though the charter operator may be using the service desk and aircraft of a major airline.

Before buying, compare charter prices with the airlines' current 'sale' fares and the cost of a discount ticket from a consolidator.

Charter operator Tower Air (see below) offers frequent service to Puerto Rico and a standard of quality on par with any major North American airline. Fares from New York start at US$267 roundtrip. You can fly to San Juan from Miami for about US$287.

A number of other charter operators fly to Puerto Rico from the USA. Check the Sunday travel sections of major city newspapers. Your travel agent should also be able to provide a listing. A good resource is *The Worldwide Guide to Cheap Airfares*, by Michael McColl, which provides a comprehensive listing of charter tour operators.

Some key charter operators to Puerto Rico include the following:

Globetrotters
   (☎ 800-999-9696)
   139 Main St, Cambridge, MA 02124

Island Flight Vacations
   (☎ 310-477-5858, 800-426-4570, fax 310-410-0830)
   6033 W Century Blvd No 807, Los Angeles, CA 90045

Sunrise Tours
   (☎ 800-872-3801)
   390 Fifth Ave, New York, NY 10013

Tower Air
  (☎ 718-553-8500, 800-348-6937)
  17 JFK International Airport, Jamaica,
  NY 11434

Courier Flights If you're willing to fly at
short notice and travel light, courier flights
are one of the cheapest ways to go – normally about half the standard fare, but often
much less.

As a courier, you are responsible for deliv-
ering an item such as a parcel or document
on behalf of a company. Usually the han-
dling of the item is taken care of by the
courier company: You merely act as its agent
by occupying a seat. The traveler is usually
allowed only one piece of carry-on baggage,
and the checked-baggage allowance is taken
by the item to be delivered.

Unfortunately, there are very few courier
options to the Caribbean. For information,
try NOW Voyager (☎ 212-431-1616), 74
Varick St, No 307, New York, NY 10013, the
leading booking agency for courier companies. NOW Voyager does book flights to the
Caribbean; you must pay a one-time US$50
registration fee.

Two good resources are *The Courier Air
Travel Handbook,* by Mark Field, and *The
Worldwide Guide to Cheap Airfares,* by
Michael McColl.

Last-Minute Flights If you can fly at very
short notice (usually within seven days of
travel), consider buying a ticket from a 'last-
minute' ticket broker. These companies buy
surplus seats from charter airlines (and
sometimes standard carriers) at hugely discounted prices. The airline would rather fill
the seat than fly empty, so you reap the re-
ward. Discounts can be as great as 40% for a
confirmed seat.

One of the leading distress-sale brokers is
Last Minute Travel Club (☎ 617-267-9800,
800-527-8646), 1249 Boylston St, Boston,
MA 02215, which specializes in air/hotel
packages to the Caribbean region. Other last-
minute ticket agencies require you to become a member of their clubs; annual fees
are about US$40, for which you receive
regular updates.

Companies to consider for last-minute
tickets include the following:

Moment's Notice
  (☎ 212-486-0500) 425 Madison Ave, New York,
  NY 10017
Worldwide Discount Travel Club
  (☎ 305-534-2082) 1674 Meridian Ave,
  Miami Beach, FL 33139

Canada
No Canadian carriers fly direct to San Juan,
but Air Canada (☎ 800-776-3000) offers connections (via Continental and American
flights) to San Juan from Montreal, Ottawa
and Toronto. Travel CUTS/Voyages Campus
(☎ 416-614-2887; toll-free in Canada 800-
667-2887) has offices in all major cities. City
newspapers such as the Toronto *Globe and
Mail* and *Vancouver Sun* carry travel agents'
ads. The magazine *Great Expeditions* (PO
Box 8000-411, Abbotsford, BC V2S 6H1)
is also useful.

Australia & New Zealand
STA Travel has offices in major cities
throughout Australia and New Zealand.
STA sells tickets to everyone but offers spe-
cial deals to students and travelers under 30.
Head offices are at STA Travel (☎ 1-300-
360-960, 3-9347-6911), 224 Faraday St, PO
Box 75, Melbourne, VIC 3053, Australia;
and STA Travel (☎ 9-309-0458), 10 High St,
Auckland, New Zealand.

In addition to STA Travel, Flight Centres
International (☎ 2-9584-9133, fax 9235-2871)
is a major dealer in cheap airfares. Check the
travel agents' ads in the yellow pages and
phone around.

The cheapest tickets to US destinations
have a 21-day advance-purchase requirement, a minimum stay of seven days and a
maximum stay of 60 days. Flying with Air
New Zealand is slightly cheaper, and Qantas
and Air New Zealand offer tickets with
longer stays or stopovers, but you pay more.

Flying from Australia to Puerto Rico is
difficult, as no one airline offers direct service to San Juan from down under. Travelers
and their travel agents will have to do a bit
of work to get a good deal. One option is to

fly from Melbourne to Mexico City with Japan Air Lines (JAL) and then fly from Mexico City to San Juan on Mexicana. The fare in low season is A$2269; in high season, it's A$2569.

The UK & Ireland

British Airways offers direct service to San Juan from Gatwick on Saturday and Sunday, with daily connecting flights through Miami. Several other airlines feed Miami and Fort Lauderdale from the UK, including American Airlines, Delta Air Lines and Virgin Atlantic. American Airlines offers connecting service to San Juan.

Trailfinders (☎ 020-7937-5400), 194 Kensington High St, London W8 7RG, produces a lavishly illustrated brochure that includes airfare details. Other good, reliable agents for cheap tickets in the UK are Council Travel (☎ 020-7437-7767), 28a Poland St, London W1; and STA Travel (☎ 020-7581-4132), 86 Old Brompton Rd, London SW7 3LQ. One of the leading air-only travel specialists is Caribbean Gold (☎ 020-8741-8491).

Look in the magazines *Time Out* and *City Limits*, the Sunday papers and *Exchange & Mart* for ads. Also look out for the free magazines widely available in London – start by looking outside the main railway stations.

Most British travel agents are registered with the ABTA (Association of British Travel Agents). If you have paid for your flight through an ABTA-registered agent that then goes out of business, ABTA guarantees a refund or an alternative. Unregistered bucket shops are riskier but sometimes cheaper.

The Globetrotters Club (BCM Roving, London WC1N 3XX) publishes a newsletter called *Globe* that covers obscure destinations and can help in finding traveling companions.

Charter Flights Puerto Rico is not nearly as popular a Caribbean charter destination from the UK as the former or remaining British colonies in the islands, but a few charter operators have contracted with airlines since Airtours first tested the market in 1988. All charter flights are into San Juan's LMM airport.

Leading charter operators serving Puerto Rico include the following:

Airtours	☎ 0706-260000
British Airways Holidays	☎ 0293-617000
Caribbean Connection	☎ 0244-341131
Caribtours	☎ 020-7581-3517, fax 7225-2491
Kuoni	☎ 01306-740888
Simply Caribbean	☎ 0423-526887
Thomas Cook Travel	☎ 020-7707-6800
Virgin Holidays	☎ 01293-562944

Continental Europe

In Denmark, Cruise & Travel specializes in travel to the Caribbean (☎ 45-33-119-500, fax 45-33-119-501), Bredgade 35C, Copenhagen, 1260 K.

In Amsterdam, NBBS is a popular travel agent. Martinair Holland flies from Amsterdam to San Juan on Monday and Saturday.

A good source in Paris is Council Travel (☎ 01 44 41 89 80), at 1, place de l'Odeon, 75006. For great student fares, contact USIT Voyages (☎ 01 42 34 56 90), at 6 rue de Vaugirard, 75006 Paris.

In Germany, try STA Travel (☎ 069-43-01-91), Berger Strasse 118, 60316 Frankfurt, or contact either of the following Council Travel offices:

(☎ 0211-36-30-30) Graf Adolph Strasse 18, 40212 Düsseldorf

(☎ 089-39-50-22) Adalbert Strasse 32, 80799 Münich

Lufthansa's subsidiary line Condor flies Frankfurt-San Juan-Frankfurt on Saturday.

If you plan to travel from Spain, Iberia offers one or two direct flights per week to San Juan from Madrid.

Asia

Bangkok and Singapore are the discount ticket capitals of the region, but their bucket shops can be unreliable. Ask the advice of other travelers before buying a ticket. STA Travel, which is dependable, has branches in Hong Kong, Tokyo, Singapore, Bangkok and Kuala Lumpur. Many if not most flights to the USA go via Honolulu, Hawaii.

The Caribbean & Latin America

Many flights to San Juan from Central and South America are routed through Miami, Houston or New York. Some countries' international flag carriers, such as Aerolíneas Argentinas, LACSA and Mexicana, fly directly to San Juan from Latin American cities.

Puerto Rico's link to Antigua, Barbados, Haiti, Jamaica and Trinidad is American Airlines. ALM Antillean Airlines also has flights to/from Puerto Rico connecting to Aruba, Bonaire, Colombia, Panama, Venezuela and St Maarten.

American Eagle is the preferred carrier for those traveling from San Juan to the US Virgin Islands. You can also take the smaller planes of Isla Nena Air Service or Vieques Air Link.

American Airlines serves San Juan from the Dominican Republic.

SEA
Cruise Ship

San Juan is the second-largest port for cruise ships in the Western Hemisphere (after Miami), with 748 home-port sailings each year. More than 25 vessels call San Juan their home port, and every year new cruise ships either originate sailings from San Juan or make San Juan a port of call. More than 1 million cruise-ship passengers pass through San Juan per year. Their ships dock at the piers along Calle La Marina near the Customs House and the Wyndham Old San Juan Hotel & Casino, just a short walk from the cobblestone streets of Old San Juan.

Per diem prices vary according to the standard of the ship, but you will be lucky to pay less than US$1500 for a seven-day cruise out of San Juan. However, this price will probably include your airfare and transfers to the ship, as well as all your meals and entertainment.

The Cruise Line International Association (CLIA; ☎ 212-921-0549, fax 921-0549), 500 Fifth Ave, No 1407, New York, NY 10110, provides information on cruising and individual lines. Or you can contact the cruise lines directly at the following toll-free numbers:

Carnival Cruise Lines	☎ 800-327-9501
Celebrity Cruise Lines	☎ 800-437-3111
Commodore Cruise Lines	☎ 800-237-5361
Costa Cruise Lines	☎ 800-462-6782
Crystal Cruise Lines	☎ 800-446-6620
Cunard Lines	☎ 800-528-6273
Holland American Line	☎ 800-426-0327
Norwegian Cruise Line	☎ 800-327-7030
Princess Cruises	☎ 800-421-0522
Royal Caribbean Cruise Line	☎ 800-327-6700
Royal Cruise Line	☎ 800-227-4534
Star Clippers	☎ 800-442-0551
Sun Line	☎ 800-872-6400

Ferry

For a true seafaring adventure, consider the oceangoing ferry between Mayagüez, on Puerto Rico's west coast, and Santo Domingo, in the Dominican Republic. Currently, the ship sails three times weekly from each port on alternating days. One-way tickets for the 11-hour trip start at US$39. See the Mayagüez section in the West Coast chapter for details.

Presently, no ferries operate between Puerto Rico and the US Virgin Islands.

Yacht

Crewing aboard a yacht destined for the West Indies from North America or Europe is a popular way of getting to Puerto Rico. You will need impressive offshore sailing experience to make (or be hired for) an Atlantic crossing. Most sailors heading to Puerto Rico and other West Indian destinations do so from Florida or the shores of other Eastern states. Winds and currents favor the passage south through the Bahamas. If you plan to travel in summer, keep fully abreast of weather reports, as July to October is hurricane season (see Climate in the Facts about Puerto Rico chapter).

Marinas are located at most major resorts and at principal ports around the Puerto Rican coast. Upon reaching the island, however, you *must* clear immigration and customs unless you are coming directly from a US port or the US Virgin Islands. You can clear customs at San Juan, Ponce, Mayagüez or Fajardo. Note that Puerto Rico's drug smuggling problem is such that you should anticipate the possibility of being boarded and searched by the US Coast Guard.

In the UK, contact Alan Toone of Compass Yacht Services (☎ 020-8467-2450) at Holly Cottage, Heathley End, Chislehurst, Kent BR7 6AB. Alan arranges yacht charters and may be able to help assist you in obtaining a crewing position.

There are now numerous online clearinghouses for those seeking yacht crew positions (both experienced and inexperienced mariners). These services usually charge a registration fee between US$25 and US$40. Two operations known for their professionalism are the Yacht Crew Registry (☎ 604-990-9901, mypage.direct.ca/y/yachtcrw) and Yacht Crew Inc (☎ 954-788-3832, www.yacht-crew.com).

During both the winter and summer seasons, there is a lot of boat traffic between the east end of Puerto Rico and Charlotte Amalie on St Thomas (US Virgin Islands), as well as the island of St Croix. Inquire at the yacht marinas in these ports if you want to take a slow boat to Puerto Rico or do some island hopping.

In early November, after hurricane season, you will find a lot of vessels bound for Puerto Rico and the US Virgin Islands from US yachting centers, including Newport, Rhode Island; Annapolis, Maryland; Beaufort, North Carolina; Charleston, South Carolina; and Fort Lauderdale and Miami, Florida.

Many of the large charter boats that work the Caribbean during the winter 'season' hole up for hurricane season around Puerto La Cruz, Venezuela, and are looking for delivery or long-term crews to take these vessels north to the US Virgin Islands and Puerto Rico in early November. Also check the notice boards at marinas; often you will find a note advertising for crew members, or you can leave one of your own. Yachting magazines are also good resources.

See Charter Yacht in the Getting Around chapter for a list of companies offering crewed or bareboat yacht charters.

Maps & Charts You'll need accurate maps and charts for any voyage through the Caribbean's reef-infested waters. British Admiralty charts, US Defense Mapping Agency charts and Imray yachting charts are all accurate. You can order them in advance from Bluewater Books & Charts (☎ 305-763-6533, 800-942-2583), 1481 SE 17th St Causeway, Fort Lauderdale, FL 33316. Consult the Books and Sailing sections in the Facts for the Visitor chapter for additional information and resources.

ORGANIZED TOURS

Tours of Puerto Rico are so numerous that it would be impossible to attempt any kind of comprehensive listing. For overseas visitors, the most reliable sources of information on the constantly changing offerings are major international travel agents such as Thomas Cook and American Express.

Package Tours

The tours that are probably of most interest to the general traveler are package deals including accommodations at a resort hotel and bus or van trips to major attractions such as Old San Juan, the rain forest at El Yunque, historic Ponce and the Cavernas del Río Camuy. Such tours can be an efficient and relatively inexpensive option for the traveler who wants to see a lot in a short time with all of the arrangements made in advance. Consult the list under Organized Tours in the Getting Around chapter for information on the island's local tour operators and offerings.

Dozens of companies offer package tours to Puerto Rico, usually using charter airlines and common carriers. The largest companies may operate on a regular basis, often every week. Many companies offer a range of hotels to choose from, with package prices varying accordingly.

Most per-person rates are quoted based on double occupancy (two people sharing a room). An additional charge (called a 'single supplement') is usually applied to anyone wishing to room alone.

The USA The following US tour operators are among those most active in the Puerto Rico market:

Adventure Tours USA
(☎ 214-360-5000, 800-999-9046)
5949 Sherry Lane, Dallas, TX

American Airlines FlyAAway Vacations
(☎ 800-433-7300, fax 817-967-4328)
Mail Drop 1000, Box 619619, DFW Airport,
TX 75261

Apple Vacations
(☎ 610-359-6700, 800-727-3400, fax 610-359-6624)
7 Campus Blvd, Newtown Square, PA 19073

Caribbean Concepts
(☎ 516-496-1678, 800-423-4433, fax 516-496-3467)
575 Underhill Blvd No 140, Syosset, NY 11791

Delta Dream Vacations
(☎ 800-872-7786)
110 E Broward Blvd, Fort Lauderdale, FL

Island Resort Tours
(☎ 212-251-1700, 800-527-5982, fax 212-545-8169)
300 E 40th St, New York, NY 10016

Travel Impressions
(☎ 516-845-8000, 800-284-0044, fax 516-845-8095)
465 Smith St, Farmingdale, NY 11735

TWA Getaway Vacations
(☎ 800-438-2929, fax 609-985-4125)
10 E Stow Rd, Marlton, NJ 08053

US Airways Vacations
(☎ 407-857-8533, 800-455-0123)
7200 Lake Ellenor Drive No 241, Orlando,
FL 32809

Canada Canadian package tour operators
include the following:

Air Canada Vacation Tours
(☎ 514-876-4141, 800-263-0882)
1440 Ste Catherine St W, Montreal, QC H3G 1R8

Canadian Holidays
(☎ 416-620-8687, 800-661-8881, fax 416-620-9267)
191 The West Mall, 6th floor, Etobicoke,
ON M9C 5K8

Sunquest Vacations
(☎ 416-485-1700, fax 485-9479)
130 Merton St, Toronto, ON M4S 1A4

Australia & New Zealand Contours
Travel (☎ 3-9670-6900, fax 9670-7558), 466
Victoria St, North Melbourne, VIC 3051, is
Australia's largest tour operator/wholesaler
to the Caribbean.

In New Zealand, contact Innovative
Travel & Promotions (☎ 3-365-3910, fax 365-
5755), PO Box 21, 247 Edgeware, Christ-
church, which is about the only tour operator
with a Caribbean specialty.

The UK Contact the Caribbean Centre
(☎ 020-8940-3399, fax 8940-7424), 3 The
Green, Richmond, Surrey TW9 1PL; or consider Uncle Sam Travel Agency (☎ 0121-
523-3141, fax 554-7315), at 295 Sotto Rd,
Birmingham B21 95A.

Japan Island International (☎ 03-3401-
4096, fax 3401-1629), 4-11-14-204 Jingumae,
Shibuya-ku, Tokyo 150, specializes in package tours and special-interest travel to the
Caribbean.

Specialized Tours

Elderhostel (☎ 617-426-8056), 75 Federal
St, Boston, MA 02110, is a nonprofit organization offering educational programs for
those aged 60 and above, and it has programs throughout the US and Puerto Rico.

Bicycling, hiking, walking, running and
multisport tours are another possibility; try
Backroads (☎ 510-527-1555, 800-462-2848),
801 Cedar St, Berkeley, CA 94710.

If ecotours are your thing, check out the
entry under Organized Tours in the Getting
Around chapter for information on ecotour
operators on the island.

Getting Around

AIR

Perhaps because Puerto Rico is a relatively small island, or perhaps because it has such a 'car culture,' the commonwealth's domestic air transportation system is rather basic. But if you are really in a hurry – or do not want to deal with a rental car – you can catch daily flights between San Juan, Ponce and Mayagüez. The bulk of Puerto Rico's domestic air traffic links San Juan to the Spanish Virgin Islands of Culebra and Vieques.

Domestic Airports & Airlines

Luis Muñoz Marín From its Isla Verde location on the eastern edge of San Juan, Aeropuerto Internacional de Luis Muñoz Marín (LMM) handles a fair amount of the island's scheduled domestic air traffic. This is the place to catch turbo-prop flights on American Eagle (☎ 787-749-1747) from San Juan to Ponce and Mayagüez. One-way fares to either city are about US$49 to US$89; roundtrip fares are US$95 to US$135.

To fly to the Spanish Virgin Islands from LMM, take Isla Nena Air Service (☎ 787-741-6362, 888-263-6213). Currently, Isla Nena charges US$90 roundtrip to Vieques from LMM, US$95 roundtrip to Culebra. Vieques Air Link (☎ 888-901-9247) also flies to Vieques from LMM; fares are US$53/100 one-way/roundtrip. See Isla Grande, below, for information on scheduled service to the Spanish Virgin Islands from that airport.

Vieques Air Link also offers service to/from the US Virgin Islands of St Thomas and St Croix. Some of these flights actually stop at Vieques.

You can charter planes from Caribair (☎ 787-791-1240) and from World Connection (☎ 787-253-7350) at LMM airport.

Isla Grande This airport in San Juan's Miramar district, on the Bahía de San Juan, is the center for private aviation as well as Puerto Rico's air taxi operations. To fly to the Spanish Virgin Islands from this convenient downtown airport, take Vieques Air Link (☎ 888-901-9247 for San Juan-Vieques flights, 787-722-3736 for San Juan-Culebra flights). Fares to Vieques are US$53/100 one-way/roundtrip; fares to Culebra are about US$45/90.

Not only is Isla Grande the operations base for Vieques Air Link, but the airport is also home to the charter services of Hill Aviation & Helicopter (☎ 787-723-3385) and of M&N Aviation (☎ 787-722-5980). Most clients of these operations are looking for a sightseeing trip or fast rides to destinations around the island.

Other Airports Out on the island, you will find long runways but only basic facilities, such as Ponce's Aeropuerto de Mercedita, about 4 miles east of town off Hwy 1 on Hwy 5506, and Aguadilla's Aeropuerto Rafael Hernández, at the former Base Ramey on Hwy 107 about 5 miles north of town.

Vieques Air Link and Isla Nena currently offer service to Culebra and Vieques from the small airstrip at the Aeropuerto de Fajardo. On Vieques Air Link, Fajardo-Vieques flights cost US$18/35 one-way/roundtrip; the Fajardo-Culebra flights cost US$20/40. For travel to/from Fajardo, contact Vieques Air Link at ☎ 787-741-3266 for Vieques flights, ☎ 787-722-3736 for Culebra flights. Isla Nena (☎ 787-643-3762) charges US$30 roundtrip to Vieques, US$40 roundtrip to Culebra.

Recently, the Puerto Rican government has built ultramodern terminals that seem ridiculously out of place at the airports on Culebra and Vieques, with the vague hope that an aircraft larger than an Islander twin or tri-motor Trilander will someday arrive to disgorge swarms of happy tourists. The airports on both islands get regular air service from San Juan and Fajardo; there are at least six flights a day to/from San Juan's Isla Grande and LMM airports, more than 10 flights a day between Fajardo and Vieques and at least three flights a day between Fajardo and Culebra.

The resorts in the beach community of Dorado, on the island's north coast, have an airstrip to serve guests who arrive by charter or private plane.

PÚBLICO

Públicos (literally, 'public cars') form the backbone of Puerto Rico's public transportation system and represent the principal means of getting around the island. For the most part, these vehicles are eight-passenger vans chock-full of bench seats. You can identify one of these vans by the letters 'P' or 'PD' on the license plate. Each van's destination is usually posted on top of the windshield.

Públicos are essentially shared taxis that run prescribed routes during daylight hours. Some públicos make relatively long hauls between places such as San Juan and Ponce or Mayagüez, but most make much shorter trips, providing a link between communities all over the island.

Públicos usually make their pick-ups and drop-offs at a van stand on or near the central plaza in each town, so you will pay extra if you want the driver to take you to a destination that is off the route, such as a hotel.

In San Juan, the principal público centers include the LMM airport, the large público station in Río Piedras and – to a much lesser extent – Plaza de Colón in Old San Juan.

Low fares are the chief attraction of público travel. A passenger will pay between US$8 and US$20 for a ride from San Juan to Ponce or from Ponce to Mayagüez, a few dollars more for the San Juan-Mayagüez haul. The fares for these trips fluctuate depending upon the number of passengers in the van. More passengers mean cheaper individual fares. The catch to traveling by público is that the vans make a lot of stops and do not always travel along the fastest routes, so that on a San Juan-Ponce run, for example, it could take you five hours or more to cover less than 75 miles.

For schedules and fares, inquire at the público stands in town plazas or at San Juan's LMM airport. You can also look under *Líneas de Carros* in the yellow pages of the telephone directory. Choferes Unidos de Ponce (☎ 787-764-0540) makes the San Juan-Ponce run; Líneas Sultanas (☎ 787-765-9377) will get you from San Juan to Mayagüez.

TRAIN

There are presently no passenger railroads on the island. Not yet, anyway. The Tren Urbano, now in the works, is a major public transportation project designed to shuttle people around San Juan. Current projections plan for the completion of about 12 miles of track – mostly above ground – and 16 stations around the city by 2004. One segment of the line, between Bayamón and Santurce, may open as early as 2001. Current thinking imagines fares to be 75¢, but that figure may rise as the project piles up cost overruns. Meanwhile, prepare yourself for traffic jams caused by construction of the rail line.

To learn the current status of the Tren Urbano, check with the Puerto Rico Tourism Company (☎ 800-223-6530) or, better yet, any of the local tour operators mentioned under Organized Tours later in this chapter.

CAR

Despite the occasional hazards of operating a car in Puerto Rico (see Driving Conditions, below), driving is undoubtedly the most convenient way to get around the countryside, see small towns, cross sprawling suburbs and explore wide-open spaces. Visitors venturing outside San Juan and other large cities will no doubt find renting a car an especially attractive option.

It's easy to list the circumstances in which you *won't* want a car. In San Juan, for example, the hassles of traffic, parking, navigating the maze of thoroughfares and the danger of being carjacked make having and using a car in the city a challenge, to say the least. To some degree, however, driving is the lesser of many evils when it comes to island transportation. Urban buses are crowded, públicos can be slow, taxis are expensive and the intra-island air service (except to the Spanish Virgin Islands) is infrequent and costly. With a rental car you can save yourself time and money while independently exploring the colorful corners of greater San Juan and the rest of the island.

Driving Conditions

Fasten your seat belt and hold on to your underwear, Maverick. Motoring in Puerto Rico is no walk in the park! Although drivers are much more competitive in many other places in the world – such as Rome, São Paulo, Bangkok and Boston, to name a few – island streets have their share of road warriors who refuse to make way for merging traffic or obey stop signs and traffic lights, especially late at night (see Security, below). Furthermore, many drivers have a terrifying habit of driving in the center of the road, particularly when the highway or street is narrow. And forget the use of turn signals for lane changes and many turns. In fact, you'll see Puerto Rican drivers use turn signals so infrequently that you might wonder if these safety features are disconnected in most cars sold on the island.

Finally, it would seem that many drivers simply cannot stand being behind another car. Hence, drivers play hopscotch with one another, overtaking their 'rivals' with daredevil folly. That these same drivers thrive on excessive speed is a fact that almost goes without saying. You will see mangled cars from fatal accidents sitting beside the road outside police stations and crosses along the highways as reminders of the consequences of reckless driving. On the other hand, some Old World courtesy does survive on the roads here: Drivers won't hesitate to stop traffic indefinitely to ensure the safety of an elderly person or mother with a baby carriage trying to cross the street.

The major problem with driving in Puerto Rico is that islanders have adopted the *yanqui* belief that it is every person's divine right to own and operate an automobile. With more than 1.5 million vehicles in the hands of

about 3.8 million inhabitants, Puerto Ricans are making real progress toward parity between cars and humans on their happy isle. In many places – particularly in greater San Juan – the sheer number of parked and moving vehicles is so daunting that it is not uncommon to see wide-eyed looks of terror or predation on the face of the average motorist.

One consolation is that Puerto Rico has the best roads in the Caribbean and probably in all of Latin America. Recent years have seen more than 100 miles of new limited-access highways open, and plans are in place to double this number in the near future. For example, with the relocation of Hwy 3 between Fajardo and Salinas, the tortured two-hour trip will shrink to less than an hour. The completion of the Hwy 22 toll road along the northwest coast takes the misery out of trips between San Juan and Arecibo.

In spite of these ongoing improvements to the number and quality of island roads, rush-hour traffic jams persist in major cities, the industrial towns west of San Juan and the towns and villages of the southeast coast, where traffic lights can slow progress to a crawl. Many mountain roads still remain narrow, twisted and prone to *desprendimientos* (landslides).

If you plan to drive in Puerto Rico, use extreme caution and drive defensively, especially at night when you should be prepared to encounter oncoming cars without headlights, or farm animals such as horses and cattle on the roads. Meanwhile, expect to be honked at as a matter of course. The honking is little more than a sign of motorists' anxiety; actual 'road rage' is far less common here than in the mainland US.

Maps & Directions A good road map is essential. The ones distributed by the car-rental companies are only adequate if you plan on staying on the main roads; buy a detailed map like the one published by Rand McNally if you plan to do any exploring in San Juan or off the beaten track. See Maps under Planning in the Facts for the Visitor chapter for details.

Islanders will be more than happy to help with directions – if you speak Spanish – but take their instructions with a grain of salt. Puerto Ricans tend to underestimate distances and can be overly optimistic about road conditions. It may also be difficult to obtain specifics on street names, probably because so many of the island's city streets are unmarked. Believe any islander, however, who tells you that a road is bad!

Spanish for the Road

The following are terms the traveler may find useful while navigating the island by car. See the Spanish for Travelers chapter at the end of this book for further language tips.

adelante	ahead
a la derecha	to the right
a la izquierda	to the left
autopista	highway
baden	speed bump
calle sin salida	dead end
carretera cerrada	road closed
carretera dividida	divided highway
carretera estrecha	narrow road
cruce	crossroads
cruce de peatones	pedestrian crossing
cuesta	hill
desprendimiento	landslide
desvío	detour
estación de peaje	toll station
lomo	bump or hill
manténgase a la derecha	keep right
neblina	fog
no entre	do not enter
no estacione	no parking
no vire	no turn
parada de guaguas	bus stop
pare	stop
peligro	danger
puente estrecho	narrow bridge
resbala mojada	slippery when wet
semáforo	traffic light
tránsito	one-way
velocidad máxima	speed limit
zona escolar	school zone

Gasoline Esso, Shell, Texaco and other major oil companies maintain gasoline stations across the island. In rural areas, stations usually close on Sunday. Almost everywhere on the island, gas stations generally stay open until 7 pm or so. Service stations sell fuel by the liter; at the time this book went to press, the price was about 26¢ a liter for economy gas, which is remarkably inexpensive by international standards. You can use credit cards for fuel purchases in all but rural areas.

Security Car break-ins and auto thefts are epidemic in some parts of the island (especially in greater San Juan). Hence, it is always best to park in hotel or other secure parking lots, especially when leaving your car overnight. If you must park on the street at any time of the day, remove all belongings if possible. At the very least, keep them locked out of sight.

Puerto Rico has a higher rate of carjackings than Los Angeles, so stopping for anyone who waves you down or approaches your vehicle carries significant risk. Letting a stranger into your car is – sadly – like playing Russian roulette. Many island drivers ignore stoplights and stop signs late at night for fear of making themselves targets for carjackers.

Road Rules

You must be at least 16 years old to drive in Puerto Rico. On the San Juan-Ponce Autopista, the superhighway traversing the island north to south, the speed limit is 70mph. You can drive 5mph over the limit without much likelihood of being pulled over, but if you are doing 10mph over the limit, you will be caught sooner or later. In small towns, driving over the posted speed limit by any amount may attract attention. Speed limits on other highways are 55mph or less, and in cities can vary from 25mph to 45mph. Watch for school zones, which can have posted limits as low as 15mph (strictly enforced during school hours). Out on the island, road signs are prevalent and helpful in finding your way around, but speed-limit signs are surprisingly rare. Most highway signs employ international symbols. One common source of confusion is that distances on island roads are measured in kilometers, while speed limits are posted in miles per hour.

Driving rules here are basically the same as they are in the US. Traffic proceeds along the right side of the road and moves counterclockwise around traffic circles at merger points; seat belts and motorcycle helmets must be worn; and children younger than four must travel in child safety seats. But aggressive drivers, unfamiliar territory and road signs in Spanish (see 'Spanish for the Road,' above) make driving on the island an experience that requires unbroken concentration and – when possible – the help of a competent navigator with a good map.

Mechanical Problems The larger car-rental agencies have 24-hour service numbers in case of breakdowns and other emergencies. If your car does break down and you must use a local mechanic, you should do so only for minor work; otherwise the car-rental company may balk at reimbursing you for work they haven't authorized. If you can't find a phone or repair service, seek police assistance by calling ☎ 911. Use common sense in dealing with unsolicited offers of help. *Never* give your keys to a stranger.

If you are a member of the American Automobile Association (AAA), the emergency roadside assistance number on the island is ☎ 787-764-4913. See Useful Organizations in the Facts for the Visitor chapter for more on AAA membership and services.

Accidents Hopefully you won't have one, but if you're involved in a *choque* (crash), there are a few rules to obey. First, do not move the vehicles, and do not let anyone else move them, including the other driver. Have someone call the police, and remain at the scene until a police officer arrives. Make sure to get the name and address of anyone else involved in the accident, as well as their license plate number and details of their vehicle. Take photos of the scene if possible, and get the names, numbers and addresses of any witnesses. Above all, do not be drawn into an argument. In situations like this,

everyone's emotions can be volatile, so you should do your best to keep things calm.

Contact your car-rental company as soon as possible to report the accident.

Rental

All of the major international car-rental companies operate in Puerto Rico, along with dozens of smaller, local firms. Most car-rental companies are reliable, although the smaller the company the greater the risks involved. Most rental companies require that you have a major credit card, that you be at least 25 years old and that you have a valid driver's license (your home license will do). Some companies may rent to drivers between the ages of 21 and 24 for an additional charge (usually around US$7 per day).

Car-rental agencies are listed in the local yellow pages and in the Puerto Rico Tourism Company's publication, *Qué Pasa*. You will find plenty of rental companies at the LMM airport, in major cities and in resort towns ringing the island's coast. Agencies in San Juan include the following:

AAA	☎ 787-791-1465
Afro	☎ 787-724-3720
Avis	☎ 800-874-3556
Budget	☎ 787-791-3685, 800-468-5822
Charlie Car Rental	☎ 787-728-2418
Discount	☎ 787-726-1460, 800-722-1460
Hertz	☎ 787-791-0840, 800-654-3131
L&M	☎ 787-725-8307, 800-666-0807
Leaseway	☎ 787-791-5600
National	☎ 787-791-1805, 800-568-3019
Target	☎ 787-728-1447, 800-934-6457
Thrifty	☎ 787-253-2525, 800-367-2277
Wheelchair Getta- ways Rent-A-Car	☎ 787-726-4023, 800-868-8028

Agencies in other cities include Popular Leasing (☎ 787-265-4848, 800-981-9282) in Mayagüez and Ponce, and Vias (☎ 787-796-6404) in Dorado and Humacao.

Puerto Rican car rentals are expensive by North American standards, and rental rates may give you sticker shock (Europeans are more likely to find prices on a par with home). In general, companies located away from airports tend to be less expensive. High-season rates begin at about US$40 per day and can run as high as US$100, depending on the vehicle you select. Of course, you can get a much better price for a weekly rental, with major rental companies offering economy cars for under US$195 a week with unlimited mileage. The prices get even better the longer you keep the car. For example, you can get a Suzuki Swift with standard transmission for as little as US$529 a month from Charlie Car Rental. You may also get cheaper rates in low season.

While some companies include unlimited mileage, others set a limit (usually 100 miles per day) and charge a fee for excess miles driven. You may be able to negotiate for unlimited mileage if this is not automatically included in your rental price. Many firms require a deposit of at least US$500 but will accept a credit card imprint. Keep copies of all your paperwork. Smaller companies may offer you what seem to be substantial savings but require a 'cash-only' transaction and a damage deposit. Beware: Once they get your money, you may have a hard time getting it back.

You can reserve a car upon arrival, but during high season you may find that most vehicles are taken and that the vehicle of your choice is not available. The best plan is to make your reservation several months in advance if you need a car during peak weeks such as the December and February school breaks and the Easter holiday. Before arrival, it's wise to reconfirm the date and time your car will be delivered to the airport (or your hotel).

Rental companies can also arrange a driver for an additional fee, if you desire.

Before signing the rental agreement, go over the vehicle with a fine-tooth comb to identify any dents and scratches. Make sure they are all clearly noted on your contract. Otherwise, you're likely to be charged for the slightest trace of damage. Don't forget to check the cigarette lighter and interior switches, which may be missing.

You can return cars to the rental office, or they can usually be left at the return stations at LMM airport. Some firms will allow you to arrange for a company representative to pick up the car at your hotel at no extra charge.

What Type of Vehicle? Most car-rental companies on the island utilize modern Japanese sedans. A small sedan is perfectly adequate for most conditions; a big car can be a liability on Puerto Rico's crowded streets and narrow, winding roads. Most companies also rent 4WD vehicles, which you may want for a bit of backcountry exploration, particularly on the islands of Culebra and Vieques.

Your options are standard (stick shift) or automatic transmission, and vehicles with or without air-con. Standard is preferable because of the constant and sudden gear changes required on the hilly, winding interior roads where kamikaze cows, horses and chickens appear out of nowhere. Automatic transmissions do not give you the control you'll need for these conditions.

Insurance There are several types of insurance to consider. Liability insurance is required in Puerto Rico as in most US states, but it is not always included in rental contracts because many drivers are covered for rental cars under their regular car liability insurance policy. Check this carefully. Don't pay extra if sufficient coverage is already included with the rental. Insurance against damage to the car, called Collision Damage Waiver (CDW) or Loss Damage Waiver (LDW), is usually optional (US$8 to US$12 per day), but will often require you to pay for the first US$100 or US$500 of any repairs. This cost, called the deductible, may be removed by paying additional premiums. Some credit card companies, like Gold MasterCard or American Express, will cover your CDW if you rent for 15 days or less and charge the full value of the rental to your card. Check with your credit card company before you leave home to determine if this service is offered and the extent of coverage.

Driver's License The minimum age to obtain a driver's license in Puerto Rico is 16 (see above for car-rental age requirements).

Most visitors can legally drive in the US and Puerto Rico for up to a year with their home driver's license. An International Driving Permit is a useful adjunct; for details see the Driver's License & Permits section under Visas & Documents in the Facts for the Visitor chapter.

MOTORCYCLE

Unlike a number of other Caribbean islands, Puerto Rico has almost no tradition of moped or motorcycle rentals to travelers. There are a number of motorcycle shops on the island, but they cater mostly to local enthusiasts who are often off-road riders.

BICYCLE

While cycling hasn't traditionally been a popular means of getting around the island, things are changing. Most resorts have at least one bicycle-rental shop, and bicycle supply shops can be found in most large towns.

The lack of shoulders on most roads, the high number of automobiles on the island and the aggressive style of drivers make bike-touring somewhat risky. Consider doing your touring or mountain biking through one of the adventure tour operators described under Organized Tours later in this chapter. The best conditions for cycling are found along the island's south coast and on the less densely populated islands of Vieques and Culebra. See Bicycling under Activities in the Facts for the Visitor chapter for more information.

For serious long-distance cycling, you'll need to bring your own bike or buy one in Puerto Rico. Some international and domestic airlines will carry bikes as checked baggage without extra charge if they're in a box. But many carriers will impose an oversize-baggage charge for any bikes that aren't disassembled first – check before you buy your ticket.

If you decide to take your own bicycle to Puerto Rico, heed this one note of caution: Before you leave home, go over your bike with a fine-tooth comb and augment your repair kit with every imaginable spare part. As with cars and motorcycles, you won't necessarily be able to buy that crucial gizmo

for your machine if it breaks down as the sun sets somewhere in the back of beyond.

Cyclists should review the caveats about road conditions and driving habits described under Driving Conditions, earlier in this chapter.

HITCHHIKING

Don't! Hitchhiking is never entirely safe in any country in the world, and we don't recommend it. Travelers who decide to hitchhike should understand that they are taking a small but potentially serious risk – creeps and criminals might see a hitchhiker as easy prey. People who do choose to hitchhike will be safer if they travel in pairs and let someone know where they are planning to go.

WALKING

Puerto Rico is small enough that it is feasible to explore on foot if you are acclimated to the warm weather or if you take to the cool mountains. See Hiking under Activities in the Facts for the Visitor chapter.

The compact area of Old San Juan is ideally suited to pedestrians. In fact, there is no better way to participate in the action along Calle San Sebastián or appreciate the local architecture than on foot. Aside from Old San Juan, some of the other areas that are best toured on foot include Condado, Isla Verde, Río Piedras (all districts of the capital) and the historic district of Ponce.

Should a sudden shower catch you without an umbrella, many shops offer plastic ponchos for less than US$1.

BOAT
Charter Yacht

All of the island's major resorts have marinas where you can charter yachts or powerboats, either with a crew or a 'bareboat.' Crewed boats come with a skipper and crew, and you don't need any prior sailing experience. With bareboat charters, you rent the boat and are your own skipper. Obviously, you must be a certified sailor to do this. Usually, you will have to give a short check-out demonstration of your skills before being allowed to sail away. Boats are normally fully stocked with linens and other supplies.

You will be expected to provision your own food, however. A security deposit is required.

Bareboat charters are usually rented by the week. Expect to pay upward of US$1200, depending on the vessel's size. Crewed charters normally cost about double that for a week or US$55 and up per person for a full day of sailing and snorkeling, including drinks and a picnic on a deserted isle.

Charter companies include the following:

Anticipation Harbor Cruises
(☎ 787-725-3500) San Juan

Brie…Z Sailing Charters
(☎ 787-850-5045) Palmas del Mar

Captain Jack Becker
(☎ 787-860-0861) Fajardo

Caribbean School of Aquatics
(☎ 787-728-6606) Condado

Caribe Aquatic Adventures
(☎ 787-724-1882) San Juan

Castillo Watersports
(☎ 787-791-6195) Isla Verde

Club Náutico Rentals
(☎ 787-860-2400) Fajardo

Connolly Yacht Service
(☎ 787-860-4421) Fajardo

El Faro SE Sailboat Charters
(☎ 787-845-7164) Sta Isabel

Erin Go Bragh
(☎ 787-860-4401) Fajardo

Spread Eagle II
(☎ 787-863-1905) Fajardo

Sun Yachts
(☎ 787-863-4813, 888-722-3500) Fajardo

Traveler
(☎ 787-863-2821) Fajardo

West Indies Charters
(☎ 787-887-4818) Fajardo

See also Sailing in the Facts for the Visitor chapter and Yacht in the Getting There & Away chapter.

Ferry

Fajardo/Culebra/Vieques There used to be a lot of jokes about untimely departures, slow going and seasickness on the passenger ferries between Fajardo and Culebra and Vieques. But no more. The Puerto Rican Port Authority (☎ 787-863-0705, 800-981-2005)

has added large, modern, high-speed vessels to these runs. In fact, the boats between Fajardo and Vieques move at such speed that passengers are required to stay in their seats during the hour-long crossings. See the Spanish Virgin Islands chapter for schedule and fare details.

Note: Don't bother taking a rental car to the islands – you can rent one there. See the Spanish Virgin Islands chapter for specifics.

For reservations, contact the Puerto Rican Port Authority at the numbers provided above or call the island offices (☎ 787-741-4761 on Vieques, ☎ 787-742-3161 on Culebra); reservation office hours are 8 to 11 am and 1 to 3 pm weekdays. If you have reservations, plan to pick up your tickets at the ferry terminal a half hour before the scheduled sailing. Note: Reservations go quickly for boats bound for the islands on Friday evening-Saturday morning and returning to Fajardo on Sunday afternoon-Monday morning, so plan ahead.

Old San Juan/Hato Rey/Cataño A commuter ferry service called the Acua Expreso (☎ 787-788-1155) connects the three main population centers around Bahía de San Juan: Old San Juan, Hato Rey and Cataño. See Ferry under Getting Around in the San Juan chapter for specifics.

TAXI

Most towns of any size on the island have taxi services. San Juan alone has seven, and none of them is cheap. All island cabs are metered, but in many cases the driver never turns the meter on. This means you must do your best to bargain for a fair rate and establish an agreed price before you get in a cab. Try to ask an islander whom you trust about reasonable taxi tariffs for the route you plan to travel, and then attempt to get that rate when you bargain. San Juan is the exception to this haggling hassle: Its so-called 'tourist taxis' have fixed rates for all their trips. Unfortunately, the prices are high enough to make you laugh (or cry) in disbelief. See the Taxi section in the San Juan chapter for specifics.

In spite of these frustrations, a taxi can sometimes be a valuable resource. As poor a value as San Juan's taxis are on short trips, they *can* be reasonable if you need to get to the east end of the island to reach a resort hotel or the Fajardo ferry terminal for a boat to Culebra or Vieques. As with most island destinations, you must bargain with the driver for a fair rate. On a good day, you may get the San Juan-Fajardo trip for as little as US$40, but expect to settle on about US$50 – plus tip (10% to 15%). Not bad, considering Fajardo is about 30 miles from the airport and you can fit four people in a cab. You could make this trip in a público for less, but it would take you three times as long.

Of course, the best reason to take a cab is to connect with island people. If you want to revive your Spanish, consider your ride a cheap language lesson: Island politics, police crackdowns on drug smugglers and the island's relationship to the US are topics that always seem to be on drivers' minds. Puerto Ricans are friendly people, and they have a fierce pride in their island that they like to share. In your US$12-plus ride from the airport to your hotel in Condado, you can pick up a lot of local knowledge about restaurants, beaches, clubs, dangerous neighborhoods and upcoming fiestas from a gregarious driver.

LOCAL TRANSPORT
Puerto Rico does not presently have an islandwide bus service. San Juan moves people via the AMA – Autoridad Metropolitana de Autobuses (Metropolitan Bus Authority; ☎ 787-767-7979) – and Metrobus (☎ 787-763-4141). AMA buses charge 25¢ to any destination on their routes; Metrobuses usually charge 50¢. See the San Juan chapter for specifics on routes and schedules. Visitors can identify bus stops by an obelisk marker that reads *'Parada'* or *'Parada de Guaguas'* (Bus Stop).

ORGANIZED TOURS
Puerto Rico has a plethora of tour operators with English- and Spanish-speaking guides. The tours are geared to meet the needs of travelers who have limited time on the island and want to see a lot. Most of these operators pick up clients at their hotels or at the cruise-ship docks in Old San Juan and whisk them off in minivans to popular tourist sites around the island, such as the rain forest at El Yunque or the Cavernas del Río Camuy. The following list includes a number of popular local operators and their destinations:

AAA Tour
(☎ 787-793-3678) El Yunque, Playa Luquillo, Old San Juan, Bacardi Rum Factory, Historic Ponce, Cavernas del Río Camuy

Colonial Adventures
(☎ 787-729-0114)
Themed walking tours of Old San Juan

Cordero Caribbean Tours
(☎ 787-786-9114)
Old San Juan, Bacardi Rum Factory, Ponce

GC International Services
(☎ 787-759-1255)
Islandwide, customized to clients' wishes

Hill Aviation & Helicopter
(☎ 787-723-3385) Helicopter tours

Hillbilly Tours
(☎ 787-760-5618) Islandwide from San Juan

Normandie Tours
(☎ 787-722-6308) All major attractions

Northwest Land Tour
(☎ 787-374-0783) Parque Ceremonial Indígena – Caguana, El Yunque, Guánica forest, Observatorio de Arecibo, Rincón, Old San Juan, Cavernas del Río Camuy

Oneida Star Line
(☎ 787-840-8435) Ponce

Sunshine Tours
(☎ 787-721-7300) All major attractions including La Parguera and its bioluminescent bay

United Tour Guides
(☎ 787-725-7605) All major attractions

VIP Coach & Tours
(☎ 787-783-6096, 800-932-9359)
All major attractions

Ecotours & Activity Tours
With the almost fad-like development of ecotourism during the 1990s, a flock of tour operators sprang up across the island to meet the demand. While nothing can compete with the adventure of planning and executing a wilderness trip on your own, these tour operators can take a lot of the

worry out of the adventure and give you a chance to interact with fellow adventure travelers:

AdvenTour
(☎ 787-832-2016) Cycling, birding, hiking, kayaking; trips to Guánica forest

Adventuras Tierra Adentro
(☎ 787-766-0470)
Camping, caving, rock-climbing, river-touring

Copladet Nature & Adventure Tours
(☎ 787-765-8595) Birding, caving, hiking, horseback riding, kayaking; trips to Isla Caja de Muertos

Encanto Ecotours
(☎ 787-272-0005) Mangroves, manatees, turtle nesting; trips to Culebra, Vieques and Isla Mona

Explora
(☎ 787-751-9647) Birding, camping, caving, hiking, river-touring; trips to El Yunque, Guánica forest

Tropix Wellness Tours
(☎ 787-268-2173) Biking, birding, caving, hiking, horseback riding, kayaking, rafting, sailing; trips to Culebra, Vieques, El Yunque, Guánica forest

Vikings of Puerto Rico
(☎ 787-823-7010)
Whale-watching (January to April)

San Juan

Havana, Cuba, is slightly larger. Santo Domingo, in the Dominican Republic, is slightly older. But no city in the Caribbean can match San Juan's sheer bravura, nor the number and variety of delights it holds for a traveler. The 300 sq miles comprising metropolitan San Juan are home to more than one-third (1.6 million) of all islanders, a concentration that speaks to the attractions of the island capital.

Simply put, San Juan has presided over the economic flowering of Puerto Rico and the rest of the Caribbean during the last 50 years. Today it is the engine of the island's economic and political life and a cultural beachhead for US influence in the Caribbean. The

Highlights

- Exploring the self-contained, walled city of Old San Juan, dominated by two dramatic fortresses and four centuries of Spanish colonial architecture

- Chilling in the serene gardens of the Casa Blanca, ancestral home of the Ponce de León family

- Plunging into the world-class restaurant, bar and shopping scene of Old San Juan

- Lounging on the broad urban beaches of Ocean Park and Isla Verde

- Immersing yourself in the scents and colors of the sprawling Mercado de Río Piedras

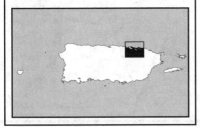

phalanx of high-rise condominiums standing guard over the shores of Isla Verde, Condado and Miramar is a powerful symbol of San Juan's prosperity, as are the city's recently expanded airport terminal, the six pages of bank listings in the telephone directory, the endless parade of ships in and out of the harbor and the shiny cars backed up in rush-hour *tapones* (traffic jams). But what the traveler is more likely to notice is the spit-and-polish care that owners lavish on their guesthouses in Ocean Park, the grandeur of new hotels such as the Wyndham Old San Juan, the variety of Caribbean and international cuisines in the city's world-class restaurants and the crowds of chic patrons in its casinos and clubs.

Of course, the undisputed crown jewel of the metropolis is the magnificent walled city that the world has come to know as Viejo San Juan (Old San Juan). As recently as three decades ago, this neighborhood of seven square blocks – pinched between the fortresses of El Morro and San Cristóbal on the steep hill at the mouth of Bahía de San Juan (San Juan Bay) – was a decaying red-light district with over 400 abandoned buildings. Today it has been largely restored, and the few ruined buildings remaining add to the Old World ambience like scratches in antique furniture.

Old San Juan is a working, breathing community rife with cobblestone streets, pastel-colored town houses, Romanesque arches, wrought-iron balconies, intimate courtyards and striking vistas that revive the look and feel of a Spanish colonial city. By day it functions as the seat of both the city and commonwealth governments. By night the old town becomes a pulsing center of nightlife. Chock-full of restaurants, clubs, bars, shops and museums, Old San Juan offers the traveler more entertainment per square foot than New York City – at a pace that is definitely laid-back and totally Latin. Beyond the walls of Old San Juan, the modern city has its hidden joys as well; look for them in

SAN JUAN

ATLANTIC OCEAN

Punta
Salinas

Isla de
Cabras

868

165

870

Ensenada de
Boca Vieja

see Old San
Juan map

PUERTA DE TIERRA

OLD
SAN
JUAN

25

1

see Condado &
Ocean Park map

165

Bahía de
San Juan

Aeropuerto de
Isla Grande

OCEAN
PARK

25

MIRAMAR

CONDADO

Ciénaga
de las
Cucharillas

888

875

24

5

Bahía de
Puerto
Nuevo

Ferry

39

35

37

26

6

SANTURCE

TOA BAJA

866

8869

869

5

CATAÑO

Expreso de Diego

5

Caño de Martín Peña

2

22

36

887

866

866

872

To Arecibo, Aguadilla

22

28

28

23

9

10

Parque Luis
Muñoz Marín

40

HATO
REY

1

167

7

Fort Buchanan
Military Reservation

8

17

18

17

25

866

864

To Arecibo,
Aguadilla

862

29

2

21

855

2

20

19

17

21

1

11

BAYAMÓN

880

861

831

174

177

GUAYNABO

841

176

167

831

833

838

177

199

840

169

199

52

199

176

(under construction)

174

20

830

837

169

176

829

830

833

Río de Bayamón

Canal Río Hondo

Canal de Bayamón

San Juan-Ponce Autopista

Río Piedras

836

To Reserva Forestal Carite, Ponce

SAN JUAN

1 Fuerte del Cañuelo
2 Bacardi Rum Factory
3 El Capitolio
4 Parques Muñoz Rivera &
   Sixto Escobar
5 Parque Central
6 Museo de Arte Contemporáneo
   Puertorriqueño
7 Luis A Ferré Parque de Ciencias
8 Caparra
9 Plaza Las Américas
10 Hiram Bithorn Stadium
11 Jardín Botánico
12 Mercado de Río Piedras

0   1.5   3 km
0   1   2 miles

Punta
Las
Marías

Punta de
Cangrejos

Punta
Maldonado

Punta
Vacía Talega

ISLA VERDE

Laguna
Los Corozos

Laguna La
Torrecilla

Bosque Estatal
de Piñones

187

To Loíza, Fajardo

37

Aeropuerto
Internacional de
Luis Muñoz Marín

Laguna de
Piñones

26

Laguna
San José

CAROLINA

Canal Blasina

Río Grande de Loíza

27

17

181

4

190

951

Universidad
de Puerto Rico

47

8

190

874

874

12

3

887

3

RÍO PIEDRAS

181

849

9959

847

848

887

845

846

8860

3

853

To El Yunque, Fajardo

844

846

181

TRUJILLO ALTO

858

859

175

Aljibe
Las
Curias

844

843

175

858

853

181

Río Grande de Loíza

Embalse
Río Grande
de Loíza

the neighborhoods where university students reside, artists paint and the songs of the next generation of *salsa* legends fill the streets.

HISTORY

Viewed from the sea or from the promenade known as Paseo de la Princesa, the 42-foot-high sandstone walls surrounding Old San Juan say it all: This city began – and thrived for centuries – as a fortress. Within a decade of colonizing the island (beginning in 1508) and scouring its mountain streams for gold, the Spanish conquistadores realized that to remain at Juan Ponce de León's first settlement of Caparra on the Río Bayamón was to invite death by Indian attack or malaria-carrying mosquitoes. The search for a healthy climate and defensible geography quickly led the Spaniards to a dramatic headland on an island about 2½ miles long and one-third of a mile wide that protected the Bahía de San Juan from the Atlantic Ocean. Ponce de León objected to leaving Caparra, but his minions prevailed against their leader's will.

Migration from Caparra began in 1511, and included some 200 Spanish soldiers and their families. The exodus to the new site ended in 1521, while Ponce de León was off getting himself fatally wounded in search of the legendary Fountain of Youth on Florida's west coast. But before the old conquistador departed on his final adventure, he named the new settlement 'Puerto Rico' (meaning Rich Port). This new epithet reflected the founding father's hopes for island wealth, which he managed to personally accumulate not from the island's disappointing yields of ore, but from selling goods to settlers who flocked here with gold fever.

The name stuck. But within a few years, Spaniards were calling the island itself Puerto Rico instead of its original name of San Juan Bautista – possibly because a Spanish cartographer had accidentally reversed the two names on a principal map. San Juan became the popular name for the new capital perched on the cliffs above the Atlantic and the Bahía de San Juan.

What a place to re-create a Spanish city in the fairy-tale mold of Toledo or Segovia! San Juan was easy to defend because of its

Founding father Juan Ponce de León

elevated island geography, more or less mosquito-free owing to the constant whir of the trade winds and a sentinel over the most protected harbor in the Caribbean.

Fortification of the City

Barricading the city against enemy attack was a first priority, and settlers quickly constructed walls, defensible entry portals like the Puerta de San Juan (San Juan Gate) and fortified houses such as the Casa Blanca and La Fortaleza. The Spanish government saw that San Juan and its harbor were the linchpin in Spain's domination of the sea routes between Europe and the Americas, and poured money into the new settlement. Soon, the gigantic fortress of San Felipe del Morro, with its 140-foot-high ramparts, began to rise above the ocean cliffs. Of course, representatives of the Catholic Church arrived in force with the architects and the military reinforcements, and the walled city quickly saw the construction of a church, a convent and a cathedral.

The British first tested San Juan's defenses in 1595 under the leadership of Sir Francis Drake, but the garrison proved stout. Over subsequent centuries, the building and rebuilding of San Juan's fortifications became a way of life. Repelling sieges by the

British, French and Dutch was the walled city's badge of honor. San Juan reached its zenith of fortification with the addition of Fuerte San Cristóbal, a massive stronghold designed to ward off land attacks. This fortress was constructed during the 18th century under the direction of Field Marshal Alejandro O'Reilly and his engineer Thomas O'Daly, both of whom were Irish mercenaries employed by the king of Spain.

During the 16th century, San Juan enjoyed being the site of the first papal see in the New World as well as a strategic colonial outpost. But the city only thrived to the extent that infusions of cash, soldiers and priests from Spain kept it going. San Juan's designation as the island's only official port of entry for three centuries actually worked against its economic development, because the Spanish mercantile system restricted trade with all but the mother country. Hence, San Juan languished during the 17th and 18th centuries while other communities on the island thrived on smuggling.

Even after the Spanish began to relax restrictions on trade between San Juan and the outside world in the 19th century, the fortress city remained a place that all but Spanish shipping preferred to work around, not through. To a degree, San Juan's exposure to arts, music, drama and politics from abroad during the 19th century made the island capital somewhat cosmopolitan. For the most part, however, the city remained little more than a monumental, remote military base.

Such was the situation when the USA claimed Puerto Rico as victor's spoils following the Spanish-American War in 1898. Initially, San Juan limped into the 20th century as little more than an American naval base. But the US government's efforts to promote free trade and its recognition of San Juan's harbor as the most secure in the Caribbean slowly began to change the face of the port. Shipping terminals grew up around the bay, new roads spread out to the rest of the island from the capital and agricultural goods such as sugar, tobacco and coffee flowed into the port from other parts of the island for shipping overseas. Meanwhile, *jíbaros* (country persons) flocked to

the city for work. Suddenly, neighborhoods sprang up beyond the little island that was colonial San Juan and began to spread in a ring around the bay, swallowing up some of the old villages such as Río Piedras.

Economic Development

WWII brought more capital and development to the port as the US beefed up its military defense of the island and the Caribbean. Following the war, a monumental economic initiative called Operation Bootstrap began changing Puerto Rico from an agricultural to a manufacturing-based economy, and in 1951 the island gained commonwealth status. San Juan boomed: Seeking to benefit from tax breaks, US factories moved in by the hundreds, particularly on the west side of the bay; foreign and US banks arrived en masse; the first high-rise buildings went up; and tourist zones took shape along the beachfront of the burgeoning city.

Growth & Restoration

The past four decades have been a constant struggle of city planners to keep up with the growing need for services, roads and housing to meet the mass migration of island residents from the country to the city. As recently as 10 years ago, much of metropolitan San Juan had the unplanned, slapped-together feel common to overnight commercial sensations such as Las Vegas or Hong Kong.

The global economic slowdown of the late 1980s gave San Juan residents a chance to pause and take stock of what was happening to their city. Citizens realized that while massive infusions of US government money had replaced squatters' camps and enclaves of makeshift shacks with concrete bunker-style housing projects called *caserios,* crime had only increased. The city seemed to be sprouting franchises of US fast-food restaurants everywhere, but there were few places to get a gourmet meal featuring the island *cocina criolla*. High-rise hotel and condo buildings had turned waterfront neighborhoods such as Condado, Miramar and Isla Verde into Miami Beach clones, while the historic restoration of Old San Juan begun in 1955 was creeping along in fits and starts. The city's public parks had become venues for drug deals.

This awakening became a call to arms for civic pride. Gradually, historic preservationists, cultural guardians, developers, city government and commonwealth officials began to pool their resources and imagination. Leaders saw an opportunity to link the private financing of the historic restoration of Old San Juan to the world's celebration of the 500-year anniversary of Columbus' 'discovery' of the Americas. By the time the fleet of tall ships arrived at San Juan from all over the world in 1992 to celebrate the Columbus voyage, San Juan had begun efforts to reduce crime in the tourist areas, spruced up the transportation system and restored nearly 80% of the buildings in Old San Juan. In addition, the city added spectacular new parks and drew a host of imaginative merchants, curators and chefs to develop a cache of shops, museums, restaurants, clubs and bars within the walls of the old city.

The energy and finesse that characterized that effort continue to this day. Not only is island pride evident in the restoration of Old San Juan, but also in the refurbishing of other tourist and entertainment zones such as Condado and Ocean Park, in the glitzy banks and office buildings of Hato Rey and in the ever-increasing number of professional sports tournaments and festivals devoted to the arts. While like any large city, metropolitan San Juan still has its poverty, crime and danger zones for the traveler, the poets hardly exaggerate when they say you can hear the streets sing.

ORIENTATION

Metropolitan San Juan surrounds the large Bahía de San Juan, filling in the coastal plain between the Atlantic Ocean and the mountains of the Cordillera Central on the northeastern coast of Puerto Rico. While navigating all 300 sq miles of greater San Juan can be daunting, most areas of interest to travelers are easy to reach and spread out along some 7 miles of Atlantic coast.

Moving west from the Aeropuerto Internacional de Luis Muñoz Marín on the city's eastern fringe, you travel from San Juan's newest neighborhood of Isla Verde through the mature *barrios* of Ocean Park, Santurce, Miramar and Condado to the city's original roots in Puerta de Tierra and Old San Juan. From the airport, two major thoroughfares head west through the city. The Expreso Baldorioty de Castro (Hwy 26) is the fastest and safest way (except during rush hour) to make the trip from the airport. The expressway intersects Avenida Ponce de León at the Laguna del Condado bridge, which links metro San Juan to Puerta de Tierra. From here, one-way traffic proceeds along the sea coast via Avenida Muñoz Rivera to Old San Juan, the city's historic colonial core. You can also make this trip via Hwy 37 and Avenida Ashford (through Condado), but there are endless stoplights and the route takes you along the edge of some dicey sections of Santurce.

Hato Rey is the name of the business district of high-rise banks and offices that flanks Avenida Ponce de León south of Santurce. Beyond Hato Rey at the threshold to the island's foothills you find the neighborhood of Río Piedras, home to the largest campus of the Universidad de Puerto Rico (UPR). The industrial zones of Cataño and Bayamón lie just a few miles west of here off the Expreso de Diego (Hwy 22). Lagoons, swamps, precious few parks, caserios and planned residential neighborhoods called *urbanizaciones* cover all the available landscape as far as the eye can see.

A traveler moving about the city can orient herself by judging her position in relation to three inland bodies of water. At the east end of the city near the airport and Isla Verde are the large lagoons (they look like one) of Laguna Los Corozos and Laguna San José. The much smaller Laguna del Condado, in the north-central part of San Juan, creates a divider between the heart of the city and the tourist zones of Condado, Puerta de Tierra and Old San Juan. The expansive Bahía de San Juan is the shipping harbor that defines the western border of the city.

Maps

Travelers will find tourist maps of Old San Juan, Condado and Isla Verde readily available through the Puerto Rico Tourism Company (see Tourist Offices under Information, below), which has offices at San Juan's LMM airport and at La Casita in Old San Juan (see that section, below). Although not to scale, these free maps are adequate for getting around the primary tourist zones on foot.

If you are driving or want a more complete view of the city, Rand McNally publishes a fold-out map of San Juan/Puerto Rico that includes a detailed overview of the metro area. These maps are widely available from most bookstores and drugstores in the city's tourists zones for under US$3. See Maps under Planning in the Facts for the Visitor chapter for maps covering other island destinations.

Once you have a map, make sure to go over it with someone who has good local knowledge about which areas to avoid because of the potential for traffic jams, damaged roads or crime (see Dangers & Annoyances later in this chapter).

INFORMATION
Tourist Offices
The Puerto Rico Tourism Company (PRTC; ☎ 800-223-6530, 787-721-2400) is the official mechanism for distributing information to island visitors and has a number of easy-to-find locations in San Juan. At the LMM airport, you can stop at the information counter between Terminals B and C or visit the PRTC's desk (☎ 787-791-1014) on the lower (arrivals) areas of Terminals B and C. Hours are 9 am to 5:30 pm daily.

Coming from a cruise ship dock, the Acua Espreso ferry dock or a taxi drop at the end of Calle La Marina near the Wyndham Old San Juan Hotel & Casino, you will find tourist information at La Casita (☎ 787-722-1709), the miniature building near the head of Pier 1 and the start of the Paseo de la Princesa. Hours are 9 am to 8 pm daily except Thursday and Friday, when the office closes at 5:30 pm. The PRTC's central offices (primarily an art gallery and a workplace for staffers) are housed in a building known as La Princesa (☎ 787-721-2400), west along the paseo.

In the past, more than a few travelers have complained about careless or inattentive treatment from PRTC receptionists, and it seems that something has finally been done to improve the quality of service at the company's visitor information desks. While PRTC workers are not exactly Disney attraction greeters, visitors can now expect a smile, courteous attention and knowledgeable service from the staff.

For information on camping, including reservations and permits, contact the Depto de Recursos Naturales (Dept of Natural Resources; ☎ 787-724-3724) or visit their office near the Capitolio on Avenida Fernández Juncos in Puerta de Tierra. The office is open weekdays.

Money
Puerto Rico's unit of exchange is the US dollar. If you are arriving by air, you can change money at the Thomas Cook Foreign Exchange (☎ 787-791-2233) at the LMM airport. This office is generally open from 9 am to 8 pm, when most scheduled international flights arrive and depart.

Unlike many cosmopolitan resorts, San Juan's hotels are not necessarily equipped to change foreign currency. If you are in the center of the city and need to change money, head for one of the overseas banks along Avenida Ponce de León in Hato Rey. Banks are open 9:30 am to 2:30 pm weekdays.

In Old San Juan you can try the Caribbean Foreign Exchange (☎ 787-722-8222), 201B Calle Tetuán, or next door at Thomas Cook Foreign Exchange (☎ 787-722-0888). Both offices are open 9 am to 4 pm weekdays; noon to 4 pm Saturday.

Post & Communications
Greater San Juan has about 20 post offices. The one likely to be most convenient for travelers is at 153 Calle Fortaleza in Old San Juan (☎ 787-723-1277). Hours are 7:30 am to 4:30 pm weekdays; 8:30 am to noon Saturday. The city's main post office (☎ 787-767-2890), at 585 Avenida Roosevelt in Hato Rey, maintains the same hours; general delivery mail comes here.

If you need to phone, fax or telex, there are a number of phone stations around Old San Juan. You will find banks of phones at

AT&T's World Service Telephone at Pier 1 and dispersed around the waterfront to serve cruise ship crews when they are in port. The city's major plazas also have many phone stations. If you want to rent a PO box, purchase a money order, send a fax or ship your treasures off the island, stop by Mail Boxes Etc at 202A Calle San Justo in Old San Juan (☎ 787-722-0040), at 1357 Avenida Ashford in Condado (☎ 787-724-8678) or at 5900 Avenida Isla Verde in Isla Verde (☎ 787-728-5623).

Travel Agencies

The metro San Juan phone directory lists hundreds of agencies under the heading *Viajes* (Trips), so you have a lot to choose from. If you need help in a hurry, try Juan José Travel (☎ 787-721-5743), conveniently located in the heart of the Condado tourist zone at 1407 Avenida Ashford.

Bookstores

Old San Juan has a couple of great bookstores. Cronopios (alias 'The Bookstore'; ☎ 787-724-1815), at 155 Calle San José near the intersection with Calle Tetuán, has one of the best collections of English-language titles on the island and networks with its branch at 124 Avenida Roosevelt in Hato Rey. Across from Teatro Tapia look for Casa Papyrus (☎ 787-722-3362), at 357 Calle Tetuán, a book and music store with a café where you can chill in the shade with a good book, soft jazz and *café con leche*. David Morgan is the helpful manager of The Book Exchange, which is primarily a used-book store at 208 Calle San Sebastián (☎ 787-725-3541, 724-8802).

Bell, Book, and Candle (☎ 787-728-5000) pulls in the vacation crowd at 102 Avenida José de Diego in Condado. Another good source for books and magazines in Condado, including English-language titles, is Scriptum Books (☎ 787-724-1123), 1129B Avenida Ashford.

As one might expect, the area around the UPR campus at Río Piedras has a number of good bookstores. Inter Books (☎ 787-751-8821) at 898 Esteban González, The Book Shop (☎ 787-287-2520) in the Monteheidra

Town Center and Librería La Tertulia (☎ 787-765-1148) at the corner of Calle Amalia Marín and Avenida Gonzalez all get high marks from the locals.

Parentesis (☎ 787-753-7140) is the well-stocked, all-purpose bookstore on the 2nd floor of the Plaza Las Américas mall in Hato Rey. Thekes (☎ 787-765-1539) is another bookstore on the 1st floor of the mall.

Libraries

San Juan's main public library is the Biblioteca Carnegie (☎ 787-722-4739), at 500 Avenida Ponce de León among the other government buildings in Puerta de Tierra just east of Old San Juan. Next door is the intimate and decorative Ateneo Puertorriqueño (☎ 787-725-3873), Parada 2 Avenida Ponce de León, a cultural association with a private library.

The UPR campus at Río Piedras is home to the great Biblioteca José M Lazaro (José M Lazaro Library; ☎ 787-763-3930). Enrolling in one of the conversational Spanish courses at the university's Multilingual Institute (see Language Courses later in this chapter) or any other classes at UPR gives you access to the library.

Universities

The main campus of the Universidad de Puerto Rico (affectionately known as 'Upi' or 'Yupi'; ☎ 787-764-0000) covers an area larger than the historic district of Old San Juan. You can find the grounds and academic buildings spreading out around La Torre (Roosevelt Bell Tower) to the east of Avenida Ponce de León.

With more than 50,000 students and regional campuses in other cities out on the island, UPR is the largest university in the Caribbean and a substantial academic institution by any standard. UPR offers degrees and graduate study in business, communications, education, humanities, law, library sciences, medicine, natural sciences, pharmacology, planning, public administration and social sciences. The medical school and university hospital lie about a mile west of the main campus (see Miramar, Hato Rey & Río Piedras later in this chapter).

Laundry

One of the largest Laundromats in Old San Juan is Norzagaray Coin Laundry (☎ 787-722-3998), 306 Calle Norzagaray. This is not in the safest area of the old city, however, and you may feel more secure washing at night at the smaller Laundromat in the Caleta building at 11 Caleta Las Monjas, where machines cost US$1 per load, or at one of several other small Laundromats you will see tucked on the first floors of apartment buildings throughout Old San Juan. In the Condado/Santurce area, try the Caribbean Laundromat (☎ 787-725-7926) at 760 Avenida Ponce de León. Río Piedras has a plethora of sites including Xtra Laundromatic (☎ 787-751-8395) at 169 Calle del Parque. To find a laundry near you, look under *Lavanderías* (Laundries) or 'Laundries – Self-Service' in the yellow pages of the telephone directory. Dry cleaners are also listed under 'Laundries.'

Medical Services

With 14 hospitals in metro San Juan, you get a lot of choice and variety in medical service. Ashford Memorial Community Hospital (☎ 787-721-2160), at 1451 Avenida Ashford in the Condado area, is probably the best-equipped and most convenient hospital for travelers. Check the San Juan phone directory for a complete list of hospitals.

You will find US drugstore chains like Walgreens all over the city. Try the Walgreens (☎ 787-722-6690) at the corner of Calles Cruz and San Francisco in Old San Juan, though you might prefer the exceedingly friendly and helpful staff at Puerto Rico Drug (☎ 787-725-2202), right across the street on Calle San Francisco. The Walgreens (☎ 787-725-1510) at 1130 Avenida Ashford in Condado is open 24 hours. If you have problems with your eyeglasses *(espejuelos)*, stop in at Ashford Óptica (☎ 787-722-0215), 30 Calle Washington in Condado, or look under *Ópticas* in the yellow pages.

Emergency

In *any* kind of emergency, call ☎ 911! But beware: You may find that the telephone directory and tourist publications list non-functioning local numbers for emergency services. At the time of this book's publication, the following numbers worked for routine inquiries. But these numbers can be frustrating to a person facing an emergency situation because of the frequency of busy signals or answering machines with messages in Spanish.

Medical	☎ 787-765-1594
Dental	☎ 787-767-4976
Police	☎ 911 or 787-793-1234
Fire	☎ 787-725-3444
Rape	☎ 787-785-2285
Weather	☎ 787-253-4588
Traveler's Aid	☎ 787-791-1054/1034
Alcoholics Anonymous	☎ 787-723-4187

Dangers & Annoyances

Before you venture into metropolitan San Juan, take some time to review the Dangers & Annoyances section in the Facts for the Visitor chapter and the companion section on Personal Security & Theft. Also consider asking someone you trust for some local knowledge about danger zones in the city.

In addition to avoiding lonely streets, unknown bars and beaches at night and taking other common-sense precautions with your money, jewelry and other belongings, there are a few specific things to consider when it comes to crime and personal safety in San Juan. The most obvious caveat is that dressing and/or behaving like a rich *gringo* (foreigner) draws attention to you and makes you a temptation to criminals. As in many Latin American cities, foreign women in San Juan who send provocative messages through their dress or actions are asking for these signals to be misinterpreted by local men who might make pests of themselves or worse.

Of course, blending in with the islanders is no guarantee that you will not be a target for a couple of punks in need of money. As every urban dweller in the world should know, the best way to escape a mugging with a minimum of hassle is to carry a US$10 bill that appears to be your only cash, and be ready to give up this bill at the onset of the assault.

Travelers should note that some neighborhoods of San Juan simply are not safe. Most of these areas are not near any attractions, but a few are. Under no circumstances should you walk into La Perla, the picturesque yet poverty-stricken enclave outside the north wall of Old San Juan. Avoid the adjacent cemetery at night as well.

Drug dealers and other bad actors hang out at the *balneario* (public beach) at Escambrón in Puerta de Tierra. The business district of Hato Rey becomes a ghost town after sunset and therefore should be avoided at night. Cataño, across the bay from Old San Juan, is another place where travelers can feel justifiably uncomfortable at night.

Travelers who visit the beaches, shops, hotels and restaurants in the Condado/Ocean Park area would do better to avoid the adjacent neighborhoods of Santurce *anywhere* south of Calle Magdalena. Calle Magdalena itself is generally safe, well-traveled and under police supervision. But in some places just a block away from the glitz, Santurce is in serious decay. Not long ago the area was a fashionable place to live, but during the last 10 years it has been overrun by unemployed males, high-school dropouts, prostitutes and all the rest.

Finally, drivers in San Juan should be aware that Puerto Rico has a high rate of carjackings, so it's best to avoid stopping for anyone who waves you down or approaches your vehicle, especially at night.

OLD SAN JUAN

Old San Juan ranks with the Rive Gauche of Paris, Barrio Gótico of Barcelona, Boston's Beacon Hill, New York's Greenwich Village, Mexico's mountain city of Cuenca and Shanghai's port area when it comes to world-class urban walks. Here is a place that treats strollers to the compound charms of a dramatic natural setting, historic architecture, fine cultural institutions and a spirited community. In Old San Juan, 500 years of Spanish colonial history blend almost seamlessly with contemporary Puerto Rican culture as you walk lamplit cobblestone streets. Colorful town houses rich with iron balconies and potted plants line your way. His-

toric forts, churches and museums open their doors to you for exploration (and most offer free admission).

Ideally, a traveler will want to devote days, weeks or even months to soaking up the tropical flavor of Old San Juan and yielding to the town's mood swings, from pensive mornings to passionate nights. Yet Old San Juan is so compact that even visitors with severe limits on their time and money can get a feel for this World Heritage Site. In fact, you can complete a tour of the old city's major sites during a three-hour walk.

The following sites are presented in the form of a walking tour, which follows the route indicated by the dotted line on the Old San Juan map. The numbers following each heading correspond to the number that each site has been assigned on the map and key. Sites without corresponding key numbers have been labeled on the map.

If you plan to enter more than just a few of the major attractions, consider a more relaxed approach and stretch this tour over a day. See the city in its various moods by breaking your walking tour into morning and late afternoon jaunts. Reserve the midday heat for a long lunch in a dark, cool restaurant, a swim or a siesta.

Visitors should note that Old San Juan is a magnet for Puerto Ricans from all over the island on weekends. Also, many cruise ships disgorge their passengers here Saturday through Tuesday. Thursday and Friday tend to be the quietest days, but the town turns wild on those evenings as flocks of night owls descend from all over the city and its suburbs.

If exploring on foot doesn't appeal to you, see the boxed text in the Getting Around section at the end of this chapter for details on the free trolley that operates through the heart of the old city.

La Casita (Key No 85)

Looking like a pink gatehouse, La Casita (Little House) greets visitors near the cruise ship docks in 'lower' Old San Juan, in the outskirts of the walled city that rises on the hill to the north. The Dept of Agriculture and Commerce built this miniature neoclassical structure with its red-tiled roof in

1937 to serve the needs of the burgeoning port. Today, La Casita is the information center for the PRTC (☎ 787-722-1709); open 9 am to 8 pm daily except Thursday and Friday, when it closes at 5:30 pm. Stop here for maps and brochures, or check out the weekend craft market on the building's threshold. Also look for the food vendors selling fruit, icy *piraguas* (snow cones) and other treats.

Paseo de la Princesa

Stretching to the west of the La Casita is the Paseo de la Princesa (Walkway of the Princess), a 19th-century esplanade lined with antique street lamps, shade trees, royal palms, statues, fountains, benches, tables, a food court, fruit vendors' carts and street entertainers on weekends. The paseo is very popular with families from all over the city who come to stroll, listen to street musicians and sample classic island treats such as coconut *tembleque* or *mavi* – a root beer-like beverage made from the bark of the ironwood tree.

This entire promenade was restored in the 1990s, and its new pink paving stones lead strollers to the brink of the Bahía de San Juan. From here you can catch the cooling breezes off the water and watch merchant and cruise ships navigating in and out of the busiest harbor in the Caribbean. The big pink building on your left as you start down the paseo is **La Aduana** (Customs House; Key No 84).

El Arsenal (Key No 88)

Take a slight detour here and follow Calle Puntilla south a short distance past La Aduana. On the point of land called La Puntilla is a low, gray fortress with a Roman proscenium entrance. This is El Arsenal (☎ 787-724-1877, 724-5949), a former Spanish naval station that was the last place to house Spanish military forces after the US victory in the Spanish-American War. Today, the Arsenal is home to the fine- and decorative-arts divisions of the Instituto de Cultura Puertorriqueña, and hosts periodic exhibitions in three galleries. Hours are 8:30 am to 4 pm, Wednesday to Sunday; admission is free.

La Princesa (Key No 64)

Farther along the paseo, poised against the outside wall of the city, is La Princesa. Once a harsh jail, the long, gray and white stone structure now houses the main offices of the PRTC (see Tourist Offices under Information, earlier) and an art gallery with welcome air-conditioning and changing shows by first-rate island artists. The gallery is free and open 9 am to 4 pm weekdays. The bronze statue in front depicts San Juan's revered mayor from 1946 to 1968, Doña Felisa Gautier.

Raíces Fountain & La Muralla (Key No 57)

As the promenade reaches the edge of the Bahía de San Juan, you will see an imposing bronze sculpture and fountain called *Raíces (Roots)*. The sculpture's figures depict the Taíno, European and African ancestors of modern Puerto Ricans.

From the fountain, follow the Paseo de la Princesa to the north along the perimeter of La Muralla (City Wall), as it squeezes along the very edge of the bay. Here you can see an excellent example of the kind of walls – with turreted guard towers called *garitas* – the Spaniards built to fortify their colonial cities. Completed in the late 1700s, the wall's 20-foot-thick sandstone construction shows one reason why British and Dutch assaults on the city failed over the centuries.

DAVID ZINGARELLI

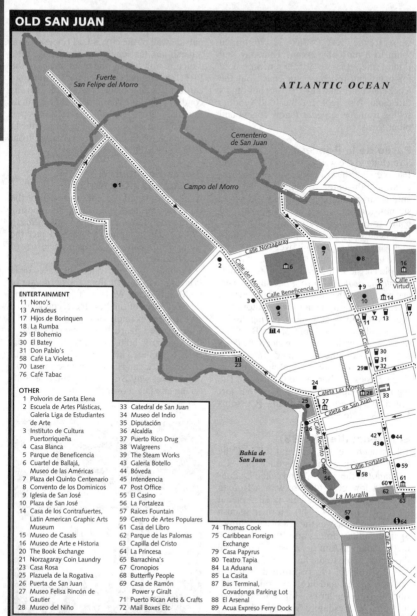

OLD SAN JUAN

Fuerte
San Felipe del Morro

ATLANTIC OCEAN

Cementerio
de San Juan

Campo del Morro

●1

Calle Norzagaray

Calle del Morro

Calle Beneficencia

Bahía de
San Juan

La Muralla

Calle Fortaleza

Calle Presidio

Calle
Virtud

ENTERTAINMENT
11   Nono's
13   Amadeus
17   Hijos de Borinquen
18   La Rumba
29   El Bohemio
30   El Batey
31   Don Pablo's
58   Café La Violeta
70   Laser
76   Café Tabac

OTHER
1   Polvorín de Santa Elena
2   Escuela de Artes Plásticas,
     Galería Liga de Estudiantes
     de Arte
3   Instituto de Cultura
     Puertorriqueña
4   Casa Blanca
5   Parque de Beneficencia
6   Cuartel de Ballajá,
     Museo de las Américas
7   Plaza del Quinto Centenario
8   Convento de los Dominicos
9   Iglesia de San José
10   Plaza de San José
14   Casa de los Contrafuertes,
      Latin American Graphic Arts
      Museum
15   Museo de Casals
16   Museo de Arte e Historia
20   The Book Exchange
21   Norzagaray Coin Laundry
23   Casa Rosa
25   Plazuela de la Rogativa
26   Puerta de San Juan
27   Museo Felisa Rincón de
      Gautier
28   Museo del Niño

33   Catedral de San Juan
34   Museo del Indio
35   Diputación
36   Alcaldía
37   Puerto Rico Drug
38   Walgreens
39   The Steam Works
43   Galería Botello
44   Bóveda
45   Intendencia
47   Post Office
55   El Casino
56   La Fortaleza
57   Raíces Fountain
59   Centro de Artes Populares
61   Casa del Libro
62   Parque de las Palomas
63   Capilla del Cristo
64   La Princesa
65   Barrachina's
67   Cronopios
68   Butterfly People
69   Casa de Ramón
      Power y Giralt
71   Puerto Rican Arts & Crafts
72   Mail Boxes Etc

74   Thomas Cook
75   Caribbean Foreign
      Exchange
79   Casa Papyrus
80   Teatro Tapia
84   La Aduana
85   La Casita
87   Bus Terminal,
      Covadonga Parking Lot
88   El Arsenal
89   Acua Expreso Ferry Dock

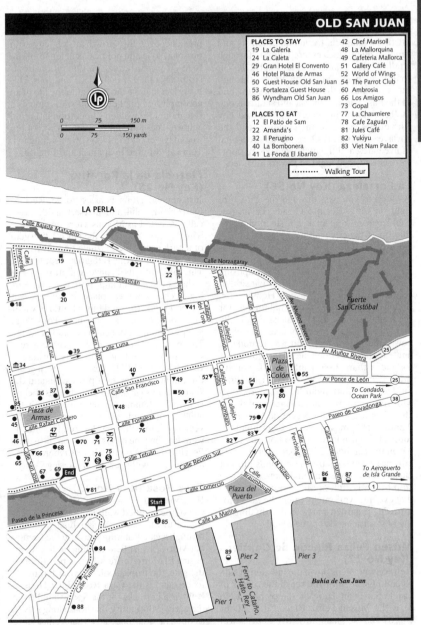

OLD SAN JUAN

PLACES TO STAY
19 La Galeria
24 La Caleta
29 Gran Hotel El Convento
46 Hotel Plaza de Armas
50 Guest House Old San Juan
53 Fortaleza Guest House
86 Wyndham Old San Juan

PLACES TO EAT
12 El Patio de Sam
22 Amanda's
32 Il Perugino
40 La Bombonera
41 La Fonda El Jibarito

42 Chef Marisoll
48 La Mallorquina
49 Cafeteria Mallorca
51 Gallery Café
52 World of Wings
54 The Parrot Club
60 Ambrosia
66 Los Amigos
73 Gopal
77 La Chaumiere
78 Cafe Zaguán
81 Jules Café
82 Yukiyu
83 Viet Nam Palace

·········· Walking Tour

Puerta de San Juan (Key No 26)

Spanish ships once anchored in the cove just off these ramparts to unload colonists and supplies, all of which entered the city through a tall red portal known as La Puerta de San Juan (San Juan Gate). This tunnel through the wall dates to the 1630s. It marks the end of the Paseo de la Princesa and stands as one of three remaining gates into the old city (the others lead into the cemetery and the enclave of La Perla). Once there were a total of five gates, and the massive wooden doors were closed each night to thwart intruders.

La Fortaleza (Key No 56)

As soon as you pass through the gate, turn right on Calle Recinto Oeste. The narrow cobblestone street makes a steep climb to the top of the city wall to the guarded iron gates of La Fortaleza (The Fortress; ☎ 787-721-7000 ext 2211 or 2358). Also known as El Palacio de Sta Catalina, this imposing building is the oldest executive mansion in continuous use in the Western Hemisphere, dating to 1533. Once the original fortress for the young colony, La Fortaleza eventually yielded its military preeminence to the city's newer and larger forts and was remodeled and expanded to domicile island governors for more than three centuries. If you are dressed in respectful attire, you can join a guided tour that includes the mansion's Moorish gardens, the dungeon and the chapel. Free guided tours generally run from 9 am to 3:30 pm weekdays except holidays; tours in English leave on the hour, in Spanish on the half hour. It's a good idea to call in advance to make sure the grounds are not closed for a government function. If you stop by La Fortaleza on a Friday or Saturday evening, you might catch the governor throwing a garden party to the rhythms of the best salsa bands on the island.

Museo Felisa Rincón de Gautier (Key No 27)

Retrace your steps down the hill along Calle Recinto Oeste until you reach the corner of Caleta San Juan. Here on the corner at No 51 is the Museo Felisa Rincón de Gautier (☎ 787-723-1897), an attractive neoclassical town house that was once the longtime home of San Juan's beloved mayor. Doña Felisa presided over the growth of her city with personal style and political acumen for more than 20 years during the Operation Bootstrap days of the 1940s, '50s and '60s. This historic home is a monument to the life of an accomplished public servant who remains a role model for women's liberation in Latino culture. The museum is open 9 am to 4 pm weekdays except holidays; free admission. Tours are offered in Spanish and English.

Plazuela de la Rogativa (Key No 25)

Just beyond Doña Felisa's house, Recinto Oeste heads uphill and intersects a side street called Caleta Las Monjas. Here on your left with a vista overlooking the bay is a tiny gem of a park called the Plazuela de la Rogativa (Small Plaza of the Religious Procession). This site, with its bronze sculpture of the bishop of San Juan and three women bearing torches, is a great place to call time-out under a shade tree and buy a bottle of water or coconut *limber* (a homemade Popsicle in a cup) from the little shop across the street. The park and statue commemorate a religious procession held in the city during the British siege of 1797. According to legend, the candle- and torch-lit procession and the simultaneous ringing of church bells tricked British lieutenant Abercromby – with his 8000 troops and flotilla of more than 50 vessels – into believing that reinforcements were flooding the city from out on the island. Fearful of being outnumbered, Abercromby and his fleet withdrew from the siege.

Casa Rosa (Key No 23)

Resuming your walk northwest along the rim of the fortified wall overlooking the entrance to the Bahía de San Juan, you pass through a gate ushering you onto the Campo del Morro, a vast field leading up to the imposing El Morro fortress. As you pass through the gate, the tropical villa to your left in the foreground is the Casa Rosa (Pink House). Built as a barracks for the Spanish militia in the early 19th century, this house long served as officers' quarters. The structure has since been restored and now serves as a plush day-care facility for government employees.

If you veer sharply left from here and follow the road that runs just inland of the top of the city wall, you will see a broad, green field ahead that spreads out as a threshold to the fortress of El Morro (see below). As you follow the road across the field toward the fort, the building with the chimney you see on your right is a 19th-century powder magazine known as the **Polvorín de Sta Elena** (Key No 1), now closed to the public.

Fuerte San Felipe del Morro

Even if forts, guns and wars don't make your blood hum, Fuerte San Felipe del Morro (☎ 787-729-6960) is impressive because of its scale, architecture and dramatic setting on the cliffs of the bold headland overlooking the Atlantic and the entrance to the Bahía de San Juan. Known simply as 'El Morro' (meaning headland or promontory), this six-level fort with its gray castellated lighthouse and 140-foot walls (some up to 15 feet thick) dates back to 1539 and claims to be the oldest Spanish fort in the New World. The National Park Service (NPS) maintains this fort and the small military museum on the premises. Displays and videos in Spanish and English document the construction of the fort over almost 200 years, as well as El Morro's role in rebuffing the various attacks on the island by the British and the Dutch.

If you do not join one of the free guided tours offered in Spanish and English, at least try to make the climb up the ramparts to the sentries' walks along the Sta Barbara Bastion and Austria Half-Bastion for the views of the sea, the bay, Old San Juan, modern San Juan, El Yunque and the island's mountainous spine. On weekends, the fields leading up to the fort are alive with picnickers, lovers and kite flyers. The scene makes an impromptu festival with food vendors' carts on the perimeter. El Morro is open 9 am to 5 pm daily; adults US$2, children and seniors US$1. Keep your receipt for free entrance to Fuerte San Cristóbal, later on the walking tour.

Escuela de Artes Plásticas (Key No 2)

Leaving El Morro by the main road (Calle del Morro), visitors will see a monumental gray and white building with a red-roofed rotunda ahead of them on the city side of the field. This magnificent neoclassical structure houses the Escuela de Artes Plásticas (Academy of Fine Arts). Built as an insane asylum during the 19th century, this grand building looks more like a seat of government with

The monumental Fuerte San Felipe del Morro

its symmetrical wings, columns, Romanesque arches, porticos, courtyards and fountains. Today it is the source of more than a few jokes by contemporary art students about the mad dreams that continue to take shape within its walls. See for yourself when student shows go on display at the end of each academic term, or take a look at the sculpture court on the right side of the building, where students can be seen chipping new images from granite.

The courtyard on the left side of the building has a food kiosk with inexpensive treats, shaded café tables and a view of El Morro.

Instituto de Cultura Puertorriqueña (Key No 3)

Just beyond the façade of the arts academy lies the Instituto de Cultura Puertorriqueña (Institute of Puerto Rican Culture; ☎ 787-724-0700), housed in another freshly restored 19th-century monument. Once a home for the poor, this buff building with green trim now houses the executive offices of the Instituto, an agency that has been shepherding the flowering of the arts and cultural pride on the island since the 1950s. Not only is this building a fine example of historic restoration, but its quiet plazas are tranquil sanctuaries. The Instituto's galleries offer changing exhibitions, including a display on pre-Columbian treasures. The galleries and museum are open 9 am to 5 pm Tuesday to Sunday. Admission to both is free.

Parque de Beneficencia (Key No 5)

Just beyond the Instituto lies a new park of paved terraces and fountains called Parque de Beneficencia (Poor House Park). On weekend afternoons this park is a major scene for roller bladers and skateboard posses, who draw crowds to watch their rail slides and kick flips.

Casa Blanca (Key No 4)

Continuing back down towards the heart of Old San Juan, beyond the far right corner of the Parque de Beneficencia you'll find the iron gateway leading to the Casa Blanca

(White House; ☎ 787-724-4102), ancestral home for 250 years of the descendants of Juan Ponce de León. Laid out before you is a secluded garden with shade trees, a chain of fountains and a courtyard. The restored 'house' – really a compound – in the heart of the garden revives the grandeur attendant on the lives of 17th- and 18th-century Spanish gentry. Ponce de León's son-in-law started construction on this house in 1521; it was intended as a retreat for the colony's founder, but the explorer died in his quest for the fabled Fountain of Youth before he could move in. This site is a 'must-tour' for travelers who enjoy poking around the quarters of the rich and famous. Otherwise, cool off in the shady garden and then move on. It's open 9 am to noon and 1 to 4:45 pm, Tuesday to Saturday; entrance to the garden is free. Self-guided house tours cost US$1 for adults, 50¢ for seniors and children; you can inquire on the premises or call ahead for a guided tour, available for an additional charge.

Cuartel de Ballajá & Museo de las Américas (Key No 6)

Heading back in the direction of Parque de Beneficencia, on the northeast side of the park you see the mammoth Cuartel de Ballajá (Ballajá Barracks), looking more like a nunnery than the former home of Spanish soldiers and their families. This restoration now houses the Museo de las Américas (Museum of the Americas; ☎ 787-724-5052) on the 2nd floor. As it expands, the museum plans to give an overview of cultural development in the New World. Current exhibits include artifacts excavated in Old San Juan, an impressive *santos* collection and displays of other traditional crafts. Hours for both the barracks and the museum are 10 am to 4 pm Tuesday to Friday, 11 am to 5 pm weekends; admission to both is free. Tours in Spanish or English are available with advance reservations.

Plaza del Quinto Centenario (Key No 7)

The barracks' eastern door opens onto the courtyard and totem-like monument crowning the recently built Plaza del Quinto

Centenario (Quincentennial Plaza), which descends in terraces from Calle San Sebastián to the fountain pool near Calle Norzagaray. Puerto Rico built this plaza at a cost of well over US$10 million in 1992 as part of the celebration and tall ships regatta commemorating the 500-year anniversary of Christopher Columbus' first voyage to the Americas. The plaza gives an unobstructed view of the Atlantic and the ship channel leading into Bahía de San Juan.

Cementerio de San Juan

Also visible from the Plaza del Quinto Centenario, this cemetery lies just outside the northern fortifications of the old city. The graveyard can be reached by following the road that leads downhill from the plaza through one of the walled city's original entry gates.

A neoclassical chapel provides a focal point among the graves of the colony's earliest citizens – as well as that of the famous Puerto Rican freedom fighter Pedro Albizu-Campos. This Harvard-educated chemical engineer, lawyer and politician led the agricultural workers' strikes in 1934 and was at the forefront of the movement for Puerto Rican independence until his arrest and imprisonment in 1936.

A number of muggings have occurred here in the past, and travelers might be wise to appreciate the tombs from afar or visit in a group.

Plaza de San José (Key No 10)

Adjacent to the uppermost terrace of the Plaza del Quinto Centenario where it meets Calle San Sebastián is the Plaza de San José. This relatively small cobblestone plaza is dominated by a statue of Juan Ponce de León, cast from an English cannon captured in the raid of 1797. The plaza is probably the highest point in this city on a hill and serves as a threshold to four cultural sites on its perimeter. A quiet open space by day, the plaza transforms into the central gathering place for San Juan's well-heeled youth on weekend nights, when they cruise the streets, bars and clubs of the old city. This is the place to come to find a world-class fiesta with *bomba*

y plena performers and drumming competitions. Until 1998, the fiestas included drinking in the streets, but things in the plaza and along Calle San Sebastián got so rowdy that the bishop and the mayor called for a police crackdown to break up the party. Carrying open alcoholic containers in the streets will now get you a hefty fine (see Legal Matters in the Facts for the Visitor chapter).

If your explorations of Old San Juan follow the sequence of this walking tour, you'll find yourself in an ideal area for some time out or even lunch following your explorations of the attractions surrounding Plaza de San José. The neighborhood around the plaza, on Calle San Sebastián and the intersecting Calle del Cristo is the original home of the restaurant, bar and café scene that began in Old San Juan more than a decade ago, and there are at least a dozen places to grab a table and a bite to eat in the shade. See Places to Eat later in this chapter for a description of your options…or just follow your nose: The smells of *sofrito* (an island seasoning), grilled chicken, garlic, fresh *dorado* and lime permeate the air.

Iglesia de San José (Key No 9)

Facing the plaza is the Iglesia de San José (☎ 787-725-7501), the second-oldest church in the Western Hemisphere. Established in 1523 by Dominicans, this church with its vaulted Gothic ceilings still bears the coat of arms of Juan Ponce de León (his family worshipped here), a striking carving of the Crucifixion and ornate processional floats. For 350 years, the remains of Ponce de León rested in a crypt here before being moved to the city's cathedral down the hill. Another relic missing from the chapel is a Flemish carving of the Virgin of Bethlehem, which came to the island during the first few years of the colony and disappeared in the early 1970s. The church is open 7 am to 3 pm weekdays (closed Thursday), 8 am to 1 pm Saturday; Sunday mass is held at noon.

Convento de los Dominicos (Key No 8)

Next to the Iglesia de San José is the Convento de los Dominicos (☎ 787-721-6866), a

Dominican convent dating from the 16th century. After centuries of use as a convent, the building became a barracks for Spanish troops and was later used as a headquarters for US occupational forces after the Spanish-American War of 1898.

Today it has been meticulously restored to its colonial grandeur and houses the arts/crafts/music/book store of the Instituto de Cultura. It's open 9 am to 5 pm Monday to Saturday. The convent also provides a venue for musical concerts.

Museo de Casals (Key No 15)

Also on the plaza is the Museo de Casals (Casals Museum; ☎ 787-723-9185). A native of Spain's proud but repressed province of Catalonia, world-famous cellist Pablo Casals moved to his mother's homeland of Puerto Rico in 1956 to protest the dictatorial regime of Federico Franco in Spain. He quickly established the respected Festival Casals for classical music, which became a principal force in the subsequent flowering of the arts on the island (see Music & Dance under Arts in the Facts about Puerto Rico chapter). This small museum celebrates the musician's life and contributions to the island with a collection of performance videos and memorabilia ranging from his favorite sweater to a cello, pipe collection, manuscripts and videotapes. Unless you love the man and his music, you can skip this place. It's open 9:30 am to 5:30 pm Tuesday to Saturday; admission US$1 adults, 50¢ children.

Casa de los Contrafuertes (Key No 14)

The final historical attraction on the Plaza de San José, the Casa de los Contrafuertes (House of Butresses; ☎ 787-724-5477), stands next to the Museo de Casals. Considered the oldest colonial residence on the island, this building dates from the 18th century. The 1st floor houses the reconstruction of a 19th-century apothecary shop, while the 2nd floor is home to the **Latin American Graphic Arts Museum**, where you can see revolving shows of local talent. The building and museum are open 9 am to 4:30 pm Wednesday to Sunday; free admission to both.

Museo de Arte e Historia (Key No 16)

After a break in the area around Plaza San José, make your way east along Calle San Sebastián (away from El Morro and all of the sites described earlier), and take your first left on Calle Virtud. This street opens onto a market square, and the former market building in front of you now houses the Museo de Arte e Historia (☎ 787-724-1875). This art and history museum is another free attraction, featuring galleries with rotating fine-arts exhibits. This is a good place to step into the air con and see a half-hour documentary about the history of San Juan (in Spanish and English). The museum is open 8:30 am to noon and 1 to 3:45 pm weekdays; 10 am to 5 pm Saturday.

La Perla

Calle Norzagaray runs parallel to the northern wall of the city here, presenting striking vistas of the Atlantic. In the foreground, accessed by a steep road and steps leading down the outside of the wall to the beach, is

---

The House that Crack Built

The area around the intersection of Calles Tanca and San Sebastián, and the alley that connects this intersection with Calle Norzagaray, is know as 'El Callejón' – a favorite haunt of drug dealers and homeless addicts that the city government seems to tolerate. Over the years, these individuals have claimed the four-story abandoned building at the corner of El Callejón and Calle Norzagaray as their own, decorating its exterior walls and gaping windows with hundreds of dolls and stuffed animals – some monstrously large. Today, citizens from all over San Juan – including local children – drop off stuffed toys to add to this folk monument celebrating lost childhood.

Although the people who linger around El Callejón may look threatening, the area is surprisingly safe except late at night.

a warren of terraced, whitewashed and pastel homes known as La Perla (The Pearl). Often called the most picturesque slum in the world, La Perla has been home to centuries of dispossessed, desperate people who have survived by their wits, creating their own microculture based on street crimes. The district gained international infamy when Oscar Lewis wrote his novel *La Vida* (1966), which detailed the tragic cycle of poverty and prostitution lived out by people growing up in La Perla. For anyone who has seen the *favelas* of Rio, the *ranchos* of Caracas or the *barrios* of Mexico City, La Perla looks innocuous by comparison. But it remains the prized turf of lawless people who will be only too happy to rough you up and rob you if given the opportunity. Wonder from afar at the social conditions that create such an enclave, and at the tenacity of this community to resist the gentrification that has overwhelmed the rest of Old San Juan. This is not a place to wander into; see Dangers & Annoyances earlier in this chapter.

Fuerte San Cristóbal

As you continue east along Calle Norzagaray, the street veers away from the ocean and the city's wall butts up against Fuerte San Cristóbal (☎ 787-729-6777), the old city's other major fortification. In its prime, San Cristóbal covered 27 acres with a maze of six interconnected forts protecting a central core with 150-foot walls, moats, booby-trapped bridges and tunnels. The fort was constructed to defend Old San Juan against land attacks from the east via Puerta de Tierra. The imaginative design for Fuerte San Cristóbal came from the famous Irish mercenary Alejandro O'Reilly and his compatriot Thomas O'Daly; construction began in 1634 and lasted well over a century.

Today the NPS maintains the fort, which includes a small museum, a store, military archives and a reproduction of a soldier's barracks. Because San Cristóbal attracts far fewer tourists than El Morro, it retains the austere ambience of its working days. It's open 9 am to 5 pm daily; US$2 adults, US$1 seniors and children. Entry is free with admission receipt from El Morro.

Plaza de Colón

Tracing its roots back more than a century to the 400-year anniversary of the first Columbus expedition, the Plaza de Colón (or Columbus Plaza) lies across the street from the lower part of Fuerte San Cristóbal. The city wall on this end of Old San Juan has been torn down, and the plaza, with its statue of the 'Discoverer' atop a pillar, stands on the site of one of the city's original gated entries, Puerta Santiago. Today, the plaza acts as a gateway to much of the traffic entering the city from Avenida Muñoz Rivera. Bus stops are along the plaza's south side.

El Casino & Teatro Tapia (Key Nos 55 & 80)

Facing the southeast corner of the plaza is El Casino. This neoclassical monument was once a social club for high society, the site of debutante cotillions and formal dancing during the 19th century. Now part of Puerto Rico's Dept of State, the building joins the Teatro Tapia (Tapia Theater; ☎ 787-722-0407) on the south side of the plaza to re-create the genteel days of the late 19th century, when sophisticated music, drama and architecture blossomed on the island. The theater takes its name from the so-called father of Puerto Rican literature, Alejandro Tapia y Rivera, a talented Puerto Rican dramatist, poet and fiction writer. Recently restored, the theater provides an intimate, regal setting for frequent concerts and drama. You can view the theater's ornate interior by attending a production (see Entertainment later in this chapter for ticket information).

Plaza de Armas

From the northwest corner of Plaza de Colón, follow Calle San Francisco back into the heart of the old city. This is the one of the busiest commercial streets in Old San Juan, and a good place to shop with the islanders in the area's many boutiques, bookstores, pharmacies, bakeries and markets.

After strolling the narrow sidewalk for several blocks, you find the street opening onto the Plaza de Armas (Army Plaza). Here you see the city's central square, which was laid out in the 16th century with the classic look of plazas from Madrid to Mexico's Mérida and San Miguel de Allende. In its time, the plaza has served as a military parade ground (hence its name), a vegetable market and a social center. Shade trees, banks of seats, open-air cafés and musical entertainment once made the plaza the destination of choice for couples making their evening *paseo* (stroll). But that was before the city declined as a result of the American military presence during the first half of the 20th century.

Today the huge shade trees are gone in favor of a gazebo and a popular food kiosk with café tables, which may be the reason the plaza swarms with pigeons. McDonalds, Wendy's, Marshalls, Walgreens and a Pueblo supermarket now line the plaza. Despite these changes, the plaza still retains a lot of its colonial image.

One of the highlights of the plaza is the recent restoration of the **Alcaldía** (City Hall; ☎ 787-724-7171; Key No 36), which dates from 1789 and has twin turrets resembling those of its counterpart in Madrid. This building houses the office of the mayor of San Juan and is also the site of periodic exhibitions. The Alcaldía is open 8 am to 5 pm weekdays, except holidays.

At the western end of the plaza, the **Intendencia** (Administration Building; Key No 45) and the **Diputación** (Provincial Delegation Building; Key No 35) are two other recently restored and functioning government office buildings adding to the charms of the plaza. Both represent 19th-century neoclassical architecture and come complete with cloisters.

Museo del Indio (Key No 34)

If you are interested in Puerto Rico's indigenous people but do not have the time to visit the related historic sites out on the island, head uphill on Calle San José one block from the plaza to No 119, site of the Museo del Indio (Indian Museum; ☎ 787-721-2864). The museum is small but not without merit because of its strong collection of artifacts, including the little stone gods called *cemíes* (see the History and the Traditional Arts sections in the Facts about Puerto Rico

chapter for more on these objects). Tours are offered in English and Spanish. The museum is open 9 am to noon and 1 to 4:30 pm Tuesday to Saturday; free admission.

Catedral de San Juan (Key No 33)

Every Spanish colonial city must have its cathedral, and the Catedral de San Juan (☎ 787-722-0861) fills the local need a block west of the Museo del Indio where Calle Luna meets the little plaza and the Gran Hotel El Convento. While not as grand as the cathedral in Ponce – or most Spanish colonial cathedrals, for that matter – the building dates back to 1521 and includes pieces of the original Gothic ceiling and staircase constructed in 1529. The current whitewashed structure is largely a 19th-century neoclassical affair, and has been lovingly restored in recent years.

Probably the chief reason to visit here is to see the marble tomb of Ponce de León and the body of religious martyr St Pio displayed under glass, before wondering for a few moments at the everlasting rewards that come to those who die in search of material or spiritual glory. It's open 8:30 am to 4 pm daily; free entry. Weekday masses are at 12:15 pm, Saturday at 7 am, Sunday at 9 and 11 am. You can get quite a show here on Saturday afternoons when the limos roll up with bridal parties putting on the ritz.

The main entrance to the cathedral faces Calle del Cristo, a shady street of posh boutiques and trendy bars and restaurants that capture the fancy of both tourists and islanders alike.

Museo del Niño (Key No 28)

Directly across the street from the cathedral is a pink and green building overlooking a small, shady park. This building is the Museo del Niño (Children's Museum; ☎ 787-722-3791). Having recently recovered from a catastrophic fire, this museum duplicates many of the interactive museums that are so popular with kids in the US. If you are traveling with a child, this museum is probably a 'must-stop' for you. Don't miss the excursion through the human heart! It's open 9:30 am

SAN JUAN

to 3:30 pm Tuesday to Thursday; 10 am to 5 pm Friday; 12:30 to 5 pm on weekends. Admission is US$2.

Parque de las Palomas (Key No 62)

From El Museo del Niño, head south on Calle del Cristo past all the boutiques and chic restaurants to the lower end of that street. Here you will see the Parque de las Palomas (Pigeon Park), a cobblestone courtyard shaded with trees at the top of the city wall. People come here for the view it affords of Bahía de San Juan and to feed the pigeons who live in the park. (You can buy bird seed from a vendor by the gate.) Devout Christians have long believed that if you feed the birds and one 'anoints' you with its pearly droppings, you have been blessed by God.

Capilla del Cristo (Key No 63)

Over the centuries, tens of thousands of penitents have come to pray for miracles at the Capilla del Cristo (Christ's Chapel), the tiny outdoor sanctuary adjacent to the park. One legend claims that the chapel was built to prevent people from falling over the city wall and into the sea. Another claims that citizens constructed the chapel to commemorate a miracle: As the story goes, a rider participating in a race during the city's San Juan Bautista festivities miraculously survived after his galloping horse carried him down Calle del Cristo, off the top of the wall and into the sea. Some historians claim the rider actually died. Nevertheless, over the years, believers have left hundreds of little silver ornaments representing parts of the body – called *milagros* (miracles) – on the altar before the statues of the saints as tokens of thanks for being cured of some infirmity. You can see the chapel any time, but the iron fence across the front is only open Tuesdays from 10 am to 3:30 pm.

Casa del Libro (Key No 61)

In this same remarkable neighborhood stands the Casa del Libro (House of Books; ☎ 787-723-0354), at 255 Calle del Cristo, yet another of the old city's tiny museums. This restored 18th-century town house contains over 5000 manuscripts and illustrated texts that date back some 2000 years. The collection includes one of the most respected assemblages of *incunabula* (texts produced prior to 1501) in the Americas, including documents signed by Ferdinand and Isabela of Spain. It's open 11 am to 4:30 pm Tuesday to Saturday (except holidays); free entry.

Casa de Ramón Power y Giralt (Key No 69)

The final leg of this walk takes you along Calle Tetuán, a block and a half east to No 155, the Casa de Ramón Power y Giralt. Once the residence of an important political reformer and representative to the Spanish court, this restored 18th-century home is now the headquarters for the Conservation Trust of Puerto Rico (☎ 787-722-5834) and a must-see for historic preservation types. The house contains limited exhibits of Taíno artifacts and a small gift shop, and the staff can be helpful in arranging your visit to some of the Trust's other island properties, including the Hacienda Buena Vista near Ponce (see the South Coast chapter for more on the hacienda). It's open 10 am to 4 pm Tuesday to Saturday; free admission.

From this stop you are just a few blocks up the hill and to the west from your starting point on the Paseo de la Princesa.

PUERTA DE TIERRA

Less than 2 miles in length and only one-quarter of a mile broad, this district occupies the lowland, filling the rest of the area that was colonial San Juan. For centuries, Puerta de Tierra was a slum much like La Perla, although far less picturesque. It was a place where free blacks and biracial people lived, excluded from the protection of the walled city where the Spaniards and *criollos* (islanders of European decent) postured like European gentry and maneuvered for political favor.

Today, the district is a hodgepodge of commonwealth government buildings, Navy and Coast Guard facilities, shipping docks and residences, along with a park, a fort, two major hotels and a dramatic coastline at the east end of the island. Puerta de Tierra takes its name from its position as the 'gateway of land' leading up to the walls of Old San Juan, which was the favored route of land attack by waves of English and Dutch invaders.

El Capitolio

This is the capitol building of the Commonwealth (☎ 787-721-6040 ext 2458), lying between Avenidas Muñoz Rivera and Ponce de León just east of Fuerte San Cristóbal. The building looks a little like the US Capitol – albeit a bit more Romanesque – monumental and out of place crushed between two highways. El Capitolio is what Puerto Rico received from the US government in 1925 instead of actual liberty or equality. The much-revered constitution of the Commonwealth, which moved the island a step closer to its citizens' dreams of freedom from colonialism in 1951, is on display inside the 80-foot rotunda. Regular sessions of the legislature meet inside while rallies in favor of and against statehood occur outside every time the government calls for an islandwide plebiscite on the issue. It's open weekdays by reservation; free entry.

Parques Muñoz Rivera & Sixto Escobar

Spanning half the width of Puerta de Tierra at the east end between the Atlantic and Avenida Ponce de León, this green space dates back over 50 years. It has shade trees, trails, recreation areas for children, and the Peace Pavilion, which sometimes hosts community events. An artisans' fair is held here and at the adjacent Parque Sixto Escobar on most weekends.

Parque Sixto Escobar was the site of the eighth Pan American Games, held in 1979, and is now home to an Olympic track, a historic powder magazine with a small museum and the Balneario Escambrón. The parks are worth a visit if you have kids or are looking for a place to jog. But despite the attractiveness of the setting, the beach continues to be a locus for drug deals and thieves. Police presence has improved here in recent years, but let the traveler beware.

Fuerte San Gerónimo

Completed in 1788, this small fort entered via the walkway (not always open) behind the Caribe Hilton barely had a chance to get up and running as a protector of the east end of Puerta de Tierra when the British ripped through during their 1797 invasion. The Instituto de Cultura controls the property and currently does not open the interior of the fort to visitors, though the exterior walls and ramparts are sometimes accessible. The chief reason to visit the site is to climb to the top of the ramparts, where you can catch a sea breeze and enjoy the vistas of Condado across the inlet.

CONDADO & OCEAN PARK

Wedged between the Atlantic and several inland bodies of water, including Lagunas Condado and Los Corozos east of the island home of colonial San Juan, these neighborhoods have been getting a bad rap from travel writers for the last two decades – more than a little of it well-deserved. But times change, and there are some good reasons for travelers to consider these areas of the city.

Certainly, the tide has turned in Condado (the name derives from the royal title for 'count' in Spain). The region was intentionally developed and promoted as the city's first tourist zone in the 1950s, and lives up to the cliché that it looks like Miami Beach. Over the decades, this strip of international-style high-rise resort hotels, casinos and apartment buildings drew an unsavory crowd of prostitutes, pimps, drug dealers and high rollers. Especially after the catastrophic fire at the Dupont Plaza (now the San Juan Marriott Resort & Casino) in the late 1980s, almost all but package tourists, gamblers and vice addicts stayed away from the Condado area. Condado's appeal was also impacted by the increasing tourist draw of Old San Juan, as the growing cruise ship business and international and local culture vultures alike sung the legitimate praises of the historic heart of the city.

As mainstream tourism declined, the long-standing laissez-faire ambience of Condado attracted both island-born and traveling gays. Reinvestment and restoration has

Top left & right: The tree-dwelling anole, and a *flamboyán* tree in bloom
Middle left: Follow your nose – puffins point the way.
Middle right: Hibiscus blossom
Bottom: The caiman, the alligator's South American cousin

THOMAS R FLETCHER

ROBERT FRIED

DAVE G HOUSER

BOB KRIST

KEVIN R DOWNEY

Ponce's Fiesta Nacional de Bomba y Plena draws performers from all over the island.

Woman preparing *pasteles*, Loíza Aldea

Roadside hot sauce

Masquerader celebrating Carnaval, Ponce

Top left & right: The tree-dwelling anole, and a *flamboyán* tree in bloom
Middle left: Follow your nose – puffins point the way.
Middle right: Hibiscus blossom
Bottom: The caiman, the alligator's South American cousin

MARK BACON

Ponce's Fiesta Nacional de Bomba y Plena draws performers from all over the island.

TONY ARRUZA

Woman preparing *pasteles*, Loíza Aldea

MARK BACON

Roadside hot sauce

MARK BACON

Masquerader celebrating Carnaval, Ponce

Wedding party, Catedral de San Juan

Puerta de San Juan and lone sentry

Bronze sculpture at Plazuela de la Rogativa, Old San Juan

Quiet side street, Old San Juan

Ponce de León's Casa Blanca, Old San Juan

Gran Hotel El Convento, Old San Juan

Sentry tower, El Morro fortress

Wrought iron and pastel, Old San Juan

Isla Verde beach, San Juan

Atlantic coastline from Cementerio de San Juan

followed. As in the renaissance of Miami Beach, what was considered tasteless, imported architecture less than 10 years ago has become kitsch. Older hotels are making way for new seaside time-share condos while the newer hotels and guesthouses hum and the nightlife howls with mixed throngs of gays and straights, islanders and travelers.

East past the Marriott is a mile of broad beach called Ocean Park, a largely residential collection of private homes and posh beach retreats that include a number of charming guesthouses.

SANTURCE

There's no question that Santurce, a thriving business and residential area during the Operation Bootstrap days of the 1950s, is in decline. Businesses are moving to the nearby money pit of shiny, new Hato Rey, while longtime Santurce residents flee to the suburbs south of the city. As discussed above in Dangers & Annoyances, Santurce and some adjacent neighborhoods are currently home to a significant number of impoverished people and street thugs. Increased police presence and a new art museum represent positive changes, however. Furthermore, affordable rents have begun attracting young artists looking for studio space. As in other cities, the arrival of artists often signals that the tide of decay has begun to turn.

Museo de Arte de Puerto Rico

Housed in the former surgery building of the Santurce Municipal Hospital at Parada 22 in Santurce, the new Puerto Rican Museum of Art (☎ 787-722-2525 ext 6097) was still under development at the time this book went to press. When finished, it will be a repository for the significant collections of art owned by the PRTC, the Instituto de Cultura and private collectors. The building is a 1924 structure of reinforced concrete with a neoclassical façade. It houses three floors of gallery space and a 4th floor of offices. The collection traces the island's contributions in the visual arts from Campeche in the 18th century to contemporary masters. Call to find out about the opening date, hours, fees and exhibits.

Museo de Arte Contemporáneo Puertorriqueño

This small museum (☎ 787-268-0049) is housed in the Barat building of Santurce's Colegio Universitario Sagrada Corazón (Sacred Heart University), just off Avenida Ponce de León south of Hato Rey on Calle Rosale. The galleries here offer changing exhibits from the museum's collection and visiting shows of modern island-made prints, posters, paintings and sculpture. It's open 9 am to 5 pm weekdays; free admission.

ISLA VERDE

For travelers who like their hotels built like modern theme parks in the vein of the resorts in Las Vegas, Jamaica and Cancún, Isla Verde is the newest and most fashionable resort area in town. Occupying the strand of beach east of Ocean Park and adjacent to San Juan's LMM airport, Isla Verde is easy to hate for its manufactured ambience and lack of traditional island culture. But many travelers find this Fantasy Island-like snap, crackle and pop to be the perfect antidote to their stressed-out lives at home. Isla Verde is all about escape, not about Puerto Rico. Take it or leave it.

MIRAMAR, HATO REY & RÍO PIEDRAS

Following one of the city's main thoroughfares, Avenida Fernández Juncos (one-way traffic), south from Condado/Ocean Park brings you into the heart of metropolitan San Juan. The first district you pass through is the upscale neighborhood of Miramar, distinguished by the yachts berthed at the *club náutico* near the Laguna del Condado bridge, the Aeropuerto de Isla Grande jutting out into the bay to the west and a mix of fancy homes and condominium towers. Looking a lot like Condado without the casinos, Miramar, by contrast, has few tourists and a significant number of financially secure expatriates, in addition to its population of Puerto Rican urban professionals. Basically, Miramar is the place to live if you work in the commercial heart of San Juan (and earn a princely salary) because you can avoid rush-hour commutes from the suburbs by taking public transportation or even walking to work.

Avenida Ponce de León skirts the southern edge of Santurce and veers south, crossing over the Caño de Martín Peña (Martin Peña Channel) where the Acua Expreso ferry arrives from Old San Juan, and landing you in the 'Miracle Mile' business district of Hato Rey. High-rise office buildings dominate the scene here, displaying the names of both local and offshore banks like Chase Manhattan and Spain's ubiquitous Banco Santander. There are plenty of business restaurants in

the area, a few business-oriented hotels and a plethora of shopping opportunities. But Hato Rey doesn't have much you haven't seen in two dozen other cities, and this district becomes a desolate place after dark.

As you head farther south, the road becomes Avenida Luis Muñoz Rivera and the landscape begins to rise above the marsh and landfill of Hato Rey. Here you enter the academic enclave of Río Piedras. Not only is this the site of the vast UPR campus (see Universities earlier in this chapter), but it is a funky indoor/outdoor discount shopping

CONDADO & OCEAN PARK

zone reminiscent of the markets and bazaars of Asia. One of the major attractions here is walking around the campus and mingling with the students who support the restaurants and bars that fan out along the streets from the intersection of Avenidas Ponce de León and Gandara.

Mercado de Río Piedras

If you like the smell of fish and oranges, the bustle of people and trading jests in Spanish as you bargain for a bunch of bananas, this market is for you. As much a scene as a place to shop, the market continues the colonial tradition of an indoor market that spills into the streets.

Four long blocks of shops and inexpensive restaurants lining Paseo José de Diego facing the market have been closed to auto traffic, turning the whole area into an outdoor mall. Here you can shop or just watch as the local citizens negotiate for everything from *chuletas* (pork chops) to *camisas* (shirts) and cassettes featuring the music of Puerto Rican pop music wonders like Menudo. *Sanjuaneros* know that the market probably has

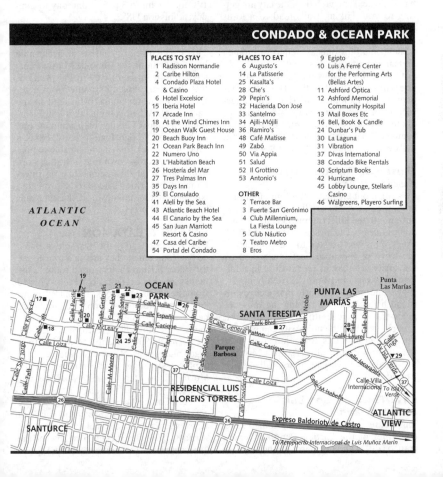

CONDADO & OCEAN PARK

PLACES TO STAY
1 Radisson Normandie
2 Caribe Hilton
4 Condado Plaza Hotel & Casino
6 Hotel Excelsior
15 Iberia Hotel
17 Arcade Inn
18 At the Wind Chimes Inn
19 Ocean Walk Guest House
20 Beach Buoy Inn
21 Ocean Park Beach Inn
22 Numero Uno
23 L'Habitation Beach
26 Hosteria del Mar
27 Tres Palmas Inn
35 Days Inn
39 El Consulado
41 Aleli by the Sea
43 Atlantic Beach Hotel
44 El Canario by the Sea
45 San Juan Marriott Resort & Casino
47 Casa del Caribe
54 Portal del Condado

PLACES TO EAT
6 Augusto's
14 La Patisserie
25 Kasalta's
28 Che's
29 Pepin's
32 Hacienda Don José
33 Santelmo
34 Ajili-Mójili
36 Ramiro's
48 Café Matisse
49 Zabó
50 Via Appia
51 Salud
52 Il Grottino
53 Antonio's

OTHER
2 Terrace Bar
3 Fuerte San Gerónimo
4 Club Millennium, La Fiesta Lounge
5 Club Náutico
7 Teatro Metro
8 Eros
9 Egipto
10 Luis A Ferré Center for the Performing Arts (Bellas Artes)
11 Ashford Óptica
12 Ashford Memorial Community Hospital
13 Mail Boxes Etc
16 Bell, Book & Candle
24 Dunbar's Pub
30 La Laguna
31 Vibration
37 Divas International
38 Condado Bike Rentals
40 Scriptum Books
42 Hurricane
45 Lobby Lounge, Stellaris Casino
46 Walgreens, Playero Surfing

the largest and freshest selection of exotic fruits in the city at the best prices. Shoppers will find the market and stores along Paseo José de Diego open from early morning to late evening, Monday to Saturday.

Jardín Botánico

This 75-acre tract of greenery is the site of the Estación Experimental Agrícola de Puerto Rico (Experimental Agricultural Station of Puerto Rico; ☎ 787-763-4408). The botanical garden is a great place for a picnic if you can't escape to the mountains or the beach when the heat and crowds of the city are getting to you. Hiking trails lead to a lotus lagoon, an orchid garden and a plantation of more than 120 species of palm. The air smells of heliconia blossoms as well as of nutmeg and cinnamon trees.

One of the reasons the garden is so serene is that it's difficult to find. The entrance is nearly hidden on the south side of the intersection of Hwy 1 and Hwy 847, a walk of about a mile from the center of the UPR campus. The garden is open 9 am to 4:30 pm daily except holidays; entry is free.

Museo de Antropología, Historia y Arte

This small but engaging museum of anthropology, history and art lies just inside the entrance to the UPR campus next to the Biblioteca Lazaro. The museum (☎ 787-764-0000 ext 2452) is worth a stop to see examples of the trove of Indian artifacts unearthed by university scholars in recent digs. In addition, this museum features revolving art shows and offers scholarly perspectives on island history. Finally, visiting the museum gives travelers a legitimate reason to be snooping around the university campus and opens opportunities for connecting with the students and faculty. It's open Monday to Saturday with varying hours (call ahead); free admission.

Casa-Finca de Don Luis Muñoz Marín

This house and farm was once home to the godfather of the Partido Popular Democrático (PPD) and the man who shepherded

Puerto Rico into commonwealth status as well as a 20th-century industrialized market economy in the 1950s and '60s. Today it is a museum (☎ 787-755-7979) honoring the memory of this legendary figure, also serving as a venue for concerts and experimental theater. Call for events, and visit if you are interested in learning more about the legend behind Luis Muñoz Marín and his astounding political career. Also take a minute to check out the great vegetation and expansive grounds. Look for the house on the east side of Río Piedras, at Km 1.3 on Hwy 181. It's open 9 am to 3 pm Wednesday to Sunday; admission US$2.

Parque Lineal Martí Coll

This park currently consists of a 1 1/2-mile boardwalk along the Caño de Martín Peña, stretching from Hato Rey to Parque Central. The park takes its name from a respected environmentalist who died in the early 1990s. When completed, it will incorporate a chain of hiking, biking and jogging paths from Old San Juan to Río Piedras, a total of 11 miles. Imagine being able to bike all the way across town free of traffic, stoplights and what now seems like an interminable bus ride! The park's projected completion was unknown at the time this book went to press.

CATAÑO & BAYAMÓN

Few travelers head to the west side of Bahía de San Juan unless they are on a tour to see the Bacardi Rum Factory or en route to the luxury resorts at Dorado Beach. Viewed from the air, the area looks like a foul, pestilent congregation of swamps, military bases, heavy industry and vast housing developments with names like Levittown. The whole area is an unbelievable mutation of historic sugar plantations. Nevertheless, the curious explorer standing on the ramparts of El Morro will inevitably wonder what she may be missing over there across the water.

Sadly, Cataño's peninsular setting and the great vistas it offers of the bay and San Juan across the water do not make it a charming seaside village. If you linger at one of the local *colmados* (convenience stores), pizza shops or outdoor bars while waiting for the ferry back to Old San Juan, you are likely to hear the loafers complaining about the water pollution from the sewage treatment facility at the head of the bay and air pollution from local factories. (Don't even think about going for a swim here, though some citizens do.) You might also hear a few choice expletives in reference to the US Army and Navy presence on the nearby 'military reservation' – a particularly spooky oxymoron imported from the US (like 'industrial park') – which really riles islanders.

But take heart, Cataño has just built a new promenade along the bay and received its first brass-and-fern upscale restaurant. Real estate speculators are eyeing the inexpensive bayside property here, as rumors spread that Cataño may be the site of a monumental statue of Christopher Columbus that will dwarf New York's Statue of Liberty. To get here, consider taking the Acua Expreso ferry from Old San Juan and enjoying a quick harbor tour along the way (see Ferry under Getting Around, later in this chapter, for details).

If you head about a mile north of town to where Hwy 165 meets Hwy 870, you can follow the latter to a secluded picnic site amidst the dramatic setting of Isla de Cabras (see below).

Eventually, explorers will turn their eye inland across the swamp to the saw-toothed hills rising above the more than 150 factories of Bayamón. Since Operation Bootstrap's push to industrialize the island in the 1950s, Bayamón has grown from a country town to a working-class city of nearly a quarter-million people, shopping malls, fast food franchises, used-car lots and video stores. The core of this city retains some of its traditional charm with an exceptional park, and Bayamón is the site of a small historic district and several museums. But the traffic here can be horrendous and the bus service convoluted. When the Tren Urbano system opens in the next few years, commuter trains will whisk you right into the center of Bayamón (see the Train section in the Getting Around chapter for details). Until then, you have to be committed to a serious mission to come here.

Bacardi Rum Factory

Called the 'Cathedral of Rum' because of its six-story pink distillation tower, the Bacardi plant (☎ 787-788-1500) covers 127 acres and stands out like a petroleum refinery across from Old San Juan, near the entrance to the bay. The world's largest and most famous rum-producing family started their business in Cuba more than a century ago, but they began moving their operation to this site in 1936. Today the distiller produces some 100,000 gallons of rum per day and ships 21 million cases per year worldwide.

The Bacardi icon is a bat, and the company serves up complimentary rum drinks under a yellow, bat-shaped tent looking out on the bay. Cynics suggest that you tank up on freebies *before* you tour the company museum and endure the tram-bus tour that guides you around the grounds for a look at the mechanics behind the big business of *ron* (rum). Some romantics claim the tour makes a decent Friday afternoon date, providing you skip the tram and just let the ferry ride, rum and bay views work their magic before heading back to Old San Juan to let the good times roll.

To get to the Bacardi factory, take a *público* (shared taxi; about US$2 per person) from the ferry terminal in Cataño along the waterfront on Calle Palo Seco (Hwy 888). At Km 2.6 north of town, look for the Cathedral of Rum and other Bacardi factory buildings to your left, rising above the landscape. Free tours of the plant leave every 30 minutes on the half hour, 8:30 am to 4:30 pm Monday to Saturday. Note that the plant's bottling line does not operate after 4 pm weekdays and is closed on Saturday.

Isla de Cabras & Fuerte del Cañuelo

Located at the end of Hwy 870 north of the Bacardi plant and the settlement of Palo Seco, Isla de Cabras (Goat Island) is perhaps the greatest seaside refuge in metro San Juan for travelers craving privacy and nature. There isn't much here except some shade trees, park benches, rocky seashore and waves. You can fish, but the offshore currents are too dangerous for swimming.

The ruins at the north end of the island mark a late-19th-century leper colony.

On the island's south end stand the remains of Fuerte del Cañuelo (Cañuelo Fort). The fort – which is nothing but ruins today – dates from 1610 and once shared the responsibility of protecting Bahía de San Juan with El Morro, which is across the channel marking the entrance to the bay. There's a US$2 entrance fee.

Luis A Ferré Parque de Ciencias

This 42-acre science park (☎ 787-740-6868) is located in Bayamón on Hwy 167 south of the exit from the Hwy 22 toll road. While this is not Bush Gardens, Lion Country or the London Museum of Science, it is a decent theme park, especially if you are traveling with children. There is an artificial lake with boat rentals for pure recreation, but the focal point of the park is education, featuring pavilions that include a new planetarium, electrical energy museum, physics museum, rocket plaza, aerospace museum, transportation museum and zoo. At US$5/3/2 for adults/children/seniors, this place is a value. It's open 9 am to 4 pm Wednesday to Friday, 10 am to 6 pm weekends and holidays.

Parque Central

In the old tradition of urban oases like New York's Central Park, this pristine park stands across from the new city hall (the industrial-looking bridge-like structure spanning Hwy 2) in the center of Bayamón. It is remarkable for its landscaping and the preserved country house located on the grounds. The train running around the park's perimeter is one of the last vestiges of the days when sugarcane railways laced the northern lowlands of the island.

Museo de Oller

Located in the former city hall on the plaza of Bayamón's historic district, this museum of art and history pays tribute to native son Francisco Oller (1833-1917), considered the first Latin American impressionist. Most of Oller's great works are displayed elsewhere, but the restored neoclassical museum building is worth a peek if you are in the area. The

collection includes some Oller portraits, Taíno artifacts and sculptures by Tomas Batista, another local artist. It's open 9 am to 4 pm Tuesday to Saturday; free admission.

Caparra

This is the site of Juan Ponce de León's first settlement on the island, established in 1508. The site was rediscovered in 1936, and only the foundations of a few buildings remain. There is a small museum (☎ 787-781-4795) featuring Taíno artifacts that is open irregularly. Located at Km 6.6 on a highly commercial section of Hwy 2 east of Bayamón in Guaynabo, the site is only worth a visit to ponder why the great conquistador ever imagined this spot on the fringe of a mammoth swamp could possibly be suitable as a location for a colony. On the other hand, this is the same guy who got himself killed in search of the fabled Fountain of Youth. Generally it's open Tuesday to Saturday with varying hours (call ahead); free admission.

BEACHES

For many travelers, San Juan is a beach. The truth is that the best Puerto Rican beaches are out on the island, and the people watching here is not anywhere near as spectacular as it is at some other seaside cities like Rio de Janeiro or Miami Beach.

By far the broadest beaches and best swimming are found at the east end of the city, in front of the beach houses at Ocean Park or farther east in Isla Verde. If you are not staying out this way, you can take a bus that runs the whole route from Old San Juan to Isla Verde (see the Getting Around section later in this chapter for details).

As mentioned earlier in the chapter, Balneario Escambrón and its associated Parque Sixto Escobar, which may seem attractive to travelers as the beach nearest Old San Juan (on Avenida Muñoz Rivera in Puerta de Tierra), has long been a favorite place for drug deals and a magnet for loafers and other bad actors. Better avoid this place. If you want a beach nearby, you can also head across the bridge over the inlet to the small Balneario Condado, a public beach in calm waters on the shore of the inlet (great for kids, but packed with local teens on weekends), or walk a little farther east to the beach in front of the hotels in Condado.

The Condado beach is steep and badly eroded in a number of places, especially at the west end; even walking here can be uncomfortable. The broader strand in front of the Atlantic Beach Hotel is popular with gays.

Rounding a point of coral at the east end of the Condado beach, you'll see the Ocean Park beach sprawling in front of you – flat, broad, sugary and uncrowded. There are a number of low-key beach concessions here. Many of the city's leisure class come here to walk, jog, swim, play paddle ball or read the morning paper.

In Old San Juan, some solitary folk follow the walkway that branches north from where Paseo de la Princesa turns east into the city through the Puerta de San Juan. This walk leads along the base of the wall and ramparts of El Morro. At low tide there are a couple of tiny beaches that appear between the rocks, and you may see people fishing, sunbathing or having a picnic on the boulders. Not a bad way to beat the heat! Note that city law prohibits swimming here as well as climbing on the rocks, and for good reason: No matter how clear and tranquil the water looks, you may be risking your health in the pollution that drains from the bay. You could also be risking your life in the substantial currents that course just offshore.

ACTIVITIES
Diving & Snorkeling
While Puerto Rico is well known for its first-class diving, San Juan is not really the best place for it because of easterly and northeasterly winds that often churn up the water. When conditions are right, you can go off the beach at Condado. This is an easy dive that takes you through a pass between the inner and outer reefs into coral caverns, overhangs, grottoes and tunnels to see the usual angel fish, jacks, blue wrasse and sergeant majors, as well as crabs and octopuses. The problem with this site is that there is only one way in and out and visibility is rarely better that 15 feet. Get a guide.

Caribe Aquatic Adventures (☎ 787-724-1882, 281-8858) keeps changing its base around the city, but you can always reach them by phone (though their phone number seems to change regularly, too). In spite of their wanderlust, the operators here are reliable and have 20 years of experience with this environment. One-tank dives cost US$45, US$85 for two.

Snorkelers and divers in need of gear should check out Mundo Submarino (☎ 787-791-5764) at the Laguna Gardens Shopping Center in Isla Verde.

Surfing
You will find the best waves and biggest *surferos* scene going east from Isla Verde, when the morning and evening breezes glass off a 4-foot swell. Popular breaks include Pine Grove, Los Aviónes and La Concha (in Bosque Estatal de Piñones) along Hwy 187.

To rent gear or for information on surfing in the San Juan area, check out Playero Surfing (☎ 787-722-4384), next to Walgreens drugstore at 64 Avenida Condado; they've also got a great website at www.playero.com.

Windsurfing
With winds from the north and east to keep you from being blown too far offshore, the beaches of San Juan are a great venue for windsurfing. The best area is off the beaches of Isla Verde, where there are fewer reefs to trip you up. Many of the beach concessions and resort hotels rent boards for around US$20 per hour, with better rates for longer periods.

Caribe Aquatic Adventures (see Diving & Snorkeling above) gets high marks for rental and instruction on Laguna del Condado, an ideal place for beginners and those who favor placid waters.

Sailing
While visitors will see a lot of sail and powerboats moored at the club náutico and San Juan Bay Marina in Miramar, Fajardo and the Spanish Virgin Islands are really the yachting and charter boat centers of the island. Any number of the charter boat operators out of those areas will be happy to

arrange to transport you from San Juan to Fajardo for a day of sailing, swimming, snorkeling and picnicking for about US$55 (see Fajardo in the East Coast chapter for details).

To rent a small sail or powerboat, contact the Caribbean School of Aquatics (☎ 787-728-6606), 1 Calle Taft, suite 10F, Condado.

For a cruise around Bahía de San Juan, call Anticipation Harbor Cruises (☎ 787-725-3500) at the San Juan Bay Marina. Their evening party cruise with free munchies, open wine and soda bar, live music and dancing is a good value at US$30/20 for adults/children.

Fishing

With the good game fishing offshore for marlin, tuna and dorado – and inshore for tarpon – charter boats leave from the San Juan Bay Marina and club náutico. Half-day trips for a party of up to six people run about US$400 before you tip the captain; double the figure for a full day. You can book through the recreation desks at the hotels. If you want one of the most experienced charter captains in the Caribbean, call Captain Mike Benitez (☎ 787-723-2292), who has carried the likes of former US president Jimmy Carter.

Yet another Mike runs Captain Mike's Sport Fishing Center (☎ 787-721-7335), which also has a reputation for bringing home the trophies. For deep-sea fishing aboard a 20-passenger vessel, call Makaira Hunter (☎ 787-397-7028).

Operated out of Miramar's club náutico in late August/early September, the International Billfishing Tournament (☎ 787-722-0177) is a world-class event in pursuit of the blue marlin. Gone are the days when the boat boys dragged in the carcasses of these 900lb monsters. One angler recently died when he was caught in a line and pulled overboard by a fish. This is a tag-and-release event drawing some very fancy boats and top-notch anglers. And guess who likes to get down and fiesta when ashore?

Golf

You won't find a golf course in town, but world-class challenges lie within 30 to 45 minutes' drive east or west of San Juan. If your hotel has an activities or recreation desk, they can make all the arrangements. For details on courses islandwide, see Golf under Activities in the Facts for the Visitor chapter.

Tennis

With court fees usually running over US$20 an hour and courts booking fast at prime time (early mornings and evenings), you have to really love this game to play in San Juan. Following is a list of the most popular hotel or club courts in the city where reservations are needed:

Carib-Inn Tennis Club & Resort (8 courts)
   ☎ 787-791-3535
Caribe Hilton (6 courts)
   ☎ 787-721-0303
Condado Plaza Hotel & Casino (2 courts)
   ☎ 787-721-1000
Condado Trio (2 courts)
   ☎ 787-721-6990
El San Juan Hotel & Casino (2 courts)
   ☎ 787-791-1000
Isla Verde Tennis Club (4 courts)
   ☎ 787-727-6490

If court fees at the hotels seem too pricey, head for the 16 lighted courts at San Juan's Parque Central (☎ 787-722-1646), on Calle Cerra. Otherwise, you might find a game at the private courts on the UPR campus in Río Piedras.

One of the best-kept secrets in Old San Juan is the pair of tennis courts on NPS land next to the Casa Rosa (along the city's western wall near El Morro). These courts are open to the public at no cost and are rarely used except on Saturday mornings. Real tennis lovers should consider staying at the Carib-Inn Tennis Club & Resort; see Isla Verde under Places to Stay, later in this chapter.

Bicycling

An avid group of mountain bikers meets almost every evening for workouts on hilly fields around El Morro. They are friendly, bilingual and mostly males who will welcome you to their evening workout if you rent from the old city's little rental shop Wheels for Fun, working out of an apartment building on Calle O'Donnell across from the Plaza Colón (look for the yellow canvas banner in English above the door).

A more complete place to rent bikes is Condado Bike Rentals (☎ 787-722-6288), 1106 Avenida Ashford. New trail bikes go for US$20 a day, US$50 for three days. The shop has trail maps for Condado/Old San Juan and sponsors mountain-biking tours.

You can also inquire about service and rentals from the Bike Stop (☎ 787-782-2282), 262 Avenida JT Piñero in Río Piedras.

See the section on Parque Lineal Martí Coll (under Miramar, Hato Rey & Río Piedras, earlier in this chapter) for details on a projected network of biking paths linking Old San Juan to Río Piedras.

Kayaking

Gary Horn (☎ 787-725-5169) runs his kayaking operation out of a van at La Puntilla in Old San Juan. With Gary as your leader you can get a good workout and some thrills as you circle the island that is home to Old San Juan and Puerta de Tierra. The two-hour trip costs about US$50.

LANGUAGE COURSES

UPR's Multilingual Institute (☎ 787-763-4122) offers a number of conversational Spanish courses on the university's main campus at Río Piedras. Most courses cost under US$200. Call, or see Language Courses under Activities in the Facts for the Visitor chapter for details.

ORGANIZED TOURS

María Alexandra Pla's Colonial Adventures (☎ 787-729-0114) offers a number of themed walking tours of Old San Juan with bilingual guides. Offerings include historic, antique/ art, shopping and mystery walks. Tours cost US$16 to US$22.

See Organized Tours in the Getting Around chapter for a complete review of area and islandwide tour operators.

SPECIAL EVENTS

Unless otherwise noted, information on the following events can be obtained by contacting the Puerto Rico Tourism Company at ☎ 800-223-6530 or 787-721-2400.

Noches de Galerías

Held on the first Tuesday of the month, February to May and September to December, Gallery Nights are sponsored by the PRTC. Fifteen galleries in the vicinity of Calle del Cristo in Old San Juan open from 6 to 9 pm; many serve refreshments and use the event to launch new shows. Sanjuaneros and travelers show up in a festive mood to bear witness, graze, drink, shop and talk about intimate imagery on the painted canvas, in the stars and elsewhere. Great for a date.

Festival La Casita

Starting at 6 pm on Saturdays and 4 pm on Sundays year-round, La Casita on Paseo de la Princesa forms the backdrop for free performances of traditional music and dance, craft exhibitions, puppet theater and sunset trio concerts. This laid-back scene provides some distraction from the substantial lure of the bars and restaurants in the old city.

Festival San Sebastián

As if this famous party street in Old San Juan really needs a reason for a fiesta! For a full week in mid-January, the street hums with semi-religious processions, music, crafts, food stalls and larger-than-ever crowds.

Festival Casals

Held during most of June, this festival is the real thing, not just another jug band fest. Renowned soloists and orchestras come here from all over the world to join the Puerto Rican Symphony Orchestra in giving night after night of virtuoso concerts, primarily at the Luis A Ferré Center for the Performing Arts. Tickets run from US$20 to US$40, but there are deep discounts for students, children and seniors.

Fiesta de San Juan Bautista

Yep, this is the celebration of the patron saint of San Juan and a summer solstice party, Latin style. Staged during the week preceding June 21, the heart of the action – including religious processions, wandering minstrels, fireworks, food stalls, drunken sailors and beauty queens (straight and otherwise) – is in Old San Juan, but the rest of the city gets into the act as well. Even some of the towns out on the island join in on the celebrating. Who's working?

Fiesta de los Artes Interamericanos

Held in late September, the Inter-American Festival of the Arts is hosted by the Ferré center and features several weeks of ballet, modern dance and musical theater as well as performances of classical, modern and folk music. Quality performances for passionate audiences. For information and tickets, call ☎ 787-725-7334.

Fiesta de Película – San Juan

Held in October, the relatively new San Juan Cinema Fest has been attracting more and more entries and attention in recent years with new films and filmmakers showing up from all over the Americas. You probably won't see Bob Redford here, but that's showbiz. Always exciting new work.

Fiesta Artisanos de Bacardi

The Bacardi Artisans' Fair, held on the first two Sundays of December, has the feel of a big county fair back in the US (complete with carny rides); it also brings together the largest collection of artisans on the island. As many as 125 crafters show up here to compete, display and sell their wares. This is a good place to see an array of folk art, including santos, and shop for bargains. The *plena* singers add a touch of tradition to the whole affair. Call ☎ 787-788-1500 ext 5240 for details.

PLACES TO STAY

The rates for places to stay in San Juan vary significantly (sometimes more than 30%) from season to season *and* from day to day as hotels adjust their rates according to the perceived demand. In general, rates are highest from December 15 to June 1. Rates are lowest from September 1 to December 14. Since these prices change so frequently, most rates listed below suggest a range for each property.

Revelers at the capital's Fiesta de
San Juan Bautista

Travelers planning on staying in San Juan for a week or longer and seeking a good value in accommodations should consider the guesthouse options in Old San Juan, some of which offer weekly rates only. Unless otherwise noted, all other rates listed in this section are per night.

Hotels have been grouped within their price categories in the order of the author's preference and recommendation.

OLD SAN JUAN & PUERTA DE TIERRA
Guesthouses

La Caleta (☎ *787-725-5347, 11 Caleta Las Monjas*) has one of the best locations in Old San Juan. Situated on a quiet street, this three-story apartment building has balconies that catch the trade winds and overlook La Fortaleza and the Plazuela de la Rogativa at the entrance to Bahía de San Juan. Michael Giessler has 17 apartments here and rents at least four to travelers staying for the week or longer. There is a small laundry on the 1st floor. A studio apartment at La Caleta usually rents for US$280 a week, but prices are negotiable. Michael also manages several other apartments around town (see Rental Agents, below).

La Galería (☎ *787-722-1808, 204-206 Calle Norzagaray*) is a series of connecting town houses overlooking the ocean from a perch near the city's northern wall. Jan

D'Sopo and her husband, Manuco Gandía, have decorated this 18th-century compound with a vast collection of their own art, and loyal guests keep returning to immerse themselves in Jan's whimsy and to buy her art. Most of the 24 rooms have air con and private bath. A light breakfast is included in the tariff, which ranges from US$95 to US$225 per night (the latter will get you a ocean-view suite). Jan also keeps a few rare parking spaces for guests.

Fortaleza Guest House (☎ 787-721-7112, *361 Calle Fortaleza*) has the cheapest rooms in the old city, with weekly rates starting at US$60. Isabela Rivera has two rooms with a shared bath. No air con; double or single beds are available. Be prepared to speak Spanish here.

Another place offering basic accommodations is the *Guest House Old San Juan* (☎ 787-722-5436, *205 Calle Tanca*). Enrique Castro has 29 simple rooms, some with balconies. All units share baths with four or five other rooms. You can get a room with a fan for US$20 per night; air-conditioned rooms cost US$30.

Hotels
Budget *Hotel Plaza de Armas* (☎ 787-722-2751, *202 Calle San José*) is the totally renovated reincarnation of the old Hotel Central. Now all of the rooms have air con, private bath, fresh paint, cable TV and new furniture. This centrally located hotel is probably the best value for the short-term visitor to the old city, with rooms ranging between US$75 and US$85 per night. Ask for a balcony room overlooking the Plaza de Armas if you want to bag the air con and catch the trade winds.

Top End *Gran Hotel El Convento* (☎ 787-723-9020, *100 Calle del Cristo*) is a newly restored 17th-century Carmelite convent with about 60 rooms. It stands opposite the city's cathedral in the fashionable west end of town, at the heart of the restaurant, bar and shopping scene. While far from cheap at US$195 to US$380, this is the place to stay if money is no object and you enjoy being surrounded by the old city. The hotel features a pool hidden atop the cloistered walls, a rooftop sundeck and several popular restaurants.

The other new attraction in the old city is the *Wyndham Old San Juan Hotel & Casino* (☎ 787-721-5100, *101 Calle La Marina*), facing the cruise ship docks. This nine-story, convention-style hotel offers 240 rooms with all the amenities for the luxury-minded, including a rooftop pool and a major casino. Rates range from US$150 to US$350.

The *Caribe Hilton* (☎ 787-721-0303; *see the Condado & Ocean Park map*), on Calle Rosales off Avenida Muñoz Rivera in Puerta de Tierra, is a better bet if you want luxury near Old San Juan as well as access to a beach and tennis courts. With 672 rooms and nine restaurants, this place is really an all-inclusive resort. Rooms cost between US$215 and US$500. The Caribe Hilton was under renovation at the time this book went to press, with a scheduled reopening date of December 1999.

Next door, more affordable (about US$200 per night) and smaller with 189 units, the *Radisson Normandie* (☎ 787-729-2929; *see the Condado & Ocean Park map*) is an art deco masterpiece. It echoes with the ghosts of the jet set who used to scandalize the island 50 years ago by cavorting nude in the pool. For a large hotel, this place has soul. Like the Caribe Hilton above, this hotel was under renovation when this book went to press, with plans to reopen in December 1999.

Rental Agents
Michael Giessler, proprietor of La Caleta in Old San Juan (see Guesthouses), manages several other apartments around town available for long-term rental. Accommodations range from basic studios with fans to upscale, restored town houses with air con. Rates range between US$280 and US$1400 per week depending on size, length of stay and season. Call Michael at ☎ 787-725-5347 for information.

CONDADO & OCEAN PARK
Guesthouses
The Condado district is home to several inexpensive but attractive lodging options.

Check out the *Arcade Inn* (☎ 787-728-7524, 8 Calle Taft), just off the beach. This place is a value at US$60 and is attended carefully by owner Aurelio Cinque; a good choice for families.

On the same street but farther from the beach is *At the Wind Chimes Inn* (☎ 800-946-3244, 1750 Calle McLeary). Occupying a restored Spanish villa, this place has 12 units and a very homey feel. Rooms cost between US$65 and US$95.

If you want to be right on the beach, try *Alelí by the Sea* (☎ 787-725-7313, 1125 Calle Sea View). In the heart of Condado, this inn has nine units with air con and private bath as well as shared living room, kitchen and seaside sundeck. Room prices range from US$55 to US$90.

A true B&B-style inn slightly more than a block off Condado beach, *Casa del Caribe* (☎ 787-722-7139, 57 Calle Caribe) has a lot to offer with original art, air con, cable TV, phone and breakfast for US$65 to US$85.

You can stay in a former consular mansion for US$75 if you choose *El Consulado* (☎ 787-289-9191, 1110 Avenida Ashford), right on Condado's main drag. There are 29 units with air con, cable TV and phone.

Just east of Condado beach in Ocean Park, *Numero Uno* (☎ 787-726-5010, 1 Sta Ana) used to be the best-kept secret on the island until a gaggle of travel writers spilled the beans in the last couple of years. Now the rates have gone up about 30%. Nevertheless, there is a lot of charm as well as a small pool in this distinctive whitewashed beach house surrounded by coconut palms. All rooms have private bath and air con. The popular on-site restaurant is an additional bonus. Rates are US$95 to US$165.

The rates are comparable at the slightly larger (17 units) *Hostería del Mar* (☎ 787-727-3302, 1 Calle Tapia), just up the beach. There is no pool here, but there's a great vegetarian restaurant in an enclosed gazebo overlooking the beach. All rooms have air con, cable TV and private bath. Of course, the cheapest rooms look out on the trash barrels, not the beach. Rates are US$88 to US$175.

Ocean Park Beach Inn (☎ 787-728-7418, 3 Calle Elena) is another option just one

house back from the beach. Catering to gay men and women, the inn features 10 rooms with private entrances and baths and ocean/garden views. Rooms cost US$80 to US$110.

A second venue popular with gay couples is next door on the beach. *L'Habitation Beach* (☎ 787-727-2499, 1957 Calle Italia) has similar rates and a restaurant-bar on the premises.

The *Ocean Walk Guest House* (☎ 787-728-0855, 1 Calle Atlantic) is another attractive place with a mixed clientele of gay and straight couples. This place has a pool and friendly beach bar-restaurant open to the public. Rates are definitely a value with an oceanfront double costing around US$100 in high season; in the off season some rooms cost as little as US$40.

If you want to be near the beach at Ocean Park and still keep your spending in check, consider the *Beach Buoy Inn* (☎ 800-221-8119, 1853 Calle McLeary). On the main drag a couple of blocks off the beach, this place offers amenities like cable TV and fridge as well as continental breakfast; the inn is also close to the area's bars and restaurants. Rooms cost US$60 to US$70.

Tres Palmas Inn (☎ 787-727-4617, 2212 Park Blvd) lies at the far east end of the Ocean Park beach in the Sta Teresita neighborhood. There is a new pool and an oceanfront sundeck with Jacuzzi. All rooms have been recently redecorated and have bath, air con and TV. At US$60 to US$140, this place is a bargain if you have a car to get you to restaurants and shopping.

Hotels

Budget *El Canario by the Sea* (☎ 787-722-8640, 4 Avenida Condado) has been the best-known player in budget accommodation in San Juan for decades. There are actually three different Canario inns around Condado – agents here at the 'By the Sea' can assist you in reserving at any one of the properties. Each of the small hotels has 25 to 40 units with air con, cable TV, phone and continental breakfast. You get a quiet, clean, well-lighted place for US$88 and up.

A gay-friendly option in the budget niche is the nice *Iberia Hotel* (☎ 787-723-0200,

1464 Avenida Wilson) in Condado. This is a Spanish-looking small hotel with 30 units in an exclusive residential neighborhood of Condado. You get all the amenities plus a terrace, solarium and restaurant for US$88 to US$99. This place offers a lot of style and attention to detail for the price.

Mid-Range The *Atlantic Beach Hotel* (☎ *787-721-6900, 1 Calle Vendig)* has been the soul of San Juan's gay community for decades. This place is truly a winner for the gay traveler: It has an attentive, knowledgeable and funny staff and 37 well-equipped rooms right on the broadest part of Condado beach. The hotel also has a rooftop deck and Jacuzzi. Too bad there aren't any balconies to catch the breeze. Room prices range between US$110 and US$135. The Atlantic Beach is also home to an on-site restaurant and a popular terrace bar (see Gay & Lesbian Venues under Entertainment, later in this chapter).

Set back from the beach is the *Portal del Condado* (☎ *787-721-9010, 10133 Avenida Condado)*. With 48 rooms that include all of the usual amenities, this international-style monolith is a reasonable backup if everything closer to the beach is full. The rates seem a little steep, however, at US$95 to US$115.

For a similar kind of experience with a better location overlooking Laguna del Condado, go for the *Days Inn* (☎ *800-858-7407, 6 Calle Clemenceau)*, where rooms cost between US$79 and US$149.

Top End The *Condado Plaza Hotel & Casino* (☎ *800-624-0420, 999 Avenida Ashford)* steals the show here in Condado. This place has it all: With a fitness center, spa, pool, bi-level suites, seven restaurants, live entertainment and great salsa all occupying two separate buildings connected by a skyway over Avenida Ashford, the Condado Plaza is not quite an adult Disney World, but close in size (566 units) and attention to detail. The hotel even has its own private beach facing Fuerte San Gerónimo across the inlet. Rooms here go for US$285 to US$1500.

The *San Juan Marriott Resort & Casino* (☎ *787-722-7000, 1309 Avenida Ashford)* rose from the ashes of the burned-out Dupont Plaza in 1995. As slick as it is with its beachfront property, two pools and 525 units, this place has not yet found its personality. Catering to all kinds of conventions and package tours keeps the house full, but many travelers think the rack rate of US$285 to US$405 is a lot to pay unless you want the absolute reliability that comes with staying in this respected chain.

Rental Agents
Esther Laugier (☎ *787-723-2941)*, 4B Ritz Condado at the corner of Calle Joffre, has several modern apartments with air conditioning and balconies overlooking the Laguna del Condado for US$1000 to US$2000 a month depending on the season.

Seabreeze Apartment Rentals (☎ *787-723-1888)* is a gay-friendly operation managing apartments all over Condado. Rentals start at around US$900 per month.

ISLA VERDE
Guesthouses
Casa de Playa (☎ *800-916-2272, 86 Avenida Isla Verde)* is a former private beach villa set amid an explosion of palms. There are now 20 units here with air con and all the rest. The beach bar and Freddo's restaurant here have a loyal following. Rooms go for between US$80 and US$160.

Several budget properties in the Villamar section of Isla Verde lie just to the south of the Expreso Baldorioty de Castro. If you don't mind the noise and smell of traffic or taking the pedestrian bridge over the expressway to get to the beach and restaurants, you might consider *Casa Mathiessen* (☎ *787-728-5749, 14 Calle Uno)*. There is a small pool and rooms come with the works – including kitchenettes – for between US$42 and US$74. This is truly one of the most attractive inns on the island for frugal travelers.

The *Green Island Inn* (☎ *787-728-5749, 36 Calle Uno)* is just up the street and has equivalent rates and lots of repeat guests. This place is within a mile of the airport and a great place to stay for little money if you are arriving on the red-eye or jetting off on the early bird.

Hotels

Budget Amid the schlock highway art, fast-food joints, car-rental agencies and condo towers of Isla Verde, *La Playa Hotel* (☎ 787-791-1115, 6 Calle Amapola) is an oasis on the beach. For US$90 to US$105 you get a room with all the comforts in a beachfront property. There is also a popular, moderately priced restaurant-bar on the premises.

Just off the beach, the *Borinquen Royal* (☎ 787-728-8400, 58 Avenida Isla Verde) is a great value at US$70. The structure is totally 1960s motor lodge and so are the rooms, but all have air con, bath and cable TV at about a third of the price of most of the places up and down the avenue.

Mid-Range For a dramatic location, the *Empress Oceanfront* (☎ 800-678-0757, 2 Calle Amapola) can't be beat. It commands a small peninsula at the water's edge of Calle Amapola. The pool and restaurant are part of a deck that stands on pilings over the ocean. Rooms here cost US$148 to US$168.

Carib-Inn Tennis Club & Resort (☎ 800-548-8217) is a block off the beach on Avenida Gobernadores. At US$110 to US$140 per night, this 255-unit hotel is one of the best values for tennis players on the island. There are eight courts with professional instructors and the pool is even shaped like a racket. Kids are welcome. There is a gym, sauna and steam room on-site.

Voted 'number one best value lodging' in the US, the *Hampton Inn* (☎ 800-426-7866, 6530 Avenida Isla Verde) chain opened its doors across the street from the chic El San Juan and the Ritz Carlton (see below) in 1997. You get all the amenities of the pricey hotels including continental breakfast, pool and fitness center for half the price: US$139.

Top End The *El San Juan Hotel & Casino* (☎ 800-468-2818, 6063 Avenida Isla Verde) has set the standard of elegance for island lodging during four decades. Now, with yet another major refit, the El San Juan is more glamorous than ever. Check out the jungle-garden setting surrounding the two pools, where the water flows like a river. The hotel's advertising claims nightlife here is reminis-

cent of 1950s Havana, and this is no lie. Bring your tux and platinum card: Rooms range from US$250 to US$2500.

The *San Juan Grand Beach Resort & Casino* (☎ 800-443-2009, 187 Avenida Isla Verde) is the reincarnation of the former Sands on the beach but also faces the heart of Isla Verde's commercial development. The big draw here is the mammoth beachfront casino overlooking the tropical gardens, pool and the Atlantic. With five on-site restaurants and the popular Martini's Cabaret (see Entertainment, later), this place is a state-of-the-art adult playground. Rates range between US$325 and US$475.

Built in 1997 with the aim of eclipsing both the San Juan Grand and the El San Juan, the *Ritz Carlton Hotel & Casino* (☎ 800-241-3333, 6961 Hwy 187) is a monster hotel (419 units) imitating European styling inside and out, with a casino that does its best to look like its Monte Carlo counterparts. Because the management keeps nonguests out of the hotel's restaurants, Puerto Ricans look down their noses at the Ritz. This is a great place to hide if you're a famous film star, oil sultan or politician. Rooms here cost US$250 to US$2000.

Rental Agents

Isla Verde is home to a number of luxury condo high-rises, villas and apartments that the owners rent out when not in use. This is especially true in the off season (May to mid-December). Many of the properties in Isla Verde are in prime resort areas and along the beach. See Rental Accommodations in the Facts for the Visitor chapter for a list of realty agents here.

MIRAMAR & RÍO PIEDRAS

While these areas have none of the seaside attractions of Old San Juan, Condado/Ocean Park or Isla Verde, the commercial heart of the city does offer a number of accommodations options.

Hotels

The *Hotel del Centro* (☎ 787-751-1335) is convenient to the UPR campus and offers 29 modern rooms at the Cardiovascular

Center (4th floor) in Río Piedras. Nightly rates at this hotel start at US$90.

In Miramar, the *Olimpo Court Hotel* (☎ 787-724-0600, 603 Avenida Miramar) offers rooms and apartments with kitchenettes in an attractive modern building with a rooftop sun deck for US$58 to US$75. The famous restaurant Chayote is on the premises (see Places to Eat, later in this chapter).

The *Hotel Excelsior* (☎ 787-721-7400, 801 Avenida Ponce de León; see the Condado & Ocean Park map) in Miramar features the respected on-site restaurant Augusto's (see Places to Eat, later in this chapter). Amenities include pool, voice mail, data ports, fitness center and Nintendo for the stressed-out business traveler. Rooms range from US$134 to US$175.

Rental Agents
Academics visiting the UPR campus in Río Piedras might want to check out the *Glorimar Apartments* (☎ 787-759-7304, 724-7440, 111 Avenida Universidad), a gay-friendly guesthouse renting studios and one-bedroom apartments near the university, usually on a three-month contract. These are basic but a good value at US$235 to US$325 per month.

PLACES TO EAT
As with restaurants in many cities, some of the high-end and more popular restaurants in San Juan have a tradition of closing on either Sunday or Monday. While this tradition is far from universal, travelers may want to call ahead on these nights before venturing out to find a tempting spot closed.

Old San Juan
Amanda's (☎ 787-722-0187, 424 Calle Norzagaray) has the best vista of any restaurant in the old city. Situated close to Fuerte San Cristóbal, this is the place to relax at a café table or take a porch seat, stare out over the Atlantic from the top of the city walls and feel the trade winds in your face. The fare is largely Mexican; gazpacho will run you US$3.50, a quesadilla US$4.50.

Los Amigos, on Calle San Jose just south of Plaza de Armas (next to Cronopios book-

store), is an old-style island cafeteria where sanjuaneros congregate for 35¢ coffee, US$1 beers, US$2 *cubano* sandwiches (chicken and cheese) and good humor. This is absolutely the best place for a frugal bite that has roots in an island tradition, not a fast-food franchise. Los Amigos is primarily a breakfast and lunch spot; it is open until 5 pm daily.

In the same vein, *Cafeteria Mallorca* (☎ 787-724-4607, 300 Calle San Francisco) is one of the city's institutions, with a soda fountain and bakery. Known for its authentic criollo cooking, Mallorca serves up chicken with rice and beans for US$6.

Half a block west on Calle San Francisco at No 259, *La Bombonera* (☎ 787-722-0658) has been a competing establishment for nearly a century. Sanjuaneros claim the baked goods here cannot be matched, and they relish the endless free refills of café con leche. This is just about the only place in Old San Juan that sells the traditional island bread called *pan criollo*, which is a bit like a fat French baguette.

Meal service here is another matter: After three separate encounters here with inattentive, impertinent waiters, we walked.

Cafe Zaguán (☎ 787-724-3359, 359 Calle Tetuán) is the chic newcomer to Old San Juan's café scene. Open until midnight Tuesday to Saturday, Zaguán specializes in soups and sandwich wraps with spinach, flour, tomato and garlic tortillas for under US$5. Try owners Diana and Billy Karmazyn's ceviche for the same price. The café tables, set among the trees in the little plaza just outside Teatro Tapia overlooking the cruise ship docks, make a great place for people watching.

Another restaurant taking advantage of a recently passed law permitting tables in the street is *Ambrosia* (☎ 787-722-5206, 250 Calle Cristo). With one of the best locations in the old town, at the foot of chic Calle del Cristo near the Capilla de Cristo, this Italian-style bistro offers up meals like fettuccine Alfredo for US$9. Look for the parasols decked out with twinkling lights.

Among the restaurant-bars at the crest of the hill on Calle San Sebastián, *El Patio de Sam* (☎ 787-723-1149) stands out at No 102 for the gauzy light of its hidden interior patio, as well as for its exceptional collection of cocina criolla specialties. *Conejo estofada* (rabbit stew) will run you US$18, or you can eat off the tapas menu for under US$7. The desserts here may be the most interesting in town: catch the tembleque (a pudding-like favorite of coconut milk and cinnamon) for US$3.75.

If you want to go vegetarian, visit *Gopal* (☎ 787-724-0229, 201 Calle Tetuán), conveniently located next to the Thomas Cook Foreign Exchange. A local Hare Krishna family run this pure veggie restaurant. Check out the vegetarian lasagna (US$6) and ask about yoga sessions and gatherings of the Krishna community.

Devotees of Asian cuisine swear by the sushi at *Yukiyu* (☎ 787-721-0653, 311 Calle Recinto Sur), on 'restaurant row' near the cruise ship docks on Calle Recinto Sur, but the new *Viet Nam Palace* (☎ 787-723-7539) a few doors down at No 332 has much cheaper entrées. You can get a bowl of *bun xao cari* (angel-hair pasta with spicy shrimp) for US$9.

In a cobblestone alley not far away, look for *World of Wings* (☎ 787-725-5521, 312 Callejón Capilla). Try the *alitas volcanicas* (volcano wings) for US$6.25.

Those looking for a fancier feast might try *La Mallorquina* (☎ 787-722-3261, 207 Calle San Justo). Over 150 years old, this restaurant serves pricey cocina criolla with entrées starting at US$15.

The trendy *Gallery Café (305 Calle Fortaleza)* has become one of the more popular dinner-date venues for sanjuaneros with a few bucks to spend. This California-style bistro is also a popular live-music venue; see Entertainment, later in this chapter, for details.

Many gourmands head for the formal courtyard where *Chef Marisoll* (☎ 787-725-7454, 202 Calle del Cristo) works her magic. You'll need reservations here to sample chef Marisoll's widely published soup recipes and to enjoy meals like stuffed pheasant. Plan on spending at least US$30.

If you're feeling really rich, head three short blocks up the hill on Calle del Cristo to *Il Perugino* (☎ 787-722-5481), at No 105. The island's rich and famous dine on Umbrian

and Tuscan delicacies like veal piccata and carpaccio in this restored town house. By the time you pay for the wine, you'll probably spend US$100 for two.

Francophiles swear by *La Chaumiere* (☎ 787-722-3330, 367 Calle Tetuán), tucked away behind Teatro Tapia. You can drop up to US$40 on the usual options like chateaubriand or veal Oscar.

Now for something a little racy: Vibrating with splashy orange, blue and yellow decor, Gigi Zafero's *The Parrot Club* (☎ 787-725-7370, 363 Calle Fortaleza) has been causing a stir with young and restless San Juan professionals since it opened in 1997 to the sounds of live jazz and the tastes of 'nuevo Latino' cuisine. The fact that the menu is written in 'Spanglish' hints at the fusion cookery that goes into recipes like crabcakes caribeños. While most dinner entrées run US$18 and up, you can 'do lunch' here for less than half the price.

At the west end of town, *La Fonda El Jibarito* (☎ 787-725-8375, 280 Calle Sol) attracts an interesting bohemian crowd of local writers and artists, hip expats and young travelers. Largely open to the quiet narrow street, the restaurant's low-lit bistro design actually re-creates the colonial façades of Old San Juan on the interior. You can watch Aida and Pedro creating their ever-changing criollo specials over the grills at the back of the room. Salad, sweet plantains and grilled shrimp will run you US$10.

Finally, all true romantics and lovers of imaginative Italian cooking must try *Jules Café*, at the foot of Calle Cruz. This 15-table establishment looks out over the docks and harbor through the tall windows of an old mercantile building. Inside, everything is linen, candlelight, vino and Vivaldi. Scents from the cooking area that fills a corner of the dining room hang in the air. The specialty of the house – pasta with mixed shellfish – runs US$19, but you can eat here for US$12. Reservations are a must.

Burger King and its fast-food competitors are all here in the area surrounding Plaza de Armas. Other great US institutions, including Ponderosa, The Hard Rock Café and Hooters, are not far afield. God bless America.

Condado & Ocean Park

Because of the prevalence of second-rate hotel restaurants, tourist traps and a host of US chain restaurants ranging from McDonald's to Chili's, a lot of travelers visiting Condado and the surrounding neighborhoods leave the area feeling ripped off and devoid of memories of any great island feasts. But take heart, it is possible to get unforgettable chow at reasonable prices in the Condado area if you know where to look. Read on.

If you're on a budget, head for *Hacienda Don José* (☎ 787-722-5880), on the west end of Avenida Ashford at No 1025, across the street from the mammoth Chili's restaurant. The chain monster is probably trying to drive this little cantina out of business, but so far the Hacienda is holding its own. Although the cooking is not really as Mexican as it claims to be, you will find good value in the *tortilla suprema* for US$3.75, or try a cubano sandwich for US$2.75. Domestic beer is only US$1.25, and you can drink up at one of the streetside café tables or on the oceanside deck.

Just next door, *Santelmo* (☎ 787-725-2950) is a 24-hour streetside café. This is a good place to stop after getting your dance on at one of the nearby clubs. Beers are US$1 here during happy hour. Food prices are low; perhaps the best deal on the menu is the *medianoche* (midnight) sandwich with pork, ham, cheese, pickle and mustard for US$2.75. Flan is US$2.50.

Veggie eaters will find a pleasant surprise at *Salud* (☎ 787-722-0911, 1350 Avenida Ashford). Both a health food store and café, this narrow little place serves up a spicy stew of roots and vegetables for US$4.50.

Right next door you'll find the Condado area's favorite pizza restaurant, *Via Appia* (☎ 787-725-8711), with its shady streetside tables. A large pizza will set you back about US$7.

If you're in the mood for something a bit more upscale, head across the street to *Café Matisse* (☎ 787-723-7910, 1351 Avenida Ashford), where US$8 will get you a chicken Caesar salad and fettuccine Alfredo costs US$12 (see also Gay & Lesbian venues, later in this chapter).

Several other restaurants are clustered along this same area of Avenida Ashford. chef Paul Carrol presides over *Zabó* (☎ 787-725-9494, 4 Calle Candina), just off Avenida Ashford near Café Matisse. The menu represents a fusion of Caribbean, Italian and Asian cuisines, all served in a restored mansion. Try the conch fritters with mango and sesame sauce for US$8.50. You'll find entrées here for under US$20.

Il Grottino (☎ 787-723-0499, 1372 Avenida Ashford) calls itself an Italian wine bar and looks the part with a 36-page wine list. You can get all of your favorite northern Italian specialties here for US$15 and up.

Ajili-Mójili (☎ 787-725-9195, 1052 Avenida Ashford) takes its name from the famous Puerto Rican sauce. This place is generally busy with an upscale crowd of sanjuaneros who appreciate some of the best cocina criolla on the island. With island-style paella going for US$22, Ajili is not cheap, but chef Mariano Ortiz is considered one of the superstar cooks on the island.

Light eaters and the upscale crowd from the surrounding condos gather at *La Patisserie* (☎ 787-728-5508, 1504 Avenida Ashford), which offers up French treats like a ham and cheese omelette between a croissant for US$3.75.

Serious Puerto Rican diners head a block south from Avenida Ashford to Avenida Magdalena (traffic splits through much of Condado, heading east on Magdalena, west on Ashford). Here you'll find *Ramiro's* (☎ 787-721-9056, 1106 Calle Magdalena), whose namesake Luis Ramiro started cooking at age eight in Valladolid, Spain. This is a totally haute cuisine establishment with a changing menu of new creations. You won't get out of this place for less than about US$30 per person.

At the east end of Calle Magdalena, gourmands will find *Antonio's* (☎ 787-723-7567, 1406 Calle Magdalena). Another restaurant in a converted mansion that drips with Old World charm, Antonio's specializes in Spanish cuisine. Paella for two costs US$38.

Farther east in Ocean Park, look for the *Hostería del Mar* (see Places to Stay, above) at the end of Calle Tapia facing the ocean.

Here visitors will find one of the island's great secrets: an intimate vegetarian restaurant right on the beach. The menu changes frequently, but plan on paying under US$10 for a tofu, brown rice and onion dish with a side salad.

Not far away on Ocean Park's main drag of Calle McLeary, follow the party crowd to **Dunbar's Pub** (☎ 787-728-2920), at No 1954. Dunbar's serves up burgers, wings and other American pub favorites; potato skins here go for US$3.50. Sunday brunch with live Brazilian jazz is a great first stop before heading to the beach nearby. See 'The Pub Scene' under Entertainment, later in this chapter, for more on this place.

Just east of Dunbar's, **Kasalta's** (☎ 787-727-7340, 1966 Calle McLeary) is a Cuban bakery that opens at 6 am for those who have watched the sun rise through the open doorway of a bar or club. Inside this old-style cafeteria with display cases filled with treats, you can order up a cubano, grilled ham and cheese, steak sandwich, omelette or one of a dozen sweet confections to eat with your steaming mug of café con leche.

Short-hitters who get out of the clubs before Kasalta's opens can rally with the other troops who come to **Denny's Restaurant** (☎ 787-725-4811, 492 Avenida Ponce de León), not far from Bellas Artes in Santurce, to gorge on pancakes and other *americano* delicacies at this 24-hour hash house. It's a big pick-up scene on weekends after the clubs close.

Pepin's (☎ 787-728-6280, 2479 Avenida Isla Verde), in the Punta Las Marías neighborhood, is a new café and tapas bar that's getting raves from both locals and expats in the area. Tapas start at US$3.50.

Almost all of the sanjuaneros and expats say that you must go to **Che's** (☎ 787-726-7202, 35 Calle Caoba), just around the corner from Pepin's, for the area's best Argentine *churrasco* and *parrillada* (grilled, marinated steak). Plan on US$15 or more for entrées.

Isla Verde

Since the commercial strip of hotels, condos, restaurants, bars and rental-car lots along Avenida Isla Verde does a nearly perfect imitation of Hwy 1 in south Florida, you can find every American chain restaurant here that you can think of…and several that you would like to forget. Sites with imaginative cuisine and ambience are few.

But pizza junkies take heart. Folks come here from all over town to dine at **Pizzaiolo** (☎ 787-268-0622, 47 Avenida Isla Verde), specializing in Brazilian-style pizza. You can get the works for under US$11.

Casa Dante (☎ 787-726-7310, 39 Avenida Isla Verde) has been a standard here for years. This family-run restaurant specializes in cocina criolla with *mofongo* for under US$15.

The **Hungry Sailor** (☎ 787-791-3017), opposite the beach in the Condado Racquet Club, is another local hangout where you can go cheap: a Monte Cristo sandwich is US$3.75. Or break the bank on US$29 paella.

Lupi's (☎ 787-253-2198), at Km 1.3 on Hwy 187 near the east end of Isla Verde, has moderately priced Mexican fare including nachos for under US$7. See also 'The Pub Scene' under Entertainment, later in this chapter.

If you are missing exceptional – we're talking world-class – Hunan and Mandarin cooking, get dressed up and head for the pagoda of **Back Street Hong Kong** (☎ 787-791-1224) in the El San Juan Hotel & Casino. Take your credit card, though, because Peking duck will cost you US$50.

Miramar & Río Piedras

Named for a flavorful island vegetable, **Chayote** (☎ 787-722-9385, 603 Avenida Miramar), in the Olimpo Court Hotel, is chef Alfredo Ayala's signature restaurant, where he combines criollo cooking with French, Hindu, African, Spanish and Central American cuisines. Like the cooking, the dining room is a golden fusion of traditional wicker and contemporary art and sculpture. Casual but elegant; entrées cost around US$20.

Austrian-born Augusto Schreiner was the executive chef at the Caribe Hilton for six years before opening his highly touted **Augusto's** (☎ 787-725-7700) in Miramar's Hotel Excelsior (see Places to Stay, earlier). Now in its second decade, Augusto's has been designated the best restaurant in San Juan six times. The menu has strong roots in all the major European cuisines. Formal and expensive, this restaurant will set you back well over US$30.

In Río Piedras, follow the trail of freshmen off the UPR campus to McDonald's, Kentucky Fried Chicken, Burger King and Taco Maker, all clustered around the intersections near the southwest corner of the campus. The more seasoned students head to **Restaurante Vegetariano Mary's** (☎ 787-753-2614, Calle Robles 53). Nothing in this clean, sweet-smelling place costs over US$4. Try the *sancocho* and rice for US$3.

Even more popular with students is **Los Mexicanos** (☎ 787-764-7241), on Avenida Universidad just a block west of Avenida Ponce de León. You can get a veggie platter here for US$2 and a quesadilla for US$1.40.

El Romano Café (☎ 787-763-9551, 8 Paseo José de Diego), on the shady end of the Mercado de Río Piedras, is full of traditional dishes, old-island cafeteria smells and good prices. A plate of chicken, rice and beans costs US$3. Pizza goes for US$1.25 a slice.

At the other end of the paseo and street market, look for **El Buen Gusto** (1117 Calle William Jones). This hole-in-the-wall cafeteria has just a half-dozen tables; the air smells of sofrito and *adobo* and the cook specializes in cocina criolla. Pork chops, rice, beans and salad cost US$4.50.

Cataño

Among the tired-looking collection of bars and open-air restaurants in Cataño, **Morgan's** (☎ 787-275-1205) stands out as the new, air-conditioned pub and grill at the north end of the *malecón* (the waterfront promenade). Although a bit pricey with lobster entrées reaching US$18, this pub offers good island dishes like *asopao de pollo* for US$9, as well as stiff drinks. A good place to stop if you want to get out of Old San Juan by ferry, or if you just did the Bacardi tour.

ENTERTAINMENT

San Juan is well known on the island and beyond for its vibrant nightlife, both its bar and club scene

and fine-arts offerings. In addition, clubs add variety to the scene by promoting different theme nights throughout the week. One night a club may be an '80s music venue for straight folks off the cruise ships; the next night the same club might fill up with a gay crowd jamming to house music. To find out where the action is in the capital, check out the weekly Entertainment Guide that comes out on Thursday in the *San Juan Star*.

Dance Clubs

Clubs in San Juan usually open between 8 and 9 pm. Since the lines at the door can get long after about 11 pm, you'll want to look sharp – cocktail dress for women, slacks and jackets for men – to catch the doorman's attention as he looks for the 'right mix' for his crowd. Otherwise, you could find yourself turned away. On Thursday to Sunday night and on holidays, most clubs stay busy until well after 3 am.

Calle Roberto H Todd is a major thoroughfare linking the districts of Miramar and Condado east of Laguna del Condado, and here at No 1 you'll find the most stylish and perhaps the most popular disco among sanjuaneros. **Egipto** (☎ 787-725-4664; see the Condado & Ocean Park map) does its best to look like a pyramid while the players work on their Cleopatra moves to a mix of rock, house,

techno and even a touch of industrial on two multilevel dance floors. For the most part this is an over-23 club (except for the 16-year-olds who get in with a wink, wiggle and big sister's ID). Wednesday is College Night; Sunday is 21-years-old and up. You can drop US$15 or more on weekends to get down with the island's young, rich and restless. While the club is very much a Latin scene, the music is curiously gringo. Of course, everybody speaks in Spanish, but their English is as good as yours, and they will prove it if you try your humble Spanish on them. Ah, but what great dancers!

Laser (☎ 787-725-7581, *251 Calle Cruz*) in the old city rocks out with a mix of the 'fun kids' on shore leave from their jobs on the cruise ships, their passengers and sanjuaneros who are too young, gay or 'alternative' to try to (or to *want* to) make the scene at Egipto. This mix makes the scene at Laser arguably more wild, crazy and cosmopolitan because these people come from all over the globe and will never see each other again… unless they want to. The music is pure New York and LA – that's hip-hop, bro. A beer can cost US$4 once the crowd rolls in after midnight. Different nights have different themes (see Gay & Lesbian Venues, later in this section).

In Condado, the wild and crazy dance scene is happening at *Club Millennium* (☎ 787-722-1900) in the Condado Plaza Hotel & Casino. There are different themes on different nights. After you meet a couple of drag queens on the dance floor who are on vacation here from New York, you get the sense that Millennium really is the harbinger of a brave new world.

Out in Isla Verde, the seriously wealthy tourist clan and the wanna-bes head to the *Babylon* (☎ 787-791-2781); formerly Amadeus), which is just one of the night spots at the El San Juan Hotel & Casino. No doubt you can picture the scene: Older men wearing Rolexes with younger women in diamonds and cocktail dresses shadow dance against an art deco backdrop. Tuxedos are not out of place for men here on weekend nights. Mainstream 1970s, '80s and '90s music is featured; plan on a US$10 cover.

A lot of night owls – both straight and gay – end their Sunday morning dance-a-thons at *Asylum* (☎ 787-723-3258, *1420 Avenida Ponce de León*).

Latin Until very recently, the best places to feel the syncopation of salsa and see the flash of legs pumping to *merengue* were in San Juan's resort hotels, and the dancers were generally middle-aged. But now *La Rumba* (☎ 787-725-4407, *152 Calle San Sebastián*) has scored a big hit by bringing back live salsa and Latin rock to Old San Juan on Thursday to Sunday nights. This is definitely a hip youth scene; things get going after 10 pm.

If you've outgrown the college set or don't want to deal with the Old San Juan weekend traffic, head to Isla Verde and check out *Martini's Cabaret*, in the San Juan Grand Beach Resort & Casino, or the *Chico Bar* nearby in the El San Juan Hotel & Casino (see Places to Stay, earlier). You will find a good mix of local aficionados and tourists in both clubs. Bands are hot and cover all the classic Tito Puente, Willie Colón, Celia Cruz and Eddie Palmieri numbers. Dress up for these places, which stay open till 1 am during the week but may go as late as 3 am on weekends.

A lot of the folks who show up here were taking dance lessons all week at the *Lobby Lounge* (☎ 787-722-7000 ext 6520) at the Marriott in Condado and brushing up on the old 'slow-slow-quick-quick' (the rumba). The *Terrace Bar* at the Caribe Hilton in Puerta de Tierra (see Places to Stay, earlier) is more casual. There is a broad range of ages here with less finesse and a lot of good humor.

A final word of advice: Drug use and sales have become commonplace in San Juan clubs, and so have undercover police trying to make a dent in the traffic. Do not think that the laid-back mood of the island and its clubs carries over to the police force. Chances are you didn't budget jail time into your island vacation.

Live Music Venues

If you want to share the liberated feeling that comes from truly making the scene, dress up and head for **The Parrot Club** (see Places to Eat, earlier) in the old city, where the music burns with Latin-seasoned jazz. This is one of San Juan's great 'date' bars. The music starts at 8 pm on Tuesday, Thursday, Saturday and Sunday, and the crowd starts lining up outside soon after. Your best bet is to come for a late dinner and stick around.

A newcomer to the bar scene, the old city's **Gallery Café** (see Places to Eat, earlier) features jazz on Wednesday night and live '80s music on Thursday. Happy hour specials run till 9 pm on Friday.

Just up a block west up Calle Fortaleza, **Café Tabac** has live jazz Thursday to Sunday starting at 8 pm, October to March. The lights are dim, the music cool and the crowd definitely upscale with prices to match: A simple beer or Bacardi costs US$4.

See Dance Clubs (above) and 'The Pub Scene' for other venues featuring occasional live music.

Gay & Lesbian Venues

If you are a gay male new to town and you have not had a chance to do your Internet homework (see Gay & Lesbian Travelers in the Facts for the Visitor chapter), point yourself in the direction of the Condado district.

You can start to get the lay of the land by stopping in at **Vibration** (*51 Calle Barranquitas*), a primo cruising bar in the Condado area with videos and all the rest. After hours, stroll next door to **La Laguna** (*☎ 787-723-3786*), which is a late-night club with guarded entrance (ring the buzzer to get in).

The terrace bar at the **Atlantic Beach Hotel** (see Places to Stay) packs in a huge crowd for its Sunday T-dance with drag revues and male strippers on most weekends.

Right next door on Condado beach is **Hurricane** (*☎ 787-725-2025, 2 Calle Vendig*), an open-air beach bar and restaurant formerly known as the Barefoot Bar. This place recently reopened under new management after suffering extensive damage from none other than Hurricane Georges. The crowd is mostly gay, but the place gets a broad mix of people for lunch and during happy hour (6 to 8 pm).

Café Matisse (see Places to Eat, earlier) in Condado is a sidewalk café, restaurant and jazz cave that sometimes features poetry readings and drag revues. The mixed crowd of straights and gays here bubbles with laughter past 3 am on weekends.

Head into Old San Juan to the men's sauna, the **Steam Works** (*☎ 787-725-4993, 205 Calle Luna*), for some R&R.

On Thursdays you can dance nearby at Laser (see Dance Clubs, earlier in the Entertainment section), which is called **Abbey 2000** on 'gay night.' Thursday is a totally gay and rowdy scene presided over by a drag queen named Monique and her blond sidekick, David. The music is 1970s and '80s disco from divas such as Patti LaBelle and Donna Summer.

If you want a place with a more Latin feel, where the disc jockey mixes some of the heavier New York house sounds with a little crazy salsa, catch **Eros** (*☎ 787-722-1131, 1257 Avenida Ponce de León*). Formerly Krash, Eros is next to the Teatro Metro in the Santurce/Miramar district. The scene starts at about 10 pm and cranks till 4 am on weekends. While basically a gay venue, this hot dance scene on Saturday nights draws free spirits from all quarters of the gay, lesbian, bi and straight world. A walk on the wild side.

Sunday is gay night at **Asylum** (see Dance Clubs, earlier in the Entertainment section).

Bars catering exclusively to women are hard to come by in San Juan, but **Cups** (*☎ 787-268-3570, 1708 Calle San Mateo*) in Santurce is a laid-back women's scene popular with couples and cruisers.

Be sure to check out the *Puerto Rico Breeze*, a weekly bilingual newspaper covering local events, arts and entertainment; the paper also has accommodations, bar and club listings for greater San Juan.

Cabarets

In its previous incarnation as the Copa Room, **Martini's Cabaret**, at Isla Verde's San Juan Grand Beach Resort & Casino, has booked headliners such as Whitney Houston and Jay Leno; performances are held on Wednesday as well as Friday to Sunday. The

The Pub Scene: Looking for the Heart of Saturday Night

San Juan is one of the best places in the world for a pub crawl west of Munich, Madrid or Dublin. But if pub crawling is your social sport, be safe, get a designated driver, take a buddy or two along and don't go wandering around deserted streets in neighborhoods you don't know. That said, here is a 'short' list of watering holes to get you started.

Students Start Here Since there are no classes at UPR on Friday, Thursday night kicks off the weekend fiesta – so heat shields up, Princess Leia. Just beyond the southwest corner of the UPR campus in Río Piedras, *El Boricua* (local jargon meaning Puerto Rican Spanish) opens its doors at 3 pm to gangs of students. The music is salsa and Latin rock, the crowd is largely gregarious humanities majors in blue jeans who will want to practice their English with you. This place rocks into the wee hours on Thursday and Friday nights, when people are shopping for Saturday night dates.

A funkier, more urban student crowd hangs out in T-shirts and baggy clothes at *Ocho de Blanco,* on Avenida Universidad just west of Los Mexicanos restaurant, to the sound of hip-hop and a half-dozen video games. During the long happy hour, you can get a Bacardi or Coors Light for US$1.

The business and marketing majors who already have their own cars and cell phones drive about 10 minutes off campus to *Shannan's* (☎ 787-281-8466), a popular Irish pub at the Centro Comercio Caribe in Río Piedras.

For those making the pilgrimage into Old San Juan, *Amadeus* (☎ 787-724-1789), on Calle San Sebastián across from the Plaza de San José, is a favorite hangout for the college crowd on weekend nights.

Enter Gringos & Other Creatures of the Night Commanding the hip corner at the top of the hill in Old San Juan where Calles Cristo and San Sebastián meet, *Nono's* (☎ 787-725-7819) is one of about a dozen cruising bars on Calle San Sebastián and its side streets. Nono's attracts travelers and a regular crowd of Old San Juan locals during the day to the camaraderie of pounding brewskis, playing video games and bouncing to the beat of great salsa. Like other bars along this strip, the façade at Nono's is more or less wide open so that when the women hit the street, it's easy for them to scope out the men who get to the bar earlier. If women like what they see, they cruise in as a group. Once you've met someone you want to talk to, head to the balconies off the 2nd-floor pool room for a little fresh air and privacy. This place is pick-up city on the weekends.

A block east at the corner of Calle San José is a little bar called *Hijos de Borinquen* (Sons of Puerto Rico) that packs them in after 10 pm to hear acoustic guitarists and singers offer up some of the island's best folk music in the spirit of the Gipsy Kings.

Heading down the hill along Calle del Cristo you'll find a big crowd at *El Bohemio* – especially on Thursday – and the connecting tapas bar. One of the bars at the Gran Hotel El Convento, El Bohemio spreads its tables from the dark and richly appointed bar onto the terrace in front of the hotel on Calle del Cristo. The scene is a mix of ages, couples and singles drinking frozen cocktails and rubbing body parts in the crowd. Things usually get busy after 9 pm, when the bar hosts a live singer or jazz combo. The crowd here dresses to kill, with some guys in suits and ties and lots of women in tight cocktail dresses (faux leopard skin is not out

The Pub Scene: Looking for the Heart of Saturday Night

of the question), major makeup and heels. Everyone carries a beeper and a cell phone, and can be seen constantly calling their less-fortunate friends back in the suburbs. The 'in' place at the moment, and a total pick-up scene, El Bohemio makes the locals roll their eyes in disgust or envy.

Quite a few of the locals are hanging out across the street at *El Batey*. This hole-in-the-wall has been a favored gathering place for Old San Juan's Puerto Ricans and expats for more than two decades; it's a good place to get a feel for what it would be like to settle down here in your sweat-stained Bogart suit, master bumper pool and do the *Casablanca* thing. The walls and ceiling (which leak when it rains) are covered with the signatures of tens of thousands of patrons. It could be Bill Clinton's autograph on the wall next to the jukebox that plays everything from Glen Miller to the Rolling Stones. When all the other bars close, party animals of all types show up here because El Batey stays open until 6 am.

Don Pablo's is next door and has that dark, blue-light, smoky atmosphere in which you would expect to find poets smoking weed and writing Dada lyrics. The crowd here is young, local, grunge and mostly Puerto Ricans getting out of their parents' apartments to play video games, hang with the *brokis* (brothers), *gufear* (goof around) and *rapear con jebas* (hit on girls) passing up and down Calle del Cristo.

Head east to Ocean Park, where *Dunbar's Pub* (see Places to Eat, earlier) has been an institution for nearly two decades with the local party crowd and serious dart throwers. Expect friendly expats, yuppies and college kids networking and looking for the person of their dreams…or at least a date. Gloria behind the bar is a trove of local knowledge.

Over in Isla Verde, step into *Lupi's* (see Places to Eat, earlier) and be dazzled by its collection of sports trophies, uniforms and memorabilia assembled by one of the owners, who was a pitcher for the New York Yankees when they were world champions in the late 1970s. This bar-restaurant turns into a jam-packed pub scene for upscale youth after 10 pm, presided over by OJ Simpson's Bill's football helmet looming eerily from its case on the wall. Lupi's has valet parking, and you'll need it.

If you are a little older and want some real *Casablanca*-style intrigue, head to the beach bar at Isla Verde's *Casa de Playa* (see Places to Stay, earlier). Word has it that things never get out of hand here because about 40% of the clientele are FBI, ATF (Alcohol/Tobacco/Firearms) or DEA (Drug Enforcement Agency) spooks chilling in their off-duty hours, trading rumors or war stories and packing their pieces.

Make Room for Lovers At the west end of Calle Fortaleza near the gated entrance to the governor's mansion, *Café La Violeta* is the place to come to cuddle in big wicker chairs, soft sofas and a collection of private alcoves spread around a courtyard while listening to sultry jazz recordings. There is exceptional privacy here for those who wish to speak of romance, and while the crowd is largely straight, Violeta gets high marks from gay couples as well.

Out in Isla Verde, the *Cigar Bar* in the El San Juan Hotel & Casino is rich in dark cabinetry and cognac. Repair to this hideaway with a date in tux or cocktail dress before trying your luck at baccarat or letting down your hair on the dance floors of Babylon or the Chico Bar on the premises (see Dance Clubs, earlier). You can wear your jewelry here!

cover charge is usually around US$30 and includes two drinks. Bringing in a mix of islanders and tourists, the scene is pure Las Vegas.

El Tropicoro is one of the many nighttime attractions at the El San Juan Hotel & Casino in Isla Verde. There are usually 9 and 11 pm shows nightly during the winter season. You won't get the big names that attract the crowds to Las Vegas shows, and the crowd here is mostly affluent tourists over 50. The shows feature a lot of dancers in tight or scant clothing working their mojo to tropical themes. Picture Havana, Cuba, in the 1950s. Cover with two drinks runs about US$22.

La Fiesta Lounge, at the Condado Plaza Hotel & Casino, wears a number of different faces, but some nights it gets very Latin and brassy. Call for the latest program and expect to find yourself with an over-40 crowd of tourists and islanders. You can hear some great salsa here from small combos. Cover charge varies.

Strip Clubs
St Tropez (☎ 787-721-5163, 521 Avenida Fernández Juncos) in Puerta de Tierra euphemistically bills itself as a 'gentleman's club': read 'mega strip joint' with 35 dancers and all the rest. *Divas International* (☎ 787-721-8270, 1104 Avenida Ashford) in Condado offers more of the same.

Wednesday is a popular girls' night out, and male dancers do the half-monty thing for ladies at *Club Millennium* (☎ 787-722-1900), in the Condado Plaza Hotel & Casino, from 5 to 9 pm. Really, who can calculate the secret desires of the human heart?

Classical Music, Opera & Ballet
Known locally as Bellas Artes, the *Luis A Ferré Center for the Performing Arts* (☎ 787-724-4747, 22 Avenida Ponce de León; see the Condado & Ocean Park map) in Santurce fills its three concert halls with bi-weekly concerts of the Puerto Rican Symphony Orchestra and appearances by international stars such as Itzhak Perlman. During the fall/winter season, Ópera de Puerto Rico and Ballet de San Juan also perform here. Built in 1981, Bellas Artes has more than 1800 seats in the festival hall, about 700 in the drama

hall and 200 in the experimental theater. Tickets cost about US$15 to US$45.

Theater
Those interested in theater should look to the Universidad de Puerto Rico in Río Piedras, the Teatro Tapia in Old San Juan and Bellas Artes (see above) for both avant-garde and Broadway style productions in Spanish and English.

Teatro Tapia (☎ 787-722-0407), on the south side of Plaza de Colón in Old San Juan, is an intimate structure in typical Spanish colonial interpretation of the neoclassical style. It dates from 1832, and has been the beneficiary of two recent restorations. Named for the famous 19th-century Puerto Rican playwright Alejandro Tapia y Rivera, this elegant theater hosts cultural productions of all types. The performances are usually in Spanish and frequently feature new works from Spain or Latin America. The acting is professional and performances attract Puerto Rico's literati and social elite. Opening night is a fashion show of who's who in San Juan. Tickets cost US$10 to US$30.

The shows at the *Universidad de Puerto Rico* (☎ 787-764-0000 ext 2505 or 2563) campus in Río Piedras are a lot less expensive (usually under US$8) as they involve student actors and productions. Sometimes lacking in finesse, these performances are still a good bet because they thrive on high energy from both the artists and the audience. Attending these shows is a good way to meet the university crowd, and it's not out of the question that your new acquaintances will invite you down to El Boricua for *una copa* (a jar o' brew, mate) or to a private party.

Dance
Visitors interested in performances of traditional music and dance should consider participating in the *LeLoLai* program (☎ 800-866-7827, 787-723-3135) sponsored by the PRTC. The program offers a week's free or discounted admission to a variety of daily cultural performances, including the country music and dance show at the Caribe Hilton or the flamenco music and dance show at the Gran Hotel El Convento in Old

San Juan. Purchase your LeLoLai membership card (US$10) at travel agencies, many hotels or directly from the PRTC. Membership cards can also be purchased over the phone by calling the numbers listed above.

Visitors can also see some exceptional modern dance concerts performed at the Burgos Amphitheater at the *Universidad de Puerto Rico* (☎ 787-764-0000 ext 2563). Call for performance schedules and ticket prices.

Cinemas

As in the US, cinemas can be found in most of San Juan's major shopping centers. The city's largest complex is *Reading Cinemas* (☎ 787-767-1363, 767-3505), in Plaza Las Américas in the Hato Rey district. *Teatro Paramount* (☎ 787-721-1101, 1313 Avenida Ponce de León) is easy to find in Santurce, as is the classic, restored *Teatro Metro* (☎ 787-722-0465) at Parada 18 on the same street edging towards Miramar. The Laguna Gardens Shopping Center in Isla Verde houses the *Humacao Cinema* (☎ 787-850-1510). In Río Piedras, check out *Teatro New Victoria* (☎ 787-765-7423, 8 Calle Robles). You can also look in the yellow pages of the phone directory under *Teatros y Cines* (Theaters & Cinemas) for the one nearest you; be sure to ask someone you trust whether the movie house is in a safe area before you go wandering around its locale after dark.

For a better selection of independent films from around the world, check out the *Fine Arts Cinema* (☎ 787-721-4288, 654 Avenida Ponce de León) in Miramar or see what's playing at one of the outdoor amphitheaters as part of the ongoing *Cultural Activities Series* (☎ 787-764-0000 ext 2563) at UPR.

Movie buffs should refer to the Special Events section earlier in this chapter for information on the city's up-and-coming annual cinema festival.

Casinos

San Juan may not be Las Vegas, but a lot of travelers and islanders come for the action. All of San Juan's casinos are associated with resort hotels, and the gaming houses have now expanded to offer Caribbean Stud Poker,

Let It Ride, Pai Gow Poker and the Big Six Wheel as well as the standard blackjack, roulette, craps, baccarat and minibaccarat.

The massive gaming facilities at the *San Juan Grand Beach Resort & Casino* (☎ 787-791-6100) in Isla Verde are reminiscent of those at the casino's Vegas namesake. The tables are new at *Stellaris Casino* (☎ 787-722-7000 ext 6759) at the Marriott in Condado.

Living up to its reputation as the most exclusive hotel on the island, *El San Juan Hotel & Casino* (☎ 787-791-1000) is a top-drawer operation where the crowd usually dresses up to play.

Most of the city's casinos are open between noon and 4 pm and 8 pm to 4 am. You must be at least 21 to enter a casino.

SPECTATOR SPORTS

To see the next generation of up-and-coming 'whiz kids,' catch a baseball game at Hiram Bithorn Stadium in Hato Rey when the *San Juan Metros* or the *Santurce Crabbers* are fighting it out with the other teams in the Caribbean League from Mexico, Venezuela and the Dominican Republic. This is a winter league with the season stretching from November to March.

November 2 is usually opening day, when tens of thousands of faithful fans show up to watch the boys of winter hit *jonrones* (home runs). While these games are not exactly Chicago vs St Louis, do not dismiss them as simply 'minor league' events. More than a few of these players are bound for the majors. For a schedule and tickets, call *Professional Baseball of Puerto Rico* (☎ 787-765-6285).

SHOPPING

Most anything that you can buy in other modern capital cities you can find in San Juan. Visitors seeking authentic Puerto Rican crafts and products should be selective about where they shop. See below for suggestions.

Old San Juan

For more than a few people, shopping in Old San Juan is a form of recreation. And with more than a dozen art galleries and 10 times that number of boutiques, jewelry shops and even big-name factory outlets such as Ralph Lauren and London Fog, there is a lot here to keep you busy. Since island merchants take exceptional pride in their sense of style, visitors will no doubt find a lot of pretty things. But don't expect a lot of bargains or the duty-free shopping of many other Caribbean destinations. Calles San Francisco and Fortaleza are the two main arteries in and out of the old city, and both are packed cheek by jowl with shops. Running perpendicular at the west end of the town, Calle del Cristo is home to many of the old city's most chic establishments.

Visitors should note that many of the craft vendors in Old San Juan are actually selling imports from South America, so do not proceed with the illusion that you are buying the produce of Puerto Rican artisans. For the real thing, check the selection at Puerto Rican Arts & Crafts at 204 Calle Fortaleza, open 9 am to 6 pm weekdays, noon to 5 pm Saturday. Another good source for santos, *mundillo* lace and Carnaval masks is the Centro de Artes Populares (253 Calle del Cristo), open 9:30 am to 4:30 pm Tuesday to Saturday (see Traditional Arts in the Facts about Puerto Rico chapter for detailed descriptions of these popular art forms).

Butterfly People (☎ 787-723-2432), across from the post office on Calle Fortaleza, is a real curiosity with its gallery, antique shop and small restaurant mixed together under walls that are covered with flurries of the little critters. (You can buy the arrangements.) Open 10 am to 6 pm Monday to Saturday.

With the visual arts in full bloom on the island, every permutation of *tropicalismo* (local color) turns up in San Juan galleries. One of the oldest, most established and avant-garde of these places that you must see even if you can't afford to buy something is Galería Botello (☎ 787-723-2879), 208 Calle del Cristo, open 10 am to 6 pm Monday to Saturday. Don't miss Angel Botello's own work, including his boiler-like sculpture of *The Three Sisters*.

Directly across the street at No 200, Linda Williams runs Bóveda (☎ 787-725-0263), one of Calle del Cristo's most imaginative arts, decoration, jewelry and clothing boutiques.

If you want to see some of the freshest expressions of island artists at affordable prices, head for the Galería Liga de Estudiantes de Arte (Gallery of Art Students' League), housed in the Escuela de Artes Plásticas building. Opening hours vary.

You can sample exotic rums for free (or buy a bottle) when you shop for jewelry and fragrances at Barrachina's (☎ 787-725-7912), at 104 Calle Fortaleza. The restaurant portion of this operation claims to have invented the piña colada. It's open 9 am to 6 pm Monday to Saturday.

Metropolitan San Juan

For more traditional shopping, head to the artisans' fair at Parques Muñoz Rivera and Sixto Escobar in Puerta de Tierra. The market is generally open on weekends, but call the PRTC ahead of time to inquire about changing hours of operation (see Tourist Offices under Information, earlier in this chapter). Of course, there's also the Mercado de Río Piedras on Paseo José de Diego for produce, meats and bargain clothing (see Río Piedras, earlier in this chapter, for specifics).

If the sun or heat get to you, you can always have a thoroughly American experience in air-conditioned comfort visiting the 200 stores at Plaza Las Américas, just off the Expreso Las Américas (Hwy 18) in Hato Rey. The mall is open 9 am to 9 pm Monday to Saturday, 11 am to 5 pm Sunday. A similar operation called Plaza Carolina lies to the east of the city off the Expreso Baldorioty de Castro (Hwy 26), offering US standards such as JC Penney and Sears among its collection of 150 shops. Plaza Carolina has the same operating hours as Plaza Las Américas.

GETTING THERE & AWAY
Air

International flights arrive at and depart from San Juan's Aeropuerto Internacional de Luis Muñoz Marín, about 8 miles east of the old city center. See the Getting There & Away chapter for information on airport services and for a list of international carriers that fly to San Juan.

Several airlines provide service between San Juan and the other parts of the island, though Puerto Rico's domestic air network is somewhat limited. See the Getting Around chapter for specifics. Private aircraft, charter services and the bulk of the commuter flights serving the islands of Culebra and Vieques arrive at and depart from San Juan's original airport at Isla Grande, on the Bahía de San Juan in the city's Miramar district. See Domestic Airports & Airlines in the Getting Around chapter for details.

Público

Travelers should note that presently there is no islandwide bus system. In the meantime, públicos form the backbone of public transportation in Puerto Rico and can provide an inexpensive link between San Juan and other points on the island, including Ponce and Mayagüez. Públicos are generally shared taxis in the form of minivans that pick up passengers along pre-determined routes.

In San Juan the major público centers include the LMM airport, the large público station in Río Piedras and – to a much lesser extent – the Plaza de Colón in Old San Juan. See the Getting Around chapter for more detailed information.

Cruise Ship

More than a dozen cruise lines include San Juan on their Caribbean itineraries, and as the second-largest port for cruise ships in the Western Hemisphere, the city is visited by more than a million cruise ship passengers a year. All ships dock at the piers along Calle La Marina near the Customs House, just a short walk from the cobblestone streets of Old San Juan. See the Getting There & Away chapter for details.

GETTING AROUND
To/From the Airport

Virtually every hotel in San Juan is within 8 miles of the LMM airport, and many are much closer. Nevertheless, you can really drop a wad of your bankroll on this trip. Consider your options before you find yourself in the rush of the terminal, and avoid taking a pricey cab unless you are traveling with at least three or more other people to share the expense.

For those that are traveling light and don't mind the wait, the bus is the cheapest option. Look for the *'Parada'* sign outside the arrivals concourse at LMM. The M7 or T1 bus will drop you in the vicinity of virtually every accommodation in Isla Verde, Ocean Park, Condado and Old San Juan (in that order).

If you have a lot of gear, feel a pressing need to reach your destination or are traveling with children, look for the airport shuttle vans or limousine kiosks on the arrivals concourse. Chances are you can join some other travelers headed your way. Once the van fills, you'll pay around US$4 to Isla Verde, US$5 to Condado and US$6 to Old San Juan. As in New York and a lot of other US cities, Carey Limousine (☎ 787-724-6281) sets the standard, but the company has a number of rivals, so inquire at the limousine kiosk for options.

Getting to LMM airport from hotels in the San Juan area is easy. Staff at virtually all of the middle and top-end hotels will arrange for a taxi or airport shuttle van to pick you up in front of your lodging at your request. Depending on how many people share the cost of the ride, you can expect to pay between US$4 and US$20. If you have time to wait, public transportation is a much cheaper alternative: You can get a bus from Old San Juan, Condado and Isla Verde to the airport for 25¢ (see the Bus section, below).

For those needing to get to/from the Aeropeurto Isla Grande for a flight to/from the Spanish Virgin Islands, taking a taxi is your only option.

Bus

The AMA – Autoridad Metropolitana de Autobuses (Metropolitan Bus Authority; ☎ 787-767-7979) – and Metrobus (☎ 787-763-4141) shoulder the task of people-moving in the city and have been maligned for decades. Recent additions to the fleet mean newer, air-conditioned and faster buses – thanks to new 'wrong-way' bus lanes on major city arteries. AMA buses cost 25¢ to anywhere on the route; Metrobuses make the crosstown run from Old San Juan to Río Piedras for 50¢. The city's main bus terminal is in Old San Juan near the cruise ship piers, beneath the high-rise Covadonga parking lot off Calle La Marina, but buses also stop at Plaza de Colón. There are other city terminals at Río Piedras, Cataño and Bayamón. Travelers can identify bus stops on the street by the obelisk markers that read *'Parada'* or *'Parada de Guaguas'* (Bus Stop).

What makes bus travel in San Juan frustrating is that printed schedules are impossible to come by and no bus stops have signs indicating the bus routes. Buses also run irregularly – if at all – after about 9 pm. The one exception is the Metrobus between Old San Juan and Río Piedras, which runs every 15 minutes from about 6 am to midnight. For route information (but not departure times) from the AMA or Metrobus, you can get a recording in Spanish and English by calling the numbers listed above.

The following are some of the primary bus routes of interest to travelers (bus numbers are followed by associated route descriptions):

M7 or T1 – LMM airport, Piñones, Isla Verde, Condado, Old San Juan

1, 2, 8 – Old San Juan, Río Piedras via various routes

A7, M2, M3 – Old San Juan, Condado

A7 – Old San Juan, Isla Verde

8 – Old San Juan, Plaza Las Américas

M1 – Old San Juan, Balneario Escambrón

Travelers should be aware that in San Juan, it's not uncommon for dangerous neighborhoods to border tourist zones, with one bus serving both zones. If you make a mistake and get off the bus at the wrong stop, you could be asking for trouble. If you are feeling uncertain about your stop or generally insecure, sit next to the driver and ask him/her to notify you when you arrive at your stop. Better yet, take a cab at night.

Train

It's coming none too soon. See the Getting Around chapter for information on projected plans for an urban train system linking major districts of San Juan. To learn its current status, check with the PRTC (see Tourist Offices under Information, earlier in this chapter) or, better yet, any of the local tour operators mentioned under Organized Tours in the Getting Around chapter.

Car

At under US$200 per week (for a subcompact), a rental car is an attractive option for travelers who do not plan on staying in San Juan. But travelers who are staying local may find their life less complicated if they hold off on renting their car until they are ready to head out on the island: Traffic, parking, the maze of thoroughfares and the danger of being carjacked make having and using a rental car in the city a challenge. If you really can't live without your own set of wheels – like most islanders – see the Getting Around chapter for tips on navigating and driving on the island.

Taxi

There are many places in the world where taxi drivers take advantage of naive, tired

---

Looking for a Free Ride?

The combination of tropical heat and humidity and the hills of Old San Juan get to more than a few travelers. The city's answer to this problem is to offer free trolley service through the old town 12 to 14 hours a day. Those arriving in Old San Juan by bus, taxi or ship can catch one of the free trolley buses that leave regularly (about every 15 minutes) from the bus terminal on Calle La Marina near the cruise ship piers, stopping at the high-rise Covadonga parking lot above the terminal.

There are two trolley routes. One takes you from the bus terminal to the center of town at the Plaza de Armas. Other trolleys depart from the terminal and take a longer route up the hill to El Morro. The trolley will stop to pick up/drop off passengers anywhere along the way.

The trolly runs from about 6 am to 8 pm on weekdays; 8 am to 8 pm on weekends.

and dependent travelers – and then there is San Juan. For decades, drivers at the airport bargained with you – using the real/imagined language barrier to their advantage – instead of giving you a metered ride. This bargaining – and the associated onslaught of touts that greeted you when you walked out the door of the LMM airport – put a bad taste in a lot of travelers' mouths.

In recent years, San Juan has tried to provide travelers with a more welcoming greeting by establishing posted rates for all trips from the city's LMM airport. So today the touts are fewer, the drivers are more friendly and you know in advance – without haggling – that you are going to pay an arm, a leg or both. Following are the fixed rates from the airport to the most popular San Juan destinations:

Isla Verde	US$8
Condado	US$12
Puerta de Tierra/ Old San Juan	US$16

The PSC (Public Service Commission) has fixed rates from the cruise ship piers, and these are even steeper:

Old San Juan	US$6
Puerta de Tierra	US$6
Condado	US$10

When the cabs actually turn on their meters (we've never seen this in San Juan), they charge US$1 initially and 10¢ for each 1/13 of a mile. Waiting time is 10¢ per 45 seconds. You'll also pay 50¢ to US$1 per piece of luggage (depending on size). There's a US$5 reservation charge; add a US$1 surcharge after 10 pm.

Another thing to know about taxis is that they are scarce after about 10 pm in the places you're likely to need them most, such as Old San Juan. If you need to return from Old San Juan to Puerta de Tierra, Condado, Ocean Park or Isla Verde after 10 pm, do not make yourself a target for a mugging by standing on a lonely street corner in Plaza de Colón (a busy hub for públicos and cabs by day). Call a cab from the Gran Hotel El Convento, in the heart of the old city. Better yet, walk down to the Wyndham San Juan Hotel & Casino, which will have taxis as long as the casino is open (until 4 am).

With more than a half-dozen cab companies in the city, you would think the competition would be stiff enough for cabs to be in a rush to get to you, but don't bet on it. Cabs have left us waiting for almost an hour…or not come at all. If you need a cab, try Major Taxi Cabs (☎ 787-723-2460) or Richdale Radio Taxi (☎ 787-721-1900); they usually come when you call.

Bicycle
Currently, the city is in the process of creating a bike trail to circumnavigate Bahía de San Juan. Contact the PRTC (see Tourist Offices under Information, earlier) for updates on the progress of this developing trail. A few hardy locals actually ride their bikes in city traffic, and you can do it too if you don't fear for life and limb, but we do not recommend this activity. Those interested in biking on the island should see the Bicycling sections under Activities (earlier in this chapter) and in the Facts for the Visitor chapter for more information.

Ferry
A commuter ferry service called the Acua Expreso (☎ 787-788-1155) connects three main population centers around Bahía de San Juan: Old San Juan, Hato Rey and Cataño. In Old San Juan the ferry dock is at Pier 2, near the Wyndham Old San Juan Hotel & Casino. The boats usually run every half hour from 6 am to 9 pm, but they leave every 15 minutes during rush hours to connect the old city with the industrial zones of Cataño to the west and San Juan's modern financial district of Hato Rey to the east. With fares at 50¢ to 75¢, the Expreso provides a cheap harbor tour and a refreshing way to cool off – if you get one of the boats with an open-air deck – as well as a means of avoiding the city's traffic snarls. But beware: This ferry can get extremely crowded on weekdays during morning and evening rush hours.

El Yunque
Playa Seven Seas or
Playa Luquillo

East Coast

The 60 miles of coastline that wrap around Puerto Rico's eastern shoulder between San Juan and Guayama offer almost endless beach, swimming, diving and boating opportunities. Furthermore, the interior Sierra de Luquillo – dominated by the anvil-shaped peak of El Yunque with its surrounding rain forest – feature exceptional attractions for hikers, bird-watchers and botanists. You can camp in the mountains and at some beaches, while a plethora of *paradores* (inns) offer less rustic accommodations at moderate prices. Upscale travelers will find three mega-resorts in the area and many of the island's best golf courses.

The region is also the gateway for ferry service to the offshore islands of Culebra and Vieques (see the Spanish Virgin Islands chapter for ferry details). Amid all these attractions, the massive US Navy base at Roosevelt Roads stands guard over the Caribbean and has functioned as a training facility for US Marines bound for the Persian Gulf or 'police actions' in Haiti and East Africa.

With so many attractions, the region's roads, beaches, trails, accommodations and restaurants can get overwhelmed on weekends as islanders and off-duty military personnel join the regular flow of travelers. At such times – as well as during Puerto Ricans' summer vacations – the natural beauty of the east coast can almost get lost beneath the traffic jams on Hwy 3 and the crowds searching for a cool breeze or the perfect place for a fiesta. Eventually, the new Hwy 66 will give expressway access to this area, bypassing the stoplights, urban sprawl, strip malls and pharmaceutical plants along Hwy 3, but as this book goes to press Hwy 66 remains a long way from completion.

The traveler's best approach to seeing the area is to follow the order of sights presented in this chapter, which leads you clockwise on a circle of the island. Starting from San Juan, take the pretty two-lane Hwy 187 along the coast to Loíza Aldea, then follow four-lane Hwy 3 from Río Grande to El Yunque, Luquillo and Fajardo.

To really get a sense of this area's natural beauty, tour it at leisure on weekdays from a local base that cuts your time on highways to a minimum.

PIÑONES

A state forest – Bosque Estatal de Piñones – and a neighborhood of its parent municipality, Loíza Aldea, farther to the east, Piñones is often called the 'Africa of Puerto Rico.' It presents an exceptional retreat from the high-rise condos and casino hotels of Isla Verde to the west and the massive pharmaceutical plants of Carolina to the south.

Of course, the Africa comparison may be public-relations code for 'black people live here.' But there is a lot more about Piñones that speaks of Africa than the faces of the descendants of the Yoruba slaves brought to

Highlights

- Hiking in the Caribbean National Forest at El Yunque

- Feasting at the beach kiosks at Piñones

- Getting tight with the saints of Africa at Loíza Aldea's Fiesta de Santiago in late July

- Taking a kayak or sailing trip for some snorkeling and a picnic on the island chain of La Cordillera, off Fajardo

- Driving along the mountain cliffs above the Caribbean coastline near Yabucoa

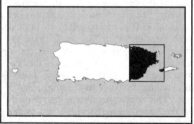

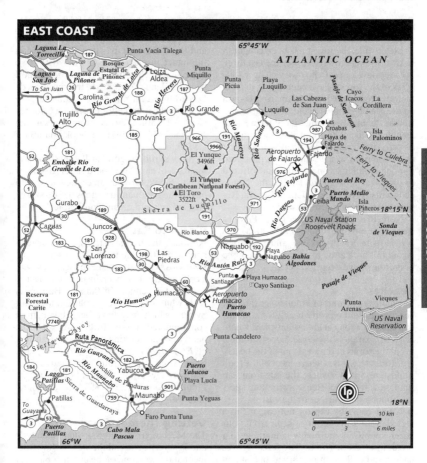

EAST COAST

this area in the 16th and 17th centuries. Driving east from San Juan along Hwy 187, you'll cross a bridge over the inlet at Boca de Congrejos. The tall plantation of coconut palms here overgrows the empty beaches and looks like places in Senegal or the state of Bahía in Brazil. Other sights reminiscent of Senegal are the pine and mangrove forest on the south side of the road, the terra-cotta-colored sandy tracks leading off Hwy 187 to secluded parking spots on the crests of dunes, and makeshift food kiosks where cooks roast plantains and skewered pieces

of seasoned pork over wood fires. A series of reefs just offshore helps create some of the best surfing conditions on the island's north coast and protect bathers from the full force of ocean swells.

In recent years, the government – thinking that the vendors' shacks mar the natural beauty of the place – has tried to force local entrepreneurs out of the forest and wildlife refuge. But the only effective agent in this 'housecleaning' has been Hurricane Georges, which leveled all but concrete structures in September of 1998. The high demand for *refrescos* at this popular beach will no doubt bring the vendors back in full force.

Meanwhile, the forest has been caught in its own struggle to survive. For the last three decades, developers (who own well over 1000 acres of the forest) have been trying to level their portion of the largest mangrove lagoon on the island – home to countless seabirds as well as the highly endangered Puerto Rican manatee – to make room for a new mega-resort. After years of legal chess, a solution may be in sight, as a developer has proposed a much smaller casino resort and offered to turn over most of the land to the Depto de Recursos Naturales (Dept of Natural Resources) to remain forever wild.

Note that the western edge of Piñones (despite the police station in the area) is a favorite site for drug deals and robberies. Avoid this area at night; more than a couple of murders have occurred here.

Beaches

The main attractions of Piñones are the wild beaches. To find a pretty beach for a picnic, you can't go wrong at almost any place where Hwy 187 parallels the coast. For swimming, avoid the corals at the west end of the beach. Unfortunately, this is where most of the food stands are, and it's where the bus from San Juan ends its route. Better swimming spots are about a mile farther to the east.

If you come by car, try not to park in a secluded area that's out of sight from your beach spot. Cars are highly vulnerable to a break-in or theft. The nearby forest groves have a sad collection of burned-out, stolen cars that testify to such goings-on.

A safer option is to park at one of the food vendors' shacks, patronize the place and ask the vendor to keep an eye on your car for a couple of dollars. Or do as the local surfers do: Travel in a pack and post a guard by your vehicle. Perhaps the best solution is to patronize the designated (but free) bathing beach at the east end of the forest.

Activities

If seeing a patch of the rarely viewed coastal wilderness catches your interest, you can join up with a kayak flotilla on a three-hour guided **ecotour** of the Laguna de Piñones. Not only does the lagoon feature fish, birds and the occasional manatee, but it also has the intact fuselage of a Convair 340 cargo plane that ditched here in 1998 after takeoff from San Juan's Aeropuerto Internacional de Luis Muñoz Marín (LMM) in the frenzy to resupply the island after Hurricane Georges. Copladet Nature & Adventure Tours in San Juan (☎ 787-765-8595) can hook you up for US$50.

If the **surfing** is good at Piñones, you will see rows of cars with board racks parked by a good break. Or you can check ahead with one of the San Juan surf shops before you go (see Surfing in the San Juan chapter).

Places to Eat

Although the ocean vistas, open-air seating and shade from the tall pine trees make the *food kiosks* a terrific place to kick back with a cold soft drink or beer, hygiene is not a top concern for vendors in Piñones. Be careful with what you eat here, particularly raw oysters, which may have been taken from contaminated waters. To be safe, get some hearty *criollo* cooking with an African flair at *El Pulpo Loco* (☎ 787-797-1747), the bright-yellow restaurant with shaded deck and sea view at the west end of the beach. Plain *mofongo* runs US$3.50. Local land crab with rice is US$11.

Getting There & Away

The M7 bus from Old San Juan, Condado and Isla Verde runs all the way to the settlement at the west end of the beach at Piñones. This is not a good place to end up, however, because you have to walk at least a mile farther east before you really get to some decent swimming beaches. Your best bet is to rent a car or catch a ride with a friend. Piñones is less than a 10-minute drive east of Isla Verde on Hwy 187.

LOÍZA ALDEA

Take Hwy 187 east from San Juan to catch some fresh air and rural scenery (and escape the hideous commerce and traffic jams on Hwy 3). The road eventually breaks out of the Piñones forest. When you cross a bridge spanning the island's largest river, the Río Grande de Loíza, the road brings you to the center of Loíza Aldea, commonly called 'Loíza.' This town is a largely rural municipality in the extensive coastal lowlands east of San Juan's LMM airport, and it includes Piñones as well as three other districts.

Loíza dates to 1719 and takes its name from the famous Taíno woman-warrior *cacique* Luisa, who controlled this fertile lowland when the Spanish arrived (see 'Woman Warriors' in the Facts about Puerto Rico chapter). But despite such a rich heritage, none of the settlements here is scenic, and most of the 29,000 residents (who are descendants of slaves) are poor. Compounding the problems of poverty, Hurricane Georges devastated Loíza in the fall of 1998, knocking down many structures and tearing roofs from about half of the houses in the community.

But what Loíza lacks in temporal bounty, it makes up for in its spirituality. At the plaza in Loíza, you will not only find the oldest active church on the island but also the site of the largest religious fiesta in Puerto Rico.

Things to See
The center of the town, known as **La Plaza**, is just east of the bridge over the Río Grande de Loíza. At the northern end of the plaza, **La Iglesia del Espiritu Santo y San Patricio** (Church of the Holy Ghost and St Patrick) appears every bit as proud and colonial as the cathedral in Old San Juan, and stands out from the humble collection of the surrounding modern buildings. The church dates from 1646 and took its name from the patron saint of Ireland to honor Puerto Rico's famous Irish mercenaries, who designed many of the fortifications of Old San Juan.

Special Events
Loíza has a fiesta celebrating St Patrick's Day (March 17), but the big event in this town is the Fiesta de Santiago. This is the town's *fiesta patronal* (patron saint's festival) and lasts nine days from the final week of July to early August. With its tradition of colorful costumes, devilish *vejigante* masks and superb *bomba y plena* drummers and singers, Loíza's fiesta patronal is probably the best-attended fiesta on the island outside of the capital's largely commercial Fiesta de San Juan Bautista.

Santiago (St James) became the patron saint of the Yoruba slaves in Loíza as a consequence of the religious syncretism that has come to be called Santería or *espiritismo* on the island (see the boxed text 'Concerning Spirits' in the Facts about Puerto Rico chapter). When the Spaniards and the Catholic church denied the African slaves the right to worship their Yoruba *orishas* (gods) and forced them to convert to Christianity, the Africans took consolation in finding that the story of some saints reminded them of legends associated with their orishas. In the case of the slaves in Loíza, the story of how Christ's follower St James descended from heaven as a vengeful warrior to help the Spaniards drive the Moorish rulers from Iberia reminded them of their proud god of thunder and lightning, Changó. So, under the guise of worshipping Santiago, the Africans worshipped Changó – and dreamed of liberation from their oppressors – drawing on their Yoruba customs of masking, ritualized drumming, entranced dancers and costumed clowns. The tradition continues to this day, focusing on parades celebrating three different effigies of St James.

And the crowds come – rich and poor, descendants of Spaniards and of slaves. They come to hear and feel the spectacle – and drink a lot of rum and beer. Sadly, as the festival has grown in popularity, it has lost much of its traditional meaning to the crowd. As one island woman from Old San Juan said,

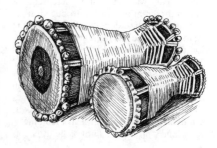

'I know it has something to do with my African roots. The music and the masks make me feel all stirred up inside – like happy and sad at the same time. But I don't know why.'

Visitors can learn why by visiting one of the *santero* priests, who read fortunes with broken pieces of coconut shells in the houses on the backroads of Loíza.

Getting There & Away

You can catch a *público* (shared taxi) to Loíza's plaza from Río Piedras in San Juan for about US$3, which is not a bad way to go during the Fiesta de Santiago, when traffic into Loíza on Hwy 187 and Hwy 188 can be more frightening than a vejigante mask. You will find públicos waiting in the plaza to return to Río Piedras, but usually only during daylight hours.

EL YUNQUE

The Caribbean National Forest in the bright-green Sierra de Luquillo mountains is popularly called El Yunque (pronounced 'El JOON-kay') for its distinctive peak, which rises about 3500 feet above sea level. This is the fabled home of the Taínos' protecting spirit, Yukiyú. Colonial Spaniards corrupted the name to El Yunque, which means 'the anvil' – a fair description of the peak when viewed from the north. Here you will find the only tropical rain forest in the US national forest system. Today, it covers approximately 43 sq miles and includes three-quarters of the island's remaining virgin forest. Some trees date back 1000 years.

El Yunque's history as a forest reserve began in 1876 when Spanish law protected the area, but under US management the forest's acreage was significantly increased, visitor and recreation areas introduced, trails cut and research stations developed. Over the years El Yunque has been designated as the Luquillo Experimental Forest and a United Nations Biosphere Reserve.

During September 1998, El Yunque suffered substantial destruction from winds in excess of 130mph when Hurricane Georges ripped across the island. In fact, the peak itself lived up to its Taíno role as the home of the island's protective spirit, actually 'steering' the eye of the hurricane to the south side of the island and away from the dense population centers of San Juan and the north coast.

Despite the damage, the forest is bouncing back. More than a million people visit a year, making this forest the most popular natural attraction on the island. And for good reason: The vegetation is Edenesque; the views of the valleys, Atlantic, Caribbean and eastern islands are inspiring; the temperatures are cool; the hiking is heart-pounding; and the streams and waterfalls are rejuvenating. Some people claim you can hear the voices of the ancient Taínos in the songs of the wind, the birds and the beloved *coquí* frogs.

Flora & Fauna

More than 240 species of trees and 1000 species of plants thrive here, including 50 kinds of orchids, as the area receives more than 200 inches of rain per year. Six major rivers trace their sources here. Most of the remaining population of the highly endangered Puerto Rican parrot – *el higuaca* – and more than 60 other species of birds live in El Yunque. The forest is also home to nine species of rare freshwater shrimp, the coquí frog, anole tree lizards, the 7-foot-long Puerto Rican boa and a substantial collection of forest rats.

Four forest zones define El Yunque. The *tabonuco* forest grows below 2000 feet and receives less than 100 inches of rain. This area is characterized by tall, straight trees such as the tabonuco and *ausubo*, many kinds of palms, epiphytes (including many orchids), flowers and aromatic shrubs.

The *palo colorado* forest grows above 2000 feet in the valleys and on gentle slopes. Here annual rainfall averages as much as 180 inches. This area is lush with ancient *colorado* trees (some more than 1000 years old), which make the nesting area for the Puerto Rican parrot. Vines and epiphytes hang from the trees.

Above 2500 feet, look for the sierra palm forest along the streams and on the steep valley slopes. The so-called mountain palm tree dominates here, with mostly ferns and mosses growing beneath.

The highest forest zone, the cloud forest, grows above 2500 feet and sees up to 200 inches of rain per year. Trees here are generally twisted from strong trade winds and are less than 12 feet tall (hence the term 'dwarf forest' commonly applied to this ecosystem). Mosses and lichens hang from trees and cover the forest floor. Red-flowering bromeliads stand out like beacons in the fog.

Orientation

You can see El Yunque from San Juan even though the mountain forest lies 25 miles to the southeast. Signs direct you from Hwy 3 to the intersection with two-lane Hwy 191, where you turn right (if coming from San Juan). Follow Hwy 191 through a neighborhood of the village of Mamayes (Palmer) and through rural pastures for about 3 miles. Just after the road starts to rise abruptly into the mountains, you enter the Caribbean National Forest. Shortly after the entrance are El Portal Tropical Forest Center and the offices at Catalina (where you can get camping permits; see Places to Stay, below).

All the forest's major attractions and trailheads appear as Hwy 191 twists, turns and climbs steeply on its way south toward the Palo Colorado Visitors Center, within a half mile of El Yunque summit. Just beyond the visitors center, Hwy 191 begins descending through the mountains toward the south side of the forest, but the road has been closed due to landslides. Mountain-bike enthusiasts get their workout on this largely untraveled section of road, which is the only route open to bikers within the forest.

If you plan on taking longer hikes or camping here, buy a copy of the waterproof Caribbean National Forest 'topo map' for US$9 (it's usually available at the visitors centers), or order it before you go from Trails Illustrated (☎ 303-670-3457, 800-962-1643), PO Box 4357, Evergreen, CO 80437-4357.

Information

See details on offerings at the forest's various visitors centers under Things to See & Do, below.

Barring closure due to maintenance or damage by storms, El Portal Tropical Forest Center is open 9 am to 5 pm daily except on Christmas. Admission to the forest is free, but it's US$3 to visit the center. This is a good place to get free basic maps and information on the forest. If you don't feel like paying the admission tariff or want to avoid crowds on weekends, head to one of the other visitors centers farther up the mountain, where you can pick up brochures and basic maps for free.

Signs throughout the forest are posted in both English and Spanish.

Things to See & Do

In addition to short and long hiking trails in El Yunque (see the boxed text), there are a few places directly accessible by road within the forest. Built in 1996 but ravaged by Hurricane Georges in 1998, **El Portal Tropical Forest Center** is once again open, and it remains the key for visitors who want to understand El Yunque and tropical rain forests in general. The facility has interactive exhibits, a 12-minute film in both English and Spanish, a walkway through the forest canopy, and a gift shop.

La Coca Falls is the first spectacular natural feature you see as Hwy 191 climbs south toward the forest peaks. There is an 85-foot cascade as the stream tumbles from a precipice to the right of the highway onto boulder formations.

Less than a half mile farther up the mountain, you see the 65-foot, Moorish-looking stone **Yokahú Tower**, which was built as a lookout in 1962. This is the first good place for vistas of the islands to the east, but there are better vantage points higher on the mountain. The tower often gets crowded with island tour groups. Pass it by unless you have a lot of time and the view to yourself.

The **Sierra Palm Visitors Center** is the first free visitors center on your way up the mountain. It is not always staffed, but its rest rooms are generally open for tour vans, and there is a picnic area.

Palo Colorado Visitors Center stands at Km 11.8 up the mountain, and it is worth enduring the switchbacks and steep road to get here. Most of the short and spectacular hiking trails leave from here. The picnicking

EL YUNQUE

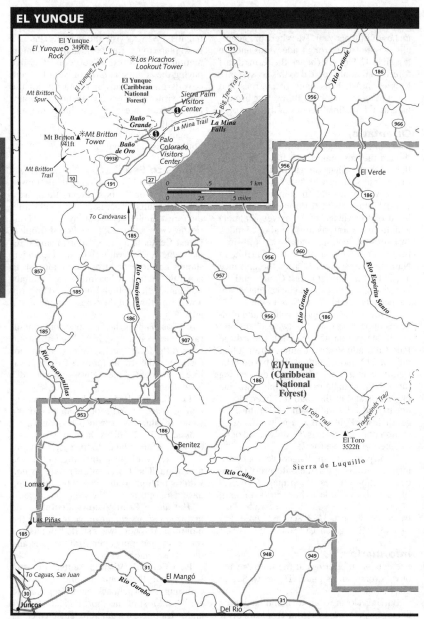

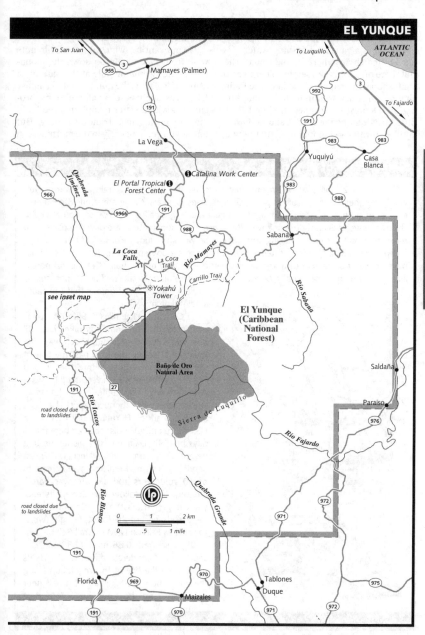

EL YUNQUE

To San Juan
955
3
Mamayes (Palmer)

ATLANTIC
OCEAN

To Luquillo

992
3

To Fajardo

191

191

983

983

La Vega

966

Quebrada Jiménez

El Portal Tropical
Forest Center

Catalina Work Center

Yuquiyú

Casa
Blanca

983

9966

191

988

988

La Coca
Falls

La Coca
Trail

Río Mamayes

Sabana

Río Sabana

see inset map

Carrillo Trail

Yokahú
Tower

El Yunque
(Caribbean
National
Forest)

191

27

Baño de Oro
Natural Area

Saldaña

road closed due
to landslides

Río Icacos

Sierra de Luquillo

Paraiso

976

Río Fajardo

road closed due
to landslides

Río Blanco

0   1   2 km

0   .5   1 mile

Quebrada Grande

972

971

EAST COAST

191

Florida

969

970

Maizales

970

Tablones
Duque

971

972

975

area – which includes a series of sheltered concrete platforms hidden in the jungle, overlooking a ravine of rushing water – is hard to match anywhere on the island. The staff here offers first-aid service. There's also a gift shop with maps and the like. The **Baño Grande**, a former swimming hole built during the Depression, lies across Hwy 191. A little farther along the road, **Baño de Oro** is another former swimming hole that now is

a very popular spot for photo opportunities with the tour-van crowd.

If you want to swim, take the 30-minute walk from Palo Colorado down the mountain to the swimming hole at the base of **La Mina Falls**. This is the quintessential Fantasy Island cascade you see in all the tourist brochures – with a water nymph in a red bathing suit posing in a tranquil setting. But unless you get here early in the morning, you

Hiking Trails of El Yunque

With at least 23 miles of well-maintained trails, plenty of rugged terrain and warm, wet, windy weather, El Yunque offers plenty of challenges to hikers. Come prepared with water, a change of clothes, a bathing suit, light rain gear and bug repellent. Of course, you will need sturdy footwear: Even though many of the short, more popular trails are paved in places and have steps on the steeps, walking surfaces can be wet and muddy. For longer treks, bring a compass or GPS navigator for satellite navigation, and a topographic map. Note that the trails have no water or trash or restroom facilities. Above all, stay on the trails. Getting lost here is as easy as daydreaming. Finally, be aware that some of the trails are lined with a particularly virulent variety of poison oak that can cause a painful, itchy rash.

La Coca Trail, 1.8 miles (2.9km), is a popular, moderate-to-strenuous hike that will take you a little over an hour each way. The trailhead is just up the road past the falls of the same name – just before the Yokahú Tower – and there is a small parking lot here. A fairly benign, low-altitude trail following streams through tabonuco forest, La Coca made its mark on El Yunque history when a US college professor disappeared here for 12 days in 1997, claiming after his rescue that he got off the trail and was lost. The Forest Service, which had enlisted a search party of 60 volunteers and aircraft, was hardly amused. If you follow La Coca to its end, you can go left (east) along **Carrillo Trail** to the eastern part of the forest, or right (west) to La Mina Falls on La Mina Trail (see below).

Big Tree Trail, 0.86 miles (1.38km), is a short trail of moderate difficulty. It gets its name from the size of the vegetation along the way. The walk takes about a half hour each way, and the route has interpretive

are more likely to find the swimming hole filled with Puerto Rican families.

Organized Tours

Most travelers come to the forest with a tour group from San Juan (see Organized Tours in the Getting Around chapter). In addition, the forest offers guided tours through the Rent-A-Ranger Program. Call for reservations (☎ 787-888-1880). It's US$35 for two hours.

Another alternative is to connect with one of the park's volunteer guides, who post themselves around the visitors centers, particularly Palo Colorado. Generally these volunteers are members of the local Boy Scout Explorer Post 919. They're knowledgeable and eager to practice their English. Jorge Dam (☎ 787-752-4266), the post's adviser, can arrange short or long guided hikes for you in advance. Sometimes he can come up with

---

Hiking Trails of El Yunque

signs along its route through tabonuco forest before ending at La Mina Falls. All these attractions make this probably the most popular trail in the park. The trailhead is at Km 10.4 on Hwy 191.

La Mina Trail, 0.7 miles (1.13km), is another popular walk. It leaves from Palo Colorado Visitors Center and heads downhill through palo colorado forest to join the Big Tree Trail at the falls. Mostly paved, this is an easy walk down but a bit of a hike back up.

If you are short on time and want to feel as if you have 'summited,' take the 45-minute climb up the **Mt Britton Trail**, 0.8 miles (1.29km) through mid-level types of vegetation into the cloud forest that surrounds this peak, which is named after a famous botanist who worked here. This is a continuous climb on paved surfaces to the Mt Britton Tower, built in the 1930s. The trailhead is at the side of Hwy 9938, which veers off Hwy 191 south of Palo Colorado. On weekends the trek up can get slowed by hikers who are physically unprepared but give it their best shot. Take a windbreaker for the rough weather on the summit.

For the more adventuresome and fit, the **Mt Britton Spur**, 0.86 miles (1.38km), connects El Yunque and Mt Britton in an invigorating walk, mostly through the cloud forest. The weather in this area (except early morning) is generally overcast and rainy, so be prepared.

The big enchilada for most visitors, the **El Yunque Trail**, 2.6 miles (4.18km), takes you to the top of El Yunque (3496 feet) in an hour and a half or longer. The trail is mostly paved or maintained gravel as you ascend through cloud forest to the observation deck, which is surrounded by microwave communication towers that transmit to the islands of Culebra and Vieques. If you want a rock scramble from here, take **Los Picachos Trail**, 0.17 miles (0.27km), to another old observation tower and feel as if you have crested a tropical Everest. Or climb Roca El Yunque, just to the south.

Serious backpackers and campers head west on **Tradewinds Trail**, 3.9 miles (6.28km). The trailhead is a bit hard to find. Park off the road near the locked gate on Hwy 191 south of Palo Colorado. Walk south on the road about a quarter of a mile until you see the trail leading from the right. Note that the trail is unmaintained and can be overgrown; bring clothes to protect your body. With four hours of strenuous trekking, you can reach the forest's highest summit, El Toro (3522 feet). This is a good place to pitch camp before hiking **El Toro Trail**, 2.2 miles (3.54km), another rugged path that leads through cloud forest and lower-level types of ecosystems along the western border of the forest near Hwy 186. These two trails are part of the National Recreational Trail System.

local accommodations, too. His prices are generally negotiable and reasonable.

Places to Stay

It's free to camp in the Caribbean National Forest, but you need a permit to do so. To get one, stop at the Catalina Work Center just after you enter the forest on Hwy 191. Camping is prohibited along many of the popular trails surrounding Palo Colorado Visitors Center and El Yunque peak. But don't be dismayed. You can camp in the wilder parts of the forest, including at its highest peak, El Toro, where it feels as if you have slipped into a primeval forest. Camping is all off-trail, and you must pack everything in and out. There are no water, trash or restroom facilities on the trails.

For less rustic accommodations in the area, see Luquillo & Environs, below.

Getting There & Away

No public transportation will carry you to El Yunque. If you don't come with a tour group, you can easily get here by car, but be aware that if you leave anything of value visible in your unattended car, it may provoke a theft or break-in. For highway directions, see Orientation, earlier in this section. Take note that some highway maps suggest that you can traverse the forest on Hwy 191 (or access El Yunque from the south via this route), but Hwy 191 south of the Palo Colorado center has been closed by landslides for years.

LUQUILLO & ENVIRONS

Calling itself the 'Puerto Rican Riviera' and the 'Capital of Sun,' Luquillo raises high expectations for travelers who have endured the traffic, pharmaceutical plants and endless strip malls as they venture east of San Juan and Loíza on Hwy 3. That Luquillo cannot live up to its grandiose promotional slogans almost goes without saying. Though Luquillo is by no means St Tropez, it is more cosmopolitan than most other resort towns on the island. And the town is literally a breath of fresh air after what you have to travel through to get here.

This community of almost 20,000 is a vast municipality that stretches all the way from the Atlantic Ocean to the edge of the Caribbean National Forest. But for most people, Luquillo's main draw is the long crescent public beach of Playa Luquillo, the associated phalanx of food kiosks and the compact urban center about a half mile away facing Playa Azul (Blue Beach). The town has a substantial collection of condo towers and vacation villas that draw a large number of long-term gringo residents in the winter and *sanjuaneros* vacationing in the summer. In addition, Luquillo is a favorite playground of off-duty US Navy personnel escaping life on the nearby Roosevelt Roads base. Four of the best golf courses on the island lie just a few miles west of town in Río Grande, which is also the sight of the new Westin Río Mar Beach Resort and Country Club.

Beaches

Although Luquillo traces its name and history to a valorous Taíno cacique and a Spanish settlement in 1797, nothing of historic value remains in the town, and almost everything you see dates from the mid-20th century or later.

Here, the beaches are the main draw. The *balneario* at **Playa Luquillo** defies the stereotype of public beaches as second-rate real estate packed with hordes of people and cluttered with trash. Set on a bay facing northwest – and therefore protected from the easterly trade winds and seas – the public part of this beach stretches in a mile-long arc to a point of sand shaded by tall coconut palms. The beach itself is a plain of broad, gently sloping white sand that continues its gradual slope below the water. Of course, the beach gets crowded on weekends, but during the week (except during school vacations) the balneario remains remarkably tranquil. There is a bathhouse, refreshment stand and security patrol. Unlike the staff and clientele at some of the island's other balnearios, those who care for and use this beach seem to take exceptional pride in keeping it trash-free. Admission is free, but parking costs US$2.

You do not have to park in the balneario lot if you want to visit the beach. Playa Luquillo extends at least another half mile to the west. If you pull off Hwy 3 by the long row of food kiosks – sometimes called *friquitines* – you can drive around to the ocean side of the stalls and park under the palms, just a few steps from the beach and more cold beer and *pastelillos* than you could consume in a year.

When this beach gets too busy, head for **Playa Azul**, east of here around the headland, on the threshold of the town proper. While more exposed to the trade winds and seas, Playa Azul is just as broad, white and gently sloping as the balneario. The crowd here is a mix of locals and folks from the condo developments. A hearty contingent of surfers hang at the east end of this beach – known as 'La Pared' (the Wall) – waiting for a flood tide and offshore breeze to glass off a 3-foot break.

Surfing
Bob and Susan Roberts have been operating La Selva Surf Shop (☎ 787-899-6205), 250 Calle Fernández García, for 18 years. This is a well-stocked, friendly place that rents surfboards and body boards and offers the latest on surf conditions at La Pared, La Selva (farther east) and around the Humacao area to the south.

Kayaking
If there is good weather, you will see the truck for Playa Azul Lagoon & Sea (☎ 787-776-0483) renting kayaks at the west end of Playa Azul. They cost US$10 per hour or US$30 a day.

For a guided kayak tour along the coast, check out a host of different day and night options beginning at US$45 from Aqua Sports (☎ 787-888-8841), a mobile operation out of Fajardo.

Diving & Snorkeling
You can join a dive trip or rent certified snorkeling gear through Divers Outlet (☎ 787-889-5721), 38 Calle Fernández García.

Golf
Visitors can play at the Bahía Beach Public Golf Course (☎ 787-256-5600). Greens fees are US$75 in the morning, US$50 after 1 pm

and US$30 after 3 pm. The Berwind Country Club (☎ 787-876-3056), on Hwy 187 in Río Grande, is open to the public weekdays. The US$50 greens fee includes a golf cart.

The Westin Río Mar Beach Resort and Country Club (☎ 787-888-8811) has two courses open to hotel guests only: the Greg Norman River Course and the Tom and George Fazio Ocean Course.

Horseback Riding
For more than a decade, the Hacienda Carabaldi (☎ 787-889-5820), on Hwy 992 south of town, has offered trail rides on Paso Fino horses along the Río Mameyes and into the foothills of the rain forest, with time-out for swimming and a picnic. Prices start at US$20 adults, US$10 children for an hour.

Places to Stay
Camping The *balneario* (☎ 787-721-2800 ext 1545) at Playa Luquillo has more than 30 campsites and a bathhouse. Sites are US$13, or US$16 with power hookups.

If you really want to get away from everything, the *Grateful Bed & Breakfast* (see below) also has campsites.

Guesthouses Rooms in one of the two houses at the legendary *Grateful Bed & Breakfast* (☎ 787-889-4919) go for about US$70 with a hearty breakfast included. You can also camp here for US$15 – and even rent a tent for US$5. But the best thing about this place is your host, Marty, who says that the fee you pay includes help in planning your itinerary, whether it be for hiking in El Yunque or water sports. While this place is not exactly a hippie commune or a crash pad for Deadheads, it does evoke memories of Woodstock, man.

An inn near the beach, *Parador Martorell* (☎ 787-889-2710, 35A Ocean View) is a block off Playa Azul in Luquillo and has only 11 units. Doubles with bath, air con, cable and continental breakfast run US$70.

An extraordinary place, the *Casa de Vida Natural* (☎ 787-887-4359), off Hwy 186 west of Luquillo in Río Grande, is a combination of B&B, health spa and spiritual center. Rooms run US$80 and up. You can meditate here with visiting yogi, get your colon flushed for US$50, have a mud bath and eat veggies all day long.

Le Petite Chalet (☎ 787-887-5802) is also on the backroads of Río Grande, with a pastoral setting and rooms for around US$75.

Hotels The *Westin Río Mar Beach and Country Club* (☎ 787-888-6000), north on Hwy 968 off Hwy 3 between Río Grande and Luquillo, is the newest player in the mega-resort trade on the island. This 600-unit high-rise facility in Río Grande opened on almost 500 acres of former plantation to a lot of fanfare in 1996. The resort tries to capitalize on the convention trade as well as ecotourism at nearby El Yunque. Rack rates vary from US$250 to US$2500 a night, but you can stay here for a lot less if you buy a vacation or convention package.

Rental Agents Doris Ramírez at *Playa Azul Apartments Realty* (☎ 787-889-3425) has her office across the street from El Flamboyán Café on Calle A, and she is doing a brisk business renting modern condos and townhouses in the surrounding vacation properties. Studios in high season start at US$57 a day, US$400 a week, US$1000 a month.

You could also call *Coral Beach Apartment Rentals* (☎ 787-889-2757).

Places to Eat
La Parilla, at kiosk No 2, stands out among the 20 or so rundown food stalls in the long line of kiosks at Playa Luquillo. This well-scrubbed, attractive place opens to the beach as well as the highway, with a deck providing shady tables in the sea breeze. The cooking and prices live up to the style. You can get a *pastelillo de chapin* (fried-fish pie) for US$1. Beer costs US$1.50. Mofongo stuffed with conch is US$9.50.

At the west end of town, *Greek Express* (☎ 787-889-4568), on Calle A in Playa Azul IV development, is another sparkling-clean place with cheap eats. You can get a full breakfast here from Nick Theologis for US$2.50 or turkey sub with salad for US$3.50.

Across the street, the *Swiss Village Café* (☎ 787-889-0276) is actually a modern bakery, with espresso for just 55¢ and a *quesito* (pastry stuffed with sweet ricotta cheese) for 90¢.

Victor's Place (☎ 787-889-5705) is a nice, small seafood restaurant next to the church on the plaza. Daily specials of criollo dishes include shrimp *empanadillas*, *tostones* and salad for US$4.

The most popular restaurant in town is *Sandy's* (☎ 787-889-5765, 276 Calle Fernández García). You can buy a burger for US$1.50, or go over the top with jalapeño peppers stuffed with shrimp or lobster for US$10.

The Mexican meals at *Lolita's* (☎ 787-889-5770), at Km 4.8 about 3 miles east of town on the south side of Hwy 3, are so popular that the owners recently moved into a building twice the original size. A soft taco costs US$1.50, and most dinners run under US$6. Imported Mexican mariachis provide the music.

Entertainment
Although you only have two options here, Luquillo is far from dull. *El Flamboyán Café* (☎ 787-889-2928), on Calle A at the west end of town, calls itself a 'cafeteria and game room.' What this means is that this wide-open patio bar has nine busy pool tables, and serves food to the gang that shows up to drink US$1 Coors. The crowd is mostly local, but both short-term and long-term expats drift in.

More gringos mix with the young, upscale local crowd just up the street at Mike McTall's *Brass Cactus* (☎ 787-889-5789). While this is a restaurant serving American pub fare on the order of Dunbar's in Ocean Park in San Juan, the Cactus does a quick change into a club with live music from 11 pm to 3 am Thursday to Saturday, when there's a US$5 cover with one drink included. Expect to meet some military types here, such as the crew of the AWACS C-130 who signed the picture of their plane.

Getting There & Away
From the capital, you can take a público (US$4) to and from the Luquillo plaza, but you really need a car to get around. Suffer the 45-minute drive from San Juan on Hwy 3 or

pray that the new expressway Hwy 66 opens sometime before you get here.

FAJARDO & ENVIRONS

Twenty-five years ago, this municipality on the northeast tip of Puerto Rico was an outpost for fishermen sailing after conch, lobster and *chillo* (red snapper) in their graceful 25- to 30-foot *nativos* (native sloops), which bear a close resemblance to the fishing smacks you still see in the Bahamas and Haiti. About half a dozen of these craft still sail out of the small harbor at Las Croabas neighborhood at the north end of town; today the nativos no longer carry fish, but passengers on picnic and snorkeling adventures.

Fajardo has a population of more than 36,000 and looks like an unplanned, dusty sprawl of shops, modest houses, marinas, vacation homes for islanders, and two shopping malls. Travelers seeing this on their way to the ferry docks (to head for the islands of Culebra and Vieques) might think that Fajardo is a town to get clear of as soon as possible. Nevertheless, you might want to pause here and look around: Some sections of the municipality still harbor extraordinary natural beauty and tranquillity, and every segment of Fajardo's irregular coastline can be the jumping-off point for a different adventure.

Las Cabezas de San Juan

This nature reserve on the northeast tip of Puerto Rico certainly deserves its title (San Juan Headlands). Here a peninsula of more than 500 acres strikes out from the end of two-lane Hwy 987 like a wedge between the Atlantic and the Sonda de Vieques (Vieques Sound). On the tip of this peninsula – part of Fajardo's Las Croabas neighborhood – you find steep, craggy cliffs crested by a restored 19th-century lighthouse.

Rescued from development by the Conservation Trust of Puerto Rico and the Depto de Recursos Naturales (Dept of Natural Resources) in the mid-1980s, Las Cabezas (☎ 787-722-5882) offers glimpses of almost all the island's ecosystems, from mangrove lagoon to dry forest to coconut plantation and coral reef.

About 2 miles of trails and boardwalks lead you through the park, but you cannot follow them on your own. You must have a guided tour, and you will probably be carted from place to place aboard a motorized trolley. Be aware that the reserve is only open to the general public Friday to Sunday, and you must make reservations in advance. There are tours in Spanish at 9:30 and 10 am and 2 pm. The only tour in English runs at 2 pm, and it can get hot. Admission, including the tour, is US$5 adults, US$2 children.

The tour, however, is not the only way to see Las Cabezas. You can get a glimpse of some of the reserve by simply walking east down the narrow beach from the Playa Seven Seas. Better yet, take a kayak tour (see Kayaking, below) around the headlands and reefs at sunset, and head into Laguna Grande after dark for the green-glowing 'fireworks' of bioluminescent microorganisms in the water.

Coming from San Juan or Luquillo, you can reach Las Cabezas (as well as the other attractions in the vicinity of Las Croabas) directly and avoid the traffic in Fajardo. Take four-lane Hwy 194 east from Hwy 3. At the Monte Brisas Shopping Center traffic light, turn left. Turn right at the next traffic light and follow this road until it intersects with two-lane Hwy 987, then turn left (north). Las Cabezas, plus the balneario, Bahía Las Croabas, and many restaurants and accommodations, lie along a 2-mile stretch of this road.

Playa Seven Seas

This is another sheltered, coconut-shaded, protected horseshoe public beach. While it may not be quite as pretty as Playa Luquillo, fear not – it is attractive. Admission is free; parking is US$2. The beach, on the southwestern shore of the peninsula of Las Cabezas, gets packed on weekends and during the summer; the rest of the time it is very tranquil (for directions, see Las Cabezas de San Juan, above).

For good snorkeling or to get off by yourself, follow the beach about a half mile to the east along the Las Cabezas property to an area known as **Playa Escondido** (Hidden Beach). The reefs are just offshore.

La Cordillera

More daring snorkelers or divers may want to rent a boat, take a kayak or book a sailing and diving tour from one of the local marinas or vendors to the islands and reefs that head east from Las Cabezas. This marine sanctuary, known as La Cordillera (the Spine), has some of the clearest, calmest water in Puerto Rico. Not only is the area alive with reef fish and lobsters, but you can see moray eels and sea turtles here. Bird colonies share the islets with reptiles such as the crested iguana.

Bahía Las Croabas

You find this spot where Hwy 987 ends at a little seaside park rimmed by funky seafood restaurants and bars looking east across the water to the cays of La Cordillera and the peaks of Culebra. There is really not much of a beach here, but the view is grand and the air blows fresh with the trade winds. The small anchorage accommodates the fishermen's co-op and the last half-dozen nativos, the graceful 'out-island' sloops that everyone around here once used for fishing and gathering conch or lobster. The fishermen here are friendly, and you can probably strike a deal with one of them for a boat ride, a trip to snorkel La Cordillera or a sail aboard a fast, able and over-canvassed (lots of sail!) nativo.

If you are in a less adventuresome mood, the bars and restaurants here are a good place to kick back with a US$1.50 beer and enjoy the same view as from the exclusive El Conquistador Resort, which is virtually just next door.

Puerto del Rey

This 750-slip marina (☎ 787-860-1000) stands behind a breakwater in a cove about 2 miles south of Fajardo. It is the largest marina on the island (and perhaps in the Caribbean). You will find a complete marina village here with restaurants, stores, laundry facilities, banking and all manner of boat-hauling and maintenance capabilities. Many yachts stop here to take advantage of the marina's courtesy car and Fajardo's inexpensive supermarkets when stocking up for a winter in the

Going Native

If you want to get a feel for how Caribbean islanders got around and fished these waters during the last 200 years, head for Bahía Las Croabas. Here the 30-foot nativo sloops, such as *Lazaro* and *Angel Negro*, swing to their moorings, and the skippers gather with their coffee every morning at the fishermen's co-op.

The going rate for a full day of sailing, snorkeling and picnicking is US$80 for six people. If business is slow, you might even make a deal with one of the captains as long as you are respectful. Try to use your Spanish and show interest in these indigenous wooden craft.

To plan in advance, Captain Freddie Rodríguez (☎ 787-863-2471) is one of the captains you can usually reach by phone.

tropics or the ride back home to the USA. Travelers will find that many of the sailing, diving and fishing charters run from here.

Boating

Almost all sailing trips advertised for travelers on the island actually sail out of one of the marinas in Fajardo. Six-hour sailing, snorkeling and picnicking trips usually cost US$55. Your only choice here is whether you want a small boat or a larger boat, a monohull or a high-speed catamaran. Here is a list of operators:

Camonix Catamaran	☎ 787-860-4421
Captain Jack's Getaway	☎ 787-887-4818
Captain Jack's Spread Eagle	☎ 787-863-1905
East Wind II	☎ 787-860-3434
Erin Go Bragh Charters	☎ 787-860-4401
Fajardo Tours Traveler	☎ 787-863-2821

More serious cruisers may want to rent a 'bareboat' (sail-it-yourself) from Sun Yachts (☎ 787-863-4813, 888-772-3502, sunyacht@prtc.net), at the Puerto del Rey marina. It offers its fleet of 36- to 51-foot boats for

US$1680 to US$5390 a week to experienced sailors who want to cruise La Cordillera, the islands of Culebra and Vieques, and the associated cays.

You can rent an outboard or sportfishing boat from Club Náutico International (☎ 787-860-2400), at Villa Marina Yacht Harbor, on Hwy 987 to Las Croabas. Plan on spending at least US$70 a day for the smallest boat.

Kayaking

Blackbeard West Indies Charters (☎ 787-887-4818) rents kayaks for about US$15 an hour, with lower rates for longer periods.

Aqua Sports (☎ 787-888-8841, 374-3723 cellular) offers guided flotilla trips to La Cordillera cays for snorkeling and a sunset trip around Las Cabezas and into the bioluminescent Laguna Grande, where microorganisms glow in the dark water (see 'Bright Lights, Black Water' in the South Coast chapter for more on this phenomenon). Rates are US$45 per person in a single, US$35 in a double. Aqua Sports also rents Jet Skis and leads Jet Ski tours for around US$70.

Fishing

There is plenty of Spanish mackerel in the Sonda de Vieques, and marlin and tuna farther offshore. Two respected local sportfishing operators running out of the marinas around Fajardo are Blackbeard West Indies Charters (☎ 787-887-4818) and Tropical Fishing & Tournaments (☎ 787-860-8551). Expect to pay about US$350 for a half day, US$500 for the day.

Diving

If you want to strap on a tank and collect some lobsters, call Palomina Island Divers (☎ 787-863-1000) or Sea Ventures Pro Dive Center (☎ 800-739-3483). One tank runs about US$40, two tanks US$70.

Golf

Only hotel guests can play at the 6632-yard course designed for the El Conquistador Resort & Country Club (☎ 787-863-1000) by Arthur Hills. Greens fee? If you have to ask, you probably can't afford it. (Try US$165 for 18 holes before 2 pm, US$95 after 2 pm.)

Places to Stay

Camping The *Playa Seven Seas* (☎ 787-863-8180) has tent sites on the beach for US$10, but make sure you reserve in advance if you plan to come during the summer or holidays.

Guesthouses If you get stuck at the ferry dock overnight, you can try the *Hotel Delicias* (☎ 787-863-1818), which is just a short block from the terminal. It has 21 rooms with private bath, air con, TV, telephone and rates starting as low as US$40 for a single. But this is a grim place in a grim neighborhood, and the staff can be indifferent to the guests.

Nearby, on the road to the ferry terminal, the tiny *Puerto Real Guest House* (☎ 787-863-0018) wasn't open the last time we were in Fajardo. Basic rooms should run about US$35.

Gregarious José Cruz runs the *Anchor Inn* (☎ 787-863-7200) at Km 2.5 on Hwy 987 on the way to Las Croabas from Fajardo. All rooms have a private bath, air con and TV. Rates start at US$55. Jose also has a beach apartment going for US$85.

La Familia (☎ 787-863-11930), at Km 4.1 on Hwy 987, is in a valley that overlooks the golf course at El Conquistador Resort, a mile from the beach. All 28 rooms have the usual amenities, and there is a small pool with a sun deck. Singles run US$69.

The *Fajardo Inn* (☎ 787-860-6000) is an attractive new hacienda-style parador on the hill overlooking the road to the ferry terminal, in the Puerto Real section of town. There are 42 units with all the modern conveniences, and some include kitchenettes. The location and ambience here make this more of a business traveler's oasis than a holiday site. Rates run US$75 to US$90.

An interesting mountain retreat nearby, the *Ceiba Country Inn* (☎ 787-885-0471) has nine units overlooking the Caribbean and the offshore islands. Picture a landscaped hillside villa with decks, BBQ grill, continental breakfast and lounge for US$70. To get there, go west on Hwy 997 from either Hwy 53 or Hwy 3 in Ceiba.

Hotels *El Conquistador Resort & Country Club* (☎ 800-468-8365) lies through the guarded gate off Hwy 987 on the way to Las Croabas. Or put another way, this 900-unit mega-resort dominates the crest of a hill looking out over its own cove to the Sonda de Vieques just south of Las Cabezas. There is even a tram that takes you down to the waterfront, and shuttle boats to carry guests out to Isla Palominos in La Cordillera. With 16 restaurants, golf, tennis courts, a spa, water sports and a casino, this 'complete destination resort' has rates starting at about US$300 and rising to US$3000. Go crazy.

Places to Eat
The most interesting places to eat in Fajardo lie along the road to Las Croabas (Hwy 987).

The *Anchor Inn* (see Places to Stay, above) has a big dining room specializing in lobster dishes that usually cost about US$22. But you can go light here with a chef's salad for about US$8.

Among the open-air bar-restaurants you see when you get to the end of the road at Bahía Las Croabas, check out *El Picazo,* where fried-fish balls cost just US$1 and the beer is about the same at happy hour.

Restaurant Croabas has grilled fish for US$8, octopus salad for US$9. *Rocar Seafood* has similar prices.

At the Puerto del Rey marina, you can sit outside with a view of the yachts and sound at *Portofino (☎ 787-860-1000 ext 4330)* or order Italian take-out. Pizza starts at US$11.50; a half-chicken with fries and garlic bread is US$6.

The marina's upscale restaurant is *La Banda (☎ 787-860-1000 ext 2443)*, where you can get lasagna or eggplant parmigiana for US$12. Beef or fish costs more.

If you get hungry waiting for the ferry, head across the street from the terminal to *Restaurante Culebra y Vieques*. This is a popular breakfast spot, with two eggs, toast and coffee for US$2.

Entertainment
The *Anchor Inn* (see Places to Stay, above) can get fired up on weekend nights when salsa, merengue or Latin rock groups perform here.

Shopping
The malls are on Hwy 3 just north of town if you need a supermarket, Blockbuster Video, Payless Shoes or Wal-Mart fix.

Getting There & Away
Air The small Aeropuerto de Fajardo lies west of town near the intersection of Hwy 3 and Hwy 976.

Vieques Air Link (☎ 787-741-3266, 888-901-9247 for San Juan-Vieques flights only, 787-722-3736 for Culebra flights) has three flights a day between Fajardo and the Spanish Virgin Islands of Culebra and Vieques. Fajardo-Vieques flights are US$35 roundtrip, US$18 one-way; Fajardo-Culebra is US$40 roundtrip, US$20 one-way. All aircraft are Islander twins or tri-motor Trilanders.

Público The main público stop is off the plaza in the center of town, but you will also find públicos at the ferry terminal and – during the summer and weekends – near the seafood restaurants in Las Croabas. Many of the públicos you find at the ferry terminal will take you to and from the Río Piedras section of San Juan for about US$10. You can get to Las Croabas for US$2; a trip south to Humacao is less than US$5.

Car If your destination is Fajardo and you are not intent on touring the island in a clockwise fashion from San Juan, you can save yourself the aggravating drive on Hwy 3 via Carolina and Luquillo by taking the four-lane expressway drive from San Juan: Hwy 52 to Caguas, then Hwy 30 to Humacao, and finally Hwy 53 north to Fajardo. Two of these roads require paying tolls intermittently at toll stations along the highway; expect to pay about US$3 total from San Juan to Fajardo.

Taxi You can always find taxis at the ferry terminal to take you to LMM airport in San Juan. The going rate is about US$55, but you might get this ride for US$40 if you call José Padin (☎ 787-887-7106, 308-2676 cellular), who runs a well-maintained van.

Ferry The Port Authority terminal (☎ 787-863-0705, 800-981-2005) for the Culebra and

Vieques ferries is about 1¹/₂ miles east of town in the run-down Playa de Fajardo/ Puerto Real neighborhood (follow the signs to either). For the ferry schedule, see the Ferry sections in the Spanish Virgin Islands chapter.

You will find two relatively secure parking lots a block from the ferry terminal that charge US$3 a day. The parking attendants may try to hit you up for an extra day, saying their definition of a 'day' is a date on the calendar, not 24 hours. In other words, if you leave a car here from 5 pm on Monday until 9 am Wednesday (just 40 hours), the attendant might charge you for three days. They tend to back off demanding money for a third day if you call their bluff, but you must have good Spanish and be persistent.

ROOSEVELT ROADS
With 8000 acres of land on the eastern tip of Puerto Rico just south of Fajardo – and an additional 25,000 acres of land on the off-shore island of Vieques – Naval Station Roosevelt Roads is the largest naval base (in terms of land area) in the world. Calling itself the 'Gateway to the Caribbean' in official publications and 'Rosie Roads' in everyday parlance, this base has a military population of 2500 and employs an equal number of local civilians. There are about 30 tenant commands on base, including Commander Fleet Air Caribbean, Commander South Atlantic Force, US Atlantic Fleet, the Atlantic Fleet Weapons Training Facility and the Naval Special Warfare Unit (the SEALs, or 'frog warriors').

No ships are actually based here, except a Coast Guard patrol boat squadron, but it is not uncommon to see an aircraft carrier with her associated battle group patrolling just off the coast, and major warships tied up at the piers for servicing. The 11,000-foot runway accommodates aircraft as large as the mammoth C-5As. While the airfield functions largely as a defense and training facility, it also serves as the principal relief and supply facility to Puerto Rico, other Caribbean Islands and even Central America after natural disasters, such as the recent killer hurricanes.

In many ways Rosie Roads is a scary place, yet it is amazing to see the base's capacity to do good. Following the 1998 hurricanes of Georges and Mitch, which ravaged the Greater Antilles and Central America, air transport and helicopter flights moved in and out of Rosie with medicine, food, water and temporary shelters. US tax dollars were spent on butter, not guns.

Roosevelt Roads, just south of Ceiba, is accessible by car by Hwy 3 or Hwy 53.

PLAYA NAGUABO & ENVIRONS
The new Hwy 53 toll road whisks most travelers away from the coast south of Fajardo and the Roosevelt Roads naval base. But if you get off the expressway, Hwy 3 will carry you south through cane fields until you find yourself in a small, tidy seaside village called Playa Naguabo. Here, a steep rock headland and the offshore island of Cayo Santiago define a dramatic bay that looks out toward the island of Vieques, 10 miles to sea.

While not Portofino, Italy, or Nantucket Town, Massachusetts, Playa Naguabo has more architectural charm than most Puerto Rican towns because of some well-positioned Victorian homes that stand like sentinels on the waterfront, such as the **Castillo Villa del Mar** (on the National Registry of Historic Places). The heart of the village has a *malecón* (waterfront promenade) with better vistas and breezes than San Juan's Paseo de la Princesa, plus a line of open-air seafood restaurants just across the street. The fishermen's cooperative and the red, white and blue launches dancing at the moorings provide the fresh chillo and *sierra* (kingfish) you smell grilling at the restaurants.

The actual waterfront of the town is rock seawall, and you will wonder why the founders ever called this place a *playa* (beach) until you follow Hwy 3 a half mile farther south, where you'll see about 2 miles of thin, tree-lined, vacant beach. Beyond this the road carries you into the low, dirty and impoverished village of **Playa Humacao**. This community obviously developed as an inexpensive seaside oasis for the more than 55,000 people who swarm the malls, factories and asphalt jungle of the city of Humacao just 5 miles inland. Dilapidated and unloved, Playa Humacao was severely battered by Hurricane Georges and is recovering more slowly than almost any other place on the island's coast. The one bright light here is the absolutely pristine balneario and the well-maintained *centro vacacional* (vacation center) at the **Punta Santiago** neighborhood south of the village.

Cayo Santiago

Lying about a mile offshore, this peaked, hazy island of 39 acres has been the source of mystery and entertainment since 1939, when primate researchers brought a troupe of rhesus monkeys and created a self-contained community for research. Today, more than 700 animals live on the island and are constantly studied by a gaggle of scientists from the Caribbean Primate Research Center, part of the University of Puerto Rico.

To a large degree, these tagged and numbered animals have been watched and videotaped by researchers interested in the social behavior the primates develop during their lifetime. But the animals have also been used in medical research for illnesses such as arthritis and diabetes.

No visitors are permitted on Cayo Santiago, but you can see the monkeys cavorting on the shore if you take a diving or snorkeling trip to the fringes of the island. Capt Frank Lopez (☎ 787-850-7881) offers fishing or snorkeling trips and sea excursions. Prices are negotiable: Start your bidding at about US$25. The Palmas del Mar resort also offers diving trips to the area (see the Humacao section, below).

Places to Stay & Eat

Centro Vacacional Punta Santiago (☎ 787-852-1660), at Km 72.4 on Hwy 3 in Playa Humacao, has a public balneario and more than 30 cabanas and condo-style duplex cottages in a coconut grove on a pristine beach. These rent for US$64 a night.

There are also more than 40 campsites here, which rent for US$10, US$20 with hookups. Make reservations through the central San Juan office of the Recreational Development Company (☎ 787-853-1660).

The *Casa Cubuy Ecolodge* (☎ 787-874-62210), in Río Blanco about 4 miles west of Naguabo on Hwy 31, has hiking trails and bathing streams right on the property. You can also get massages here. Expect to pay at least US$75 for a double.

Among the open-air seafood restaurants facing the promenade in Playa Naguabo, *Bobby's Place* (☎ 787-643-0058) stands out for its friendliness, fresh food and reasonable prices. A plate filled with grilled kingfish, coleslaw and coconut-flavored *arepas* costs US$6.

Getting There & Away

The público vans in Playa Naguabo park near the promenade. They go to Naguabo (US$1) or Humacao (US$2), from whence you can move on to the greener pastures of Fajardo or San Juan.

By car, follow Hwy 3 if you are traveling the coast from San Juan or Fajardo. You can also take the Hwy 53 toll road, then Hwy 192 from Naguabo to Playa Naguabo.

HUMACAO

Like Bayamón, Fajardo and so many other old island towns, Humacao has grown into a city thanks to the urban population explosion brought on by Operation Bootstrap and the industrialization of Puerto Rico. Really, it is not worth braving the traffic, heat and pollution from auto emissions to find the narrow streets, shady plaza and the few historical buildings that may once have given Humacao some charm. For the affluent traveler, the attractions of this town of about 20,000 really lie in the well-known Palmas del Mar mega-resort nearby, which – as a thoughtfully planned leisure community – stands in sharp contrast to the city pushing toward its gates.

Palmas del Mar

Set on more than 2700 acres of former coconut and sugarcane plantations, the *Wyndham Palmas del Mar Resort* (☎ 787-852-6000, 800-725-6273), off Hwy 3 about 5 miles south of Humacao, really is a world unto itself. There are banks, real estate offices and a shopping center, as well as police, fire and medical facilities. All this is dedicated to people living the life of leisure for either a week or a lifetime.

The core of this resort consists of privately owned villas and time-share units built around a marina, beach and golf course. But there are a casino and two hotels here as well: the Candelero and the Palmas Inn, with more than 120 rooms. Surprisingly, rates start as (relatively) low as US$166, and you may do better if you get a golf or tennis package.

Palmas, with its Iberian architecture, looks a lot like one of those resort communities that you see in southern Spain or the Balearic Islands. Here you get a total fantasy island experience where tan, attractive people ride around on golf carts, speedboats or horses.

Unlike some of the other mega-resorts on the island, Palmas does not totally lock the public out. As long as you have a destination, such as one of the sports facilities, you can enter the property.

Diving Coral Head Divers (☎ 800-635-4529) is one of the most experienced dive operations on the island. They operate out of the Marina de Palmas and will take you to Cayo Santiago and the deeper sites offshore. It's US$45 for a one-tank dive.

Golf You can make reservations at either of the resort's two courses (☎ 787-285-2256). The greens fee for the newer, 6800-yard Gary Player course is US$155 for nonguests; the old course (called 'the Palms') is US$140.

Tennis There are 20 courts here, but you will need reservations (☎ 787-852-6000 ext 51). Court fees are US$22 an hour during the day, US$26 at night.

Horseback Riding The Rancho Buena Vista (☎ 787-852-6000 ext 10310) boards about 40 horses, including hunters and jumpers. One-hour-plus trail rides cost about US$40; it's closed on Monday.

Getting There & Away The resort will arrange for a minivan to haul you to and from LMM airport in San Juan, about a 40-minute trip in normal traffic. During peak season the scheduled trip is US$25 a person; otherwise it's US$72 for one to four people.

The entrance to Palmas is a well-marked road off Hwy 3 a couple of miles south of Humacao. Driving from San Juan, take Hwy 52 south to Caguas and Hwy 30 to Humacao – all expressway, toll-road driving.

YABUCOA & ENVIRONS

If you are traveling south from the Humacao area, take the Hwy 53 toll road to avoid the traffic on Hwy 3. The expressway is your escape route to fresh air and a sense of open space, as this lightly traveled section of road bisects miles of sugarcane fields and estuary where three mountain rivers meet east of Yabucoa. The scenery gets grand here as the steep, forested mountains of the Cuchilla de Panduras stretch right to the water's edge. The town of Yabucoa lies in the uplands between the mountains and the estuary, perfectly poised to be the processing and distribution point for the coffee grown on the mountain slopes to the north and the sugarcane raised in the lowlands to the south.

The actual town of Yabucoa has nothing to offer the traveler but traffic jams (don't even think of trying to get through here in a hurry on a Saturday), plus a chance to provision and refuel. And the serenity of the adjoining estuary and its bay have been marred by an oil tanker facility called Puerta Yabucoa and a Phillips Oil refinery whose tanks and towers rise from the cane like hissing, metallic tombstones.

However, travelers will enjoy area attractions, including the public beach at Playa Lucía, the old haciendas and the lighthouse.

Things to See & Do

The balneario at **Playa Lucía**, near the intersection of Hwys 901 and 9911 in Yabucoa, has great shade under its coconut trees and several little beach-bar/restaurants just off its premises. Parking is US$2. **El Cocal** is one of the few good surfing spots in the area (ask for directions at the balneario).

There are many things to see off Hwy 901 along the coast (see Scenic Drives, below). You can explore the ruins of **Hacienda de Santa Lucía**, an old sugar plantation, about a mile north of Playa Lucía off Hwy 901. **Central Roig** is the still active but old-time sugar hacienda and mill on the same road.

Lovers and solitary types like the peace and the view from the base of the **Faro Punta Tuna**, the lighthouse just southeast of Maunabo. From Hwy 901, take Hwy 760 toward the ocean. The lighthouse is off Hwy 760 in Maunabo.

Scenic Drives Puerto Rico's **Ruta Panorámica** (scenic drive) begins here and climbs through coffee country into mountain wilderness via Hwy 182, before threading its way across the tops of the island's highest peaks in the Sierra de Cayey and the Cordillera Central. This spectacular drive follows some 165 miles of narrow, twisting roads before descending into Mayagüez at the west end of the island (for more on the drive, see the Central Mountains chapter).

Before rushing out of Yabucoa to the mountains, however, take the time to follow the easy-to-miss **coastal road**, Hwy 901, as it heads southwest toward Patillas. Although the road signs have been missing every time we have passed this way in the last 10 years, Hwy 901 to Maunabo actually takes up where the Hwy 53 expressway stops (eventually the toll road will run all the way along the southeast coast to Guayama and join Hwy 52, the San Juan-Ponce Autopista). Just go straight from the end of Hwy 53 – don't be tempted by a bad map to turn left or right – and follow this spectacular shoreline drive. Hwy 901 scales mountain cliffs that fall to the sea, in a fashion reminiscent the crazy hairpin roads along Spain's Costa Brava. Almost 20 miles of scenic seaside driving lie ahead as the road becomes Hwy 7760, then Hwy 3. Guesthouses, seaside cantinas and campsites dot your way.

Places to Stay

Guesthouses You will find the **Playa de Emajaguas Guest House** (☎ 787-861-6023) at Km 2.5 on Hwy 901 as the road descends (westbound) to the beach from the mountains of the Cuchilla de Panduras. The attraction of this funky and well-used inn is its sense of space: It sits in the middle of a field and orchard like an old plantation house on a rise above a narrow beach. There are seven efficiency apartments here renting for about US$70.

Hotels *Palmas de Lucía* (☎ 787-893-4423) is on Playa Lucía at the intersection of Hwys 901 and 9911 in Yabucoa. Here you will find a friendly staff and a new, well-scrubbed hotel. Each of the rooms has all the usual modern conveniences, plus a private balcony with a view of the pool and beach. Rates start at US$74.

Farther west, where Hwy 3 runs along the seashore between Maunabo and Patillas, you will find the *Caribe Playa* (☎ 787-839-6339). Tucked right on the shore under a slanting plantation of coconuts, this inn has 29 units, many with beachfront balconies and full kitchens. There is also a restaurant on the premises and a natural pool carved into the rocky coast. Owner George Engels has an interesting collection of parrots and iguanas to keep you company. Rates start at US$75.

About a mile farther west on this same stretch of road, the attractive beachfront *Villa de Carmen* (☎ 787-839-7576) has just 12 units, all with kitchenettes, air con and laundry service. There are also two pools on the premises, which is a good thing because the beach along the coast between Maunabo and Patillas is narrow and eroded. Rates range from US$50 up to US$125 for a three-bedroom suite.

Rental Agents A number of agents rent beach houses in the beach resort neighborhood of Bajos de Patillos (a couple miles west of Villa Carmen off Hwy 3). Try *Esmeralda del Sur Rental Apartments* (☎ 787-839-6173). Rates are usually around US$200 for a weekend.

Places to Eat

At Playa Lucía in Yabucoa, check out the cheap beer and empanadillas at *Coco Mar* and *Bar Ortiz*.

Just a mile or two west of these bars, the view rarely gets better than it does from *El Nuevo Horizonte* (☎ 787-839-6173), at Km 9.8

on Hwy 901. This restaurant is perched on a hairpin turn on a mountainside overlooking the Caribbean. You can smell the *asopao de langosta* (lobster stew) cooking 200 yards before you get here. A caldron of the stew will set you back about US$18 and serves at least two people.

Once the road returns to sea level (going to the west), look for ***El Mar de la Tranquilidad*** (*☎ 787-839-4870*), on the seaward side of Hwy 3 west of Villa Carmen. Beer on the outdoor terrace costs US$1.75, and you can get *salmorejo de jueyes* (land crab in tomato sauce) for under US$10.

South Coast

Until Hwy 52 (the San Juan-Ponce Auto-pista) opened in the late 1980s, the south coast of Puerto Rico had been more or less a kingdom unto itself for more than 450 years. Now, the once-difficult journey over the mountain range of the Cordillera Central takes about an hour and a half as the sweeping curves of the highway snake across the island from north to south.

But while travel to the south coast today takes less time than some commuters spend getting to work in the traffic jams of metro San Juan, old attitudes die slowly. You are likely to detect a sort of 'them and us' distinction between the 'two Puerto Ricos' – the north and the south – almost like the old stereotypes between the north and the south in the USA.

Typically, *sanjuaneros* describe *ponceños* (residents of Ponce) and other southerners as 'romantics.' According to the island stereotypes, southerners are traditionalists preoccupied with religious mysticism, social class and old colonial conventions of civility that favor excessive friendliness and familiarity. Ponceños often generalize about the sanjuaneros as well, calling them rude, arrogant and materialistic – slaves to current American fashions.

While such stereotypes are gross exaggerations, the traveler will definitely notice some cultural differences between the north and south. Coming from San Juan, you may be surprised by the number of people – of all ages – holding hands as they stroll the historic district of Ponce. You may wonder at the spiritual proclivities of a city that erects a giant cross as a lookout tower and has no fewer than three *botánicas* (shops selling herbs, potions, charms and statues of saints) in the central market. If you have spent some time in eastern Spain, you may recognize the genetic footprint of the south's Catalan ancestors: high cheekbones, sharp features and natural red or blond hair. You may also notice that southerners in general have lighter skin than many of the Puerto Ricans

in the north and that communities and neighborhoods in the south seem somewhat segregated according to race.

But these changes in culture will probably seem just subtle nuances compared to the changes in the landscape between the north and south. On the north side of the mountains you see houses everywhere – not just the high-rises of San Juan or the endless suburbs of Guaynabo and Trujillo Alto, but clinging to the sides of the mountains as well. On the southern side of the Cordillera Central what hits you is the green of the mountain forests, the agricultural fields and the cattle pastures that stretch as far as you can see. Even a city like Ponce seems to blend with the landscape

Highlights

- Strolling the historic district of Ponce
- Losing yourself to the spirit of Ponce's Carnaval in February
- Learning about colonial life at Hacienda Buena Vista
- Exploring the old sugar towns, especially Aguirre with its huge wildlife preserve, Bahía de Jobos
- Hiking dry-forest trails or sunbathing and swimming at Bosque Estatal de Guánica
- Taking a snorkeling or diving trip to the offshore reefs of La Parguera – and seeing the bioluminescent Bahía Fosforescente

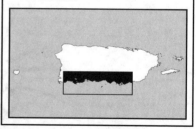

because few of its buildings exceed three stories in height. In the south, it is easy to forget that Puerto Rico is one of the most densely populated areas in the world.

The south is the place to explore historic towns, notably Ponce, Arroyo and Aguirre. Linger longer if you love poking around coastal nature preserves such as the mangrove estuary at Bahía de Jobos, the dramatic hills and dry forest of the Bosque Estatal de Guánica and the Bahía Fosforescente at La Parguera. Also, if you want to squeeze the most out of your travel budget, come to the southern side of the island. Hotels, restaurants and pubs run 30% to 50% less than in San Juan. How does a waterfront hotel room for US$75 sound? A gourmet meal for US$8, or 50¢ beers in a lively pub? All are here in spades.

PONCE

A public-relations executive once observed that Ponce is as different from San Juan as New Orleans is from New York. While there may be a little Madison Avenue hype in such a statement, the comparison is largely apt, particularly as it associates Ponce with New Orleans. Like New Orleans' French Quarter, Ponce's historic district of more than 1000 buildings is a textbook collection of 19th-century *criollo* architecture. In Ponce you see blocks of buildings that blend rococo and neoclassical elements with a Latin flare for opening up interior spaces to the tropical climate with patios, high ceilings, broad doorways and balconies.

During the nights of Carnaval in February, Ponce looks very much the part of the Big Easy on the Mississippi Delta. Parades of masked *vejigantes* and crowds of revelers fill the gaslit streets around the Plaza Las Delicias in the center of town. Adding to this sense of a strange and wonderful place, you have the lighted Fountain of Lions, the racket of the *bomba y plena* drummers, the warm scent of rum and the red-and-black Parque de Bombas (firehouse, now a museum) standing next to the plaza's cathedral like the fortress of Satan.

In the evening, Ponce is often a quiet place where grand buildings painted in pas-

tels eye each other across serene streets like dowagers lost in remembrances of things past. Meanwhile, the flower vendors court the couples strolling down the Callejón de Amor (Alley of Love) southeast of the Plaza Las Delicias.

By day these same streets swirl with color as ponceños take to the streets, strolling down the broad sidewalks. Flocks of children pass back and forth to their schools in neat uniforms and shoppers come to buy fruits, vegetables and meat at the central market. Career women pause to check out the latest bargains as merchants trundle racks of discount apparel onto the sidewalks and promenades like Paseo Atocha. Schoolboys stop at the street vendors' stands to consider a new pair of sunglasses or a coconut ice-cream cone.

You get the feeling of time and space to spare here – an attitude of *que será será* (what will be will be). Nobody seems in a hurry to make a dollar. No one seems anxious that, on an island where most towns have doubled in size during the last 20 years, Ponce's population of about 187,000 has actually declined. No one seems distressed that Ponce is no longer 'Puerto Rico's Second City,' having been eclipsed in the number of residents by industrial monsters to the north like Bayamón, Carolina and Caguas.

For proud ponceños, their city is still 'La Perla del Sur' (Pearl of the South). And many travelers agree. They will tell you that in Ponce a traveler can find a well-planned city that feels like a small town (unlike most towns on the island, where the opposite is true). The historic district has seen some significant restoration since the early 1990s. And there is culture here in the form of a half-dozen specialized museums, a historic theater, a major university, an orchestra that gives free outdoor concerts every Sunday and the best art museum in the Caribbean. In addition, you can find attractive, moderately priced accommodations in the historic district and an interesting collection of restaurants that will keep your travel budget intact.

Finally, in recent years Ponce has developed a waterfront pavilion, boardwalk and beach south of the city at a site called Paseo

Tablado La Guancha, often simply called 'La Guancha.' There are dozens of new, attractive restaurants and cafés here, live salsa music on weekends and one of the liveliest weekend scenes for families and youths on the island.

History

The story of Ponce's rise to wealth and prominence as the longtime center of island culture is the story of benign neglect by centuries of Spanish colonial rulers. The first settlers came here in the 16th century to raise cattle and horses for the Spanish colonial expeditions in Mexico and South America. We know that they had established a hamlet on the narrow plain between the mountains and Caribbean by 1630, when they built the first incarnation of the current cathedral and named it for the patron saint of Mexico, the Virgen de Guadalupe. But it was not until 1692 that Spain recognized Ponce as a town, named after the great-grandson of the island's infamous first colonist and governor.

In some ways the layout of the town was already set in those early years. One of the primary entrances to town came from the

mountains along Calle Atocha, which led to the plaza and the cathedral (just as it does today, though part of Atocha is now a pedestrian mall). If you came from the east, on what is now Hwy 1, your landmark for the entrance of the town was a huge ceiba tree (called 'La Ceiba'), which still stands on Calle Comercio near Río Portugués.

During the first century of the colony, the lifeblood of Ponce flowed through the easy-to-approach harbor defined by the headlands of La Guancha, which afford ships shelter from the easterly trade winds. While this was a disastrous place for ships to get caught during hurricane season, most of the year it was an easy stop and a perfect crossroads for vessels bound west with goods from the spice islands or ships traveling to and from Mexico and South America. Ostensibly the port was only open to Spanish vessels trading directly with Spain, but the island governor and his legions lay a universe away, over the mountains in San Juan. With no one to enforce the law, commerce flourished in this free-trade environment with money, culture and a mix of people flowing into and through Ponce from around the Americas.

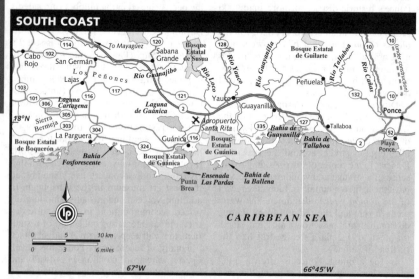

And folks got rich during the 16th and 17th centuries. When the slave revolts began to shake neighboring French-held Saint-Domingue (Hispaniola) in the 1790s and South America (between 1810 and 1822), many of the wealthy refugees fled to Ponce, bought land and introduced new, more efficient ways of growing coffee and sugarcane. Soon they were importing former slaves from the British colonies in the Caribbean to meet the local demand for labor and ever-increasing demands from American ships for sugar, coffee and rum. Production and profits from agriculture and trade rose exponentially throughout the 19th century as aristocrats with Catalan names financed the import of art, music and fashion from Europe and America. Merchants built homes and business structures around the Plaza Las Delicias to showcase their wealth and sophistication. Meanwhile, the black West Indian immigrants shared their traditional drum music and blended their own spiritual beliefs with Catholic adoration of the saints and ancient Catalan traditions of a masked celebration at Carnaval. With such wealth, growing sophistication and a multicultural

population, Ponce achieved its golden age in the second half of the 19th century.

But Ponce's boomtown days were numbered. The Spanish-American War resulted in American military occupation of the island, bringing uniformly enforced trade laws and an end to Ponce's freebooting days. In addition, hurricanes devastated the coffee industry, sugar prices dropped and the US fixated on developing San Juan as a port. Then came the Great Depression in the 1930s, and Ponce fell into an economic hibernation. Bad news for the citizens of the city at the time, but an event that deterred developers from destroying the city's historic building stock.

In the midst of this decline, revolutionary forces took hold across the island, especially with the many intellectuals and students who had been drawn to Ponce because of its reputation for culture and sophistication. On Palm Sunday, March 21, 1937, students protesting in favor of Puerto Rican independence staged a march on the plaza in Ponce. Originally they had a parade permit, but at the last minute the governor of Puerto Rico withdrew his permission for the political march. Angered, the nationalists defied the

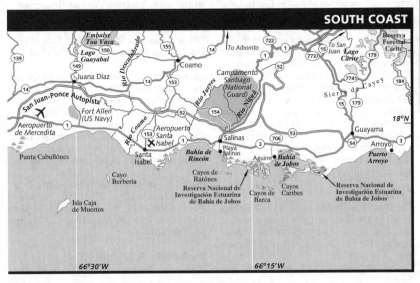

SOUTH COAST

prohibition and marched. Slightly less than 100 young men and women faced off with 150 armed police near Plaza Las Delicias. When the nationalists started singing 'La Borinqueña' – the national anthem – a shot was fired and then the entire plaza erupted in gunfire. Seventeen marchers and two police officers died. Not one civilian carried a gun, and most of the 17 died from shots in the back. While the US government chose not to investigate, the American Civil Liberties Union did and confirmed that the catastrophe warranted its popular name, 'Masacre de Ponce' (Ponce Massacre).

Since then Ponce has limped along with lots of civic pride and an economy relying on textiles, plastics, oil and rum. The nearly US$500 million pledged to the city for historic restoration in the early 1990s brought a rush of optimism in the city and truly worked magic by burying utilities and reclaiming more than 600 buildings. But the funds dried up before a lot of the money pledged to the project Ponce En Marcha (Ponce on the Move) came to completion. Many ponceños claim that the program got shelved because of a long-standing feud between the city's mayor and Governor Pedro Rosselló, who comes from an opposing political party. Lawsuits filed against the Commonwealth have repeatedly endorsed Ponce's right to the rest of the redevelopment money, but so far the current island administration is making no move to compensate the city.

So Ponce languishes in its history and architectural beauty, content in knowing that at least it has cooler, clearer and drier weather than the current governor and his minions will ever see in San Juan.

Note that many of the city's museums and historic sites are closed on Monday and Tuesday; come on other days if you really want to get under Ponce's skin.

Orientation

The Plaza Las Delicias (Plaza of Delights) stands at the heart of the city, surrounding both the Catedral Nuestra Señora de Guadalupe and the Parque de Bombas. The cathedral's five-story, blue-and-white bell tower is the beacon leading you to the historic district, no matter what highway brings you here. Navigating within the city is easy because all of the historic district lies within a boxed grid of streets. The only difficulty is that street signs are often missing or hard to find; carry a map and keep yourself oriented to the cathedral tower. This is even easier than it sounds as almost all the attractions, accommodations and restaurants lie within three blocks of Plaza Las Delicias.

Note that you do not have to drive through the center of town to get to from one side of Ponce to the other. Two bypass roads circle the city to the south. The inner road is Avenida Emelio Fagot/Avenida Las Américas (Hwy 163). The faster route is the outer road, called the 'Hwy 2 bypass.' You will find the city's biggest mall and all the fast-food franchises along Hwy 2. To reach the port area, take Calle Hostos (Hwy 10) south from the center of town or its successive intersections with Hwy 163 and Hwy 2.

Information

Tourist Offices See Judith Pacheco Santos at the Ponce Tourism Office (☎ 787-841-8160) on the 2nd floor above Citibank facing Plaza Las Delicias. She has superb local knowledge and lots of helpful brochures on the city. The office is open 8 am to 4:30 pm weekdays.

The Puerto Rico Tourism Company (☎ 787-840-5695) has a desk on the 2nd floor of the Fox Delicias Mall, just north of the plaza.

Money With no fewer than five banks on the perimeter of Plaza Las Delicias, it's no problem finding someone to meet your financial needs in Ponce. Most of the banks are open 9 am to 2:30 pm weekdays, plus Saturday mornings. The ATM at Citibank is a convenient stop if you're on your way to the tourist office on the 2nd floor of the building.

Post The most central of the city's four post offices stands on Calle Atocha, three blocks north of Plaza Las Delicias. It's open 7:30 am to 4:30 pm weekdays, 8:30 am to noon Saturday.

Bookstores & Libraries Sadly, there are no great bookstores to be found in downtown

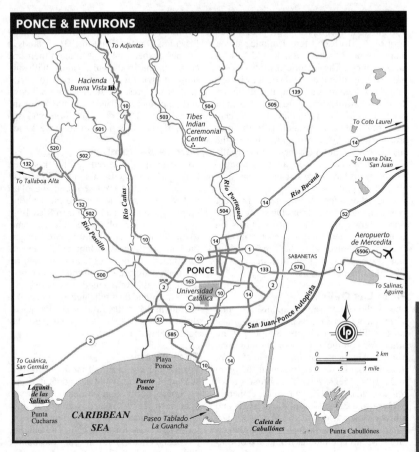

PONCE & ENVIRONS

Ponce. But you can find a limited selection of novels (mostly in Spanish) and a good collection of newspapers and magazines at Isabela II, a block east of the plaza on Calle Reina Isabel.

For a more substantial collection, check the Centro Libros de Puerto Rico (☎ 787-840-2796) in the Plaza Caribe south of town. Another place to look is Librería Educativa (☎ 787-284-2443), on the Avenida Las Américas marginal road south of the historic district. The library serves the Universidad Católica (Catholic University) community.

Laundry If you are planning on doing it yourself, head for Coin Machine (☎ 787-841-6464), 8 Calle Pampano. Most guesthouses and hotels offer laundry service. Expect to pay US$4 for a medium-size load.

Medical Services Hospital Manuel Comunitario Dr Pila (☎ 787-848-5600), on Avenida Las Américas east of Avenida Hostos, is recommended. In an emergency, call ☎ 911.

For a pharmacy in the historic district, head to Farmacia El Amal (☎ 787-842-1180), 67 Calle Union.

Dangers & Annoyances While Ponce has fewer areas attracting desperate people than a lot of Puerto Rico's larger municipalities, there are places where you should be cautious at night. The historic district can get pretty lonely after dark, and you may be setting yourself up for a mugging if you venture down a deserted street more than a block or two in any direction from Plaza Las Delicias.

Another place to be alert is in the port area near La Ancla restaurant and in the vast parking lot at La Guancha's boardwalk. However, both areas seem a lot safer now – with very visible police patrols – than they were in the past.

One other thing: Ponce's genteel veneer masks an underground sex club scene. These clubs migrate around the city, and as soon as the vice squad stamps one out, another appears someplace else. Both male and female travelers should keep their distance for all of the obvious reasons.

Plaza Las Delicias ✓

This is the quintessential Spanish colonial plaza, and it lives up to its name, which translates as 'Plaza of Delights.' Simply put, no other plaza on the island – or perhaps in all of Latin America – can measure up. Picture the lush, manicured vegetation of the plaza in Mérida, Mexico, with its horse-drawn *calesas* (carriages). Then mix in the cathedral of Oaxaca, the fountains of Mexico City and a firehouse right out of the *Wizard of Oz*. Surround the whole picture with monumental 19th-century buildings from Paris or Barcelona, and you have some sense of Ponce's colonial heart. On a warm night, violet and pink lights dance in the waters of the Fuente de Leones (Fountain of Lions), a monument rescued from the 1939 World's Fair in New York. Couples holding hands seem drawn here like moths to a lantern. In the shadows, statues of island legends like Luis Muñoz Marín and famous *danza* composer Juan Morel Campos fix their eyes on eternity.

Catedral Nuestra Señora de Guadalupe ˅

Painted a soothing blue and white with twin bell towers that blaze silver in the midday sun, this cathedral (☎ 787-842-0134) is actually a newcomer to this site in the center of Plaza Las Delicias. Built in 1931, it stands in the place where colonists erected their first chapel in the 1660s, which (along with subsequent structures) succumbed to earthquakes and fires. The stained-glass windows and pipe organ can help you block out the material world. The cathedral is open 6 am to 3:30 pm weekdays, 6 am to noon weekends.

Parque de Bombas ✓

An Arabian-styled, red-and-black-striped building, Parque de Bombas (☎ 787-284-4141 ext 342) stands back-to-back in the plaza with the cathedral and is the most photographed building in all of Puerto Rico. Built as part of an agricultural exhibit that came to the city in 1882, the building later became the home of the city's volunteer firemen and functioned as a firehouse until 1990. Now it has been restored as a museum to highlight the fires that have plagued the city over the last century and the firefighters who struggled to contain the conflagrations. The Parque de Bombas is open 9:30 am to 6 pm every day but Tuesday. Admission is free.

Casa Alcaldía ✓

Ponce's current city hall (☎ 787-284-4141) started life in the 1840s as a general assembly house, but it soon became a jail. If you head into the courtyard, which was once used for public executions, you will see galleries that were formerly cells. The building has been Ponce's civic center for most of the 20th century. Its balcony has seen speeches by four US presidents, including Teddy Roosevelt, Herbert Hoover, Franklin Roosevelt and George Bush. The lord of misrule and head of Carnaval, El Rey Momo, also makes his pronouncement from here, and local wags sometimes speculate that more of Ponce's hot air derives from this spot than from the warm Caribbean. The Alcaldía is open 8 am to 4:30 pm weekdays.

Casa Armstrong-Poventud

With its caryatid columns, Casa Armstrong-Poventud (☎ 787-840-5695) looks like a gingerbread house as it faces the cathedral

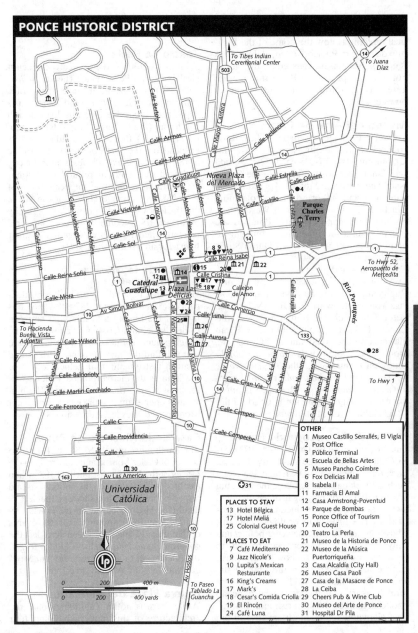

PONCE HISTORIC DISTRICT

To Tibes Indian
Ceremonial Center
503

To Juana
Díaz
14

Calle Bertoly

Calle Arenas

Calle Tricoche

Calle Mayor Cantera

Calle Bettances

14

Calle Guadalupe

Nueva Plaza
del Mercado

Calle Estrella

Calle Olivieri

●4

Calle Union

Calle Atocha

Calle Leon

Calle Mayor

Calle Virtud

Calle Salud

Calle Castillo

Parque
Charles
Terry
🏛5

Calle Loma (El Tren)

Calle Victoria

3●

Paseo Atocha

Calle Vives

14

Calle Washington

Calle Molina

Calle Sol

7▼●▼10
8 9
🏛️6

Calle Reina Isabel

14

1

1

To Hwy 52,
Aeropuerto de
Mercedita

Calle Progreso

Calle Reina Sofia

11●
12🏛️

ℹ️15
🏛14

20●
🏛️21

🏛 22

Río Portugués

Calle Mora

Catedral
Guadalupe

13

Plaza Las
Delicias

Calle Cristina
▼17 ▼19
16▼ 18▼

1

Callejón
de Amor

Calle Trujillo

To Hacienda
Buena Vista,
Adjuntas

Av Simón Bolívar

Calle Torres

Calle Salud

▼24

●23

Calle Comercio

133

Calle Wilson

Calle Marueño-Vega

Calle Mayor Mercado Montalvo Concordia

25■

🏛26

Calle Luna

●28

Calle Roosevelt

Calle Baldorioty

Calle Martín Corchado

Calle Marina

🏛️27

Calle Aurora

Av Hostos

To Hwy 1

Calle Ferrocarril

10

14

Calle Gran Vía

Calle La Cruz

Calle Numero 1

Calle Numero 2

Calle Numero 3

Calle C

Calle Providencia

Calle Campos

Calle Numero 4

Calle Numero 5

Calle Numero 6

Calle A

Calle Molina

10

Calle Campeche

🚩29
🏛 30

Av Las Americas

163

Universidad
Católica

⊕31

Av Hostos

To Paseo
Tablado La
Guancha

0   200   400 m
0   200   400 yards

SOUTH COAST

OTHER
1 Museo Castillo Serrallés, El Vigía
2 Post Office
3 Público Terminal
4 Escuela de Bellas Artes
5 Museo Pancho Coímbre
6 Fox Delicias Mall
8 Isabela II
11 Farmacia El Amal
12 Casa Armstrong-Poventud
14 Parque de Bombas
15 Ponce Office of Tourism
20 Teatro La Perla
21 Museo de la Historia de Ponce
22 Museo de la Música
    Puertorriqueña
23 Casa Alcaldía (City Hall)
26 Museo Casa Paoli
27 Casa de la Masacre de Ponce
28 La Ceiba
29 Cheers Pub & Wine Club
30 Museo del Arte de Ponce
31 Hospital Dr Pila

PLACES TO STAY
13 Hotel Bélgica
17 Hotel Meliá
25 Colonial Guest House

PLACES TO EAT
7   Café Mediterraneo
9   Jazz Nicole's
10 Lupita's Mexican
    Restaurante
16 King's Creams
17 Mark's
18 Cesar's Comida Criolla
19 El Rincón
24 Café Luna

across the street on the plaza. Built in 1900 as the home of a Scottish banker, this whimsical building is now the home of the Instituto de Cultura Puertorriqueña del Sur. This is not really a museum geared for the public, but you can pick up cultural information here. It's open during regular business hours on weekdays.

Museo del Arte de Ponce ✓

Set across from Universidad Católica, about 10 blocks to the southwest of the plaza, this art museum (☎ 787-848-0505), 25 Avenida Las Américas, is without rival in the Caribbean. There are more than 850 paintings, 800 sculptures and 500 prints in this collection, which represents 500 years of Western art. Former governor Luis Ferré donated the collection and the magnificent building to house it in 1959, and Edward Durell Stone (architect of Washington, DC's Kennedy Center) designed the space.

Among the collection are exceptional pre-Raphaelite works and Italian baroque paintings. You will see works by Diego Velázquez, Peter Paul Rubens, Benjamin West and Eugène Delacroix, along with Puerto Rican masters Francisco Oller and José Campeche. Don't miss Campeche's *Dama a Caballo* (Lady on Horseback), Oller's *La Ceiba de Ponce*, Delgado's *Giannina* or Lord Leighton's erotic *Flaming June*. It's open 10 am to 6 pm every day. Admission is US$4 adults, US$2 children, US$1 students.

Museo de la Historia de Ponce

This history museum (☎ 787-844-7071), 51-53 Calle Isabel, is large for a city this size. Located in the Casa Salazar, near Teatro La Perla a block east of the plaza, the museum has 10 galleries displaying artifacts donated by the local citizenry to document centuries of the city's history in ecology, economy, education, architecture, medicine, politics and daily life. This is an excellent place to come to get a clear perspective on how Puerto Rican culture has evolved from the time of the Taínos. The building (1911) is an architectural treasure that blends typical ponceño criollo detailing with Moorish and neoclassical elements. It's open 10 am to 6:30 pm

every day except Tuesday. Admission costs US$3 for adults, US$1 for children.

Teatro La Perla

With its six-columned entrance, the neoclassical Teatro La Perla (Pearl Theater; ☎ 787-843-4399) is as beautiful an example of a small music hall as you could imagine (its capacity is 1000). Designed by Juan Bertoli Calderoni (the father of Puerto Rico's neoclassical style), the original building took its origins from the 1860s but fell victim to the 1918 earthquake. Twenty years later the city gathered the funds to rebuild this monument with acoustics that duplicate those of New York's Carnegie Hall. You can check out the lobby 8 am to 4 pm weekdays. But by all means try to come here for a play or a concert when Ponce's elite gather in their finery for an 8 pm curtain.

Museo de la Música Puertorriqueña

Housed in a pink villa (also built by Calderoni), this museum (☎ 787-848-7016) fills most of the block on Calle Salud between Calles Isabel and Cristina. It showcases the development of Puerto Rico's music. Here you will find displays of Taíno, African and Spanish instruments that helped to evolve the island's distinctive bomba y plena folk music as well as the formal danza. The museum is open 9 am to 4 pm every day except Monday and Tuesday. Admission is free.

Casa de la Masacre de Ponce

This small museum (☎ 787-844-8240), at the corner of Calles Marina and Aurora, held the offices of the Nationalist Party in 1937 when a confrontation between the nationalists and armed police ended in a shooting that left 19 dead (see History, earlier in the Ponce section). Today, this museum recalls the events of that tragedy, 'the Ponce Massacre,' lest the government and nationalists of today forget. It's open 9 am to 4 pm every day but Monday and Tuesday. Admission is free.

Nueva Plaza del Mercado ✓

While there is nothing stunning about the architecture of this modern building, four blocks north of the plaza on Calle Mayor, the interior is full of fresh produce, food vendors and great smells. If you are in the mood for some of the freshest fruit on the island, do not miss this place. You also may want to check out the market if your health or luck has been running a little thin: Stop by one of the botánicas in the market to see what kind of charms the local *curanderos* (healers) can prescribe to change your astral energies.

Fox Delicias Mall

On the north side of the plaza, this building has art-deco motifs combined with Mediterranean red tile, which marked this former palace of film as the place to be in the 1930s. It now has been restored as an air-conditioned mall with lots of fast-food vendors. You can get cheap beer or expensive fruit juices to drink at café tables in front of the vendors' kiosks in the small plaza.

Calle Reina Isabel

If you head east from the plaza, past the restaurants and museums you will see storefronts and residences built in seven different ponceño styles: Spanish colonial, European neoclassical, Ponce criollo, residential-town criollo, town criollo, neoclassical criollo and superior neoclassical.

Museo Pancho Coímbre

This museum (☎ 787-284-4141 ext 463), on Calle Lolita Tizol, is in a sense Ponce's sports hall of fame. It honors the achievements of ponceño Pancho Coímbre (one of baseball's greats) as well as lesser luminaries with Ponce roots. It's open 9 am to 5:30 pm every day except Tuesday. Admission is free.

Escuela de Bellas Artes

This building (☎ 787-259-7373) lies a little way beyond the Museo Coímbre. It is one of the few remaining buildings of the Spanish Crown in the city and was known as 'El Castillo' when used to garrison soldiers. For most of the 20th century it served as a courthouse and jail before receiving a nearly US$10 million restoration to become the fine arts school in 1992. Now there are work-shops here for music, drama and plastic arts, as well as a theater that seats 600.

El Vigía

At the beginning of the 19th century, the Spanish Crown posted lookouts on this hill north of town to watch for smuggling activities in the port and off the coast. Today it is still a lookout site, and you can catch the view of Ponce, the coastal plain and the Caribbean from the top of a 100-foot reinforced concrete cross, which you can ascend by elevator. Depending on your spiritual point of view, the cross is either inspiring or not. But one thing is certain: Neither the cross nor the vista can stack up against their counterparts on Corcovado in Rio de Janeiro. It's US$3 to go to the top.

Museo Castillo Serrallés

If you decide to make the trip up to El Vigía, and you are curious about the lifestyles of Puerto Rico's rich and famous, duck into the Museo Castillo Serrallés (Serrallés Castle Museum; ☎ 787-259-1774). The Moorish-style castle's red-tile roof, turrets and verandahs date to the 1930s, when the baron of the island's Don Q rum empire decided to build a monument to his wealth. This is a decent house tour if you are interested in how completely a Puerto Rican family might recreate the golden age of Spain for themselves. There is also an informative display on the history of the sugar and rum industries. No free booze, though there is a café on the premises. It's open 9:30 am to 5:30 pm every day except Monday. Admission is US$3 adults, US$2 seniors, US$1.50 children. Tour guides are bilingual, and tours last 45 minutes.

Paseo Tablado La Guancha

In the spirit of waterfront restorations in Boston, Baltimore, Miami, San Francisco and St Louis, Ponce built this great half-mile boardwalk in the mid-1990s to overlook the town's yacht harbor and *club náutico*. Today there is a seaside concert pavilion with dozens of bars and restaurants, often great live salsa, an obligatory observation tower and a well-maintained public beach.

Except on a quiet Monday or Tuesday night, this is where the action is. It's a great place for people-watching and cool breezes.

People may give you a lot of complicated directions if you ask them how to get to the beach and boardwalk at Paseo Tablado La Guancha. The simple route is to head east from the center of town until you hit Hwy 14. Go south until you see the lights, pavilion and parking lot of La Guancha.

Pontificia Universidad Católica de Puerto Rico

Officially known as Pontificia Universidad Católica de Puerto Rico, this Catholic university (☎ 787-841-2000) spreads out across a large area on the south side of Avenida Las Américas across from the art museum. The university serves about 10,000 students with programs in all major undergraduate disciplines as well as graduate programs and a law school. While this is a commuter campus (like all universities on the island), the students play a major role in shaping the entertainment scene in Ponce.

Isla Caja de Muertos

Maybe it is good that the Port Authority discontinued ferry service to this mile-long island, about 3 miles off the coast of Ponce. It is a wildlife refuge of rare value. It has a nearly pristine reef system and one of the driest environments in Puerto Rico, which supports a number of endangered plants and reptiles.

If you come to this island on a low-impact tour (see Boating & Snorkeling, below), you will see the outpost for resident biologists, a restored lighthouse and a mix of rocky and sandy coastline, lowlands and hills reminiscent of southern California's Channel Islands.

The name Isla Caja de Muertos (Coffin Island) probably derives from an 18th-century French author's observation that the island's silhouette looked like a body in a coffin. Of course, there are legends that give more color to the name, including tales of piracy, star-crossed lovers and necrophilia that are supposedly associated with this salty patch of land.

Swimming

There really used to be no good beaches in Ponce, but about five years ago the municipality poured a lot of money into building a beach on the east side of the Paseo Tablado La Guancha. Because this small beach is so close to all of La Guancha's cafés and restaurants, it is not a bad place to come for a few hours of sun and sea (though rarely surf). But for these same reasons the beach gets packed on weekends.

Boating & Snorkeling

Until a few years ago a government ferry took people to the wild beaches on Isla Caja de Muertos, several miles offshore, but the authorities decided they needed this ferry for the Fajardo-Vieques-Culebra runs, and public access to the island has been all but cut off. Recently, Island Venture (☎ 787-842-8546) has begun offering 'Day at the Beach' trips to Caja de Muertos with chair, umbrella, lunch and refreshments for US$20.

Island Venture also offers snorkeling trips to the island for US$35. The trip includes everything you get with the 'Day at the Beach' package plus snorkeling gear and a tour of the reefs. If you want to add a two-tank dive to the experience, the price is a bargain at US$60.

Special Events

Carnaval Held the week leading up to Ash Wednesday in February, Carnaval is composed of seven days of serious partying with each evening offering new festivities. Events kick off on Wednesday with a masked ball and follow with a series of parades on successive nights: the first introduces El Rey Momo, the festival's lord of misrule who has a huge, comical papier-mâché head.

On the following nights there are parades that end with the coronation of the Carnaval queen and the child queen. For most of Sunday afternoon, a huge parade fills the streets with floats, vejigantes and other maskers, and musicians. Monday evening entails a formal danza competition. Tuesday brings an end to the whole shebang with one last parade, concluding with the burial of a sardine and the onset of Lent. Each parade and all of the critical activities take place in Plaza Las Delicias in front of Casa Alcaldía.

Note that if you are planning to visit Ponce during Carnaval, make your hotel and transportation reservations at least three months in advance to make sure you beat the crowd.

Fiesta Nacional de la Danza During this mid-May festival (☎ 878-284-4141), chamber orchestras perform under the lights in Plaza Las Delicias. Men in tails and women in silk gowns offer waltzlike arabesques for the crowd, in this town where high society and composers made danza a distinctive art form at the turn of the 20th century.

Fiesta Nacional de Bomba y Plena Each November, this fiesta brings in drummers and *pleneros* (plena singers) from all over the island to compete in and demonstrate the singing, dancing and drumming that evolved in Ponce from citizens of African descent who came en masse to work the cane fields.

Fiesta Patronal de la Virgen de Guadalupe Held the week preceding December 12, this festival may make you feel that you are in Mexico. The town long ago adopted Mexico's patron saint – the Virgen de Guadalupe – as a result of the constant cultural and human exchange between the island and Mexico during the colonial era. And while this celebration does not match up with the one in Mexico City, a lot of fireworks are exploded, alcohol consumed and songs sung during this week. The climax is at midnight on December 12, when Mexican mariachis called the Cantata Las Mañanitas arrive to lead a procession of singing citizens through the streets.

Places to Stay

Guesthouses The six-room *Colonial Guest House* (☎ 787-843-7585, 33 Calle Marina), a block south of the plaza, is an absolutely charming place. Here you get the feel of colonial Ponce amid patios, art and antiques. Rates run US$70 and up, including breakfast.

Texan Guest House (☎ 787-843-1690) lies east of the center of town, on Hwy 1 in the

Ponceños have adopted Mexico's patron saint, the Virgen de Guadalupe, as their own.

Sabanetas neighborhood. There are nine rooms here with private baths and air con. Rooms cost US$55.

Hotels Just off the southwest corner of the plaza stands the *Hotel Bélgica* (☎ 787-844-3255, 122 Calle Villa). This 20-room hotel has character oozing from its European-style high ceilings and iron balconies. Of course, you get air con to cool things off when you get tired of looking down on the street from your private balcony. Rooms run US$60.

The *Hotel Meliá* (☎ 787-842-0260, 2 Calle Cristina), just east of the plaza, reminds some guests of favorite three-star hotels in Spain and Portugal. Everything is clean and functional, the building is monumental, the staff is friendly and helpful and the decor seems to be aging with grace. A rooftop sundeck and the free continental breakfast are attractive bonuses. The 80 rooms on four floors each rent for US$70 to US$80.

You have three modern hotel options on the periphery of town. *Days Inn* (☎ 787-841-1000) is on Hwy 1 on your way to the airport, offering 120 rooms with a lot of surrounding

SOUTH COAST

amenities for the price. There is a courtyard pool, Jacuzzi, restaurant and laundry on the premises. This is a good place for a family on a budget; rooms go for US$80 or US$90.

The *Holiday Inn & Tropical Casino* (☎ 787-844-1200) sits on a hill west of town on Hwy 2. Attractions include a small casino and a pastoral setting with a good view of the mountains and the distant Caribbean. Room rates start at US$122.

The most deluxe accommodation in town, the 153-room *Ponce Hilton & Casino* (☎ 787-259-7676), is off Hwy 14, the road to the La Guancha boardwalk on the Caribbean. The hotel is seaside, but there is no beach as this is a rocky shore. The hotel offers a swimming pool, golf range, fitness center, two restaurants, a casino and a disco. Rooms go for US$190 and up, but a lot of people get a much better deal as they come here as part of the hotel's significant business and convention trade.

Places to Eat

Café Medeterraneo (66 Calle Isabel), just east of Plaza Las Delicias, is set back in the courtyard of a colonial office building, which is becoming a headquarters for the FBI. All of the food comes out of a hole-in-the-wall kitchen while you sit at café tables. Get a gyro sandwich served with wedges of watermelon or roasted veggie chips for less than US$4. Also, there's excellent cappuccino.

Another good cheap-eats place is *Café de Tomás*, at the end of this same block as you head east. The menu here is *cocina criolla* with all of the standard offerings. Many full meals cost less than US$5.

A block south on Calle Mayor, past the Museo de la Historia and Teatro La Perla, you find two more notable low-cost restaurants. *El Rincón*, at the corner of Calles Mayor and Cristina, has a US$1.25 ham, eggs and toast breakfast. *Cesar's Comida Criolla* is virtually next door, with 30¢ coffee and *pollo asado* (roast chicken) for US$3.

There are upscale restaurants in this neighborhood on the east side of the plaza as well. *Lupita's Mexican Restaurante* (☎ 787-848-8808, 60 Calle Isabel) is the same kind of ersatz cantina as Lupi's in Isla Verde and Old San Juan. And while the Corona

signs make the place feel touristy, it actually thrives on a loyal local crowd. Entrées seem a little pricey: expect to pay about US$9 for a big burrito platter. Next door, *Jazz Nicole's* offers a more authentic and intimate ambience. This is a storefront restaurant with international dishes, tablecloths, flowers and candlelight. Nothing is overstated, and there is live jazz on weekend evenings. Entrées are in the US$12 range.

One of Ponce's favorite spots for haute cuisine is also in this same corner of town. *Mark's* (☎ 787-842-0260) is on Calle Cristina in the Hotel Meliá. The entrées here are an imaginative fusion of international cooking styles. Splurge on seared salmon for US$25.

A block south of the plaza behind city hall, *Café Luna* is a popular breakfast and lunch spot as well as a bar. A large American breakfast with ham, eggs and toast costs US$2.50. Medalla beer is US$1 at happy hour.

King's Creams is the ice-cream emporium facing the Parque de Bombas on the east side of Plaza Las Delicias. You can get huge coconut and passion-fruit ice-cream cones here for less than US$1. Of course, you will find the usual chains of fast-food places scattered around the plaza as well.

If you are up for a drive to the port area, ponceños will point you to a couple of traditionally popular seafood places with white tablecloths, water goblets, an armory of silverware and waiters in vests. *Canda's* (☎ 787-843-9223, Calle Comercio 38) will serve you fresh *chillo* (red snapper) for US$17.

A hundred yards away, *La Ancla* (☎ 787-840-2450, 9 Avenida Hostas Final) has paella for two for US$27 and chicken breast with garlic for US$13. You can go light here with fish croquettes for US$6.

If you want to save some money and are looking for informal seaside dining, head to the Paseo Tablado La Guancha, where dozens of open-air cafés, restaurants and bars await you in a fiestalike atmosphere (see Orientation, earlier).

Entertainment

Pubs Thursday night is the biggest scene for the college crowd at *Cheers Pub & Wine Club* (☎ 787-848-7217, 35 Avenida Las Américas)

MARK BACON

Verdant rain forest of El Yunque

STEVE SIMONSEN

Locals near Humacao

THOMAS R FLETCHER

Along Big Tree Trail, El Yunque

DAVID ZINGARELLI

MARK BACON

TONY ARRUZA

Top left: Staying dry near Playa Luquillo
Top right & bottom: Revelers parade in devilish *vejigante* masks and dance to traditional bomba at the Fiesta de Santiago, Loíza Aldea

Ponce's Catedral Nuestra Señora de Guadalupe

Festival in Plaza Las Delicias, Ponce

Hacienda Buena Vista, north of Ponce

Friendly waves from workers in a municipal 'bus,' Ponce

BOB KRIST

Sunrise over Bahía Fosforescente, La Parguera

MARK BACON

Dry forest of Bosque Estatal de Guánica

BOB KRIST

La Parguera's secluded mangrove estuaries

near Universidad Católica. *Puerto Santiago* is a bar-restaurant at No 27 on the boardwalk at La Guancha that gets pretty packed with a young crowd listening to live salsa and Latin rock Wednesday through Saturday.

If you are staying in the historic district, try *Jazz Nicole's* and *Lupita's* (see Places to Eat, above) for Thursday and Friday happy hours (before 10 pm) and the weekend scene. Nicole's gets some great local jazz while Lupita's is pretty much a guzzle and giggle scene for a crowd packed around the bar on the back patio. You won't find many gringos in either of these places, and the scene at Lupita's may feel a little cliquey as some bartenders and patrons may sport a kind of in-crowd arrogance.

Café Luna gets packed for its live Latin rock, but the crowd in this venue seems a little more open to meeting the new gringos in town. There is a patio off the back here, too, where you can get away from some of the smoke and look for the stars through the hazy glow of the city.

The *Hollywood Café* (☎ 787-843-6703), near the car dealerships at Km 125.5 on Hwy 1, is an upscale bar-restaurant with bar food such as chicken wings (US$5). But this place has outdoor porch seating and a cavernous interior with pool tables and a sound system that can wither your ears with mainstream American rock.

A certain segment of ponceños love the *Hollywood*, which lures them with live Latin rock and US$1 Don Q rum drinks Thursday to Sunday. Some visitors reject the Hollywood as a pickup scene with a careless staff and a fair number of drunk teenagers out to wreck their parents' flashy cars. Maybe you have to be under 22 to catch the thrill.

Dance Clubs One of Ponce's weekend hot spots is the *Pavilion* disco at the Ponce Hilton (see Places to Stay, above). Another popular venue on Friday and Saturday nights is *Holly's* (☎ 787-841-1200), in the Holiday Inn. Techno dominates the music at both places.

Gay & Lesbian Venues At the *Cave* (15 Barrio Teneria), behind Ponce Candy Weekends, there's a fresh weekend scene for club

kids and cruisers. There is lots of dancing and often a drag show here as well.

Michelangelo's is another popular spot. You will find this on Hwy 10 at Km 13.7 between Ponce and Adjuntas.

Concerts The *Banda Municipal de Ponce* gives free outdoor concerts at 8 pm every Sunday in Parque Dora Colón Clavell.

Spectator Sports
The beginning of November usually opens the season for the *Leones de Ponce (Ponce Lions;* ☎ 787-848-4717) at the Parque Paquito Montaner stadium, just off Avenida Las Américas southwest of the center of the city. Try to catch a game against their arch rivals, the San Juan Metros. US$5 will get you in.

Shopping
Paseo Atocha and Fox Delicias Mall lie just to the north of the plaza. The upscale shops are in the mall, which has been carved out of the old Fox movie theater. Paseo Atocha is a street that has been closed to traffic and spruced up as a pedestrian mall. Here, and along the associated cross streets, merchants create a street-bazaar feel by displaying racks of clothing and leather goods on the sidewalk amid the costume jewelry displays and food vendors' carts. This has to be one of the best places on the island to shop for everyday streetwear like shorts, jeans and T-shirts.

To buy vejigante masks or *santos*, stop in Mi Coquí (☎ 787-841-0216), on the east side of the plaza. Another vendor of these popular items is nearby Utopia (☎ 787-848-8742), 78 Calle Isabel. To go to the source for mask making, visit master craftsman Miguel Perez at his home and shop on Calle Arias near Canda's restaurant in the port area.

Getting There & Away
Air About 4 miles east of the town center off Hwy 1 on Hwy 5506, the Aeropuerto de Mercedita (Mercedita Airport) looks dressed for a party but is still waiting for the guests to arrive. American Eagle currently has two San Juan-Ponce flights a day on Monday, Tuesday and Wednesday, and one flight a day the rest of the week. Fares for the half-hour

flight run anywhere from US$49 to US$89, depending on the season and promotions. But if you want to fly to Ponce on an overseas ticket via American Airlines and change planes in San Juan, your flight to Ponce only costs US$15 more than the fare to San Juan.

Público The stop is on Calle Union just a couple of blocks north of the plaza. You can get vans from here to all of the major towns on the south coast and the mountains. There are also plenty of long-haul vans headed to Río Piedras in San Juan (about US$10) and Mayagüez (about US$8).

Getting Around

To/From the Airport You should expect to pay around US$10 for the 4-mile trip to or from the airport (see Taxi, below).

Trolley Ponce has free trolley buses and a fake train that runs on the roads to carry citizens and travelers around the city 8 am to 8 pm daily. There are four routes: each runs toward a cardinal point on the compass, leaving and returning to the stop in front of Casa Armstrong-Poventud on the east side of Plaza Las Delicias. Trolleys appear about every 15 minutes and the complete loop takes between a little over an hour and two hours, depending on the route.

The Este (East) trolley goes to Teatro La Perla, Museo Pancho Coímbre and Escuela de Bellas Artes.

The Oeste (West) trolley's stops include the Museo del Arte, Universidad Católica and Casa de la Masacre.

The Norte (North) trolley mounts the steep hill up to El Vigía and Museo Castillo Serrallés.

The Sur (South) train stops at the Museo del Arte, the Universidad Católica, Paseo Tablado La Guancha, Museo de la Música Puertorriqueña and Museo de la Historia.

Car Ponce has a good supply of rental car agencies, including the following:

Avis   ☎ 787-842-6184
Hertz   ☎ 787-842-0357
L&M   ☎ 787-840-9729

Popular   ☎ 787-843-8995
Thrifty   ☎ 787-843-6940

Taxi The city has six cab companies. Cabs charge US$1 initially and 10¢ for each $1/13$ of a mile; waiting time is 10¢ per 45 seconds. Try Ponce Taxi (☎ 787-642-3370) or Cooperativa de Taxis (☎ 787-848-8248).

AROUND PONCE

Two extraordinary, meticulously preserved historic sites lie just to the north of Ponce, and any traveler with the time and the interest in native Caribbean and colonial hacienda life should not miss these marvels.

Tibes Indian Ceremonial Center

While Tibes lacks the dramatic ruins of a place like Uxmal in Mexico, it is nonetheless one of the most important archaeological sites in the Caribbean because it has evidence of both Igneris and pre-Taíno cultures.

History Tropical storm Eloíse hit Ponce in 1975, causing the Río Portugués to overflow its banks. When flood water retreated from local farmland, it exposed the ruins of this ancient ceremonial center. The municipal government quickly expropriated more than 30 acres, and a team of archaeologists, historians, engineers and geologists moved in. To date they have excavated slightly more than 5 acres of the property.

Information Tibes (☎ 787-840-2255) is open 9 am to 4 pm every day except Monday and major holidays. Visits entail a tour, which takes about an hour including a movie and a visit to the small Tibes museum where you can see Indian ceremonial objects, pottery and jewelry. Sometimes the tour gets sold out, so you should make reservations in advance. The cost is US$2 adults, US$1 children and senior citizens.

The Site Current excavations have uncovered seven *bateyes* (ball courts), two ceremonial plazas, burial grounds, at least 180 skeletons, pottery, tools and charms. As you tour the manicured pastoral setting – with its bateyes and plaza rimmed by bordering stones (some with petroglyphs) – guides explain that the first settlers on this spot were Igneris who probably migrated from the Orinoco Valley in Venezuela and arrived at Tibes about 300 AD. They were farmers and sought out fertile river valleys like Tibes to grow their staple crop of cassava. As part of their cassava culture, the Igneris became fine potters, making vessels for serving and storing their food. Many of these bell-shaped vessels have been found buried with food, charms and seashells in more than 100 Igneri graves, where individuals were buried in the fetal position in the belief that they were bound back to the 'Earthmother' for rebirth.

Many of the Igneri graves have been discovered near or under the bateyes and walkways constructed by the pre-Taínos who probably came to the site around the first millennium. You can see many of the axes, dishes, *cemíes* (deities), spoons and adzes that they used in a well-developed museum on the property. You will also see some reconstructed pre-Taíno *bohíos* (huts) amid this natural botanical garden with its fruit trees, including the popular *guanábana*. There's a cafeteria at Tibes if you get hungry.

Getting There & Away Tibes lies about 2 miles north of Ponce at Km 2.2 on Hwy 503. The easiest way not to get lost is to follow the brown signs leading to Tibes: you will pick these up on Hwy 14 (Calle Fagot) on the northeast side of town.

An easier way – if you don't mind waiting for a van to fill – is to take a *público* to and from the station on Calle Union in the historic district. Vans to and from Ponce run about once an hour (sometimes more often) and cost US$3.

Hacienda Buena Vista

This is the place to come if you want to see a 19th-century coffee plantation and corn mill restored to its former glory by a team of island researchers and artisans as well as Smithsonian Institute specialists. Perhaps Buena Vista is not quite Thomas Jefferson's Monticello, but it is a splendid natural and historical heirloom, and an extraordinary piece of historic restoration.

History The hacienda's name, meaning 'beautiful view,' aptly describes its 482 acres embracing a tropical forest and waterfall in the steep Río Cañas valley. Salvador de Vives was the patriarch of the family, which owned the hacienda from its founding in 1833 until the government expropriated the land in the 1950s. Vives was a Spanish loyalist who fled to Puerto Rico in 1821 as a refugee of the revolutionary war in Venezuela.

While Vives and his family made their principal residence in Ponce, they used slave labor to develop this agricultural *estancia*, a sort of truck farm producing corn, yams, plantains, pineapple and coffee. Vives prospered along with all of Ponce, which was booming from sugarcane and contraband trade during the first half of the 19th century. Intrigued by the industrial revolution unfolding in Europe and America, Vives purchased a corn mill, rice husker, cotton gin and coffee de-pulper.

His son Carlos was also fascinated by machinery and the cheap productivity it could afford a farm, and when Carlos took over the hacienda he won approval from the island's governor to divert part of the Río Cañas through a series of flumes to power a water wheel to drive his machinery. Eventually, Vives added a water turbine from New York to increase the hacienda's production of corn meal.

Subsequent generations brought in a large coffee crop and modified the mill to husk and polish the beans. After a hurricane devastated the coffee plantation, the resourceful Vives family planted a large orange grove. But during the Depression and the following years of WWII, the hacienda could no longer support itself, and the government took over and divided up the land.

In 1984 the Conservation Trust purchased Buena Vista and spent the next decade researching and restoring the buildings and machinery as living proof of a way of life that once put its stamp on Puerto Rico.

Information Hacienda Buena Vista (☎ 787-722-5882, 284-7020 on weekends) may only be visited with reservations made in advance. It's open every day but Monday, Tuesday and major holidays. Admission, including a guided tour, is US$5 adults, US$2.50 senior citizens, US$2 children under 12. Tours take 1¹/₂ hours.

The Site One of the charms of the hacienda today is its subtropical forest setting, which is home to birds such as the Puerto Rican screech owl, mangrove cuckoo and humming-birds. Then there is the Río Cañas, rushing through the flumes and plunging over a 60-foot waterfall.

Amid this setting you can visit a fully restored two-story manor house – furnished with period antiques (some donated by the Vives family), plus the waterworks, mill and machinery, which is now functioning in like-new condition. Here, you can watch the milling of corn and take a turn at de-pulping and grinding your own coffee beans.

Getting There & Away The hacienda sits about 10 miles north of Ponce at Km 16.8 on Hwy 10 (the road to Adjuntas). Go west from the Plaza Las Delicias on Avenida Simón Bolívar, which becomes Hwy 10.

ARROYO
If you are circumnavigating Puerto Rico's coastline in a clockwise fashion starting from San Juan, you officially reach the south coast (from the east coast) when you reach the small coastal town of Arroyo. Here the island's geography changes: to the east steep mountains verge almost to the edge of the sea; to the west a marshy coastal plain – more than 5 miles broad – spreads between the coast and mountains and stretches 50 miles farther west to Ponce. For centuries this plain was the heart of the south coast's lucrative sugar industry. Today most of the cane fields have gone to seed, and the local population finds work at oil refineries, electricity plants and factories scattered among the flatlands of old sugar plantations with romantic names like Hacienda Aguirre, Hacienda Josefa and Hacienda Amadeo.

The town of Arroyo is one relic from the days of 'king sugar.' The commercial development and the tract housing that has gobbled up many island towns have made few inroads here. And as you enter the village via Calle Morse from Hwy 3, you will be struck by the number of traditional, 19th-century, Caribbean-style buildings made of wood, with porches, verandahs, shuttered windows and gently sloping tin roofs. Dilapidated brick-and-stucco warehouses – some now harboring bars and seafood restaurants – overlook the small harbor and short *malecón* (waterfront promenade).

Like Ponce, Arroyo developed as a smugglers' port during the colonial days, but this town achieved some measure of respectability when the American inventor of the telegraph, Samuel Morse, showed up in 1848 to oversee the installation of telegraph lines. Electronic communication put Arroyo on the map and won it recognition as a distinct municipality in the 1850s.

While the town is far from being a museum piece, it has a funky charm that has recently made it something of a local tourist attraction. The big draws here are the *balneario* and *centro vacacional* at Punta Guilarte and the Tren del Sur, which is the only working railroad left on the island (outside the one in the park at Bayamón). On weekends a trolley carries railroad passengers from the station on a tour of the town.

Orientation
Hwy 3, the old southern coastal road, skirts the edge of town. Hwy 753 brings you to the center and becomes the main street, Calle Morse, named after you know who.

Things to See & Do
The long, narrow strand adjoining the centro vacacional at Punta Guilarte is the public **balneario** and the only decent beach around. Parking is US$2.

The **Antigua Casa de Aduana** (Old Customs House), Calle Morse 67, is now a cultural center and local museum. Hours are irregular, but it is open most days. You can get a useful brochure here that clues you into the town's history and the stories behind how New England sea captains built many of the colonial wooden houses on Calle Morse and adjacent streets.

The tourist **trolley** and the **Tren del Sur** are both just to the west of town at the restored railway station on Hwy 3. The trolley makes a short circle around town detailing some of the architecture and lore about the days when 'king sugar' reigned and Morse brought his telegraph to town to speed up business communications. The 3-foot, narrow gauge Tren del Sur makes the 4-mile trip west to Guayama and back over the tracks that used to bring the sugar to Arroyo for shipping. The railway equipment – a little diesel switch engine and passenger cars built from old cane gondolas – are survivors of the railroad that the Central Aguirre sugar company operated until 1990 (see Aguirre & Bahía de Jobos, later in this chapter).

The trolley and train are weekend-only operations, and are most active during the summer vacation months.

Places to Stay

The *Centro Vacacional Punta Guilarte* (☎ *787-839-3565*), at Km 126 on Hwy 3 about 2 miles east of Arroyo, has 28 cabins, 32 villas, 40 campsites, a pool and all the well-maintained facilities you have come to expect from these government facilities. Cabins sleep six and rent for US$65; the villas go for US$109; tent sites cost US$10. It's advised to reserve early through the San Juan office (☎ 787-724-2500, 722-1771).

Places to Eat

If you can stand waiting in the noon-time line, you will love the food and value at *La Familia* (*53 Calle Morse*), next to the great old-time general store. Here a burrito runs US$1.25; a huge ham-and-cheese sandwich is US$1.50.

Travelers and residents looking for a fancier meal head down to the line of old warehouses facing the malecón and Caribbean. *La Llave del Mar* (☎ *787-839-6395*) is the most popular of the seafood emporiums here. Expect to pay US$14 for variations on red snapper. Check out this place and its neighbors for a small-time pub scene on weekend nights.

Getting There & Away

The público terminal is in the center of the town, on Calle Morse near the town hall. You can get a público to Guayama for 50¢, and find a connecting ride there to Río Piedras in San Juan or Ponce.

GUAYAMA

For centuries Guayama was Arroyo's partner in crime. But while Arroyo did the day-in, day-out dirty work of shifting smuggled goods and sugarcane aboard the ships that came to call from places like New England, Guayama grew fat on the profits. Lying about 5 miles northwest of Arroyo, Guayama stands several hundred feet above sea level in the foothills of the mountains. Clearly, this was a cooler and more salubrious place to live than Arroyo, lying in the mosquito-infested lowlands. And so Guayama became one of the island's first upscale suburbs (like Guaynabo today) as smuggler-merchant princes erected their mansions.

Today, Guayama is a town of more than 40,000 people. And like many of the island's other overdeveloped municipalities, it is prone to traffic jams that make you wish Puerto Rico would either finish construction on the toll road (Hwy 53) that bypasses the town – or just shoot you before you die of exhaust fumes as you sit stuck in the traffic bleeding in and out of the local mall.

However, if you catch this town on a quiet weekday morning before most of the local drivers are off to the races, it can be worth the stop. Long called the 'City of Witches,' probably because of Santería worship brought to the area by African laborers in the cane fields, Guayama now prefers to be called the 'Cleanest City in Puerto Rico.' And judging by the well-scrubbed, manicured central plaza, the town lives up to the claim. Facing the plaza stands a museum made from one of the mansions of a local robber baron, and also a branch campus of Ponce's Universidad Católica, whose students – mostly female – often claim the plaza's benches for study breaks. One of the campuses of the Universidad Interamericana stands near the edge of town.

Horse lovers make it to town the first weekend of March for the upscale Feria Dulce Sueño (☎ 787-834-1988), a Paso Fino horse race.

Museo Casa Cautiño

Housed in a white criollo-style townhouse on the north side of the plaza, this museum (☎ 787-864-9083) takes its origins from 1887 when the wealthy Cautiño family erected this monument to the wealth they garnered from cane, cattle and tobacco. Almost 100 years later the government claimed the property for back taxes (a common event on the island, which has saved many heirlooms). Now the house has been restored to its Victorian splendor with period pieces (including the plumbing) and Oriental carpets. It's open 10:30 am to noon, 1 to 4:30 pm every day except Monday and Tuesday. Admission is US$2.

Places to Eat

If you get stranded in the center of Guayama waiting for a público or want a bite after visiting the museum, check out *King's Pizza* (☎ 787-866-4331, Calle Vinente Pales 2 Este). This place is popular with both the high school and college crowds. A medium pizza costs US$6.

Getting There & Away

To find a público, look for the van parking lot just off the plaza. You can get local service to neighboring towns such as Patillas and Salinas for about US$3, or longer hauls to Río Piedras in San Juan or Ponce for about US$6. Just check the decals on the windshields of the públicos to reckon their destinations.

Coming by car, you can't miss this place – it's at the junction of Hwy 3 and the Hwy 53 toll road.

AGUIRRE & BAHÍA DE JOBOS

If you need a reason to follow dusty, two-lane Hwy 3 west through the old cane fields along the southern coast instead of taking the new, parallel toll roads, the nearly unknown town of Aguirre and the neighboring Reserva Nacional de Investigación Estuarina de Bahía de Jobos (National Estuarine Research Reserve at Bahía de Jobos) may be the compelling factors. No other settlement in Puerto Rico turns back the clock 100 years as powerfully as Aguirre does – not Old San Juan, not Ponce's historic district, not San Germán in the west. In fact, Aguirre is so lost in time and space that it does not even appear on many of the most popular contemporary maps of the island. But if you get here, you'll find a totally intact early-20th-century sugar town complete with mill, company stores, hospital, movie theater, hotel, bowling alley, social club, golf course, marina, executive homes and narrow-gauge railroad.

This was the planned private community of the Central Aguirre sugar company, and at its height (around 1960) it processed 12,500 tons of sugarcane per day. But since then, declining prices for sugar, foreign competition and escalating production costs drove the company under. In 1990 the mill closed along with the hotel, stores, hospital, cinema, social club, bowling alley and railroad. Aguirre became a virtual ghost town. Well, except for the local families who rented some of the former executives' homes, golfers who knew about the town's quaint little nine-hole course and a few naturalists drawn to explore the enormous Bahía de Jobos estuary along the surrounding coast. When the company's creditors sold off the railway locomotives for use on the tourist line in Arroyo, somebody painted on the engine's cab a message in Spanish: 'Good-bye, Aguirre…until we meet again!'

If you visit today, you will find Aguirre tucked under its tree shade like a Puerto Rican Brigadoon – a town waiting to wake up after a long sleep. And on first seeing this haunting place, you may find yourself wondering how it is that shadowy forces in island politics and industry have so far prevented Aguirre from earning a place on the National Register of Historic Places to assure its preservation as the island's most complete legacy of its sugary past. You may see the effects of environmental decay (which spreads so quickly in the tropics), and know that soon it will be too late to save Aguirre from the wind and rain and termites. You may feel like grabbing the governor of the island or the directors of the Conservation Trust and the Instituto de Cultura by the lapels and shouting, 'Look what you are about to lose!'

But after you cool down in the shade of the overgrown plaza, you realize that there is more here than the ghostly evocation of a time gone by. In the former bowling alley, a new visitors center introduces you to the estuarine reserve where you can hike or kayak to sites where hundreds of manatees play free, untroubled by the comings and goings of humans.

As of yet, there are no places to stay in the town of Aguirre.

Bahía de Jobos

This big mangrove bay is one of the largest patches of pristine coastal wilderness on the island and surely the least known. The reserve

Manatees steal the show at Bahía de Jobos.

covers 2883 acres of brackish water and includes the associated coastal wetlands and 15 offshore mangrove keys known as Los Cayos Caribes. West of the research reserve, the Reserva Forestal Aguirre adds even more undeveloped coastal land to this wilderness.

In appearance, the area looks like the Ten Thousand Islands and Cape Sable area of the Florida Everglades. Bird life abounds – all the superstars of the marine estuary are here: brown pelicans, great blue herons, black-crowned night herons, snowy egrets, ospreys, peregrine falcons and American oyster catchers. This is probably the best place to see manatees in Puerto Rico. Well over 100 feed here, along with dolphins and hawksbill sea turtles.

Environmental Threats With Aguirre's sugar factory closed and boat traffic into the Bahía de Jobos reduced to a trickle, you might think that this sanctuary has escaped the meddlesome hands of humans. Sadly, that's not the case. Some years ago the power company sited a thermoelectric plant less than a mile east of Aguirre. Then, in recent years, plans were made to build a fossil fuel-powered (coal) plant nearby as well. This would no doubt entail the building of a major shipping terminal for importing the fuel and the use of a large amount of bay water. Environmentalists are outraged, but nothing yet has really derailed this project.

Information The visitors center, offices and lab for the Bahía de Jobos reserve (☎ 787-853-4617, 853-3569) are on Hwy 705 at Km 2.3 in Aguirre, in the restored bowling alley next to the hotel ruins. They are open 7:30 am to 4 pm weekdays, 9 am to 2 pm weekends. Here you can see attractive displays that explain how estuaries like the Bahía de Jobos are the nurseries of the ocean. Admission is free.

Reserve manager Carmen Gonzales is exceptionally helpful and friendly. If you are a marine scientist, call her when you have a project in mind for the bay because Carmen may be able to arrange accommodations for you in a dormitory on the premises (it can hold 16 visiting researchers). Carmen can also grant you permission to camp in the reserve and point you to the best hiking or bird-watching trails.

While there are currently no vendors offering kayak tours of the bay, the reserve is ripe for this kind of investigation, and you can launch right at the small marina at Aguirre. If you do not have a kayak, the visitors center may be able to point you to rentals or a guided tour as vendors come on the scene.

Golf

Spread over rolling fields and knolls, this nine-hole, 3201-yard course at the Aguirre Golf Club (☎ 787-853-4052) was built in 1926, making it the oldest on the island. The greens fee is US$10 weekdays, US$18 weekends. Look for the sign near the closed hospital on the west side of the village.

Places to Eat

There is only one restaurant in town, but it's a gem. Nelson Santos has kept alive *El Batey Restaurant* (☎ 787-853-3386), in the center of town near the closed movie theater. You can get 'Siete Potencia' (Seven Powers) – a seafood stew – for about US$6, along with incredible anecdotes about the history of Aguirre from Nelson.

Getting There & Away

The only way to visit Aguirre is by car. Take Hwy 705 south from Hwy 3. Watch for the barely visible sign pointing to 'Historic Aguirre.'

SALINAS & PLAYA SALINAS

Five miles east of Aguirre, Hwy 3 brings you into Salinas – a dirty, broken-down, larger, poorer copy of Arroyo. In other words, Salinas is where many sugar plantation laborers lived while the bosses enjoyed the good life back at Aguirre. There is nothing for the traveler in this town except the stomach-churning scent of human misery.

However, the subdivision of Playa Salinas (Salinas Beach), a mile south of town, is one of the most important harbors for cruising sailors in all of the northern Caribbean. The name 'playa' is a misnomer here as this waterfront has almost no beach. What it does have is deep water surrounded by a coastal mangrove forest and a collection of reefs and mangrove islands that offer nearly total protection from bad weather to boats at anchor here. In other words, Playa Salinas is a 'hurricane hole' of the first magnitude, and dozens of cruisers proved its worth when they rode out the 110mph winds of Hurricane Georges here. All the boats survived, while most of the vacation houses and restaurants onshore were devastated.

Travelers looking for a berth aboard a cruising sailboat headed north to the Dominican Republic, the Bahamas or the US will do well to check in at the sailors' bar at the Marina de Salinas in late March and early April. You might even find a boat leaving for Cuba or Jamaica.

Places to Stay & Eat

Witness the *Marina de Salinas & Posada El Náutico* (☎ 787-752-8484). This is it, folks: lodging, food and entertainment. Yes, Playa Salinas does have more than 20 beat-up seafood restaurants packed among the mangroves along its twisting, crowded, narrow streets. But as one local confided, 'Frankly, I would not trust the cleanliness of any of them.'

You will find the marina on Hwy 701 south and a little west of Salinas proper. There may or may not be a sign with the route number, but there is definitely a green sign pointing to Playa Salinas. The marina is about a mile down the tortuous road where it makes a sharp bend to the left. You can't miss its well-kept facade and parking lot. Attractive, modern rooms with air con range from US$55 to US$125. You can get sandwiches and US$1.25 beers at the bar near the pool where the cruising fraternity hangs. The restaurant *Costa Marina,* built in two stories on stilts over the harbor, has some very pricey seafood, but you can get fried chicken for US$8.

If you stay at the marina, you can take swimming or snorkeling trips to the offshore cays on their launch for free. The other way to get out on the water – which is the best part of Playa Salinas by far – is to rent a kayak from the marina. The first hour costs US$15, additional hours are US$10; you'll pay US$40 for the day.

Getting There & Away

Público As usual, you cannot miss where the vans gather in the lot near the town plaza. You can get to Guayama for about US$1.50 or Ponce for US$3. To get to Playa Salinas and the marina, you have to walk (about 1¹/₂ miles) or ask around for a local to drive you over – a risk we would not take or recommend.

Car From the east, Hwy 3 becomes Hwy 1 as it passes through Salinas (see directions to Playa Salinas and the marina above). From Ponce, take Hwy 1 east or the Hwy 52 toll road to Las Marias, then take Hwy 1 south.

COAMO

If you are traveling the south coast to or from Ponce and are feeling a little crusty and enervated from your trip along the coast, consider inland Coamo. This town, in the foothills of the Cordillera Central – just a few miles north of the San Juan-Ponce Autopista (Hwy 52) – claims to be the home of the third-oldest colonial settlement on the island as well as a Taíno village. Coamo also boasts to be the site of the 'decisive battle of the Spanish-American War' (something of note, as hardly a shot was fired during the American invasion).

If such tales are not yet enough to lure you to spend time and money here, then the town's publicists will point out that the Catholic church has paintings by the island masters Campeche and Oller, including one of Oller's girlfriends being tortured in Purgatory. Coamo also hosts the island's premier foot race, the 20K San Blas Marathon, which takes place every February. Finally, as in Guayama, Coamo has converted an old mansion on the plaza into a museum, which opens on request through town hall.

The one truly exceptional thing that Coamo has to offer is south of town at the *baños* (baths) – thermal springs that have hosted luminaries such as US President Franklin Roosevelt.

But enough hype. Today, Coamo is one of the major chicken-processing centers on the island and the town is busting out of its britches with more than 30,000 people and probably half that many cars. But there are no real attractions in the town proper, unless you come on marathon day, when the town is a zoo.

Los Baños de Coamo

Maybe you have been to Hot Springs, Arkansas, or Calistoga, California, and found the commercialism surrounding the thermal pools off-putting and disappointing – more like a visit to massage parlor than a natural high. Banish those memories. Coamo has the real thing. Yes, there is a hotel here, but it does not overwhelm the scene.

To get here, take Hwy 153 from Hwy 1 or Hwy 52. There is not always a sign announcing this exit on Hwy 52, so keep track of where you are on a map so you do not miss it. Head north for about 3 miles and look for the sign that points off to the left (west) to the *parador*. The road passes through fields for a little more than a half mile to the parador parking lot. The parador has its own bath, but you can reach the public facility by taking a path down to the river, which flows near the right side of the parador's fence. Walk less than 100 yards down the nearly dry riverbed; after you pass the parador's thermal pool on your left, you will see some ruins and then two pools built high on the side of the riverbank.

You will need a swimming suit here as nudity is not the fashion with local bathers, but otherwise you are in for an exceptional natural experience, especially if you take a dip early in the morning, during a rain shower or perhaps at dinnertime when you may have the place to yourself. The upper pool has thermal water at about 110°F. When you get too hot, move to the lower pool to cool off and just take in the scene as trade winds blow across the fields and mountains and the Río Coamo rustles past on its way to the sea. It's open 8 am to 6 pm daily. It's free to use the public baths.

Presently, no public conveyance brings you to the baños.

Places to Stay & Eat

The **Parador Baños de Coamo** (☎ 787-825-2239) is the most recent incarnation of hotels that have stood on this site for 150 years. This attractive and shaded two-story facility has a courtyard, open-air bar and swimming pool. You can use the hotel's swimming and thermal pools for US$5 adults, US$3 children; hours are 10 am to 5:30 pm.

Rooms here go for US$70 to US$90, and you can eat cocina criolla at **Café Puertorriqueño** in the parador for less than US$10 if you go with the chicken dishes.

GUÁNICA & ENVIRONS

If you are heading west of Ponce on the Hwy 2 toll road, consider a detour upon the less-traveled Hwy 116, which swings south toward the coastline from Hwy 2 to the site where the US military landed its troops in 1898 during the Spanish-American War. And reaching the waterfront in the town of Guánica, you will see why the US Navy picked this spot for an invasion. The Bahía de Guánica is one of the most unusual coastal features on the island – a tropical fjord poised between rugged hills covered with dry forest. The bay is barely more than a quarter of a mile wide but stretches 2 miles from its mouth on the Caribbean to the town. And the bay is deep enough to accommodate ocean-going ships. All of these features make the Bahía de Guánica the most protected and secluded anchorage on the south coast.

The town itself is a funky fishing village with a well-kept malecón reminiscent of Arroyo's short strand of seaside restaurants and bars facing the bay. And like Arroyo, Guánica has not yet been surrounded by faceless housing developments, strip malls and the associated traffic. So you may want to call time-out for lunch along Guánica's quiet waterfront or visit the nearby Bosque Estatal de Guánica.

But you probably will not be tempted to sink roots here for much longer – unless you thrive on a sense of melancholy. Hurricane Georges hit the town hard and you can still see the pain in the residents' eyes – and in the industrial ruins west of town.

Pausing in town for *empanadillas* stuffed with lobster and a cold Medalla at a café, you may notice how many locals are ashamed of the large animal-food factory, which mars the bayside hill to the east. Mention it and many Guánica residents are likely to stare at the floor and mumble. Ask about the large tropical dry forest reserve (the Bosque Estatal de Guánica), however, and their eyes are likely to brighten up. Some folk may even become enthusiastic, offering (in their best English) suggestions to hike among the cactus forest, swim in the 'Whale Bay' or take a boat to Gilligan's Island. Guánica owes much of its pristine beauty – on the hills and coast on both sides of the bay – to the reserve.

Bosque Estatal de Guánica

Also known as the Guánica Biosphere Reserve, this 9500-acre forest has been called by some botanists 'perhaps the best example of subtropical dry forest vegetation in the world.' Since scientists estimate that only 1% of the earth's dry forest remains, Bosque Estatal de Guánica is a rare sanctuary indeed. And finding it within a two-hour drive of the rain forests of El Yunque and the Cordillera Central on this lush, tropical island makes the dry forest seem a truly unexpected natural treasure.

With 36 miles of trails and over 10 miles of undeveloped Caribbean coastline, Guánica is a first-rate attraction to nature lovers. This is the place to visit for a half-hour hike to a beach through three different kinds of forests, tramping the coast until you find a secluded cove for sunning and hiking back to your car by a different trail than led you here. And all of this takes place in an arena where birds, bullfrogs, the pale blue Caribbean and the sunshine make music together.

History This protected forest got its start in 1919 with the acquisition of about half the property. Over the years the government has continued to add to the reserve and efforts to buy adjacent land still continue. During the 1930s the Civilian Conservation Corps (CCC) cut many of the roads and built the essential buildings here, as they did at parks across the US and Puerto Rico. Since those

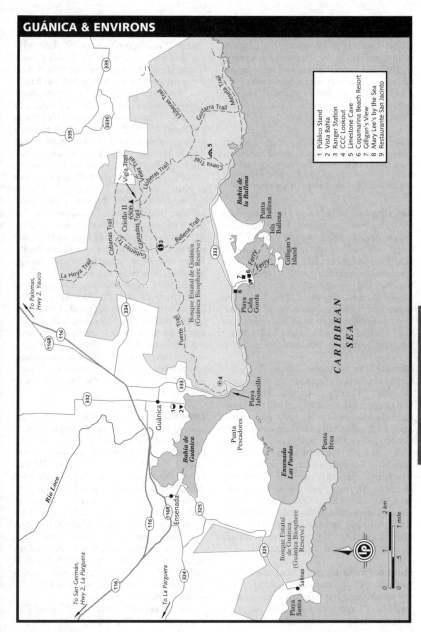

GUÁNICA & ENVIRONS

1 Público Stand
2 Vista Bahía
3 Ranger Station
4 CCC Lookout
5 Limestone Cave
6 Copamarina Beach Resort
7 Gilligan's View
8 Mary Lee's by the Sea
9 Restaurante San Jacinto

Masvidal Trail
Guilarte Trail
Llúperas Trail
Vigía Trail
Vélez Trail
Llúberas Trail
Cueva Trail
Cobanas Trail
Granados Trail
Gutiérrez Trail
Ballena Trail
La Hoya Trail
Fuerte Trail

Criollo II
650ft ▲

5

3

Bahía de la Ballena

Punta Ballena
Isla Ballena
Gilligan's Island

333

Ferry
Ferry

7
8
9
6
Playa Caña Gorda

Bosque Estatal de Guánica
(Guánica Biosphere Reserve)

To Palomas,
Hwy 2, Yauco

334

116R
116

332

Guánica

1
2

4

333

Playa Jaboncillo

Bahía de Guánica

Punta Pescadores

CARIBBEAN SEA

Río Loco

116R
Ensenada

325

116

Ensenada Las Pardas

Punta Brea

To San Germán,
Hwy 2, La Parguera

116

324

To La Parguera

325

Bosque Estatal
de Guánica
(Guánica Biosphere
Reserve)

Salinas

Playa
Santa

0   1   2 km
0   .5   1 mile

N

days, the forest has continued to expand while the Puerto Rico forest service has protected it with prohibitions against charcoal cutting, goat grazing and subsistence farming. In 1981 the United Nations acknowledged the value of this dry forest by designating it a UNESCO 'biosphere reserve.' This accolade, UNESCO says, makes it one of only 285 such preserves in the world

where government decision-makers, scientists, managers and local people cooperate in developing a model programme for managing land and water to meet human needs while conserving natural processes and biological resources.

Geography The Bahía de Guánica divides the forest into two sections. The highest elevation here is 650 feet, and many of the forest's hills rise abruptly from the coast to nearly equivalent heights. The terrain can be described as undulating, with steep slopes in the east and moderate slopes in the west. Limestone underlies most of the forest and is overlaid by several yards of calcium carbonate. Erosion from both water and sun have created sinkholes, caves and a forest floor that often looks like brittle Swiss cheese.

Climate The dry forest owes its distinctive and unusual microclimate to the presence of the nearby Cordillera Central. This mountain range creates, guides and exhausts tropical rainstorms as the easterly trade winds drive warm, moist air over the cool peaks. As a consequence, the cordillera gets inundated with rain while Guánica to the south gets very little – usually about 35 inches a year, mostly from June to September. Meanwhile, December through April is so sunny, hot and dry that the deciduous trees shed all of their leaves. Temperatures fluctuate from 80° to 100°F, virtually tropical desert conditions. The flora and fauna that survive here must be hearty and attuned to the seasons.

Flora & Fauna More than half the forest – the uplands – consists of deciduous forest while more than 1000 acres of semievergreen forest and scrub forest are near the coast, with mangroves at the waterline. One of the most unusual plants here is the squat melon cactus with its brilliant pink flowers that attract hummingbirds. Another plant, with the unseemly name of the Spanish dildo cactus, grows into huge treelike shapes near the coast and attracts bullfinches and bats.

The forest's uneven rainfall and drainage patterns have created an unusual variety of habitats for more than 700 varieties of plants (48 in danger of extinction), which attract a large number of birds. Some studies claim that at least 40 of the 111 species of birds found in Puerto Rico turn up in Guánica. Other studies say that you will see more types of birds here than at El Yunque. Everyone agrees that Guánica is a preferred habitat for nine of the island's 14 endemic species, which include the Puerto Rican woodpecker, the Puerto Rican emerald hummingbird, the Puerto Rican lizard cuckoo and the Puerto Rican nightjar, which is one of the island's highly endangered species.

Scientists come here to see the crested toad (*Bufo lemur*), the *Amelva wetmorei* lizard with its iridescent tail, blind cave shrimp and the purple land crab. Green and leatherback turtles still lay their eggs here, but their hatchlings may be in a losing contest against the predation of mongooses, which have overrun the island since their introduction to control the rat problem in the cane fields.

Orientation & Information To get to the eastern section of the reserve and the ranger station, which has trail maps and brochures, follow Hwy 116 south toward Guánica from Hwy 2. Turn left (east) onto Hwy 334 and follow this road as it winds up a steep hill through an outlying barrio of Guánica. Eventually, the road penetrates the forest, and after cresting the hills it ends at the ranger station, a picnic area and scenic overlook of the forest and the Caribbean to the south.

The southern extent of the eastern section of the forest – including Bahía de la Ballena (Whale Bay) and the ferry to Gilligan's Island – is also accessible by Hwy 333, to the south of Guánica.

The forest and office (☎ 787-821-5706) are open 9 am to 5 pm daily. Make sure you pick up a copy of the *Guide to the Trails of Guánica* (US$1), a photocopied pamphlet by Beth Farnsworth offering excellent local knowledge and illustrations. (There are no guides available for the forest, so it's well worth taking the map.) Hikers should carry drinking water and wear protective clothing against very strong sun as well as insects, thorns and the poison *chicharron* shrub with its reddish spiny leaves.

Admission and parking are free.

Beaches

The **Playa Caña Gorda** (Stout Cane Beach) is the public balneario (☎ 787-821-6006), adjacent to the southern edge of the dry forest on Hwy 333. After being run down from constant use, this facility was recently refurbished. A new high fence and a distinct, guarded entranceway clearly separate it from the surrounding coastline and forest. Weekends, holidays and summer vacations here can be a mob scene. Parking is US$2.

On the Trails of Guánica

Of the 36 miles of old roads and trails in the forest, all of those developed for public exploration lie in the eastern section of the forest. Most of the trailheads lead away from the parking lot at the ranger station at the end of Hwy 334. You can also access many of these trails from Hwy 333 along the coast, if you are willing to park on the roadside and trust your car's security to fortune.

Slightly longer than a mile, the **Ballena Trail** (actually an old road) is the most popular in the forest. It is an easy hike downhill (from the ranger stations) toward Bahía de la Ballena through a mahogany plantation, deciduous forest and coastal cactus forest. Along the way you will see a sign pointing you to a 700-year-old guayacán tree (6 feet in girth) before you reach Hwy 333, which leads to the beach.

If you came to the bay via the Ballena trail, consider walking to the east end of the cove and heading back to the ranger station on the **Cueva Trail** or **Guitarra Trail**. Both of these trails climb through cactus forest that is often alive with butterflies. The shorter of the two, the Cueva Trail, passes by a large limestone cave that is home to two species of bats and an unusual type of blind shrimp, but respect the fragility of the environment and do not enter the cave without permission from park rangers.

Eventually both of the trails join the **Llúberas Trail**, the longest trail in the forest. If you turn west here, it's 2 miles back to the ranger station. Go east here and the trail goes along an old road through different forest types to the ruins of a cane plantation and sugar mill, where the trail dead-ends.

For a different kind of extended hike, take the 3-mile **Fuerte Trail**, which follows an old road along undulating ridges to a perch above the Bahía de Guánica. Here you will find a circa-1930s CCC lookout tower built on the ruins of a 19th-century Spanish fort that failed to protect this coastline from the 1898 American invasion. If you cross Hwy 333 from its southwestern terminus, you will find trails leading down to Playa Jaboncillo and other swimming spots at the mouth of the bay. The trail offers great views of the bay, the sea and rolling hills.

If you want a landlocked hike, head north from the vicinity of the ranger station on the short (generally under a mile) connecting paths: **Granados Trail**, **Cobanas Trail** and **Gutierrez Trail**. Making a convenient loop, these shaded highland trails – the Granados especially – are good for bird-watching. From the Granados, take the **Velez Trail**, then the **Vigía Trail** north for an easy ascent of Criollo II (650 feet), the highest hill in the forest. Here on the lip of a sheer cliff, you can look north across the Río Loco valley to the thunderstorms brewing over the Cordillera Central.

SOUTH COAST

Gilligan's Island, made up of sand and mangrove cays, lies just a few hundred yards off the tip of the Caña Gorda peninsula. It's actually part of the dry forest reserve, but open for recreational use. And like the public beach, Gilligan's gets a lot of use on weekends, holidays and summer vacation. Nearby **Isla Ballena** (Whale Island) is less crowded. There are some snorkeling opportunities at both islands, but they are not spectacular.

To get to Gilligan's or Ballena, look for the signs pointing south off Hwy 333 right after you pass the Copamarina resort. The small ferry leaves from in front of Restaurante San Jacinto every hour from 10 am to 5 pm every day barring bad weather. The ride costs US$4 roundtrip.

If you bypass the turn to the ferry landing and keep heading up the road, the dry forest and its spectacular cactus stands will be to your right. In less than a mile the road passes along the long crescent of mixed rocky and sandy shore bordering **Bahía de la Ballena**. The road ends at the east end of the bay, and you can park anywhere along the road to picnic and sunbathe. If the seas are calm, you can also find good snorkeling among the rocks, but do not risk it if there is much of a surge.

Another local beach, **Playa Santa**, lies on the western side of the Bahía de Guánica. It's at the very end of Hwy 325 in the western segment of the forest reserve. Park along the road and follow the trail down to the water.

Water Sports

Part of the Copamarina resort, Dive Copamarina (☎ 787-821-0505 ext 729) has one and two-tank wall dives 15 to 30 minutes away for US$75; it's US$15 extra to rent equipment. Weather conditions often prevent afternoon dives. They also rent snorkeling gear and small boats.

At Playa Santa west of town, Pino's Boat & Water Fun (☎ 787-821-6864) rents kayaks and paddle boats for about US$15 an hour. You can also arrange boat tours and banana boat thrill rides here.

Places to Stay

As of yet, there are no campsites in the Guánica area, including the forest and beaches.

There has been some talk of carving out campsites at Playa Caña Gorda, but don't hold your breath. And if the campsites come to pass, do not expect any privacy unless you come off-season or mid-week.

Guesthouses The little community of vacation houses called San Jacinto dominates the highlands of the small Caña Gorda peninsula. Set away here on a steep hillside overlooking the mangrove cays, you will find one of the most charming guesthouses in Puerto Rico: ***Mary Lee's by the Sea*** (☎ 787-821-3600). This compound of rambling houses is the fanciful creation of long-time American expatriate Mary Lee Alverez (she's from Flint, Michigan), who offers eight apartments, each of which feels like its own villa with decks, hammocks, barbecue and sea views. One even has a bathroom that opens into a private garden shower.

In addition to the charming setting, Mary Lee spares no expense with fabrics and furnishings to create the feel of luxury. Her rates are excellent for what you get: Studios start at about US$90, and a three-bedroom apartment runs US$200. One single, interior bedroom (still quite spectacular) goes for US$70. Mary Lee has boats and kayaks for rent from her dock (your front door), but be forewarned – she does not take credit cards.

If you can't get a place at Mary Lee's, consider her new rival, ***Gilligan's View*** (☎ 787-821-4901). This modern vacation house, just up the street from Mary Lee's, has a couple of apartments for rent at competitive rates.

Hotels The ***Copamarina Beach Resort*** (☎ 800-981-4676) lies on Hwy 333 just east of the public balneario. This is a 'boutique' resort and has recently doubled in size by adding a new wing of condo suites. But even with 106 units, the place still seems small and clubby in the best sense of the words. There are tennis courts, water sports, two pools and two restaurants on-site. Rates start at US$176.

Places to Eat

If you are tempted to stop in town for a stroll along the malecón and a bite to eat, consider

Vista Bahía (☎ 787-821-4402, *83 Avenida Esperanza Idrach*), facing the water. This friendly bar-restaurant has an active pool table and offers the usual seaside fare, including empanadillas with *chapin* (trunk fish) for US$1 and 95¢ Medalla beers. Of course, you can spend close to US$20 here on lobster.

At the Gilligan's Island ferry landing, the *Restaurante San Jacinto* has sandwiches, seafood and chicken. Pollo asado runs US$9.

To put on the ritz, head out to the Copamarina's popular new restaurant, *Wilo's Coastal Cuisine* (☎ 787-821-0505). Try the fillet of red snapper for US$19 or the double-cut pork chops for US$25. Note that this is not your average hotel dining room and Wilo prepares all of his entrées with imaginative marinades and sauces.

Entertainment
Though stargazing is by far the most popular nighttime activity in Guánica, you will find local night owls at such bars as *Vista Bahía* along the malecón in town or crowding a table at *Restaurante San Jacinto* (see Places to Eat, above). A small upscale crowd of vacationers and locals gathers in the lobby at the *Copamarina Beach Resort* to listen to live salsa, merengue or tropical standards.

Getting There & Away
Público vans stop on the plaza in Guánica from Ponce (US$5), Mayagüez (US$5) and towns nearby such as Yauco and Sabana Grande. During the summer and on sunny weekends you may be able to catch vans to the beach at Caña Gorda and Playa Santa or the ferry dock to Gilligan's Island. But do not count on this service.

If you're driving to Guánica, follow Hwy 116 south from the Hwy 2 expressway.

LA PARGUERA
Explorers will probably take the backroad (Hwy 324) along the coast as they head west from Guánica. Destination: La Parguera, whose Bahía Fosforescente (Phosphorescent Bay) has been one of the most ballyhooed tourist attractions on the island. (A quicker, less depressing way than Hwy 324 is via Hwy 116, then south on Hwy 304.)

If you come by Hwy 324, you'll probably feel like the victim of a cruel hoax as you pass between salt flats, foul-smelling mangrove swamps and dilapidated settlements. In other words, it may look a lot like you are on a slow road to the end of the earth, not one of the seven natural wonders of the Caribbean.

And you may still be perplexed when you reach La Parguera because your map calls it Playa La Parguera (Parguera Beach), yet there is definitely no beach in sight. Just more mangrove swamp, a bright green iguana squatting in the middle of the road stopping traffic and a monkey or two racing up a coconut tree.

Keep going. The road suddenly veers through a wooded valley and then hits the actual town, poised on a hillside sloping to the mangrove coast. Now you see a host of signs heralding freshly painted guesthouses, paradores and restaurants. Dive and windsurfing shops dot the short main street; boat docks jut south into watery canals lined with mangroves. And now and again you catch glimpses of whimsical wooden houses built on stilts along the canals like houses on the *klongs* in Thailand. Several vacation condo developments spread across the upland fields beneath a tall steep hill.

Clearly not really earth's end, there is something of value here. Yes, part of the attraction is the Bahía Fosforescente east of the town, but its bioluminescence is only La Parguera's drawing card. The people who fall in love with this village – really just a barrio of the distant town of Lajas – have discovered that once you launch into this watery world on a kayak, sailboard, small outboard or dive boat, La Parguera becomes a maze of mangrove canals, bays and islands to rival the coastal wilderness of Louisiana's bayous. Five miles offshore at 'the Wall,' you can find some of the best diving in Puerto Rico.

If nightlife is your thing, La Parguera has a collection of pubs that get packed with folks of all ages throughout the summer vacation season (Easter to early September). Weekends draw crowds of college kids and lovers on getaways year-round.

Information

Carlos Quiñones, who works at Parador Villa Parguera, is an enthusiastic and knowledgeable ambassador for his town. Check out his website (elshop.com) for photos, maps, activities, menus and prices.

✳ Bahía Fosforescente

This is La Parguera's big enchilada. It's really two bays: Bahía Monsio José and Bahía La Paguera. Both lie east of town and are nearly encircled by mangroves. You reach them via narrow canals through the mangrove forest, and if you come here at night, bioluminescent microorganisms in the water put on a funky light show as your approaching boat sends fish racing around like undersea meteors.

If you have already read the Fajardo section of this book (in the East Coast chapter),

you know that there are actually a number of places – like Laguna Grande north of Fajardo and on the offshore island of Vieques – in Puerto Rico where you can see this phenomenon. While the light show here at La Parguera is the most famous, it probably no longer can claim to be the best. (You have to go to Vieques for that. See the Spanish Virgin Islands chapter for details on the phosphorescent bay there.) Pollution from illegal building, boating and dumping of sewage have diluted the concentration of the little lights in the sea. Nevertheless, the US$5 you pay Cancel Boats (☎ 787-899-5891), at the town docks, for a ride to the Bahía Fosforescente aboard the *Fondo Cristal II* (Glass Bottom II) is the least expensive way to witness this phenomenon in Puerto Rico.

Bright Lights, Black Water

The bioluminescence you see in a few of Puerto Rico's sheltered mangrove bays depends on ocean-born microorganisms known as dynoflagellates. There are a number of these organisms in tropical waters, but the most abundant in Puerto Rico's 'phosphorous' bays is *Pirodinium bahamense*. (The term 'Pirodinium' comes from 'pyro,' meaning fire, and 'dinium,' meaning rotate.)

When any movement disturbs these creatures, a chemical reaction takes place in their microscopic bodies that produces the flash. Scientists speculate about the purpose of the flash; many think that the dynoflagellates have developed this ability to give off a sudden green light as a defense mechanism to ward off predators.

You can see these microorganisms flashing in Atlantic waters as far north as New England in the summer, but never in the brilliant concentrations appearing in Puerto Rico. As it turns out, enclosed

Puerto Rico's mangrove estuaries are the birthplace of the island's phosphorescent phenomenon.

mangrove bays, where narrow canals limit the exchange of water with the open sea, are the places that let the dynoflagellates breed and concentrate. In a sense, the bay is a big trap, and vitamins produced along the shore provide food for the corralled microorganisms.

Islas Mata la Gata & Caracoles

These two mangrove keys lie less than a half-mile offshore. The sandy strands on the seaside are really the only places in La Parguera to spend a traditional day at the beach. You can come here in your own rental boat or kayak, but the boat vendors at the town docks can take you for US$5 roundtrip.

Isla de Magueyes

You can see this large island lying about 200 yards south of the boat docks. Magueyes is the research station for the marine science division of the Universidad de Puerto Rico (University of Puerto Rico) in the city of Mayagüez, and you will probably see one or two research boats tied up at the docks. The island is closed to the public, but you may see some scientists cruising around town. Over the years, large iguanas and rhesus monkeys that were held on the island for research purposes have escaped (particularly when hurricanes passed through). Now the happy critters are breeding ashore – a source of embarrassment to the university and its scientists, but a great source of amusement to children and local wags.

Bosque Estatal de Boquerón

About 5 miles of the mangrove coast here, plus the islands and canals that wind among them – including the waterfront of the town and Bahía Fosforescente – are legally part what locals often call the La Parguera forest reserve. Actually, this mangrove estuary is just the eastern section of the Bosque Estatal de Boquerón. But nomenclature aside, the fact is that this estuary is an important and protected breeding ground for fish, marine mammals and sea birds – and it is threatened.

Dumping sewage here is illegal, as is clearing mangroves, building waterfront houses and anchoring boats. In other words, much of the community of La Parguera stands in violation of the law. For decades the government has been fighting to get people to remove the houses built illegally on the banks of these mangrove canals. But no one has moved out yet, and even after devastating hurricanes you still see these squatters re-building. Meanwhile, the quality of the water and the rest of the natural habitat decays.

Boating

Travelers have a number of vendors to choose from in this town. Cancel Boats (☎ 787-899-5891), at the town docks, has a lot of loyal customers renting their 15-foot whaler-type boats with 10hp engines for US$15 an hour. Competitor Torres Boat Service nearby has similar prices.

On an adjacent dock you will find Aleli (☎ 787-899-6086), which rents one/two-person kayaks for US$10/15 an hour, US$30/40 a half day, US$50/60 a full day.

Diving & Snorkeling

There are two good dive shops in town that rent snorkeling gear (US$10) and diving equipment. For US$35, Paradise Scuba Center (☎ 787-899-7611), in the Hotel Casa Blanca, will take you offshore to Cayo Enrique or Cayo Laurel on a four-hour snorkeling excursion that includes drinks and snacks. For US$50, you can take a sunset snorkeling trip that includes swimming after dark in Bahía Fosforescente.

Paguera Divers (☎ 787-899-4171), at the Posada Porlamar, is the oldest dive operation in the area, and many scuba fanatics return to this operator again and again to dive places like the Wall and Trench Alley to see big morays, barracuda and sea turtles. A two-tank dive at the Wall is US$70.

The Boquerón Dive Shop (☎ 787-851-2155), 58 Calle Muñoz Rivera, offers one-tank night dives for US$40 and also rents snorkeling gear for US$10 a day.

Fishing

You can fish the reefs for grouper, snapper or mackerel or head into deeper water for blue marlin, tuna or dorado. Parguera Fishing Charters runs half and full-day trips on their 31-foot Bertram out of the same dock as the Boquerón Dive Shop. Rates start at about US$250.

Windsurfing

Because of the area's sheltered waters and good breezes, board sailing is one of the most popular water sports here. See Eddie 'Gordo' Rodríguez at Ventolera water sports shop in the Muelle plaza, or head to the other end of town to Viento y Vela (☎ 787-899-4689). Expect to pay US$45 a day for your rig.

Horseback Riding

You can hire a horse for as little as a half hour or as long as a day to tour the 209-acre ranch called Gaby's World, off Hwy 2 in Yauco, which is 10 miles east of La Parguera. Prices start as low as US$15, and Gaby's actually has a racecourse for those who want to do the *National Velvet* thing.

Special Events

As La Parguera is a fishing port taking its name from the abundant pargo fish, a fiesta to celebrate the patron saint of fishers is in order. The Festia de San Pedro, held in the middle of June, packs the town and closes the main street with live music, food and artisan kiosks, puppets for the kids and enough beer to pollute the harbor.

Places to Stay

When you drive into La Parguera, you will see a lot of signs advertising rooms and apartments for rent, and if you are coming here off-season in the fall or spring, you might easily find a good deal at one of these places (perhaps US$250 a week for an apartment). On the other hand, you may find that a lot of these places are closed or waiting for the weekend to bag the college crowd that comes here to party. The places listed here are reliable and proven.

Guesthouses The *Guesthouse Viento y Vela* (☎ 787-899-3030) is the wood-framed windsurfing shop and hostel on the hill, on Hwy 304 at Km 3.2 across the street from Randy's Supermercado as you approach the center of town. You can get rooms with fans or air con. Rates are US$55. *Hostal Casa Blanca* (☎ 787-899-4250) is near the docks with about 20 basic rooms and private baths. Rates are US$68 weekdays, US$85 weekends.

The *Restaurante Pagomar* (☎ 787-899-4545), next to Randy's Supermercado, has several rooms upstairs with good views of the lagoon, the islands and the Caribbean. Expect to pay about US$40 for these basic rooms.

Hotels About two blocks east of the center of town, you will find a good value at *Andino's Chalet and Guesthouse* (☎ 787-899-0000, 133 Calle 8). You are some distance from the water here, but you do get a breezy terrace, air con, private bath, color TV and library. Some rooms go for as little as US$35, and US$90 will get you an apartment for five.

The *Nautilus Hotel* (☎ 787-899-4004) faces the parking lot and mangrove lagoon just east of the piers and restaurants in the center of town. This is a new modern place with air con, private baths, pool and Jacuzzi. There are 18 rooms, which rent for US$50 during the week, US$65 and up weekends.

Parador Villa Parguera (☎ 787-899-7777) is on the main street across from the church. This two-story hotel with 63 units comes closest to a luxury accommodation in town with its waterfront dock, private balconies, harbor views, landscaped seaside grounds and large swimming pool. There is also a gourmet restaurant and nightclub on-site. The rates – US$75 to US$85 – are a good value for what you get.

Just up the road to the west, the *Parador Posada Porlamar* (☎ 787-899-4015) is a tall building that lost part of its 3rd floor in Hurricane Georges. However, the hotel is back together with more than 24 units up and operating. Divers and fishers like this spot because a number of the charter boats work out of the Posada's private dock. Rooms start at US$75.

Parador Villa del Mar Hotel (☎ 787-899-4265, 3 Avenida Albizu Campos) is outside of town at the top of a hill with a view of the Bahía Fosforescente. There are 25 rooms here with the usual modern conveniences and a swimming pool. Rooms are US$80 to US$85.

Places to Eat

You will find many cheap-eats venues in this town. *La Lucerna Bakery*, in the same building as Restaurante Pagomar on Hwy 304 near Randy's Supermercado, is a gem with a friendly staff and good prices. Pancakes cost

US$1.50. The bakery's sandwiches, such as a *medianoche*, run less than US$2.

Among the bars and food kiosks at the waterfront by the docks, check out *El Karacol* for fresh *empanadillas de chapin* (US$1).

Tony's Pizza is in the facing building. A medium pie runs US$6.

Dave's Deli is the fresh new place in the Muelle shopping center where a grilled cheese sandwich costs US$2. Don't miss the stuffed baked potatoes for US$1.50.

La Parguera now has a Chinese restaurant in the Muelle shopping center as well: *Golden City* (☎ 787-899-5644) does a big take-out as well as eat-in business. The sweet-and-sour chicken is only US$5.

Among the more formal restaurants along the main street, locals favor *La Casita* for criollo-style seafood (entrées are around US$15) and *Parguera Steakhouse*, just up the road, for *churrasco* (US$14). The restaurant in the *Villa Parguera* (☎ 787-899-7777) is on the Puerto Rico Tourism Company's *mesones gastronómicos* list of the island's top dining spots, so make reservations.

Entertainment

You will find *Mar y Tierra* among the cluster of bars and restaurants that are packed together between the main street and the commercial docks. This place is more of a pavilion (with indoor and patio seating) than a traditional bar, and it pumps out live Latin rock and salsa on the weekends. The crowd gathers early, when happy-hour prices for Budweiser are 75¢ a can. And the gang stays late: Many are college students from Universidad Interamericana in San Germán, but the mix includes locals and students from other colleges as well. Some make the commute back to the schools or home after

the party, but a lot stay here for the weekend, packing as many people as they can into rented apartments or rooms in the less expensive hotels and guesthouses.

Up the road about 200 yards from the church in the center of town, you will see the new Muelle shopping center (really more of a strip mall). On its south end, the *Blues Café* has become another popular young person's scene, and both the inside and patio deck fill up many nights a week. Thursday is 'Ladies Night,' when women drink free for an hour and everyone tries to set dates for the weekend. Friday through Sunday, there is live jazz, salsa, rock and reggae.

An older crowd – including many couples – gathers at the parador *Villa Parguera* (☎ 787-899-7777), where there's always dancing and a show on Saturday night. The shows usually include well-known island singing stars and comedians. Expect to pay US$20 and up for the night.

Among gay and lesbian venues, *Milagro's Place* draws a mixed crowd on Hwy 116 between Lajas and La Parguera.

Getting There & Away

Público Vans come and go irregularly from a stop near the small waterfront park and boat piers in the center of the village. Service is basically local to nearby towns such as Lajas (US$1), where you can move on to bigger and better van stands in bigger and better municipalities.

Car As mentioned in the introduction to this section, you might not want to take the depressing Hwy 324 to get to La Parguera. The fastest way here is Hwy 2 via Hwy 116 from Guánica or San Germán. Follow the signs for the last couple of miles on Hwy 304.

West Coast

Even the briefest glance at a map of Puerto Rico can tell you a lot about the island's west coast. With its back to a thicket of mountains and the rest of the island, the long, bold coast faces the roily waves of the Pasaje de la Mona (Mona Passage). No place in Puerto Rico is farther from metropolitan San Juan. Of course, this seclusion is part of the region's charm, making it something of a frontier. In some ways, Puerto Rico's west coast is not unlike the Wild West of American fame. The cattle farms on rolling upland pastures south of Lajas have the look of northwest Texas. The mix of salt flats, bold cliffs and lack of human development on the peninsula of Cabo Rojo (not to be confused with the inland town of the same name) may remind travelers of Baja California. The colonial architecture and hillside plazas of San Germán recall the highlands of Mexico. Resort towns such as El Combate and Boquerón bring to mind the sights and smells of Baja California's Ensenada, with its long beaches and scents of grilled fish and beer, or the fiesta-happy beach towns in Mexico's state of Oaxaca.

The industrial waterfront in Mayagüez – with its tuna canneries and oceangoing ferry to the Dominican Republic – may put you in mind of Long Beach, south of Los Angeles. And for some travelers, the Universidad de Puerto Rico campus here conjures images of the University of Southern California.

Then there's Rincón, which has become a gringo oasis. Picture the north coast of Oahu in Hawaii, and you won't be far off the mark: rugged coast, big waves, humpback whales, emerald hills, coconut palms – the whole deal. And from the hilltops of Rincón you may be able to see the islands of Mona and Desecheo like mirages in the haze over the Pasaje de la Mona, looking more than a little like the island of Catalina, west of Los Angeles.

And while your mind is on LA, you may as well realize that Puerto Rico's west coast has its pockets of traffic, pollution and commercial and industrial development, too. If it starts to get to you, just pull on your darkest pair of shades and drive on to the next attraction of the region.

CABO ROJO

The name 'Cabo Rojo' can be a little confusing to the traveler because it appears twice on a map of the island's west coast, identifying two sites about 10 miles apart. Cabo Rojo (Red Cape) takes its name from the hue of the limestone cliffs at land's end – the extreme southwest tip of the island. Here, the Faro de Cabo Rojo (Red Cape Lighthouse; 1881) flashes its warning out to ships leaving and entering the Pasaje de la Mona. In a literal sense, these cliffs are the original and true Cabo Rojo.

But the colonists who settled the region claimed the entire southwest tip of Puerto Rico, and in 1771 likewise named their municipality Cabo Rojo. Today, that municipality includes the cape itself, more than 12 miles

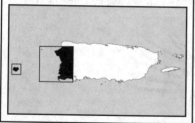

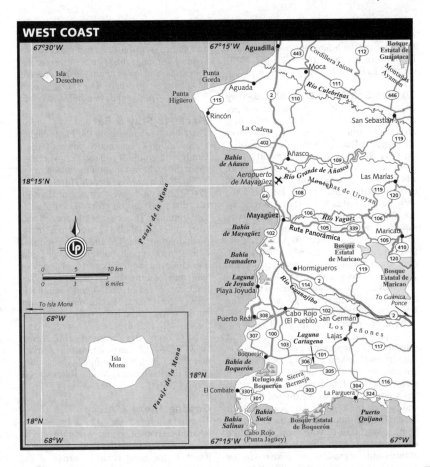

WEST COAST

Isla Desecheo
Punta Higüero
67°30'W
67°15'W
Aguadilla
443
Cordillera Jaicoa
112
Bosque Estatal de Guajataca
Montañas Ayamen
Punta Gorda
Aguada
Moca
115
2
111
110
Río Culebrinas
446
Rincón
La Cadena
402
San Sebastián
119
Bahía de Añasco
Añasco
109
18°15'N
Aeropuerto de Mayagüez
Río Grande de Añasco
Las Marías
64
108
Montañas de Uroyan
119
120
Pasaje de la Mona
Mayagüez
106
Río Yagüez
106
Bahía de Mayagüez
102
Ruta Panorámica
105
339
Maricao
105
Bahía Bramadero
Bosque Estatal de Maricao
410
120
Hormigueros
119
Bosque Estatal de Maricao
Laguna de Joyuda
Playa Joyuda
114
2
Río Guanajibo
To Guánica, Ponce
0   5   10 km
0   3   6 miles
To Isla Mona
68°W
Puerto Real
308
Cabo Rojo (El Pueblo)
102
San Germán
2
307
100
Laguna Cartagena
Lajas
Los Peñones
Isla Mona
103
101
117
Boquerón
306
Bahía de Boquerón
18°N
305
Refugio de Boquerón
Sierra Bermeja
El Combate
3301
303
La Parguera
304
324
301
Pasaje de la Mona
Bahía Salinas
Bahía Sucia
Cabo Rojo (Punta Jagüey)
Bosque Estatal de Boquerón
Puerto Quijano
18°N
68°W
67°15'W
67°W

of western coastline and miles of adjacent inland territory. To distinguish the cape from the municipality, colonists added the name Punta Jagüey to describe the rocky headland. The villages of El Combate and Boquerón – both of significant interest to travelers – are actually part of this large municipality as well (see those sections, later in this chapter). The seat of municipal government, however, is an inland village known locally as El Pueblo but often labeled as 'Cabo Rojo' on maps. The village is near the intersection of Hwy 102 and Hwy 100.

Basically, the town of Cabo Rojo is a country market community that holds little attraction for the traveler save a small museum dedicated to local heroes, including Ramón Betances, the father of Puerto Rico's independence movement. The area's real attractions – and lodging options – are found closer to the water's edge. The following sections primarily focus on the remote corner of the island known as Cabo Rojo, which includes the cape itself and the headland at its southernmost tip known as Punta Jagüey.

You can get good brochures covering local and islandwide entertainment and accommodations at the branch office of the Puerto Rico Tourism Company (☎ 787-851-7070), south of El Pueblo on Hwy 100, Km 13.7.

Corozo Salt Flats & Punta Jagüey

For a truly serene drive through undeveloped coastal plain – or even better – a refreshing cycling adventure, approach Cabo Rojo from La Parguera (see the South Coast chapter) via Hwy 304, Hwy 305 and Hwy 303. Then follow Hwy 301 south until it turns to dirt, where you'll traverse a narrow spit of sand between Bahía Salinas (Salt Bay) and the aptly named Bahía Sucia (Dirty Bay). Vast salt flats surround this narrow peninsula, especially to the east; humans have been gathering salt here since 700 AD. When the first Spaniards arrived, they quickly took over the evaporation pools used by the Taínos to collect salt and expanded the business, making it a sustaining force in the local economy until efficient sugarcane farming arrived in the 18th century.

At the Corozo Salt Flats, you'll see pools of evaporating brine and mounds of salt waiting to be shipped to market alongside the dirt road as you proceed south toward the headland of Punta Jagüey, where scrub forest sets in and the land rises to the steep limestone cliffs. Go to the end of the road and park on the left near the vacant crescent beach. The lighthouse and surrounding cliffs lie up a sand trail to your right. If you like windblown settings, fraught with the screech of birds and the crash of surf (like navigator Prince Henry's lookout on the cliffs of Sagres in Portugal), this place is for you. Also, the bathing is good in the very salty cove, off the beach to the east.

Refugio Nacional Cabo Rojo

This refuge (☎ 787-851-7297, 851-7258) is on Hwy 301 at Km 5.1, about a mile north of the Hwy 3301 turnoff to El Combate. The visitors center at Refugio Nacional Cabo Rojo (Red Cape National Refuge) contains displays on local wildlife and wildlife management techniques. Outdoors you will find bird-watching trails among the ruins of an old farmstead in the Valle de Lajas (Lajas Valley). This area around the coastal plains and shores of Cabo Rojo is a major winter ground for migratory ducks, herons and songbirds, and more than 130 bird species have been sighted here. The refuge is open 7:30 am to 4 pm weekdays; admission is free.

Places to Stay & Eat

There are no campsites in the Punta Jagüey area, though occasionally you will see a family or a group of college kids who have spent the night in a tent on the beach.

The *Bahía Salinas Beach Hotel* (☎ 787-254-1212) is on the western side of Hwy 301 (the dirt road) as you cross the salt flats to the lighthouse. This is a recently opened one-story place with all the usual trimmings (including air con, TV and kayak rentals), housed in a compound of rancho-style buildings clustered around a courtyard and pool. With only 24 units, you get plenty of privacy. Rack rates start at US$80, but some packages go for US$62. The *seafood restaurant* on the terrace here is the only place to eat for miles. There's live music on weekends.

Next door, the *Punta Aguila Resort* (☎ 787-254-4454) rents out efficiency apartments in a multilevel, condo-style building facing the Pasaje de la Mona. Rates start at about US$100.

Getting There & Away

Travelers touring the island by *público* (shared taxi) must be aware that there is no regular van service to the Punta Jagüey area, which is the most remote corner of the island. Some days there is a morning *público* that runs between the town of Cabo Rojo (El Pueblo) and the point, but you can't count on it. A more reliable option is to come by rental car or bike (particularly the route from La Parguera via Hwy 304, Hwy 305 and Hwy 303).

EL COMBATE

Signs on Hwy 301 point westward to Hwy 3301 and the somewhat battered beach town of El Combate (the Battle), named after a Spanish colonial turf war held here centuries ago for control of the lucrative salt

Zorro Goes to Sea: The Obligatory Pirate Tale

As far as many Puerto Ricans are concerned, the famous foreign privateers (including the likes of Francis Drake, John Hawkins and Henry Morgan) who plundered shipping off the coast of Puerto Rico and took refuge on offshore islands were scoundrels, thieves and murderers. But Puerto Rico's own homegrown freebooter, Roberto Cofresí y Ramirez de Arellano, constitutes a virtual maritime Robin Hood or Zorro of the 19th century.

As the story goes, poor Roberto came into this world in the *barrio* of Guaniquilla (a neighborhood of Cabo Rojo) under some daunting handicaps in 1791: He was the youngest of four brothers (no chance at inheritance), and his mother died when he was only four. His father sent him to primary school, but Roberto didn't take much to schooling, preferring to read stories of maritime heroics and buccaneers – and re-create them in his little boat *El Mosquito*.

In keeping with the nature of folk heroes, the young Roberto was strong and agile, with an agreeable personality that won the sympathy and confidence of his contemporaries. He was a *buen chico* (good boy), according to the residents of Cabo Rojo, admired for his bravery and leadership as a mariner.

And while his fellow countrymen were busy circumventing Spanish colonial law and trading their sugar, rum, cattle and coffee with ships from all over the Atlantic, young Roberto and a crew of his neighbors from Cabo Rojo got themselves some guns and a fast boat to ambush the fat, happy foreign vessels as they lumbered through the Pasaje de la Mona, just like in the good old days of the 17th century. Since Roberto and company only attacked vessels flying foreign flags – and the pirate shared his loot with local citizens of Cabo Rojo – he thrived with impunity. But not for long.

A host of foreign governments complained to Spain, and in 1825 the governor of Puerto Rico received orders from the Spanish government to put an end to this embarrassment known as 'El Pirata Cofresí' (Cofresí the pirate). Consequently, according to island historians, local Spanish forces 'were obliged to pursue and capture' troublesome Capitano Roberto. March 29, 1825, saw the pirate-hero executed in San Juan with 11 of his compatriots. His remains rest in the Cementerio de San Juan, outside the northern wall of the old city. Back in Cabo Rojo, people lamented that their darling Roberto had been born a century too late for such out-and-out piratical daring. Then everyone went back to their smuggling.

Today, the US Drug Enforcement Agency (DEA) maintains a radar surveillance blimp tethered over Cabo Rojo to watch for drug smuggling in Roberto's old waters. According to local observers, the only thing the blimp ever sees are the boatloads of illegal immigrants headed to Puerto Rico from the Dominican Republic. The drugs get through; contemporary Robertos don't fly the skull and crossbones.

---

flats to the south. But the only fighting you might see these days is over the last bottle of Medalla or Coors Light. On weekends and holidays, high school and college kids pour into town with coolers full of beer and Bacardi, bound for the water's edge to re-create the rites of spring ad infinitum. Once

the gang gets liquored up, things can get a little crazy around here.

El Combate's sole attraction is what is reputed to be the longest beach in Puerto Rico. Locals claim the beach runs more than 3 miles along the Pasaje de la Mona. And it's a good thing that it's long: A whole lot of people want to use it, including many Puerto Rican families. Gringos and other visitors rarely frequent this stretch of sand.

The town is packed with rather temporary-looking guesthouses, trailer-camping sites, beach houses and bars that look even less substantial and attractive since Hurricane Georges whipped through town.

Places to Stay & Eat

Villas Mojacasabe (☎ 787-254-4888) is the big operator here. This place is inside a sturdy fence on the north side of the village. There are rows of little air-conditioned cabins for rent, an amusement hall with a bar, a boardwalk and a launch ramp for your Jet Ski. The crowds pile in here to listen to live Latin rock, salsa and merengue on weekends. A wooden or concrete cabin that sleeps six costs US$100 per night.

Among the more than half a dozen guesthouses in the area, your best bet for cleanliness is probably *Caribbean Connection Apartments* (☎ 787-254-2358), at the south end of town. Rates start around US$55.

Annie's Place is a bar-restaurant across the street on the beach (but with no view). This popular watering hole has reasonable prices: A cup of fish soup goes for 50¢; beer is US$1.

Getting There & Away

Públicos run frequently to/from the town of Cabo Rojo (El Pueblo) from April to the end of August. The fare is US$1.50. In Cabo Rojo you can connect to Mayagüez (US$4) or Ponce (US$7).

If you're arriving by car, El Combate is at the bitter end of Hwy 3301. Go west at the turnoff from Hwy 301.

BOQUERÓN

If El Combate is a little too rough around the edges for you – or if you're in search of people who speak English – head 2 miles north on Hwy 301 and then west on Hwy 101 to Boquerón. This is one of the places historians claim Columbus may have landed when he 'discovered' Borinquen in 1493 – and renamed it Puerto Rico. When you look out from the palm-shaded *balneario* onto

this deep bay – protected by hills and forests on three sides – you can see why a mariner might have found this anchorage attractive.

Sailors still do. Boquerón is a popular year-round port for both local sailors and foreign cruisers. But the bay really fills up with boats around the end of March when cruising sailboats that have spent winter all over the Caribbean use Boquerón as a staging area to provision and find companion vacation vessels before starting the long trip back north (toward the USA) through the Pasaje de la Mona, along Hispaniola and through the Bahamas.

Members of Puerto Rico's moneyed class are also attracted by Boquerón's engaging natural setting, and recent years have seen a plethora of private luxury vacation villas rise on the hillsides around town. To be sure, Boquerón is not the world's greatest beach town. But it is an attractive middle-class resort village that is becoming trendy and upscale. The crowd here is much more likely to include professional families and yuppies than the college and high school posses at El Combate, and prices rise accordingly. But if you like to rub shoulders with a cosmopolitan crowd in a party mood, Boquerón could work for you, and there are still some reasonably priced accommodations here.

One word of advice: Do not come to Boquerón on a major holiday such as the Fourth of July or Puerto Rican Constitution Day (July 25). The police close the downtown area to cars, and traffic backs up for miles in all directions as everybody scrambles to get here in search of their own piece of *la dulce vida* (the sweet life).

Refugio de Boquerón

If you have read about La Parguera in the South Coast chapter, you know that much of the mangrove estuary there (about 12 miles from Boquerón) is part of Bosque Estatal de Boquerón. The western section of that forest carries the name Refugio de Boquerón and is made up of more than 400 acres of mangrove wetlands, about 2 miles south of town between the coast and Hwy 301. This is an excellent area for bird-watching; more than 60 species are commonly sighted. A number of duck species migrate here in the winter, as well as osprey and mangrove canary. An excellent way to see this sanctuary is to rent a kayak and paddle south across Bahía de Boquerón (Boquerón Bay), but there's a boardwalk trail off Hwy 301 as well.

Beaches
You can't miss the sign to Balneario Boquerón on Hwy 101, which heads south a quarter of a mile from town to the beach. Parking is US$2.

Playa Buyé is a smaller beach that's about 2 1/2 miles north of town off Hwy 307.

Diving & Snorkeling
Mona Aquatics (☎ 787-851-2185), on Calle José de Diego next to the *club náutico* west of the center of town, has a 43-foot dive boat – *Orca Too* – which can take you to Isla Mona, 50 miles out at sea, for a day dive (US$65) or a weekend dive (US$115). Local night dives run US$50. Mona Aquatics also rents snorkeling gear and operates US$7 boat tours of Bahía de Boquerón.

Note that nearby La Parguera has good diving and snorkeling opportunities as well (see Diving & Snorkeling under La Parguera in the South Coast chapter).

Kayaking
Kaipo Kayak Rentals (☎ 787-254-3413) is on Boquerón's short main street – Calle de Diego – north of the landmark Shamar Bar-Restaurant & Hotel (see Places to Stay, below). Boats go for US$15 an hour, but you can get better rates for multiple hours.

Golf
Club Desportivo de Oeste (☎ 787-851-8880), near the intersection of Hwy 102 and Hwy 308 in Cabo Rojo (El Pueblo), is a Jack Bender-designed nine-hole course with a panoramic view along its 3360 yards. Greens fees are US$20 and up, depending on the time you play.

Places to Stay
Guesthouses Roberto 'Bob' Sancho and his wife Cat run the **Shamar Bar-Restaurant & Hotel** (☎ 787-851-0542), located right at the center of the village. In fact, Shamar is the oldest commercial building in Boquerón and has been a working bar for more than 50 years. Except for the *centro vacacional* (see below), it is also the only place to rent a room on the water in Boquerón.

Bob has rebuilt the structure himself (concrete sheathed in wood), and you can rent his simple but attractive rooms with seaside balconies over the bar and restaurant for US$70 off-season. Prices go up from Easter through summer, and people book years in advance for major fiestas such as the Fourth of July. Stay here if you like to party, because the crowd downstairs is all fired up from late on Wednesday to Sunday night.

Locals say that a quieter option is up the street at *El Muelle Guest House*, but it was closed during our last pass through town.

Centros Vacacionales The *Boquerón Centro Vacacional* (☎ 787-851-1900) is right on the beach at Balneario Boquerón. Each of the 158 modern apartments (in two-story duplex units) holds six people and comes with bath, kitchen, bunk beds and ceiling fans. (Plans for 42 additional units have been drawn up.) Activity rooms, a convenience store and first-aid station are on the premises. The rate is only US$65 a night, but the place gets booked a year in advance for summer and holidays.

Hotels The *Parador Boquemar* (☎ 787-851-2158) has more than 60 rooms in a three-story building. You will see the *parador* on your right as you head north on the main street of Calle de Diego (really an extension of Hwy 101). Rooms have air con, private bath, color TV, telephone and balcony. There is a small pool and restaurant on the ground floor. Rates start at US$65.

Adamari's Apartments (☎ 787-851-6860) is the tall building right next to the parador, with a Laundromat on the 1st floor. While this place is not state of the art, it does have nine clean efficiency apartments (many with ocean views). Rates are US$65.

You will get a lot more luxury at the *Cofresí Beach Club* (☎ 787-254-3000), on Hwy 101 as you approach the center of the village from the south. Recently opened, this three-story building has one-, two- and three-bedroom apartments. The one-bedroom sleeps four and goes for US$79 in the fall, US$99 in the winter and US$119 during the spring and summer. Each unit is fully equipped, including a microwave and TV with VCR. There's a view of the bay from the pool.

Slightly farther out of town (to the south, at the turnoff for the balneario and the centro vacacional), the **Boquerón Beach Hotel** (☎ 787-851-7110) has 35 units. This place has the feel of a roadside motel because it borders busy streets on two sides. There is a pool, however, and the rates are reasonable at US$59 to US$107. The actual beach is at least a quarter of a mile away.

The **Cuestamar Hotel** (☎ 787-851-2819) is on the north side of town at Km 7.4 upon Hwy 307. Here you will find another three-story apartment hotel (must be a zoning thing). You'll have to drive to the beach from here, but the hilltop location affords a good view, and there is a small pool. Rates for the 25 units start at US$55.

The **Lighthouse Inn** (☎ 787-255-3835), at the intersection of Hwy 102 and Hwy 100, lies about 5 miles north of Boquerón near Cabo Rojo (El Pueblo). This roadside mini-resort has 31 units, a pool, outdoor bar and restaurant. It looks like something right out of a 1960s brochure for some huge Atlantic beach resort such as Ocean City, Maryland, or Myrtle Beach, South Carolina. Rates range from US$65 to US$125.

Rental Agents Riosun (☎ 787-851-5468) rents out scores of vacation homes and condos in the area. Expect to pay US$300 to US$1000 a week.

Places to Eat

Pizzeria Lyken (☎ 787-851-6335, 28 Calle de Diego) is in the middle of town. You can eat on the patio or carry out. A large cheese pizza costs US$10.

Shamar Bar-Restaurant & Hotel (see Places to Stay, above) also has some good cheap eats like burgers for US$4.50. The Sanchos, who run Shamar, also run the **Bistro**, which is the intimate café just across

the street facing the little park. The cuisine here is actually a couple of imaginative jumps beyond basic *cocina americana y criolla*. Try the *chillo almondén* or the *torta rústica* (a spinach pie with ham, salami and three cheeses) for US$6.50.

Galloways (☎ 787-254-3302) extends out over the water on a 2nd-story deck across from Adamari's Apartments. This place does a popular fern-bar imitation of seafood restaurants in Sydney or San Francisco. The management prices the entrées accordingly. Light pub fare runs under US$9; real dinners cost US$14 and up.

The **Paradise** (☎ 787-851-5003, 210A Calle de Diego), on the north end of the main street, is a very popular patio restaurant. The Paradise specializes in seafood that owner Elvin Comacho either catches himself or buys from fishers in Puerto Real. The lobster dinner price here (US$16) is the lowest in Boquerón.

You will find more formal dining for couples and families across the street on the water at the **Club Náutico**. Comacho owns this place too, so the cuisine and prices are similar to those of the Paradise.

Entertainment

Considering that Boquerón is one of the few towns on the island that puts a cap on serving alcohol – midnight on weekdays, 1 am on weekends – the place remains a major party scene.

Shamar Bar-Restaurant & Hotel (see Places to Stay, earlier in this section) has the most popular pool table at this end of the island, and many of the talented wait in line to try their skills. The college crowd and local yuppies (not really viewed as a pejorative term on the island) jam into this place to watch the events at the pool table, drink happy-hour specials, listen to live salsa or merengue on weekends and grope each other. This is not totally a straight scene either, especially on Thursday and Friday nights when Shamar is a popular cruising ground for lesbians.

Galloways (see Places to Eat, above) drops all pretense of being a restaurant by 9 pm on weekends, when a yuppie crowd shows up for live music and Medalla. You might meet an interesting gringo calling himself 'ELM,' who has painted a lot of the art you see on the walls here.

The patio at the *Paradise* (see Places to Eat, above) also fills with the beautiful-people-who-love-cell-phones crowd on weekend nights. You can hear live jazz and Latin rock here.

Shopping

In addition to a few of the usual boutiques you find in upscale resort villages, Boquerón offers some good local art. Amil Droz (☎ 787-849-1027) is a Newyorican painter and sculptor who has returned to his roots to specialize in indigenous art. He makes exceptional Taíno *cemíes* and *vejigante* Carnaval masks (see Traditional Arts in the Facts about Puerto Rico chapter for details on these art forms). Inquire at the Paradise restaurant, where Amil works part-time.

Getting There & Away

The easiest way to get here by público is via the town of Cabo Rojo (El Pueblo). From April to August, it's easy to find one for about US$1.50. From El Pueblo, you can catch a van to Mayagüez (US$4), Ponce (US$7) or San Germán.

If you're driving from El Pueblo or Mayagüez, follow Hwy 100 south to Hwy 101, and turn right (west). From San Germán, it's a straight shot west on Hwy 101 south of Lajas.

PUERTO REAL

Another coastal village that is part of the Cabo Rojo municipality, Puerto Real lies about 4 miles north of Boquerón (follow Hwy 307 north and then head west on Hwy 308) and is frequently referred to as 'the biggest fishing port on the west coast.' That's not saying much on an island where fishing brings in less than 1% of the GNP, and Puerto Real itself is not much either. For dirt, decrepitude and foul smells, this place stacks right up with some of those pirate dens you might have seen on the east coast of peninsular Malaysia.

But there are two excellent reasons for adventuresome travelers to pass this way: whale-watching or taking a boat out to the marine sanctuary of Isla Mona 50 miles offshore. (For details, see the Isla Mona section, later in this chapter.)

Whale-Watching

Every winter the *Viking Starship* (☎ 787-823-7010) makes the long trek down to the Pasaje de la Mona from its summer whale-watching base on Long Island, New York. It follows the humpback whales that feed all summer in the New England waters, then come here to mate and calve during the winter. This 140-foot, high-speed vessel can carry 300 passengers and offers great day trips from Puerto Real. During your trip, the naturalist onboard speaks about the whales and other sea life you'll encounter. The sundeck Tiki Bar serves drinks and light food.

Whale-watching trips depart from mid-January to mid-April. Weekend trips are for the general public; from Wednesday through Friday, the boat generally takes school trips, but the public is welcome. Boarding time is usually at 10 am; the boat departs at 11 am and returns around 5 pm. You will find the boat at the wharf at Pescadería Rosas. Rates are US$25 adults, US$12 children. Reservations are suggested.

Diving & Snorkeling

The Caribbean Reef Dive Shop (☎ 787-254-4006) is in one of the warehouses facing the docks in the center of the village. You can get certified through these folks (starting at US$200) or go on a half-day snorkeling trip including a picnic lunch (US$35). A two-tank dive from the 28-foot *Delta Dive Boat* runs US$75. Expect to pay at least US$120 for a weekend dive trip to Mona (see the Isla Mona section at the end of this chapter for details on the island).

WEST COAST

Getting There & Away

You can access Puerto Real via público from the station on the eastern fringe of Cabo Rojo (El Pueblo) for US$1.50. Be advised that these vans don't leave in a timely fashion, so don't depend on them if you are planning to make a date for a diving or whale-watching excursion.

PLAYA JOYUDA

This is the last of Cabo Rojo's diverse coastal villages that you see as you head north to Mayagüez, and there is little here for a traveler to get excited about. Clearly, this beach-resort community's proximity to Mayagüez contributed to its development as a retreat for middle-class citizens of the city when it was an industrial and shipping boomtown 100 years ago. The settlement is laid out in a long line on both sides of Hwy 102 as it parallels the coast south of Mayagüez, and one gets the impression that a railroad might once have run along this route from Mayagüez to bring holidaymakers out to the beach.

The problem is that years of coastal erosion have left Joyuda with little more than a dirt bank and desperately constructed seawalls where once there was a sandy beach. Meanwhile, as the beach was washing away, development was crowding the land with tourist-related businesses: beach houses, condos, hotels and restaurants, restaurants and more restaurants. With 35 family-owned seafood restaurants along this 3-mile stretch of highway, Joyuda claims the nickname 'Capital de los Mariscos' (Shellfish Capital).

Many of the oysters, crab and shrimp served up here come from the neighboring Laguna de Joyuda, which provides an exceptional nature retreat just a few hundred yards from the center of town.

Reserva Natural Laguna de Joyuda

The heart of this over-300-acre wildlife reserve is a saltwater lagoon a mile long and a half-mile wide, with a depth that rarely exceeds 4 feet. The sanctuary is of great importance to waterfowl and other migratory birds that come here to prey on more than 40 species of fish. Humans come here for the same reason.

The reserve is also home to another of Puerto Rico's famous bioluminescent bodies of water, like its famous cousins in La Parguera and Vieques, but free of commercial tourism. After dark, dynoflagellate microorganisms give the dark water a green glow. Travelers with access to a canoe or kayak can launch a nighttime exploration of the lagoon; watch for the access road off Hwy 102 near Parador Pirichi's. For more on this bioluminescent phenomenon, see 'Bright Lights, Black Water' in the South Coast chapter.

Places to Stay

Joyuda Plaza (☎ 787-851-8800), at Km 14.7 on Hwy 102, is across the street from the beach and is one of the best values in this area. Friendly and helpful Rita Acosta runs this modern multistory hotel, which has 55 rooms and two pools. You get all the usual amenities here for US$55; a studio apartment costs US$75.

Nearby, **Parador Pirichi's** (☎ 787-851-5650), at Km 14.3 on Hwy 102, has long been a popular family vacation spot. There are 41 rooms with balconies and air con here, with a restaurant and large pool downstairs.

Farther up the road at Km 11.7, the **Parador Joyuda Beach** (☎ 787-851-5650) is right on the narrow strand of beach. The beach is not much, but the snorkeling right offshore is OK, as long as the wind stays southerly. The hotel has a restaurant, pool and 41 rooms. Rates start at US$70.

Places to Eat

Local seafood addicts swear by **El Bohio**, **Raito** and **Vista Bahía**. All these restaurants are on the strip and specialize in grilled lobster (about US$18) and *mofongo* stuffed with seafood (about US$16).

SAN GERMÁN

There has been so much balderdash written about the historical significance and architectural charms of San Germán that many travelers find themselves a little disappointed when they actually visit. This hillside country town lies about 10 miles inland from the Cabo Rojo coast, and 36 acres of its historic center are on the National Register of

Historic Places. San Germán's four-square-block center offers a haunting evocation of Puerto Rico's colonial past. But don't expect a Williamsburg, Virginia; Paratí, Brazil; or San Miguel de Allende, Mexico – places where residents strive to turn every corner into romantic specters from the past, peppering the streets with inns, restaurants and businesses to match. Most inhabitants of San Germán seem to ignore the town's historic core, sticking instead to the main street of Calle Luna, which is packed with fast-food restaurants, tacky commercial signs and a modern new city hall.

Nevertheless, you may still find a trip to San Germán a welcome break from west-coast beach scenes. This is the island's second-oldest settlement (1512), and it owes its name to Germaine de Foix, the second wife of Spain's King Ferdinand. Surrounded by sharply peaked hills, the town has been nicknamed the 'Ciudad de las Lomas' (City of Hills). Even the two plazas in the center of the historic district – divided by the old town hall (1839) – slope downhill.

At the high end of the Plaza Francisco Quiñones, the 18th-century Catedral de San Germán de Auxerre rises monumentally against the sky and looks downhill on ranks of *criollo*, neoclassical and Victorian structures. At the foot of Plaza Santo Domingo stands Iglesia de Porta Coeli. The striking thing here – besides the architecture – is that both plazas are unnaturally quiet; there's virtually no traffic or commerce in the area, in stark contrast to the colonial plazas of Old San Juan and Ponce. The plazas and historic churches of San Germán (like the quiet lanes of the dormant sugar town of Aguirre) seem lost in time.

All of that changes, however, when the sun goes down and several pubs and restaurants around the plazas open to serve the students who attend the Universidad Interamericana,

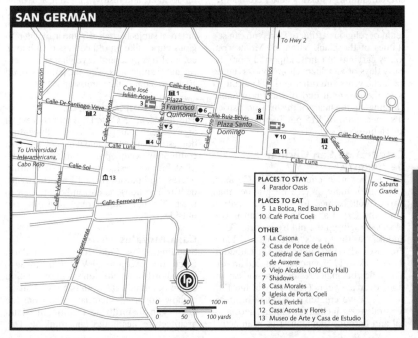

SAN GERMÁN

PLACES TO STAY
4 Parador Oasis

PLACES TO EAT
5 La Botica, Red Baron Pub
10 Café Porta Coeli

OTHER
1 La Casona
2 Casa de Ponce de León
3 Catedral de San Germán
    de Auxerre
6 Viejo Alcaldía (Old City Hall)
7 Shadows
8 Casa Morales
9 Iglesia de Porta Coeli
11 Casa Perichi
12 Casa Acosta y Flores
13 Museo de Arte y Casa de Estudio

WEST COAST

which is situated on a pastoral campus less than a half mile to the west. The truth is that, in its ordinary daily life, San Germán defines itself much more as a college town than as a historic place. And for college travelers and the young at heart, this town can rock.

Iglesia de Porta Coeli

Constructed between 1606 and 1607 as the chapel for the Dominican Monastery (itself demolished in the 1860s), this small but dramatic church (☎ 787-892-5845) is poised at the crown of a long, steep flight of steps and is the oldest house of worship outside of San Juan. It is also one of the best surviving examples of early colonial construction techniques on the island. Porta Coeli ('Heaven's Gate' in Latin) has an interior with *ausubo* pillars and roof beams and a ceiling made from palm wood, which is typical of construction in Puerto Rico during the 17th and 18th centuries.

Today, Porta Coeli is no longer an active church (although mass is held here on special occasions). The building belongs to the Instituto de Cultura and functions as a museum of religious artifacts. Here you can see statues of the black Virgin of Montserrat, folksy carvings of Christ imported from the early days of San Juan, choral books dating back 300 years and other curios. The church is at the downhill end of the Plaza Santo Domingo in the heart of the historic district. It's open 9 am to 4:15 pm Tuesday to Sunday; admission is US$1.

Catedral de San Germán de Auxerre

This is the 'other church' in San Germán, and it is actually quite a bit grander than Porta Coeli. Named for the town's patron saint, the Catedral de San Germán is two blocks straight up the hill from Porta Coeli, and it faces the town's 'other plaza' – Plaza Francisco Mariano Quiñones. The cathedral dates back to 1739, when it replaced an earlier edifice, but major restorations and expansions over the years (especially in the 19th century) have created a mélange of architectural styles, including colonial, neoclassical and baroque elements. This is an active

DAVE G HOUSER

San Germán has a wealth of ornate architecture.

parish; if you visit for a Saturday or Sunday service, take note of the crystal chandelier that helps to light the main nave and the *trompe l'oeil* fresco.

Museo de Arte y Casa de Estudio

Built in 1903, this memorable example of patrician residential architecture now houses the local art and history museum, at 7 Calle Esperanza, which is typical of most proud Puerto Rican towns. Rooms are dedicated to different subjects, such as Taíno artifacts, religious curios like an old confessional booth, colonial furniture and revolving shows featuring graphic arts. The museum is open 10 am to 3 pm daily; admission is free.

Casa de Ponce de León

This house, at 13 Calle Dr Santiago Veve, is an excellent example of local 17th-century domestic architecture, and it may be the most continually occupied house in the town. Its most famous resident was a 19th-century poetess and patriot named Lola Rodríguez de Tió. The house is currently not open to the public, but you can observe it from the outside.

Casa Morales

Standing across Calle Ramos from Porta Coeli, this exceptional Victorian house – built shortly after the American occupation of the island in 1898 – offers a visual image of how imported Victorian taste from the US began to infiltrate traditional island architecture, aesthetics and thinking. This house is currently a private residence and can be admired only from the outside.

Casa Acosta y Flores
Built in 1917, this house is one of the best examples of the art-nouveau era in Puerto Rican architecture. Today a private residence, Casa Acosta y Flores is located a block east of Porta Coeli on Calle Dr Veve.

Casa Perichi
This 1920s-era estate, at 94 Calle Luna, is yet another architectural monument that can only be viewed from the outside. It has been on the National Register of Historic Places since 1986. The house contains remarkable examples of what has been called 'Puerto Rican ornamental artisan architecture.'

La Casona
This mid-19th-century house, on Calle José Julián Acosta at Calle de la Cruz, was once the meeting place for an elite San Germán social group known as the Círculo de Recreo. The house is not open to the public.

Viejo Alcaldía
A classic example of 19th-century colonial municipal buildings, Viejo Alcaldía (Old City Hall) is not only remarkable for its architecture, but also for its location dividing the two historic plazas and churches. (Or viewed from another perspective, the eyes of the Catholic church watch over both the front and the back doors of the government.) The departure of the municipal government for new headquarters on Calle Luna has blessed the historic district with a new solitude. Unfortunately, changing mayoral regimes cannot decide what to do with this beautiful old building, thus it stands empty – some say it's a metaphor for the town.

Universidad Interamericana
Founded in 1912, the Universidad Interamericana (☎ 787-892-3090) is now the largest private university in the Western Hemisphere. Today, the Interamericana has branch campuses in San Juan, Arecibo, Barranquitas, Bayamón, Fajardo, Guayama and Ponce. Tens of thousands of students work toward degrees at Interamericana in both its Spanish and English programs.

The 267-acre campus in San Germán is without a doubt the most attractive college setting in Puerto Rico, and it draws about 6000 students from the island and all corners of the globe.

Special Events
If you're here for the Sugar Harvest Festival (☎ 787-892-5574), held late in April, you'll be able to drink huge quantities of rum (which is distilled from sugarcane) while learning about the farming process.

Places to Stay
If you're planning to spend the night in San Germán, your only choice is the *Parador Oasis* (☎ 800-981-7575, 72 Calle Luna), the convent-like building with Romanesque arched windows in the heart of the historic district. Although there are 52 units in this place, the small lobby, intimate dining room and bric-a-brac Victorian decorations make it seem as homey as your grandmother's house. And the staff is just as casual and nurturing. All rooms have air con and TV. The pool on the property is small but a welcome oasis here in the middle of town, and the restaurant serves full American breakfasts for about US$3. Rooms run about US$60.

Places to Eat
You probably will not take all of your meals at the *Oasis* (see above), even though it is a gourmet establishment. If you are on a tight budget, follow Calle Luna west over the crest of the hill toward the university campus, where college folk parade in and out of all the favorite fast-food franchises. The most interesting of these is *Food Escape*, where a large pizza costs US$7.

You can catch a cheap dessert just up the hill at *Columbo Frozen Yogurt (35 Calle Luna)*. A small serving costs US$1.

If you are looking for a romantic place to refuel, head into the heart of the historic quarter. *La Botica (☎ 787-892-5790)*, on Calle de la Cruz near Calle Dr Santiago Veve, is a steakhouse with dim lights and sharp scents amid the decor of a restored pharmacy. Beef entrées like *parrillada* and *churrasco* are in the US$15 range.

Café Porta Coeli is a trendy California-style eatery just across the street from the famous chapel. You will find an international mix of things here. The salads are good and cost around US$7.

Entertainment

Los Tigres (☎ 787-264-5505), a popular bar-restaurant next to the campus gate, draws a student crowd most afternoons and evenings. It has a lively jukebox, pool table and a good porch for drink-sipping and people-watching. You can get 50¢ beers and 75¢ rums at the Thursday happy hour, when it gets difficult to shoulder up to the bar.

The ***Red Baron Pub*** (☎ 787-892-5770) is underneath La Botica steakhouse, and this place rocks and rolls almost all week long. On Tuesday, Wednesday and Thursday evenings, college kids form a line to get into this tight, smoky bistro and get pumped up to live music. Beers cost 1¢ from 4 to 5 pm during midweek. Sunday is 'Sport Night.'

Shadows is a disco-bar in the next block on Calle Ruiz Belvis, across from the old city hall. Things go late here.

The ***Hacienda Villa Coquí***, at Km 38 on Hwy 102, has a country-club setting for gay couples and cruisers. Things get wilder at the ***World*** (formerly the World Upside Down), another gay club on the same road.

Getting There & Away

San Germán enjoys frequent público service to/from Ponce (US$6) or Mayagüez (US$4).

San Germán lies just south of the Hwy 2 expressway, so if you are driving here from the west coast, follow Hwy 102 from the town of Cabo Rojo (El Pueblo).

MAYAGÜEZ

The 'capital' of the west coast has seen more prosperous days, and its decline may ultimately be its blessing. For centuries of colonial rule, Mayagüez was the guardian of the Pasaje de la Mona and the best deepwater port outside of San Juan. It was the gateway to commerce with Hispaniola across 'the Mona,' a major agricultural exporter of coffee

grown in the nearby mountains and – after the American takeover – one of the island's first industrial centers. A lot of people got rich here, and you can still see the magnitude of personal wealth accumulated in Mayagüez in the gated palaces – some of the most lavish on the island – that dot the mountaintop in the neighborhood of Las Mesas, west of the city.

But central Mayagüez is in obvious decline. Older citizens say it started with a catastrophic earthquake in 1918, which reduced much of the city to rubble. Middle-aged citizens say their city was overlooked for decades as US attention and capital investment shifted to San Juan. Younger citizens think the city's problems are rooted in the recent closing of more than half of the area's tuna canneries, which once packaged more than half of the tuna sold in the US. Everyone agrees, however, that Mayagüez has been further hurt by its exclusion by road builders who have brought new, limited-access expressways to the gates of virtually all of Puerto Rico's other population centers.

Whatever the causes of the decline, Mayagüez has actually fallen far below its long-time status as Puerto Rico's third-largest city, with a population of about 100,000. And in spite of some half-hearted civic attempts to restore monumental central buildings (such as the Teatro Yagüez, the post office and city hall), businesses and their customers have departed the heart of town in favor of the malls north and south of the city. Families have moved out of central city housing for life in the 'burbs. Today, the beautiful and shady city plaza is home to pigeons and skateboarders by day and drag-queen prostitutes by night.

But a subtle and interesting transformation is taking place amid this urban decay. As one transplanted academic says about her adopted home, 'It takes a while before you find the energy in this place, but it's here.'

Where that energy roots specifically is in the attractive architecture and landscaped green spaces of the Mayagüez branch of the Universidad de Puerto Rico (UPR). This branch enjoys the evocative nickname of RUM (an acronym for Recinto Universitario

Mayagüez). In recent years, student demand for housing has spread south from the university campus and pushed its way through a low-rent neighborhood called Barrio Paris. Now the student district – with its pizza spots, bookstores and bars – is creeping south right to Plaza Colón, where a new student pub has taken over a large, vacant commercial loft. Meanwhile, the campus is underwriting a steady stream of cultural and entertainment events, which include appearances by Nobel Prize winners such as Derek Walcott.

Mayagüez may not be for every traveler, but if you are a student or an academic, you may want to check it out. But come during the middle of the week when the university students and faculty are in top form, because – like all UPR campuses – RUM empties on weekends, when the action moves to the beaches.

Note that Mayagüez also offers the only zoo on the island and a tropical agricultural research station that is like a massive botanical garden. Mayagüez is also the jumping-off point for one of the Caribbean's all-time great adventures: A ferry (more like a cruise ship) sails from Mayagüez on the 11-hour trip across the Pasaje de la Mona to Santo Domingo in the Dominican Republic. This trip is by far the longest ferry voyage (in time and distance) in all of the Caribbean, and the size of the vessel, open sea and length of passage give you the feeling of having traveled to a different world.

Recinto Universitario Mayagüez

Over 10,000 students are enrolled at RUM (☎ 787-832-4040) in a host of disciplines. But over the years, RUM has become the premier math and science campus of the UPR system and boasts internationally respected programs in agriculture and engineering as well as in the physical and biological sciences. The campus lies just north of town off Calle Post (Hwy 2). With its gated entrance, green lawns, rolling landscape and modern international-style concrete buildings, this is the kind of place most people picture when they hear the word 'university.' It's a great place to take a stroll and escape the noise and exhaust fumes of town.

Estación Experimental Agrícola Federal

Strolling is even more of an attraction at the Estación Experimental Agrícola Federal (☎ 787-831-3435), the tropical agricultural research station of the US Dept of Agriculture, and the adjacent city park, known as Parque de los Proceres (Patriots' Park). These grounds lie just east of the RUM campus. The best way to enter is from Hwy 65 (Avenida Paris), via Spur 2, where the road bisects the two natural retreats. Pick up a map from the administration office, then head off for adventures with green things.

At the agricultural station you will see plantations of yams, plantains, bananas, cassavas and other tropical 'cash crops' as researchers evaluate new hybrids and species introduced to the island (including a cinnamon tree from Sri Lanka). The gardens have one of the largest collections of beneficial tropical plants in the world. The research station is open 7 am to 4 pm weekdays only; admission is free. The Parque de los Proceres, on the south side of Hwy 65, has more verdant walkways and is open daily during daylight hours.

Zoológico Zoorico

The only serious zoo (☎ 787-834-8110) on the island is in the same neighborhood, just to the northeast of the university off Hwy 108. Here you will find 90 acres of landscaped grounds surrounding a lake with islands and a children's park. There are 300 species of reptiles, birds, amphibians and mammals. In the past some visitors have complained that this was an 'old-fashioned' zoo with lots of cages and bars. Recent years have seen a lot of money spent on trying to give the animals something like the habitats they would know in the wild. While this place certainly is no match for the zoos of San Diego, California, or Singapore, it is worth a visit if you have the time.

The zoo is open 9 am to 4 pm Wednesday to Sunday; admission is US$3.

Teatro Yagüez

This beautiful theater (☎ 787-834-0523), with its red-and-black dome, stands a block west of the Plaza Colón on Calle McKinley. The building has undergone a US$4 million restoration. It blends neoclassical and baroque styles in a way that recalls the days when wealth and opulence were trademarks of this city. Today this national monument is a venue for concerts, drama and – yes – the beloved Puerto Rican beauty pageants.

Barrio Paris

Don't expect Paris' Left Bank here, or even Berkeley, California, but this funky, five-square-block area – around the público station north of Plaza Colón – is definitely a vibrant student quarter with bookstores, boarding houses, rowdy bars and cheap food. Many establishments line Avenida Méndez Vigo.

Places to Stay

Hotels RUM operates the *Hostal Colegial* (☎ 787-832-4040), on campus, for visiting faculty and students. You may need to be here for some official reason (not spring break) to get a room, but if you are on a botany field trip to study the variety of tropical palms at Estación Experimental Agrícola Federal, or research concentrations of *Pirodinium bahamense* in Laguna de Joyuda, you may be able to stay in this modern highrise for under US$35.

If you can't get a place at the Hostal Colegial, consider *Hotel Embajador* (☎ 787-833-3340, 111 Este Ramos Antonio), which has gained a literary reputation. A number of years ago, when the world-famous Caribbean poet Derek Walcott visited RUM for a reading, the English faculty put him up at the Embajador. While the hotel is a rather sterile, four-story concrete structure, being here got Walcott's creative juices going, and he actually composed some of *Omeros* here, the work that won him the Nobel Prize in 1992. You can catch the magic in this motel setting for as little as US$35 or as much as US$95. If you find Walcott's room, let us know: Someone should put up a plaque.

The *Parador El Sol* (☎ 787-834-0303, 9 Este Calle Ramiro) is another value spot downtown, with 52 rooms. But unlike its competitors, this high-rise tower looks brand new. Prices here start at US$55, and you get all the amenities plus a fridge and a pool downstairs.

Just a few blocks away, and also in the center of town, *Hotel La Palma* (☎ 787-834-3800) is right off the plaza at the corner of Calles Méndez Vigo and Peral. This is a classic Spanish-colonial hotel with iron balconies, shuttered doors and 12-foot ceilings. There is also air con, cable TV, a restaurant and parking. Rooms run US$59.

For a more bucolic setting, some travelers choose the *Holiday Inn Mayagüez* (☎ 787-833-1100), at Km 149.9 on Hwy 2. This boxy, six-story, international-style hotel has lots of glass and all the goodies you expect from this chain. Everything seems geared to the business traveler, including the rates: US$120 to US$150.

The *Best Western Mayagüez Resort & Casino* (☎ 787-832-3030) is at Km .3 on Hwy 104, off Hwy 2 north of town. This 140-unit property – with tennis courts, pool and casino – is the closest thing to a luxury resort in the city. Surprisingly, it is not on the water, but rather on 20 acres of tropical gardens – actually an adjunct to the nearby agricultural research station. Rates range from US$135 to US$175.

Rental Accommodations Almost every house you see in Barrio Paris has apartments or rooms for rent to students. They do not advertise, but ask around at such places as the Red Baron Pub (see Entertainment, below).

Places to Eat

Travelers coming to town in search of the university scene but hoarding their grub stake should head into Barrio Paris to *Fun & Pizza (66 Norte Calle Post)*. Students and locals gather here for happy hour to play pool, munch pizza (US$1 a slice) and drink the locally made India brew for 50¢ a can.

There are a number of restaurants in the vicinity of Plaza Colón, a few blocks to the south. For light, inexpensive fare, check out *Brazo Gitano (101 Calle Méndez Vigo)*, about two blocks east of the plaza. This is an extremely popular bakery and deli. There are tables where you can sip coffee or eat a pastry or sandwich, and you can get a ham-and-cheese sandwich here for US$2. Unlike a lot of other restaurants in town, this bakery is popular with groups of women.

Across the street, **Restaurant Estoril** (☎ 787-834-2288) is a formal, smoky businessmen's haunt by day and a 'big night out' stop for local couples in the evening. Chicken entrées can run over US$12; fettuccine Alfredo is US$15.

You will find another popular dining spot for couples and groups of women and men a block up the street. **Restaurante Don Pepe** (☎ 787-834-4941, 58 Este Calle Méndez Vigo) draws a hip young crowd, especially academics who teach at the university. The menu is eclectic and international. Dinner entrées run about US$12.

After a stroll up to the plaza to see if any of the drag queens, including local legend Charytín, are out and about in some outrageous new gear, you can get an ice-cream cone (80¢) for dessert at **Rex Cream**, across from city hall on Calle Méndez Vigo.

Entertainment

Unless you want to get dressed up and head over to the Best Western for the casino and bar scene, the action (for students and the academic community) in Mayagüez mostly revolves around the university. To get up to date with what is going on in town in the way of concerts, films and the like, check out the RUM website (rum.upr.clu.edu). Look for the weekly activities blotter called *La Cartera Semanal*, or call ☎ 787-833-5100. The campus film club also has a page on this website.

If you want to party during the week, Mayagüez is a pretty good place to get down. **Red Baron Pub** (☎ 787-265-5770, 73 Oeste Calle Post), in Barrio Paris, is a two-story landmark, and you can't miss it because there is usually a banner across the street announcing the latest promotion. Yes, this is a brother of the place you may have come to love in San Germán, and things may get even crazier here. There's live Latin rock most nights.

The hard-drinking crowd also hangs out at **El Garabato**, in the same neighborhood.

Mayagüez Café (57 este Calle McKinley) is a more recent hot spot. This cavernous loft is in a green building on the north side of Plaza Colón and has beer banners flying from the balcony. It has pool tables, US$1 beer, live rock and conga lines.

There is a popular gay scene south of town at **Faces Pub**, at Km 164 on Hwy 2 in the community of Hormigueros.

Sweet Things in Sweet Lips

If you work your way down to the waterfront warehouse and red-light district known as Dulces Labios (Sweet Lips), you will find the most famous place to eat in Mayagüez. For more than a century, *sanjuaneros* have been making regular pilgrimages to the **Repostelría y Cafeteria Franco** (☎ 787-832-0070, 3 Calle Manuel Pirallo) just for the local confection *brazo gitano* (gypsy's arm).

Eating here is truly a sensuous experience. This is a cheerful place with parquet floors, checkered tablecloths, flower arrangements and bakery display cases to tempt you out of your socks. Some people say they get their satisfaction just sitting in Franco's and inhaling.

An associated little pleasure is the twinkle in the eyes of the waitstaff, who seem to assume when you order your sweets that you and your tablemate are here fresh from some sumptuous and indecent liaison. A visitor might wonder about the actual motives of the wayfarers that come here from San Juan, and the double entendres latent in the district's name and the names of the confections. But clearly the hedonists know good food.

Later, while you and your alleged partner-in-sin are enjoying a *cubano* and a beer (about US$5), you will have time to ruminate upon the improbable history of this place: The man who started it, Don Enrique, was the great-uncle of Spain's long-time dictator Francisco Franco. Some people love guns; some love butter.

WEST COAST

Getting There & Away

Air The Aeropuerto de Mayagüez is about 3 miles north of town, just off Hwy 2. American Eagle (☎ 800-433-7300) currently has only two flights (down from five) a day to and from San Juan. Fares are no bargain for this half-hour flight: Expect to pay US$120 roundtrip.

Público You will find the terminal in Barrio Paris about two blocks north of Plaza Colón. Públicos make the trip to the west coast beach towns and the long trek to San Juan (US$15; plan on four hours at least).

Car Hwy 2 brings you to town from the north or south. While this is a four-lane road, it is plagued by traffic lights. Hwy 105 is the west end of the Ruta Panorámica, which leads from Mayagüez into the mountains and to Maricao.

Ferry Quite a few travelers arrive in Mayagüez as a gateway between Puerto Rico and the Dominican Republic. Ferries Del Caribe (☎ 787-832-4800), on the docks of Mayagüez north of the tuna canneries, offers the serious 'off-island' adventure across the Pasaje de la Mona. The massive rainbow-colored ship sails every other day across the Pasaje de la Mona for Santo Domingo in the Dominican Republic. On board you will find a restaurant, cafeteria, bar, casino and disco as well as conference rooms, private cabins, sauna and Jacuzzi. There is room for 250 cars along with 550 passengers.

The 11-hour trip always runs during the night, leaving both Mayagüez and Santo Domingo at 8 pm. Currently, the ship is sailing from Mayagüez on Monday, Wednesday and Friday; from Santo Domingo on Tuesday, Thursday and Saturday.

One-way tickets cost as little as US$39; it's US$30 more for a cabin. You pay US$10 to take a bike or US$60 for your car.

Getting Around

To/From the Airport A few taxis usually show up at the airport when the flights arrive from San Juan; if none is there, or if you need to get to the airport, call Taxi Mr

Special (☎ 787-832-1115, 832-1154 cellular). The one-way fare to town is about US$6.

Car To rent a car to get up into the mountains or out to the beaches, you will find the following vendors at the airport:

Avis	☎ 787-833-7070
Budget	☎ 787-831-4570
Hertz	☎ 787-832-3314
Popular Leasing	☎ 787-265-4848

RINCÓN

You may hear a Puerto Rican snort *'paraiso gringo'* (gringo paradise) if you mention Rincón, as if the place harbors some kind of North American cooties that could contaminate the beloved island. Not only are most visitors to Rincón gringos, but most of the town's innkeepers and many restaurateurs are as well. The lingua franca here is English, and this fact challenges the sensibilities of a lot of *puertorriqueños* who are proud of their island culture.

But a lot of gringo travelers love this place! Yes, English is spoken here and you can bump into people from back home (an undeniable attraction after weeks or months of absorbing a different culture), but more enticing are Rincón's great surfing, diving and whale-watching opportunities. Not to mention Rincón's overall barefoot ambience, its lack of traffic, environmental activism, eclectic paradores, tempting bakeries, green mountains and cow pastures pushing up against the Caribbean.

Yet Rincón is no Margaritaville. Sure, the town of about 13,000 has its share of beach bars and expats drifting around looking for their lost shakers of you-know-what. But while Rincón may be laid-back, it also has a youthfulness, energy and athleticism that engages most of the community and lifts it out of the mold of a stereotypical tropical oasis.

Situated along a box-shaped peninsula halfway between Mayagüez and Aguadilla on the northwest coast, Rincón traces its history to the 16th century and a few low-key sugarcane plantations. And while many people believe it gets its name from the

Spanish word *rincón* (corner) because of its shape, the municipality is actually named after one of the area's original planters, Don Gonzalo Rincón. For most of its history, the community's energy came from the gusto demanded by cane farming and cattle raising. But things changed in the mid-1960s as surfing grew in popularity and many discovered that Rincón's winter surf puts Malibu, California, to shame. When the world surfing championships came here in 1968, glossy images of Rincón were plastered all over international magazines and TV – and the word was out.

Every year since then has seen successive generations of wave riders make the pilgrimage. They have heard tales of over-15-foot breaks that match those on the north shore of Oahu. In the early days of the surf scene, Rincón was little more than a collection of US$5-a-night bunkhouses spread along the beaches of a small agricultural town. But eventually the surfers looked for ways to support themselves – beyond washing dishes, cooking and painting houses. And while they pursued an endless summer, they began to invest in the community, building their own restaurants, guesthouses and bars.

As the baby-boomer generation of surfers got older, they continued to harbor romantic images of Rincón. But when they traveled with their own children, they demanded better accommodations, slicker restaurants and a broader variety of activities. And the town responded. Today, you can rent distinctive vacation homes or stay in one of the most luxurious hotels on the island. While the old-style bunkhouses are all but gone, imaginative and moderately priced guesthouses remain a staple in Rincón.

Today, 'Little Malibu' – as Rincón is often called – still has its youth scene composed of both local hotdoggers and surfers from all over the globe. But now Rincón also has a mature community of expatriates who still thrive on the area's climate, dramatic topography, marine life and water sports.

Orientation

The actual municipal center is only about four square blocks, encircling the Catholic church and the Presbyterian church that face each other across the small Plaza de Recreo. While this urban core has many essential services, most of the inns, restaurants and beach attractions lie north or south of the town.

The best swimming beaches are south of the village, as are many of the larger hotels. A number of different snorkeling and surfing sites lie off Hwy 413 along the west side of the peninsula (the actual 'Little Malibu'), as it runs north to the lighthouse and the sideroad to BONUS, the closed nuclear power plant. Moving farther north, Hwy 413 climbs into steep hills. There is a strong representation of guesthouses and a few bar-restaurants in this area, especially on a loop of road that circles down to the north-facing beach and rejoins Hwy 413 a mile farther to the northwest. Another group of accommodations lies south of town along Hwy 429.

Maps The Tourism Association of Rincón (see below) puts out a great, amusing map complete with site descriptions, cartoon drawings and essential phone numbers. You can get one from your innkeeper, or call the Lazy Parrot Inn (☎ 787-823-5654). Sometimes you can get a map for free; sometimes it's US$1.

Information

Tourist Offices On the northern border of town at the junction of Hwy 413 and Hwy 115, the Tourism Association of Rincón (☎ 787-823-5024) is a one-person show that is usually open 10 am to 4 pm weekdays. If the office is not open when you visit, most essential information is included on its widely available map.

Money Both Banco Popular and Western Bank are downtown near the plaza, and both have ATM machines. The banks are open 9 am to 2:30 pm weekdays, plus Saturday mornings.

Post The post office (☎ 787-823-2625) is a mile north of the plaza on Hwy 115. It's open 7:30 am to 4:30 pm weekdays, 8:30 am to noon Saturday.

RINCÓN

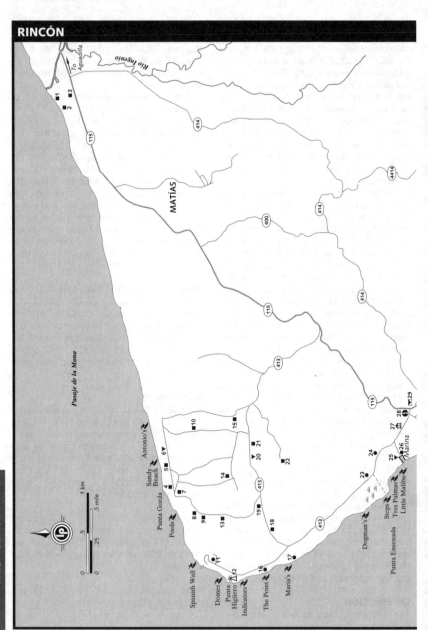

Pasaje de la Mona

To Aguadilla

Río Ingenio

MATÍAS

414
414
4414
400
115
413
413
413

1 km
.5 mile
.5
.25
0
0

Sandy Beach
Antonio's
Punta Gorda
Pools
Spanish Wall
Domes
Punta Higüero
Indicators
The Point
Maria's
Dogman's
Punta Ensenada
Steps
Tres Palmas
Little Malibu
Marina

1 2 3
6 5
4
7
8 9
13
14
10
15
20 21
22
19 18
17
16
11
12
23
24
25 26
27 28
29

RINCÓN

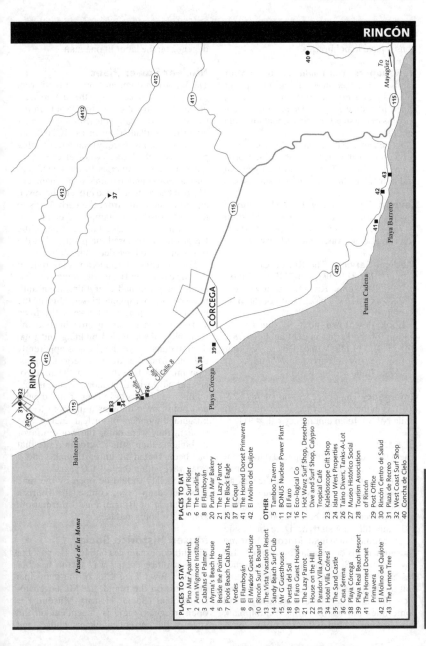

PLACES TO STAY
1 Pino Mar Apartments
2 Ann Wigmore Institute
3 Cabañas el Palmer
4 Myrna's Beach House
6 Beside the Pointe
7 Pools Beach Cabañas
   Verdes
8 El Flamboyán
9 El Mirador Guest House
10 Rincón Surf & Board
13 The Vista Vacation Resort
14 Sandy Beach Surf Club
15 Mr G Guesthouse
18 Puesta del Sol
19 El Faro Guest House
21 The Lazy Parrot
22 House on the Hill
33 Parador Villa Antonio
34 Hotel Villa Cofresí
35 The Sand Castle
36 Casa Serena
38 Playa Córcega
39 Playa Real Beach Resort
41 The Horned Dorset
   Primavera
42 El Molino del Quijote
43 The Lemon Tree

PLACES TO EAT
5 The Surf Rider
6 The Landing
8 El Flamboyán
20 Punta Mar Bakery
21 The Lazy Parrot
25 The Black Eagle
37 El Coquí
41 The Horned Dorset Primavera
42 El Molino del Quijote

OTHER
5 Tamboo Tavern
11 BONUS Nuclear Power Plant
12 El Faro
16 Eco-logical Co
17 Hot Wave Surf Shop, Desecheo
   Dive and Surf Shop, Calypso
   Tropical Café
23 Kaleidoscope Gift Shop
24 Island West Properties
26 Taíno Divers, Tanks-A-Lot
27 Museo Histórico Social
28 Tourism Association
   of Rincón
29 Post Office
30 Rincón Centro de Salud
31 Plaza de Recreo
32 West Coast Surf Shop
40 Concha de Cielo

WEST COAST

Libraries No entrepreneur has opened a bookstore in Rincón yet, but most guesthouses have loan libraries.

Newspapers You might try to get your hands on the free little tabloid newspaper called *El Chavito Nuevo* (☎ 787-890-1258), which has some helpful display advertising and lots of classifieds for apartment and villa rentals.

To get up to speed on ecological issues, get a copy of the Liga Ecológica Puertorriqueña's *Boletín Informativo*, which you can find in many restaurants and guesthouses.

Laundry Try Nilsa's, on Hwy 115 south of town, or Pueblo Laundromat & Garden (☎ 787-823-3266), on Calle Comercio, where you can also get wash-and-fold service.

Medical Services The Rincón Centro de Salud (☎ 787-823-5171, 823-2795, 823-3120), at 28 Calle Muñoz Rivera, is in town next to Paco's Grocery, a block south of Plaza de Recreo.

Look downtown next to the Texaco station for the Farmacia del Pueblo (☎ 787-823-2540), 33 Calle Muñoz Rivera. Another option nearby is Farmacia Nogueras, at 11 Oeste Calle Muñoz Rivera.

Emergency The police station (☎ 787-823-2020) is in the south corner of the village off Calle Nueva. In an emergency, call ☎ 911.

El Faro

The lighthouse at Punta Higüero dates from 1892 and rises almost 100 feet above the terrain. It has survived countless hurricanes, an earthquake and a tidal wave (though it was razed and then rebuilt in 1922). The 26,000-candlepower light has been automated since 1933 and still helps ships navigate the Pasaje de la Mona. The small **Rincón Maritime Museum** is inside, displaying artifacts recovered from Spanish galleons and other vessels wrecked in the surrounding waters. But the principal reason to come here is the view. Five great surf breaks are nearby, and sometimes during the winter, humpback whales come within 100 yards of the coast.

The museum is generally open in the winter only, from about 10 am to 2 pm, as it totally depends on the labor of one man.

Nuclear Power Plant

The big green dome just up the road from the lighthouse once housed the first nuclear-powered electrical generating facility in the Caribbean. Basically, the Boiling Nuclear Superheater Plant (known as BONUS, an acronym laden with irony) was a test facility producing only 16,000kW of electricity to introduce Latin America to the benefits of nuclear power and to train visiting engineers. The plant never functioned properly, however, and in its short life from the early 1960s to the early 1970s it contaminated employees and suffered a reactor failure. Finally, the US government closed the plant and at the time claimed to have decontaminated it.

For 20 years it became a rusting relic of the nuclear age and a favorite venue for graffiti writers, who had everything from anti-nuke to pro-marijuana biases. During the mid-1990s cooperation between the town and the electrical company brought about the reopening of the sealed building and total decontamination of the site – as apparently the folks from the Atomic Energy Commission missed a few things on the first go-around. Now, with the building 'clean,' untold numbers of dollars have been spent to paint and polish everything as a museum to the misguided pioneers of nuclear energy, who thought they were doing the world a favor by building their little reactor in a site that has been visited by an earthquake and a tidal wave within the last 100 years.

The facility should be open by the time you visit; drop by, or contact the Tourism Association of Rincón (see Information, above) for hours and fees.

Museo Histórico Social

This little museum lies on Hwy 413 past the tourism office on the way to the beaches north of town. Like a lot of the municipal museums on the island, the Museo Histórico Social (Social History Museum) is open irregularly and is dependent on the state of the current municipal budget and volunteerism. We have never been able to get in, but you may have better luck.

Isla Desecheo

Looking a lot like Shangri-la in the film *South Pacific*, this 360-acre peaked island lies 13 miles offshore and has a habit of taking on a rosy or violet glow (according to the position of the sun) in the haze of the Pasaje de la Mona. Desecheo is a wildlife preserve; landing here is not permitted, but the fringe reefs around the island are spectacular, with visibility up to 100 feet (see Diving & Snorkeling, below).

Surfing

Not all 'surf shops' in Puerto Rico really cater to the sport, but in Rincón you get the real thing. West Coast Surf Shop (☎ 787-823-3935) is downtown across from the Catholic church, with expert staff and lots of gear. Hot Wavz Surf Shop (☎ 787-823-3942) is on the lighthouse road. Both of these places can hook you up with whatever you need, or rent you a surfboard to fit conditions for US$20; boogie boards run about US$12.

Diving & Snorkeling

Rincón has three good dive shops thanks to the popularity of diving the pristine reefs of Isla Desecheo and Isla Mona.

Desecheo Dive and Surf Shop (☎ 787-823-0390) is on the lighthouse road near the Calypso Tropical Café.

Tanks-A-Lot Dive Shop (☎ 787-823-6301) is at the little marina west of the center of town, near the Black Eagle restaurant. Greg Carson's Taíno Divers (☎ 787-823-6429) is in the same location.

All of these operators rent snorkeling gear for about US$10 a day. They also offer serious diving adventures like three-day trips to Isla Mona for US$200. One-tank dives are as low as US$30.

Snorkelers head for Steps beach in calm conditions. Steps lies off Hwy 413, just north of town.

Swimming

At many times of the year, the surf is too rough for swimming at many sites along the coast. Fortunately, there's a safe balneario with a southerly exposure. (It's just south of town, off Hwy 115 near the school and the old railroad water tank.)

There is also good, safe swimming on the adjacent strand in front of Parador Villa Antonio and Hotel Villa Cofresí.

Kayaking

You can rent kayaks at West Coast Surf Shop (see Surfing, above) and the Sandy Beach Surf Club (see Places to Stay, below) for about US$15 an hour, less for longer periods.

Fishing & Whale-Watching

Desecheo Dive and Surf Shop (see Diving, above) will take you fishing offshore for marlin, *dorado*, wahoo and king fish on their dive boat. Five-hour trips run US$425, eight-hour trips cost US$525 for a party of four. Other dive operators offer similar deals, and you can take a charter boat to go whale-watching during the winter months.

Tennis

Make reservations to play at the Concha de Cielo (☎ 787-826-5261), south of town off Hwy 115. Courts run US$10 during the day, US$12 at night, US$20 with lessons.

Golf

Rincón is only a 15-minute drive from Punta Borinquen Golf club, the best golfing bargain on the island (for details, see the Aguadilla section in the North Coast chapter).

Places to Stay

Camping At *Playa Córcega* (☎ 787-823-6140), south of town at Km 10.8 on Hwy 115, you can get a tent site. Depending on the season, campsites are US$10 to US$15 without power hookup, about US$20 with hookup.

Guesthouses – North of Town The *House on the Hill* (☎ 787-823-5306), off Hwy 413 on Calle Sector Collazo, is a small guesthouse in the area that mostly caters to youths. A bunk in a four-person dorm room is US$20; the private double room is US$35. (The whole house can be rented for a minimum of three days for US$150 a night.)

Beaches, Code Words & Surf Wars

Surfers have given Rincón's beaches a wild collection of names, which they can shout out when passing one another on the roads while searching for the freshest break and the perfect wave. Now everybody in town uses these code words. Unless you know this local argot, you will be lost. Here's the skinny on the beaches and the breaks, dude, going north along the coast from the southwest.

Barrero – This spot takes its name from the seawall along the narrow beach near the Horned Dorset Primavera hotel. There is no surfing here, but it's great for a stroll past the beached fleet of small fishing boats that stretch all the way to the balneario. You will find good kayaking and windsurfing along here, especially in the area by the Hotel Villa Cofresí.

Balneario – This public swimming beach (about 600 yards long) is south of town, where you pay US$2 to park.

Little Malibu – This surfing site on the west-facing strand runs north from the marina. It's a decent surfing spot in the winter, with generally 4-foot breaks.

Tres Palmas, Steps & Dogman's – The next three breaks, as you move north along the west coast, are mostly winter breaks that can get quite a bit bigger than Little Malibu. Tres is definitely the biggest of all the breaks in Rincón, and in the right conditions waves go well over 25 feet. But be cautious: Several surfers have died here in recent years. The rule here is that if the surf is too big at one of these spots, look for smaller conditions at spots to the south.

Maria's – It rarely breaks evenly here, off the beach near the Calypso Tropical Café. But about three times a year you get a monster swell from the north and a strong southerly wind, and then it's time for the war boards because the surf can go higher than 20 feet.

The Point – Basically in front of the lighthouse parking lot at Punta Higüero, this break is definitely not for amateurs. It can get big at times when nearby Maria's is flat or confused.

Indicators – You have a point break here right off the lighthouse. Winter conditions usually run around 6 to 8 feet here, but like the Point, Indicators can get suicidal because the waves break in about 5 feet of water.

Domes – This place takes its name from the nearby nuclear reactor, and Domes is one of the most consistent sites; when everything else seems flat, Domes may still have surf. The currents running around Punta Higüero tend to shape a wave, and you can get an offshore breeze falling off the hills in the morning and evening. Note that this place can be dangerous in a heavy northerly swell; if it's too rough, head south.

Spanish Wall, Pools, Sandy Beach & Antonio's – These beach breaks line up west to east along the north shore of the peninsula. This is where you most consistently get the big stuff in the winter. It can be particularly fabulous the day after a cold front, when you still have a big northerly swell and the wind fills in at midday from the south. These breaks are also good spots for winter boogie boarding.

The guesthouse has shared bath, kitchen and common room with cable TV, laundry facilities and an outdoor deck with barbecue.

Up on the ridge above the north-facing beaches, Steve and Francia Lantz's *Lazy Parrot Inn* (☎ 787-823-5654), at Km 4.1 on Hwy 413, has grown with the expatriate community for over a decade. Now, this attractive hilltop inn has a pool, outdoor bar and restaurant deck. A room with private bath, air con and TV runs US$65.

Rincón Surf & Board (☎ 787-823-0610), in the Sandy Beach area north of town (down the hill from the Lazy Parrot), advertises basic apartments 'over the jungle' for US$20 to US$75. This is a favorite haunt of the 'surf trolls' who show up to ride the waves all winter.

Another classic surfers' palace is *Sandy Beach Surf Club* (☎ 787-823-1146), in the same neighborhood. Dorm rooms are US$20. Studios begin at about US$70.

Mr G Guesthouse (☎787-823-4621), off Hwy 413 on the road down to Antonio's beach, has two rooms with shared bath and no air con. Rates start at US$20.

Beside the Pointe (☎ 787-823-8550) is right on Sandy Beach by the Landing restaurant. Jay and Fred Douglass have eight rooms here, some with air con. All have cooking facilities, private bath and cable TV. Rates range from US$60 to US$125.

Pools Beach Cabañas Verdes (☎ 787-823-8135) has four fully equipped, private studios with rates starting at US$70 a night.

There are a number of other guesthouses in the area on the north side of the Rincón peninsula, including *Myrna's Beach House* (☎ 787-823-4450) and the *Vista Vacation Resort* (☎ 787-823-3673), both of which seem to have a mixture of rustic rooms and apartments for rent at prices that are competitive with Rincón Surf & Board and the Sandy Beach Surf Club.

Mike and Cathy Trahan run *El Mirador Guest House* (☎ 787-823-5481), near the BONUS dome. Bunk-style rooms with shared bath go for US$30. A room with air con and a private bath is US$65.

The *Puesta del Sol* (☎ 787-823-2787) is a similar place with competitive rates in the same area on Hwy 413, as is the *El Faro Guest House* (☎ 787-823-5247).

Way north of town on Hwy 115 (on the way to Aguadilla), you will find *Pino Mar Apartments* (☎ 787-868-8269) and *Cabañas El Palmer* (☎ 787-868-7808). These places have efficiencies for US$75 and up.

You will also find the *Ann Wigmore Institute* (☎ 787-868-6307) on the beach in the same area. This retreat and spa draws its clients here for wheat-grass therapy, 'internal cleansing' and lots of organic gardening. Expect to pay over US$1700 for two weeks of therapy and a private room with bath and meals.

Guesthouses – South of Town The *Casa Serena* (☎ 787-823-2026) and the *Sand Castle* (☎ 787-823-0162) both lie on the good swimming beach at the end of Calle 14 off Hwy 115 at Km 11.4. Rates are US$65 and up.

If you continue southeast from here on Calle 8 (which becomes Hwy 429 as it passes the ruins of the old Cocega sugar mill), you will find the hospitable *El Molino del Quijote* (☎ 787-823-4010) on the wild beach. The manager, Arturo, has cabañas in the US$75 range.

Farther up the road you will find luxury-end waterfront rentals at *Lemon Tree* (☎ 787-823-6452). Paul and Mary Jeanne Hellings have four units here that range from a simple bedroom with cathedral ceiling and 2nd-floor waterfront deck to a three-bedroom house. Rates run from US$100 to US$150.

Hotels Two of Rincón's most popular hotels stand right next to each other southeast of town on a swimming beach off Hwy 115. The *Hotel Villa Cofresí* (☎ 787-823-2450), at Km 12.3, has 42 units with kitchenettes and air con. There is a pool, restaurant, bar and water-sports concession stand on the property. Rates are US$75 to US$140.

Next door, the *Parador Villa Antonio* (☎ 787-823-2645) has a loyal following of families and older couples. There are 55 rooms here, a playground for kids and two tennis courts in addition to the pool and game room. Rooms run US$75 to US$100.

The ***Playa Real Beach Resort*** (☎ 787-823-2800) is a mile southeast of the parador on Calle 8. This resort is of the same ilk as the two mentioned above, but with fewer rooms. Rates start at US$75.

Possibly you have heard of the crown jewel of the island's small resorts, the ***Horned Dorset Primavera*** (☎ 787-823-4030), at Km .3 on Hwy 429. It claims to offer the 'epitome of privacy, elegance and service,' and it delivers. There are 30 suites here in private villas, antiques galore and chamber-music concerts. This is also a place with no children under 12, TV or activities. Rates start at US$340 per night.

Rental Agents If you have dipped into Puerto Rico's websites, you have probably already seen the home page for Susan Cravey's ***Island West Properties*** (☎ 787-823-2323, islandwest@coqui.net). The office is on Hwy 413 about a mile out of town toward the lighthouse. Susan can show you modern, waterfront three-bedroom houses for as low as US$132 a night.

Places to Eat
There are two good options for groceries: ***Rincón Cash & Carry***, across from the plaza in the center of town; and ***Econ's***, next to the Texaco station on Hwy 115 in town. (Both stores close at 6 pm during the week, 4 pm on Sunday.)

Other cheap options for food can be found at Rincón's plethora of good bakeries, including the popular and well-stocked ***Puntas Mar*** bakery, next to the Lazy Parrot on Hwy 413 north of town. In town, try ***Mandin*** or ***Ricoeña***, both by the plaza next to Rincón Cash & Carry.

A lot of Rincón's guesthouses and hotels also serve food, so the complete list of restaurants in this small municipality is surprisingly daunting.

For rock-bottom prices, head to ***Family Pizza*** (☎ 787-823-1090, 15 Calle Progreso) by the Presbyterian church. Eat in or take out; a tasty 20-inch cheese pizza costs US$8.

Two other bargain spots in the village include the ***Healthfood Store*** (☎ 787-823-1746), on Calle Muñoz Rivera, where a baked potato with cheese and veggies costs US$2. ***El Jardín*** (☎ 787-823-5829, 33 Calle Santa Rosa) is the local Chinese restaurant. Cashew chicken and rice runs US$5.50.

If you are in the Sandy Beach area north of town, consider the ***Surf Rider*** at Beside the Pointe (see Places to Stay, above). Bobby and Raquel make some of the best food in town according to the surfing crowd and returning travelers. Prices are excellent for waterfront dining: Try the rice and beans, or chicken fajitas for US$4.

El Flamboyán, on the cliff near here, is a total *cocina criolla* place, where folks come for inexpensive fish and chicken dishes. Entrées start around US$6.

On this same stretch of beach, you also have Rincón's hottest new restaurant, the ***Landing*** (☎ 787-823-3112). Here you will find the latest creation from the owner of Luquillo's popular Brass Cactus. This is definitely an American-style fern bar – but with all of the vegetation waving in the breeze off the seaside deck. A lot of people come for the baby-back ribs (US$20), but you can go light with a jerk-chicken salad for US$8 or buffalo wings for US$7.

Up on the hill, the ***Lazy Parrot*** (see Places to Stay) got famous for its cheeseburger-in-paradise cooking, but now the new chef is taking some risks, and you can get things like sushi for US$6 or stick with the old favorites.

If you are at the lighthouse to watch surfing action or whales, you can catch a bite at ***El Faro***, at the base of the lighthouse, where an *empanadilla de chapin* costs US$1.75 and a conch dinner runs US$13.

The place to go in Rincón for seafood has long been the ***Black Eagle*** (☎ 787-823-3510), at the marina off Hwy 413 north of town. A red snapper supper is US$16.

Open only on weekends, ***El Molino del Quijote*** (see Places to Stay) is a romantic choice for those who want to sip Carmencita's sangria over paella for two (over US$20).

If you are game for a bit of a drive up into the mountains, try ***El Coquí***. To get to this extremely laid-back criollo spot with a great perch for watching the sunsets and sea, take Hwy 115 south out of town; turn left on

Hwy 412, then take the next right (look for the sign) and head up the winding road about a mile. Expect to pay US$10 and up.

For the opposite extreme in formality, you can head to the dining room at the **Horned Dorset Primavera** (see Places to Stay). Candlelight and serious gourmet recipes from French-trained chefs will cost you around US$50 for the fixed menu. The *crème brûlée* may be the best you ever taste, but a second helping will cost you another US$12.

Entertainment
The action here is all on the weekends when the college crowd and city folk show up to hit the beaches.

The **Calypso Tropical Café** (☎ 787-823-4151) has probably the oldest pub scene in Rincón, and they pull in a big mix of locals, expats and travelers with live bands covering American rock, reggae and even calypso classics. It's US$1.50 for a Medalla.

You get the same kind of action at the **Landing** (see Places to Eat, above), but the crowd at the 75-foot bar is more upscale and likely to be packing cell phones.

The **Tamboo Tavern** is the patio bar at Beside the Pointe (see Places to Stay). You may not always get live music here, but the sound system is plenty good, and this is *the* place to be if you are a gringo surfer – or love the scene. Beer seems a little steep at US$1.75 for the local Medalla.

Shopping
A number of Rincón's gift shops have more thoughtful collections than what you are used to seeing around the island.

The Kaleidoscope Gift Shop (☎ 787-823-3070) is on Hwy 413 north of town. Wendy Restrepo carries a lot of traditional island products including *santos*, masks, gourmet coffee and jewelry. There are also art openings and book signings here.

The Lazy Parrot Tropical Gift Shop in the inn of the same name is a must stop for parrot-heads. You will also see Lisl Wright's handmade seaglass jewelry here.

Eco-logical Co is the gift shop near the lighthouse park with guess what kinds of treasures.

Spectator Sports
Held in June, the Rincón Triathlon is an iron-human contest that's starting to draw some quality international athletes and make for a serious fiesta for spectators.

Getting There & Away
Air Rincón doesn't have an airport, but there are two in the area. If you are coming from San Juan, fly into Mayagüez (see the Mayagüez section earlier in this chapter). Aguadilla's Aeropuerto Rafael Hernández, generally has a couple of flights a day from New York or Miami (see Aguadilla in the North Coast chapter).

Público The van stand is just off the town plaza on Calle Nueva. Expect to pay about US$4 if you are headed north to Aguadilla or US$1 to go south to Mayagüez (you can access San Juan from either of these cities).

Car Painful experience has taught us that all roads into Rincón are far from equal. While it looks easy to approach Rincón via Hwy 115 to the north, the town of Aguada is a major bottleneck, and you may feel like slitting your throat before you escape the traffic there.

There is no problem with traffic (unless you get behind a loaded truck) on the spider-web of roads that approach Rincón from the east, but they all scale major mountains, which reduce your effective speed to about 20mph, and they can be dangerously slippery when it rains.

Clearly the easiest way to approach the town is via the valley roads of Hwy 402 and Hwy 115, both of which intersect Hwy 2 south of the Rincón peninsula.

Getting Around
You will pay US$15 or more for a taxi from either the Aguadilla or Mayagüez airport, and you will still be stuck with no way to get around Rincón unless you already have friends here with wheels. You definitely need a car to move around to the various attractions in Rincón. But don't worry if you didn't want to splurge for a car in San Juan: There are four rental car sites at both the

Mayagüez or Aguadilla airports (see the Getting Around sections under Mayagüez, earlier in this chapter, and under Aguadilla in the North Coast chapter).

ISLA MONA

There is no greater wilderness adventure in the Caribbean than a trip to Isla Mona, Puerto Rico's 'Jurassic Park,' 50 miles to the west of the main island in the Pasaje de la Mona. And although very, very few Puerto Ricans or travelers actually ever visit Mona, this nearly circular island of 14,000 acres

looms large in many people's imagination. A nature reserve since 1919 and uninhabited for more than 50 years, Mona is so full of history, dramatic geological formations and wildlife that it can overwhelm your senses and pique your curiosity in ways you cannot even imagine.

You suddenly begin taking the 'long view' of our planet's history when you see the violet cliffs of the tabletop island rising like a fata morgana above the deep blue waves or a collection of giant iguanas scrambling onto a trail to sniff your scent. Puerto Rican traffic

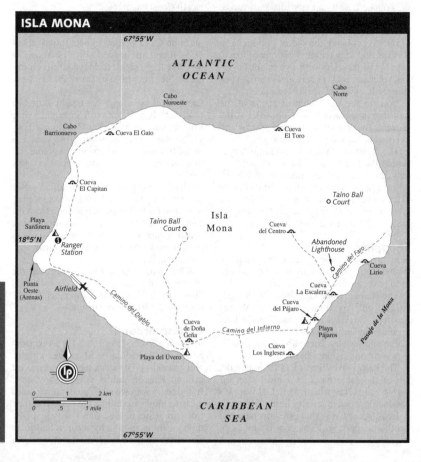

ISLA MONA

67°55'W

ATLANTIC OCEAN

Cabo Norte

Cabo Noroeste

Cabo Barrionuevo — Cueva El Gato

Cueva El Toro

Cueva El Capitan

Taíno Ball Court

Playa Sardinera

Taíno Ball Court

Isla Mona

Cueva del Centro

18°5'N   Ranger Station

Abandoned Lighthouse

Camino del Faro

Cueva Lirio

Punta Oeste (Arenas)   Airfield

Camino del Diablo

Cueva La Escalera

Cueva del Pájaro

Cueva de Doña Geña

Camino del Infierno

Playa Pájaros

Pasaje de la Mona

Playa del Uvero

Cueva Los Ingleses

0   1   2 km
0   .5   1 mile

CARIBBEAN SEA

67°55'W

jams and decaying Air Force bases seem like only the tiniest wrinkles in time when a pod of humpback whales begin breaching in front of you, a nurse shark surprises you beneath some antler coral, or you scramble through one of the island's limestone caves toward a point of light until you come to a hole that opens in the side of a cliff 100 feet above the sea.

Then there are fish-eating bats, wild goats and pigs, Taíno petroglyphs on cave walls and the stories – stories of enslaved Indians, sunken galleons holding treasures of gold, skeletons of 18th-century pirates uncovered on Playa Pájaros, buried buccaneer loot and a government-sponsored search for the same that ended abruptly when a member of the search party committed suicide.

All this serves as ample food for thought when you are sitting around your campfire in the starlit night – and a reminder that a trip to Mona cannot be undertaken on a whim. While the Depto de Recursos Naturales (Dept of Natural Resources) provides toilets and saltwater showers at Playa Sardinera, Mona is basically a backcountry camping experience, and boat trips here can take more than five hours in rough seas. The rangers and police detachment here (in their small station at Playa Sardinera) can provide basic first aid and have radio contact with the main island, but beyond this you are on your own in a beautiful (but potentially hostile) environment.

History

Scholars believe that Arawaks (the pre-Taínos) probably arrived at Mona about 1000 years ago as their migration spread northwest through the Caribbean archipelago. Petroglyphs in some caves and the ruins of *batey* courts are the chief remnants of the Indian presence. Another remnant is the island's name, a corruption of the original Arawak name 'Amona.' Most likely the Indians used Mona as a way station in their travels between Puerto Rico and Hispaniola, and owing to the rich soil on the island, the Indians developed farms of cassava and sweet potatoes here to replenish the larders of voyagers.

Following in the tradition of native Caribbean mariners, Columbus stopped at Mona on September 24, 1494 (at the end of his second New World voyage), and remained several days to gather water and provisions for the long trip back to Spain. When the Spaniards returned in 1508, Mona had become a sanctuary for Taíno people escaping the slavery that the Spanish were impressing on the islanders of Hispaniola. But, like Columbus, this small group of Spaniards had not come to conquer the island people, but simply to trade with them for water, cassava and sweet potatoes. This group of voyagers – led by Juan Ponce de León – was on its way to start a colony in Puerto Rico. In successive years Mona served as the 'bread basket' for the new Puerto Rican colony that Ponce de León called Caparra.

The Spanish government eventually claimed control of the island to guard the ship traffic through the Pasaje de la Mona, which was fast becoming the highway to and from the gold coast of the Americas. But after two decades of enslaving and decimating the population of Indians throughout the New World, the Crown found its resources of men and money stretched too thin and withdrew. Abandoned and defenseless, Mona fell into the hands of pirates by the late 1500s, when French corsairs used Mona as a staging ground and refuge in their attacks on the Spanish colony at San Germán.

During the next 300 years Mona became the refuge of a host of privateers, including Sirs Walter Raleigh and Francis Drake, John Hawkins, William Kidd and the Puerto Rican buccaneer Roberto Cofresí (see 'Zorro Goes to Sea,' earlier in this chapter). The 1832 execution of the freebooter Almeida, known as 'El Portugués,' brought an end to Mona's days as a pirates' den.

Throughout the next century, Mona went through cycles of activity and decline as various entrepreneurs tried to get rich mining the bat guano from Mona's caves. Rich in phosphate, the guano made exceptional agricultural fertilizer, but by 1924 the mines went dry and the citizens left (except for the family of Doña Geña Rodríguez, who lived in a cave – called Cueva de Doña Geña – on the south end of the island until 1943). It was about this time that a German submarine fired on the island (thinking it was a post for the Allies), probably scaring the living daylights out of the unarmed iguanas, goats and pigs.

Following Civilian Conservation Corps activities on the island, the comings and goings of treasure hunters, WWII and a scam to turn Mona into an airbase, the government of Puerto Rico slowly began to take seriously its duty to protect the island as a nature preserve and eventually prohibited development. Finally, after almost 500 years of queasy human frenzy, Mona returned to her wild state.

Flora & Fauna

Although Mona's dry, semitropical climate might suggest an area with little variety in vegetation, Mona claims about 600 species of plants and 50 species of trees. Four of the plant species here are endemic, unknown to the rest of the world. Over the years many exotic species have been introduced to the island. Mahogany and coconut palms are two such species that still thrive. If you are exploring here, wear protective clothing. Mona has four types of venomous trees and bushes: *indio, papayo, manzanillo* and *carrasco.*

Almost 3000 acres of the island consist of cactus thickets, while 11,000 acres are in forest.

Of course, the stars of the island's wildlife menagerie are the giant rock iguanas, *Cyclura stejnegeri* (similar to the iguanas at Anagada in the British Virgin Islands and Allan's Cays in the Bahamas). These guys can grow a body the size of a very large tomcat with a tail that makes them 4 feet long. But it is their large heads and powerful jaws that are most fascinating, giving the iguanas the appearance of small-scale Tyrannosaurus rexes. Generally, these critters hunt and nest among the limestone ruts of the

coastal plain, but you may see their tracks on the island's trails or beaches.

Do not offer food to these animals, and keep your distance. They have sharp teeth and claws, and they could charge if they feel cornered.

This advice also holds true for the feral pigs, goats and cattle whose ancestors got left behind by former settlers. There is a hunt here every winter to thin the herds, but there are still plenty around. Store your food out of their range or you may find your campsite invaded.

Humpback whales breed during the winter around the Pasaje de la Mona, and, during a trip to or from Mona, it is not uncommon to see pods of these gregarious animals breaching, spy-hopping with their heads out of the water to look around, and slapping their pectoral flippers on the water. There are also schools of dolphins and pygmy sperm whales here.

Between May and October, Isla Mona's beaches are important nesting grounds for a number of species of marine turtle, including the chronically endangered Carey turtle.

If you are a bird-watcher, you will no doubt be attracted to the osprey, pelicans and hawks that hunt here, as well as about 100 other species.

Mona is also loaded with all kinds of bugs, so be aware and prepared. Fifty-two species of spider, three kinds of scorpion and four types of centipede are here for your pleasure. Several are venomous, including the black widow spider.

Orientation

Isla Mona is almost a perfect oval, measuring about 7 miles from east to west and 4 miles from north to south. Most of the island's coastline is made up of rough, rocky cliffs, especially along the north side. The south side, meanwhile, has a number of narrow beaches, which fringe the highlands. The most approachable of these beaches is

Don't Mess with Mona

Isla Mona, the site of numerous shipwrecks and violent deaths, claimed another victim in 1998. As Hurricane Georges approached the island of Puerto Rico, the Aguadilla detachment of the US Drug Enforcement Agency (DEA) thought it would be a good idea to move two twin-engine aircraft that it uses for surveillance off the main island.

The two planes took off from Aguadilla, bound for safety in the Dominican Republic. But for some reason, the planes flew over Mona at extremely low altitudes and were so close to each other that they collided. One of the aircraft landed safely on the airstrip at Mona, but the other veered out of control and crashed in shallow water off the beach. A passenger escaped, but the pilot died in the crash.

Perhaps embarrassed by the accident, the DEA refused to answer all questions related to the crash and took cover from the press under the bigger story of Hurricane Georges' ensuing devastation of the island. Nevertheless, local aviators and mariners have not forgotten the crash. 'Strange things happen out there on that island,' one aviator says. 'It doesn't pay to mess around with Mona.'

Playa Sardinera, where you will find toilets, showers and the concrete living quarters of the rangers and police detachment. The airfield lies about a mile farther east.

The island's terrain consists of a broad rim of coastal plain that rises gently to a central mesa, and because the land is relatively flat and overgrown with vegetation, it is difficult to find landmarks on the horizon. More than a few people have gotten lost here – including the pirate William Kidd. If you're planning to venture off the main roads, try to get a good map of the island (not just the basic photocopy you can get from the Depto de Recursos Naturales in San Juan); the USGS publishes one of the best (US$4). Better yet, go in company with a knowledgeable guide.

Caves

Mona has 18 named caves, which tunnel through the limestone in every part of the island. Many, like Cueva Lirio (Lily Cave), were mined for their guano, and some caves contain remains of railway tracks and machinery. Cueva de Doña Geña (Doña Geña Cave) was inhabited by a family for many years. A number of the most dramatic caves lie near the southeast cliffs, including Cueva La Escalera (Stairway Cave, in English), the

Cueva del Pájaro (Bird Cave) and the Cueva Los Ingleses (English Cave).

Diving

You will find spectacular 150-foot visibility in the waters around the island. And although the area has been heavily fished, there are excellent barrier and fringe-reef dives filled with lagoons and ruts on the south side of the island with eight different kinds of coral. Wall dives lie farther offshore.

Places to Stay

The only option for staying overnight on Mona is to camp. The Depto de Recursos Naturales (☎ 787-723-1616, 721-5495) in San Juan is the only place that issues permits to camp on Mona (in designated areas on the south side of the island) for a maximum of three days. It's best to apply at least a week in advance. Campsites cost US$1 per night per person.

If you are on a diving expedition, you will probably camp at **Playa Sardinera** on the west end of the island. Head up to the old grass airstrip at Punta Oeste (Arenas) to get away from the detachment of rangers and police who are here to protect the environment and watch for a steady stream of illegal immigrants crossing from the poorer

Dominican Republic. With time to trek, you can hike across the island on the Camino del Diablo (Devil's Road) to rough it at the camping areas of **Playa del Uvero** (south side), or farther on the Camino del Infierno (or Hell's Road) to **Playa Pájaros** on the southeast side of the island.

Getting There & Away

Air Aero Borinquen (☎ 787-890-5400), at the airport in Aguadilla, is a good bet to take you on the 20-minute flight to Mona's dirt strip. Figure at least US$350 for drop-off and pick-up service in a five-passenger light twin aircraft.

Boat Mona Aquatics (☎ 787-851-2185), next to the *club náutico* on Calle José de Diego in Boquerón, has weekend trips to Mona, leaving Friday at 7 am and returning Sunday at 11 am. Day dives on the 43-foot boat are US$65, weekend trips are US$115. Expect similar prices from the Caribbean Reef Dive Shop (☎ 787-254-4006), on the waterfront in Puerto Real. In Rincón, there are a number of outfits offering three-day dive trips to Mona, including the Desecheo Dive and Surf Shop (see Rincón, earlier in this chapter), or try Encanto Ecotours in San Juan (☎ 787-272-0005).

An excellent guide and Mona veteran working out of San Juan is Jaime Vives at Scuba Centro (☎ 787-781-8086), at 1156 Avenida Roosevelt. His 48-foot catamaran *Club Aquarius*, with twin diesel engines, carries 48 passengers and can get you to and from Mona in $2^{1}/_{2}$ hours from the west coast. Jaime offers six-day diving vacations, which include four days of camping and diving at Mona for US$1195.

North Coast

From a vessel navigating the north coast of Puerto Rico, the shore appears like a place in a strange dream. In the foreground lies a surf-strewn mix of reefs, rocky promontories, dark mangrove estuaries and ribbons of beach guarded by coconut palms. Behind this shore, a weird jumble of craggy hills tower over the scene like a thicket of green pyramids laced with narrow canyons. In the distant haze, the 4000-foot summits of the Cordillera Central appear to be the lower slopes of the thunderclouds that billow up to 20,000 feet above the sea.

But the average traveler or islander passing along this coast sees little of this drama. The driver on the four-lane commercial artery of Hwy 2 witnesses a sea of traffic, industrial plants and housing developments. And if the car windows are down, the air probably reeks of auto exhaust and industrial emissions. The passenger aboard a plane at night sees a relentless, bright belt of light, just as they might see looking down on the densely populated US East Coast between Washington, DC, and New York.

Such is the paradox of Puerto Rico's north coast: It is a region of extraordinary shorelines and uplands bisected by a band of urban sprawl. Just 50 years ago, sugar plantations and a few small towns composed the northwest coastal plain; now the region is home to the bulk of Puerto Rico's population and industry. And yet it still has places where you can travel for miles and see only cows, mongoose, hawks, snowy egrets, caimans and remnants of Taíno civilization.

To appreciate this part of the island, you must learn to skirt its main roads and the towns that clot the coastal lowlands from San Juan to Arecibo. One solution is to jump on the recently opened four-lane Hwy 22 toll road and breeze past the congestion (and everything else) at 65mph until you find an exit onto a road that leads directly to a secluded beach or mountain retreat. The other alternative is to meander through the north coast region along a network of

those little gray roads on your map that twist like snakes into the hills or along the coast, and find your Puerto Rican oasis of choice. There are many beach sanctuaries in this region, but you probably will be most surprised and delighted by karst country: Beaches are commonplace on the island, but karst formations of the size and extent found on the north coast of Puerto Rico are an exceedingly rare geological phenomenon (see the boxed text 'Karst Country' for more information).

Highlights

- Riding horses on the empty Atlantic beaches of Isabela

- Exploring backroads through karstic ravines and peaks

- Spending a few nights in a cabaña amid the wilderness of Bosque Estatal de Río Abajo

- Visiting the Observatorio de Arecibo to see what 'contact' earth has made with the stars

- Riding the passenger launch around Lago Dos Bocas in the early morning

- Taking the tour at the Cavernas del Río Camuy or – better yet – making a rappelling, spelunking and body-rafting trip down the Río Camuy

- Playing the excellent and cheap seaside golf course at Punta Borinquen in Aguadilla

The north coast also features some of the most challenging natural adventures on the island, ranging from surfing and hiking to caving, body rafting and rappelling.

AGUADILLA

If you've read the Bottom 10 list of places on the island in the Facts for the Visitor chapter, you know that this place suffers from commercialism. Nonetheless, Aguadilla is hard to avoid. If you are traveling along Hwy 2 between the west coast and San Juan, you can count on getting caught in Aguadilla's traffic even though the road passes east of the actual urban center. But the city does offer travelers a few attractions, plus good accommodations and great golf.

The city's name is a Spanish corruption of the Taíno word meaning 'garden' – and 'corruption' is exactly what Spanish explorers and, later, Americans brought to what was once a heartbreakingly beautiful coastline

of cliffs, coves and hidden beaches. Like Boquerón, Mayagüez and Aguada, Aguadilla claims to have been the place where Columbus 'discovered' Puerto Rico. Maybe if the great 'Admiral of the Ocean Sea' could have imagined the crumbling waterfront, decaying air base, computer factories and strip malls that came in the wake of his discovery, good old Cristóbal might have kept quiet about this place or settled here to eat *lotos* (lotus) with the Taínos, never to return to his home across the seas.

If you need more information on the region, the Puerto Rico Tourism Company (☎ 787-890-0022) has an office at the Aeropuerto Rafael Hernández, north of town.

Base Ramey

If you're curious about what a Cold War-era Strategic Air Command base looks like, here is your big chance. The base has been closed for military operations for over 30 years, and

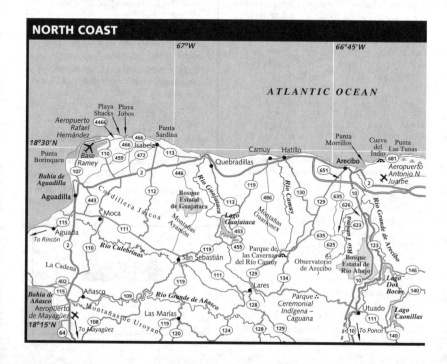

NORTH COAST

the land was turned over to the Common-wealth of Puerto Rico to use as a ready-made town. Today, the old government buildings give visitors a chilling vision of the massive military development that once existed here.

To get to the base from the south, take Hwy 107 north from Hwy 2. This route brings you through what is called Gate One. The traffic can get a little nutty on this road, so you may want to approach from the east via Hwy 110 (the route to the airport), which brings you through Gate Five. Once you're in, have fun getting lost on the maze of roads that lead you around the shopping center (still partially open), airfield, administration buildings and the nearly endless plots of former base housing that have been sold off to local families.

Beaches

For swimming and snorkeling, the most popular place to go is **Crash Boat Beach**. It

got its name because the Air Force used to keep rescue boats here to pick up crews from the Strategic Air Command's heavy bombers that didn't make the runway. The beach lies off Hwy 107, halfway between town and the former airbase. You will see a sign for Crash Boat that directs you west on the short Hwy 458.

If you are more adventuresome and want to avoid the crowds, follow Hwy 107 past the Crash Boat turnoff and onto the base. Eventually, you will see the golf course on your left and a road that heads west through the golf course. Follow this road as it winds down to rough, lonely **Wilderness Beach** and the ruins of what must have been Air Force recreation clubs. You get great sunsets and views of Punta Borinquen here.

Golf

This may the best reason to visit Aguadilla and the only good thing the US government

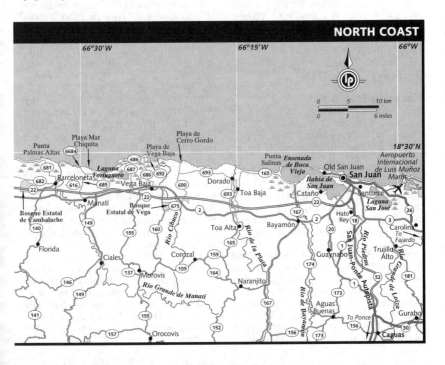

Karst Country

Puerto Rico's karst formations, or 'karstic landscapes,' began when carbonic acid in rainwater, streams and rivers drained into the cracks and fissures of the island's limestone. During various ice ages, much of Puerto Rico was under the sea, and decaying plants and marine life built up a layer of limestone over the island's volcanic core. When the ice ages came to an end and the sea receded, Puerto Rico's limestone was exposed to the weather. Over millions of years, the carbonic acid in rainwater wore away the more soluble parts of the limestone, leaving deep, narrow canyons where once there were only tiny fissures. The erosion cut deep *sumideros* (sinkholes) and exposed craggy *mogotes* (conical peaks) hundreds of feet high where once there were upland slopes.

Streams and rivers burrowed through the rock to make a honeycomb of caves. In Puerto Rico's tropical climate – fueled by cloudbursts and mountain runoff – this process eventually yielded the third-largest cave network in the world.

Nowadays, on the surface of the north coast, narrow, twisting roads and streams go on for mile after mile through lost valleys that look like sets for such Hollywood classics as *King Solomon's Mines* or *The African Queen*.

did for the town. Punta Borinquen Golf (☎ 787-890-2987) is a 6800-yard, 18-hole course on the former Air Force base that was designed for US President Dwight D Eisenhower in the 1950s. The course offers a cafeteria, pro shop, practice range and lessons. Greens fees are only US$18.

Places to Stay & Eat

If you really must stay in Aguadilla (on business, for a flight out of Aeropuerto Rafael Hernández, or out of desperation), it is possible to find attractive, reasonably priced accommodations (just don't leave your lodgings if you want to stay in a good mood).

The *Hacienda El Pedregal* (☎ 787-891-6068) is at Km .1 on Hwy 111, which cuts north (coming from Rincón) through Aguadilla, then away from the port area. There are 27 rooms but no restaurant here. Rooms range from US$50 to US$70.

Nearby on Hwy 111, the *Cielo Mar Hotel* (☎ 787-882-5959, 84 Avenida Monemar) is set on a hilltop perch, with a panoramic view of the Pasaje de la Mona and the Atlantic. It's a great escape from the surrounding dirt and decay. All rooms have private balconies with sea views. The Cielo Mar also features a pool, restaurant and bar. Rates start at US$70.

There are several inland accommodations of note as well. *El Faro* (☎ 787-882-8000) stands at Km 2.1 on Hwy 107, the route to Gate One of Base Ramey. This place has won a number of design and service awards, all of them well deserved. With lush grounds, 50 units and a pool, El Faro has a country-club feel. Rates start at US$67.

El Faro's management also runs the *Parador Borinquen Hotel* (☎ 787-891-0491), just off Hwy 107 on Hwy 467, south of the base. The Parador is probably best for a budget-conscious family. Rooms run US$50; there is a pool and children's playground.

Some business travelers prefer to be on the east side of Base Ramey, nearer the industrial park. *La Cima Hotel* (☎ 787-890-2016), on Hwy 110, meets their needs with a three-story concrete motel-like building. There are two restaurants on the property, along with a pool and gym. Rates vary from US$55 to US$100.

For more luxury (in a pastoral and secluded setting), try the *Parador JB Hidden Village* (☎ 787-868-8686), on Hwy 416 in Aguada, which is 5 miles south of Aguadilla on the way to Rincón. You will find 33 rooms, a restaurant and a pool. Rooms run US$69 to US$129.

Entertainment

The *Cielo Mar Hotel* (see Places to Stay & Eat, above) features live rock and salsa bands on weekends for dancing.

The gay club *Factory* (☎ 787-890-1530), in the Punta Borinquen shopping center at Base Ramey, is great fun, and there are a lot of gay *sanjuaneros* and travelers here on weekends for the drag shows and all-night dancing.

For other nearby entertainment options, see the Isabela & Environs section, later in this chapter.

Getting There & Away

Air Until recently, KIWI International Air Lines (☎ 800-538-5494) offered scheduled service from New York and Miami to the bomber strip at Aguadilla's Aeropuerto Rafael Hernández. Unfortunately, at the time this book went to press the airline had suspended its service indefinitely. Call in advance to check on the carrier's current status and service.

Aero Borinquen (☎ 787-890-5400) offers charter flights to nearby Isla Mona; see the Isla Mona section in the West Coast chapter for details.

Público There is a terminal in town right off the central plaza, if you really want to wait around for a ride to your next destination. Expect to pay US$11 to San Juan.

Car If you are driving between San Juan and the west coast (and want to avoid rush-hour traffic), consider taking the backroad Hwy 443, which breaks off Hwy 2 just east of town, then rejoins it to the south.

Getting Around

If you have reached Aguadilla by *público* or plane, you will definitely need a car to explore the interesting backcountry of the surrounding area. The following vendors will rent you vehicles at the airport:

Aguadilla Car Rental	☎ 787-895-5020
Avis	☎ 787-890-3311
Budget	☎ 787-890-1110
L&M	☎ 787-890-3010

Do not count on taking a taxi from the airport. Virtually everyone who flies into Aguadilla uses private ground transportation.

MOCA

If you really want to avoid Aguadilla's traffic and you are headed back east to San Juan from the west coast, you can take Hwy 111 and Hwy 110 through this town. Moca is not a picture-postcard settlement, but because it is set in a pastoral valley at the foot of the Jaicoa and Tuna mountains, it does have some charms. During the 19th century and early 20th century, Moca thrived as a center for the sugarcane industry. Native son Dr Enrique Laguerre wrote his celebrated novel *La Llamarada* about the area and chronicled the hard life of the *agregados* (farm workers) bent to the iron will of North American sugar companies.

The town has several historic homes that recall the hacienda life of the old sugar barons and their cohorts. Most of all, Moca is noted for preserving the tradition of *mundillo*, an intricately woven lace. Barbara Bush, the wife of former US President George Bush, came to Moca in the early 1990s to learn the secrets of mundillo.

Mansions

While you are in Moca, you may want to take a look at three mansions from the hacienda era of Puerto Rico. You will pass the **Hacienda Enrique** on your way into town from the west on two-lane Hwy 111. This is now the private home of Dr Elueterio Loperana, who maintains part of the house as a museum of colonial artifacts. He allegedly opens the hacienda to visitors on occasion, but his unpublished phone number makes it difficult to find out when he is giving tours. Ask in town.

If you approach Moca from the north via two-lane Hwy 110, you will pass **Los Castillos Meléndez**, which resemble medieval castles. **Palacete Los Moureau** is a beautiful yellow French-provincial chateau in Barrio Aceitunas and is currently being restored as part of an ambitious municipal project that is adding parks, gardens and sports facilities to the town. Call the town's public relations office

(☎ 787-877-6015) for information on the status of the chateau's opening.

Mundillo Stores & Workshops

If you are looking to learn about how mundillo is made, or you want to buy some, head to the **Tienda Bazaar María Lasalle**, just off the plaza, or visit the **Leonides shop**, at 114 Calle Ramos Antonini. You can also ask around town for directions to a number of the home workshops where women practice this antique lacemaking art.

ISABELA & ENVIRONS

While the town of Isabela, near Aguadilla and the northwest tip of the island, is probably not a place you can fall in love with, it is far enough off the beaten track of Hwy 2 that it's relatively free of traffic jams and the bland housing developments you see surrounding other north coast towns.

What Isabela has going for it is plenty of wild, dramatic surrounding countryside, plus two absolutely first-rate supermarkets (which you will likely need for provisioning). In fact, there may be no more striking contrast in Puerto Rico than leaving Aguadilla's Base Ramey on Hwy 110, and then taking Hwy 4466 east from the base and 'over the edge.' This is a 200-foot escarpment that rises from virtually the water's edge to the coastal plain above. On the plateau (where the base is), you'll find shopping centers and car dealerships, but below the escarpment, another world awaits – one of dunes, coral islets, a lush narrow savanna and salt flats pressed between the beaches and cliffs.

Here, along 7 miles of coast, you can beachcomb or go horseback riding and rarely see another person. The 1989 world surfing championships were held here at Playa Jobos, where a big, mean point break protects a crescent cove with beach bars and restaurants overlooking the scene from the dunes. A cluster of rental homes and two resorts lie farther east.

A 20-minute drive from the beach transports you to yet another world. Follow two-lane Hwy 113 east out of Isabela and then head south on Hwy 446, which leads you into a web of backroads that meander through

dark-green valleys where the air smells of cool moss and dairy cows – and into some of the most dramatic hills and valleys of karst country. This is the site of the forest reserve of Bosque Estatal de Guajataca as well as a serene fishing lake, Lago Guajataca.

Beaches

The dramatic, crescent **Playa Jobos** is protected by a large headland of dead coral to the east, and the surf breaks pretty consistently off this point. The site of the 1989 world surfing championships, Jobos is a good place to surf or watch professional-caliber athletes doing their wave thing. There is also good swimming off the eastern beach, where the point protects you from the surf. The bar-restaurants on the south side of the cove are popular places to kick back, especially on weekends.

Another beach, **Playa Shacks**, lies less than a mile west of Jobos, near Base Ramey on Hwy 4466. There are good submarine caves here for snorkeling.

Bosque Estatal de Guajataca

While this forest, southeast of Isabela on Hwy 446, has only about 2300 acres of land, it is truly a dramatic setting in the thick of karst country. The terrain rises and falls between 500 and 1000 feet above sea level, punctuated by towering *mogotes* (conical peaks) that look like a spilled box of giant green gumdrops. The reserve has about 25 miles of hiking trails and the **Cueva del Viento** (Cave of the Wind), which is rich with stalactites and stalagmites. There is also an observation tower and plantations of blue mahoe trees. The area is a favorite habitat of the endangered Puerto Rican boa as well as 45 species of birds.

Trails here are well-marked, but don't head off on any extended expedition unless you have a map. Unfortunately, the ranger station near the trailheads in the center of the forest is not always open, and the rangers do not necessarily have maps. The best bet is to call the Aguadilla office of the Depto de Recursos Naturales (Dept of Natural Resources; ☎ 787-890-4050, 890-2050) to secure a map before you arrive at the forest, find things closed and feel a little lost. (Another possibility is picking up a map at Lago Guajataca; see below.)

Lago Guajataca

This lake and wildlife refuge is like a 4-mile-long blue rift between the pastureland of the dairy farms south of Quebradillas and the mogotes of San Sebastián and Lares. The easiest approach from Hwy 2 and the coast is via Hwy 119. But this area is really beautiful country, and you may want to get off the main road to explore. Do not miss driving along the north side of the lake, where there are two clubs for anglers hoping to hook fish such as the tucunare, which is stocked in this lake. The view from the dam here looks into a dramatic 'lost valley' of conical peaks.

If you want to fish, stop by the Depto de Recursos Naturales office (☎ 787-896-7640), at Km 22.1 on Hwy 119 near the lake, for permission. The office is open 6 am to 6 pm Tuesday to Sunday and sometimes has maps on hand for the nearby forest reserve of Bosque Estatal de Guajataca.

⚞ Horseback Riding

A horseback ride along a nearly deserted beach is one of the true joys of the region. There are two options in the area. You can take a ride along the fields, dunes and beaches from Villas de Mar Hau near Playa Jobos (see Places to Stay, below). Rides are US$15 for a half hour, US$25 for a full hour.

A second option for horseback riding is Tropical Trail Rides (☎ 787-872-9256), which works out of stables at Km 1.8 on Hwy 4466 near Playa Shacks.

Places to Stay

Camping It is not legal, but surfers and beach-lovers have been camping on *Playa Jobos* since the surfing championships were here more than a decade ago.

At the Bosque Estatal de Guajataca, there are 10 campsites at *La Vereda*, on Hwy 446, 5 miles south of Hwy 2. Call the forest reserve's central office in San Juan (☎ 787-724-3724) for a permit and to make reservations, or try the Aguadilla office at ☎ 787-890-4050. It's US$4 per person.

Guesthouses *Cabañas Gonzales* (☎ 787-872-7048), at Playa Jobos, offers some basic efficiency apartments in a concrete, motel-style building for US$60.

Hotels The *Villas de Mar Hau* (☎ 787-872-2045) lies on the beach off Hwy 466 about a mile east of Playa Jobos. This classic cabaña village sits on a dramatic coast where offshore coral islets create bathing lagoons. The down-home resort has 36 units in wooden or concrete cabañas facing the sea; there are also some recreational shelters and a horse pasture. To the east lie 4 miles of undeveloped sand dunes. Puerto Ricans love the old-time feel of this place, and it tends to get packed with summer vacationers, but during other seasons the villas can be one of the most tranquil places on the island. You can ride a horse, take a bike tour, kayak, snorkel or hike the beach and see almost no one for hours. The hotel has inexpensive rentals for all of these activities. Cabañas cost US$80 to US$110.

At the east end of the dirt road that snakes behind the barrier sand dunes between Villas de Mar Hau and the edge of Isabela, the modern *Costa Dorado Beach Resort* (☎ 787-872-7255) has 52 rooms housed in three-story, condo-style buildings set around landscaped grounds, two pools and two restaurants. Rooms run US$90 to US$125.

Villa Montaña (☎ 787-872-9554) offers luxury accommodations at Playa Shacks. Here the accommodations are in individual or duplex modern villas, and there are tennis courts, a guarded gate and a pool. Rates start at US$200 for a one-bedroom villa.

In Quebradillas, about 5 miles east of Isabela, the *Parador El Guajataca* (☎ 800-964-3065), at Km 103.8 on Hwy 2, is a chain of buildings with 38 units spread out along the edge of a cliff above the Atlantic. The inn has a pool, a tennis court and a restaurant. Rates start at US$80.

Less than a mile east, the *Parador Vistamar* (☎ 787-895-2065), at Km 102 on Hwy 2, has 55 rooms in two hilltop buildings overlooking the Atlantic. Most rooms have private decks and ocean views as well as all the amenities. There is a pool, tennis court and gourmet restaurant on-site. Rates here range between US$69 and US$90 per night.

Places to Eat

Among the collection of bar-restaurants overlooking Playa Jobos, *Restaurante Sonia Rican* has a bar that looks out over the surfing action. A serving of fish soup with *mofongo* costs US$5.

Less than 100 yards west, *Happy Belly's* (☎ 787-872-6566) is a very popular eating and drinking spot for both gringos and Puerto Ricans. A big burger goes for US$5; a grilled chicken sandwich runs US$6; fish and chips cost US$9.

If you are exploring karst country, head down two-lane Hwy 453 along the east side of Lago Guajataca and stop for a bite at *Cafeteria Vista al Lago* (☎ 787-895-6877), where you can get grilled chicken or pork for US$5 and eat at a picnic table with a view of the lake and dairy farms.

Entertainment

At Playa Jobos, you can catch live Latin rock and salsa at *Happy Belly's* (see Places to Eat, above), where the crowd is a real mix of ages and ethnic origins. Just up the street, the *Sunset Café* (☎ 787-872-2117) has the same kinds of music starting on Thursday night.

In karst country, the *Cafeteria Vista al Lago* (see Places to Eat, above) has live music Saturday and Sunday.

Getting There & Away

The easiest way to access the region, from San Juan or the west coast, is via four-lane Hwy 22. But to really enjoy this area (and its lack of traffic), you need to get off the main highway and explore the backroads. To do so, you'll need a car.

But be careful. More than a few happy motorists have been breezing along these roads after a tropical downpour only to wind up stuck in a mud hole or loose, wet sand in the beach areas. In karst country, the danger is coming face to face with landslides that block or dangerously mire the roads.

No públicos serve these backroads or beach areas such as Playa Jobos.

ARECIBO & ENVIRONS

With almost 100,000 residents, Arecibo can easily claim to be the commercial capital of the north coast, and such a claim may well keep you away. But those willing to venture beyond the traffic of Arecibo's sprawling outskirts will discover a mid-size coastal port (about 50,000 folk in the urban center) that has a bit more charm than you might expect after close encounters with Aguadilla or Mayagüez.

Fresh paint and the relative cleanliness of Arecibo are clear signs that it is prospering. The best parts of the town are its long, cliffside *malecón* (waterfront promenade) and its compact plaza. Before Hurricane Georges, you could access this area – and avoid about a half hour of crawling traffic – by turning north toward the sea at either side of town and taking Avenida Victor Rojas along the malecón. But floods caused by the hurricane washed out the center span of the bridge, and it is taking more than a little time to repair the damage. Ask a local about the condition of the bridge before you attempt this route.

If the bridge is open (and you are circumnavigating the island in a clockwise direction and heading east on Avenida Rojas), you can cross the bridge over the Río Grande de Arecibo. Here you connect to Hwy 681, which takes you to the *balneario* (public beach), the Faro de los Morrillos lighthouse and 10 miles of rural coastline.

Another option for adventure is to avoid Arecibo completely and head south through rugged karst country into the mountains of the Cordillera Central on Hwy 10. The scenery along this drive rivals anything you may see descending toward Ponce on Hwy 52 or following the Ruta Panorámica along the island's spine. And Hwy 10 is also the smoothest drive on the island because it is a new three-lane, limited-access highway with no toll booths or traffic.

A reasonable day trip would carry you south toward the mountain town of Utuado. Along the way, take a detour to see the famous Observatorio de Arecibo (Arecibo Observatory; see below), a 15-minute drive off Hwy 10. Near here are the forest reserve of Bosque Estatal de Río Abajo and two lakes – Lagos Dos Bocas and Caonillas.

From Utuado, head west on Hwy 111 and cross the ridges to the Parque Ceremonial Indígena – Caguana (the Indian Ceremonial Park at Caguana), then go on to the town of Lares, where Puerto Rico's independence movement began. If you have the time, and prior reservations, you might join a trip offered by a local outfitter for a climbing, caving and body-rafting expedition (see Organized Tours in the Getting Around chapter for activity-tour operators). Leaving Lares, take Hwy 129 north back down to the coast, stopping for a tour of the Parque de las Cavernas del Río Camuy.

Observatorio de Arecibo

The drive south on four-lane Hwy 10 from Arecibo to this observatory (☎ 787-878-2612), home to the world's largest radio telescope, is almost as exciting as the site itself. From Hwy 10, follow the roller-coaster ride through mogotes on narrow, two-lane roads. Hwy 626 and Hwy 623 cross the Río Tanamá valley to meet Hwy 625, which leads to the observatory. (For a gentler ride, take Hwy 129 south from Arecibo to Hwy 635 and Hwy 625.)

Either way, your arrival here has a touch of drama and science fiction to it as the road crests a steep mogote. Ahead you see the immense telescope support towers gleaming in the sun above the hills, while the road in front of you descends toward a line of high fences and a guarded gatehouse that look like something out of the *X-Files*.

After entering and parking, you follow a walkway down to a space-age glass-and-concrete building set on the steep side of a mogote. From here you can see the 20-acre 'dish' set in a sinkhole between a cluster of hills. This radio telescope's silver dish (unlike smaller telescopes) is a fixed receiver for radio waves and does not rotate to improve reception. The actual receiving and transmitting instruments – which do rotate – are suspended by cables 50 stories above the dish. They weigh more than 600 tons and look to some people like the Federation starship USS *Enterprise*. On-site scientists from the National Astronomy and Ionosphere Center (administered by Cornell University) have used this facility to prove the existence of pulsars and quasars, the so-called 'music of the stars.'

Astronomers also examine things closer to home, such as the earth's ionosphere, the moon and the planets of our solar system. But, yes, there is an ongoing SETI (Search for Extraterrestrial Intelligence) program here like the one Jodi Foster obsesses over in the movie *Contact*, some of which was filmed here.

A new building has exhibits explaining astronomy and the function of the telescope. There is also an observation deck, panoramic elevator, video presentation and gift shop.

When the scientists are not searching for decaying star systems or ET, the observatory is open noon to 4 pm Wednesday to Friday, 9 am to 4 pm weekends and holidays. Admission is US$3.50 for adults, US$1.50 for seniors and children.

Bosque Estatal de Río Abajo

This 5000-acre forest (☎ 787-721-5464), just off Hwy 10 south of Arecibo, has some of the most rugged terrain on the island. Situated in the heart of karst country, the forest's altitude jumps between 700 and 1400 feet above sea level. The steep sides of the mogotes are overrun with vines, and the forest is a jungle of tropical hardwoods and bamboo. Rifts between the mogotes often seem like canyons rather than narrow valleys.

And yet most of this land was once logged bare. In the mid-1930s, the US government and the Civilian Conservation Corps (CCC) stepped in with their plan to reforest the island. The remains of the roads cut by the loggers and the CCC workers have now become trails. In fact, 24 trails wind through the canyons, around the edges of sinkholes and over the sides of the mogotes.

If the trails tempt you, buy a USGS topo map before you head off into the dense jungle. (The maps that are sometimes available at the reserve's ranger station are unreadable photocopies.)

The ranger station is near the entrance and the rental cabañas (see Places to Stay & Eat, later in this section) as Hwy 621 snakes into the forest. At the end of this road, there is a picnic and recreation area and an aviary, where the Depto de Recursos Naturales is working to rescue the Puerto Rican parrot and other endangered species.

Lagos Dos Bocas & Caonillas

These two lakes – each more than 2 miles long – fill a deeply cleft valley at a point where karst country gives way to the actual mountains of the Cordillera Central, east of Hwy 10 and about 12 miles south of Arecibo. The lakes are the principal reservoirs for the north-central part of the island, and for years they caused anxiety to communities downstream, which worried that the lakes could not absorb a torrential rainfall without overflowing or bursting a dam.

As it turned out, drought was the first plague to hit the lakes. At one point the water dropped so low at Lago Caonillas that the bell tower of a 1930s-era chapel was exposed. The chapel had been built in the valley before the Aqueduct and Sewer Authority claimed the land and flooded it with their reservoir. Thousands of islanders flocked to the site, hoping for a miracle, as if the image of the bell tower rising above the water was the sign of the second coming of Jesus.

But the miracle was short-lived. When Hurricane Georges passed over Puerto Rico in 1998, upward of 25 inches of rain fell on the Cordillera Central, and a lot of that water found its way to Caonillas and Dos Bocas. The dams did not break, but the reservoirs overflowed, sending a wall of water down the Río Grande de Arecibo valley. The flood destroyed crops, houses, possessions and even the bridge over the river's mouth in Arecibo. No one is talking about miracles anymore, and an immense lawsuit against the Aqueduct and Sewer Authority is working its way through the courts.

In calm weather, you can ride Dos Bocas' free launch, which serves as a taxi service to the residents in the area. The boat landing is on Hwy 123 on the west side of the lake. Boats leave almost every hour. You can disembark at restaurants around the lake (generally open only on weekends) or just sit back and enjoy the two-hour ride. It can make for a sublime experience when the winter sun is just creeping over the top of the Cordillera Central.

Parque Ceremonial Indígena – Caguana

Like the archaeological site at Tibes near Ponce, this Taíno ceremonial site (☎ 787-894-7325), off Hwy 111, is not dramatic in the sense of having monumental ruins. The power of the place comes from its first-rate setting in a natural botanical garden of ceiba, *ausubo* and *tabonuco* trees shading the midslopes of the Cordillera Central. There are also 10 ceremonial *batey* (ball) courts, which date back about 800 years (see the boxed text for details on batey). Stone monoliths line many of the courts; some weigh up to a ton, but most are small. One court, however, measures 60 feet by 120 feet. Quite a few have petroglyphs, such as the famous Mujer de Caguana, who squats in the pose of the traditional 'earth mother' fertility symbol.

The discovery of this site dates to the beginning of the 20th century, when it was originally excavated by the respected archaeologist J Alden Mason. He and subsequent archaeologists have concluded that the size and number of the ball courts suggest that Caguana was not much of a village, but rather a central ceremonial site, perhaps one of the most important Taíno sites in the Caribbean.

Caguana is a place to walk and reflect, not to be stimulated by exhibits. Nevertheless, there is a small museum with artifacts and skeletons on the property, and a gift shop that sells inexpensive but attractive reproductions of Taíno charms, including the statues called *cemíes*.

The site is open 9 am to 4 pm daily. Admission is free.

Parque de las Cavernas del Río Camuy

This park (☎ 787-763-0568) is home to one of the largest cave systems in the world, and although a visit costs more than mere peanuts, the Cavernas del Río Camuy are definitely worth the trip.

Your visit begins with a film about the caves at the visitors center. Then you take a

At Play in the Fields of the Lord

Scholars now think that the popular Taíno game *batey* (both the name of the game and the court on which it was played) was not simply a sports pastime, but was also a socioreligious endeavor that had significant community-wide implications and involved a transcendental experience for the players.

Ten or more players composed a team. Generally players were male, but females were often participants, too. The cost of playing – the court fee, in a sense – was determined by teams before the game, and the 'fees' usually included quantities of foodstuffs, such as sweet potatoes or fish. Naturally, the winning team took all.

When the game began, teams of equal numbers took the court, and each team had its own territory that could not be entered by the opposition.

The game was simple enough: Teams kept a solid ball – made of woven rubber, about 16 inches in diameter – in the air; if the ball fell to the ground on one team's side of the court, the opposition won a point. Teams agreed upon the winning number of points before playing.

In a sense, batey was something like playing volleyball without a net, but with one big exception: In batey, players could use any part of their bodies to keep the ball aloft except their hands and feet.

Scholars have actually pieced together some of the Taíno vocabulary associated with the game, so that today's Puerto Rican schoolchildren can play the ancient game with some semblance of authenticity. Rumor has it that one imperative, *daca batú* (pass me the ball), can sometimes be heard at the rowdier island sports pubs when local soccer hunks show up after a big game and want a few cans of Medalla real fast.

---

trolley bus that follows a spiraling road down through the jungle into a 200-foot-deep sinkhole to Cueva Clara de Empalme (Clear Cave Junction), where you take a 45-minute guided walk through the cave. Here you walk past enormous stalagmites and stalactites and into rooms littered with boulders. At one point, the ceiling of the cavern reaches a height of 170 feet; at another, you can see the Río Camuy rushing through a tunnel.

After leaving the cave from a side passage, you take another tram to the Tres Pueblos sinkhole, which measures 650 feet across

and drops 400 feet. Newer attractions at the park are the 42 petroglyphs found in Cueva Catedral (Cathedral Cave) and the Mina del Río Camuy, a touristy invention where you can sluice for semiprecious stones.

The park is at Km 18.9 on Hwy 129, a few miles north of Lares on the road to Arecibo. The caves are open 8 am to 4 pm Wednesday to Sunday (and holidays). The last tour leaves at 2 pm if you want to see all three areas, or at 3:45 pm if you want to see just one sinkhole. Admission is US$10/7/5 for adults/children/seniors. There's a US$2 fee for parking.

Cueva de Camuy

This privately owned cave (☎ 787-898-2723) is in Barrio Quebrada, south of Camuy on Hwy 486 at Km 11.1. While the cave itself is an attraction here – you get a lighted walk amid hundreds of stalactites and stalagmites – it gets a bit lost under the topside, which is thoroughly developed with a water park, go-cart track, pony rides and the like. The cave is open 9 am to 5 pm Monday to Saturday, 9 am to 6 pm Sunday and holidays. Admission varies, but plan on US$8.

Faro de los Morrillos

This lighthouse, on the hill at Punta Morrillos, east of Arecibo on Hwy 681, is an excellent example of the Spanish neoclassical architecture used for lighthouses around the island. Dating from 1897, the Faro de los Morrillos was one of the last lighthouses

---

Bat World, Mole People & the Undiscovered Country

Experts today estimate that Puerto Rico has at least 1000 caves, only 250 of which have been explored. Most of these caves lie in the karstic zone where rivers draining the rain forest of the Cordillera Central have tumbled into sinkholes and carved tunnels on their way downhill to the sea. One such system of sinkholes and tunnels is the Cavernas del Río Camuy, which spreads over an area about 10 miles long and has 17 entrances in the area between the towns of Hatillo, Camuy and Lares. Another big network is the Sistema del Río Encantada, which runs almost totally underground for about 10 miles between the towns of Ciales, Florida and Manatí. A third system, in the same area as the other two – more wild river than caves – is the Río Tanamá.

Over the centuries, the caves have been important shelters for indigenous people, home to millions of bats that help keep the island's insect population under control, and a source of fertilizer. But no modern explorers went to the trouble of making a thorough investigation of the caves until 1958. This was when Russell and Jeanne Gurnee and Bob and Dorothy Rebille accompanied José Limeres (a Puerto Rican doctor) into a Río Camuy sinkhole. The upshot of this trip was a suggestion that the government purchase 300 acres of land around the Río Camuy caves as a nature preserve. Later, the Speleological Society of Puerto Rico explored and mapped the caves, eventually proposing that the government develop the Cueva Clara de Empalme (at the site of the Cavernas del Río Camuy) for tourism, and in 1986 the attraction opened.

Although what you see here is spectacular, veteran spelunkers say it is the tip of the iceberg. If you want to see more – and you crave a first-class adventure – Puerto Rico now has several experienced outfitters who have caving adventures that combine technical climbing and body rafting to meet the skills of either novices or seasoned explorers. One such trip is the 'Angeles.' This trip starts with a zipline ride (with you in harness and sliding down a cable) into the forest, followed by a 200-foot rappel into a sinkhole. Later, you explore the cave on foot and by swimming an underground lake before exiting down a mudslide and body rafting through the canyons of the Río Camuy.

The Angeles rappelling, spelunking and body-rafting trip costs US$85 with Adventuras Tierra Adentro (☎ 787-766-0470). Even longer trips on the Río Tanamá, in the same area, go for about US$100.

You can get similar prices from two other outfitters: Explora (☎ 787-751-9647) in San Juan, and Expediciones Tanamá (☎ 787-894-7685) in the village of Angeles. All guides are bilingual and use the most modern equipment.

built in the colonial period, and it shows a more elegant and gracefully refined shape than do many of the older lighthouses around Puerto Rico.

After the lighthouse became automated in the 1970s, vandals and the weather took their toll on the lighthouse keeper's house at the base of the tower. Finally, the city found funds for restoration, and in recent years the lighthouse has become a museum (☎ 787-879-1625). If you stop here, you will see revolving shows of island artists' work, artifacts pertaining to the history of Arecibo, and stamp collections. It's open 8 am to 4 pm Wednesday to Sunday. Admission is free.

Cueva del Indio

Heading east from the Faro de los Morrillos, Hwy 681 takes you along a rugged coastline, punctuated by coral outcroppings, dunes and lagoons. The countryside is largely rural, but clutches of beach houses have grown up along sections of the road. You will find the Cueva del Indio (Indian's Cave) near one such settlement about 2 miles east of the lighthouse. There may be a sign (that is, if a hurricane or vandals haven't made off with it) on the side of the road pointing you north to the oceanfront cave, but if it's gone, your landmark is the derelict gas station on the right. You can park here and follow the well-worn path across the road to the shore.

The surf crashes around the cave's entrance, which leads to a descending staircase and a substantial collection of Taíno petroglyphs on the walls. Bring a flashlight and good footwear.

Simple Taíno petroglyph typical of those found in island caves

Beaches

You will find two good beaches in the area of the Faro de los Morrillos. On the cove side, south of the point and the commercial pier, just off Hwy 681, you will see the manicured facilities of a **town beach** with broad sand and totally protected water. This is a great place for families.

If you follow the road past the lighthouse (less than a quarter of a mile), you come to the **Morillo** balneario. There is a big parking lot and all the usual facilities. The beach is about a half mile of low dunes and white sand, and it usually gets plenty of surf.

Places to Stay & Eat

In the heart of the *Bosque Estatal de Río Abajo* (☎ 787-878-0297), you will find a rustic camping village with a cluster of cabañas. Each holds 10 to 12 people and has a private bath and hot water. The cabins rent for US$100 to US$120 on weekdays, US$150 to US$180 on weekends and holidays. You need to bring your own bedding, and you can take meals in the cafeteria, where breakfast runs US$2 and other meals cost US$5.

If you are looking for an actual B&B, the *Posada el Palomar* (☎ 787-898-1060), south of Camuy at Km .5 on Hwy 119, may work for you. The owners promise a romantic room with 'music therapy,' as well as the use of a pool and Jacuzzi and 'the feel of the country.' Rooms start at US$65.

For even more of a country feel, check out *Casa Grande* (☎ 888-343-2272), at Km .3 on Hwy 612, which is off Hwy 140 east of Utuado. This inn is a former coffee plantation with 20 rooms in the vicinity of Lagos Dos Bocas and Caonillas. You won't have to venture out on the mountain roads at night because *Jungle Jane's* restaurant is right at the inn, as is a hillside swimming pool surrounded by woods. Rooms start at US$75.

For a base closer to Arecibo, consider *El Buen Café Hotel* (☎ 787-898-1000), at Km 84 on Hwy 2 in Hatillo. This modern concrete building has 20 rooms with air con and the other goodies. Rates start at US$80. Across the street, the restaurant of the same name is on the Puerto Rico Tourism Company's exclusive Mesones Gastronómicos list.

Alamar Restaurant & Sports Bar (☎ 787-878-5658), near Arecibo's commercial pier, is a good stop for lunch or dinner when you are in the area, or if you want to go to the beach or visit the lighthouse and Cueva del Indio. It's US$17 for the paella (enough for two to split), or you can go light with chicken wings for US$6.

Entertainment
Alamar Restaurant & Sports Bar (see Places to Stay & Eat, above) draws a big crowd to its patio deck and bar on Friday and – sometimes – Saturday when they offer live salsa, merengue and boleros.

Getting There & Away
Arecibo is accessible from San Juan or Aguadilla by Hwy 2, or from Ponce by Hwy 10. The público stop is just east of the plaza. Públicos to San Juan run about US$8; US$6 to Aguadilla.

MANATÍ & ENVIRONS
You can skip the town completely: It is an industrial hub for workers in the local pharmaceutical factories, which were the sole producers of Valium until the exclusive patents ran out. The attractions of the area form a constellation of sites in a 15-mile radius around the town. In a sense, the town's name, Manatí (manatee), is an indication of the watery attractions here.

The network of backroads that head north from the town lead to a series of beaches, balnearios and vacation home settlements. In the midst of all of these coastal retreats is Laguna Tortuguero, one of the largest estuaries on the island.

At one time, all these coastal lowlands were sugarcane haciendas, and one of the best (Hacienda Esperanza) has been saved as a wildlife preserve with virgin beaches. Farther inland are two small forest reserves, Bosque Estatal de Cambalache and Bosque Estatal de Vega, set among the sinkholes and limestone mogotes of karst country.

Hacienda Esperanza
This former sugar plantation stretches over 2200 acres from the inland mogotes of karst country to the sea, northeast of the town of Barceloneta. The hacienda traces its origins to the early 19th century. By the time of the US invasion in 1898, Hacienda Esperanza had become the richest and most technically advanced sugar operation on the island. At one time the steam-driven mill here was the only one of its kind in the world.

The Márquez de Esperanza (Marquise of Esperanza) founded the hacienda, but after the decline of the sugar industry, the Conservation Trust of Puerto Rico purchased the property in 1975. The trust quickly got the hacienda, its buildings and machinery listed on the National Register of Historic Places, and by the 1980s had begun restoring the buildings and machinery while the land became a natural reserve.

The Trust restoration is still incomplete, however, and the manor house and mill are not yet open to the public. But you can explore the grounds and wonder how one family could have owned so much beautiful land on this small island. The empty beaches are a big attraction here, and the interior wetlands are rife with fish (such as tilapia), blue crab and shore birds.

Traditionally, there have been two ways to approach the hacienda – from the south or east. Coming from the east, travelers used to follow Hwy 6684 from the Mar Chiquita area. A trail still leads from the end of Hwy 6684 onto the hacienda property and the deserted beaches and surfing site, but recently the Conservation Trust posted 'Do Not Enter' signs at this trailhead.

Reaching the hacienda by the legal route adds a bit of grandeur to the scenery. Follow Hwy 685 north out of Manatí and turn left when you get to Hwy 616. After going through a barrio that was probably once a hamlet for the agregados or slaves who worked in the cane fields, the road sets out on a long dogleg through the savannas of the hacienda's old cane fields. If you meet anybody along this road, it is likely to be a girl or a boy out exercising a horse. You pass the ruins of another sugar plantation and mill before the road approaches the coast and curves through a gate leading onto the hacienda's land.

Yellowfin is the catch of the day at Crash Boat Beach, Aguadilla.

TONY ARRUZA

Warm sands of Rincón

RANDALL PEFFER

Giant rock iguana, Isla Mona

KEVIN R DOWNEY

Future major leaguers at play, Mayagüez

ROBERT FRIED

Participants in the time-honored tradition of dominoes, Rincón

Sunset over the Caribbean and mangrove wetlands, Bosque Estatal de Boquerón

Punta Morrillos, near Arecibo

Karstic landscape near Utuado

TOM BEAN

Ancient Taíno *batey* (ball court), Parque Ceremonial Indígena – Caguana

BOB KRIST

Exploring the vast Cavernas del Río Camuy, part of the third-largest cave network in the world

The hacienda is open during daylight hours every day except Monday. Currently it's free to enter the property, but expect that to change to something like the US$5 fee charged at the Hacienda Buena Vista (outside Ponce), which is also owned by the Conservation Trust.

Beaches

Unlike most public beaches, the **Playa Mar Chiquita** is not right alongside a main thoroughfare, and therein lies part of its charm. There's a hardly visible sign to the beach off Hwy 685, about 2 miles north of Manatí and just beyond the entrance to the town of Boquillas. If you miss the sign, go north on Hwy 648 (about a mile east of Boquillas). This road takes you over a steep hill to the beach. The beach lies at the bottom of an escarpment where the plateau of the coastal plain has been hollowed out into caves. When you get to this point, you'll see a parking area, a grove of trees and a huge promontory of dead coral protecting the beach.

There is tranquil swimming and decent snorkeling here. And the scene may be sublime unless you happen to get here after a junk car or a horse has fallen off the escarpment (apparently not uncommon) and has not yet moldered away. There are rarely crowds here, and parking is free.

As you continue east on the seaside road (which has now become Hwy 686), you'll pass through a coastal forest. When the road creeps back to the edge of the coast, the long strand of **Playa Tortuguero** will be on the left. And you may think you have found Eden until you come to the new balneario called Playa Los Tubos: Picture a tarmac parking lot surrounded by a green lawn populated with large-as-life concrete creatures, many painted in pastel colors. An elephant, shark, whale and manatee have all come to this party, but there is really no reason to join them.

A couple of miles farther east is a normal balneario, **Playa Puerto Nuevo** – a narrow crescent of sand sheltered by a broad headland to the east and surrounded by clusters of beach homes.

If this place seems too tame for you, head east from here upon Hwy 692, a road that comes to a halt in a mile or so at the spot where the Río Cibuco joins the sea. The beach along this road is exposed and punctuated with reefs and rocks. To the south lie cow pastures and savannas that have remained unchanged for centuries. This beach is known variously as **Playa de Vega Baja** and **La Costa Roja**, and strong riptides here make it dangerous for swimming. But the surfing can be excellent, and the peace you get sitting here under a coconut palm may be as good as it gets in Puerto Rico.

After a long detour inland (to clear the swampy mouth of the Río Cibuco), the network of coastal roads takes you to one more surprising beach as you head east. **Playa de Cerro Gordo** lies at the end of Hwy 690. This is like a giant version of the protected crescents of sand you saw at Mar Chiquita and Puerto Nuevo. Here is a long, broad beach with a glade of trees to protect you from the sun and the moundlike peninsula of Cerro Gordo to break the ocean swell. You can camp here or rent a place in the small beach community (see Places to Stay, later in this section). Parking is US$2. Note that the beach is teeming with vacationing Puerto Ricans during holidays and summer vacations.

Laguna Tortuguero

When you see this place, you'll probably think 'Africa' because of the heat, coastal marshes, brown water and flocks of wading birds. This lagoon stretches for more than 2 miles behind the barrier beach of Playa Tortuguero and holds 708 million gallons of water. No doubt this estuary once teemed with manatees, but the gentle 'sea cows' have all but disappeared in the wake of hunting and the introduction of exotic species, the most notable of which is the alligatorlike caiman.

The best way to see the lagoon is to visit the recreation area at the east end, off of Hwy 687. Look for the sign reading 'Facilidades de Pesca' (Fishing Area) and try to catch some tilapia off the dock.

Bosque Estatal de Cambalache

The entrance to this small forest reserve (☎ 787-878-7279) of just over 1000 acres lies west of Barceloneta at Km 6.6 on Hwy 682,

Look, Mom, No Hand!

Scientists believe that *Caiman crocodilus*, a South American cousin of the crocodile and alligator, arrived at Laguna Tortuguero in the 1970s after island pet shops had sold a lot of these baby animals as exotic pets. Unlike other reptile pets (such as snakes and iguanas), caimans are not necessarily docile. Nor do they stop growing until they reach more than 6 feet in length and are 150lb or more. Their bite is quick, sharp and savage. Even the bite of a baby caiman of less than a foot in length can instantly perforate your skin with dozens of little holes. Watch out!

No doubt more than a few of the critters snapped some flesh from the local collectors (or their neighbors or kids) before they found themselves flushed down a toilet or released. For some caimans, that meant ending up in the lagoon – a perfect habitat, full of fat fish to eat.

For the last 15 years, government wildlife officials have been trying to stop the proliferation of the animals at Laguna Tortuguero. Nothing has really worked except natural selection. Current estimates place the lagoon's caiman population between 500 and 1000. You probably will not see one, however, unless you come at night, when they are active, but you are better

off staying clear because the same kinds of folks who bought and released these animals in the first place are now making extra money snaring the caimans and butchering them for their meat. Some islanders say that the hunters are as vicious and territorial as the caimans themselves.

in front of the Job Corps facility. Karstic formations characterize this forest; countless mogotes pop straight up from the landscape to heights of 160 feet. Its many caves provide homes for fruit bats, which often swarm like bees into the evening sky.

The forest has a picnic area, some hiking trails, two designated trails for mountain bikes and two camping areas (see Places to Stay, below). Note that a permit is required for cycling (US$1) and for camping (free, but there's a US$4 charge per site). Call ☎ 787-724-3724 to obtain one.

The forest is also home to a nursery for ornamental trees, open to visitors 7:30 am to 3 pm weekdays.

Bosque Estatal de Vega

This is another small forest of approximately 1000 acres, among the mogotes south of the Hwy 22 expressway and just to the northwest of the town of Vega Alta. You enter off

Hwy 676, where you'll see the forest office. There are picnic shelters and a few modest hiking trails, but the forest isn't very developed. Its principle function is to preserve some of the aquifer that lies beneath the sinkholes and to offer a green sanctuary for the residents of San Juan's outer suburbs, which are pressing toward the forest borders.

Places to Stay

Camping The balneario at *Playa de Cerro Gordo* (☎ 787-883-2730) has 81 campsites, which rent for US$13. Like most public beaches, this one is serene – except during weekends, holidays and the summer.

To camp in karst country at the *Bosque Estatal de Cambalache* (☎ 787-724-3724), you need to make reservations. There are two campsites here: La Boba holds four tents, and La Rosa holds eight. It's US$4 per person per night. A free permit is required; see Bosque Estatal de Cambalache, above.

Rental Agents The coastline of Barceloneta, Manatí and Vega Baja claims quite a collection of vacation homes and apartments, mostly clustered near the balnearios. If you drive this way, you will find a lot of posted signs offering these places for rent. The problem is that unless you are here during the summer or on holiday weekends (when the place is already packed and you have no chance of getting a room, on the fly anyway), you probably will not find anyone to answer your knocks on doors.

You probably will have to make your inquiry over the telephone, and do it in advance of seeing the place – tricky business to say the least. However, if what you have read about this area makes you ready to commit to renting a place for a weekend (or longer), go for it. The going rate for a beach house apartment (excluding the high season) is about US$200 for the weekend or for Monday to Thursday, but prices are always negotiable.

At Playa de Vega Baja, try **Blankimar Apartments** (☎ 787-855-3412). At Playa de Cerro Gordo, call **Beach House Rentals** (☎ 787-883-0356, 883-8251).

Places to Eat

There used to be a couple of popular restaurants – traditional family stops – along the backroads to the beaches, but 'the well's done dried up.'

One great find is the funky seaside spot known as **Restaurante Costa Roja**, east on Hwy 692 along the edge of Playa de Vega Baja (see Beaches, earlier in this section). The road bumps along for about a half mile between palm trees and surf-strewn coast on one side and the cow pastures on the other until you see the restaurant, looking a bit like a Mexican cantina in *Night of the Iguana*. There is a good surf break here, and surfers hang out on the patio and eat when they want a break from the waves. A *pionono* (spicy ground beef fried in plantain batter) is only US$1, as is a beer; a cup of fresh conch salad goes for US$4.

At Playa de Cerro Gordo, you can survive on US$1 pizza slices at **Pizza Mar**, across from the entrance gateway to the balneario.

Sometimes you can get *cocina criolla* dishes just up the street along the beach at **Bar Salimar** (☎ 787-883-2354), which has a great patio with a sea view.

And if you are lucky, maybe **Restaurante Manatuabón** will have reopened under new management on Hwy 690 (the road to Cerro Gordo); this place used to have some great eggplant dishes.

Getting There & Away

While you can get to and from Manatí by público, you'll need wheels to avoid being stuck in the undesirable town with no way of getting around the sites. By car, Manatí can be reached from the east or west via Hwy 2, or by taking Hwy 149 south from Hwy 22.

DORADO

Several miles of white-sand beaches at the mouth of the Río de la Plata attracted gringo investors to this area at the turn of the 20th century. The investors quickly set up a large plantation west of town for growing grapefruit and coconuts. Eventually, developers convinced the plantation's heirs of its tourist appeal, and so began the development of Puerto Rico's oldest resort community beyond San Juan. Today, the name Dorado, which means 'golden,' has become synonymous with vacationing US presidents and a leisure class who measure their days by golf holes, tennis sets and polo chukkas.

The long-time keystone of this life has been the Hyatt Dorado Beach Resort & Casino, which opened in the late 1950s. And now this mega-resort has been complimented by the high-rise Hyatt Regency Cerromar Resort & Casino. Together, the two resorts cover well over 1000 acres of prime real estate and include four 18-hole championship golf courses and possibly the largest freshwater swimming pool in the world.

Over the years, this once remote community has developed easy highway access to San Juan and grown more attractive to both expats and Puerto Ricans. Wholesale residential development has ensued. And while the area is not yet Palm Springs, California, or Naples, Florida, a traveler – after eyeing strip malls, guarded housing developments and real estate banners – might get the sense that Dorado harbors such dreams.

Unless you have the money, reservations or connections to get you through all of Dorado's locked gates to uncover its mysteries, there is not much here for the independent traveler, though the moderately attractive town of Dorado rivals Guayama for being the cleanest settlement in Puerto Rico.

Beaches

Although nobody is advertising it, there is, in fact, a public beach in Dorado where you can swim. To get to the rocky shore, head west from town on Hwy 693. Pass the shopping center, turn right at the Gulf gasoline station and keep going until you hit the entrance to the balneario. Parking is US$2.

Golf

You have four great 18-hole courses to choose from here at the Hyatt resorts, but the one not to miss is the East Course at the Hyatt Dorado (☎ 787-796-1234). Its major-league water hazards have helped it earn its rating as one of the best in the world by *Golf Digest*. Guests play for about US$90, nonguests pay US$105 for tee-off times before 1 pm; after 1 pm the greens fee drops to US$50, but the heat and sun can be brutal.

Tennis

The Hyatt properties have more than 20 courts available to guests only. The daytime rate is US$15. Prime-time rates (from 6 to 8 pm) are US$22 per hour.

Windsurfing

Once again, it's 'guests only' at Lisa Penfield's Windsurfing School (☎ 787-796-2188) at the Hyatt Dorado. Semiprivate lessons are US$45; half-day rental is US$50.

Places to Stay

Although the Dorado area is known for its pricey accommodations, one exception is the *Hotel Campomar* (☎ 787-784-7295). This small beachfront property is on Hwy 165 between the town of Dorado and the Bacardi factory to the east. During the week (Monday through Thursday nights), rooms are US$40, including continental breakfast.

In the good old days, respectable-looking travelers, expats and Puerto Ricans used to cruise into the *Hyatt Dorado Beach Resort & Casino* (☎ 787-796-1234, 800-233-1234), on Hwy 693 west of town, and use the facilities with impunity. No more! You will be turned away at the gate unless you have reservations at the Hyatt Regency Cerromar's Swan Café (though for lunch only) or you are on the tee-off list at one of the golf courses.

If you fancy staying at this all-inclusive, 298-unit resort where the rich and famous sometimes come to relax, it costs US$500 for the simplest unit during the winter season.

On the adjacent property farther east, the *Hyatt Regency Cerromar Resort & Casino* (☎ 787-796-1234, 800-233-1234) offers all the same amenities as the Hyatt Dorado, except that here you stay in a monumental high-rise with 506 rooms and several wings. The big attraction here is the 1779-foot swimming river composed of a chain of free-form pools, falls and grottoes. It's enormous, but don't worry: There is a swim-up bar where you can stop, have a toddy and ask directions if you get lost. Winter rates start at US$340, but you can stay here from June to October for US$185.

Places to Eat

For years it was difficult to find good cheap eats in Dorado; the fast-food franchises around the shopping center west of town drove the old cocina criolla places out of business and the new or established restaurants catered to the big spenders from the resorts.

So, if you wanted to stuff yourself for a dollar or three you had to head to the *food kiosks* set up along Hwy 165. These little shacks, which are still a popular stop, fill the space between the edge of the highway and the rock beach more than a mile east of town. If you are not counting calories or fat intake, you can get a *pionono* with a beer (in a brown paper bag) for US$3, sit on the hood of your trusty Suzuki and have a little party.

There is also a recently opened modern food court near the town's center on Calle

Mendez. Check out the kiosk *El Criollo*, where you can get rice and beans or *lechón asado* (roasted pork) for US$5.

Just east of here is another new place, the *Country Cheese Sports & Oyster Bar* (☎ 787-278-2015), also on Calle Méndez Vigo. This venture is an upscale fern bar with a pool table, large-screen TV and exotic salsa CDs, but the prices are not pretentious. They have a lot of burgers (including the 'Holandés Burger' – Dutch cheese, lettuce and tomato) in the US$3 to US$4 range.

Serious gourmands head across the street to *El Ladrillo* (☎ 787-796-2120, 224 Calle Méndez Vigo), which is on the Puerto Rico Tourism Company's list of Mesones Gastronómicos. Generally open only for dinner, the restaurant serves international cuisine as well as some fancy cocina criolla. Expect to pay more than US$20 for an entrée.

Most meals are cheaper a block west at the recently opened Cuban restaurant *El Navigante* (☎ 787-796-7177, 385 Calle Méndez Vigo). Here fettuccine Alfredo runs US$9; chicken curry is US$10.

Two places on the way out of town are old favorites for upscale islanders and resort guests. *El Malecón* (☎ 787-796-1645), on the marginal street parallel to Hwy 693, serves international and island recipes at moderate prices; both *asopao de pollo* (chicken stew) and lasagna are US$9. Virtually next door, *La Terraza* (☎ 787-796-1242) usually opens only for dinner and has a lot of high-end entrées; lobster is more than US$30.

In the same neighborhood is a rather pricey Chinese restaurant. *Jewel of China* (☎ 787-796-4644) specializes in Szechwan and Cantonese recipes. There is very little on the menu for under US$10.

Entertainment
You used to be able to go to the resorts to find nightlife in Dorado, but now the no-nonsense security folks at the gates have gotten real picky about letting nonguests on the property.

But fear not, underprivileged traveler, the *Country Cheese Sports & Oyster Bar* (see Places to Eat, above) opens its doors to you – and a lot of islanders too. In fact, this gin mill has become something of the 'local' for a cosmopolitan group of under-35 folks who want to party but do not feel like making the trek to San Juan. Thursday has live rock and roll; Friday is folk music or a trio; Saturday offers a mix of live music.

Getting There & Away
It is easy to get a van to and from Río Piedras in San Juan (or the ferry terminal in Cataño). Expect to pay about US$2. The van stand is in the center of town off the main street, Calle Méndez Vigo.

Caribe Limousine (☎ 787-796-7687) and Dorado Transport Coop (☎ 787-796-1214) offer service to and from Aeropuerto Internacional de Luis Muñoz Marín (San Juan) for about US$15 per person, with a minimum of three people.

Central Mountains

Travelers headed south on the San Juan-Ponce Autopista (Hwy 52) often crest the mountains of the Cordillera Central to a sight that takes them by surprise: As they look south, they see the highway surrounded on three sides by steep green peaks folding shaded valleys into their creases. And far below in the distance lies the Caribbean like a pale-blue mirror. From here, Puerto Rico looks like a totally different world – far removed from the sophisticated and populated place they left behind on the island's north coast.

On your first visit to Puerto Rico, you may be astonished to learn of the island's diverse landscapes and hidden charms. Some of Puerto Rico's attractions – Old San Juan, historic Ponce, the rain forest of El Yunque and the island's countless beaches, dive sites and golf courses – are well known and much visited. But less talked about are the island's central mountains, the Cordillera Central, which rise more than 4000 feet in places and encompass a jagged hodgepodge of peaks and valleys. The mountains have a back-country charm – a sense of wilderness and timelessness – that is uncommon in Puerto Rico and the rest of the Caribbean. The Cordillera Central is also a source of the music, literature and political vision that have defined Puerto Rico. Many Puerto Ricans who live in the urban centers still think of the mountains as their real homeland and spiritual center. And the Cordillera Central is also home to the wild *flamboyán* tree, the scent of coffee, the taste of *lechón asado* (suckling pig roasted on a spit) and the chorus of *coquí* frogs.

For centuries the central mountains have been known as the domain of the witty and self-sufficient *jíbaro* – the rural mountain dweller often cast as the archetypal Puerto Rican. Today, the jíbaro is more a mythical figure than a reality. Satellite TV and better roads import San Juan and US culture 24 hours a day, homogenizing styles and ways of talking, especially among the mountain

youth. Nevertheless, if you venture into mountain towns, you can easily see that the jíbaro's characteristic resourcefulness, constant play of dry humor and love of a party are still the means to help contemporary mountain folk weather the weeks and even months without electricity and water that can follow a natural disaster such as Hurricane Georges. Of course, the Spanish spoken here – especially among the older generation – retains the jíbaro's characteristic predilection to slur words and drop consonants such as 'r' and 's.'

While some of the mountain towns, such as Barranquitas and Maricao, have a certain charm (largely dependent on their dramatic settings), do not expect an endless array of quaint alpine villages. The real attractions here are the cool temperatures and the constantly changing vistas presented by forest

Highlights

- Hiking one of the trails – particularly Relámpago – at Reserva Forestal Carite

- Making a morning trek down into the Cañón de San Cristóbal

- Wandering the byways of the mountainside town of Barranquitas

- Camping in the cloud forest at Reserva Forestal Toro Negro

- Spending a night at one of the old coffee haciendas/inns in the mountain towns of Maricao or Jayuya

reserves such as Carite, peaks such as Cerro de Punta – Puerto Rico's highest mountain, at 4389 feet – and chasms such as Cañón de San Cristóbal. Come here to hike, camp or discover small mountain hostels and exceptional restaurants.

The Puerto Rico Tourism Company created the **Ruta Panorámica**, a chain of 40 mountain roads that cover 165 miles across the roof of Puerto Rico, from Yabucoa in the east to Mayagüez in the west. This chapter takes you along the Ruta Panorámica from east to west. Do not fear getting lost on your drive; the route is well marked with distinctive road signs and highlighted on almost all commercial maps of the island, as well as the maps in tourist booklets such as the Puerto Rico Tourism Company's *Qué Pasa*, a comprehensive bimonthly magazine for Puerto Rico-bound travelers. The Ruta Panorámica is also indicated on the map at the start of this book.

Getting There & Around
If the mountains intrigue you, as they probably will, be advised that while some *públicos* (shared taxis) pass this way, they can be infrequent, and they are always slow. Most likely you will see the mountains in a rental car.

Roads here are so steep and twisting that you should rarely drive faster than 25mph. So plan accordingly. If you have only one day for the mountains, plan to cover just the eastern, central or western section. The central section of the mountains, around Aibonito, Barranquitas and Adjuntas, is the most taxing drive because of frequent changes in altitude brought on by what sometimes seems an endless array of steep peaks and valleys. Take at least three days to drive the entire Ruta Panorámica, and do not drive at night. You could hit a stray cow – or just sail off a cliff into thin air.

RESERVA FORESTAL CARITE
Less than an hour south of San Juan, the Reserva Forestal Carite (Carite Forest Reserve; ☎ 787-745-4545) is the closest mountain reserve to the metro area, and it can get packed on weekends and during the summer when *sanjuaneros* (residents of the capital) come here to enjoy the 72°F temperatures, green shade, calls of birds and whir of the trade winds in the Honduras pines.

Carite is so popular that at least a dozen *lechonerías* (restaurants specializing in suckling pig) line Hwy 184 as it approaches the northern forest entrance, not far from the San Juan-Ponce Autopista. From miles away,

The Ruta Panorámica traverses 165 miles of the Cordillera Central's dramatic peaks and valleys.

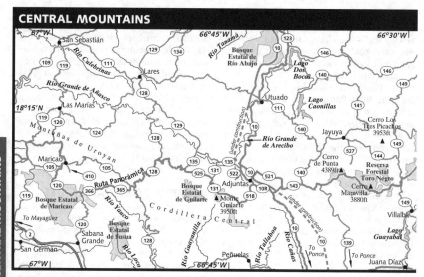

CENTRAL MOUNTAINS

you can smell the suckling pigs and chickens roasting on spits over open fires. And the scents attract the city folk in search of their jíbaro roots like bees to honey. Since lechón asado is the typical meal for a Puerto Rican feast such as Christmas or Easter, the Carite lechonerías become a total mob scene during the weeks surrounding such holidays. Of course, traffic jams ensue.

But if you come to Carite midweek in the fall, winter or spring, you will find an exceptional oasis for hiking, camping, fishing, toe-dipping (in pools and streams) and birdwatching. There is natural drama here, in Carite's more than 6000 acres spread over the slopes and peaks of the Sierra de Cayey. Among these forested mountains you will find the headwaters of some of the island's most important rivers, including the Río Grande de Loíza, the Río Grande de Patillas and the Río de la Plata. In 1935 the government established the forest to protect the watershed from erosion that had developed as a consequence of logging and agricultural ventures. They also began building a series of five dams on the rivers, creating reservoirs to better provide potable water for the

island's population and irrigation for agriculture. Two-mile-long Lago Carite, on the southern edge of the forest, is one of these reservoirs.

As the population on the island has burgeoned and people have begun craving green space for recreation, Carite has developed picnic sites, two camping areas and 25 miles of trails. This is the place to come if you want to go off by yourself and see some of the 49 species of bird – including the endangered native *falcón de sierra* (mountain hawk) – that call the area home. If you are passing through the forest on the Ruta Panorámica, you may want to stop for a picnic at the Area Recreativa Charco Azul, a recreation/camping area near the southeastern entrance on Hwy 184, and take a short walk to the Charco Azul natural pool. Of course, if you are in a festive mood, you can follow your nose to the lechonerías on the north side of the forest.

Orientation

The only way to enter the forest is by car. From the north, take the San Juan-Ponce Autopista (Hwy 52) to the Cayey Este exit

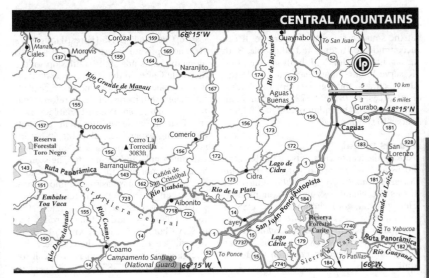

CENTRAL MOUNTAINS

to Hwy 184. Or from the south, take the Ruta Panorámica from Yabucoa. You can also reach the forest from Patillas on the south coast via Hwy 184.

Hiking

Charco Azul Trail The most popular trail in the reserve is Charco Azul, which takes you to the swimming hole and camping/picnic area of the same name. It is an easy half-mile walk from Hwy 184 near the southeast corner of the forest. You can't miss the signs marking the trailhead.

Doña Jovita Trail Another easy/moderate walk is the Doña Jovita trail. It begins near the northwestern entrance to the forest on Hwy 184 and makes a loop around the headwaters of the Río Guavate for about a mile. The charms here include the running water and excellent bird-watching.

El Radar Trail El Radar trailhead departs to the south off Hwy 184 near the northwest corner of the forest and makes a steep, 1-mile climb to the peak of Cerro Balíos (about 3000 feet above sea level). There is a

Doppler radar weather station here, plus vistas of the north and south coasts as well as toward El Yunque.

El Seis Trail This trail is about 3 miles one way, but it is a tough hike with steep climbs and descents. The trailhead leaves from the Area Recreativa Real Patillas at the southwest end of the forest, scales the ridges and valleys cut by the headwaters of the Río Grande de Patillas and rejoins Hwy 184 in the middle of the forest. Along the way you get spectacular vistas of the south coast. Note: If you want to walk this trail only one way, bring friends and two cars, and leave one car at each end of the trail.

Relámpago Trail This is another longer trail – about 4 miles roundtrip – for fit, experienced hikers. It heads south from Hwy 184 near the middle of the park and traces the headwaters of the Río de la Plata and its merger with the Río Guavate.

Places to Stay

The forest has two camping areas. At the northwest corner of the reserve is *Guavate*, with room for six tents and 30 people. *Charco Azul* is the pond-side camping area at the southeast end of the reserve. It can accommodate 10 tents and 50 people. Both areas have toilet and bathing facilities. Reserve 15 days in advance with the Depto de Recursos Naturales (Dept of Natural Resources; ☎ 787-724-3724) in San Juan. Sites cost US$4 per adult per night. Children under 10 stay for free.

Places to Eat

Among the lechonerías outside the Reserva Forestal Carite's north gate, *El Rancho Numero Uno* (☎ 787-747-7296) stands out for its size, cleanliness and welcoming staff. Here you can get lechón asado for US$6 a pound. Most diners calculate a half pound per person when ordering. *Lechonera El Monte*, just across Hwy 184, has similar prices and gets high marks from the forest staff.

CASA DE LA SELVA

Lying just to the south of Reserva Forestal Carite, Casa de la Selva (Forest House) is a 1000-acre private forest reserve. It spreads along the highlands of the south slope of the Sierra de Cayey in the Río Grande de Patillas watershed. There was once a coffee plantation here, but its owners have reforested it in hopes that it can be a sustainable-growth tree farm. The reserve offers half- and full-day hiking experiences that inevitably involve trekking along a streambed to a swimming hole and picnic site. The scenery here is memorable; the trekking is rough. The reserve also has basic accommodations: US$40 gets you a room and breakfast.

To find the Casa de la Selva, follow Hwy 184 southeast toward Patillas through the Reserva Forestal Carite to Km 16.1, where you will see a turnoff for the reserve. Note: The gate will be locked unless you call for reservations (☎ 787-839-7318). Expect to

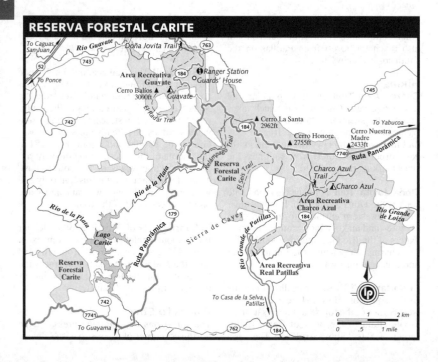

RESERVA FORESTAL CARITE

pay around US$20 for the half-day experience, US$50 for the whole day with meals.

AIBONITO

If you are heading west on the Ruta Panorámica from Reserva Forestal Carite, your travels will take you just south of a place residents like to call the 'Switzerland of Puerto Rico' – an extreme paradox. Once the de facto capital of Puerto Rico, after the Spanish Governor Romualdo Palacios González established residence here in 1887, Aibonito has long been a popular retreat for the island's political leaders, its religiously devout and the most wealthy. The town has a number of other claims to fame that include being the island's highest town (at about 2000 feet), the site of the island's lowest recorded temperature (40°F in 1911) and the home of an impressive flower festival. For all these reasons, and because it's on the Ruta Panorámica, Aibonito is no doubt the most visited mountain town in Puerto Rico.

The town has a euphonious name that suggests a Spanish exclamation meaning 'Wow, how beautiful.' But the name is probably derived from a Taíno word that the first Spanish settlers heard when they arrived here to start ranches in the 1630s. And today, travelers should associate Aibonito with beauty only in very specific ways. The town itself, which shelters at least half of the municipality's 25,000 residents, is no Geneva. It sprawls across a high plateau in a slight rift between surrounding peaks. There are traffic jams every day on the old, narrow roads at the center of town, as rural families gravitate here for shopping, banking and – naturally – a pass through the drive-through at McDonald's. Thriving flower-growing and poultry-raising and -processing industries have brought prosperity to the region in recent years, with little thought to urban planning and only belated attention to the area's natural gifts.

Yet there are two extraordinary natural treasures here. One, La Piedra Degetau, is a cluster of boulders on a peak bordering the Ruta Panorámica; there are great views from this place. Even more spectacular than La Piedra Degetau, the Cañón de San Cristóbal (St Christopher Canyon) lies north of town in a deep volcanic rift cut into the rolling fields between Aibonito and the neighboring town of Barranquitas.

Aibonito-lovers claim that the weather in their town is perpetually spring-like. They are not exaggerating: The average temperature here is 72°F, and gentle showers are common.

Orientation

Most drivers approach Aibonito via the Ruta Panorámica. A less-traveled and more dramatic route (if you like hairpin turns) is to take Hwy 173 and Hwy 14 south from Cidra.

Cañón de San Cristóbal

The canyon is so unexpected in both its location and appearance that it may take your breath away. The deep green chasm with its rocky crags and veil of falling water looks like something Samuel Taylor Coleridge would have described in a poem crafted after an opium dream. Lying less than 5 miles north of Aibonito, the canyon is a fissure that cuts more than 500 feet down through the Cordillera Central. But you probably will not see it even as you approach its edge, because the rift is so deep and narrow that the fields and hills of the surrounding high-mountain plateau disguise it. In fact, it is difficult to get a clear view of the canyon unless you have local knowledge of how best to do so.

The highest waterfall on the island is here, where the Río Usabón plummets at least 500 feet down a sheer cliff into a gorge that is deeper, in many places, than it is wide. For fit mountaineering enthusiasts, the descent into the canyon is a first-class thrill whether they take steep trails or make it a technical descent. Not so long ago, San Cristóbal was a garbage dump, but the Conservation Trust of Puerto Rico saved the canyon by buying up most of it for preservation.

You can catch a glimpse of the canyon from a distance by looking east from the intersection of Hwy 725 and Hwy 162. But to get close, you would have to take one of the side roads off Hwy 725 or Hwy 7725, and then cross private land to approach the rim of the canyon. Do not try this: You will be trespassing unless you actually get permission to cross private property, and you could easily put yourself at risk if you do not know the terrain. Cañón de San Cristóbal has sheer cliffs that are prone to erosion and landslides, and the trails into the canyon are so steep as to be an invitation for suicide when they get wet (and it rains a lot around here).

The best way to visit the canyon is to plan ahead, make reservations and join an organized trek with a capable local guide. During fair weather, groups usually gather early on Saturday morning at La Piedra restaurant (☎ 787-735-1034; see Places to Eat, below) for an 8:30 am departure into the canyon. The steep descent into the canyon and the return trip will take all morning. Wear secure shoes and appropriate clothing that you can take off at the canyon floor, where temperatures can be more than 10°F warmer than up on the brink. Of course, you will need water and maybe some energy bars to get you back up the canyon wall.

To make sure that a trek is leaving on a particular Saturday, or to make arrangements for a personally guided trip, call one of these guides: Ricky López (☎ 800-759-1255) or Felix Rivera (☎ 787-735-5188). Expect to pay US$10 and up for the group trip. If you have no luck reaching these men, call La Piedra restaurant directly (see above) and inquire about dates and times for treks.

La Piedra Degetau

This nest of boulders lies on a hilltop alongside the Ruta Panorámica (Hwy 7718 here) at Km .7, just south of Aibonito. Once this was the 'thinking place' of Ponce-born writer Federico Degetau y González, who became the island's first resident commissioner in Washington, DC, from 1900 to 1904. This must have been a truly sublime place, with its views of the mountains, the Atlantic and the Caribbean. From here on a clear evening, you can actually see cruise ships leaving San Juan (more than 20 miles north) as you look through a cleft in the mountains. If you turn your head south, you can see the flash of the sunset over the Caribbean and the lights of Ponce beginning to glow.

Sadly, the natural beauty of the site has been marred by a new park and lookout tower that dwarf the actual rocks, which huddle together like a nest of massive eggs. Now, in addition to the vistas and the sound of the humming wind, you get picnic shelters, a playground for the kiddies and a paved parking lot. So much for inspiration.

La Casilla

This is the yellow, circa-1880s lodge on the edge of town, at Km 51.8 on Hwy 14 from Cayey. This building was once part of a network of 27 such huts that housed 'road keepers' (in this case, convicts). Today the building has been restored as a monument for 'the benefit of the cultural heritage enclosed in these walls' (Resolution 2392 of the Puerto Rican House of Delegates).

The 'cultural heritage' you witness here, however, is not necessarily a positive one. This lodge stands on the old 'pick and shovel' road built by slaves of Spanish landowners and later maintained by convicts – generally poor black convicts impressed into work on the roads – over the centuries. In the last years of Spanish colonization, decadent *criollo* landowners of Aibonito used to boast that the government had killed all of the town's people of African descent by forcing them to build the road. (Today's visitor to Aibonito will observe people of all skin tones here as elsewhere on the island, but perhaps as a result of this colonial legacy of racism, there is still a much larger percentage of fair-skinned people here than on the coast.)

Special Events

The Festival de Flores (Flower Festival) at Aibonito has grown into a major rite of summer during the last 30 years. Today it draws hundreds of commercial growers and amateur horticulturists and tens of thousands of flower lovers to see the town and the surrounding countryside ablaze with roses, carnations, lilies and begonias. Of course, along with the flowers there are food and craft stalls as well as the ubiquitous Puerto Rican beauty pageant. This event takes place at the end of June and often runs into the July 4th holiday (US Independence Day), so get here before the crowds or expect to spend your holiday in a traffic jam.

Places to Stay
The Catholic seminary *Seminario Salesino* (☎ 787-735-24860), on the edge of town, will rent basic rooms to persons looking for a retreat in a spiritual setting; rooms cost less than US$40.

Las Casitas Hotel (☎ 787-735-0180) is outside of town and near the Ruta Panorámica at Km 4.8 on Hwy 162. It has bungalows packed around a swimming pool that's decorated in something like a Polynesian theme. Rates are about US$75 for a room that will accommodate two.

Hostal Aibonito (☎ 787-735-1034) is in the works across from La Piedra Restaurant (see below) on Hwy 7718, the Ruta Panorámica. This place is the longtime brainchild of La Piedra's owner, WOSO radio personality José 'Joe' Esterás, who hosts the island's popular gardening show on Saturday mornings. The permits to build this ecotour hostel have been in place for years, but construction has been slow. Nevertheless, the project is moving along and the facility may well be finished by the time you read this book. Anyone interested in mountain lore and island flora and fauna should endeavor to visit Hostal Aibonito: Joe is an expert in island tales and wildlife and is known island-wide as a gregarious host. Expect to pay US$75 and up.

Places to Eat
La Piedra (☎ 787-735-1034), on the Ruta Panorámica (Hwy 7718 here) right next to the Piedra Degetau park, is probably the most famous mountain restaurant in Puerto Rico. This has been Joe Esterás' baby for decades, and he is visited regularly by movers and shakers who arrive by helicopter to feast for hours. The draw here is threefold: the superb view, Joe's welcoming personality, and the gourmet cooking that produces a mix of traditional and continental recipes. One specialty is *pollo a monte* (chicken and veal in a wine sauce) for US$17, which includes soup and salad made with homegrown

vegetables and spices. You can get lighter fare, such as chicken broth and *mofongo* (fried plantains with pork rind and spices) for US$8.

Getting There & Away
Públicos will take you to Aibonito from Cayey or Caguas for about US$3. These cities have connections to the Río Piedras district of San Juan for another US$3. See Orientation, earlier in this section, for suggested driving routes.

BARRANQUITAS
If you have time to see only one of Puerto Rico's mountain towns, Barranquitas is the one to choose. Lying on the north side of the Cañón de San Cristóbal, about a 20-minute drive out of Aibonito on Hwy 162 (or an even shorter detour off of the Ruta Panorámica via Hwy 143), the town clings to a steep mountainside surrounded by vegetation. It might remind a traveler of Cuenca in Spain or Mexico's Guanajuato. The view you get from the mountain road descending into town is truly memorable, particularly when the golden afternoon sun sets the church tower ablaze above the shadowy and thickly settled town.

This is, however, not a fairy-tale village of architectural heirlooms. Hurricanes and fires have destroyed the town several times, and the oldest structures, such as the church, date only from the first decades of the 20th century. Barranquitas' charm is its narrow streets, tightly packed with shops and houses, which fall away into deep valleys on three sides of the town plaza. Alleys with steep steps often connect parallel streets. In addition, the rugged terrain has so far prevented the demon of urban sprawl from gobbling up this compact hamlet. But maybe you should come soon, before the crowds get here: A Burger King recently appeared, and you never know when a housing development might be constructed in what is currently a cow pasture.

But maybe potential developers will pay heed to the town's cautionary name – which translates as 'Place of Little Mud Slides' – and turn away, leaving the streets filled with the laughter of old men playing dominoes at a curbside table and young mothers pushing baby strollers in circles around the plaza, the only level spot in town.

Come to Barranquitas if you like the idea of restaurants with US$3 meals. Hang around to observe that many of the early settlers who came here were English and bestowed their surnames, fair skin, freckles and red hair on many of today's citizens. Take some time to meet the lively students at the branch campus of the Universidad Interamericana, south of town. Finally, when you are in a pensive mood, wander along Calle Padre Berrios. Here you will find a small museum and the mausoleum that holds the bones of the island's two greatest statesmen, Barranquitas native Luis Muñoz Rivera and his son Luis Muñoz Marín – truly the grandfather and father of modern Puerto Rico. In terms of the political legacy these two men left the island, Barranquitas is the Windsor Castle or Mount Vernon of Puerto Rico.

Orientation
The easiest way to get here from the Ruta Panorámica is to take Hwy 143 northeast after you pass Aibonito.

Casa Museo Luis Muñoz Rivera
This house (☎ 787-857-0230), at the corner of Calles Muñoz Rivera and Padre Berrios, honors the father of Puerto Rico's autonomy movement and the 20th-century architect of the Puerto Rican commonwealth. This is where Luis Muñoz Rivera was born in 1859, and it contains a collection of furniture, letters, photographs and other memorabilia. The museum is open 8 am to noon and 1 to 4:30 pm daily except Monday and Thursday. Admission is free.

Mausoleo Familia Muñoz Rivera
Just south of the plaza at 7 Calle Padre Berrios is a family tomb that holds the remains of Muñoz Rivera, his famous son Luis Muñoz Marín and their wives. Photographic displays at the tomb evoke the funeral of Luis Muñoz Marín. It's open in the same hours as the museum; admission is free.

Museo de Arte y Antropología
Just to the north of the mausoleum, you'll find this small museum (☎ 787-857-2065), which displays the painting and sculpture of local artists. It's open by appointment and for exhibitions; admission is free.

Colección Toño Vélez
This is another small museum (☎ 787-857-3576), just south of the mausoleum. It has a small pre-Columbian collection as well as documents, money, machinery and works of art depicting life in colonial Barranquitas. The museum is open by appointment; admission is free.

Places to Stay & Eat
Hacienda Margarita (☎ 787-854-0414), at Km 1.7 on Hwy 152, is currently the only game in town when it's time to get some sleep. Just south of town, this old plantation house on the mountaintop has a pool and on-site restaurant as well as guest quarters. The hacienda was badly damaged by Hurricane Georges and is recovering slowly. Call for rates.

Bar Plaza (☎ 787-857-4909), at the corner of Calle Barcello and the west end of the plaza, is really a classic Puerto Rican cafeteria. You can get great rice and beans here for US$3, roast chicken for US$4.

Entertainment
Check out **Bar Ortiz**, across from the plaza on Calle Barcelo. Known as a *bar típico*, this is a place to rub shoulders amid shadows, smiles and cheap beer. There is a 1960s jukebox packed with salsa classics and *boleros* (love songs). On busy weekend nights, young men often play *americano* music on the jukebox – for example, Lionel Ritchie singing 'Hello' – to set the mood for romance when groups of young women wander in to size up the Romeos over a US$1 can of Medalla.

Getting There & Away
Vans to and from surrounding towns stop on Calle Padre Berrios, three blocks south of the plaza past the Mausoleo Familia Muñoz Rivera.

RESERVA FORESTAL TORO NEGRO

As the Ruta Panorámica (Hwy 143 in this section) heads west from Barranquitas, it makes a steady ascent to the rooftop of Puerto Rico, twisting and turning to follow the ridgeline of the Cordillera Central. If you come here during the dry midwinter, the views into the mountain valleys and to the distant north and south coasts can be exhilarating. But clouds may gather year-round in this high country, and in all probability you will be driving in and out of fog and/or showers. Be careful: Landslides are a constant problem in these mountains when the ground is saturated, and wet, mud-slick roads can reduce auto traction to zero in a heartbeat. If ever there were a place to travel with a cellular phone, this section of the Ruta Panorámica is it; there is little traffic and you are a long way, in terms of travel time, from civilization and assistance.

But if you are cautious and prepared for your journey, a great adventure lies ahead as you climb 3000 feet above sea level and approach the Reserva Forestal Toro Negro (Black Bull Forest Reserve). Your route bisects this 7000-acre reserve for about 10 miles and carries you through some of the wildest territory on the island, which includes Puerto Rico's highest peak, Cerro de Punta (elevation 4389 feet), and others such as Monte Jayuya and Cerro Maravilla – the lattermost has a violent history (see 'Murder on Cerro Maravilla,' below).

For the hiking and camping crew (and other travelers as well), this is a good place to call time-out from the taxing drive. The

CENTRAL MOUNTAINS

Murder on Cerro Maravilla

You will see this peak with its communication towers looming over the north side of the road once you pass Lago El Guineo (the highest lake on the island), several miles west of the Area Recreativa Doña Juana. Finding the route up to this nearly 4000-foot summit is difficult unless you have a local guide, but in 1978 enough people got here to stage a messy little massacre.

Now, more than 20 years later, the events of July 25, 1978, remain shrouded in mystery, myth and rumor. But some facts are clear. Two young men who backed the island's pro-independence political party died from police gunfire on this mountain. Many people and publications have argued that undercover agents posing as revolutionaries enticed the youths here. According to the story, they did so under the pretense of bombing a communications tower to protest what looked like ballot box fraud in a closely contested governor's race. When the young activists arrived, the police shot them for trespassing and allegedly plotting against the state.

Unfortunately for the police who pulled the triggers, for the government officials who allegedly plotted the assassinations, and for the FBI, which supposedly tried to cover up the mess, one of these boys was not just a faceless revolutionary. Carlos Soto Arriví was the son of the famous Puerto Rican author Pedro Juan Soto and the relative of another prominent writer, Francisco Arriví. And these popular authors and their influential friends would not let the story or the investigation of the massacre rest. The controversy toppled the regime of Governor Carlos Romero Barceló in 1984. Curiously, the ex-governor then got himself appointed Puerto Rico's resident commissioner (a nonvoting member of the US House of Representatives) and has been serving in this prestigious capacity for more than 15 years.

Members of Romero Barceló's progressive party still cringe when someone mentions Cerro Maravilla, and complain that people should let the dead rest in peace. Others say that such platitudes have been used to dismiss political crimes since time immemorial.

CENTRAL MOUNTAINS

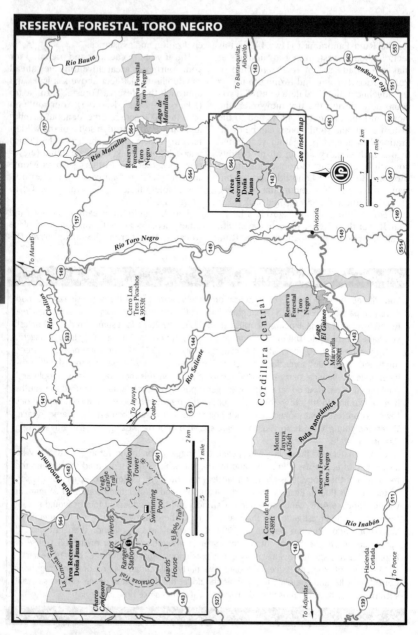

RESERVA FORESTAL TORO NEGRO

region is full of steep landscapes, escarpments and cascades. There is a designated picnic and camping area here that you will find empty unless you come in the summer or during the Christmas or Easter holidays. The Depto de Recursos Naturales maintains only about 12 miles of trails here, but if you have a topo map of the area, you will discover trails leading to the summits, as well as secluded waterfalls such as Salta Inabón.

Flora & Fauna
As these mountains were long a coffee-growing region and were reforested only in the 1930s by the US Dept of the Interior, almost all of Toro Negro's woods are second or third growth. At the lowest levels you encounter the *tabonuco* forest, with a large variety of tall trees including the white-bark tabonuco tree that gives this forest zone its name. Here the flora is similar to that of El Yunque. Higher elevations are largely covered with sierra palms, while the cloud forest around the peaks resembles El Yunque's dwarf forest, the highest forest zone, where trees are generally less than 12 feet tall and liverworts and mosses grow on both the ground and on vegetation. The difference at Toro Negro is that the dwarf forest here is far less tortured by the wind.

With only 30 recorded species of bird, Toro Negro is not a birder's paradise, but on a clear day you will see the highly endangered falcón de sierra wheeling on the thermals above the ridges. Your best sense of the animal kingdom in these mountains comes at night, when 20 different kinds of frogs and other reptiles start their chirping and croaking and eight species of bat flutter among the trees.

Orientation & Information
The Ruta Panorámica (Hwy 143 here) is your artery to and from the forest, and it is none too wide. Honk your horn when approaching blind curves.

All of the forest's public facilities lie at the east end of the reserve in the Area Recreativa Doña Juana, clustered in the vicinity of the ranger station at Km 32.4 on Hwy 143.

The ranger station (☎ 787-844-4051) is open irregularly except during the summer,

when it is open from 8 am to noon and 1 to 4 pm weekdays. The office has blurry photocopies of park literature, and some of this material is extremely misleading: The trail map lacks a compass rose and has been rotated so north is not at the top of the page. You're not likely to get anything better in San Juan from the Depto de Recursos Naturales, nor is it easy to get USGS maps on the island without ordering through a bookstore. You can get a USGS map from your favorite map supplier in the US or mail-order one on the island. Otherwise, the map in this book is the best you will find.

Area Recreativa Doña Juana
This is the area of about 3 sq miles at the eastern end of the park surrounding the ranger station. You will find picnic sites, toilets, showers, the camping area and a half-dozen short trails branching off Hwy 143. One trail leads to the swimming pool (open summers only). Three others lead to the observation tower, less than a half mile south of the highway.

Cerro de Punta
If you want to climb to the 4389-foot summit of Puerto Rico's highest peak (with yet more communication towers, alas), Cerro de Punta lies near the western end of the forest – almost 10 miles of tortured driving from the Area Recreativa Doña Juana. The short pedestrian approach takes you up an unmarked paved road north from Hwy 143 to the summit. If you want an extensive trekking experience, start at the Hacienda Gripiñas in the town of Jayuya (see Places to Stay, below) and make a day's adventure out of summiting.

Places to Stay & Eat
The designated camping area, *Los Viveros*, is just north of the forest office on Hwy 143 at Km 3.2 in the Area Recreativa Doña Juana. There is space for 14 tents, but part of the area is often reserved for larger groups such as the Boy Scouts. You need a permit from the Depto de Recursos Naturales (☎ 787-724-3724) in San Juan. Apply 15 days in advance. Rates are US$4 per person.

Consider a detour to the north on Hwy 140 to Jayuya, where you will find the former coffee plantation, **Hacienda Gripiñas** (☎ 787-828-1717) at Km 2.5 on Hwy 527. This is a fully restored hacienda with alpine surroundings. Rates start at US$66.

If you are lingering in this area of the central mountains, you'll want to bring your own food along as there are no easily accessible restaurants along the Ruta Panorámica between the towns of Barranquitas and Adjuntas. If you bring charcoal and lighter fluid, you can cook your food over one of the open-air picnic grills at the Area Recreativa Doña Juana near the east end of Reserva Forestal Toro Negro.

ADJUNTAS

This town of 20,000 is variously known as the 'town of the sleeping giant' (because of the silhouette created by the surrounding mountains), the 'Switzerland of the Caribbean' and the 'citron capital of Puerto Rico.' Because of these fetching nicknames, and because the Ruta Panorámica skirts the town west of the Toro Negro forest, you may be tempted to have a look. But be advised that unless your chief reason for heading into Adjuntas is to buy camping provisions or find a bed for the night, you will probably be disappointed and frustrated.

The problem is that Adjuntas marks the spot where one of the island's major north-to-south arteries (Hwys 123/10) crests the Cordillera Central. In other words, Adjuntas has trucks creeping toward it and backing up traffic from two directions. Some of these trucks are just passing through; others are here to pick up shipments of citron and coffee. Of course, like other mountain towns (such as Aibonito) with thriving agricultural industries, Adjuntas has a burgeoning population that has long outgrown its narrow streets.

Fortunately, you can bypass most of this if you stay on the Ruta Panorámica, which becomes Hwy 522 as it approaches the town from the east. As you go west from here, the highway numbers change with startling frequency, but the Ruta Panorámica signs are always there to guide you. At any rate, the road soon brings you to the real attraction in this area, the Bosque Estatal de Guilarte, with the seventh-highest peak on the island and a lake and cabins for rusticators (see the section on the forest, below).

Places to Stay & Eat

The **Monte Río Hotel** (☎ 787-829-3705) stands not far from the Ruta Panorámica, one block south of the plaza of Adjuntas. There are 23 rooms here with fresh air (you don't need air con), TV and mountain views. The restaurant and bar on the 1st floor are as good as they come in this town, with *cocina criolla* dishes starting at less than US$7. Rooms cost US$40 to US$60.

To the northwest of town lie the **Villas de Sotomayor** (☎ 787-829-1717). This 'tourist complex' features 26 condo-like units with a central swimming pool, basketball courts, cooking grills and bike rentals. It is extremely popular with island families in the summer. Rates are US$80 to US$200.

BOSQUE ESTATAL DE GUILARTE

This forest, west of Adjuntas, actually consists of a number of parcels of land totaling about 3600 acres. Most of it is rain forest dominated by sierra palms. Coming from the east, you first see Lago Garzas, a popular fishing site. West of the lake, the road rises toward the park's ranger station, near the intersection of Hwy 518 and Hwy 131. Here you will find a picnic area with shelters, cooking grills and toilets. There is also a trail that leads to the top of Monte Guilarte (3950 feet) and five *cabins* you can rent for overnight stays.

The Depto de Recursos Naturales maintains the cabins, toilets and shower facilities. Each cabin sleeps six; cooking facilities are outdoors. Make your reservations 15 days in advance with the Depto de Recursos Naturales (☎ 787-724-3724) at their offices close to El Capitolio on Calle Fernandez Juncos in Puerta de Tierra, just east of Old San Juan. Cabins cost US$4/2 for adults/children.

See Adjuntas, above, for accommodations and dining options in and near that town.

MARICAO

With a population of fewer than 7000 citizens, Maricao is the smallest municipality on the main island of Puerto Rico, and a gem of a mountain retreat near the western end of the Ruta Panorámica. This is a town of little commerce, with rushing streams, gorges, bridges, terraced houses, switchback roads, and temperatures so cool and damp that houses have stone fireplaces to take the nip out of the air. Outside the town, you will find dramatic vistas, coffee plantations and the largest state forest in Puerto Rico, the Bosque Estatal de Maricao.

With its peaks, dark forests and fog, Maricao is just the kind of place in which legends take root. Admirers of Maricao like to claim that it was the strong coffee grown here that woke up the devil on the island. Another old story claims that 2000 Taínos survived here into the 19th century, centuries after the last of the native Puerto Ricans were thought to have disappeared.

Yet another myth tells how the town takes its name from the demise of a local Taíno princess, María. According to legend, María was in love with a Spanish conquistador, and she told her beloved of Indian plans to attack the local Spanish encampment. When the Taínos discovered her treachery, the princess was tortured to death. The Spanish honored her by naming the town after a fusion of María's name and the suffix 'cao' (from *sacrificio*) to signify her sacrifice for love. Less romantic scholars say the town's name comes from the Taíno name for a local tree.

But whatever the source of its name, Maricao seems more like the kind of place you find lost in the folds of the Venezuelan or Peruvian Andes than in Puerto Rico. Stopping here for a day or two is probably as close as a traveler can come to experiencing the charms of the legendary jíbaro's existence, or to understanding why the Puerto Rico Tourism Company promotes the nickname Isla Encanta (Enchanted Island) for Borinquen.

Maricao hosts a popular coffee harvest festival in mid-February, with local crafts and traditional coffee-making demonstrations.

Orientation

In addition to approaching Maricao from the east or west on the Ruta Panorámica,

you can get here by heading south on Hwy 119 from San Sebastián (then going east on the Ruta Panorámica to Maricao; about two hours' drive) or driving north from Sabana Grande on Hwy 120 (about one hour's drive). Both routes involve a spectacular climb into the mountains on twisting roads.

Bosque Estatal de Maricao

This forest of more than 10,000 acres lies along the Ruta Panorámica south of Maricao, and you will bisect the forest before you reach town. The drive is spectacular, with sharp curves snaking over ridges as the mountainsides fall away into steep valleys. Vista points overlook the south and east coasts of the island. As you make this drive, you will see places to pull your car off the road at trailheads that lead into the woods or traverse down steep inclines.

Curiously, few of these trails are maintained or mapped by the Depto de Recursos Naturales. In fact, guides to Bosque Estatal de Maricao are difficult to come by both at the department's office in San Juan and in Maricao. So if you are coming here to hike, get yourself a topo map of the area from a map supplier in the US, ask an island bookstore to order one from the USGS, or get some local knowledge.

While the landscape is generally categorized as high-mountain rain forest, scientists note that the 845 species of plant here are less 'exuberant' than they are in a tropical rain forest such as El Yunque. Other observers think that the flora at Maricao looks like the vegetation you see in karst country on the island's north coast. This forest has many introduced species, such as the tropical hardwoods you also see in lower-altitude karstic forests on the island.

Birds are the most-studied fauna here, with 44 identified species. Tanagers, cuckoos and warblers are some of the remarkable types spotted in the forest.

Los Viveros

Follow the signs south out of the center of Maricao to Los Viveros (Fish Hatcheries; ☎ 787-838-3710), on Hwy 410 at Km 1.7. Or take the short trail off of Hwy 120 if you want to see the buildings and streamside reservoirs where the commonwealth raises the tilapia and bass that stock the freshwater lakes of the island. To say the least, this place is a quiet attraction. There is little to see here other than thousands of small fish, little to hear besides the sounds of the surrounding woods, the hum of a few pumps and the hush of running water. But all of this is totally in keeping with the ambience of Maricao. The hatchery is open 7:30 am to noon and 1 to 4 pm weekdays, 8:30 am to 4 pm weekends. Admission is free. Call if you want a tour.

Places to Stay & Eat

The **Centro Vacacional Monte de Estado** (☎ 787-873-5632), at Km 13.1 east of Maricao on Hwy 120, has 24 cabins to rent in the state forest. Each cabin holds six and has a refrigerator, fireplace and hot water. The area also has a swimming pool, basketball courts, a picnic area and an observation tower. Make reservations as far in advance as possible by calling the Compañía de Fomento Recrea-

tivo in San Juan (☎ 787-722-1551, 722-1771), a government agency of the commonwealth. Cabins rent for US$65 per night.

If you really want a piece of the jíbaro lifestyle, check out the **Hacienda Juanita** (☎ 787-838-2550), at Km 23.5 on Hwy 105 about 2 miles west of town. This is a working coffee plantation that dates from the 1830s. There are 21 units here in a rustic *parador* (inn) that is somewhat reminiscent of a retreat in New York's Adirondack Mountains – no phone, TV or air con. But there is an excellent restaurant (often with live folk music Sunday afternoons), which is on the Puerto Rico Tourism Company's list of *mesones gastronómicos* (see the Facts for the Visitor chapter), as well as a pool, tennis court and hiking trails. Rooms run US$75.

Getting There & Away

Público vans leave the town's plaza on the Maricao-Mayagüez run and charge US$4. As is usually the case, the vans leave when they are full or on the driver's whim.

Vieques - Bana Mosquito
Culebra - Playa Flamero

Spanish Virgin Islands

For the traveler wanting to discover truly undeveloped Caribbean islands where sun, sea, wilderness and wildlife are the big attractions, there is simply no better place to look than the islands of Vieques and Culebra and the more than 30 surrounding cays. These peaked islands – carved with bays, coves and scores of empty beaches – lie halfway between mainland Puerto Rico, to the west, and St Thomas in the US Virgin Islands, to the east.

Ironically, Vieques and Culebra owe their wild state to persistent (but sporadic) 'invasions' by the US Navy and Marine Corps, who have used the islands for target practice and to rehearse 20th-century military actions

Highlights

- Making a night trip to Bahía Mosquito (Phosphorescent Bay) on Vieques and swimming in liquid stars

- Biking the roads on US Navy land to any of Vieques' wild beaches

- Snorkeling the reefs of Cayo Afuera in Esperanza harbor

- Hiking to Playa Carlos Rosario, on Culebra, for a day of snorkeling, sun and picnicking

- Taking a water taxi – or better yet, a kayak – to one of Culebra's offshore cays

- Putting on your party hat with all the islanders at El Batey on Culebra

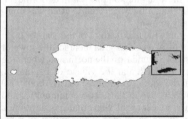

on other shores, such as Grenada, Haiti and Kuwait. Because the US military claimed large chunks of these islands, much of their land has been protected from development. Today, the Spanish Virgins remain islands where boys ride their horses down the main streets and roosters – not alarm clocks – wake local fishing folk. Many long-term cruising sailors say that Vieques and Culebra still retain the pristine qualities that drew sailors to the nearby US and British Virgin Islands 40 years ago, before tourism brought substantial development to those island groups.

Vieques and Culebra rarely saw travelers until the final decade of the 20th century because the military presence on the islands kept the populations low and civilian development limited to small pockets of land. Meanwhile, in spite of occasional bombing practices and phony invasions, the flora, fauna and sealife of the islands have flourished. The vast fringe reefs have remained largely undisturbed, and the islands' mangrove swamps are still nurseries for rare birds and fish. Sea turtles such as the hawksbill lay their eggs on the beaches, and herds of wild horses roam freely. Today, a large national wildlife refuge on Culebra and vast tracts of Navy-owned lands on Vieques preserve the natural habitat and wild 'feel' of these islands.

Another blessing of the Spanish Virgin Islands is their climate – it's even more congenial than that of Puerto Rico itself. Vieques and Culebra are constantly cooled by the easterly trade winds and receive less than 50 inches of rain per year. One benefit of the low rainfall is that the visibility for diving here is often significantly better than in the waters around Puerto Rico proper.

Long a stronghold for pirates, Culebra and Vieques have traditionally been home to independent folk accustomed to the comings and goings of colonial powers like the English, Dutch, French, Spaniards and Americans (most of these visitors, with the exception of the Americans, left little trace

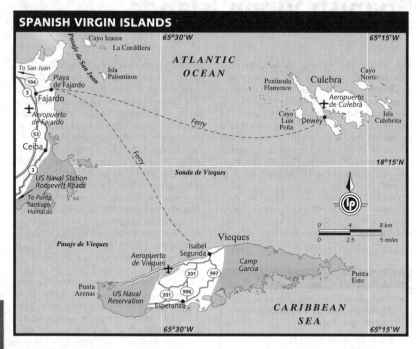

SPANISH VIRGIN ISLANDS

upon the islands). And in recent years, the Spanish Virgin Islands have been a magnet for free-spirited expatriates who have contributed to the flowering of low-key eco-tourism and guesthouse-building across the islands. Vieques in particular has become popular with gay and lesbian expats and travelers looking for an oasis free of prejudice and prying eyes. Straight travelers linger here for the same reason. Meanwhile, the islands' economies lope along on modest agricultural endeavors, some small-scale manufacturing, cattle raising, fishing and tourism.

Inexpensive government ferries and commuter flights from San Juan make both Vieques and Culebra easily accessible from the main island.

VIEQUES

Twenty-one miles long and 5 miles wide, Vieques is the largest of the Spanish Virgin Islands, and it lies just 6 miles southeast of

the main-island naval base at Roosevelt Roads. The name 'Vieques' is a 17th-century Spanish colonial corruption of the Taíno name *bieque* (small island). The Spaniards also called Vieques and Culebra *las islas inútiles* (the useless islands) because they lacked gold and silver. But over the centuries, residents and visitors who share an affection for this place have come to call Vieques 'Isla Nena,' a term of endearment meaning 'Little Girl Island.' The name implies that Vieques is the daughter of the sea and Borinquen (the name by which Puerto Rico was originally known).

Only the middle third of the island is open for local use. This area includes the town of Isabel Segunda, on the north side, where the ferries dock, and the village of Esperanza, on the south (Caribbean) coast. About 9000 citizens live in these two communities and in a collection of villas that has developed on the upper slopes of the mountain ridge dividing the island's northern and southern sides. The western and eastern thirds of the island are US Navy lands.

Although there are some fine beaches on the Caribbean side of the island within walking distance of Esperanza, many of the island's most famous and deserted beaches lie on Navy land. When the island is not 'hot' – when there are no military maneuvers here (about 90% of the time) – the Navy permits the public to pass through its guarded gates to visit popular sites like Green, Red and Blue Beaches or to do some trail riding and exploring by bike. You must bring an ID to pass through the gates. The Navy also permits herds of Brahma cattle and wild horses to roam free on government land, perhaps to distract or entertain the 'invading' US sailors and marines.

Although the Navy's control over wide stretches of Vieques may seem more than a little bizarre, this system keeps the population size under control, limits development and provides uninterrupted vistas of forests and pastures inclining to a turquoise sea. Almost everybody here claims to hate the US Navy, but only the fools and the developers want the military to leave.

History

Indians & Spaniards Archaeological discoveries on the island have included a burial site with human remains dating back 4000 years (see the Indian Burial Site section, later in this chapter, for more information). Taíno people lived here when Columbus sighted the island in 1493 during his second voyage, on which he 'discovered' Puerto Rico.

As the Spanish colonization of Puerto Rico expanded under Ponce de León, many Taíno people fled to Vieques (still undisturbed by the Spaniards) from the mainland, seeking the protection of a powerful *cacique* (chief) here named Cacimar. In 1513, Cacimar led an army of Indians in an attack on the Spaniards near Canóvanas (on Borinquen). Many Spaniards died, but so did Cacimar. His brother continued the fight by forging an alliance with the Caribs, who were his former enemies. Vieques remained a sanctuary for militant Taínos and Caribs

until Spanish soldiers arrived en masse on Vieques to kill, enslave and drive off the local population.

The Free Port Era Although Spanish explorers surveyed the island as early as 1524, colonists did not develop a notable settlement on Vieques for another 50 years. And even after this settlement, Spanish control over the island remained tentative at best. In succeeding years, both the British and French tried to claim the island as their own. But in reality, Vieques remained something of a free port, thriving as a smuggling center through which ships and traders could pass goods without paying duty to the various European colonial powers vying for control of the Caribbean. (Some say such smuggling continues here to this day.)

In 1647, 1718 and 1753, Spanish Crown soldiers sailed to Vieques from Puerto Rico to drive the British from the island, but as soon as the armed forces left, the island was once again open to the control of robber barons of any nationality. The Spaniards decided to fortify the island in 1839, but the plan came too late. A Frenchman named Don Teofilo Le Guillen had already established himself as governor of Vieques. At last, the Spaniards came to the island in force, deposed Le Guillen, built their Fortín Conde de Marisol (a fort named after the governor of Puerto Rico at the time) and reclaimed the island in 1854.

As elsewhere in Puerto Rico, the colonial economy turned on sugarcane plantations, and 'king cane' still ruled Vieques when the island fell to the Americans as spoils from the Spanish-American War in 1898. During the first half of the 20th century, the island's cane plantations failed. Vieques lost more than half of its population and settled into near dormancy; the remaining locals survived as they always had, by subsistence farming, fishing and smuggling.

The Navy & the Tourists Arrive In 1948, everybody was more than a little surprised when the US Navy showed up on Vieques and grabbed 70% of the island, claiming rights to the land based on a little-known Act of

Congress passed in 1942. Immediately, the Navy fenced off both the east and west ends of the island for military use.

Although the remaining inhabitants of the island were dismayed by the Navy's usurpation of the land, there was still more than enough land to go around. The Navy granted locals cattle-grazing rights on 'its' land and began pouring lots of money into the local economy. Eventually, the Navy even brought a freshwater pipe across the ocean floor from its base at Roosevelt Roads to supply the *viequenses* (islanders).

However, recent generations of viequenses have not been enthusiastic about the military presence, perhaps because of the periodic bombardments of the east end and the occasional discovery of a cow blown to bits by mortar fire: 'No Navy' is a slogan commonly scribbled on the walls of abandoned sugar mills. So these days, the military tries to maintain a very low profile on Vieques,

keeping its marines and sailors out of the island's restaurants and bars.

Ecotourism, construction, cattle raising, fishing and some light manufacturing, such as the General Electric assembly plant, bring money and jobs to the island. While statistics show that more than 50% of Vieques' residents are unemployed, no one on this island seems to live in desperate circumstances. A curious paradox, unless the recent arrests of five island police officers for drug trafficking are clues that Little Girl Island still hasn't given up her piratical ways.

Orientation

Vieques is shaped somewhat like a long fish, with a spine of mountains dividing it lengthwise from east to west. The west end of the island, including the island's tallest peak, Monte Pirata, is largely a jungle known as the Naval Reservation. Here the US Navy stores munitions and wild horses clog the

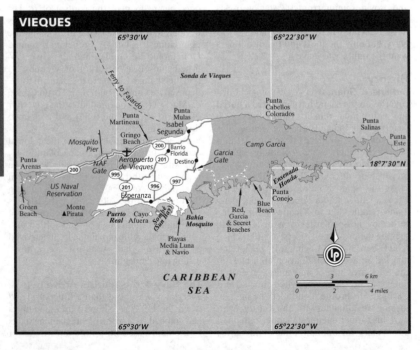

paved access road. You can reach this wilderness through the Naval Artillery Facility (NAF) Gate on Hwy 200, which leads along the north shore and passes the airport. Like all the other roads on the island, Hwy 200 originates in the town of Isabel Segunda, near the middle of the island's north coast, where the ferries from Fajardo land.

To reach the other community on the island, the south-coast village of Esperanza, you can take either of two routes south over the mountains, Hwys 201/996 or Hwy 997. If you take the latter route, you will pass along the Navy Fence as you descend from the summits. Look for the gate to Camp Garcia on your left. Beyond this gate, you can access miles of wild beaches that end at a restricted area at the eastern end of the island, where marines zoom around in tanks and Humvees and offshore warships lob live shells at the heights during military exercises.

Some of the best cycling is along Hwy 995, Hwy 996 and Hwy 201, which wind through the countryside north and west of Esperanza.

Maps The *Vieques Times* (see Information, below) produces a map that is widely available at restaurants and guesthouses around the island; your host will probably send you one if you reserve your room in advance, or you can pick up one at the tourist office (see below).

Information
You will find the tourist office (☎ 787-741-5000) in the town hall on the plaza in Isabel Segunda. It's open 9 am to 4 pm weekdays.

The island's sole ATM machine is at the Banco Popular on Calle Muñoz Rivera in Isabel Segunda.

Isabel Segunda's post office is on Calle Muñoz Rivera near the Banco Popular. Esperanza has no post office.

18 Degrees North, on the Strip in Esperanza, has a good selection of second-hand novels.

Charlie Connelly publishes the *Vieques Times* (☎ 787-741-8508) monthly in both English and Spanish. The little paper takes on tough issues such as struggles between environmentalists and local government and

The US Navy has maintained a strong presence on Vieques since 1948.

claims it has 'no secret backers.' Subscriptions to the paper cost US$20 a year.

To get your clothes washed in Isabel Segunda, try the Vieques Laundromat & Dry Cleaner, on Calle Victor Duteil.

The island's health center, the Centro de Salud de la Familia (☎ 787-741-2151), is just south of Isabel Segunda on Hwy 997, which goes by the Garcia Gate. In Isabel Segunda, you will see the Farmacia Antonio (☎ 787-741-8397) on Calle Benitez Guzman, across the street from the town hall.

In an emergency, call ☎ 911 to reach the police in Isabel Segunda; you are on your own in Esperanza.

Isabel Segunda
This is the town you'll see first when arriving by ferry from Fajardo. As the ferry pulls in, the town may seem like another bustling, rural Puerto Rican town, with a crush of trucks, *públicos* (shared taxis), cars and people crowding around the ferry dock. But should you return to the dock when the ferry isn't loading or unloading, you'll find a town that is exceptionally tranquil by Puerto Rican standards. In fact, you are likely to see more pigeons and stray dogs than people in the town's sun-swept plaza, even though about half of the island's 9000 residents live in or around Isabel Segunda.

Set on a hillside and overlooking a rather exposed cove in the center of the island's northern shore, Isabel Segunda is the oldest settlement on Vieques (1843) and takes its name from the queen who ruled Spain between 1833 and 1868. With its general serenity, 68-foot lighthouse, terraced shops and

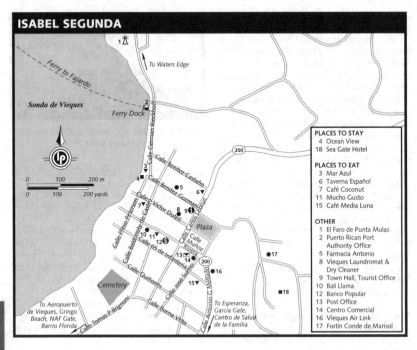

ISABEL SEGUNDA

Ferry to Fajardo

To Waters Edge

Sonda de Vieques

Ferry Dock

0   100   200 m
0   100   200 yards

Plaza

Cemetery

To Aeropuerto
de Vieques, Gringo
Beach, NAF Gate,
Barrio Florida

To Esperanza,
Garcia Gate,
Centro de Salud
de la Familia

PLACES TO STAY
4   Ocean View
18 Sea Gate Hotel

PLACES TO EAT
3   Mar Azul
6   Taverna Español
7   Café Coconut
11 Mucho Gusto
15 Café Media Luna

OTHER
1   El Faro de Punta Mulas
2   Puerto Rican Port
    Authority Office
5   Farmacia Antonio
8   Vieques Laundromat &
    Dry Cleaner
9   Town Hall, Tourist Office
10 Bali Llama
12 Banco Popular
13 Post Office
14 Centro Comercial
16 Vieques Air Link
17 Fortín Conde de Marisol

homes along the waterfront, and colonial fort standing guard on the hillside to the south, Isabel Segunda has a certain aesthetic appeal. But until a few years ago, the town had little to offer travelers except a handful of basic services. Most travelers simply passed through Isabel Segunda, seeing the town as the gateway to their planned *Blue Lagoon*-type fantasies that they'd embark on elsewhere on the island. But things seem to be changing. Isabel Segunda has recently gained two new, attractive restaurants, more accommodations options and the most lively nightlife on Vieques.

Esperanza

Most travelers first see Esperanza through the windows of cars or públicos carrying them south over the island's mountains from the Isabel Segunda ferry dock or the airport, and the vista may disappoint. Set on the edge of Brahma cattle pastures, Esperanza

might remind Australians of a dusty outpost in Queensland where horses roam the streets freely and abandoned buildings are in ready supply.

But seen from the deck of an arriving sailboat, Esperanza looks magical. The harbor is deep, clear and well sheltered on the east and south (the directions of the prevailing winds) by two tall, lush islands. The white concrete railings of the modern *malecón* (waterfront promenade) rise above the town's narrow beach. And if you arrive at sunset, you will see twinkling lights and hear music (Paul Simon's *Graceland* is popular) pouring from the cafés and restaurants that line the Calle Flamboyán 'Strip' of seaside businesses facing the Caribbean.

Fifteen years ago, Esperanza was a desolate former sugar port with a population of about 1500. Its residents survived by fishing, cattle raising and subsistence farming. But then a couple of expatriate Americans in search of the *Key Largo*, Bogart-and-Bacall life discovered the town. One of the expats set up a B&B in an old sugar hacienda; the other started a bar and guesthouse that he called Bananas. Gradually, word spread among independent travelers, and they began to check out this hole-in-the-wall village where prices are cheaper than anywhere else in the Caribbean. The dramatic beaches, snorkeling reefs and one of the world's best phosphorescent bays (illuminated by microorganisms) became additional draws for travelers.

The rest is history. Guesthouses and restaurants come and go here – witness the ruins of a failed resort at the east end of town – but at any given time Esperanza usually has about 10 inns and an equal number of interesting restaurants up and running. To be sure, Esperanza is not the place for travelers who want a spit-and-polish, Bermuda-style destination. But independent travelers willing to overlook a little trash in the streets can find kindred spirits in Esperanza and a real sense of the wild, laid-back Caribbean, and they love the frontier feel of the place. And they know that when they swim, snorkel, kayak or sail off Esperanza and look back at the south coast, the island gleams like Shangri-la.

El Faro de Punta Mulas

This classic lighthouse (1896) stands on the hilly point just north of the Isabel Segunda ferry dock. It was restored in 1992 and contains a small museum that is open irregularly. Come for the vista and sunset, not the exhibitions – a rather paltry collection of photos and artifacts depicting local maritime history, island history and natural history of the coast. Admission is free.

Fortín Conde de Marisol

This small fort (☎ 787-741-1717), on the hill above Isabel Segunda, is the last Spanish fort constructed in the Americas (1840s). Although never completed, the fort has ramparts and a fully restored central building that houses a history and art museum. This place is definitely worth a stop if you want to see exhibits on the island's 4000-year-old Indian

culture or learn about its colonial history under four flags. Here you can discover the story of sugarcane farming on Vieques and read about how Venezuelan liberator Simón Bolívar got stranded for a while on the island. Of course, the museum also includes displays on the Navy's presence. Art-show openings at the museum are major social events on Vieques. It's open 10 am to 4 pm Wednesday to Sunday; admission is free.

Museo de Esperanza

This tiny museum, on the Strip in Esperanza, is operated by a private trust and contains exhibits on the island's natural history and its early Indian inhabitants. The museum claims to be open 10 am to 3 pm Tuesday to Saturday and 1 to 3 pm Sunday. But we have always found it closed for one reason or another. Check it out if you are cruising the Strip. Donations are welcome.

Indian Burial Site

You will find this site off Hwy 997, east of Esperanza. About a quarter mile east of the entrance to Sombé (Sun Bay), take the dirt road on your left (it heads inland). Drive for about two minutes until you find the burial site of the Indian known as the 'Hombre de Puerto Ferro,' which is surrounded by a fence. Islanders say you can climb through a hole in the fence and walk right to the big boulders that identify a grave where a 4000-year-old skeleton (now on exhibit at the Fortín) was exhumed. Little is known about the skeleton, but archaeologists speculate that it is most likely the body of one of Los Arcaicos (the Archaics), Puerto Rico's earliest known inhabitants; this racial group made a sustained migration as well as seasonal pilgrimages to the Caribbean from bases in Florida. Until the discovery of the Hombre de Puerto Ferro, many archaeologists imagined that the Arcaicos had reached Puerto Rico sometime shortly after the birth of Christ; the presence of the remains on Vieques could push that date back nearly two millennia if controversy surrounding the skeleton is resolved.

Some islanders make the trek to the tomb regularly at around 5 pm for great light and a spiritual feeling. Maybe they can convince the curators of the Fortín to return the bones to this place.

Beaches
Playa Esperanza The great thing about this narrow strand is that it is a very short walk from most of the guesthouses, restaurants and bars in Esperanza. In addition, there is good snorkeling in front of the Trade Winds guesthouse, under the ruins of the government pier, and across the little harbor at **Cayo Afuera** (you'll see dramatic antler coral, nurse sharks and, occasionally, manatees).

Sometimes this beach is clean, but hurricanes and fall storms can make it a catchall for seaweed, beer cans and plastic trash. Playa Esperanza was at its best when the little resort near the east end of the beach was open, with its popular beach bar and cookouts. When that resort went belly up, the beach fell into decay. Recent rumors say that the resort may rebuild and reopen. If it does, you may discover beach-bum heaven.

Sombé This long half-moon-shaped bay, also known as Sun Bay, is less than a half mile east of Esperanza. It's the island's *balneario* (public beach), with all the facilities you have come to expect in Puerto Rico. It's sheltered and popular with families, campers and wild horses. It is also not always staffed, so you can drive in without paying the usual US$2. If the gate is locked, take the easy walk east along Playa Esperanza, and then walk across the narrow sand spit to Sombé.

Playas Media Luna & Navio If you continue east on the dirt road that leads you through the public beach at Sombé, you'll enter a forest. Go left at the fork in the road. In a couple hundred yards, you will see Playa Media Luna, a very protected, quiet beach. If you keep bearing left on this road, you will come to Playa Navio, where the surf rolls in. Both of these beaches served as sets in the 1961 film version of the novel *The Lord of the Flies*. If Vieques has a specific beach that attracts gays and lesbians, Navio is the one.

If you climb the rocks at the right (west) end of Playa Navio, you'll find a path along

the shore that you can follow to find petrified clams and corals dating from 50 million years ago.

Red, Garcia, Secret & Blue Beaches All these south-shore beaches, which are on Navy land (and named with the usual military sense of imagination), can be reached by entering the Garcia Gate on Hwy 997. You can do this only when Camp Garcia is not 'hot' (when no military exercises are in progress).

At Camp Garcia, turn south on the dirt road to Red Beach, which is the best kept of the bunch because the Navy grooms the property and maintains cabanas to shade bathers from the sun. Garcia Beach and Secret Beach are the next coves along the road. They are more protected from the surf, more natural and less visited than Red Beach. You will find good snorkeling at Secret Beach.

Blue Beach, at the east end of the Camp Garcia road, is long, open and occasionally has rough surf. This beach is so popular with viequenses (and their relatives from the mainland) that they come here three to four weeks before the Semana Santa (Holy Week) vacation and reserve spots by placing signs and string perimeters on the sand. When Semana Santa comes, the hordes descend on the beach, where they camp and party in honor of the death and resurrection of Jesus Christ. If the Navy ever closes this beach during Semana Santa, expect a riot.

Gringo Beach This is the site of the new Martineau Bay Resort, near the airport. It is your closest beach if you are staying in Isabel Segunda, and you will find a great reef for snorkeling just 10 yards offshore.

Green Beach To get here, pass through the NAF Gate and head west for about 20 minutes through pastoral landscapes and herds of wild horses. At the western tip of the island, the road turns to dirt; here you'll find clearings among the trees for parking near the beach.

The sand here is not very broad and is punctuated with coral outcroppings, but there are plenty of shade trees and great vistas of El Yunque rain forest and mainland Puerto

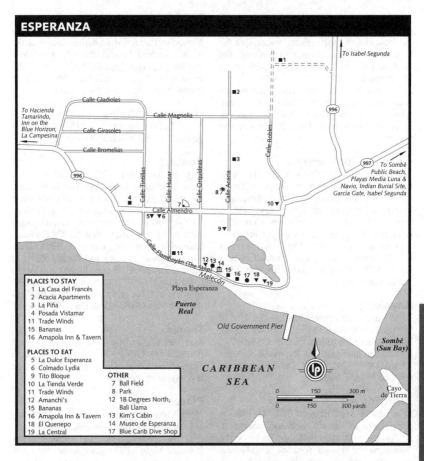

ESPERANZA

To Isabel Segunda

To Hacienda
Tamarindo,
Inn on the
Blue Horizon,
La Campesina

Calle Gladiolas

Calle Magnolia

Calle Girasoles

Calle Bromelias

Calle Robles

To Sombé
Public Beach,
Playas Media Luna &
Navio, Indian Burial Site,
Garcia Gate, Isabel Segunda

Calle Tintillas
Calle Hucar
Calle Orquídeas
Calle Acacia

Calle Almendro

Calle Flamboyán (The Strip)
Malecón

Playa Esperanza

Puerto
Real

Old Government Pier

Sombé
(Sun Bay)

CARIBBEAN
SEA

Cayo
de Tierra

0   150   300 m
0   150   300 yards

PLACES TO STAY
1 La Casa del Francés
2 Acacia Apartments
3 La Piña
4 Posada Vistamar
11 Trade Winds
15 Bananas
16 Amapola Inn & Tavern

PLACES TO EAT
5 La Dulce Esperanza
6 Colmado Lydia
9 Tito Bloque
10 La Tienda Verde
11 Trade Winds
12 Amanchi's
15 Bananas
16 Amapola Inn & Tavern
18 El Quenepo
19 La Central

OTHER
7 Ball Field
8 Park
12 18 Degrees North,
    Bali Llama
13 Kim's Cabin
14 Museo de Esperanza
17 Blue Carib Dive Shop

SPANISH VIRGIN ISLANDS

Rico. Snorkeling reefs extend for miles, and you can expect to have this place pretty much to yourself except on summer weekends, when a lot of yachts out of Fajardo come here on day trips. Since this beach is generally sheltered from the trade winds, you definitely want bug repellent here.

Bahía Mosquito

Locals claim that this bay, a designated wildlife preserve about 2 miles east of Esperanza on the south coast, has the highest concentration of phosphorescent dynoflagellates not only in Puerto Rico, but in the world. Indeed, it's also known as Phosphorescent Bay.

Before we took the tour, we thought these boasts were just a scam to get us to spend US$15 for a boat ride on a dark, buggy bay. But we could not have been more mistaken. While we cannot confirm local claims, we can say that never have we seen such dramatic bioluminescence anywhere else in Puerto Rico or in our travels elsewhere in the world.

The trip through the lagoon, on a pontoon boat piloted by Captain Sharon Grasso (☎ 787-741-0720) of Island Adventure, is nothing short of psychedelic, with hundreds of fish whipping up bright-green contrails as the boat charges through the water. But the best part of the trip is when Sharon stops the boat and lets you swim: The experience is like bathing in stars.

For more information, check out the Island Adventure website (www.biobay.com), which gives you pictures and detailed scientific descriptions in English, Spanish and German.

Diving & Snorkeling

The Blue Carib Dive Shop (☎ 787-741-2622), on the Calle Flamboyán 'Strip' in Esperanza, near the Amapola Inn & Tavern, is under the leadership of retired Navy SEALS Tom Keith and Denny Johnson. They offer gear rental and all levels of certification. One-tank dives cost US$50 (your gear) or US$75 (their gear). Snorkel/mask/fins rent for US$10 a day. For good snorkeling sites, see Beaches, above.

Kayaking

Blue Carib (see above) has kayaks: US$10 for the first hour, US$5 for each additional hour. Bahía Mosquito trips cost US$20.

You can also call Tim Raymond at Aqua Frenzy (☎ 787-741-0913). Kayaks usually go for US$25 for a half day.

Bicycling

Don't Yank My Chain (☎ 787-741-3042) is the place to go. This is a back-door operation, so don't expect an actual shop as Tuffy, the owner, moves around from one rental house to another in Esperanza. If you can't reach anyone by phone, look for Tuffy at the Trade Winds guesthouse in Esperanza (see Places to Stay, below), where he tends bar. Bikes cost US$10 a day, and Tuffy will deliver your bike to wherever you are staying.

In addition to the quiet country rides along Hwys 995, 996 and 201, you'll find plenty of good trail riding at Camp Garcia and on the Navy land (through the NAF Gate) at the west end of the island. Mind the signs designating restricted zones, however, or you may find yourself surrounded by a platoon of armed US marines.

Fishing

Lots of viequenses and travelers head for Mosquito Pier, on the northwest end of the island, reached through the NAF Gate. You can buy gear (lure and line) at Centro Comercial in Isabel Segunda for US$5. Plan on catching yellowtail and barracuda.

Horseback Riding

Steve Valazquez (☎ 787-741-2607) offers guided trail rides. Rates start at US$20.

Boating

Captain Richard (☎ 787-741-1980) is your man for charter boats. He also runs island nature tours and is a knowledgeable and articulate naturalist. Prices are negotiable.

If you plan to sail these waters, try to get your hands on Bruce Van Sant's *Cruising, Snorkeling & Diving Guide to the Spanish Virgin Islands*. It has good sketch charts of the anchorages, GPS coordinates and lots of local knowledge. It's available at marine retailers or through Cruising Guide Publications (☎ 800-330-9542), in Dunedin, Florida.

Tennis

Martineau Bay, the new five-star resort planned for Gringo Beach (see Places to Stay, below), will offer tennis courts when it opens in early 2000.

Places to Stay

Note: Vieques is an open-minded and tolerant community, and you can safely assume that all tourist accommodations are gay friendly. Many of the guesthouses and restaurants on the island are owned or staffed by lesbian or gay expats.

Camping Just east of Esperanza, pitch your tent at the *Sombé balneario* (☎ 787-741-8198) for US$10. Make reservations.

Guesthouses Guesthouses are found in both of Vieques' main towns as well as around the island.

Isabel Segunda The *Sea Gate Hotel* (☎ 787-741-46610) is near the Fortín on the hill above Isabel Segunda. The owner, Penny, has 15 rooms, mostly suites and efficiencies, starting at about US$65. This place is for dog lovers – Penny started the local humane society, which shelters stray canines.

The **Waters Edge** (☎ 787-741-1128) is northeast of the ferry dock, past the lighthouse. It has 10 units and an adjoining villa. Rates start at US$70 for a single room on the courtyard and run higher than US$100 for a room with an ocean view. Those who need a video fix will appreciate the TV/VCRs in all rooms.

The **Crow's Nest** (☎ 787-741-0033) is west of Isabel Segunda, in the barrio of Florida. It's on the hill off Hwy 201. It has 13 efficiency apartments (some are being changed into condo units), a pool and a respected restaurant. Rates are US$65 and up.

Esperanza On the Strip, **Bananas** (☎ 787-741-8700) is the place where island legend Hugh Duffy started the guesthouse craze more than 15 years ago. Hugh has moved on (twice), but he left a popular open-air bar and restaurant with eight rooms out back. This is the place if you want to be at the heart of Esperanza's action (not quite an oxymoron). The rooms are basic, and the front rooms can be noisy. Rates are US$45 and up.

The **Posada Vistamar** (☎ 787-741-8716) has five rooms with private bath for around US$60 apiece; there's a restaurant downstairs. This place is on a hill at the west end of Calle Almendro, a block from the waterfront.

Trade Winds (☎ 787-741-8666) was Duffy's second guesthouse, restaurant and bar on the Strip (west end). Harry and Janet Washburn now run this popular place. There are 10 rooms, including three terrace rooms that have a harbor view and catch the breeze. Most rooms have air con; prices range from US$50 to US$75.

Jürgen Meuser and Manfred Kissel run the **Acacia Apartments** (☎ 787-741-1856, acaciaapts@aol.com), on the upland end of Calle Acacia. There are four airy apartments here in a three-story, towerlike building, which offers spectacular views of mountains and sea from its 2nd and 3rd-floor decks as well as its rooftop patio. Jürgen and Manfred have another apartment at their mountain-

top house in the barrio of Destino. Prices for these one and two-bedroom units start at US$65 and include full kitchens. All are modern, well equipped and meticulously cared for. Although there is no air con here, you will not miss it because the apartments catch the trade winds. In our experience, these apartments represent an exceptional accommodations value for Vieques as well as Puerto Rico itself.

Amapola Inn & Tavern (☎ 787-741-1382) is the newest player on the Strip. It has five small rooms with queen beds, air con and private bathrooms for around US$80.

La Casa del Francés (☎ 787-741-3751) is an old hacienda mansion that Roger Greenblatt reclaimed from the termites almost 20 years ago and turned into one of the most eclectic guesthouses in the Caribbean. Set in the middle of a cow pasture about a half mile east of central Esperanza (near Sombé), La Casa has more than a dozen rooms decorated with Roger's sense of whimsy. You get a pool, gift shop ('the Mall') and continental breakfast for around US$100.

La Piña (☎ 787-741-2953) is another inexpensive, small guesthouse on Calle Acacia (about halfway up the hill). Elswith Petrocovik has three apartments in this modest two-story house; rates start at US$55 and rise to over US$120.

Hacienda Tamarindo (☎ 787-741-8525) is one of the largest guesthouses (15 rooms) on the south side of the island. It lies along Hwy 996 about three-quarters of a mile west of Esperanza, on a hill looking across fields to the Caribbean. You get air con, a private bathroom, pool and American breakfast here for US$115.

The **Inn on the Blue Horizon** (☎ 787-741-3318) is on the seaside bluff just down a dirt road from the Hacienda Tamarindo. With a spectacular natural setting, nine rooms in separate bungalows and the most elegant restaurant/bar (outdoor) on the south side of the island, these are luxury accommodations. Rooms cost US$175.

Around the Island The **Finca Caribe** (☎ 787-741-0495) is a mountain-ridge oasis on Hwy 995. It was once the New Dawn, a women's retreat featuring great vistas, fresh air, pastures and horseback riding. All the old attractions of this place remain, but it is now under the ownership of a straight couple and attracts a wide range of guests, including families. Rates are US$55 and up.

Hotels The *Ocean View* (☎ 787-741-3696) is on the cliff in Isabel Segunda, 200 yards south of the ferry dock. With 35 rooms, this hotel is currently the largest on the island. Its convenience and price (rooms cost US$40) make this place a good deal.

Martineau Bay is a new five-star resort hotel opening on Gringo Beach near the airport in early 2000. The hotel features 48 suites, three restaurants, pools, tennis courts, convention facilities and a children's activities area, plus all the amenities you'd expect from a luxury resort. Managed by prestigious Rosewood Hotels & Resorts (☎ 800-928-8889), which runs the Caribe Little Dix Bay and Caneel Bay resorts in the Virgin Islands, Martineau Bay promises to be a stunner. The rack rate on its rooms is in the US$300 range, but look for packages and discounts.

Rental Agents Lin Weatherbie runs gay-friendly *Rainbow Realty* (☎ 787-741-4312). Jane Sabin (☎ 787-741-0023) can also help you out, as can *Beach Chalets* (☎ 787-720-2461) and *Laurel Real Estate* (☎ 787-741-6806). All these agents represent a variety of vacation properties ranging from apartments to villas. You should expect to pay US$650 to US$2500 per week.

Places to Eat
Isabel Segunda The *Mar Azul* (☎ 787-741-3400) is near the ferry dock and is a good place to get a beer (US$1.50) and a turkey sandwich (US$4.50) while waiting for the boat.

Café Coconut (☎ 787-741-1051) is on Calle Victor Duteil. This is the breakfast place of choice for gringos who live or rent houses in the barrio of Bravos de Boston. Get a full American breakfast here for around US$2.50.

Mucho Gusto (☎ 787-741-3300) is next to the Banco Popular and offers up some great

bargain grub: *arroz con habichuelas* (rice and beans) goes for US$4.50.

Taverna Español (☎ 787-741-1175) is on Calle Carlos LeBrun, near the town hall. Try paella for around US$14.

Café Media Luna (☎ 787-741-2594) is the new upscale trattoria across from Vieques Air Link. It serves dinner only and features an eclectic international cuisine. Mahi mahi runs around US$24.

The *Crow's Nest* (see Places to Stay, above), in the barrio of Florida, features a 2nd-story terrace with great views of the main island. Its inexpensive, tasty chicken breast in sesame with salad is US$14. It serves dinner only.

The *Morales Supermercado* is the largest market on the island. It is located outside Isabel Segunda on the road to the airport (Hwy 200).

Esperanza If you want a good, open-air lunch spot serving breaded shrimp and sandwiches for less than US$4, try *La Central* (☎ 787-741-0106), on the east end of the Strip.

El Quenepo, also on the Strip, is a good place to go when you are low on cash. Rice and beans costs US$4.50.

La Dulce Esperanza (☎ 787-741-0085), on the west end of Calle Almendro, serves Danish pastry (under US$1), fresh bread and large pizzas (US$11).

Bananas (see Places to Stay, above) specializes in sandwiches, skins and wings (under US$6). Islanders claim Bananas now has the best pizza on Vieques.

Amanchi's (☎ 787-741-1325) is the Mexican grill in the same cluster of buildings as 18 Degrees North and Bali Llama on the Strip. It serves dinner only. Burritos cost less than US$8.

Cook David Donavan sometimes has a special lasagna night at *Trade Winds*: all-you-can-eat (US$10) includes salad. Conch fritters cost US$6.

Amapola Inn & Tavern, on the Strip, has international and *criollo* dishes like *pollo asado* and *arepas*. Meals cost less than US$10.

To get away from the gringo crowd in Esperanza, head to *Tito Bloque*, at the foot of Calle Acacia next to the mangroves. This

Señor Mislavega at work in his tobacco fields, Isabela

The ubiquitous roadside stand, purveyor of island *cocina del kiosko* (food-stand cuisine)

Rural landscape along the Ruta Panorámica, Sierra de Cayey

Coffee harvest, Yauco

Early morning fog in Sierra de Cayey

Playa Flamenco, Culebra's most popular beach

Flourishing corals and sponges

Playa Esperanza, Vieques

Aerial view of Isla Culebrita

MARK BACON

Traditional bait fishing, Culebra

DAVE G HOUSER

View from abandoned lighthouse, Isla Culebrita

RANDALL PEFFER

Souvenir courtesy of Uncle Sam, Playa Flamenco

RANDALL PEFFER

Kim's Cabin, on the Strip in Esperanza (Vieques)

raised outdoor patio draws a local crowd and is known for its good, cheap grilled lobster (cost varies, but expect to pay US$15).

Head west of Esperanza on Hwy 996 past Hacienda Tamarindo and look to your left for *La Campesina* (☎ 787-741-1239). You can get leg of lamb (US$18) in a romantic setting with outdoor dining amid twinkling lights.

At the *Inn on the Blue Horizon*, west of Esperanza, we're talking casual, elegant gazebo dining with a view like the name implies. Fresh trout goes for US$18.

You can get groceries at *La Tienda Verde* (Green Store), on Calle Robles, and at the *Colmado Lydia*, on Calle Almendro near the ball field in the center of town.

Around the Island Visit *Chez Shack* (☎ 787-741-2175), on Hwy 995 in the center of the island, to see Hugh Duffy's latest creation. This place really is a shack, but the food is excellent. Monday is the big night, with live reggae and an outdoor grill: Chicken/ fish/steak costs US$15 to US$18.

Entertainment
Café Media Luna (see Places to Eat, above), in Isabel Segunda, has salsa, jazz and Latin rock on weekends and draws a mixed crowd of gringos and locals, straights and gays. You will find a similar scene, plus a pool table and a seaview deck, at *Mar Azul*, also in Isabel Segunda.

On Monday, *Chez Shack* has live reggae. *Bananas*, in Esperanza, always has a lively pub scene with an active dart board. The *Inn on the Blue Horizon* has a friendly gringo crowd, especially on Friday night.

Shopping
Kim's Cabin (☎ 787-741-3145), on the Strip in Esperanza, has island-made dresses and shorts. Spice from Paradise (☎ 787-741-0848), in Barrio Florida – but with products on sale at island stores – is Puerto Rico's only maker of gourmet hot sauces and mustards. Try the pineapple-chili mustard for less than US$4.

You can get local honey from Miguel Díaz at Vieques Bee Farm (☎ 787-741-2132), who will also give you a tour of his apiary.

Bali Llama (☎ 787-741-0520) has shops selling jewelry and designer clothing in both Isabel Segunda and Esperanza.

Getting There & Away
Air The island has excellent air service from San Juan and Fajardo, provided by Isla Nena Air Service (☎ 888-263-6213) and Vieques Air Link (☎ 888-901-9247 for San Juan-Vieques flights, 787-741-3266 for Fajardo-Vieques flights). There are at least six flights a day to/from San Juan's Isla Grande and Luis Muñoz Marín (LMM) airports, and more than 10 flights a day between Fajardo and the island. Currently, Isla Nena charges US$90 roundtrip to fly to/from LMM; Vieques Air Link charges US$100 roundtrip to/from Isla Grande. Fajardo flights cost US$35 roundtrip. All aircraft are Islander twins or tri-motor Trilanders.

Vieques Air Link also has several flights a week between Vieques and St Croix in the US Virgin Islands. The airline has an office in Isabel Segunda.

Ferry The Puerto Rican Port Authority's modern, high-speed ferries run between Fajardo and Vieques several times a day. Generally the passage takes slightly more than an hour, but the actual time depends upon the ferry you are aboard, the weather and – possibly – the last time the engines had an oil change. One-way fares are US$2. The passenger ferry schedule was as follows at the time this book went to press:

route	weekdays	weekends
Vieques-Fajardo	7 am	7 am
Fajardo-Vieques	9:30 am	9 am
Vieques-Fajardo	11 am	1 pm
Fajardo-Vieques	1 pm	3 pm
Vieques-Fajardo	3 pm	4:30 pm
Fajardo-Vieques	4:30 pm	6 pm

Call to confirm the schedule and to make reservations (particularly for trips on Friday, Saturday, Sunday and Monday). You can also request departure times for the cargo ferry if you must take a car (not a great idea). You can reach the Puerto Rican Port Authority office in Fajardo at ☎ 787-863-0705, 800-981-2005; the Vieques office, at the ferry dock in Isabel Segunda, can be reached at ☎ 787-741-4761. Both offices are open 8 to 11 am and 1 to 3 pm weekdays.

Getting Around

The island has about a half dozen rental-car operations. Almost all rent Suzuki Samurai jeeps for about US$35 a day. Although Vieques is a big island, you may not need a car for your whole stay. However, plan ahead and make reservations early, because if you come during holiday periods, you will find all the cars rented. Here are the current vendors:

Diaz Car Rentals	☎ 787-741-0720
Dreda & Fonsin Rent-a-Car	☎ 787-741-8163
Island Car Rentals	☎ 787-741-1666
Marco's Car Rentals	☎ 787-741-1388
Maritza Car Rental	☎ 787-741-0078
Vieques Car Rental	☎ 787-741-8691

CULEBRA

A T-shirt sold on this island heralds it as 'the island where the chicken still crosses the road.' With more space, the artist might have added 'horses, cows, goats, lizards, pelicans and crabs' to the parade. And it would take another shirt to list everything that swims over the reefs, including angelfish and barracudas. Humankind has not yet wrecked this place.

Lying 17 miles east of Fajardo, on Puerto Rico's east coast, Culebra is geologically more a part of the Virgin Islands (St Thomas is 12 miles east) than of the 'mainland.' And it looks the part when viewed from an approaching ferry – lush, irregular peaks are fringed by beaches and rugged offshore cays. The island and its satellites are small enough for the eyes to take in at a single glance. Culebra's main settlement is small enough for a visitor to circumnavigate in 10 minutes.

Despite its distance from the main island, Culebra culture remains strongly Puerto Rican, with a veneer of Key West-style Margaritaville imported by expatriate entrepreneurs. Two thousand people live here; most

are born-and-bred *culebrenses*, but several hundred expats run the bulk of the restaurants, guesthouses and tourist services. The common bond here is eccentricity. As one islander said, 'If we wanted to do things the way they do in San Juan or New York, we wouldn't be on this island.'

So when you get to Culebra, be prepared for the fact that things get done a little differently here. Notice the yard that one woman has decorated with ocean flotsam, nautical memorabilia and recovered military matériel (including bombs!) instead of conventional grass or shrubs. Realize that a restaurant owner may open her doors only when she is in the mood. Don't be surprised when your rental-car guy tells you to just leave his jeep on the street somewhere, with the keys in it, when you depart, or your guesthouse host puts you in charge and heads off to St Croix for a couple of days to research desalination plants. Don't be too upset if your favorite breakfast place is out of pastries because the baker went kayaking. Privately built docks here are legally public facilities, and squatters simply build their homes on any unpurchased, untitled public land. Only new and uptight gringo immigrants complain, because they haven't yet learned the system here.

Beyond the amusing eccentricities of the culture, Culebra's most endearing charms are its natural resources. You could snorkel, kayak, hike, fish or sail here every day for a year and still not feel like you had 'done' Culebra. And while the island is threatened to a certain extent by development, much of Culebra has been designated a national wildlife refuge, protected by both the Dept of Natural Resources and the US Fish and Wildlife Service. Large chunks of Culebra's 7000 acres – including all of the coastline and the offshore cays – are owned by the federal government, and much of the interior land that has not already been developed is zoned 'RO25,' which means that a 25-acre plot cannot be subdivided and can contain only one residential unit. Many beaches here are closed during the summer, when they are important nesting grounds for endangered sea turtles.

History

Early Peoples A shadow of mystery covers Culebra's history prior to the latter half of the 19th century, as the island had no continuous settlement or permanent inhabitants to keep records before that time. It seems that shifting, itinerant populations have been the story of Culebra for at least 500 years.

Taíno people told the early Spanish expeditions that the islands east of Puerto Rico, including Culebra, were disputed territory between the Taínos and the Caribs at the beginning of the 16th century, and that groups from both tribes came and went from these islands according to the season – probably to hunt the turtles that nested here. But it seems that no one stayed here long, as nearby Vieques had more fertile, flatter land for farming. Probably the first real settlement came to Culebra during the early 16th century, when Taíno and Carib refugees from Borinquen gathered here and on Vieques to make peace with each other, pool their resources and mount a fierce (but unsuccessful) campaign to drive the Spaniards from the big island.

Pirates & Spaniards Once the Spaniards had annihilated the Indians, Culebra became a place forgotten by all but privateers such as Captain Henry Morgan, who could hide his ship and weather hurricanes in the long, deep bay of Ensenada Honda. There was, however, no secure source of fresh water on the island, such as pirates found on the island of Mona, off Borinquen's west coast. So the pirates came and left, probably after catching and killing as many turtles as they could carry.

Although the Spanish Crown claimed Culebra as part of its Puerto Rican colony, the Spaniards showed no interest in it for hundreds of years. Meanwhile, English cartographers charted Culebra as Pasaje (Passage) Island, because Culebra marks the first safe

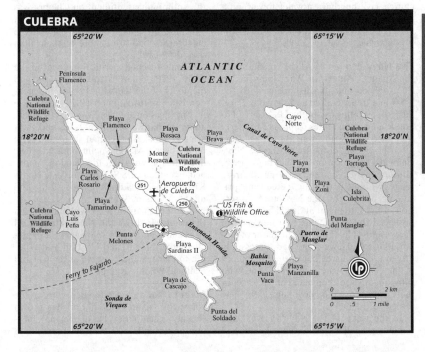

CULEBRA

deepwater route through the Antilles chain (from the Atlantic to the Caribbean) east of the Mona Passage. The Culebra Passage no doubt proved an attractive route to British, French and Dutch mariners heading to or from their Caribbean colonies.

By the mid-19th century, Spain had lost all its vast holdings in the Americas except Cuba, Puerto Rico and their satellite islands. Fearful of losing these as well, Spain ordered Culebra colonized under the authority of the newly installed military government on nearby Vieques. Colonists arrived in 1880 and built their settlement on the eastern side of Ensenada Honda (near the current office of US Fish and Wildlife). They called their community 'San Ildefonso de la Culebra' after a famous Spanish bishop, but in local usage the name was often shortened to 'Culebra.' In the years just prior to the Spanish-American War (1898), the settlement expanded to include more than 500 colonists who built more than 80 houses, a church, civil buildings, a water tower and a dock. They survived by exporting livestock, a variety of garden vegetables, and turtle by-products such as oil and shells.

The Navy Moves In At the conclusion of the Spanish-American War, Spain ceded Puerto Rico and its offshore cays to the USA in a treaty crafted and signed in Paris. According to this treaty, the USA agreed to honor all citizens' titles to private property they held before the war. But three years after the signing of the treaty, the US Navy claimed a large portion of Culebra for use in military maneuvers and as a naval firing range. Without regard for the citizens' private property rights, the Navy took possession of the settlement at San Ildefonso and displaced the inhabitants to a new site on the western side of the bay. In honor of Admiral George Dewey, who had successfully driven the Spaniards out of the Philippines in the Spanish-American War – and who subsequently took command of US forces in the Caribbean – the Navy named the new refugee camp Dewey.

In the wake of the Navy's arrival, the remaining civilians on Culebra languished under the rule of politically appointed delegates (later called 'mayors'). Ostensibly, the other creatures on the island fared slightly better after US President Theodore Roosevelt signed a law in 1909 establishing Culebra as a wildlife refuge.

But with the onset of WWII, living conditions worsened further on Culebra as the US Navy began using the island for naval bombardments and aerial bombing practice. Culebra had the misfortune of looking a lot like the South Pacific islands on the front lines of the war with Japan. US military anxiety over the Cold War and the Vietnam War kept up persistent military assaults on the island throughout the 1950s and '60s.

During the same era, the culebrenses won the right to elect their own mayors and municipal delegates. Political activity began to build as residents protested the Navy's illegal usurpation of island land and its destruction of an environment that was supposed to be a wildlife sanctuary. In a sense, the antimilitary sentiment on Culebra was a manifestation of the antiwar movement sweeping through the US at the time, but the culebrenses had a lot more at stake than their draft cards.

Events reached a critical moment in the early 1970s when island protesters and members of the left-wing Partido Independentista Puertorriqueño (PIP) derailed a marine invasion at Playa Flamenco by blockading the harbor with local boats and gathering at a makeshift chapel at 'ground zero' on the beach. At some point, both sides detonated explosions, but the standoff continued. Eventually, US Secretary of State Henry Kissinger, who had just negotiated the end of the Vietnam War, used his talents to broker a permanent Navy withdrawal from the island. In 1975, the Navy returned all its island land to private owners, the municipal government, and US Fish and Wildlife to manage and preserve as the Culebra National Wildlife Refuge.

Culebra Today Since the departure of the Navy, the island's population has grown steadily as ecotourism has opened new business opportunities for both culebrenses and expats. Today, the population stands at about 2000 people, and Culebra can claim one of the lowest unemployment rates in Puerto Rico (about 5%, in contrast to its sister island Vieques' rate of about 50%). The largest employers are various arms of the local/commonwealth government, RD Medical, where workers assemble IV units, and tourist services.

But even with the Navy out of the picture, illegal land use and environmental destruction continue to be Culebra's biggest problems. Corruption at both the municipal and commonwealth levels of government has allowed wealthy individuals to redefine restrictions on development and to build without permits on untitled land. Once the houses are up, there is no way to remove them – there's no governmental agency nearby that can go through all the trouble it takes to evict the squatters, and few islanders are willing to risk a confrontation with their neighbors.

Flora & Fauna

Large coastal mangrove forests – particularly at Punta de Manglar on the east end of the island – provide breeding grounds for crustaceans and small fish. Fringe and barrier reefs around the island and its offshore cays create rich feeding areas for mature fish. And when the fish are here, the birds follow to hunt them. Sooty terns, roseate terns, bridled terns, sandwich terns, royal terns, brown noddys, ospreys, martins and – of course – the endangered brown pelicans.

For these birds, Culebra is heaven. The fishing is superb, and the nesting, on thousands of undeveloped forest acres, is almost as good. More than 160,000 sooty terns nest on the Península Flamenco alone.

And birds are not the only creatures that lay their eggs here. Biologists believe that the Culebra giant anatole (a 4-foot-long lizard once thought to be extinct) survives among the boulders and the jaguey trees of Monte Resaca. Meanwhile, the extremely endangered leatherback turtle (one of the largest sea reptiles in the world) lays its eggs on the beaches of Isla Culebrita, a large cay east of the main island. The endangered loggerhead

Culebra's beaches are important nesting grounds for endangered sea turtles.

lays its eggs here, too, as well as on the north-coast beaches of Playas Zoni, Larga, Brava, Resaca and Flamenco. The hawksbill turtle and the green turtle, which are also threatened species, nest here as well. Turtles usually come ashore and lay their eggs at night during the late winter and early spring. The eggs hatch in May, June and July, and the armies of perfect little critters scramble out of the sand and parade to the sea to start their lives as mariners. To protect the hatchlings, US Fish and Wildlife closes the beaches during hatching season.

Orientation

Culebra looks like a crab claw, 7 miles long and no more than 4 miles wide, opening to the southeast. In many ways, the long bay of Ensenada Honda (between the pincers of the claw) shapes the island's character. Most of Culebra's commercial development – residences, baseball field, airport, etc – clusters around the head of the bay.

The heavily populated area of the island has three distinct neighborhoods. The commercial center of the island, where the ferry lands, is formally named Dewey, but nobody acknowledges the admiral – culebrenses call the island center either 'El Pueblo' (Town) or

'La Puebla'; the gringo expats usually call it 'town.' North of town, the neighborhood of houses on the hill above the baseball field is Barriada Clark (Clark Neighborhood). This is the first land that the municipality subdivided into tiny housing lots after the Navy gave up its claims on the island. East of the airport runway is another development of small homes, called Villa Muñeco. The municipality subdivided this land for housing to give islanders safer places to live after their waterfront and lowland homes were destroyed in Hurricane Hugo (1989).

Beyond this population nucleus, Culebra is largely overgrown with a variety of forest types. At 650 feet above sea level, Monte Resaca is an imposing peak on this small isle.

Five main roads fan out across the island, but most stop short of the island's many beaches. The exceptions are the roads to Punta Melones, near town, and the popular balneario and camping area at Playa Flamenco, on the north side. To get to all the other beaches, you have to hike. Road and street signs are almost nonexistent here, but the island is so small, the topography so distinctive and the roads so straightforward that there is little chance of getting lost.

Maps The *Tourist Times*, an adjunct publication of the island newspaper (see Newspapers & Magazines, later in this chapter), includes a map of the settlement and a basic island map that highlights essential roads.

The *Isla de Culebra Tourist Guide*, published by La Loma gift shop (see Shopping, below), on the hill in town, offers more detailed maps.

Information

Tourist Offices There is a small tourist office (☎ 787-742-3288) in the town hall on Calle Pedro Márquez, just east of the ferry dock. But the information you get here is of the most basic kind. You can pull much more information off the Internet from websites run by local businesses, guesthouses and vacation-home rental companies. Everybody agrees that Bruce Goble of La Loma gift shop runs the island's best website (www .culebra-island.com).

Money You can tell that the economy is on the move on Culebra because the old, basic Banco Roig has given way to Banco Popular (☎ 787-742-3572), with a new ATM machine (which was introduced to the island in 1997 with music and beauty queens) on Calle Márquez. And now Citibank (☎ 787-742-0220) has set up shop just up the street.

Banco Popular is open 8:30 am to 2:30 pm weekdays except Tuesday. Citibank has the same hours on weekdays.

Post The post office (☎ 787-742-3862) is right in the center of town on Calle Márquez. It's open 8:30 am to 4:30 pm weekdays, 8:30 am to noon Saturday.

Libraries Sorry, folks, Culebra doesn't yet have any bookstores. But many of the guesthouses have their own loan libraries of paperbacks. The collection of books at Club Seabourne (see Places to Stay, later in this chapter) is exceptional.

Newspapers The *Culebra Calendar* (☎ 787-742-4816) is the island's first and only newspaper. It began publishing in late 1995 and usually publishes about six editions a year with features on local issues like ecotourism and plans for a pipeline to bring water from the mainland. It also offers profiles, event listings, a police blotter, classifieds, perspectives and letters to the editor. The *Calendar* really is your best source of print information on the island, and you can buy back issues for US$3 each.

Head to the Paradise Gift Shop (☎ 787-742-3569), in town on Castelar, to obtain an English version of the *San Juan Star*.

Laundry The Wash & Wear Café (☎ 787-742-0758), in the Hotel Kokomo across from the ferry dock, is the place to go. The café is open 6:30 am to noon Tuesday to Friday, but the laundry's hours differ slightly.

Medical Services Despite its small population, Culebra has good heath services. The clinic (☎ 787-742-3511), in town on the road to Punta Melones, has drugs and resident doctors. The island also keeps a plane on emergency standby at the airport overnight for medical transport. In a recent emergency, when a diver was struck by a powerboat, the Navy sent a helicopter to the island from the nearby base at Roosevelt Roads.

There is no pharmacy on the island, so culebrenses call Walgreens in Fajardo (☎ 787-860-1060), and the pharmacy ships drugs to the island on Vieques Air Link flights.

Emergency Culebrenses will tell you repeatedly that if you have an emergency on the island, you will get a much faster and more professional response by calling the island detachment of the Puerto Rican Police (☎ 787-742-3501) than by contacting the municipal police.

Dangers & Annoyances The municipal police love to issue tickets to travelers who make the mistake of cruising around town in their rented jeeps without using their seatbelts or wearing shirts. Buckle up, and *pa-lease* cover those indecent bare shoulders before they rend the moral fabric of the community.

On the other hand, it is perfectly acceptable on Culebra for local adults to romance 14-year-olds. Community standards are indeed strange and wonderful things to observe.

Dewey

Alias: 'El Pueblo' or 'Da Town' (as in 'da plane' and 'da island,' from TV's *Fantasy Island*, which is apparently an old favorite of Culebra expats).

OK, this place used to get low marks from the 'pretty city' beauty pageant judges. But today the town seems fresher, cleaner, more brightly painted and – best of all – perkier than the place that once seemed a clone of some Mosquito Coast outpost. Now, you can actually find places to shop, bank, eat and drink that are open and staffed by a collection of diverse and friendly folk. Now, you can hear music as you walk through the streets of the settlement instead of just the buzz of biting insects.

Beaches

Punta Melones There is only one bathing/snorkeling site you can walk to from town,

and this is it. Take the road past the clinic about a half mile north until you reach a development on the hill to your right. Ahead on your left, you'll see the rocky Melones point, with a navigation light; to the right of the point is a stony beach. If you head down to this beach, you will find good snorkeling at both ends. The point's name comes from the prevalence of a species of melon cactus in this part of the island.

Playa Flamenco This is the public beach about 2 miles due north of town. If you like a deeply indented horseshoe beach, lined with palms and cupped between mountain ridges; if you like clear water, no surf, manicured sand and public bath/toilet facilities; and if you like camping in a seaside grove, make a date for Playa Flamenco.

The beach, which is named for the flamingoes that usually winter in the nearby lagoon, could be close to paradise, except that it has been discovered by so many people. Hordes of Puerto Ricans from the mainland descend on this place during weekends and holidays to camp and party with a passion. But come on a weekday in any season except summer and you will have Flamenco pretty much to yourself. The snorkeling is not great here, but you can find reefs at either end of the beach to entertain you.

Playa Carlos Rosario If you follow a path west from the parking lot at Playa Flamenco, a 12 to 15-minute hike over the hill will bring you to Playa Carlos Rosario, one of the best snorkeling areas in Puerto Rico. But don't get confused: Playa Carlos Rosario is not the first beach you'll reach along this path. This first nameless beach, however, is one of the few places in Puerto Rico where you'll see nude or topless bathers, taking the sun in privacy.

To reach Carlos Rosario, head north from this first beach, cross the narrow peninsula and head down to the sandy basin and shade trees. A barrier reef almost encloses this beach, and you can snorkel on either side of it by swimming through the boat channel – look for the white plastic bottle marker – at the right side of the beach. But be *very*

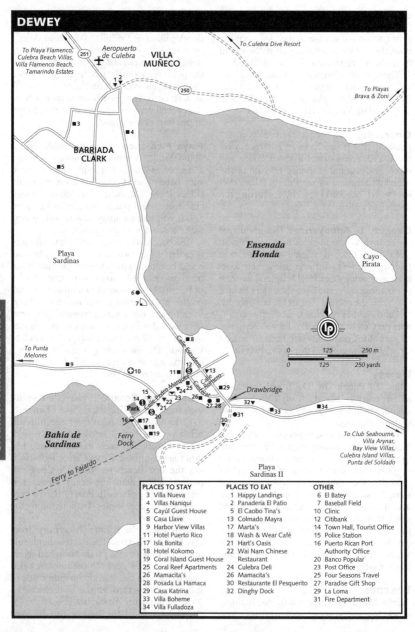

DEWEY

To Playa Flamenco,
Culebra Beach Villas,
Villa Flamenco Beach,
Tamarindo Estates

Aeropuerto
de Culebra

VILLA
MUÑECO

To Culebra Dive Resort

251

250

To Playas
Brava & Zoni

BARRIADA
CLARK

Ensenada
Honda

Cayo
Pirata

Playa
Sardinas

SPANISH VIRGIN ISLANDS

To Punta
Melones

Calle Escudero

Calle Pedro Marquez

Calle Romero

Calle Escudero

Drawbridge

0   125   250 m
0   125   250 yards

Park

Bahía de
Sardinas

Ferry
Dock

Ferry to Fajardo

Playa
Sardinas II

To Club Seabourne,
Villa Arynar,
Bay View Villas,
Culebra Island Villas,
Punta del Soldado

PLACES TO STAY	PLACES TO EAT	OTHER
3 Villa Nueva	1 Happy Landings	6 El Batey
4 Villas Naniqui	2 Panadería El Patio	7 Baseball Field
5 Cayúl Guest House	5 El Caobo Tina's	10 Clinic
8 Casa Llave	13 Colmado Mayra	12 Citibank
9 Harbor View Villas	17 Marta's	14 Town Hall, Tourist Office
11 Hotel Puerto Rico	18 Wash & Wear Café	15 Police Station
17 Isla Bonita	21 Hart's Oasis	16 Puerto Rican Port
18 Hotel Kokomo	22 Wai Nam Chinese	Authority Office
19 Coral Island Guest House	Restaurant	20 Banco Popular
25 Coral Reef Apartments	24 Culebra Deli	23 Post Office
26 Mamacita's	26 Mamacita's	25 Four Seasons Travel
28 Posada La Hamaca	30 Restaurante El Pesquerito	27 Paradise Gift Shop
29 Casa Katrina	32 Dinghy Dock	29 La Loma
33 Villa Boheme		31 Fire Department
34 Villa Fulladoza		

careful: Water taxis and local powerboats cruise this channel and the reef, and in 1998 a longtime Culebra resident and diver was struck and killed by a boat.

For really spectacular snorkeling, work your way along the cliffs on the point south of the beach, or head about a quarter mile north to a place called **the Wall**, which has 40-foot drop-offs and rich colors. By the way, a lot of local gringos call Carlos Rosario 'Impact Beach' because of all the shelling it took back in the Navy days, and you may see ordnance in the water. It could be live; don't mess with it!

Playa Resaca A *resaca* is an undertow and a metaphor for a hangover, so you can probably picture the state of the water on this beach and the way you will feel after climbing up and down 650-foot Monte Resaca to reach it. US Fish and Wildlife maintains the trail here, and you should call them for permission as well as directions to the trail head (☎ 787-742-0115).

Playa Brava As the name *brava* (rough) implies, this beach east of Playa Resaca has plenty of surf, so watch yourself. You can just about be sure that there will be no one here to help you if you get pummeled by a wave or sucked out to sea in a rip tide. But it is just this sense of life on the edge that makes Brava attractive.

To get here, travel around to the eastern side of Ensenada Honda. Pass the Km 4 marker and turn left a little way past the cemetery. Follow this road until the pavement ends and you come up against a gate. This is the entrance to a cattle farm, but it is also a public right-of-way, so park your car or bike and head due north on the trail beyond the gate. The second half of the trail leads through a grove of trees that are often rife with butterflies.

Playa Zoni Here is another secluded beach, near the extreme eastern end of the island. The snorkeling is only fair at both ends of the beach, so you will need other compelling reasons – like romance or a picnic – to make the nearly half-hour drive on a rough road

to get here. The route is straightforward (go east until you can't go any farther), so navigation is not the problem. The condition of the road is what you worry about. If there have been recent rains, this road can snare you like the tar pits trapped the dinosaurs. Check with your car-rental person to see if the road is safe before you venture this way.

Punta del Soldado This site on the extreme southwestern tip of the island has a rocky beach and terrific snorkeling. To get here, follow the road south across the drawbridge for about 2 miles, passing Club Seabourne and finally scaling a steep hill. Here the pavement stops, so pull over to the side of the road and park. Walk down the dirt road to the beach at the bitter end (about 10 minutes). You will see the reef about 50 yards offshore to the southeast.

Culebra National Wildlife Refuge

More than a third of Culebra's 7000 acres constitute a national wildlife refuge that President Theodore Roosevelt signed into law almost 100 years ago. Most of this land lies along the Península Flamenco and from Monte Resaca east to the sea, and includes all of the coastline as well as more than 20 offshore cays. US Fish and Wildlife (☎ 787-742-0115) administers these lands. Monte Resaca, Isla Culebrita and Cayo Luis Peña are open to the public from sunrise to sunset daily. Stop by the office, on the east side of Ensenada Honda, for maps, literature and permission to visit other sections of the refuge. This is also the place to come to find out what beaches may be closed for turtle nesting or to learn about being a volunteer on an overnight turtle watch.

Note: Fish and Wildlife is basically a one-woman show, so it is not always easy to find someone around the office.

Isla Culebrita If you need a reason to rent a kayak or hire a water taxi, Isla Culebrita is it. This small island, just a mile east of Playa Zoni, is part of the wildlife refuge. With its abandoned lighthouse, six beaches, tide pools, reefs, and nesting areas for seabirds, Isla Culebrita has changed little in the past

500 years. The north beaches, such as the long crescent of Playa Tortuga, are popular nesting grounds for sea turtles, and you may see these animals swimming near the reefs just offshore. Note: Bring a lot of water, sunscreen, a shirt and a hat if you head for Isla Culebrita, because there is little shade here. See the Kayaking and Boating sections, below, for details on renting and hiring boats to reach this island.

Cayo Luis Peña Less visited than Isla Culebrita, Luis Peña is the island of peaks, rocks, forests and coves you'll pass just a few minutes before the ferry lands you at Culebra's town dock. This island is another part of the wildlife refuge, and it has a collection of small sheltered beaches. Luis Peña is a short kayak or water-taxi trip from town, and the snorkeling all around the island is good.

Diving & Snorkeling
You can rent snorkel gear for about US$10 a day from the following shops:

Culebra Dive Shop	☎ 787-742-1932
Culebra Divers	☎ 787-742-0803
Club Seabourne	☎ 787-742-3169

Reef Link Divers (☎ 787-742-0581) has gear and snorkeling/boat trips for US$25 for a half day, US$50 for a full day with lunch. See Beaches, earlier in this chapter, for good snorkeling sites.

The same vendors offer dive instruction and trips. One-tank dives cost around US$50; two-tank trips run about US$75.

Kayaking
Jim Petersen's Ocean Safaris (☎ 787-379-1973) kayak trips have been featured in a number of magazine articles on Culebra – and for good reason. For just US$45, you can get instruction and a half-day guided tour to places such as Isla Culebrita or Cayo Luis Peña; a full day costs US$75. Jim also rents kayaks for US$25/40 for a half/full day. And as this book went to press, Jim was developing a floating ecotourism resort that will offer beach camping, kayaking and snorkeling for less than US$100 a night.

Reef Link Divers (see above) also offers kayaks for rent at competitive prices.

Bicycling
With its hills, dirt trails, low-volume traffic and attractions spread miles apart, Culebra is an excellent place to bike for transportation, exercise and sport. Culebra Bike Shop (☎ 787-742-2209) has serious mountain bikes for rent; US$12 a day, with discounts if you keep your wheels more than four or five days. Sun Moon Tours (☎ 787-742-1948) and Dick & Cathy (☎ 787-742-0062) will also rent you wheels. Prices are usually less than US$15 a day. Make reservations early if you're visiting during a major holiday.

Fishing
The real fish hawk on the island is Chris Goldmark (☎ 787-742-0412). He can take you out to the flats for some superb bonefishing, or offshore for the big stuff. Figure on US$225 for a half day.

Boating

You've got a lot of choices here. You can rent small boats from Scott's (☎ 787-742-0419). Or charter a 50-foot Gulfstar sloop for a five-hour sail from Paradise Day Sail (☎ 787-742-0328) for US$45 per person. For water taxis, try the following:

Captain Jack's	
Muff the Magic Fun Boat	☎ 787-742-7494
Guilin's Water Taxi	☎ 787-742-9575
Tanama the Glass Bottom Boat	☎ 787-413-0325

Sea Turtle (☎ 787-742-0591) is a 27-foot dive boat that does double duty as a water taxi. Expect to pay about US$4 each way to be dropped off at Cayo Luis Peña or the west coast beaches. The trip to Culebrita will probably cost you US$10 (each way), but prices vary depending on the size of your party.

See the Boating section under Vieques, earlier in this chapter, for sailing guidebook recommendations.

Places to Stay

Camping You can camp for US$10 a night at the camping area on the west side of *Playa Flamenco* (☎ 787-742-0600). Depending on when you visit, this experience can be bucolic or chaotic. On major holidays and during summer vacations, Puerto Ricans from the mainland descend on this camping area in droves. In an area that might sensibly contain 50 campsites, you may see far more than 200 tents and several thousand people. Always call to make reservations, and be patient: The staff may not be near the phone the first or the fifth time you call.

Guesthouses Almost all the accommodations (slightly more than 200 rooms) on Culebra fall into this category, even when they call themselves villas, hotels or B&Bs, and the range of what you get for your dollar is broad.

Dewey The *Hotel Puerto Rico* (☎ 787-742-3372), across from Citibank in the center of town, has the shabby look of a legendary Heartbreak Hotel. Here you share a bathroom and get a no-frills room for less than US$30. Be warned that it can be hot.

Coral Island Guest House (☎ 787-742-3177) is a total budget place across from the liquor store and ferry dock. It can be noisy, as construction and ferry traffic seem a way of life here. US$30 will get you a room with shared bath, except for when the island is packed with tourists, at which time you might expect a rate hike.

Hotel Kokomo (☎ 787-742-0719) is an old-time tropical hotel that puts you in the midst of the village scene. It has various restaurants and shops on the ground floor, which faces the ferry dock, and its accommodations are clean and basic, with shared bathroom; US$40 and up.

At *Isla Bonita* (☎ 787-742-3575), by the ferry dock, Quique Canovanas has two rooms over his wife Marta's restaurant for about US$50.

Casa Llave (☎ 787-742-3559) is a B&B just north of town on Ensenada Honda. This inn offers breakfast, separate entrances, air-conditioning and bayside living, with rates that start at about US$50. It also has a hand-crafted glassware shop. From here you can easily walk into town or to the bars/restaurants north of town, such as Tina's, El Batey, Happy Landings and Panadería El Patio.

Mamacita's (☎ 787-742-0090) has several small apartments over its bar-restaurant on the canal in the center of town. Bring your bug repellent because this area can be rife with mosquitoes. Rooms cost US$65.

Posada La Hamaca (☎ 787-742-3516), close by, is similar to Mamacita's, but it has nine units (some with kitchens), less style and no bar-restaurant. A terrace overlooks the canal; rates are comparable to those of Mamacita's.

Coral Reef Apartments (☎ 787-742-3885) is in the same building as Four Seasons Travel, in the middle of town. There is no discernible character to this building, but its three floors can get you up out of the mosquito zone, US$85.

Harbor View Villas (☎ 787-742-3171) are Druso Daubon's modified A-frames, sitting on a steep hill overlooking Cayo Luis Peña and the ferry dock. It has great views and breezes. The place feels pleasantly isolated but is only about a three-minute walk away from town. Rates are about US$95, but some units cost less.

Casa Katrina (☎ 787-742-3565) is in town above La Loma gift shop. Here Bruce and Kathie Goble rent two fully furnished apartments for US$350 a week. They have been on the island for more than 20 years and can really fill you in on local lore. There is a three-day minimum; no children or pets.

Barriada Clark The *Cayúl Guest House* (☎ 787-742-0206) stands by El Caobo Tina's restaurant on the hill. Rates are about US$40.

At *Villa Nueva* (☎ 787-742-0257), Ernesto Villanueva has four meticulous rooms with private bathrooms and air conditioning for US$50.

Villa Naniqui (☎ 787-742-3271) is near the airport, on the water at the head of Ensenada Honda. You can get several styles of accommodations here, with water views, for about US$60.

South of Dewey The *Villa Fulladoza* (☎ 787-742-3576) is one of the first guesthouses you'll reach on the road past the Dinghy Dock restaurant. You will know this place by the cream-colored Model A Ford roadster parked outside. Location and style make this a good value, with rooms starting at less than US$70.

Villa Boheme (☎ 787-742-3508) is the attractive violet building with arches, right on Ensenada Honda past the Dinghy Dock restaurant. And this place is another good value, with air con, views and proximity to town for about US$75.

Club Seabourne (☎ 787-742-3169) definitely ranks at the top of the island's luxury accommodations list. It lies 1¹/₂ miles south of the drawbridge (past the Dinghy Dock restaurant), on the Punta del Soldado road. Erica and Dan Gilmore are the engaging young hosts of this operation, which includes a collection of villas positioned on a hillside above a central building with a pool, outdoor bar, library, video lounge and one of the best restaurants on the island. You can even rent snorkel gear here (US$10 a day).

Rates range from US$95 for an inside room to US$125 for an attractive hillside villa (no kitchens).

Villa Arynar (☎ 787-742-3145) is an attractive place, offering a view of Ensenada Honda from its hillside south of town, on the same road as Club Seabourne. A retired career Navy couple runs this place with spit and polish. Their rates start at about US$70.

Much farther down this road, *Bay View Villas* (☎ 787-742-3392) has actual vacation houses for rent for about US$1000 a week.

Culebra Island Villas (☎ 787-742-0333) is an operation in the same style, area and price range as Bay View Villas.

Around the Island The *Culebra Beach Villas* (☎ 787-742-0319) has 32 condo units on the east end of Playa Flamenco, with rates starting at US$95 for studios and one-bedroom apartments with full kitchens.

Right next door, *Villa Flamenco Beach* (☎ 787-742-0023) is the 'beach digs' of Quique Canovanas (who also owns the Isla Bonita guesthouse and Marta's restaurant, at the ferry dock). This is an airy three-story building with efficiency apartments at the same price as the neighboring competition.

Tamarindo Estates (☎ 787-742-3343) is on lovely, remote Playa Tamarindo, overlooking Cayo Luis Peña. The site is hard to find because it is on a dirt road that veers west off the road to Playa Flamenco. This place has a pool, restaurant and bar and competes with Club Seabourne for upscale travelers. Rooms start at about US$110.

Culebra Dive Resort (☎ 787-742-0129) is on a hill above Villa Muñeco, east of the airport. It has great views, a small pool and four units. For less than US$200 a day, you can stay here and go on daily diving excursions.

Rental Agents Jim and Cheryl Galasso run *Pelican Enterprises* (☎ 787-742-0052), which is a very professional real-estate/property management/vacation-rental operation. They rent houses and apartments at prices ranging from US$600 to more than US$2000 a week.

Cathy West at *The Culebra Connection* (☎ 787-742-31120) is a long-time island expat who has traded in her guesthouse-manager keys to become a booking agent for island accommodations and just about anything else you might need.

Places to Eat

Dewey *Hart's Oasis* (☎ 787-742-3175) is in the center of town, across from the town hall. This is the only place on the island to get pizza. Tasty stuff, but not cheap: You pay US$12 for an 18-inch cheese pizza, and the price can approach US$20 with add-ons.

Culebra Deli (☎ 787-742-3277), in the center of town, is a hangout for schoolkids. Locals joke about the 'open-air dining' as a lot of patrons eat sitting on the low wall next door. The place is good for barbecued rotisserie chicken (about US$4).

Wai Nam Chinese Restaurant is next to the post office, in the center of town. This establishment is basically a take-out place, but, curiously, it has no phone. The *egg foo yong* (US$6.50) is popular among culebrenses.

Marta's (☎ 787-742-3575) is right on the corner across from the ferry pier at the town dock. She is not always open, so call in advance to learn about her *criollo* specials, such as chicken breast (US$7). One of the island's characters, Marta has endeared herself by becoming something of an ad hoc protector for many of Culebra's stray dogs and cats.

Mamacita's (☎ 787-742-0090), on the canal in town, is the kind of open-air restaurant and bar most people picture when they think of the tropics. The best value on the menu is the chicken wings (less than US$5). Chef Jerry Rosario is duly proud of the spicy guava sauce he uses to baste his pork chops and dorado (US$12). Check out the bar if you want to meet a lot of the local expats as well as island legends. One of these titans is 'Cuba' (and his dog, Fidel, who rides in a shopping cart), who has been fishing for sharks for most of his 70-plus years. Some people claim that Cuba was the prototype for Santiago in Hemingway's *The Old Man and the Sea*; they are mistaken, but Cuba fits the part.

Wash & Wear Café (☎ 787-742-0758) is in the front of the Hotel Kokomo, by the ferry landing. This is a popular coffee spot among local expats. You can get a bagel with cream cheese here for about US$1.50 and do your laundry at the same time.

Colmado Mayra (which everyone calls 'Che Lee's' for its owner), atop the hill on Calle Escudero near La Loma gift shop, is Culebra's largest grocery store.

Barriada Clark *El Caobo Tina's* (☎ 787-742-3235), commonly known as Tina's, is north of town in the hillside settlement of Barriada Clark, above the baseball field. This place has excellent and inexpensive *cocina criollo*. Tina's is definitely the place to come when you want a lot of food for your dollar. A mound of arroz con habichuelas will cost you less than US$4.

Happy Landings, at the end of the airport runway, is another popular and economical restaurant with criollo cooking. Try the pork chops (less than US$6).

Panadería El Patio (☎ 787-742-0374) is also at the end of the runway. Come here for fresh *pan criollo* and sandwiches for around US$3.

South of Dewey Try the *Dinghy Dock*, (☎ 787-742-0581) on the water, just south of the drawbridge on the Punta del Soldado road. Every Tuesday night, the Silver Truck shows up to sell veggies here. A lot of people come to buy produce and then head into the restaurant, which offers a US$6 pasta dinner special.

Restaurante El Pesquerito sounds a bit grander than it looks. This small place is in the fishermen's co-op, to the right after you cross the drawbridge. While there are just a few tables here, it is the place to come for fresh fish and the island's best *empanadillas* stuffed with *sierra* (kingfish).

Club Seabourne (☎ 787-742-3169) is the upscale, attractive inn 1½ miles south of town toward Punta del Soldado (see Places to Stay, earlier in this chapter). Its conch fritters are a great find (less than US$5). One of chef Barbara Petersen's specialties is fish and chips (about US$13), which is not listed on the menu. Many islanders claim that her seafood stroganoff (US$19) is the best meal on the island.

Around the Island Quique Canovanas, husband to Marta of Marta's restaurant, runs *Coconut's Beach Grill* at the Villa Flamenco Beach (see Places to Stay, earlier in this chapter) on weekends. His thick burgers and fries go for less than US$5.

Tamarindo Bar & Grill (☎ 787-742-0345) is at the Tamarindo Estates guesthouse, at the end of the dirt road that takes you to Playa Tamarindo. It is open only during the winter season, and often just on weekends. Travelers and locals come here for the sunsets and lobster (US$18).

Entertainment
El Batey (☎ 787-742-38280) is on the road that leads north from town to the airport. This is largely a local place that pulls in just about everybody on the island on Saturday night, when a DJ cranks the salsa and merengue and the crowd works a little magic on the dance floor. Islanders say El Batey has the best burgers in town (under US$4). If you get a chance to talk to the owner, Digna, ask her about her personal experience as a 'noncombatant' in the so-called Battle of Culebra, which forced the US Navy to retreat from the island in 1975.

Happy Landings (see Places to Eat, above) also draws a crowd on weekends for salsa. A number of the habitués claim to have made up a new drink called the 'Monica': it requires the wearing of a blue dress and the drinking of an El Presidente beer.

Mamacita's also has a lively happy hour. On weekends, local gringos, many travelers, and yacht crews from the harbor favor this place, with its open-air deck and selection of reggae, calypso, Buffett, etc.

Shopping
Bruce Goble's La Loma gift shop (☎ 787-742-3565), at the corner of Calles Escudero and Romero in town, has an inventory of all-handcrafted goods that ranges from T-shirts and jewelry to watercolors and jams. Its useful tourist guide costs US$1.50.

The Blue Moon Spice Company sells various spices at the Hotel Kokomo. Look for the Barefoot Contessa, who usually sells her jewelry under the mahogany tree in the little park near the ferry landing on Thursday, Friday and Saturday.

Getting There & Away
Air Culebra gets excellent air service from San Juan and Fajardo on the two commuter carriers that also serve Vieques: Isla Nena Air Service (☎ 888-263-6213) and Vieques Air Link (☎ 787-722-3736). There are at least six flights a day to/from San Juan's Isla Grande and Luis Muñoz Marín (LMM) airports, and three flights a day to/from Fajardo. Currently, Isla Nena charges US$95 roundtrip to fly to/from LMM, and Vieques Air Link charges US$90 to/from Isla Grande. Fajardo trips are US$40 roundtrip. All aircraft are Islander twins or tri-motor Trilanders.

Pro Air (☎ 787-721-2866) flies charters in its Aztec based on Culebra. Expect to pay at least US$200 an hour.

Ferry Puerto Rican Port Authority ferries travel between Fajardo and Culebra several times a day. Generally, the passage takes slightly more than an hour. One-way fares are US$2.25. The passenger ferry schedule was as follows at the time this book went to press:

route	weekdays	weekends
Culebra-Fajardo	–	7 am
Fajardo-Culebra	9:30 am	9 am
Culebra-Fajardo	11 am	2 pm
Fajardo-Culebra	3 pm	4 pm
Culebra-Fajardo	4:30 pm	5:30 pm

Call to confirm the schedule, to make reservations (particularly for weekend travel), or to request departure times for the cargo ferry if you must take a car (which is not a great idea). You can reach the Fajardo Puerto Rican Port Authority office at ☎ 787-863-0705, 800-981-2005; the Culebra office, at the ferry dock in Dewey, can be reached at ☎ 787-742-3161. Both offices are open 8 to 11 am and 1 to 3 pm weekdays.

Getting Around
Most of the island's natural attractions are not near the center of town, and chances are

good that your guesthouse or other rental isn't either. So you will need a ride, by either rental car or taxi.

Biking, kayaking and water taxis are good options for reaching far-flung attractions around the island. See Activities, earlier in this chapter, for details.

Car Old Culebra hands will tell you this is the way to go, even though car rentals are not cheap at US$45 per day. You should also know that with more than 200 guestrooms and several dozen vacation villas for rent, Culebra's 60 rental cars (mostly Suzuki Samurais) cannot meet the demand during the peak vacation months in winter and summer. So reserve your car (at least for part of your visit) when you book your accommodations, and pick a reliable vendor recommended by your guesthouse, because some companies have been known to overbook.

Jerry Beaubien of Jerry's Jeeps (☎ 787-742-0587) braved a flash flood to get us our jeep on time and capped off the delivery with a half-hour briefing as well as a guided tour of the island. He claims to work on the honor system, and he told us to just park our jeep at the airport or ferry dock with the key in the ignition when we left.

Other rental agencies on Culebra include the following:

Coral Reef	☎ 787-742-0055
Dick's	☎ 787-742-0062
Prestige	☎ 787-742-0587
Rancho Ruvy	☎ 787-742-0237
Tamarindo	☎ 787-742-3343
Willie's	☎ 787-742-3537

Taxi There is taxi service on the island, but the taxis are basically público vans designed to get large parties of people back and forth between the ferry dock and Playa Flamenco (where they will be partying or camping) for a couple of dollars per person. However, the públicos are not radio dispatched, so getting a timely pick-up has been a problem for many people heading to or from dinner at a restaurant.

If you get stuck for a ride, try Romero (☎ 787-378-2787) or Willie (☎ 787-742-3537).

Spanish for Travelers

Many seasoned Spanish speakers initially find themselves a little off balance with the Spanish they hear on their first visit to Puerto Rico. In fact, two very different forms of Spanish are spoken on the island. Every Puerto Rican learns in school to speak Standard Modern Spanish with the crisp pronunciation of the language spoken in the highlands of Bolivia, Colombia and Ecuador as well as the salons of high society throughout Latin America. This is the language you will hear from hotel and restaurant staff (*if* you address them in Spanish); it is also the idiom in which you will converse with business, legal and medical professionals and intellectuals. And you should use the polite *usted* when addressing anyone with whom you have no emotional ties.

But the Spanish you hear in the plazas, markets and mountain towns and on the beaches is something else: Boricua – the language of Borinquen. And for a number of reasons, the rhythm and sound of spoken Boricua take a little time to process for an ear trained in Castilian, Mexican or South American dialects.

Boricua 101

Most of the original Spanish colonists of Puerto Rico came from Andalucía, Extremadura or the Canary Islands and brought with them the regional tendencies to relax or devoice consonants. This style persists to the extreme on the streets of the island. When you hear two well-acquainted Puerto Ricans of any social class speaking together, you will notice their strong tendency to totally drop the pronunciation of final consonants like 's' and 'd,' and sometimes articles like *el* or *la*. A standard Spanish sentence such as '*Vamos a la ciudad*' (Let's go to the city) becomes '*Vamoh a ciudá*' in Boricua; '*nos vemos*' (see you later) becomes '*noh vemoh*'; '*muchas gracias*' (thanks a lot) is '*mucha gracia*'; '*adiós*' becomes '*adió*.'

What seems to be going on here is that Puerto Ricans love vowels and diphthongs with a passion that grows not only from the dialects of Andalucía and Extremadura, but also from the Arawakan language spoken by the indigenous Taínos, who gave the world words like *hamaca* (hammock) and *huracán* (hurricane; from the Taíno god Juracán). Islanders constantly strive to fill their speech with sonorous vowel sounds by dropping or changing the sounds of consonants in the middle of words as well as at the ends. A classic example is the tendency to drop the 'd' in past participles, so that the standard Spanish *asopado* (stewed or stew) becomes *asopao*, which is the accepted name and spelling for a traditional Puerto Rican stew. In Boricua, when an 'r' appears next to another consonant in the middle – and sometimes the end – of a word, island speakers tend to pronounce that letter like an 'l.' So *farmacia* (pharmacy) becomes *falmacia* in Boricua; *comprar* (to buy) becomes *compral*.

Furthermore, some islanders – especially those from the interior – reverse this transliteration, replacing the written 'r' next to another consonant in the middle or end of the word with a spoken 'l.' In this situation, a word like *dulce* (a sweet or candy) becomes *durce*; *hotel* changes to *hoter*. Put this whole mix of dropped and changed consonants together and the standard Spanish sentence '*El asopado de este hotel es salado, y eso es la pura verdad*' (This hotel's stew is salty, and that is the pure truth) changes into '*El asopao de este hoter eh salao, y eso eh la pura veldah*.' Note: *pura* does not change to *pula* because the 'r' in *pura* comes between two vowels.

To spice up their rhythms even more, islanders run their words and sentences together with breathless speed, even when compared to Spanish spoken in many other places around the world such as Madrid or Caracas.

Several other variants characterize Boricua as well, and these variations extend throughout much of Latin America. *Seseo* is the pronunciation of the soft 'c' sound as an 's' rather than the 'th' of Castilian Spanish.

For example, the word *placer* (pleasure) gets pronounced 'pla-thair' in Madrid but 'pla-sair' in San Juan. *Yeísmo* is the tendency to pronounce the trilled 'll' of a Spanish word like *amarillo* (yellow) as an English 'y' or even a 'j,' so the word in Boricua sounds like *amariyo* or even *amarijo*. When Puerto Ricans come across a word like *carro* (car), they change the trilled 'rr' to an 'h'; hence *cahro* or *pehro* for *perro* (dog). Then there is the letter 'v,' which is always pronounced like a 'b,' as is now the case in most Spanish-speaking countries. Hence, *venga* (you come) sounds like 'benga.'

Finally, when it comes to pronunciation, Puerto Ricans love to stress an initial consonant and stretch out a vowel sound to give their speech a funky syncopation unlike Spanish spoken anywhere outside the Caribbean. Some linguists see this syncopation as vestiges of the rhythms of languages like Yoruba brought to the islands by African slaves. Whatever the source, Boricua has a rhythm as distinct as a song by Tito Puente.

You get some really colorful speech on the island when you mix in some street slang known as *cafre*. The term reputedly derives from the name of an African tribe whose members were brought as slaves to the island, but today it refers to a hip-looking urban youth wearing baggy clothes and a ball cap on backward. In cafre, a standard Spanish locution such as '*Mira, hermano: esa chica está muy bonita*' (Look, brother: that girl is very pretty) becomes '*No' bemo, broki: esa jeba está brutaaaal.*'

Some Puerto Rican slang seems to come from standard Spanish, as in expressions like '*qué chavianda*' (what a drag), '*qué chulito*' (how cute) and '*eah madre*' (wow). But a lot of island slang comes from the influence of English, which filters to the island from the Puerto Rican barrios in the US as well as from TV, radio, film and advertising. Puerto Ricans have taken the stems of many English words and turned them into Spanish-sounding verbs and nouns. To eat the midday meal, islanders *lonchar*. To goof around or hang out is *gufear*. '*Vamo a rapear*' means literally 'Let's rap,' but on the street it means 'Let's hit on girls.' A male can be a

tipo (type) or *mano* (buddy), as in '*Hola, mano*' (Hey, buddy). *Playeros* (beach bums) *surfear* or *snorklear* all day long. Urban families in a hurry stop by Kentucky Fried Chicken to pick up *una Kentukita* (a bucket of wings).

Of course, the bilingual experience promotes widespread code-switching in Boricua, so that within the everyday life of a Puerto Rican household you are likely to hear things like '*Se está brushing his teeth*' or '*Tú miras funny.*'

Finally, Puerto Ricans tend to keep themselves company both at work and at play by carrying on a running dialogue with their alter egos for anyone to hear, often punctuated with either actual or invented lyrics sung to the tune of a favorite *bolero* (love song).

For a look at the history of the bilingual tradition on the island, see the Language section in this book's Facts about Puerto Rico chapter.

The traveler hoping to submerge herself in the island's rich culture needs to have some command of basic Spanish vocabulary as well as some sense of the significant distinction between Puerto Rican Spanish and the language spoken in places like Madrid or Bogotá. However, even if travelers speak Spanish well, they can expect Puerto Ricans who are proud of their hard-earned English skills to perceive visitors as *gringos* and to address them accordingly. Admittedly, it can be a little deflating when you initiate a conversation in Spanish and someone responds to you in English. Some bilingual cultures are infamous for exhibiting this behavior as a power trip to make travelers feel unsettled and simply 'foreign.' While such power tripping is not below some Puerto Ricans, the vast majority of islanders are choosing to speak English to a visitor out of pride in being bilingual and consideration for the language they perceive to be most welcoming for their guest.

If one of your goals in coming to Puerto Rico is to immerse yourself in the Spanish language as well as the island's culture, an acknowledgment of your host's bilingual talents, a smile and a simple explanation of your hopes to practice your Spanish are an effective and congenial way to set a clear agenda for conversation in Puerto Rico's mother tongue. One of the great rewards for many travelers to Puerto Rico is remaining long enough at a destination for the local citizens to feel comfortable addressing you in Spanish.

Pronunciation

Pronunciation of Spanish is not difficult, given that many Spanish sounds are similar to their English counterparts, and there is a clear and consistent relationship between the pronunciation and the spelling. Unless otherwise indicated, the English words used below to approximate Spanish sounds take standard American pronunciation.

Vowels Spanish has five vowels: **a**, **e**, **i**, **o** and **u**. They are pronounced something like the highlighted letters of the following English words:

a as in 'f**a**ther'
e as in 'm**e**t'
i as in 'f**ee**t'
o as in the British 'h**o**t'
u as in 'b**oo**t'

Diphthongs A diphthong is one syllable made of two vowels, each of which conserves its own sound. Here are some diphthongs in Spanish and their approximate English pronunciations:

ai as in 'h**i**de'
au as in 'h**ow**'
ei as in 'h**ay**'
ia as in '**ya**rd'
ie as in '**ye**s'
oi as in 'b**oy**'
ua as in '**wa**sh'
ue as in '**we**ll'

Consonants Many consonants are pronounced much as they are in English, but there are some exceptions:

c is pronounced like 's' in 'sit' when before 'e' or 'i'; elsewhere, it is like 'k'
ch as in 'choose'

g as the 'g' in 'gate' before 'a,' 'o' and 'u'; before 'e' or 'i,' it is a harsh, breathy sound like the 'h' in 'hit.' Note that when 'g' is followed by 'ue' or 'ui,' the 'u' is silent unless it has a dieresis (ü), in which case it functions much like the English 'w':
    guerra   'GEH-rra'
    güero   'GWEH-ro'
h always silent
j a harsh, guttural sound similar to the 'ch' in Scottish 'loch'
ll as the 'y' in 'yellow'
ñ a nasal sound like the 'ny' in 'canyon'
q as the 'k' in 'kick'; always followed by a silent 'u'
r is a very short rolled 'r'
rr is a longer rolled 'r'
x is like the English 'h' when it follows 'e' or 'i' – otherwise it is like the English 'x' as in 'taxi'; in many Indian words, 'x' is pronounced like the English 'sh'
z is the same as the English 's'; under no circumstances should 's' or 'z' be pronounced like the English 'z' – that sound does not exist in Spanish

There are several other distinct pronunciation differences and a lot of slang that is typical of the Spanish spoken in Puerto Rico. Obviously, the longer you stay on the island, the easier these peculiarities will become.

The letter *ñ* is considered a separate letter of the alphabet and may follow 'n' in alphabetically organized lists and books, such as dictionaries and phone books.

Stress There are three general rules regarding stress:

* In words ending in a vowel, 'n' or 's,' the stress goes on the penultimate (next-to-last) syllable:
    naranja   na-RAHN-ha
    joven   HO-ven
    zapatos   sa-PA-tos
* In words ending in a consonant other than 'n' or 's,' the stress is on the final syllable:
    estoy   es-TOY
    ciudad   syoo-DAHD
    catedral   ka-teh-DRAL

- Any deviation from these rules is indicated by an accent:

México	MEH-hee-ko
mudéjar	moo-DEH-har
Cortés	cor-TESS

Gender

Nouns in Spanish are either masculine or feminine. Nouns ending in 'o,' 'e' or 'ma' are usually masculine. Nouns ending in 'a,' 'ión' or 'dad' are usually feminine. Some nouns take either a masculine or feminine form, depending on the ending; for example, *viajero* is a male traveler and *viajera* is a female traveler. An adjective usually follows the noun it modifies and must take the same gender as the noun.

Greetings & Civilities

Hello/Hi.	*Hola.*
Good morning/Good day.	*Buenos días.*
Good afternoon.	*Buenas tardes.*
Good evening/Good night.	*Buenas noches.*
See you.	*Hasta luego.*
Goodbye.	*Adiós.*
Pleased to meet you.	*Mucho gusto.*

How are you? (to one person)
  ¿Cómo está?
How are you? (to more than one person)
  ¿Cómo están?

I am fine.	*Estoy bien.*
Please.	*Por favor.*
Thank you.	*Gracias.*
You're welcome.	*De nada.*
Excuse me.	*Perdóneme.*

People

I	*yo*
you (familiar)	*tú*
you (formal)	*usted*
you (plural formal)	*ustedes*
he/it	*él*
she/it	*ella*
we	*nosotros*
they (m)	*ellos*
they (f)	*ellas*
my wife	*mi esposa*
my husband	*mi esposo,*
	mi marido
my sister	*mi hermana*
my brother	*mi hermano*
friend	*amigo(a)*
Sir/Mr	*Señor*
Madam/Mrs	*Señora*
Miss	*Señorita*
young girl	*la nena*
young boy	*el nene*

Useful Words & Phrases

For words pertaining to food and restaurants, see the Food section in the Facts for the Visitor chapter.

Yes.	*Sí.*
No.	*No.*
What did you say?	*¿Como?*
good/OK	*bueno*
bad	*malo*
better	*mejor*
best	*lo mejor*
more	*más*
less	*menos*
very little	*poco* or
	poquito

I am…(location or temporary condition)	*Estoy…*
here	*aquí*
tired (m/f)	*cansado/a*
sick/ill (m/f)	*enfermo/a*
I am… (permanent condition)	*Soy…*
a worker	*trabajador*
married	*casado*

Shopping

How much?	*¿Cuánto?*
How much is it worth?	*¿Cuánto vale?*
I want…	*Quiero…*
I do not want…	*No quiero…*
I would like…	*Quisiera…*
Give me…	*Deme…*
What do you want?	*¿Qué quiere?*
Do you have…?	*¿Tiene…?*
Is/are there…?	*¿Hay…?*
market	*mercado*
convenience store	*colmado*

How much does it cost?
  ¿Cuánto cuesta esto? or *¿Cuánto se cobra?*

Nationalities

American (m/f)	*(norte) americano/a*
Australian (m/f)	*australiano/a*
British (m/f)	*británico/a*
Canadian (m & f)	*canadiense*
English (m/f)	*inglés/inglesa*
French (m/f)	*francés/francesa*
German (m/f)	*alemán/alemana*

Languages

I speak...	*Yo hablo...*
I do not speak...	*No hablo...*
Do you speak...?	*¿Habla usted...?*
Spanish	*español*
English	*inglés*
German	*alemán*
French	*francés*
I understand.	*Entiendo.*
I do not understand.	*No entiendo.*
Do you understand?	*¿Entiende usted?*

Please speak slowly.
   Por favor hable despacio.

Immigration & Customs

birth certificate	*certificado de nacimiento*
car-owner's title	*título de propiedad*
car registration	*registración*
customs	*aduana*
driver's license	*licencia de manejar*
exit permit	*permiso de salida*
identification	*identificación*
immigration	*immigración*
insurance	*seguro*
passport	*pasaporte*
visa	*visado*

Getting Around

avenue	*avenida*
block	*cuadra*
corner (of)	*esquina (de)*
corner/bend	*vuelta*
road	*camino*
street	*calle*
this way	*por aquí*
that way	*por allí*
north	*norte*
south	*sur*
east	*este*
west	*oeste*

short route	*vía corta*
Where is...?	*¿Dónde está...?*
the airport	*el aeropuerto*
the bus station	*el terminal de guaguas*
a long-distance phone	*un teléfono de larga distancia*
the post office	*el correo*
bus	*guagua*
minibus, shared taxi	*público*
city bus stop	*parada de guaguas*
taxi	*taxi*
train	*tren*
ticket sales counter	*taquilla*
waiting room	*sala de espera*
baggage check-in	*(recibo de) equipaje*
toilet	*sanitario, baño*
departure	*salida*
arrival	*llegada*
platform	*andén*
left-luggage room/ checkroom	*guardería, guarda de equipaje*

How far is...?
   ¿A qué distancia está...?
How long? (How much time?)
   ¿Cuánto tiempo?

Driving

gasoline	*gasolina*
fuel station	*gasolinera*
unleaded	*sin plomo*
regular/leaded	*regular/con plomo*
fill the tank	*llene el tanque; llenarlo*
full	*lleno*
oil	*aceite*
tire	*goma*
puncture	*agujero*

How much is a liter of gasoline?
   ¿Cuánto cuesta el litro de gasolina?
My car has broken down.
   Se me ha descompuesto el carro.
I need a tow truck.
   Necesito un remolque.
Is there a garage near here?
   ¿Hay un garaje cerca de aquí?

For highway signs in Spanish, see 'Spanish for the Road' in the Getting Around chapter.

Accommodations

hotel	*hotel*
guesthouse	*casa de huéspedes, pensión*
inn	*posada*
room	*cuarto, habitación*
room with one bed	*cuarto sencillo*
room with two beds	*cuarto doble*
room for one person	*cuarto para una persona*
room for two people	*cuarto para dos personas*
double bed	*cama matrimonial*
twin beds	*camas gemelas*
with bathroom	*con baño*
shower	*ducha*
hot water	*agua caliente*
air-conditioning	*aire acondicionado*
blanket	*manta*
towel	*toalla*
soap	*jabón*
toilet paper	*papel higiénico*
the check (bill)	*la cuenta*
What is the price?	*¿Cuál es el precio?*

Does that include taxes?
  ¿Están incluidos los impuestos?
Does that include service?
  ¿Está incluido el servicio?

Money

money	*dinero*
traveler's checks	*cheques de viaje*
bank	*banco*
exchange bureau	*casa de cambio*
credit card	*tarjeta de crédito*
exchange rate	*cambio*

I want/would like to change some money.
  Quiero/quisiera cambiar dinero.
Is there a commission?
  ¿Hay comisión?

Telephones

telephone	*teléfono*
telephone call	*llamada*
telephone number	*número de telefóno*
area code	*clave*
local call	*llamada local*
tone	*tono*
operator	*operador(a)*

collect (reverse charges)	*por cobrar*
dial the number	*marque el número*
please wait	*favor de esperar*
busy	*ocupado*
toll/cost (of call)	*cuota/costo*
time and charges	*tiempo y costo*
Don't hang up.	*No cuelgue.*

prefix for long-distance call
  prefijo
long-distance call
  llamada de larga distancia
long-distance telephone
  teléfono de larga distancia
coin-operated telephone
  teléfono de monedas
long-distance telephone office
  caseta de larga distancia

Dates & Times

Monday	*lunes*
Tuesday	*martes*
Wednesday	*miércoles*
Thursday	*jueves*
Friday	*viernes*
Saturday	*sábado*
Sunday	*domingo*
yesterday	*ayer*
today	*hoy*
tomorrow	*mañana*
right now	*ahorita*
already	*ya*
morning	*mañana*
tomorrow morning	*mañana por la mañana*
afternoon	*tarde*
night	*noche*
What time is it?	*¿Qué hora es?*

Numbers

0	*cero*
1	*uno* (m), *una* (f)
2	*dos*
3	*tres*
4	*cuatro*
5	*cinco*
6	*seis*
7	*siete*
8	*ocho*
9	*nueve*
10	*diez*

11	*once*	40	*cuarenta*
12	*doce*	50	*cincuenta*
13	*trece*	60	*sesenta*
14	*catorce*	70	*setenta*
15	*quince*	80	*ochenta*
16	*dieciséis*	90	*noventa*
17	*diecisiete*	100	*cien*
18	*dieciocho*	101	*ciento uno*
19	*diecinueve*	143	*ciento cuarenta y tres*
20	*veinte*	200	*doscientos*
21	*veintiuno*	500	*quinientos*
22	*veintidós*	900	*novecientos*
30	*treinta*	1000	*mil*
31	*treinta y uno*	2000	*dos mil*
32	*treinta y dos*		

Glossary

See 'Spanish for the Road' in the Getting Around chapter for transportation-related Spanish terms and useful phrases. See the Food section in the Facts for the Visitor chapter for a list of common food terms.

agregados – farm workers; landless free laborers
aldea – village, hamlet
Arcaicos – Archaics; first known inhabitants of Puerto Rico
areytos – epic songs and ceremonial dance of the Taínos

babalawo – male priest who practices the rites of Santería
bahía – bay
balneario – public beach
bar típico – bars frequented by locals
barrio – neighborhood or city district
batey – Taíno ball court
bohíque – Taíno word meaning 'shaman'
boleros – ballads/love songs
bomba – musical form and dance inspired by African rhythms and characterized by call-and-response dialogues between musicians and interpreted by dancers; often considered as a unit with *plena* (see below), as in *bomba y plena*
Boricua – Puerto Rican Spanish
Borinquen – traditional Taíno name for the island of Puerto Rico
bosque estatal – state forest
botánica – shop specializing in herbs, icons and associated charms used in the practice of Santería

cacique – Taíno chief (male or female)
callejón – narrow side street; alleyway
capilla – chapel
caretas – traditional masks worn at island festivals (see also *vejigantes*)
Caribs – original colonizers of the Caribbean islands, for whom the region was named
casa – house
caserios – government-sponsored, low-income housing projects
catedral – cathedral

cayos – cays; refers to islets in the Caribbean
cemíes – small figurines carved from stone, shell, wood or gold representing deities worshipped by the Taínos
centros vacacionales – literally, 'vacation centers'; form of rental accommodation popular with island families, with facilities ranging from basic wooden cabins on the beach to two-bedroom condos
cerro – hill or mountain
Changó – Yoruba god of fire and war believed to control the thunder and lightning; one of several principal deities worshipped in Santería (see also *orishas*)
cocina criolla – traditional island cuisine
Colón, Cristóbal – Christopher Columbus
convento – convent
coquí – a species of tiny tree frog found only in Puerto Rico and beloved as the island's mascot
criollo – island-born person of Spanish parentage; in colonial times considered inferior by peninsular Spaniards (see also *mestizo)*
culebrenses – residents of Culebra
curandero – healer

danza – form of piano music and stylized figure-dance with origins in Spain, fused with elements of island folk music
Depto de Recursos Naturales – the Dept of Natural Resources

espiritismo – spiritualism
estado libre asociado – free associated state or commonwealth

fiestas patronales – the annual celebrations staged in Puerto Rican cities and towns to honor each community's patron saint
fortaleza – fortress
fuerte – fort

galería – gallery
garitas – turreted sentry towers constructed at intervals along the top of Old San Juan's fortifications
gringo – term used on the island to describe Americans

hacienda – agricultural estate, plantation

iglesia – church
Igneris – Indian group of the Arawakan linguistic group; early settlers of Puerto Rico
independentistas – advocates for Puerto Rican independence

jíbaro – rural mountain resident, often cast as archetypal Puerto Rican

laguna – lake or lagoon
lechonería – restaurant specializing in roast suckling pig
LMM – acronym for San Juan's Aeropuerto Internacional de Luis Muñoz Marín

malecón – pier, waterfront promenade
máscaras – masks (see also *caretas, vejigantes*)
mercado – market
Mesones Gastronómicos – a Puerto Rico Tourism Company-sponsored program involving a collection of restaurants around the island that feature Puerto Rican cuisine
mestizo – person of mixed ancestry (usually Indian and Spanish; see also *criollo*)
monasterio – monastery
mundillo – traditional form of intricately woven lace, made only in Puerto Rico and Spain
municipios – town and city government units comprised of mayors and assemblies
muralla – wall; sandstone fortifications surrounding much of present-day Old San Juan
museo – museum

Newyoricans – island term developed in the 1950s to describe Puerto Ricans who migrated to the US, many of whom settled in New York City
NPS – National Park Service

orishas – Yoruba deities worshiped in Santería, often associated with Catholic saints (see also *Changó*)

palacio – palace
parador – country inn
parque – park
pasaje – passage
pava – typical straw hat of the *jíbaro*
playa – beach

plazuela – small plaza
plena – form of traditional Puerto Rican dance and song unfolding to distinctly African rhythms beat out with maracas, tambourines and other traditional percussion instruments; often associated with *bomba* (see above)
pleneros – plena singers
ponceños – residents of Ponce
públicos – shared taxis, usually minivans equipped with bench seats, which pick up passengers along a prescribed route and provide low-cost local transport islandwide
puerta – gate/door
puerto – port

reserva forestal – forest reserve
ron – rum
Ruta Panorámica – network of scenic roads across Puerto Rico's mountainous spine

sanjuaneros – residents of San Juan
Santería – Afro-Caribbean religion representing the syncretism of Catholic and African beliefs, based on the worship of Catholic saints and their associated Yoruba deities, or *orishas* (see above)
santero – an artist who carves santos (see below); one of many names for practicioner of the rites of Santería (see also *babalawo*)
santos – small carved figurines representing saints, enshrined and worshiped by practitioners of Santería
sonda – sound

tabonuco – forest ecosystem growing below 2000 feet and characterized by tall, straight trees such as the *tabonuco* and *ausubo*, palms, epiphytes, flowers and aromatic shrubs
tropicalismo – contemporary art movement celebrating the flora and fauna of the tropics

UNESCO – the United Nations Educational, Scientific, and Cultural Organization
urbanizaciones – planned residential neighborhoods
USFS – US Forest Service
USGS – US Geological Survey

vejigantes – traditional masks crafted from papier-mâché or coconut husks, usually depicting many-horned diabolical figures
viequenses – residents of Vieques

LONELY PLANET

Phrasebooks

Lonely Planet phrasebooks are packed with essential words and phrases to help travellers communicate with the locals. With color tabs for quick reference, an extensive vocabulary and use of script, these handy pocket-sized language guides cover day-to-day travel situations.

- handy pocket-sized books
- easy to understand Pronunciation chapter
- clear & comprehensive Grammar chapter
- romanization alongside script to allow ease of pronunciation
- script throughout so users can point to phrases for every situation
- full of cultural information and tips for the traveller

'...vital for a real DIY spirit and attitude in language learning'
– Backpacker

'the phrasebooks have good cultural backgrounders and offer solid advice for challenging situations in remote locations'
– San Francisco Examiner

Arabic (Egyptian) • Arabic (Moroccan) • Australian *(Australian English, Aboriginal and Torres Strait languages)* • Baltic States *(Estonian, Latvian, Lithuanian)* • Bengali • Brazilian • Burmese • Cantonese • Central Asia • Central Europe *(Czech, French, German, Hungarian, Italian, Slovak)* • Eastern Europe *(Bulgarian, Czech, Hungarian, Polish, Romanian, Slovak)* • Ethiopian (Amharic) • Fijian • French • German • Greek • Hill Tribes • Hindi/Urdu • Indonesian • Italian • Japanese • Korean • Lao • Latin American Spanish • Malay • Mandarin • Mediterranean Europe *(Albanian, Croatian, Greek, Italian, Macedonian, Maltese, Serbian, Slovene)* • Mongolian • Nepali • Papua New Guinea • Pilipino (Tagalog) • Quechua • Russian • Scandinavian Europe *(Danish, Finnish, Icelandic, Norwegian, Swedish)* • South-East Asia *(Burmese, Indonesian, Khmer, Lao, Malay, Tagalog Pilipino, Thai, Vietnamese)* • Spanish (Castilian) *(also includes Catalan, Galician and Basque)* • Sri Lanka • Swahili • Thai • Tibetan • Turkish • Ukrainian • USA *(US English, Vernacular, Native American languages, Hawaiian)* • Vietnamese • Western Europe *(Basque, Catalan, Dutch, French, German, Greek, Irish)*

LONELY PLANET

Guides by Region

Lonely Planet is known worldwide for publishing practical, reliable and no-nonsense travel information in our guides and on our Web site. The Lonely Planet list covers just about every accessible part of the world. Currently there are nine series: travel guides, shoestring guides, walking guides, city guides, phrasebooks, audio packs, travel atlases, diving and snorkeling guides and travel literature.

AFRICA Africa – the South • Africa on a shoestring • Arabic (Egyptian) phrasebook • Arabic (Moroccan) phrasebook • Cairo • Cape Town • Central Africa • East Africa • Egypt • Egypt travel atlas • Ethiopian (Amharic) phrasebook • The Gambia & Senegal • Kenya • Kenya travel atlas • Malawi, Mozambique & Zambia • Morocco • North Africa • South Africa, Lesotho & Swaziland • South Africa, Lesotho & Swaziland travel atlas • Swahili phrasebook • Trekking in East Africa • Tunisia • West Africa • Zimbabwe, Botswana & Namibia • Zimbabwe, Botswana & Namibia travel atlas
Travel Literature: The Rainbird: A Central African Journey • Songs to an African Sunset: A Zimbabwean Story • Mali Blues: Traveling to an African Beat

AUSTRALIA & THE PACIFIC Australia • Australian phrasebook • Bushwalking in Australia • Bushwalking in Papua New Guinea • Fiji • Fijian phrasebook • Islands of Australia's Great Barrier Reef • Melbourne • Micronesia • New Caledonia • New South Wales & the ACT • New Zealand • Northern Territory • Outback Australia • Papua New Guinea • Papua New Guinea (Pidgin) phrasebook • Queensland • Rarotonga & the Cook Islands • Samoa • Solomon Islands • South Australia • Sydney • Tahiti & French Polynesia • Tasmania • Tonga • Tramping in New Zealand • Vanuatu • Victoria • Western Australia
Travel Literature: Islands in the Clouds • Sean & David's Long Drive

CENTRAL AMERICA & THE CARIBBEAN Bahamas and Turks & Caicos • Bermuda • Central America on a shoestring • Costa Rica • Cuba • Dominican Republic & Haiti • Eastern Caribbean • Guatemala, Belize & Yucatán: La Ruta Maya • Jamaica • Mexico • Mexico City • Panama • Puerto Rico
Travel Literature: Green Dreams: Travels in Central America

EUROPE Amsterdam • Andalucía • Austria • Baltic States phrasebook • Berlin • Britain • Central Europe • Central Europe phrasebook • Czech & Slovak Republics • Denmark • Dublin • Eastern Europe • Eastern Europe phrasebook • Edinburgh • Estonia, Latvia & Lithuania • Europe • Finland • France • French phrasebook • Germany • German phrasebook • Greece • Greek phrasebook • Hungary • Iceland, Greenland & the Faroe Islands • Ireland • Italian phrasebook • Italy • Lisbon • London • Mediterranean Europe • Mediterranean Europe phrasebook • Paris • Poland • Portugal • Portugal travel atlas • Prague • Romania & Moldova • Russia, Ukraine & Belarus • Russian phrasebook • Scandinavian & Baltic Europe • Scandinavian Europe phrasebook • Scotland • Slovenia • Spain • Spanish phrasebook • St Petersburg • Switzerland • Trekking in Spain • Ukrainian phrasebook • Vienna • Walking in Britain • Walking in Italy • Walking in Switzerland • Western Europe • Western Europe phrasebook
Travel Literature: The Olive Grove: Travels in Greece

INDIAN SUBCONTINENT Bangladesh • Bengali phrasebook • Bhutan • Delhi • Goa • Hindi/Urdu phrasebook • India • India & Bangladesh travel atlas • Indian Himalaya • Karakoram Highway • Nepal • Nepali phrasebook • Pakistan • Rajasthan • South India • Sri Lanka • Sri Lanka phrasebook • Trekking in the Indian Himalaya • Trekking in the Karakoram & Hindukush • Trekking in the Nepal Himalaya
Travel Literature: In Rajasthan • Shopping for Buddhas

LONELY PLANET

Mail Order

Lonely Planet products are distributed worldwide. They are also available by mail order from Lonely Planet, so if you have difficulty finding a title please write to us. North and South American residents should write to 150 Linden St, Oakland, CA 94607, USA; European and African residents should write to 10a Spring Place, London NW5 3BH, UK; and residents of other countries to PO Box 617, Hawthorn, Victoria 3122, Australia.

ISLANDS OF THE INDIAN OCEAN Madagascar & Comoros • Maldives • Mauritius, Réunion & Seychelles

MIDDLE EAST & CENTRAL ASIA Arab Gulf States • Central Asia • Central Asia phrasebook • Iran • Israel & the Palestinian Territories • Israel & the Palestinian Territories travel atlas • Istanbul • Jerusalem • Jordan & Syria • Jordan, Syria & Lebanon travel atlas • Lebanon • Middle East on a shoestring • Turkey • Turkish phrasebook • Turkey travel atlas • Yemen
Travel Literature: The Gates of Damascus • Kingdom of the Film Stars: Journey into Jordan

NORTH AMERICA Alaska • Backpacking in Alaska • Baja California • California & Nevada • Canada • Chicago • Deep South • Florida • Hawaii • Honolulu • Los Angeles • Miami • New England USA • New Orleans • New York City • New York, New Jersey & Pennsylvania • Pacific Northwest USA • Rocky Mountain States • San Francisco • Seattle • Southwest USA • Texas • USA • USA phrasebook • Vancouver • Washington, DC & the Capital Region
Travel Literature: Drive Thru America

NORTH-EAST ASIA Beijing • Cantonese phrasebook • China • Hong Kong • Hong Kong, Macau & Guangzhou • Japan • Japanese phrasebook • Japanese audio pack • Korea • Korean phrasebook • Kyoto • Mandarin phrasebook • Mongolia • Mongolian phrasebook • North-East Asia on a shoestring • Seoul • South-West China • Taiwan • Tibet • Tibetan phrasebook • Tokyo
Travel Literature: Lost Japan

SOUTH AMERICA Argentina, Uruguay & Paraguay • Bolivia • Brazil • Brazilian phrasebook • Buenos Aires • Chile & Easter Island • Chile & Easter Island travel atlas • Colombia • Ecuador & the Galapagos Islands • Latin American Spanish phrasebook • Peru • Quechua phrasebook • Rio de Janeiro • South America on a shoestring • Trekking in the Patagonian Andes • Venezuela
Travel Literature: Full Circle: A South American Journey

SOUTH-EAST ASIA Bali & Lombok • Bangkok • Burmese phrasebook • Cambodia • Hill Tribes phrasebook • Ho Chi Minh City • Indonesia • Indonesian phrasebook • Indonesian audio pack • Jakarta • Java • Laos • Lao phrasebook • Laos travel atlas • Malay phrasebook • Malaysia, Singapore & Brunei • Myanmar (Burma) • Philippines • Pilipino (Tagalog) phrasebook • Singapore • South-East Asia on a shoestring • South-East Asia phrasebook • Thailand • Thailand's Islands & Beaches • Thailand travel atlas • Thai phrasebook • Thai audio pack • Vietnam • Vietnamese phrasebook • Vietnam travel atlas

ALSO AVAILABLE: Antarctica • Brief Encounters: Stories of Love, Sex & Travel • Chasing Rickshaws • Not the Only Planet: Travel Stories from Science Fiction • Travel with Children • Traveller's Tales

LONELY PLANET

Lonely Planet Journeys

JOURNEYS is a unique collection of travel writing – published by the company that understands travel better than anyone else. It is a series for anyone who has ever experienced – or dreamed of – the magical moment when they encountered a strange culture or saw a place for the first time. They are tales to read while you're planning a trip, while you're on the road or while you're in an armchair in front of a fire.

These outstanding titles explore our planet through the eyes of a diverse group of international writers. JOURNEYS books catch the spirit of a place, illuminate a culture, recount a crazy adventure or introduce a fascinating way of life. They always entertain, and always enrich the experience of travel.

FULL CIRCLE
A South American Journey
Luis Sepúlveda (translated by Chris Andrews)

'A journey without a fixed itinerary' with Chilean writer Luis Sepúlveda. Extravagant characters and extraordinary situations are memorably evoked: gauchos organising a tournament of lies, a scheming heiress on the lookout for a husband, a pilot with a corpse on board his plane ... *Full Circle* brings us the distinctive voice of one of South America's most compelling writers.

WINNER 1996 Astrolabe – Etonnants Voyageurs award for the best work of travel literature published in France.

GREEN DREAMS
Travels in Central America
Stephen Benz

On the Amazon, in Costa Rica, Honduras and on the Mayan trail from Guatemala to Mexico, Stephen Benz describes his encounters with water, mud, insects and other wildlife – and not least with the ecotourists themselves. With witty insights into modern travel, *Green Dreams* discusses the paradox of cultural and 'green' tourism.

DRIVE THRU AMERICA
Sean Condon

If you've ever wanted to drive across the USA but couldn't find the time (or afford the gas), *Drive Thru America* is perfect for you. In his search for American myths and realities – along with comfort, cable TV and good, reasonably priced coffee – Sean Condon paints a hilarious road-portrait of the USA.

'entertaining and laugh-out-loud funny'– *Alex Wilber, Travel editor, Amazon.com*

SEAN & DAVID'S LONG DRIVE
Sean Condon

Sean and David are young townies who have rarely strayed beyond city limits. One day, for no good reason, they set out to discover their homeland, and what follows is a wildly entertaining adventure that covers half of Australia.

'a hilariously detailed log of two burned out friends' – *Rolling Stone*

Lonely Planet On-line
www.lonelyplanet.com *or* AOL keyword: lp

Whether you've just begun planning your next trip, or you're chasing down specific info on currency regulations or visa requirements, check out Lonely Planet On-line for up-to-the minute travel information.

As well as mini guides to more than 250 destinations, you'll find maps, photos, travel news, health and visa updates, travel advisories, and discussion of the ecological and political issues you need to be aware of as you travel. You'll also find timely upgrades to popular guidebooks which you can print out and stick in the back of your book.

There's also an on-line travellers' forum where you can share your experience of life on the road, meet travel companions and ask other travellers for their recommendations and advice.

And of course we have a complete and up-to-date list of all Lonely Planet travel products including travel guides, diving and snorkeling guides, phrasebooks, city maps, travel atlases, travel literature and videos, and a simple on-line ordering facility if you can't find the book you want elsewhere.

Lonely Planet Diving & Snorkeling Guides

Beautifully illustrated with full-color photos throughout, Lonely Planet's **Pisces Books** explore the world's best diving and snorkeling areas and prepare divers for what to expect when they get there, both topside and underwater.

Dive sites are described in detail with specifics on depths, visibility, level of difficulty, special conditions, underwater photography tips, and common and unusual marine life present. You'll also find practical logistical information and coverage on topside activities and attractions, sections on diving health and safety, plus listings for diving services, live-aboards, dive resorts and tourist offices.

Lonely Planet Travel Atlases

L onely Planet has long been famous for the number and quality of its guidebook maps. Now we've gone one step further and produced a handy companion series: Lonely Planet travel atlases – maps of a country produced in book form.

Unlike other maps, which look good but lead travellers astray, our travel atlases have been researched on the road by Lonely Planet's experienced team of writers. All details are carefully checked to ensure the atlas corresponds with the equivalent Lonely Planet guidebook.

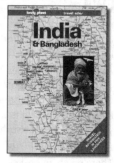

- full-colour throughout
- maps researched and checked by Lonely Planet authors
- place names correspond with Lonely Planet guidebooks
- no confusing spelling differences
- legend and travelling information in English, French, German, Japanese and Spanish
- size: 230 x 160 mm

Available now: Chile & Easter Island • Egypt • India & Bangladesh • Israel & the Palestinian Territories • Jordan, Syria & Lebanon • Kenya • Laos • Portugal • South Africa, Lesotho & Swaziland • Thailand • Turkey • Vietnam • Zimbabwe, Botswana & Namibia

Lonely Planet TV Series & Videos

L onely Planet travel guides have been brought to life on television screens around the world. Like our guides, the programs are based on the joy of independent travel, and look honestly at some of the most exciting, picturesque and frustrating places in the world. Each show is presented by one of three travellers from Australia, England or the USA and combines an innovative mixture of video, Super-8 film, atmospheric soundscapes and original music.

Videos of each episode – containing additional footage not shown on television – are available from good book and video shops, but the availability of individual videos varies with regional screening schedules.

Video destinations include: Alaska • American Rockies • Australia – The South-East • Baja California & the Copper Canyon • Brazil • Central Asia • Chile & Easter Island • Corsica, Sicily & Sardinia – The Mediterranean Islands • East Africa (Tanzania & Zanzibar) • Ecuador & the Galapagos Islands • Greenland & Iceland • Indonesia • Israel & the Sinai Desert • Jamaica • Japan • La Ruta Maya • Morocco • New York • North India • Pacific Islands (Fiji, Solomon Islands & Vanuatu) • South India • South West China • Turkey • Vietnam • West Africa • Zimbabwe, Botswana • Namibia

The Lonely Planet TV series is produced by: Pilot Productions
The Old Studio
18 Middle Row
London W10 5AT, UK

FREE Lonely Planet Newsletters

We love hearing from you and think you'd like to hear from us.

Planet Talk

Our FREE quarterly printed newsletter is full of tips from travellers and anecdotes from Lonely Planet guidebook authors. Every issue is packed with up-to-date travel news and advice, and includes:

- a postcard from Lonely Planet co-founder Tony Wheeler
- a swag of mail from travellers
- a look at life on the road through the eyes of a Lonely Planet author
- topical health advice
- prizes for the best travel yarn
- news about forthcoming Lonely Planet events
- a complete list of Lonely Planet books and other titles

To join our mailing list, residents of the UK, Europe and Africa can email us at go@lonelyplanet.co.uk; residents of North and South America can email us at info@lonelyplanet.com; the rest of the world can email us at talk2us@lonelyplanet.com.au, or contact any Lonely Planet office.

Comet

Our FREE monthly email newsletter brings you all the latest travel news, features, interviews, competitions, destination ideas, travellers' tips & tales, Q&As, raging debates and related links. Find out what's new on the Lonely Planet Web site and which books are about to hit the shelves.

Subscribe from your desktop: www.lonelyplanet.com/comet

Index

Text

Bold indicates maps.

Boxed Text

MAP LEGEND

BOUNDARIES

- International
- State
- County

HYDROGRAPHY

- Water
- Coastline
- Beach
- River, Waterfall
- Swamp, Spring

ROUTES & TRANSPORT

- Freeway
- Toll Freeway
- Primary Road
- Secondary Road
- Tertiary Road
- Unpaved Road
- Pedestrian Mall
- Trail
- Ferry Route
- Railway, Train Station
- Mass Transit Line & Station

ROUTE SHIELDS

- (52) Territorial Highway

AREA FEATURES

- Park, Garden
- Ecological Reserve
- Cemetery
- Building
- Plaza
- Golf Course

MAP SYMBOLS

- ✪ NATIONAL CAPITAL
- ◉ State, Provincial Capital
- ● LARGE CITY
- ● Medium City
- ● Small City
- ● Town, Village
- ○ Point of Interest

- ■ Place to Stay
- ▲ Campground
- ⛺ RV Park

- ▼ Place to Eat
- ⬛ Bar (Place to Drink)
- ☕ Cafe

- ✚ Airfield
- ✈ Airport
- ∴ Archaeological Site, Ruins
- ⑤ Bank
- ⚾ Baseball Diamond
- ⛱ Beach
- ⬤ Transportation (Bus, Ferry)
- ⛪ Cathedral
- ⌒ Cave
- ✝ Church
- ⬛ Dive Site
- ◗ Embassy
- ⤢ Foot Bridge
- ✿ Garden
- ⛽ Gas Station
- ⛳ Golf Course
- ✛ Hospital, Clinic
- ❶ Information
- 🗼 Lighthouse
- ✳ Lookout
- ▲ Monument

- ☪ Mosque
- ▲ Mountain
- 🏛 Museum
- ⌂ Observatory
- ← One-Way Street
- ⚘ Park
- P Parking
-)(Pass
- ⊼ Picnic Area
- ★ Police Station
- 🏊 Pool
- ✉ Post Office
- ⚓ Shipwreck
- ❖ Shopping Mall
- 🏛 Stately Home
- ⚓ Surfing
- ⬛ Tomb, Mausoleum
- 🚶 Trailhead
- ⬛ Windsurfing
- ⛲ Winery
- 🐾 Zoo

Note: Not all symbols displayed above appear in this book.

LONELY PLANET OFFICES

Australia
PO Box 617, Hawthorn 3122, Victoria
☎ (03) 9819 1877 fax (03) 9819 6459
email talk2us@lonelyplanet.com.au

USA
150 Linden Street, Oakland, California 94607
☎ (510) 893 8555, TOLL FREE (800) 275 8555
fax (510) 893 8572
email info@lonelyplanet.com

UK
10A Spring Place, London NW5 3BH
☎ (0171) 428 4800 fax (0171) 428 4828
email go@lonelyplanet.co.uk

France
1 rue du Dahomey, 75011 Paris
☎ 01 55 25 33 00 fax 01 55 25 33 01
email bip@lonelyplanet.fr
3615 lonelyplanet *(1,29 F TTC/min)*

World Wide Web: www.lonelyplanet.com *or* AOL keyword: lp
Lonely Planet Images: lpi@lonelyplanet.com.au